The Arcane Schools

The Arcane Schools

John Yarker

ADULTBRAIN

CONTENTS

Adultbrain Publishing is dedicated to breathing new life into timeless literary works by resurrecting old classics for the modern age. We meticulously curate and convert these masterpieces into high-quality digital and audio formats, making them accessible to a new generation of readers and listeners. Our commitment to preserving the essence of these works, while enhancing them with today's technology, allows us to offer immersive experiences that retain the authenticity of the original texts. Whether rediscovering a beloved classic or experiencing it for the first time, our editions invite readers to start using their Adultbrain today.
Published by Adultbrain Publishing.
ISBN: 978-1-998614-02-8
eISBN: 978-1-998614-03-5
Title: The Arcane Schools
Start using your adultbrain today.
For more information, visit: www.adultbrain.ca

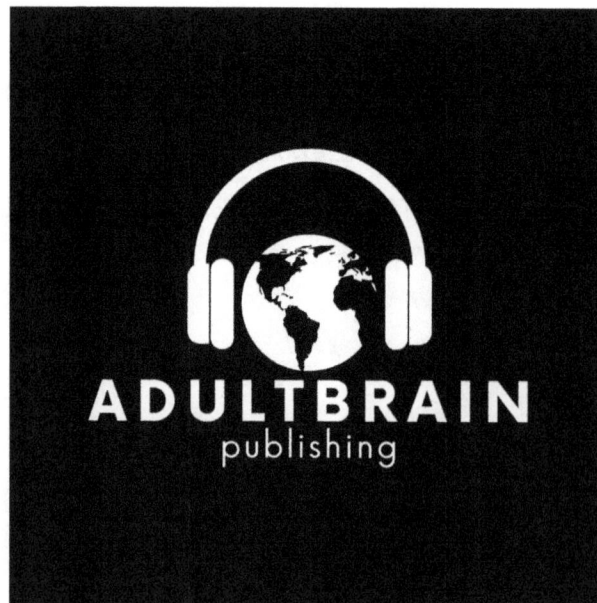

PREFACE

IN the following pages I have sought to satisfy a request, often made to me, to give a short but comprehensive view of the whole fabric of the Arcane mysteries, and affinity with the Masonic System; and I here take the opportunity of recording my protest against the sceptical tendencies of the present generation of the Moderns who are Masons, and against the efforts that are made, in season and out of season, to underrate the indubitable antiquity of the Masonic ceremonies. These efforts, which tend to lower the prestige of our ancient Craft, are not altogether without good results, as they have led to a more careful examination of our Masonic legends and of ancient documents, and I have therefore added, to a general History of the Arcane Schools, a view, sufficiently explicit, of the ancient rites of the Masons, leaving the intelligent Freemason of our day to trace the relative bearing of these. It is no compliment to the Masons who founded the Grand Lodge of England in 1717, and who, however ill informed they may have been in London, yet, as is amply proved, accepted old customs of the Guilds with discrimination, to suppose that they unanimously undertook to impose upon the public, a system as ancient which they themselves were engaged in concocting. Nor is it any compliment to the intelligence of their imagined victims. Whether or not I succeed in convincing the candid reader of the great antiquity of the Institution must be left to time; those of my readers who are pledged to the views of these Moderns will no doubt adhere {v} through life to the ideas in which they have indoctrinated themselves, but enquiry is progressing and there is still a very large substratum of the Craft whose belief is yet strong in the good-faith of their predecessors, whether, in what was last century, termed Ancients or Moderns, and it is to such that I more particularly address myself. The best reward for my labours would be to find that the study of our Craft and analogous societies was making progress, and that others are supplying new facts from old books, that may aid in bridging over any chasms that may be noticed in the following pages. My endeavour has been to print well authenticated matter only, in order that the information supplied may be reliable. Every paragraph is a fact or deduction from facts, and however much condensed nothing of moment,

known to the present time and having a bearing upon Freemasonry, has been omitted. The works of the learned Brother George Oliver, D.D., lack critical cohesion, and have consequently fallen into undeserved neglect, but sufficient will be found in these pages to show that his theories are not devoid of method, and will admit of an authentic construction being put upon those claims which he advances for the antiquity of the Masonic Institution.

Those who obstinately deny the existence of anything which is outside their own comprehension are fully as credulous as those who accept everything without discrimination. There are certain in-tellects which lack intuition and the ability to take in and assimilate abstruse truths, just as much as there are people who are colour-blind, or deaf to the more delicate notes of music; this was well known to the ancient theologians and mystics, and the reasons which they assigned for the mental incapacity will appear in the following pages.

I cannot allow the opportunity to pass, in closing my labours, without thanking my publisher for his invariable kindness, courtesy, and general care; and the reader is also much indebted to him for the compilation of the Index. We have considerably exceeded the 500 pages {vi} with which we made the announcement to the public, hence the slight delay in publication.

I have also to thank our subscribers for their unwearied patience in waiting for the appearance of this work, which, except for modern revisions, has lain dormant for 10 years.

JOHN YARKER.

WEST DIDSBURY, MANCHESTER,

"17th April, 1909."

INTRODUCTION

THE object of the following chapters is to give a broad but condensed view of the various traces which are to be found amongst the ancients, in their religion, in their Art, and in their buildings -- civil, sacred, and military -- of a speculative system, such as is now professed under the designation of Freemasonry. The work is necessarily a compilation of suitable information gathered from books upon history, mystery, mysticism, and Freemasonry; but it embraces the most recent views upon these subjects which have been evolved by a close critical examination, and generally accepted by the learned.

In the "first and second chapters" will be found the proofs of a system of most ancient sacerdotal grades and mysteries which in the earliest or proto- Aryan, civilisation added to their ceremonies those emblems of geometry and art which have been transmitted by Freemasonry.

In the "third and fourth chapters" we see more clearly the advance which the Aryan civilisation introduced into the primitive association; the development of a caste organisation, and the reduction of the more ancient civilisation, by invasions, to a subject state, which in time created an independent system of Art-Mysteries, combined with natural religion, or what we now term Freemasonry.

In the "fifth and sixth chapters" we have attempted the elucidation of the doctrine and symbolism of the Ancient Mysteries and their relationship with the minor schools {x} of Philosophy which sprang from them, as for instance the Pythagorean and Platonic schools, proving that all these possessed much in common -- in doctrine, rites, and symbols, not only with each other but with Free Masonry of our own days, without the distinguishing features of the latter as an operative art; whilst, side by side, the Arcane schools of Philosophy passed onwards through the centuries of Christianity, in numerous branches, with the old rites and symbols.

In the "seventh and eighth chapters" we have, for convenience, a recapitulation of proofs of the existence and transmission of Art Mysteries and symbols from the most ancient times to our own days, with details of the Constitutions of a Fraternity, speculative in its teaching and operative in its application, for the conservation of Arts and Sciences in their tripartite application to houses, churches, and fortications, and which entering this country in British and Roman times from Egypt was modified by Culdee monks and learned clerics, and so continued as Folc-motes or Guilds in the time of the Anglo-Saxons.

In the "ninth and tenth chapters" some space is devoted to an enquiry as to the origin of the Semitic legends of Free Masonry which entering this country in Anglo-Norman times, with an Eastern system of work, of marks, and symbols, were engrafted upon the older Constitutions; together with some account of the esoteric marks, emblems, and rites of the organised Building- brotherhood who erected our noble Gothic edices, and references are made to many of these edifices in illustration of Free Masonry. We see the end of the Gothic and revival of the Classic Arcanum.

The remaining "eleventh, twelfth, and thirteenth chapters" give a short account of the principal points in the history of Modern Freemasonry from 1717 to our own days; and which includes a chapter upon the design, origin and history of what has come to be termed high-grade Free-masonry, {xi} and out of which sprung the distinction between Ancient and Modern Masonry, a dissension which continued until the union of these two sects of Masons in 1813.

Lastly in the "Appendix" we have added a full series of Constitutional Charges which continued in force from Saxon times until the year 1717 and even much later; these we have slightly modernised for the ease of the reader.

CHAPTER I. ARCHAIC LEGENDS

IT may reasonably be supposed that the advancement of mankind which we term civilisation had made great progress in hot climates before the Arts, science, and more especially the mystery of building temples and houses of stone, brick, or wood was developed. Religious mysteries, the rudiments of science, and open and secret worship, if not innate, which we believe them to be, would arise, and as the erection, first of temples, and then of houses, indicates a knowledge of geometry and constructive tools, it implies a more advanced culture.

The tradition which has reached us through the ages is that mankind contracted very slowly the protoplasm which forms our natural body, after which a variety of wants became apparent that were in earlier ages unfelt. Whether we accept or reject this view, we can realise that the united intellect of thousands of years has been unable to supply any better idea of the creation and progress of humanity upon earth than that handed down to us from the ancient sages. As man s material nature increased his spirituality decreased, and as his intuition tended to become dormant means were sought which might restore his ancient status. The discipline necessary for this purpose was

neither suitable nor agreeable to the majority, and this led to the establishment of secret or esoteric {1} schools for those who sought the higher spiritual development. Of an unpretentious nature at first and possessing but moral trials or proofs, these schools gradually assumed a magnificent exterior under State control, with even proofs dangerous to life, and were designated THE MYSTERIES. The natural wants had now come to be provided for; the Arts and Sciences were developed: Architecture, Metallurgy, Ship-building, Astronomy, Agriculture, etc., were added to Theosophia, and religious ritual. This is the tradition of the Mysteries.

There are certain ancient legends in regard to a lost or sunken continent and a deluge which, though not absolutely accepted as history, are too probable to be passed over in silence. It is admitted by scientists that the surface of our earth is continually wasting away, with the result that the bed of the ocean is being slowly raised, and the geographical position of the land is changing: we see in one locality that the ocean is washing the land away, whilst in another the sea is receding. Equally great climatic changes are slowly developing; thus Greenland was at one time a torrid clime, which at a later age, to be reckoned only by tens of thousands of years, was succeeded by intense cold, and when our own island was depopulated by a deluge of ice and frost.

These changes are attendant upon what astronomers term the "Precession of the Equinoxes"; there is a gradual displacement of the poles of the earth, occurring in cycles or periods of 25,000 years, and the last of which reached its extreme point about 12,500 years ago, when it is held that a great cataclysm occurred which changed the face of the entire globe. It follows of necessity that men s habits must change with climatic changes. The Hindu priests have a complicated series of cycles within cycles, which are not altogether imaginary but are grounded upon recondite astronomical calculations. When we remember that there is a great central sun round which the entire galaxy of planets and suns revolve, we may draw the analogy that in immense cycles what we may term seasonal {2} changes or states are produced, even on these planets and suns, similar to those which occur on our earth.<< Vide "Notes and Queries" (S. C. and L. M. Gould, Manchester, N.H.), xi, p. 203.>>

There exists in Thibet and India a "Secret Doctrine" which is of unquestioned

antiquity, and of which analogical confirmation may be found in the writings of the ancient Philosophers. This doctrine allows for the existence in extreme antiquity of a sunken continent in the Pacific ocean, of which the present islands are mountain tops, and in the Atlantic ocean of seven islands, the last of which sank beneath the waters about the period which we have assigned for a great cataclysm, or 12,500 years ago.

Behind this account, which in the East is considered historical, lies the cyclical doctrine of a Day and Night of Brahm, or by whatever other word the impersonal Deity is designated. These cycles are the Outbreathing and Inbreathing of the Unknowable deity, or everliving Spirit and primal Matter; the gradual progress of all created matter is the divine Day which proceeds from the etherial or cometary to the concrete by means of the Tatwas, which will correspond with the Genetic Days of Moses, and these again with the gestation of the ordinary foetus; in the divine Night everything again reverts to the etherial state, to be again followed, in immense cycles, by a reversed action.

The mythological account of the Hindu Paradise places Mount Meru at the North-pole, or the imperishable land ; a circular island upon which is the "City

of the Gods," which is supposed to be a perfect square guarded by a wall protected by eight circular towers, and the holy mount, which is of conical shape, rises in the centre of the city<<"Anacalypsis," i. p. 507>>.

Temples have been designed to represent this legendary Meru, and it has also formed the basic plan of cities, which we may mention later. It is also noteworthy that the Egyptian legend of the Mystery God, Osiris or Heseri, is applicable to 68 Degrees north latitude, or where the sun dies {3} for 40 days, and which was then a hot climate, according to the legends. We know that the Mammoth existed there and fed on tropical herbage. The north they consider to have been torrid owing to the then nebulous or cometary state of our globe, which had neither cooled down nor hardened. Humanity, of a sort, existed in that land, but was moon-bred, etherial, globular, gigantic, sexless, generated as are atoms by self-multiplication. To these succeeded a second race, giants, of whom the later and more material were inspired by the Solar gods, these were dual-sexed or hermaphrodite, as many forms of life yet are, and more compact than the first race.

The Arabs and Persians have legends of such a race, and represent that it

was ruled by 72 kings of the name of Suleiman, of whom the three last reigned one thousand years each. It does not seem that these Suleimans, who are, par-excellence, the rulers of all Djins, Afreets, and other elemental spirits, bear any relationship to the Israelite King, that being a more modern application. We find the name as one of the gods of the ancient Babylonians, and the late Doctor Kenealey, who as a Persian scholar translated the poems of Hafiz, asserts that the earliest Aryan teachers were named Maha-Bodhs or Solymi, and that Suleiman was an ancient title of regal power, synonymous with Sultan in Asia, Pharaoh in Egypt, Khan in Tartary, Tsar in Russia. There is also a Persian legend which alleges that in the mountains of Kaf, which can only be reached by a magic ring (that of Suleiman), there is a gallery built by the giant Arzeak where the statues of the ancient men are preserved who were ruled by the Suleimans, or wise Kings of the East. Many an Eastern storyteller laments the departed glories of the throne of Suleiman, located near the present Aden in Arabia, which it has been suggested may have been populated by Kushites from the Hindu Kush. There is a very wonderful structure hewin out of solid rock on the confiness of Afghanistan and India called the Takht-i-Suleiman, or throne of Solomon, its ancient Aryan name {4} being Shanker Acharya, fabled to have been erected by supernatural means, and known to have been a great rendezvous for two thousand years of merchants caravans. It is on the western side of the Suleiman Mountains. Leaving this slight digression we return to the Secret Doctrine, which goes on

to relate that in course of time a third race of men were produced with bones and divided into sexes, and who are practically the first race of Adamic men, for the rib of Adam is a euphemism alluding to the division of sex. These are said, after developing a monosyllabic language, now represented by Chinese, to have spread over the long lost Pacific continent; here they became great builders, developed the religious Mysteries, and spread from north to south, populating the Atlantic continent, who are considered a fourth race, after the Pacific continent had disappeared. Here was the home of the proto-Aryan race of a brown-white complexion. A colony of these settled in Egypt in remote ages, where they introduced the astronomy and zodiac of Asura-Maya of Romakapura, and the pupil of Narida, of whose books the Indians claim to have

some fragments. Another colony of educated priests settled upon an island, where the desert of Gobi now exists, but then an inland lake, which held in its bosom 12 smaller islands. These priests, or at least some of them, allied themselves with a red-yellow Mongoloid race possessing great intuitive powers, a race of which the Chinese are a branch, for it is claimed that there were seven sub-races in each of the 3rd and 4th races.

The intermarriage of these two races, which we may compare with that of the sons of God with the daughters of men, gave rise to a fifth race of Aryans, who sent out civilising missions over the world, and it is asserted that there are records which show that these priests travelled into Europe to superintend the erection of religious structures such as existed amongst the British Druids, and it is not impossible, as the Eastern civilisation had a lengthy precedence over that of Europe. {5}

When the island of Atlantis sank a pass was reft which drained the Desert of Gobi, and caused the Aryans to take refuge in the mountains and high table- lands, and the change of climate may have sent out others to seek a warmer home; others being forced outwards by the increase in population, and thus compelled to colonise new regions. Thibet has preserved many details of the wars of this lost Atlantis, charging the cause of its destruction to the cultivation, by a portion of its tribes of black magic, or the left-hand path. It may be mentioned that there yet remains between Cabul and Balkh, or the ancient Bactria, some five immense statues from 120 to 60 feet high, said to symbolise this doctrine of these successive races<<The Secret Doctrine, of H. P. Blavatsky.>>. It is curious that on Easter Island there are some similar statues, ranging from 70 to 3 feet high, mentioned by Cooke as equal to our best masonry, and of which investigation has been made by the Smithsonian Institute, and which are said to have been wrought in lava with iron tools.

The Egyptian priests had a chronology vastly in excess of the ordinary computation, and the accounts dovetail with what we have already related. Herodotus, who visited Egypt about 450 B.C., states that the following were careful records of time preserved by the priests. Before any King, a dynasty of gods ruled in Egypt; the First of these were the 8 great gods, sometimes enumerated as 7; then followed the 12, who were produced from the eight, of which the Egyptian and Tyrian Heracles was one, and who ruled 17,000 years before the historian s time; Horus, the son of Osiris, who the historian tells us is identical with Bacchus and his son with the Grecian Apollo, ruled 15,000 years before his own visit. From the time of Menes, the first human king and founder of Memphis, the priests read over to him the names of 330 kings, and also showed him the statues of 34I hierophants, which the historian estimates, at 3 to a century, as representing 11,340 years from the foundation of Memphis. Herodotus {6} was prohibited from giving any esoteric information, but we may point out that there is an affinity between the twelve zodiacal signs and the labours of the Grecian Heracles whom Herodotus considers to be much more modern than the Heracles of Egypt and Tyre, and whose labours were applied to the Hercules of the Latins. The great gods may refer to the Cabiric culte, the lesser gods to the Aryan, but we shall see more of this as we proceed. The former are represented by the planets, and the latter by the zodiacal signs. The birth of the gods may indicate the introduction of their worship into a country or district, their marriage the era when one worship was associated with another, whilst their death may be explained on the doctrine of an alleged

reincarnation. The Egyptians, Herodotus says, were the first who erected altars, shrines, and temples, and who engraved the figures of animals in stone; the first to divide the year into twelve months, and to give names to the 12 gods; the first to defend the doctrine of the soul s immortality; the first to develop geometry.

It is worthy of note that 3, 7, and 12 are prominently represented in Hebrew. There are 3 mother letters, 7 double, and 12 simple characters, which actually bear a planetary and zodiacal signification. The Hebrew alphabet is but an adaptation from an older one, but the arrangement proves that the inventor was an Initiate of the Mysteries, of which this alphabet is the synthesis. It is asserted that in the most ancient times there were two secret zodiacal signs and ten that were known as also 10 simple characters. It is now impossible to fix with mathematical precision the dates of such zodiacs as exist. Of the Egyptian that at Dendara might refer to 13,000 B.C., but there is one at Esne which might refer to 15,000 B.C. Without doubt the ancient Hierophant who designed these figures embodied therein a secret doctrine, and it has been supposed that the system was intended to symbolise the destinies of humanity for the 2,500 years which each sign represents, or for the period which the sun occupies in over-running {7} a sign. The chronology here set forth is much in excess of that allowed by the more extravagant archaeologists, but, in some confirmation of it, Baron Bunsen admits traces of buried pottery which may be 20,000 years old, estimated upon the deposit which the Nile leaves at each annual flow.

The Aryan legend of the sunken Atlantis is said to have been recorded in
Egypt. Plato indirectly informs us in the "Timaeus" that when his ancestor Solon visited Egypt the priests of Neith at Sais informed him that many catastrophes had occurred to mankind in remote times, the most remarkable of which was one contained in the records of the temple. That some 9,000 years before this visit, which took place about 600 B.C., a large continent and some adjacent islands had perished in one night by earthquakes, and that from these islands was the way to the true continent; that the inhabitants of this Atlantis were a race who recognised that great advantages sprang from a just and righteous commerce; that they had conquered and colonised Greece, and extended themselves on one side as far as Lybia, and on the other to Tyrrhenia. But a part of the island s inhabitants had given themselves up to selfish aggrandizement, and had made war upon the well disposed people, and to subvert the good regulations which had been established by Poseidon and his son Atlas. Whereupon the incensed gods, in one night, sank the country of Atlantis beneath the waves of the ocean. It is further stated that the country had temples of black and white stones, decorated within and without with precious metals. The shrine of Poseidon and the palace of the King was surrounded with three sheets of water, forming three parallel concentric circles, and a temple existed roofed with gilded copper. Theopompus in his "Meropis" attributes a similar account to the priests of Phrygia, and tells us that the island contained a fighting and a contemplative race; the former knew how to make themselves invulnerable to iron, so that they could only be wounded by stone or wood. Proclus quotes Marcellus on the subject. {8} Blavatsky says that they had a written character and used it with the tanned skins of monstrous animals now extinct. Professor Bowdler Sharpe thinks that allied forms of birds point to a lost continent which stretched from South

America to Australia with an arm extending to Madagascar, and this would meet the account of Plato.

We have another account, similar in its essentials to that recorded. "The Popul-Vul," or "Book of the Azure Veil" of the Mexicans, tells us that these Atlantians were a race that "knew all things by intuition," and repeat the charge of sorcery, or black magic, as the cause of the destruction of their country by the gods. This book allegorises and personifies the forces of nature. The "Troano MS." records the same matter with special mention of the geological changes which the catastrophe caused. Dr. le Plongeon translates a passage thu: -- "In the year 6 Kan, on the 11th Muluc, in the month Zac, there occurred terrible earthquakes which continued without interruption until the 13th Chuen." The MS. goes on to say that the land of Mu disapeared and that ten countries were scattered, and that this occurred 8,060 years before the book was written. This writer advances still more extraordinary matter confirmative of the statements of the book.

We find in the grave-mounds of a prehistoric race<<See "Ars Quatuor Coronatorum," v, part II.>>, as well as in the architectural sculptures of the Mayaux, the cross in its various forms; the tau cross {T} of Egypt, on the breast of numerous statues throughout America, the equilimbed cross {+}, and the so- called Latin cross {symbol: a Latin cross}, a form equally found in Egypt in pre- Christian times. There is the winged-egg with a symbolic explanation same as was given to it in Egypt<<"Sacred Mysteries of the Mayas and Quiches 11,500 Years Ago.">>. Brother George Oliver, D.D., asserts that these races used a cube of pure crystal in their temples, and Dr. le

Plongeon, who spent twelve years in overhauling the ruins of Yucatan, has found cubical dice upon which is engraved a human hand, as well as crystals of a globular form, arrows of jade, the {9} hardest of stones, etc. The hand, as a symbol, held an important place amongst these people, as it is found stamped on the inside of buildings as if it was done with the actual hand of the architect as a mark of approval, or as a modern Indian Rajah stamps his own hand on the standard given to one of his troops; the same custom appears in the Temples of India. Le Plongeon further found an altar which is a facsimile of one at Anger-thom in Cambogia, and he also claims that he has discovered the tomb, statue, and cremated body of Prince Cay Canchi, the High-priest; in the centre of his mausoleum was represented 12 serpent heads, and the statue which he disinterred at Chichen Itza, the city of the Sages, possesses a carved apron on which is figured an open human hand. The number seven is an important factor in their secret symbolism.

The Doctor, who found a difficulty in getting into print because the publishers saw no money in the subject, claims that the following account is sculptured upon the ruined temple of Uxmal, and confirmed by the "Troano MS." as the veritable history of the country, but which has become mythologised in the old world: the history of an Empire more ancient than Atlantis, embracing three continents peopled by a red and black race, that is including North and South America and Atlantis; that this empire was symbolised by the trident, and the three-peaked crown of its kings, and alluded to in mythology as the kingdom of Poseidon, Kronos, or Saturn.

There was, says the author, a deified king named Can, whose totem or emblem was the serpent, and a rule of his kingdom, as in some Asiatic countries, was that the eldest son should marry his youngest sister. This Can

had 3 sons and 2 daughters, thus making a famly of 7, each of whom ruled one of seven cities. Following the rule already mentioned, one of the brothers named Coh, chacmol or leopard, took to wife his sister Moo, but their brother Aac, whose TOTEM was the turtle, out of love for his sister slew her husband treacherously. According to {10} the custom of the country he is represented as offering her fruit, whilst she is seated under a tree upon which is perched a macaw as the "totem" of Moo; the serpent, or her husband s emblem, is twined in the branches of the tree, whilst a monkey stands by as if representing a councillor. The tree is the emblem of the country, and the representation is in close conformity with the legend of Genesis as to the temptation of Eve. Moo refuses to accept this symbol of the love of Aac, and he puts her to death, as well as her elder brother Cay Canchi, or Hunacay, the wise-fish, the high- priest.

It is noteworthy that in the sculptured representations of this legend, or history, whichever it may be, the murderer Aac is represented as a Sun- worshipper, whilst Coh and his sister Moo venerate the serpent. A curious analogy to this is to be found in Egypt, it is in a statue of Typhon or Set as described by Plutarch. It is the representation of a hippopotamus, which corresponds to the turtle of Aac, and on the back of the animal is a hawk and a serpent in the act of fighting. Le Plongeon again affords another correspondence with Egypt in the description of the 12 kings descended from the 7 of the race of Can, who ruled before the destruction of Atlantis; for we have here the 12 minor gods and the zodiac, and the 7 greater gods or planets. The account may be veritable history, as Le Plongeon maintains that it is, but it is possible that the author may have mistaken for history a still older mythology carried from Atlantis to Pucatan.

The temple of Chichen Itza is itself an interesting study. It is built on a

ground plan of three apartments which {Symbol on two lines of text: A Greek cross with a short horizontal bar at the top and bottom of the vertical arm} make a triple cross. In one peculiarity it corresponds 1 with some ancient temples in Egypt and Cambodia where a keyed arch was then not known. It has a triangular arch constructed by the overlapping of large stones, in which the three sons of Can are symbolised; by taking in the sides we have five to include the two sister; and adding the ends we have seven or the whole family; numbers which are sacred both in Central America and in {11} the East. Over the door of the sanctuary is represented both the cross-bones and a skeleton holding up its two fleshless arms in the form of two squares, a position which is sometimes represented in Egypt as that in which the soul appears before Osiris. Here again it is singular that a corresponding doctrine is found in India as to the symbolism of the walls and floors of their temples. There are other temples in Yucatan which were intended for sun-worship, the ground plan being three concentric circles, like the lakes we have mentioned as surrounding a palace in Atlantis

But the most extraordinary part of the claims of Le Plongeon is that he has

discovered the interpretation of the hieroglyphical inscriptions and finds that the character used, with the exception of a very few letters, is absolutely identical with the hieratic alphabet of Egypt, whilst the language which these characters bespeak is yet found in almost pristine purity in the dialect of Patan, a language which is perfectly constructed and strikingly resembles the Coptic. As in Egypt and Chaldea the ground plan of a temple was the oblong

square {symbol of a horizontal rectangle}, which was again the symbol both in Yucatan and Egypt of the letter M or "Ma", which implies the earth, and the word Maya. In the names of the Greek alphabet Le Plongeon finds a poem, the Patan words of which gives the history of the great catastrophe.

The Mayaux had their religious Mysteries which were governed by 12 priests, with initiations and carefully guarded sacred rites, of which some account may be gathered in the writings of the Quiches, a neighbouring race at Xibalba: in passing through these initiations the Neophyte had to undergo most severe bodily trials, which Le Plongeon compares with certain descriptions in the Chaldean "Book of Enoch". It is not, however, shown that in these Mysteries Art symbolism exists such as we shall find in Thibet and China and in Freemasonry. We learn elsewhere from some researches made at the instance of the Smithsonian Institute that these, or similar Mysteries, {12} are yet preserved by the Zuni people and consist of twelve orders of priests, into some degrees of which Mr. Frank H. Cushing has recently obtained admission after undergoing severe bodily trials. Historical and religious analogies with Yucatan are to be found amongst the Japanese who represent the first seven gods by the same symbols as the Mayas, and Brother George Oliver sets forth that a Japanese candidate, in initiation into their Mysteries, represents the sun s passage through the twelve Zodiacal signs. It is singular that the Mayaux legends or Mythology should contain so much in common with Egypt, Asia, and India. Persia has the tradition of one brother slain by another. The Hindu "Ramayana" represents that the king of the monkey race, perhaps an inferior aboriginal tribe such as the Andamans, had two sons, Bali and Sougravia, each of whom desired the same wife, and Sougravia, by the aid of the divine Rama, treacherously slew his brother Bali. It is alleged, in confirmation of Solon s statement, that Atlantian emigrants settled in Egypt and Greece, that they equally settled in the Dekkan. Indeed, the "Ramayana" states that Maya, the magician and architect of the Davanas, took possession of South India and navigated the ocean from west to east and from the south to the north; the word Maya here meaning a dweller upon the sea.

In the Atlantic Islands, or mountain tops of Atlantis, there is a general belief

that a system of secret Mysteries prevails, and this seems to have been established as a fact by several recent Masonic experiments.<<"Canadian Craftsman", xvii, No. 4; also A.Q.C.>> The natives of Virginia have a society of Initiates designated Huseanawer. The mother prepares a funeral pyre for her son of whom a simulated sacrice is to be made, as in the case of Isaac, and during the preparation she weeps him as dead. A tree is cut down and a crown made from its boughs: the initiate is given a powerful narcotic by which he is thrown into a state of somnambulism, and after a protracted retirement he {13} is looked upon by his tribe as a new man. Again, the negroes of Guinea have certain Mysteries called the Belly Paaro; the candidate is led into a wood where he is divested of all clothing and metals; here he passes five years in absolute seclusion; after this he is initiated into the most secret doctrines of the sect.<<"Secret Societies of All Ages and Countries". Jno. Hogg, 1875, by Heckethorn.>> The object of their worship, as with the Maoris, is Rangi and Papa, or the heavenly Father and the earthly Mother

Even in the Pacific islands, or the mountain tops of a great sunken continent

which has been denominated Lemuria, there exists a system of religious Mysteries. Heckethorn mentions that at Tahiti and scattered over Polynesia, is

a society called Areoiti, which has seven degrees of initiation, which none but the king may pass over all at once. One of their ceremonies is practised at the winter solstice, and it is a funereal ceremony resembling that in honour of Osiris, Bacchus and Adonis. The meaning underlying this initiation is the generative powers of nature, and laymen have to undergo severe bodily trials.<<"Secret Societies of All Ages and Countries". Jno. Hogg, 1875, by Heckethorn.>>

There are cave pictures in Australia of a race more ancient than the Bosjesmen, one of these caves has a robed figure with a rainbow round the head which the Rev. J. Matthew considers to be identical with the chief god of Sumatra.<<"Lucifer", xiv, 1894.>> There are many general assertions that a system of signs identical with modern Freemasonry exists amongst the native Australians, and one such account appears in "Ars Quatuor Coronatorum."<<Vol. x. Bro. F. Jones.>> But the most precise account is a paper in the "New Zealand Craftsman" of 8 Feb., 1898, by Brother Henry Stowell, whose grandmother was a Maori. The paper deserves to be fully copied.

"The Maori in their traditions, "Fangitawhiti" (epic poems), and language show conclusively that ages ago there was at Hawaiki, a grand temple known as Wharekura, {14} at which temple meetings were regularly held and presided over by Tohunga, or initiates of a very high order, and wherein was taught and practised a perfect system of principles in an esoteric form, with exhaustive and appropriate rituals, also symbols, signs, and passwords, and that these were kept and preserved on tables of stone, which latter were deposited in the temple. The ritual and symbols were entrusted by the Ariki-Ranji (divine and supreme head) to the various officers in order to properly carry out the ceremonials connected with these meetings, whereat only those others who were entitled to be present had the happiness of listening to the recitals, and of observing the uses of the higher symbols. Regarded from a Maori point of view this Masonry is neither more nor less than the relation of the main features of creation and the origin and history of the higher destiny of man, which relation was accompanied with appropriate symbols. TANE was the G.A.O.T.U., he may or may not be identical with the Chaldean Oannes. The language in which this wisdom religion was embodied is extremely archaic, but thanks to my having been taught in my youth by an aged Tohunga, and relative, some of the symbols and mysteries, I understand many of the allusions and am acquainted with various signs. A knowledge of astronomy being absolutely essential to a proper realisation of the principles of the order, its Adepts -- Tohunga- Kokorangi -- constantly taught in observatories its elements and phenomena, to those who were accepted for qualification.

"Under the Maori system the two main Pillars, together with their Chapters,
were represented before the dome of the sky. These were divine. A subordinate pillar was the Pillar of the Earth ; at certain points the Nagana or centre was traced. These were two great circles which intersected and which had their corresponding circles. The square was taught upon four points of the visible universe. Moral teachings were more or less {15}} associated with the Figure of the Ripeka cross, the type of good and evil, or enlightenment and ignorance by two opposing lines. It appears that there is a universal tendency to restrict, thwart, or delimit its beneficial functions. Hence, "He waewae tapeka ta ta ara Ripeka." (A foot which diverges from the good or pure to the

evil or impure path.) The figure of the triangle, Tantora, formed the basis of, or for, the most elaborate calculations in connection with astronomy and geography.

"The term Mason, Masonry, Masonic, are used in the English sense and for convenience. Days and months were measured by successive phases of the moon, while the year was marked by the heliacal rising in June of the star Puanga, Rigel in Orion, due east, this being the star of the Maori new year, and the first sign of the Awahio-Rangi, or zodiac.

"I have no knowledge of the use of such a thing as the 24 inch gauge, but can vouch that calculations of length or distance were worked out with nice exactitude. The signs in use varied from those of the Europeans. Still in some important respects, so far as a mere M.M. is able to compare, there is astonishing agreement, and the agreement suggests "a variation on the European scale," owing to the incorporation or blending therein, of the terms of the Oath. The ordinance of the Tapu sanctity was its (Masonic) very essence: any infringement thereof, or neglect of its observance, by whomsoever, resulted in sure and speedy death, which was the true penal sign, silent and awesome. Then again Speculative Masonry was not advanced or urged, and each one appears to have used his enlightenment for the purpose of furthering his knowledge along these ancient lines, which embraced the complete system, offering that fulness of happiness granted to mortals who were enabled to penetrate the very depths of nature, and by revelling in her mysteries attain the threshold of the divine."
There are numerous other archaic legends which might have appeared in this
chapter but which it will be more {16} convenient to refer to hereafter by way of illustration. Those of Genesis, for instance, come within this category. The Adamic legend of Genesis has the appearance of being the esoteric caste mythology of a tribe which settled in the Caucasian highlands,

holding the Aryan doctrine of divine incarnations, to which they gave the expression of a coming Messiah, or divine reincarnation, who was to redeem and rehabilitate their own fallen race alone, and we have seen that the serpent was equally an esoteric emblem in America. Analogous legends to those of Genesis appear also in Vedaic literature. A clergyman recently advanced in his book entitled the "Fall of Adam" that it allegorised the intercourse of the higher spiritual or Adamic man with the lower and soulless race of pre-Adamites, and as we are not bound down by the Rabinical chronology we may carry such a theory back to the "Moon" and "Sun" races of Thibet.

In the American Can we may have a coincidence with the Tartar title of Khan,
and perhaps with the Biblical Cain. In the scriptural account it is Cain, the eldest son, who, like the Thibetians, offers a sacrifice of the fruits of the earth, slays his younger brother Abel who offers a sacrifice of blood, and who leaves no progeny. The continuance of a spiritually minded line devolves upon the third son, or race of Seth. It is after the marriage of these sons of God with the daughters of men that we find the union of the worldly arts of the line of Cain with the more spiritual line of Seth. According to the Talmud Lamech marries the two daughters of Keenan, to whom it assigns the stone tablets of prophecy; the progeny of these marriages become men of renown -- Jabal, Jubal, Tubal Cainl, &c. In Egypt owing either to a racial inversion of the legend, which may have either been the production of some very old racial war, or later to mark their detestation of the Hyksos, or Shepherd Kings, the priests made of the god

Set, or Seth, a devil identical with Typhon who murdered his brother Osiris. There existed in Africa, contemporary with the beginning of {17} Christianity, a sect of Abelites, and it is not improbable that the Syrian Baal, the Cretan Abelios, the Celtic Abellio, and the Greek Apollo, were modified versions of the Hebrew Hebel or Abel.

It is worth while to note that the Jewish Bible makes the line of Cain to be the first to build a city, which may mean a series of wooden huts analogous to those which originated the trabeated, or beam style of stone work, prevailing amongst the early Egyptians, Greeks, and Romans in their temples and coming down even to Christian times; found as well in the cave temples of India, which are richly and wonderfully carved to represent woodwork. After the flood it is the descendants of Ham who become the great builders, and Japhet is to "dwell in the Tents of Shem," which tent is the prototype of the Pagodas of China, Persia, and Japan.

As these legendary accounts of an art which spread from a sunken continent are scarcely more than prehistoric tradition, we need not follow the subject further in this chapter; widely spread as these traditions are, they can scarcely be altogether baseless. Some confirmation has been found by scientific sea- soundings, and further corroboration is afforded in the accepted fact that all the Pacific islanders are of the same race, and speak dialects of the same language, and this at a distance from each other which is impassable to their small boats; all equally say that their forefathers dwelt in a land over which the waves of the ocean now sweep.

We are, for these various reasons, justified in a belief in the veritable existence of such continents, and, by the same parity of reasoning, as we find sacred and secret mysteries existing amongst them, in the Pacific, Atlantic, and in Australia, we are justified in supposing that these sacred schools are as old as the race that inhabited these continents. We see, however, that these mysteries have no architectural aims, and are a part of the conjecture with which we began this chapter, as to the relative position of religion and art. If the reader places no {18} confidence in these traditions, until science has pronounced upon them, he can forget that he has read them, and pass on to what is more generally accepted.

In the following pages closer proof will be found of the existence of a system resembling Free Masonry, and though we have not a minute book to prove that primeval man invented Free Masonry, under a more ancient name, and then established Lodges in Tartary, Egypt, Babylon, Greece, Italy, Britain, etc., yet the fact that similar societies existed in all these countries is indisputable, and there is no doubt that other and more important links will yet be brought to light by a diligent perusal of old classical authors, by someone who has the intuitive ability to understand the language of Mystery.

CHAPTER II PROTO-ARYAN CIVILISATION AND MYSTERIES

PHILOLOGISTS seem to be fast arriving at the view that when the whole earth was of "one language and of one speech" it was a primitive monosyllabic or Turanian tongue. The word Turanian is most indefinite, for it is taken to include the small, dark, long-headed Dravidian race of India, which penetrated Britain before the Aryan Celt and of which the Basques of Spain are a survival; the long-headed white race of Scandinavian hunters; and the white, broad- headed Mongoloid, whom we chiefly term proto-Aryan, as an early branch of the Aryan race; a race which in prehistoric times spread from Lapland to Babylon, and from India to Egypt and Europe.

The modern discoveries of archaeologists, in the countries occupied in remote times by this once powerful proto-Aryan race, have scarcely yet had time to filter down into the ordinary Masonic channels, but they must in course of time considerably modify the views of older writers upon our Masonic Mysteries. It would seem from what can be gathered that we owe advanced building in stone and brick to this race, and the assimilation of their so-called Turanian speech is indicated by this, that, Monsieur Lenormant traces the remotely connected Proto-Median and Akkadian of Babylon to the Ugro-Altaic family of languages, traces the Aryan to the same Finnic race of the Ural mountains, and the anthropological evidence is as conclusive as the language of the Ugro-Altaic origin of the Aryan race. It may have taken {20} tens of thousands of years for the development of the proto-Aryan into the Indo-Iranian tongue, Zend, Sanscrit, Pushtu, Baluchea, as well as the Aryo-European languages, including Greek, Latin, Sclavonic, Lettic, and Teutonic. From it also sprang, at an earlier period, the Celtic of Europe, and from it, by a probable mixture with a black or Hamitic speech, the Semitic tongues spoken in Assyria, Phoenicia, Arabia, and Palestine.

Even with the comparatively slight knowledge which we possess of the ancient Turanian and proto-Aryan speeches it may be taken for granted that a race which had founded a language which embraced certain roots equally found in Teutonic, Greek, Celtic, Semitic, and Sanscrit, and their cognate dialects, before separating into colonies, and which embraced terms in art, agriculture, jurisprudence, family life, religion, etc., had even then made progress in geometry, in the building of temples and houses, and architecture generally. In this chapter, however, we are dealing more particularly with an earlier phase of culture, but it is necessary to say some little of Aryan advancement.

A high state of civilisation was developed in the highlands of Europe and extended to other centres in Northern India which included Thibet. The Indian Vedas assign the centre of their culture to the

Himalayan source of the Ganges, "the abode of the Gods." The Persian Avesta seems to point to the northern plateau of Pamir. We have no certain information in regard to the departure of colonies from their parent home, but no doubt the causes were various. The continuous increase of population would, of itself, make it a necessity. The Zend Avesta attributes their departure from their original home to climatic changes: Ahriman, the evil spirit, who is mentioned both in the Avesta and the Vedas, introduced cold. The nomadic habits of the people as breeders of cattle led them into Europe. In the Himalayan centre or that of the Hindu, a war arose between those who had assumed divine powers in virtue {21} of their,

orally acquired, knowledge of the sacred hymns, and the warrior or Maharajah class, who were subdued by a divine being who incarnated as Rama, upon which the priests allowed favourable terms and permitted the warriors to receive a limited amount of sacred knowledge, and to "hear" the Vedas, when collected in writing, read. A previous incarnation is alleged for the benefit of the "monkey race," by which is perhaps meant some low-caste tribe, but that of Rama represents some prehistoric reformer of the Turanian culture, to whom a divine origin is assigned.

At the period when the advance into India began, some 6,000 to 8,000 years ago, a race existed under the name of Tchandalas, probably partly Aryan, and partly Hamitic and other conquered Turanian races. These migrated to other parts, and some are believed to have originated the Semitic tribes. Such of the Tchandalas as remained were treated with the greatest barbarity by the Rishis or ancient Brahmin rulers, and were compelled to submit to a slavery which reads like that of the Hebrews in Egypt.<<"Mackenzie s Royal Masonic Cyclopaedia," also "Blavatsky s Secret Doctrine.">> There were ex-Brahmins amongst them, and a caste system was established amongst the tribes which the Rishis did their best to suppress.

It is not possible to give any reliable estimate of the centuries that elapsed before the reduction into writing of the ancient hymns, and the conversion of the rocks into temples of Cyclopian architecture. The late Baron Bunsen deemed that the date 4,000 B.C. might be a very suitable era for what we may term the "manifestation of light," or the beginning of recorded history, and the desire to transmit the same upon monuments, in Egypt in hieroglyphics, in Chaldea upon slabs in the cunieform. The Iran and the Hindu had developed the Avesta and the Vedas; the Babylonian an epic upon the journey of the sun through the signs of the Zodiac; the Egyptian the Book of the Dead, and the books of Hermes. But the nomadic Aryans of Europe had not made the same {22} progress, the Celt was the most advanced but used bronze tools until about 2,000 B.C. Hence the Esoteric claims deserve serious consideration. Their earliest buildings are subterranean caves wrought with infinite labour and perseverance. We should have liked to enlarge upon these wonderful cave temples wrought in solid rock but space forbids. An interesting visit to some of these is recorded in the late H. P. Blavatsky s book entitled "The Caves and Jungles of Hindustan." That of Elephanta is a threefold construction, and it is alleged that all castes, and even kings wrought with the chisel in its construction. Whilst the oldest cyclopean architecture is attributed in Europe to the Pelasgians, in India it is attributed to the Pandus who were a pre- Brahmin tribe, and Ferguson regards the analogy of this style with that of the Incas of Peru as one of the most remarkable facts of history. It was in these prehistoric times that the symbols of the two creative forces of nature developed, represented by crux-ansata, lithoi, or lingam, and the vesica piscis, or yoni. They are equally the signs of a dogma which lay at the root of all religions in regard to fire, not the fire burning upon the altar, but the fire which that symbolised and was termed "divine darkness," a spiritual or magical fire, seen by gifted seers, of which the earthly symbols are the pyramids, the obelisk, and the church spires.<<"The Rosicrucians," Jennings.>>

The oldest of the Turanian, or proto-Aryan, races had an organised
priesthood of three grades, as in that of the Art school. It is true that we cannot now give proof that such a system is as ancient as humanity, but we

may accept its extreme antiquity from the fact that in the most ancient historic times there was a widespread system of three degrees of Theosophy amongst people hopelessly separated.

The Finlanders from the most ancient times to the present day have had a magical system of three grades which are termed Tietajat (learned), Asaajat (intelligent), {23} and Laulajat (incantators). The Babylonian Chasdim were termed Khartumim (conjurors), Chakamim (physicians), and Asaphim (theosophists).<<"Chaldean Magic," by Lenormant.>>

There yet exists in India certain Kolarian and Dravidian tribes who possess a magical system similar to that of the Finnic and Babylonian races, and they practise a system of secret initiation which they claim has descended to them from a time more ancient than the invasion of their plateau in central India by the Aryans, a conquest occurring thousands of years ago, but we purposely abstain from following European dates as they are altogether unreliable. Their grades are Najo (witches and wizards), Deoni or Mati (wizards), and Bhagat (diviner). It is said that in the grade of Bhagat the Master priest goes through a part of the initiation alone with the aspirant, and that the ceremony is completed at night time with a corpse, near to some water. Amongst these tribes are the Gonds, sprung from Dravidians, who in early times reached a high degree of culture; in Chanda are the ruins of a palace and town with a perfect network of underground passages, which have never been explored by Europeans, and which, tradition states, lead to a series of halls where secret conclaves were formerly held.<<"The Kneph," v, p. 40 See also Mr. E. D. Ewen s paper (who resided several years amongst these people) in "Five Years of Theosophy.">> Mr. James Ferguson, F.R.S., in a lecture read before the Bengal Institute of this country maintains that the original occupiers of India were a Turanian race of builders who were tree and serpent worshippers, and that the Pelasgian inhabitants of Greece possessed the same features, in each case before the Aryan invasions and conquest of these countries. The full comprehension of this is the key to much that is puzzling in the transmission of Masonry and the Mysteries. There are important distinctions between the Hindus and these aboriginal hill-tribes; the latter have no caste divisions, they eat flesh food and offer live victims in sacrifice to their {24} gods; and are essentially either of a Mongolian or Turanian type, like the Burmese and Japanese.

The Median Magi, or sacerdotal class of the proto-Medes were originally a so-
called Turanian priesthood. But at some remote period there arose in the region north of Bactria a monotheistic reformer whom his followers termed Zaradust, the first of the name, and who is probably the same prophet whom the Hindus term Parusha-Rama, and it is this reformed Median civilisation which constituted the religion of the most ancient Babylonians; and of the somewhat more

modern Persians. It is clear that the race worked metals and built in brick and stone from their earliest migrations. In the time of Cyrus I. these Magi consisted of three classes, thus named by the
learned German scholar Heeren -- Harbed, or disciple; Mobed, or master; Destur-Mobed, or complete Master. These constituted a sacerdotal College over which presided a Rab-Mag, or chief magian. The word Magi, or Mahaji in Sanscrit, means great or wise. Their distinguishing attributes
were the Costi or girdle; the Havan, or sacred cup; and the Barsom, or bundle of twigs grasped in
the hand; a symbol not properly understood but supposed to represent staves that were employed

in divination, but it is much more probable that it was a symbol of that union which was to give
strength to their order. The cubical dice were said to be used by them for divinatory purposes. Aristotle asserts that this Magian pontificate was more ancient than the foundation of Egypt; and Plato,
who had an exalted opinion of the purity of its doctrines, confirms this antiquity. Hermeppius says
that the primitive Zoroaster was initiated by one Azanaces 5,000 years before the Trojan war, or, as is
supposed, 8,168 years ago; Endoxes says that he lived 6,000 years before the death of Plato, or 8,237
years ago. In its proper place we will take the rites of the Aryan Mysteries of Mythras. Heckethorn
asserts that the Indian Gymnosophists were the disciples of the early Magi, and that these Magi had
{25} put forth 5,000 years before the Iliad was written the three grand poems of the Zend Avesta,
the first ethical; the second military; and the third scientific. They taught the duality of nature as
exemplified in light and darkness, heat and cold, summer and winter, good and evil, of which two
principles, in the revolving cycles, the good would become paramount.
Ernest de Bunsen says that it is proved that the three grades of the Jewish
Rabbinical school are an exact parallel of the three grades of the Magi; that it was a secret school of
Scribes, its highest teaching embracing the doctrine of the indwelling Holy Spirit in man, and that
Jesus was a Rabboni. The Babylonian Rabu corresponding with the Hebrew Rab, the Mobed with
the Rabbi, and the Destur Mobed with the Rabban or Rabboni. The Persian Mazda is equally styled
Ahmi yat Ahmi -- I am that I am.<<"Miscell. N. & Q." (Gould, 1894), xii, p. 304.>>
The British or Celtic Druids were a priesthood that had features common to the Eastern Magi, and
were divided into three classes denominated Bards, Ovates, and Druids. Michaelet says that it is
wonderful the analogy which the names of the gods of Ireland -- Axire, Axceavis, Coismaoil, Cabir,
bear to the Cabiri.<<"Freemasons Mag.," 1860, i, p. 166.>> The evidence of Strabo is to the same effect, as he says that the British Druids practise the same religious rites as existed at Samothrace. They
cause their ancient progenitor to exclaim: "I am a Druid, I am an architect, I am a prophet, I am a
serpent." We shall see that the Cabiric Rites were the prerogative of priests and architects, embodying the drama of a murdered god. There can be small doubt that the Irish legend of Gobham-Saer,
the son of Turibi of the Strand, who was murdered with his
12 companions by 12 robbers, is a vulgarised exoteric reference to the murdered Cabir and the 12
signs of the Zodiac. O Brien says that he was a Guabhres or Cabiri, and that Saer has the signification
of son of God. He advocates in his {26} "Round Towers" the Phoenician origin of these buildings
with their appropriation by later Christian Monks; often, as at Glendalough, seven small chapels, or
altars, are attached. It is possible, as has been maintained, that north Europe was the centre whence
the Orientals derived their legends, and that Chaldean, whence Culdeean, was as appropriate to the

Druids as to the Babylonian, and that as the Essenians were Babylonians, the Culdees were Essenes, as held by the venerable Bede, and thus the Essenes, or Assidiana, were Culdees.

The chief British gods were Hu and Ceridwen, or the Ouranos and Ghe of the Cabiri; and it is worthy of mention that there are Druidical unhewn stones and temples in cruciform, the one in the island of Lewes consists of 12 stones each limb having three, and the subterranean of New Grange in Ireland is also

cruciform. Higgins in his "Celtic Druids," mentions in Scotland as prechristian, a crucifix on one side of which is a lamb, and on the other an elephant.

There is nothing very remarkable in the prechristian existence of such cruciform structures, in Italy it predates architecture, and the Rev. Baring Gould points out that there are in South Italy lakedwellings of an immense antiquity where the cross-form is of greater antiquity than the bronze age. The cyclopean temple at Gazzo is built on the basis of a Latin cross, and hence it was a religious emblem of the Cabiri. It is found in India in the most ancient cave of Elephanta, and is equally an emblem in central America. There are also two prechristian caves in Ireland of this form.<<See "Freemasons Magazine," 1857. p. 276.>> We mentioned its use by the Maori race.

Toland points out that the three divisions of the Druidical system which we have mentioned must not be taken as progressional degrees. They were three classes corresponding to Soothsayers, Physicians, and Prophets. The last, or the Druid class, had four degrees conferred at intervals of 3, 6, and 9 years. The Bards and Ovates {27} were each divided into three classes with special functions.<<"Toland," quoting Jones.>> Taliesin as an initiate exclaims -- "Thrice was I born, now I know how to acquire all knowledge by meditation." The emblem of the Druid was a vitrified egg, chased in gold, and hung from the neck, and which held up to the light shewed a sacred token; the "Serpents," or Druids, prepared it.

It is generally accepted that the theology of these sacred Colleges, even in the most ancient times, taught the existence of one sole power or creator of the visible universe, though triplicated in His manifestations, and that from Him proceeded the minor gods, angels, and demi-gods. He, the one, was Dyaus in Sanscrit, Zeus in Greek, Tiu in Teutonic, the ancient inscriptions and books of the Egyptians place it beyond doubt; the Chinese, the Magi, Hindus, Hebrews, etc., all add confirmation, and various other proofs are adduced in the work entitled "Natural and Revealed Religion" of our brother the Chevalier Ramsay. It is immaterial by what name the prophet, or outteller, who revealed this doctrine whether Taut, Fohi; Zaradust, Rama; Enoch or Edris whose pupil Abram, or great-father, was; the doctrine of one God, uncreated, incorporeal, all-seeing, all-powerful, everywhere present, and dwelling incomprehensibly in his own unity, gleams out through the darkness of the ages. And though the doctrine admits of minor deities as agents of the Supreme the dogma of unity formed the background of all the ancient religious Mysteries, coupled with that of divine incarnations, and that indwelling holy spirit in men, which makes him equal with the minor gods.

The examples which we have given of an arcane society divided into degrees, so widely separated by locality, by language, and by manners, from data existing some thousands of years ago, unmistakably point to a much more ancient derivation from a common centre, unless we admit an intuitive need for some such system. We {28} find equally the same widespread distribution of geometrical symbols intended to typify Theosophical truths, and embracing cosmogony and creation. It is held that each symbol represented a letter, a colour, a number and a sound, thus constituting an esoteric hieroglyphic understood by the Initiates of every country. As an example we might easily arrange a set of very ancient symbols forming little understood Masonic emblems, and equally carved by operative masons on the ancient ruins of Asia, India, and Egypt, and these might again be applied on the plan of the old

Philosophers to the recondite mysteries of nature. Take the following as numerals
I, II or V. {equilateral triangle with apex to top, square. Pentagram.
Hexagram. hexagram circumscribed. cube. cube circumscribed.} 10.
In mystic crosses of equal antiquity with all our other emblems we find the following forms, namely, {Symbols: reverse swastika. T. Ankh. X. Latin cross. Earth. Latin cross composed of two transparent rectangles}.
each having special application to a dogma.
We have already made slight allusion to the Cabiri, and all authorities are agreed that the Mysteries practised under this name were allied with the Cyclopean Masonry and its builders, and that those Rites and Buildings, in all countries, were the religion and architecture of a primitive race which preceded the Aryan invasions of Media, Babylon, India, Greece, and Egypt. The primitive inhabitants of Babylon, whom it has been agreed to term Akkadian, were more nearly allied in blood, language, and religion, with the Finlanders, Mongolians, early Egyptians, proto-Medes, Pelasgi, Etruscans, perhaps also American Indians, all so-called Turanian, than they were with the Elamites, Ethiopians, Arabians, and other Semites, or with the Hindu, Persian, and other Aryan races, that appear later on in the pages of resuscitated history. Yet there are actual traces of speculative Freemasonry, intimately allied with the religious Mysteries, amongst these primitive proto-Aryans. A clear explanation of these particulars does not admit of being printed, but every intelligent Free-Mason will be able to read, {29} what we may write, between the lines, and thus supply for himself what we may leave unexplained.
Recent discoveries go to prove that Palestine had its Cabiric or Magian Rites,
and that long before the invasion of the "brigand Joshua," the son of Nun, as an old inscription is said to term that scriptural warrior, Akkadian civilisation existed in Syria, and the legendary Cain, Abel, and Seth of Genesis, and their progeny, find their analogies in other of the religious Mysteries. But the Talmud or Mishna, which is a very ancient explanation of the Law, differs materially from "Genesis;" thus it is said that in the days of Cain s son Enoch, and in the days of Seth s son Enosh, the people made images of copper and wood to worship, and it is to Keenan the son of Enosh that the Talmud attributes the prophecies of the destruction of the world, which he wrote upon tablets of stone. Enoch is represented as a Hermit, and the word implies Initiation. Lamech when blind by age is said to shoot his progenitor Cain by the accident of an arrow, and further, in his grief, kills by accident his own son. Hence the traditional Lament of Lamech in Genesis which has been supposed to be a veiled confession of Initiation. The scriptural Tubal-Cain who was son of Lamech by the daughter of the Sethite Keenan seems to be equally a Cabiric legend in the Crysor of Sanconiathon the Phoenician historian, who is supposed to have lived as a contemporary of King

Solomon. Equally Tubal- Cain, and Crysor, is the Vulcan of Greek mythology. Sanconiathon says of this Crysor: -- "Men worshipped him as a god after his death and they called him Diamachius, or the great inventor, and some say his brother invented the making of walls and bricks. After these things, of his race were born two young men, one of whom was called Technites or the artist, the other Geinos Autochthon or earth born, or generated from the earth itself. These men found out to mix stubble with the brick earth, and to dry the bricks so made in the

sun."<<Cory s "Ancient Fragments," 1876, p. 8.>> {30} Sanconiathon further states that Upsistos was deified after he had been torn in pieces by wild-beasts, and that he was the father of Ouranos who invented sculpture, and of Tautus who invented hieroglyphics, and represented the constellations by pictures; he says also that in the third generation two Pillars were erected which were dedicated to "Fire" and "Wind."

According to F. von Schlegel there exists a tribe in Eastern Asia, in the mountains, that possesses an inverted history resembling the Cain and Abel legend, but with these people it is the youngest brother who out of envy at the success of his elder brother, in mining for gold and silver, drives him out of the fatherland into the East. This writer, in his "Philosophy of History" thinks that the wars of races, the giants and the Titans, may be traced in the Biblical legends, and he is inclined to identify the holy Sethite race with the seven holy Rishis of Brahminical tradition. He also supposes that the confession of Lamech may hint at the beginning of human sacrifice. As Cain s offering was the fruits of the earth, animal life ought to have been as sacred to him as to the Budists. As Cain was the eldest son Schlegel s view would make him the prototype of the Turanians, whilst Seth would represent the prehistoric Aryan; and these races the Talmud would again reunite in the posterity of Lamech, which does actually point to the union of religion and art.

As a matter of fact the Babylonian, Phoenician, and Jewish legends of the invention of the arts can only be looked upon as an attempt to explain the remote origin of these, something invented to please the curious, and to point out the early period at which these were supposed to have successively originated; the Persians have similar legends applied to their own people. But we are not without some proof to shew that an esoteric Masonic system was known to these early races, from which proceeded the "hundred families" that founded the Chinese culture. Owing to the researches of Professors de Lacomperie, {31} Douglas, and Ball, it has been established that the Bak tribes, which entered China about 4,000 years ago, had the archaic cuneiform character, and the customs of the tribes of Elam and Chaldea, which alone is sufficient to establish a community of race. The Yh-King, or Book of Changes, in its original form was about a sixth of its present extent and termed the Ku- wen, and is a vocabulary of the primitive cuneiform thus uniting with the other countries which used it. There can be no doubt that the primitive Mysteries were held in Groves, and that the Initiates, as in the Druidical Rites, were received "in the eye of day," the trials being rather moral than physical, the latter being a later stage, when the schools had somewhat degenerated, and temples specially adapted for the physical proofs began to be built.

Before we enter upon the nature of the CABIRIC MYSTERIES, and the Architecture termed CYCLOPEAN, we will endeavour to prove that in the most ancient times there was in existence an actual Society such as we now term Freemasonry. We will take first the

Chinese, who are the most primitive of civilised races, and still retain their monosyllabic language, represented by hieroglyphics of which each is the picture of a root-word, of such value that the characteristic meaning is understood throughout the Empire, even where the spoken language is mutually unintelligible. It is a culture concreted thousands of years ago amongst a race closely allied in language, religion, mythology, and astronomy with Akkadian Babylon. Moreover the archaic tablets of Thibet have

mystical allusions in consonance with the Mysteries, but we will allude to these in a later chapter. There occurred in the year 1879 in the District Grand Lodge of China a discussion upon the subject we have mentioned above, from which we learn that about 4,000 years ago this people had a symbolism identical with the Masonic Craft. An altar in form of a perfect cube was used to typify the earth, and this may be read in conjunction with what we wrote in our last chapter on the Maori {32} rites, the circle being an emblem of heaven, and "earth" and "heaven" in union were Cabiric deities. The N.E. and S.E. are relatively used to imply the beginning and conclusion of an object in view. One of the oldest words in the language is literally "square and compasses" and signifies right conduct. The skirret as an hieroglyphic signifies the origin of things. When the Emperor of a new dynasty succeeded he began the erection of a new temple under the oversight of a Grand Architect. Aprons were used which bore emblems denoting religious office -- there is a plant, an axe, and another not clear. The Shu-King, which is one of the oldest books in the language, gives the representation of two jewels in jadestone, which is one of the hardest and most valuable of all stones and the most difficult to work; these two are the square and the plumb-rule. The same book speaks of Chien jen, magistrates, which is literally "level men," implying what is expected of them; and the three chief officers of State are called the San chai, the three houses or builders; and one of the most ancient names of deity is the "First Builder." The Emperor Shun, about 3,000 years ago, had amongst his attributes the circle and rule; and the hammer in the hands of their kings was an emblem of authority. When a monarch died the emblems of authority were returned for the purpose of reinvestiture.<<The "Masonic Magazine" (Kenning).>> In Masonry this is done on election of a new Master.
We learn from the "Book of Odes" that when an Emperor sacrificed he
divested himself of his Imperial robes, was barefooted and bareheaded and girt with a lambskin. At the spring festival, which has much in common with the rites of the Grecian Ceres, we see following the procession a boy with one foot bare and the other shod, but which they apply to the "yang" and "yin," or the positive and negative principles of nature. Brother Chaloner Alabaster, from whom we copy some of these illustrations, says that this building symbolism was continued by the Chinese philosophers of the 5th century B.C. Thus we
{33} read in the "Great Learning" that "a man should abstain from doing unto others what he would not they should do unto him"; and the writer adds, "this is called the principle of acting on the square." Other similar expressions are used by Confucius 481 B.C.; and his later follower Mencius says, "that a Master Mason, in teaching his apprentices, makes use of the compasses and square; ye who are engaged in the pursuit of wisdom must also make use of the compasses and square."<<"Ars Quat. Cor.", ii, p. 12O, and iii, p. 14.>> Every trade in Japan has a Guild, and they are said to have been derived from China, by way of Korea, 3,000 years ago.

At the present time we are not thoroughly informed whether a system identical in all respects with that of China existed in Babylon, but there are indications that such was the case, as well as in Egypt, and we have already pointed out that Yh-King is an Akkadian vocabulary of root-words. Mr. St. Chad Boscawen has afforded us a note, where he treats of the ancient Calneh, about 3,800 B.C.<<"Modern Thought," 1883.>>; in this article he represents

the Viceroy Gudea as Patesi, or sceptre-bearer, subservient to the King of Erech, and terms him the chief priest and architect as well, his palace indicating the art influence of Egypt. His statue represents him as seated and having the right arm and shoulder bare; on his knees is a tablet containing a plan, or what Modern Masons term a Tracing-board, of his palace or temple; the edge of this tablet is divided into a scale of 20 3/10 inches to the cubit, a measure corresponding with that used in Egypt. Brother W. H. Rylands deems that this cubit may have divided the plan into chequered squares though not shewn thereon. Pure copper images of the Cabiri have been disinterred at Calneh.

Very strong philological grounds have been shewn by Dr. Miller in his "Har- moad" for identifying the Chinese Masonic system with Babylon, and this must be read in the light of the remarks we have made thereon. {34}

One of the earliest Akkadian Kings named Lik-baga was a pyramid builder and, like Melchisedek, a king and priest of the Most High; he uses as a title the term Pa-teshi, which is thus literally translated "Pa" -- anoint, "te" -- corner stone, "shi" -- to strike; and the same term is used by his successors. Patasso is a hammer, and the term Patoeci was the habitual designation of the images of the gods of the Cabiric Mysteries. Lik-baga seems to have modified Akkadian theology and was the crowned architect and apostle of Sin (moon), Samas (sun), Bel, and Anu. Another term used by these kings, and applied by Nebuchadnezzar to the most ancient kings, is Pa-teshi tsi-ri, which is translated Sublime Master by Dr. Schrader; it is connected with the Hebrew Pat-tish, a hammer, or the Cabiric hammer in the hand of Tubal-Cain or the Greek Vulcan. With the Akkadians the god of coppersmiths had the same name as the god of ironworkers amongst the Laplanders, and the words for iron and copper are the same respectively.<<"Chaldean Magic" -- Lenormant.>> It is, however, through the Aryan Sanskrit that we can more particularly trace the assimilation of Akkad to a building fraternity, for the word Ak means to pierce, Akra is a sharp point, Akri is corner, Akana is a stone, Aktan is the number eight or the angles which are in a cube. Akman in Sanscrit is a stone and in Persian heaven, and as a cube symbolises the eight cosmogonical powers, the word comes to imply the whole heavens. In Greek, which is an Aryan tongue, the name of the father of Ouranos is Akmon, and Diodorus makes Ur, or Ouranos and Ops children of Akmon and parents of the Titans, who are again the Cabiri. Akmon is also an anvil, which means a meteorolite, from which iron was first made, for in Greek Sideros is iron and related to the Latin Sidus, a star. The word Ak in the Akkadian signifies to build or to make, hence we have ta-ak, tak, tag, a stone or mountain, and akka, a building temple or sanctuary; these significations further connect Akkad, or proto-Aryan, with the Hindus and their architecture. {35} Ak is also the monogram of Nabu who is Mercury, Marduk, whence Nimrod; Nabu is therefore Mercury, and the Hermes of Egypt, the revealing God. In Semitic Assyrian abn is stone, abni stones, banah (Heb. benah) is to build. The learned Alexander Wilder<<Gould s "N. & Q.", xiii, p. 296.>> expresses an opinion that Nimrod, founder of Babylon, was of Tartar descent, in which language the word means "spotted," and may point to the leopard skin in which the Assyrian priests of Dionnisi were clothed. If Nimrod personates Kronos, as some hold, he was in that case a Cabiri or king of the race of Cyclopean builders.

From all this it is argued, with much soundness, that the first kings were both priests and architects, or the Grand Masters of these, and of the class of Cabiri who were first workers in stone and brick, and afterwards in metals, and that they transmitted a traditional doctrine of the temple, based upon cosmogony and the creation of the world.<<"Ars Quat. Cor.," v, pt. 2.>> It explains why Genesis assimilates the worldly arts with religion, and shews the high respect the Hebrew priests had for art, though deficient in practice. The Babylonians must have afforded information to Ezra who revised the Jewish Bible, and it may be pointed out that these people were builders in brick rather than stone, and hence that the practice of art would vary in a country with that in which stone was used.
CABIRIC MYSTERIES AND CYCLOPEAN WORK.

When we approach historic times we find that the actual Cabiric Mysteries were of Grecian continuation and perpetuated at Samothrace where they had been in existence, from a remote era, far into Christian times, and where they were held in great veneration, not only for their antiquity but for the purity of their doctrine. They are said to have retained much of their technique in the Chaldean language, and to have preserved much of the Masonic symbolism which we have seen in Chinese practise, {36} for the aboriginal inhabitants of Greece, Pelasgians, were an allied race, and Dr. Petrie asserts that pre- Hellenic, or proto-Aryan Greeks, were in Egypt, either as friends or captives, 2,500 B.C., with a civilisation all their own. Barbarous wars arose, the Aryan Hellenes devastated the country, and during an era of oppression reduced the old inhabitants to subjection; we find them denominated Pelasgi with a succession of 26 kings followed by 7 priests. Egypt eventually sent them rulers who restored their country to prosperity, founded cities and gave them laws. Upon this we learn that the Cabiric Mysteries were in practice at Samothrace, and that they were, or had been, a fraternity which combined art with religion. Herodotus says that Samothrace had these Mysteries from the Pelasgi, and that they taught the initiated by a sacred tradition, why the figure of Hermes, Mercury, or Casmillus was constructed in a peculiar manner, from which we gather that they used Phallic symbols as emblems of the generative powers of nature; and this historian, who wrote 450 B.C., tells us that the names of their gods were derived from Egypt, as anciently they used the general term "Disposers."
The views of all authorities are in unison with those of Frederick von
Schlegel, who says that this primitive people were the constructors of the Cyclopean buildings of Greece and Italy, being the original inhabitants who were conquered and overrun by the Aryan immigration of Deucalion, that they were a people who had the traits in common with those of many other countries, at a remote period.<<"Philosophy of History," p. 234.>>
Before we consider their Mysteries we will say something of their architecture; a style which is of prehistoric antiquity. It was very massive, and built of irregular and well-bound blocks of immense size, so well knit that though without cement a knife blade would not enter the joints, and so placed that a large block might be withdrawn without endangering the structure. The French {37} Institute, in 1804, traced about 150 towns which were in part, at least, Cyclopean, and 127 of these were

in Europe. Strabo says that the

builders were from Syria in Asia Minor, by which he means Assyria; the same writer mentions vast caverns in Argos which had been converted into a Labyrinth by the Cyclops; and here was a statue of the father of the gods, which had a third eye in the middle of the forehead, and which was said to have been brought from the palace of Priam at Troy, an Asiatic city intimately connected with Assyria.

Pliny states that in the island of Lemnos, the home of the Cabiric Mysteries, there was a Labyrinth of 150 columns, each stone of which might be moved by a child; hence we learn that they resembled the rocking stones of the Druids; and Dr. Daniel Clarke found a stone circle at the top of Mount Gargarus, where the gods, according to Homer, assembled at the siege of Troy.<<"Anacalypsis.">> Pliny attributes the working of iron to their invention, and the first inhabitants of Sicily are said to be of this race. Achilles Statius, bishop of Alexandria, mentions a statue in a temple on Mount Cassius, between Syria and Egypt, which held a pomegranate in the hand; it is a temple which Sanconiathon deems to have been built by the descendants of the Cabiri.<<Mackey s "Cyclo. Art. Pomegranate.">>

This peculiar Masonry is found upon the summits of mountains, a position in which Homer places the Cyclops and the Lastragons, and Theocritus the establishments of the old Pelasgi. As it demanded a large exertion of physical strength the later, but still ancient, Greeks attributed the work to giants who had an eye in the middle of the forehead as had Priam s statue of their deity. Mythology makes them sons of Neptune and Amphitrite, whom Jupiter overthrew and cast into Tartarus where they become the assistants of Vulcan; thus assigning a sea-pedigree to these workers in iron and stone, and typifying an enforced slavery by their {38} Aryan conquerors. They are fabled to have made the sickle of the Greek Kronos or Saturn, whom the Latins made the god of agriculture, in whose reign a ship grounded at Samothrace, where the passengers settled and erected a temple for their Mysteries. It is further pretended that these Cyclops constructed for Jupiter a cubical altar of brass upon which the father of gods took his oath before attacking the Titans, and upon this altar was engraved the name of Deity. Three principal Cyclops are mentioned -- Brontes, Steropes, and Paracmai. We see that like Hiram, who has credit for building the temple of Solomon, the Cyclopean Cabiri were not only skilled builders in stone but workers in brass and iron, a race subject to Vulcan, and that all this long preceded the introduction into Greece of a Masonry of flat and squared stones, which came into use about the time of the Egyptian colonisation, after the ages of barbarism occasioned by the Aryan wars.

Besides India, which we have mentioned in its cave temples, and Greece,

other nations have this ancient style of Masonry, and Syria, under Babylonian influence, has many traces of it, older than the invasion of Joshua and the Abri, and it is quite possible that the Hebrew invaders had much of their special bias from the school of Melchisedek, King of Salem.

It has been shewn by Monsieur Perotti that some of the most ancient ruins in Palestine are Cyclopean, or as he terms them Pelasgian, and he instances some at Ephrata or Zelzah, in other places are later ruins of a mixed style, built compositely of polygonal and squared blocks; at Rama is a doorway resembling, on a small scale that of Atreus at Mycenae;<<"Freemasons Mag.," 1862, viii, p. 384.>>

Cyclopean ruins exist also at Bashan and Baalbec. The Rev. Brother

Fosbrooke says: "The abacus of the gate of lions at Mycenae, which was built by the Cyclops, supports four balls or circles, which are again surrounded by a second abacus, similar to the first. They are supposed to be {39} derived from the worship of Mythras, the lion being his symbol. The triangular form of the stone had a special signification. The Cyclops were worshippers of fire, Vulcan, and the sun."

Older and still more important than Mycenae is the recent discovery in Crete of the palace of Minos at Knossos, with its works of art, and its Dedalian labyrinth of passages and rooms, but more remarkable still tablets and records partly in hieroglyphics, and partly in alphabet.

In an article in the "Builder" in 1865, Monsieur Renan states that this style is the most ancient in the world, except it be the Pyramids, and he points out that Homer mentions the great strength of the walls of Tiryns and Mycenae in Argolis, the former of which is said to be 20 feet thick: the Etruscan style, he says, is derived from it, but when it had made a decided advance, as it indicates improved architectural knowledge. He also points out that wherever this Masonry is found there exists a tradition of an ancient race of giants, who have passed away or been destroyed, and he attributes the remains of this style in Palestine to the Anakim, Rephaim, and the Canaanitish tribes.<<Ibid, 1865, xii, p. 146.>>

"Britain." The Cyclopean architecture of the British isles is prominent and may range from 4,500 to 1,500 years antiquity,<<WEH NOTE: Carbon dated in modern times to be up to 8,000 years old as to wooden precursors.>> and are well described by Toland as they existed 200 years ago. Numerous circles of stone were dedicated to the sun: that in the isle of Lewes has 12 obelisks and a 13th in the centre representing the rudder of a ship, and reached by a passage of double obelisks each of 19 stones with a 39th guarding the entrance of the avenue. We have here the 12 signs of the Zodiac, the Sun, and the Druid cycle of 19 years. At St. Burien in Cornwall is a temple of 19 stones, each 12 feet distant, and a 20th of greater height in the centre, this may refer to the 19 years cycle of 12 months. In these temples a large altar was erected near which stood {40} the Cruimthear or priest, and adjacent are found prodigious stones which can be moved by a touch at the right place, whilst elsewhere they resist all the strength of man. Toland mentions one of these Cromleachs at Cruich, in Cavan, placed in the midst of 12 obelisks, covered with brass, on which stood statues of the gods, whilst the bowing-stone was covered with gold and silver.

The Circles of Stonehenge are 3,600 years old, according to the calculation of Professor Norman Lockyer, founded upon its orientation as a Sun-temple 1680 years B.C. This calculation is confirmed by the discovery in 1901, when making some repairs of the chippings from the two descriptions of stones, of which the two circles are composed, together with rude flint axes and hammers of the pre-bronze age, "i.e.", 1500 to 2000 B.C.

In the face of the varied authorities we have quoted it is not possible to come to any other conclusion than that the Cyclops were the primitive builders and workers in metals, and that their descendants the Cabiri were until we approach Christian times a religious and operative brotherhood which then became entirely speculative. There is a mythological groundwork for the assimilation of the various nations that practised the Cyclopean style. Plutarch quotes Anticlides as affirming that Isis was the daughter of Prometheus, who as

a revelator of arts was a Cabir, and wife to Dionysos or Bacchus, and Dionysius Halicarnassus says that Atlas left his habitation on Mount Caucasus and became King of Arcadia. Apollodorus affirms that this Atlas was son of Japhetus and brother to Prometheus. Pausanius informs us that the Arcadians were all Pelasgi, as were also the inhabitants of Argos, and that the Pelasgians had that name from a King Palagius.<<Bishop Cumberland; "Origenes.">> Dionisu is Assyrian, and also Indian as Dionysos, whilst admittedly Egyptian as Bacchus; hence the Dionysian artificers of Greece may have sprang out of the Cabiri. Raol Rochette considers that the Cyclop Palaemonius, to whom a Sanctuary was raised, was {41} the Tyrians Heracles.

H. P. Blavatsky says that the -builders of the sacred columns at Gadir covered them with mysterious characters and figures, of which the same is still found on the walls of Ellora, that gigantic ruin of the temple of Visvakarman styled "the builder and artificer of the gods." It is quite likely that the physical and superior strength of the Cyclops has a foundation in fact. Apart from the testimony of ancient writers, collected by men of the stamp of Grotius, in regard to the existence at one time of a race of giants, there has recently been discovered at Piedmont in Moravia the skeleton of a human family, side by side with the bones of the Mammoth, that of the man being of "extraordinary size."

At the Grotto of Rochers Rouges, Mentone, skeletons have been found under

29 feet of limestone stalagmite, which may be reckoned to represent 8,000 years, that of a male was 7ft. 9in. without head, and that of a female 6ft. 3in.

"Cabiric Mysteries." In order to arrive at an idea of the Cabiric Mysteries and their several great gods, or powers, we must recognise their antiquity, and the fact that their chief constellation was the Great Bear, the seven stars. Of the Pleiades a seventh star is said to be lost, "the six present the seventh hidden." We must also consider the most striking facts of nature, which led to the division of time into days, months, and years. The first measure of time is a contest between light and darkness, a day and a night, or what is now known to be a revolution of the earth round the sun. The next measure of time was the birth and death of the moon, or what we know as a monthly revolution of the moon round the earth. It would next be noted that the seven stars of the Great Bear makes a complete turn round in 365 days or thereabouts. The 13 lunar and 12 solar months in the annual birth and death of the sun is a later and more complicated calculation of a year, though it corresponds with the annual revolution of the seven stars round a polar centre, which was what the Cabiri plainly commemorated. {42}

The Sun was the Semitic, rather than the Cabiric symbol, and may possibly

be indicated in the archaic hymn of the Akkadian victory of Hea over the seven- headed serpent. Other changes of the symbolism succeeded and we have the seven gods applied to so many spheres, or to the planets, and finally anthropomorphised into seven gods of arts. We read<<II "Kings" xvii., v. 30.>> "The men Of Babylon made Succoth Benoth," which is understood to be the image worship of the Pleiades. The late Doctor Walker Arnott asserted that none could comprehend Masonic ritual without a full knowledge of Hebrew astronomy. These considerations tend to prove the greater antiquity of the Cabiric system, as preceding the Mysteries that made a dying god of our solar orb; and it has also a higher scientific basis, as implying the origin of systems from that far distant central sun, round which all the globes revolve. It is on these natural phenomena, spiritualized in the Mysteries, that their ceremonies

are founded. Apollodorus and Varro say that the Cabiri adored the heavens and earth under the names of Ouranos and Ghe as the creators of mankind: Hindu spirit and matter.

According to Sanconiathon and the Phoenicians, the Cabiri were the eight sons of Sadyk, of whom the youngest, named Eshmun or Akmon, or in the Greek version Cadmillus or Casmillus, was slain by the others. Misor, the brother of Sadyk, was father of Taut, and received the inheritance of Egypt, and the Cabiri record it, a claim that the most ancient inhabitants of Egypt were of this ritual. Of these eight, three were most noted, and were termed by the Greeks Axieros, Axiochersos, and Axiocheres, and as "xi" is but the Greek "chi" it has been suggested<<Dr. Tytler, in "F.M. Mag.">> that these names may be transmuted into Chaldean as Ahea, Ashur, Ahea, which is equal to I am that I am. Mr. Edward C. King<<"Akkadian Genesis," p. 59; "Exodus" iii. v. I4; Ahih Ashr Ahih.>> reads these words Aya, Asher, Aya, and {43} when Theodoret asked a Jew the true pronunciation of the sacred name HB:YH YH, the Jew said "ya," and wrote "aya," for he was not permitted by his law to pronounce the sacred name. Equally in Masonry there is a Word which can be written but not pronounced, and there is a mode of uttering that word which cannot be written. Some writers suppose that the three Cabiri, or Corybantes, symbolise sun, moon, and earth, in the contest between which one is supposed to be slain in eclipse, and quote the words of Hesiod -- "Stained with blood and falling by the hands of two celestial bodies." One of the gods was named Eubulos, pronounced very similarly to three words used in "Ancient" Masonry, which had a reference to Solomon s temple, which all ancient writers admit was a type of the universe.

The slain Casmillus had the same signification as the Osirian sun-god, and

in the Phoenician, Babylonian, and Egyptian books, and cosmogonies are some curious references which may typify circumcision, the Mythraic baptism of blood, and the Taurobolium or baptism of bull s blood, which is referred to in the Phrygian version of the Cabiric rites. Thus, on the authority of Philo Byblus, we have it in the legend of Kronos that he sheds his son s blood as a propitiation to his father Ouranos and circumcised his family, and from the words used it would seem that this was symbolically acted in the Mysteries. In another legend, El castrates his father Ouranos in order to fertilise the rivers, in which is found the first germ of life. Again Bel Merodach cuts open the dragon Tiamat, or chaos, from which he proceeds. In the Egyptian "Ritual of the Dead" it is said: "the blood is that of the sun as he goes along cutting himself."

Masonic writers tell us that the Initiated symbolically embrued his hands in

the blood of the slain Casmillus. These murdered gods, as in the case of Osiris and Adonis, usually suffer in the generative parts, indicative of the transfer of the life principle, and it is said mythologically that when the two other gods slew Casmillus they fled {44} with a chest containing his genitals to Etruria, in which we have doubtless a notice of colonisation.

The Cabiric gods were held to be the instructors of mankind in all useful knowledge; magical rites, building, smelting and working in metals, shipbuilding, music, etc., and were denominated Technites or artificers. Sanconiathon says that Ouranos was the father of Sculptors, as was Hiram the father or Abiv of Masons, metal workers, carvers, and dyers, and in verity a Cabir. Faber considers that the term Fabri by which the Latins designated

Artificers in general is derived from Cabiri, and he also asserts that "all the most ancient remarkable buildings of Greece, Egypt, and Asia Minor were ascribed to Cabirian or Cyclopean Masons."<<Faber, "Cab." i. p. 35.>>

As the rites also professed to instruct the candidate in incantations such as we know were used by the Akkadians of Babylon that alone would indicate identity of origin. The learned Hyde attributes the name Cabir to Gabri, Guebri, fire or sun worshippers; and as the slain god is named Akmon, which word also means a cube of eight angles, heaven or Ouranos, it is therefore equivalent to the Semitic Ur and Urim, and remotely to Hiram, whose father Josephus says was named Ur.

It is said that the Initiatory ceremony into the Mysteries of Samothrace lasted three days and was termed "Enthronement," and that mystic dances representing the motions of the heavenly bodies were performed round the throne, which connects the rite with astronomy. A white-stone was presented to the Initiate as a symbol of membership. Hives of bees were preserved in the temple, and the interior cavern or Sanctuary contained a pyramidical chamber as its most sacred place. Heckethorn asserts that in the Phrygian branch of these Mysteries they had a pine tree cut to form a cross, with the figure of a man upon it, and the same thing is asserted of the British Druids. The tomb of Midas in Phrygia is adorned with the, equal-limbed cross, or the modern Greek

{45} form. Eusebius, who can see only the worst side of the Mysteries, writes of them in the same style as the modern secularist upon the scriptures. Ection, he says, founded the Samothracian Mysteries, and Venus sprang from the member of Uranus which was thrown into the sea, wherefore a lump of salt is the symbol of generation. These are what the Phrygians celebrate as the rites to Attys, Cybele, and the Corybantes. Certain signs were, "I have eaten out of the tambourine. I have drank out of the cymbal. I have carried the mystic salver. I have slipped into the bed." Similar expressions are found amongst the Druids, and were known to the Eleusenian initiates. They are but allegories and not actual rites.

Clemens of Alexandria speaking of these Mysteries says: -- "Know that having killed their third brother they covered the head of the dead body with a purple cloth, crowned it (or encircled it with a chaplet), and carrying it on the point of a spear (or bearing it on a brazen shield), buried it under the roots of Olympus. The Mysteries are in short murders and funerals."<<"Ars Quat. Cor." v., p. 173.

-- "Exhort," ch. ii., also "Eiusebius," prep. "Gos." c. iii., b. 2.>> Where two gods murder a third the reference may be to two seasons and winter.

"Babylon." We will now glance at the Babylonian contemporaries of these Cyclops or Cabiri. Berosus the Chaldean historian records that the civilisation of Babylon was derived from a god who was half man and half fish, and who rose each day out of the Erythrean sea, and Lepsius has expressed the opinion that the legend points to Egyptian sources. The faith of the old Akkadians was of a magical nature in which amulets, as in the Cabiric Mysteries, played a leading part. They adored the spirits of nature and the elements, whom they believed to be ruled by three great gods -- Anu the supreme; Hea the ruler of the earth from his heavenly boat; and Mulgi the lord of the underworld or Hades. Each of these had his feminine consort. Hea is the counterpart of the Hebrew {46} Jehovah, he walks with, talks with, and instructs mankind; and a hymn, which is possibly the most ancient in the world, describes his power and might and his victory over the seven-headed serpent, a metaphor equally found

in Lapland, Thibet, Egypt, India, Greece, and even Yucatan. These Akkadians were, like the Egyptians and Mayaux, pyramid builders, and the ruins of Babel or Borsippa is of this nature. It came to be called the temple of the Bit-zida or of the right hand, and there is an ancient cylinder which represents a seven- stepped pyramid, at the top of which is a colossal hand, and eight worshippers, corresponding to the Cabiric gods surround the pyramid in worship.

The locality of Babylon gave them in speculation two "Great Pillars," the "Mount of the world," in the northeast, or Ararat, which they also termed "the abode of the gods," and which was to them what Meru was to the Aryans, and a corresponding mount in the south west, whence was the descent to the domain of Mulgi the ruler of the dead; which descent was alleged to be guarded by seven concentric walls, with one gate in each wall. All the great mountains of the East are represented as the residences of a spiritualised race.

At a remote period the priests had composed an epic in twelve books answering to the Zodiacal signs over which the sun-god journies -- in Akkadian Isdhubhar, in Egyptian Heracles, in Tyrian Melcarth. It commences the first book or month with the siege of Ghizdubar or Isdhubhar in Erech -- it is light which overcomes darkness. In the second and third the hero resorts for comfort to the prophet Heabani. In the fourth and fifth there is war, figuring the elemental storms. In the sixth and seventh we have the lives and disorders of the hero and Ishter, believed to refer to the moon s changes. Ishtar descends into Hades, like Ceres of Greece, to seek aid from Mulgi, and is divested of some portion of her apparel at each gate of the seven walls. In the eighth and ninth we have the wanderings of the hero and a Paradisical garden. In {47} the tenth the hero is ferried over the Styx that he may be restored to health by Tamzi, the translated Sage. The eleventh is a similar account of the deluge to that in Genesis. The twelfth commemorates the death of Heabani.

In analogy with this sacred number seven, the tower of Babel had seven stories, and Herodotus informs us that Ecbatana in Media was guarded by seven concentric walls, each of which, as were the stories of Babel, was painted to represent one of the seven spheres or planets. The Mythraic Mysteries though proto-Median in their conception, were Aryan when we become historically acquainted with them, and they had seven caverns of Initiation approached by gates in a pyramid of seven landings, and the trials of Initiation are doubtlessly allegorised by the ancient Persian poet Ferdusi, in the Heft- Khan or labours of Rustam. In this the implication is obvious that the mythology was more ancient than the erections which symbolised it, old as these are in the world s history. The tower of Babel or Borsippa, "which had been left unfinished since the deluge," was completed by Nebuchadnezzar with the addition of an eighth story "according to the original design"; this last consisted of a "cubical chamber" as a shrine for the god, the appointments being of gold.

The oldest temple in the world is said to have been discovered by excavators at Biaya in Central Babylonia. The walls of the tower were first uncovered and the summit cleared. The first inscription on the surface was brick stamped with the name Dungi of 2750 B.C. A little lower appeared a crumpled piece of gold with the name Param Sim who lived in 3750 B.C. ("Freemasons Chronicle," 15 Aug., 1908.)

In his "Seven Great Monarchies," Professor George Rawlinson terms the Tower of Babel the "Birs-i-Nimrod," the ancient temple of Nebo at Borsippa. It

was a perfect square of seven ascents or stages, 272 feet at base, each way, the four corners facing the Cardinal points, and the {48} seven stages occupying a height of 156 feet, the highest of all was a perfect cube and the Sanctuary of the God. Rawlinson s arrangement of these is as follows: --

STAGE. COLOUR. PLANET.

Basement, Black, Saturn. Second Stage, Orange, Jupiter. Third " Blood Red, Mars.

Fourth " Golden, Sun. Fifth " Pale Yellow, Venus. Sixth " Azure, Mercury. Seventh " Silver, Moon.

A similar symbolic plan existed in India, for we find Seven Courts of which the last, or central ones, have no canopy, but that of the heavens. In Egypt, the most ancient of the Pyramids, that of Saccarah, consisted of Seven Stages, the same thing equally existed in Mexico.

All the wonderful works wrought by the god Hea upon earth were performed by virtue of an omnific Word, which would seem to have been lost to the Magi, though the ancient priests of Egypt appear to have claimed that they possessed it, and they had a god "whose name is hidden." The Jewish belief as to the power of the Ineffable name of their God JHVH -- Yahvah, Yihvah, or as we, incorrectly, use it Jehovah, would seem to be based on these beliefs. Yahvah reads, He causes to bring forth.

"Assyria." A complete fusion of the Akkadian and Semitic faiths had taken place before 2500 B.C., and the population had become known as Chaldean. Assyria, civilised from Babylon, rose into power, though its precise beginning has not been traced. About 1820 B.C., Samsi-Vul built at Assur a temple to Anu and Vul, and Iritak built one called the "House of Salvation." Samsi-Vul also repaired the temple of Ishter then at Nineveh. About 1350 B.C. Budil built a palace at Assur which his successor Vul-Nerari I. enlarged and which his son Shalmaneser 1300 B.C. still further extended; he also restored the great temple called the "Mountain of the world"; he further built the new city of Caleh, about 18 miles from Nineveh, founded a palace at the latter place, and repaired the temple of Ishter there. His son Tugulti-Ninip {49} assumed the title of "King of Nations, King of Sumar and Akkad, and conqueror of Karduniyas" (Babylon). The next great builder was Tiglutli-Pileser, 1120 B.C., he rebuilt the temple of Assur, after a lapse of 701 years and raised there two pyramidical towers; he also improved the palaces of Assur and Nineveh, and left his country one of the foremost monarchies of the world. His tablet, in the British Museum, represents him with a Maltese cross which hangs from the breast, and there is also one of another king having the like decoration.

There is a somewhat remarkable Assyrian confirmation of the antiquity of the

Masonic system of consecration to be found in the inscriptions. When Cyrus King of Persia discovered the foundation of his early predecessor in Assyria, Assur-bani-pal, he says -- "I laid the foundation and made firm the bricks; with beer, wine, oil, and honey."<<"Records of the Past," iv, p. 171.>> Other inscriptions mention oil, and the sacrifice of animals. The foundation cylinder of

Naboniadus, a Babylonian King conquered by Cyrus, speaks of the discovery

of the foundation-stone of the temple built by Naram-sin, son of Sargon of Akkadia the Semitic conqueror of Babylon 3,200 years earlier. Recent digging is said to carry Babylonian data to 8000 B.C.

Something of the nature of caste initiation must also have existed amongst the Augurs and Sacred Scribes. Professor Sayce in his "Hibbert Lectures" has to this effect -- A tablet states that an Augur must be, "of pure lineage unblemished in hand or foot," and speaks thus of the vision which is revealed to him before he is "initiated and instructed, in the presence of Samas and Rimmon, in the use of the book and stylus," by "the Scribe, the instructed one, who keeps the oracle of the gods," when he is made to descend into an artificial imitation of the lower world and there beholds "the altars amid the waters, the treasures of Anu, of Bel, and Hea, the tablets of the gods, the delivery of the oracle of heaven and earth, and the cedar tree, the beloved of the great gods, which their {50} hands have caused to grow." It is thought that each sign of the Babylonian Zodiac had its special order of priests, in all twelve.

In very many countries the eternal stability and power of the deity was

represented by a square block or cube stone. Maximus Tyrius speaking of the worship of some god by the Arabians says -- "The statue that I saw of him was a square stone." Phurnutus speaking of the figuration of Hermes or Mercury says -- "As the square figure betokens his solidity; so he wanted neither hands or feet to execute what he was commanded by Jove."<<Toland s "Druids.">>

Some approximation of the very ancient flourishing period of the Cabiric Mysteries may be formed upon consideration that the Nagon-wat of Cambodia contains Cabiric sculpture in its architecture; the fish-man or Dagon of Babylon, and equally with every nation, including the Mayas of America, the monkey god. No one now knows what people erected the place, but Blavatsky, who is good testimony on a point of this nature, maintains that whoever built Nagon-wat were of the same religion and race as those who built the ancient Pagodas, the Egyptian pyramids, and the ruins of Ellora, Copan, and Central America.

"Egypt". If we now turn to Egypt we find it accepted by scholars that its earliest known population were allied with the Akkads of Babylon, by language and religion. Besides the affinity of the ancient Coptic to the Chinese and Chaldean speech, it is admitted that before the Osirian worship became general, and it is as old as Menes the first King of Egypt, there was an identity of religion; and that the seven gods of Memphis represented in the worship of Ptah -- the potter who creates the world out of the mundane egg -- and his minor gods, are identical with the gods of the Cabiri. The greater antiquity of Egypt would seem to be proved by the mutations of the methods of writing, for the Egyptians besides their Hieratic and Domatic alphabet, reserved the hieroglyphic system for {51} sacred things; the Domatic was then used for secular matters, and the Hieratic for their sacred manuscripts. This latter alphabet they transmitted to Phoenicia, whence through Greece and Rome, in a gradually modified state, it forms the characters of our own times. But when the Akkadians settled in Babylon they were already possessed of the cuneiform alphabet, and although the exact locality where this was developed has not yet been settled, it is possible that they carried it with their language and religion by way of Bactria from their primitive home in the Caucasian highlands, or those of central Asia. The Egyptian Sesun, the Babylonian Nabu, the Akkadian and Aryan Ak, and the Chinese diagrams called the Kouas, introduced into the

primitive Yh-King at a later period, all have the same relation and are equally represented by eight parallel lines in two fours. The "Ritual of the Dead" or Manifestations of Light, contains allusions to the Cabiric constellation of the Great Bear or seven stars, who are equally the seven sons of Ptah; the seven spirits of Ra; the seven companions of King Arthur; the seven Hohgates of America; the seven Lumazi or leaders of the star flock of Assyria; they may also be applied to the seven Amashpands of Persia, the seven Rishis of India, and seven spirits that surround the throne of God. Mr. W. St. Chad Boscawen asserts that at a remote period, a close intercourse existed between Egypt and Chaldea, the point of junction of the two civilisations being the peninsula of Sinai. The old legends of Chaldea and the old hymns of Eridu which, on the evidence of silt, are assigned a period of 6,000 years B.C., betray a culture derived from a maritime people; Eridu, like Memphis, was called the "Holy City," and in Chaldea we find a god named Asari and in Egypt Heseri or Osiris, whilst in India we have Iswari.

At the remote period of which we are writing we have no written account of
the nature of the Mysteries practised either in Egypt or Chaldea, and we must judge the secret rites, by what we can ascertain of them at a later {52} period; we know, however, that that which was applicable to the Cabiric gods of Greece and Chaldea was also applicable to the seven sons of Ptah at Memphis. Sanconiathon informs us that in the time of one of the most ancient hierophants, they had corrupted their Mysteries by mingling cosmogonical affections with the historical traditions; from which we see that before his time they had diverged from the Cabiric ritual. It is very noteworthy that Egypt was the most prosperous during the eras which followed the accession of Menes their first King. Most of the arts known at this day, and some which we do not know, are pictured in the earliest tombs, and these include gold mining and smelting, Cabiric claims, of which we accept Tubal-Cain as the father on Hebrew evidence.

It was the custom of the priestly caste to confer Initiation upon a new
Pharaoh, as was the case in Babylon, and there are traces of art symbolism to be found in the earliest times. Thus the Cubit rule was the sacred symbol of Truth; and we are told by Diodorus that the ancient Hieratic alphabet, distinguished from the Domatic or common, was of this nature, as it made use of the tools of carpenters, and he instances the hatchet, pincers, mallet, chisel, and square. The most ancient ruins contain Masons Marks, such as the point within a circle, the triangle, the trowel, the tau, and triple-tau. We give here a part of the first chapter of the "Book of the Dead;" the work is of a composite character and commingles the Memphian theology of Ptah with that of the Theban Amen, and the Osirian theology. The copies also vary according to the social position of the dead for whose burial the copies were intended.

"I am a Priest in Abydos in the day that the earth rejoiceth, I see the secret places of the winding region,
I ordain the festival of the spirit, the Lord of the abiding land, I hear the watchword of the watchers over me,
I am the Architect of the great barge of Sochais, (Ptah.) Building it from the stocks   (a temple Sym-

bol.)

Oh! ye Liberators of Souls, ye Builders of the house of Osiris, {53} Liberate the Soul of the Osirian (Name of deceased.)

He is with you in the house of Osiris, He sees as you see, hears as you hear, He stands as you stand, sits as you sit, O! ye that give meat and drink,

To the souls built into the house of Osiris, (living stones.) Give seasonable food and drink to the Osirian . . . (Name.) I do not compute my justification in many parts,

My soul stands up square to the face of tbe Judge, It is found true on the earth." (Guild Symbolism.)

Another passage says -- "As the sun died and rose again yesterday, so man dies and rises again." There are many passages in the Ritual which clearly imply secret Initiation. The representations of the Judgment Hall of Osiris -- the living one, the Master of life, the Master of all, in all his creation, names, functions, diadems, ornaments, palaces, etc., is of a very impressive character, and has been incorporated with the Christianity of later times. In some of the papyrus MSS., both in hieroglyphic and hieratic characters, 3- 4,000 years old, the spirit appearing for justification stands between Isis and Nepthys pictured with the sign of a Fellow Freemason; in others he is holding up both arms, representing two squares; in this following the written statement that he stands "square" before his judge.

Each district of Egypt had its Trinity of Gods: -- Thebes, in the 14th century

B.C. had the "hidden god," Amen, "Maker of all things; Thou only one"; Muth (mother) Mother Nature; Khensu (the child): in the 4th century B.C. we have Amen or Khepura (creator); Tefunt (humidity); Shu (light). Abydos had Osiris, Isis, and Horus. Elephantine -- Khnum or Chnoumis; Anuka or Anocuis; and Hak. Heliopolis had Tum or Harmachis; Nebhetp; Horus. Memphis had Ptah by Merenphtah; Nefer; Atum.

Though this chapter has run to great length something must be said of the architecture of this extraordinary people. The oldest structures which remain are the {54} pyramids, and the most ancient of these is possibly 8,000 years old, and may be described as a mere cairn of stones. Next follows the great pyramid of Ghizeh, which has been termed a stone bible, the Masons might call it that wonderful religious, scientific, and astronomical Tracing-board. According to Herodotus it was built by Cheops, whom the priests held in detestation, as he had caused all the temples to be closed during its erection, its date variously estimated at 3324 to 4325 B.C. It is said that the architect was Khufu-ankh, an Osirian, who was buried near to it. Cheops was certainly an Osirian, whilst the priests were opposed to that worship.<<"Egypt," Wm. Oxley, p. 87.>> All the pyramids had their official priests attached, and even in the earliest times fabulous sums were lavished upon these structures, and upon their temples. These latter were divided into three portions: -- 1, an outer court, not always roofed; 2, the body of the temple; 3, the Holy-place and the shrine of the god in whose honour the temple was built. The temple of Jerusalem was of analogous character. Archaeologists consider that the pre-historical nucleus was the holy-place, and that gradually other chambers began to be erected around it. The pyramid was the model upon which the builder acted, the walls sloping and narrowing upwards.

There are grave discrepancies amongst the learned in regard to the chronology of this nation, owing to disagreement as to whether certain

dynasties of kings were reigning contemporaneously; but the great pyramid of Ghizeh, whatever its real age, shews a marvellous knowledge of geometry, astronomy, and operative Masonry. The hardest granite has been chiselled with such mathematical accuracy that a knife blade will not enter the joints, and men of science suppose that they have discovered in its construction the evidence of a learning equal to that of the present day. The number 5, and its multiples, is the radical basis of its measurements; precisely as the Israelitish Tabernacle is set up with the like {55} multiple of 5, whilst the Temple of Solomon works upon its exact double or 10. The pyramid is found to be an exact mathematical expression of the proportion which the diameter bears to its circumference, that is as 1 is to 3.1459{SIC}. It is accurately oriented, that is its four sides are opposite the cardinal points; and it occurs that twice in each year, at a period of 14 days before the spring, and 14 days after the autumnal equinox, the sun for a short period seems to be resting upon the very apex of the pyramid, as if it was its pedestal. It is so constructed that five hundred million pyramid inches, or twenty million cubits, represent the polar axis of the earth. The height multiplied by ten to its ninth power gives the distance of the sun from the earth (about 92 1/2 million miles). If the length of each of its four base lines is divided by cubits of 25 inches it gives the exact length of a solar year, in days, hours, minutes, and seconds. The length in inches of the two diagonal lines, drawn across the base, gives exactly the number of years occupied in a full procession of the equinoxes, or 25,826 1/2 years. The entrance is so designed that it indicates the obliquity of the polar axis of the earth, and the stones of the Masonry above the entrance form the monogram of Osiris, it is a cube over which are two squares. The chambers are equally based upon intricate mathematical calculations, and various astronomical facts are symbolised in the arrangements of its several parts, but for these particulars the reader must consult some of the works which have been specially written on the subject. The coffre in the King s Chamber is generally considered a "pastos" of Initiation, but is said also to constitute a standard of dry measures. Even a prophetical bearing is said to be found in its measurements, but as this is the least certain of these various uncertain correspondences we will not enter into it here. Herodotus says that it took 300,000 workmen to build the structure in 30 years, and that one-third of the men and of the time were employed in making a causeway {56} for the blocks. Noting its splendid work, we may ask, if this pyramid is only 5,000 years old, of what age is Cyclopean work?

But the pyramid of Cheops has a much more important bearing on Speculative Freemasonry than anything that we have yet said; and though the secrecy of the priests of Egypt was absolute, yet is not altogether impenetrable. This secrecy was equally stringent at Memphis, Thebes, and Heliopolis, and when Pythagoras applied for initiation he was referred from one to the other. The architect of Cheops embodied the Osirian Mysteries in imperishable stone, as did also the builder of the Babylonian Borsippa, and the designer of the Persian cave of Mythras. And now for something of the Mysteries of Egypt, as represented by this pyramid. The entrance and its passage conform to the letter Y, or "two paths" of Pythagoras and the broad and narrow way of the Greek Mysteries. The descending path leads to an underground chamber, the floor of which is rough and unhewn, as is the rough Ashlar of a Freemason. The ascending passage leads first to a middle chamber named the

Queen s, or

that of our Lady Isis, and above that is the King s chamber with the empty sarcophagus of Osiris; over all are five secret chambers of small dimensions. Dr. Oliver asserts that the "vesica piscis" enters into the constructive design of the Queen s chamber.<<"Freemasons Treasury," p. 241.>> The whole of the internal structure covers an all-important allegory. It has been recently shewn by Brother W. M. Adams, and having the general approval of Professor Maspero, that there is a relationship between the internal structure of the pyramid and the "Ritual of the Dead," or as Maspero says, "both the one and the other have reference to an ideal house which Horus was conceived to have erected for his father Osiris," and Adams points out that the Well, the hidden lintel, the north and south passages apply equally to the heavenly temple, and the earthly counterpart. It is in fact the embodiment, perhaps 6,000 years ago, of a {57} speculative and operative Masonry consonant with the spiritual faith of Osiris.

The religious symbols of Egypt, according to Mr. William Oxley s work on
Egypt, changed with the progress of the sun through the signs of the zodiac, an assertion confirmed by much evidence. The era of Osiris and Isis is mythical, yet they are represented as parents of the twins Horus and Harmachis. In the year 4,565 B.C. the sun entered Taurus, and the Bull became the emblem of Osiris. It entered Aries 2,410 B.C., and the Ram becomes the emblem of Amen at Thebes. It entered Pisces 255 B.C., and we have crocodile-shaped gods, and the fish is a Christian symbol. The Egyptians conveyed something of this nature to Herodotus, who records it in a curious fable: Heracles desired to behold the highest god, he being one of the 12 minor gods; at length to meet his prayers, the supreme one revealed himself clothed in the skin and with the head of a Ram. The late Godfrey Higgins supposes in his "Anacalypsis" that when the sun entered Taurus he found man a negro such as the black Budha, and when he entered Aries he found him still black but with aquiline nose and straight hair as in the handsome Chrishna.

The recent discoveries of Colonel Ram indicates that the Sphinx is one of the
most ancient monuments of Egypt, as it was old in the days of Cheops, and there is a tablet which shows that it was repaired by Pharaoh Chephren. It represents, as facing the rising sun, the god Ra-Harmachis and has at its base several chambers hewn in the rock, the tombs of kings and priests devoted to the worship of Harmachis.

During the 5th dynasty of Kings several small temples were erected, as at Esneh, some pyramids, and an Osirian temple at Dendereh. There is an inscription of the 6th dynasty in the Ghizeh Museum, in which Una, a man of the people, describes how he had been sent by Pepi I. to cut, and then convey, a block of stone for the royal {58} tomb; he details the mode in which he accomplished this, with much engineering skill, about 3,400 B.C., and styles himself "chief of the royal workmen." Usertesen I., perhaps 3,000 B.C., laid the foundation of the temple of the Sun at Heliopolis, and assumes himself to be son of the double Harmachis; the same king built the front part of the temple of Karnak, which measures 1,200 feet by 348 feet; he also enlarged the temple of Ptah at Memphis. Professor Norman Lockyer, F.R.S., considers that as Karnak is oriented to receive the direct shaft of the sunlight at the season when it touched the horizon, opposite the temple gateway, that it was built 3,700 B.C.

The superintendence of Egyptian Craftsmen by higher officials is shewn in
the rockcut temple of Rekhmara, as 3,400 years ago the Vizier of Thebes is

represented with all his attendants, "inspecting all the handicrafts made in the temple of the house
of Amen, and teaching each man his duty concerning his trade." His inscription concludes: "I have
left no evil deeds behind me, may I be declared just and true in the great judgment." (Boscawen in
"Globe," Aug., 1900.)

A few centuries later the famous Labyrinth was erected; it represents the twelve Zodiacal signs, and
the twelve great gods, and contains 3,000 chambers with a lofty carved pyramid as adjunct. As proof
that the priests had a monotheistic creed we quote the following words from over the gate-way of
the temple of Medinet-Abou: -- "It is He that has made all that is, and without Him nothing has
been made." The temple of Luxor is the largest upon earth, but space fails us to record a tithe of the
mighty works of this wonderful race. The names of numerous architects are preserved and Brugsch,
Leiblein, and Lepsius, give the names of thirty-four, some of whom were allied with the reigning
Pharaohs. Commercial intercourse existed with China, as pottery, and other works of art, have been
found in very ancient tombs.

There is the record of an Artist of the name of Iretsen, of about 2,800 B.C., in which he says: -- "I
know the {59} mystery of the divine Word; the ordinances of the religious festivals, and every rite
performed therein, and I have never strayed from them. I know how to produce the form that is-
sueth forth and cometh in, so that each member goes to its place. I know the contemplating eye,
without a second, which affrights the wicked; also the posing of the arm that brings the hippopotamus low. I know the making of amulets, by which one may go and the fire will not give its flame, nor
will the water destroy. I am an artist wise in his art, a man standing above all men by his learning."
One passage here can only refer to the egress and ingress of the soul in trance, as in the Yogism of
India, and the amulets against fire and water would seem to refer to the trials of the Neophyte by
fire and water in the Mysteries. But in our days very extraordinary tales are told about the priests of
Japan, and other less civilised people, walking unharmed over hot coals. We wonder how this artist
would interpret the following symbolic design upon an ancient monument? A lion holds in one
paw a crux-ansata {Symbol: Ankh}, and with the other takes the hand of a recumbent man, whose
head is near an altar, as if the lion intended to raise the man; at the altar stands a god with the hailing
sign of a Craftsman.<<Vide Pike s "Morals and Dogma," p. 80.>>

The highest development of Egyptian civilisation was during the patriarchal
times extending from the 4th to the 12th dynasty, say from 7,000 to 2,400 B.C., and before Egypt
began to be affected by foreign influence. The kings had their "Court Architects," the profession being held in such honour that this officer often mated with the royal family. During the whole period
that we have named the highest positions of the State were open to intellect, and the humblest man
might aspire to become a General, a Court Architect, or a royal Scribe: the Kings were the fathers
of the people, and accessible to their subjects, and a successful soldier or architect might become, as
the highest prize, a "Royal Companion," or a "True royal {60} Companion," and be intimately associated with the King.<<W. St. Chad Boscawen.>>

Running contemporaneously with the Egyptian culture was that of the great Scytho-Hittite Kingdom, the equal of Egypt, in metals, buildings, and art, and Captain Conder points out that the point within a circle, {Symbol: Circle with point in center}, was their phonetic symbol for "An," or God; the five-pointed

star, {Symbol: Pentagram}, the symbol of "to," which implies either down, or to descend, and that the cypriote symbol of two triangles joined at their apex,
{symbol like "X" with the top and bottom chevrons closed to triangles}, but without the bottom line, {symbol as last, but with the lower chevron left open}, was the Hittite character for man or protection.<<"Lucifer," ix.>>

A long period of historical darkness now supervenes, and it has been discovered that a race totally distinct from the Egyptians had taken possession of the highlands to the north of Thebes, between the 7th and 9th dynasty. They were a tall, powerful race, resembling the Lybian and Ammonite people, had wavy brown hair, prominent aquiline noses, and used flint axes and copper implements. They were accomplished potters, stone workers, and metallurgists. In a ritualistic sense they were cannibals, and broke the bones of human bodies to extract the marrow. Near to the home of this recently discovered race was Nubt, a town which was devoted to the worship of the execrated Set and which is mentioned in one of the Satires of Juvenal, as the origin of horrid wars, and cannibal orgies. Following upon this, as if in some measure due to it, was the domination of the Hyksos, or Shepherd Kings, who overran Egypt, between 2500 and 1600 B.C., perhaps dependent in part upon the ferment which arose in Central Asia when the Elamites invaded Babylon, and these Hyksos seem to have followed the religious views of the Semitic tribes, though some writers have thought that they were old believers who were opposed to the ritual of Osiris, which we shall mention in our next chapter as an Aryan ritual, the weight of evidence is altogether in favour of a foreign origin of {61} the invaders. Manetho, an Egyptian historian who was employed by the Greek Ptolomies to investigate the annals of Egypt, asserts that the Hebrews were of this race.<<Josephus, "Against Apion.">> Simplicius asserts that what Moses taught the Hebrews he had learned in the Mysteries. These Hyksos were at length expelled by a Theban of the name of Aahames and the Osirian temples were re-opened.

Very recently the mummy of Menephtah was discovered at Luxor, and on
examination at Cairo was held to be the Pharaoh who pursued the Israelites; he was the 2nd king of the 19th dynasty.

Thothmes III., about 1,600 B.C., relates the ceremony which he observed in laying a foundation-stone at Buto, but the tablet is imperfect. The first stroke of the hammer thereon appears to be intended to conjure the keeping out of the water; a document was deposited in the stone containing the names of all the great gods and goddesses, "and the people rejoiced." There is also an inscription of this period on the Statue of Semut, in which he is styled: "First of the first, and Master of the works of all Masters of work."

There are also Geometrical diagrams of this period indicating the knowledge of the square, and in the great pyramid there yet exists a workman s diagram indicating the method of making a right angle; the "vesica piscis" exists in a recess over the King s Chamber. Some of the drawings yet exist of a Canon of proportion for the construction of the human figure, which Vitruvius represents by this

{X}, the navel being the centre; and though from the earliest to the latest times, the Canon varied, the relative proportions were fixed by forming a chequered diagram of perfect squares. Clement of Alexandria says that the temples of Jerusalem and Egypt separated the congregation and the Sanctuary by a large curtain of four colours, drawn over five pillars, the one alluding to the cardinal points of the compass, the other to the elements. The

Pyramids were worked from the centre by the angle {62} 3, 4, 5. The Guilds say that this symbol {Neteru: Three vertical lines with a horizontal right angle line at the top of each one to right}, indicates the presence of 3 G.M.M. s.

There followed upon this era the introduction into Egypt of a large amount of Babylonian influence, but to render this comprehensible some explanation is necessary. At some remote period races of conquering Cushites from Ethiopia, followed by Semites, settled in Elam, had planted themselves in Babylon. The first of them was probably a worshipper of the god Marduk, or Mercury who is also Thoth and Hermes, for the Biblical Nimrod is one with Marduk, the beginning of whose kingdom was Babel and Erech and (Ur in) Accad, and Calneh in the land of Shinar. These new comers accepted the religion of the earlier Akkadians, whence we may assume either that there had arisen no great distinctions in the mode of worship, or that the latter had influence as a race of higher culture. The conquerors, however, changed the names of the gods to adapt them to their own Arya-Semitic tongue, and as astronomical terms are in that language the inference is drawn that that science was a Semitic development.<<"Chaldean Magic," -- Lenormant.>> The chief gods of the assimilated race were Samas the sun-god; Sin the moon-god; and Yav "the inundator," who is probably Hea of Akkad. They accepted the doctrine of the soul s immortality.<<"Records of the Past" -- translated hymn.>> The early Assyrian King Asir-nasir-pal claims all the diabolical conquests which he relates in his inscriptions from these gods, and proclaimed himself as the "exalter of Yav." The Semitic names of Beth-Yakin and Yakin, as names of places and persons are found in these early inscriptions. The remains of this theology exists to-day amongst the Yezids of Asia, the sun is worshipped by its old name, and the moon and bull receive equal veneration amongst some of the tribes, and with the worship have been transmitted secret modes of recognition, which a writer who was acquainted with them terms Freemasons {63} signs.<<"Ars Quat. Cor." iv. -- Yezids (Yarker).>> It equally constitutes an argument for the possibility of the uninterrupted transmission of Freemasonry from century to century; and it is impossible to overlook the many striking points of similarity to the primitive Mysteries which it possesses; and the inference which we may draw from this is that an educated priesthood had added art and science to their curriculum, and that all temples yet continued to be erected under their supervision.

The Chaldean civilisation about 4,000 years ago dominated Syria, and its tongue became the diplomatic language of the known world, whilst commerce was maintained extensively between Egypt, Babylon, India, and China. About 1500 B.C. an Egyptian King of the name of Amenophis III., a worshipper of the Theban god Amen, married an Asiatic woman who surrounded the throne with her kindred, and a Babylon Scribe was established at the Court, for Chaldean legends were copied and sent to Egypt. Their son Amen-hotep adopted the Chaldean faith and changed his name to

Khu-en-aten, withdrawing from Amen, then one of the oldest priesthoods in the world. He built in eight years the vast city of Tel-el-amarna, where for seventeen years he enforced the worship of the "Solar disc," or its vitalising rays. It was in fact the worship of the sun s vital rays as the source of all vital life, power and force. Probably in some respects it was a restoration of the faith of the Hyksos but it terminated again with the death of the King. In the erection of his new city, Bek, the hereditary successor of a long line of Egyptian architects, is described as -- "the

artist, the overseer of the sculptors, the teacher of the King himself." His assistant, or what we should now term, his Deputy or Warden, was Potha, who is described as -- "Master of the Sculptors of the Queen," by whom no doubt the Asiatic is meant. These valuable records have only recently been disinterred, and in the house of the Master, trial-pieces were found in various stages exemplifying {64} the cutting of hieroglyphics, and as well, perfectly finished portraits and statues, without any admixture of foreign style, and which are equal to any work of the moderns. It is noteworthy that the ground plan of the tomb of the Queen of Amenophis III., about 1470 B.C., is a cross of the Latin form, and as Mr. William Oxley says, "exactly on the plan of a Christian church."

The Ramiside dynasty, in which the priests of Amen came again into power, did much in the 14th century B.C. to adorn Egypt with stately buildings, and Beken-Khonsoo describes himself as the architect of Rameses II., "the friend of Amen," and the restorer of Karnak, and Dr. Wm. Birch informs us that the twins Suti and Har were Mer-kat, architects, who had charge of Karnak. Rameses III. makes a record of the numerous temples which he restored. He built at Thebes a temple to Khons, of good hewn sandstone and black basalt, having gates whose folding doors were plated with gold and itself overlaid with electrum like the horizon of heaven.<<"Records of the Past," vi.>>

It is unfortunate that we have so little that is authentic in regard to the rites of the Mysteries, though the doctrine is fully embodied in the "Ritual of the Dead," we only begin to have details after they had been carried to Greece by Orpheus, Cadmus, and Cecrops in the 16th century B.C. All the Egyptian Kings were initiated into them, and are represented as adorned with very handsome aprons. There are also representations, in paintings, of scenes which may equally apply to the earthly Mysteries, or to the passage of the soul in the after life, which was in reality the object of the sacerdotal mysteries, and it was a firm custom in Egypt to adapt their whole life to their faith in the future, or to enact in their religious rites, that which they believed would follow on quitting the body.

In our next chapter we may be able to form a more solid opinion upon the changes made in the Cabiric Mysteries, which were clearly the most ancient of the great Mysteries, by the advanced Aryans, and as to the alleged {65} changes made in ancient Egypt by the substitution of cosmogonical or natural effects, for such traditional history as that recorded by Sanconiathon, Berosus, etc., a natural consequence, for the Egyptians were undoubtedly a nation of mixed blood. They seem first to have been of the Negro or Hamitic type with a polytheistic creed, they saw God in all nature and in all forms. As proto-Aryans they developed greatly the arts and sciences. Lastly, reinforced by purer Aryans they became the Apostles of the conditional immortality of the human soul. During the thousand years rule of the Hyksos, or Shepherd Kings, they were in constant contact with a monotheistic creed, but no sooner had they driven out these oppressors than the rites of the doctrine of immortality, under a Father, Mother, and Son, arose in their old splendour.

By way of closing this chapter it may be pointed out that we have first a
series of Mysteries, which amongst people who, living in hot climates, had little need of art, and confined themselves rather to speculative views of the creation of the world and the relations that exist between heaven and earth. To these, in the next stage were added the whole circle of arts and science, the older

Mysteries as to the creation of the world and the affinity between heaven and earth were retained, but a superior race of Cabiri added an improved architecture, agriculture, metallurgy, shipbuilding, and all the arts. The third stage which followed was the separation of the Mysteries of Religion and Art into two branches.

CHAPTER III. ARYAN CIVILISATION AND MYSTERIES

IN the long series of ages which it took to develop the Ugro-altaic monosyllabic language into proto-Aryan, and in the centuries which it took to convert the Aryo-European into Celitc, Latin, Sclavonic, Lettic, German; other branches into sub-dialects as, for instance, Indo-Aryan into Sanscrit, Persian, Greek, Armenian, Pushtu, Kurd, Baluchi, Hindustani; and again the Semitic speech into Babylonian, Assyrian, Phoenician, Arabic, etc., need we feel surprised if the Rites of the Theosophical and Art Mysteries underwent a variation also. Thus the primitive Mysteries known as Magian and Cabiric, were denominated Osirian amongst the Copts; Tammuz and Adonis amongst the Semites; Dionysian amongst the Assyrians and the Greeks; and applied to Bacchus amongst the Latins. Yet all had the same primitive origin in a remote Arcane School, and varied but by a gradual development in technique.

And notwithstanding such departures from an exact form of transmission,
with the change of scene, in passing from one country to another by colonists, the social customs of Oriental nations are most unchanging. We have already instanced the practice to-day of Babylonian rites by the Yezids. The sacred springs and trees of the old worship are venerated with the ancient rites of music and the dance. The priests of Christianity may be seen practising their ceremonials with the serpent staff of Mercury or Esculapius in their hands; and also personating the High priest of Zeus of Vanessa. The ancient {67} Artemis of the Lakes, the Ephesian Aphrodite who is Ishter in Chaldea, and Astarte in Phoenicia, has been succeeded by the Virgin of the Lakes, with a special society called the Takmorei which has consolidated into a species of Freemasonry termed the "Brotherhood of the Sign." Even in this country many curious customs of the Druids have been preserved in the three kingdoms. And as Free Masonry can unquestionably be carried up to very ancient times in England, and, beyond, its legends into Oriental lands, what right can be adduced to condemn its traditions as altogether false? The sacred Mysteries spread with the various colonies into many lands and in the lapse of ages began to apply their traditional knowledge to their new home, under the supposition that their ancestors had occupied this residence in all time.
The late Lord Beaconsfield, in his "Lothair," speaks of the MADRE NATURA as
the oldest and the most powerful of the secret societies of Italy, whose mystic origin, in the idealised worship of nature, reaches the era of paganism, and

which, he says, may have been founded by some of the despoiled professors of the ancient faith, which as time advanced has assumed many forms. Its tradition that one of the Popes, as Cardinal de Medici, became a member of the Fraternity is accredited upon some documentary grounds, and it accepted the allegorical interpretation which the Neo-Platonists had placed upon the Pagan creeds during the first Ages of Christianity.

It is necessary to say that in dealing with the chronology of the ancients we have no certain era which enables us to give dates with the least precision. We saw in our last chapter that from North Europe colonies spread over Asia, Arabia, and Chaldea, erecting some wonderful structures in their passage and introducing art into their new settlements. The Celts, Persians, and Greeks continued together a sufficient length of time to merit the title of true Aryans, but of the main branch the Hindu undoubtedly made the greatest progress in architecture, {68} literature, and early civilisation. There is a record, which we will allude to later, that a whole army of pure Aryans entered Egypt. The cradle of the Hindu is traditionally held to be the high-table-land between Thibet and India in the region of the lake Mansurawara. Before their advance into India three chief peoples were in possession of that country: the Dravidians of the north west, who have some affinity with the aborigines of south and west Australia, use the boomerang as a weapon, and have the same words for I, thou, he, you, etc., these now use a language represented by Tamil, Malayalam, Telugu, Kanarese, Tulu, Kudugu, Toda, Kota, Gond, Kandh, Urain, Rajmahal, etc. A second tribe was the Kolarians driven from the north-east against the Dravidian, and so broken up into Santals, Savars, Kurkus, Juangs, Hos, etc. A third race were the Tibeto-Burman tribes who have an affinity with the Mongolians. Lastly, and after the invasion of India, Scythic tribes, as the Jats or Getae, and the Ghakkars, secured a footing in the country; our Gypsies seem to spring from the Jat race.

As Aryan civilisation was but an advance upon what we have termed proto-
Aryan, so also it follows that the art of building with squared and levelled stones, wrought by the use of square, level, and plumb was the gradual improvement upon the Cyclopean system of irregular blocks; and mingled with the most ancient level architecture of India, equally with various other countries, are walls which resemble the Cyclopean method of building;<<"Philosophy of History." and from this, and other circumstances, we may draw the conclusion that Aryan culture was the medium of advanced architecture. This improvement had birth in north India and one of the oldest cities was the Aryan colony of Balkh where are vast ruins, colossal images, of which the number of prominent figures, or recesses, amount to twelve thousand, in subterranean temples hewn out of the solid rock.

At a remote period there arose a contest for supremacy {69} between the warrior and the priest, who had the oral hymns that now compose the Vedas; also termed the wars of the solar (warrior) and lunar (Brahmin) races. The priests or Brahmins obtained a victory over the Maharajahs who were of a different branch of the Aryan family, and were both warriors and agriculturists. An alliance was formed, and the warriors were permitted to receive a limited amount of religious instruction, and at a period later than the oldest Vedas, a system of hereditary caste was established in three chief divisions, the Brahmin, warrior, and artisan, which may be now considered three distinct Rites of the Mysteries.

It has long been thought that some of these ancient wars were the result of a dispute as to the relative power of the two forces of nature. In prehistoric times a system had spread over the world in which creative spirit was represented by the Phallus, and first or primordial matter by the Yoni, or the male and female organs of generation, but it is somewhat doubtful whether the most ancient hymns accepted these emblems; the emblems are older than any of the hymns when committed to writing, but the probability is that when the hymns were written they had not then been sectarianly adopted. Primordial matter, upon which the action of spirit is supposed to take place, is not ordinary matter as we designate it, but its originator; and it is a scientific fact, well known to the ancients, and embodied in the "Divine Poemander" of Hermes, that matter, such as we know it, cannot be destroyed, we can only change its form, and under all that we see lies this primordial matter, as the vehicle of spirit.

Both spirit and primordial matter are eternal, and in the recondite aspect of

Aryan philosophy, all creation springs from the union of these two indestructible principles, which is Para-Brahm, or Deity without form. In Egypt the conjoint worship of the two active principles, or latent forces, is found emblemised in the crux ansata {Symbol: Ankh} which embraces both attributes; separately they appear {70} also in the obelisk and the vesica-pisces, but also in various other emblems in all countries. In remote times sects arose that made a separate symbol of one or other of the principles.

It has been shewn by Dr. Inman<<"Ancient Faiths in Ancient Names.">> that most Hebrew names have reference to the male principle. On the other hand the Greeks, who are designated Yavans in Hindu literature, with other tribes that it was said were expelled the Aryan home with them, were worshippers of that female nature, or principle of nature, which in Egypt was adored as Isis; in Babylon as Ishter; in Samothrace as Ghe; in Britain as Ceridwen; in Italy as Cybele; in Greece as Ceres; in Armenia as Anaitis; in Germany as Hertha; in Persia as Mythra; and we may even add, in Christian times as the Virgin Mary.

The learned Brother Dr. George Oliver, in his "History of Initiation," professes to give the ceremonials of Initiation into the Brahminical Rites of Mahadeva, but as we know of no evidence of their accuracy we shall refrain from quoting the account. There is a very interesting legend in Porphyry, which he gives upon the authority of Bardesanes, an Initiate and Gnostic, who had it from the Brahmins. There was a very lofty mountain which had in it a cave of large dimensions. It contained a statue of 12 cubits with its arms extended in form of a cross, the face was half male and half female; on the right breast was represented the Sun, and on the left the Moon; the arms had figures of the sky, the ocean, mountains, rivers, plants, and animals; on the head of the figure was a god enthroned. Beyond this was a large extension of the cavern, guarded by a door from which issued a stream of water, but only the pure in mind could pass this door; but upon doing this they reached a pellucid fountain. The writer supposes that it is to this cavern of Initiation that Apollonius of Tyana alludes to the letters which he addressed to the Brahmins, where he is wont to say, "No! by the Tantalian water by which you Initiated me into {71} your Mysteries." The description of this cavern has some points very similar to the Peak cavern in Derbyshire, which Faber supposes was used by the Druids for like purposes. The late H. P. Blavatsky asserts that every ancient and modern Initiate takes the following oath: "And I swear to give up my life for the salvation of my brothers, which constitute the whole of mankind, if called upon, and to die in the defence of truth."

A system of caste initiation does exist amongst the Hindus at this day. Thus a Brahmin youth is first invested with a sacred symbolic cord worn from the left shoulder to the right hip, which is done at about 8 years of age; for a Brahmin the thread is cotton; warriors of flax; traders of wool. As the Parsees are of Aryan race, a similar custom prevails amongst them; the cord in this case goes thrice round the waist. It is three yarns twisted into one thread, and three of such threads knotted into a circle, symbolising "one in three, and three in one"; it also signifies these conquests, over speech, thoughts, actions. The Hindu youth is from this time instructed in the Mysteries of the Vedas, and when he comes of age he is formally bound in the Goparam to the service of his temple and instructed in the science and higher Mysteries of his religion; it is practically analogous to Christian baptism, and confirmation. But the instruction of a Hindu is sometimes compared to a "nine-storied house," and they speak mystically of nine spiritual grades, represented by nine jewels upon a string, or in the hands of a beggar. A Hindu Mason thus allegorises the practices of a Brahmin: "With the sacred Word of a Brahmin on his lips, the Yogi closes his eyes to the visible creation, that in abstraction he may erect the symbolic temple, looking heartfully upon his body as a temple with nine gates, governed by three principal officers, supported by three subordinate agents. The temple of Truth is thus built in the heart, without the sound of metal tool." The symbol of a Pranayani Yogi, as an emblem of the prolongation of life beyond the ordinary time, is the 5 pointed star in a circle, {Symbol: Pentagram in a circle}. {72}

Then again there are degrees of Aspirants who are taught by Brahmins of different degrees of learning, and these again by ascetics or Mahatmas of different degrees of spiritual knowledge. The Buddhists of Thibet recognise four degrees of spiritual advancement; and amongst the Moslem sects of India, Persia, and Turkey, the system is sometimes of four, and with others of seven degrees. Much of this is spoken mystically and with secrecy, and has its counterparts in the esoteric side of Freemasonry.

There is a symbolic doctrine taught by the Brahmins to their disciples in respect to the construction of their temples, and given orally; their basic symbol is the equilateral triangle, the first corner represents "birth," the next "death," and the apex "immortality;" the four walls, floor, etc., are typical of their doctrinal teaching; the entrance must be either south or west so that the worshipper may face either the north where the gods are said to reside and whence knowledge comes, or the east whence rites and ceremonies are derived; the body of the temple represents our human body, and the central image, which has its emblem, much resembling the "Seals" of the Rosicrucians, symbolises our own "jivatma," or immortal spirit, but the aspects or faces are only explained fully to competent Initiates.<<"Mis. Notes and Queries," x, p. 279.>> This species of instruction has been equally applied to our own cathedrals. There is also supposed to be what we may call an invisible tyler, represented by a statue.

That the ancient Brahminical system of Initiation was fearfully secret is evidenced by the "Agrouchada Parikshai" or manual of Hindu caste-initiation, which makes death the penalty of indiscretion. Every initiate of the first class who betrays the secret instruction to members of other castes must have his tongue cut out, and suffer other mutilations. Again, it is said that: "every Initiate, to whatever grade he may belong, who reveals the great sacred formula must be put to death." And, "any Initiate of the third class who reveals, before the prescribed time, {73} to the Initiates of the second class, the superior truths, must be put to death." Blavatsky states that if an aged Brahmin was tired of life he might give his own blood, in place of an animal sacrifice, to the disciple whom he was initiating. She makes no reference to her authority, but the act is probable enough.

We shall allude shortly to the Mysteries of Mythras, Dionysos, and Osiris, as systems practised by the Aryan race, but it must be borne in mind that the Hindus teach that the Persians and Greeks were of the warrior and agricultural caste, who were only allowed partial instruction in Vedaic learning, but it is possible that they branched from the parent stem before the establishment of caste, and others refused caste arrangement. The Maharajahs of India identify themselves with the legislation of Bacchus or Dionysos, whom the German savant, Heeren, believes to be the Parusha-Rama, or incarnated priest who aided the Brahmins. The basis of the Devanagari character of the Hindus, called the "Alphabet of the Gods," is the square {symbol of a carpenter s square: a vertical line with horizontal line at top from left to apex only}, termed "the pillar of knowledge entwined with the garland of thought."

But besides the Initiatory ceremonies of Brahmins, and warriors, there has existed from remote times a succession of members of an Art Fraternity, using the investiture of the sacred thread, and with an Initiation of their own intended to embrace all castes. The god whom they recognise is Visvakarman, the great builder, or Architect of the Universe, and Lord of the Art Fraternity. Mythology says that he crucified his son Surya (the sun) upon his lathe, which is esoterically the Jain cross, {Symbol: Swastika}, or four squares joined at the ends; and the Pagodas of Benares, and Mathura are built as an equal-limbed cross, as an many others, of which we mentioned some in our last chapter.

In a lecture of 1884 Bro. Nobin Chand Bural speaking of the existing Hindu sect of Visvakarma says that all description of Artizans observe the last day of the month Bakdra as a close holiday sacred to Visvakarma, and will {74} not even touch a tool, and says: "Mr. Ferguson, the celebrated archaeologist, who is a good authority on these matters, connects the sect with some of the old temples abounding in those parts, and by reason of these temples bearing Masonic symbols and devices sculptured on their walls, competent authorities connect the sect with Masonry."

When Jacolliot, the celebrated French savant and author, was studying the antiquities of India, he was informed by the priests of Benares, that, in very remote ages, "thousands of ages before our era," he says, the Artisan caste formed two divisions the one of which adopted as its mark or sign the plumb- rule, and the other the level. They eventually united into one, in order the more effectually to resist the confederacy between the two higher castes; and all the great works of remote ages were executed by this confederacy. As this confederacy is evidently a mixed caste, and as the two higher castes, refused them equal recognition, it seems evident, that these builders were a mixture of Aryans and aborigines, who had their existence as a Fraternity before caste existed, and from the evidence adduced in our last chapter, and the splendour of their labour, a branch of the Cabiric fraternity.

A remnant of this confederacy was recently brought to light by a very ridiculous mistake of our Government in India by interpreting "mystical" language as "to the repair of their temple," by Yogis, "literally." It is located in Cochin where the "dynasty" is of Dravidian origin. They claim, in a pamphlet, equal right to the sacred cord with the Brahmins, and even dispute their authority, claiming that their privileges and special symbolic instructions were conceded by the Rishis who founded the Brahminical caste Initiation, in those remote ages when hereditary caste was first established. Whilst the Brahmins use "nature" symbols to embody divine truths, they express the esoteric truths of the Vedas by "art" symbols, plans, and measurements. (The reader should note this because it is the {75} essential difference between Modern Free Masonry and the church.) All temples and even private houses are erected according to traditional symbolism, which conveys a secret and esoteric doctrine. An Anglo-Indian Officer who had the duty of inspecting the Guilds at the date of the Mutiny says they have all which Masonry possesses.

We have here an Art Society springing out of the old religious Mysteries but

becoming by conquest an independent organisation, tolerated for its great services. Such were the Dionysian Artificers of Greece, whence originated the Roman Colleges of Artificers, and we shall assign good reasons for believing that it was this creation of caste that made Artists into a separate society.

Brother C. Purdon Clarke, who has had practical experience amongst these Master builders, confirms the general truth of these claims.<<"Vide Ars Quat. Cor.," vi, p. 99.>> He says that the Hindu carpenters and masons, who are also carvers, constitute a body that claims peculiar privileges of divine origin, which, though often prejudicial to the Brahmins, were usually conceded. To these artizans belong 32, or as some reckon 64, of the Shastras of which they are the custodians. At the great temple of Madura, in 1881, whilst one of these Shastras were read out, an architect drew from the details the representation of one of their deities. The record seemed but a string of meaningless figures resembling a table of logarithms, but when these were marked down in off-set lines, on both sides of a centre stem, it produced a representation of Vishnu with his flute, standing upon one leg. He noticed that the centre stem was divided into 96 parts, and he further states that the Pagoda at Cochin in Travancore has a special room set apart for the temple architect, the walls being decorated with full size figures of temple furniture. All this seems to be an advance upon the chequer designs which were used in ancient Egypt. Ram Ras, in his work upon the building caste, says that jealous of the Brahmins and of trade competitions, they took care to conceal from {76} the rest of the people the sacred volumes which have descended to them. The Shastra on civil architecture says that, "an architect should be conversant in all sciences, ever attentive to his vocations, generous, sincere, and devoid of enmity or jealousy."

The late Brother Whymper states that the key-stone used in erections by the

earliest Aryan builders was tau-shaped {symbol: A squared hollow "T" composed of two rectangles and shown by outline only} and that the wedge- shaped key-stone, though of old date, is of a more modern form.<<Ibid. vi. >> According to the Vastu Shastra, the ancient Hindu temple consisted of seven courts, as at Srirangam and Mavalipuram, their seven walls referring allegorically to the seven essences of the human temple. In the centre of these courts was a raised seat without any covering. At entrance the worshippers had to undergo purification before a fire, kept burning for that purpose. The

Goparams, or towers at the entrance, represent the mountain over which Deity presides, surrounded by seven classes of angels and purified beings. The palace of the King of Siam has seven roofs, and he only can occupy the highest stage.

If we rely upon the Hindu tradition, as we may, that the Persians and the Greeks were members of the Maharajah caste, coupled with what seems to be historical fact that certain parts of India refused caste laws, we find a reason for the special characteristics of the Mysteries, so far as applies to Brahmin governed countries but not therefore of general practice. It leads to this conclusion that in the Rites of Maha-deva we have the Brahmin caste; in the Mythraic, and their equivalents, we have the Maharajah caste; whilst in the followers of Visvakarman we have the Artizans, and this combination tends to prove the contentions of the last named, coupled with the evidence of the priests of Benares, that they were sanctioned when the warriors combined with the Brahmins to confine each profession in a close fold, and make hewers of wood, and drawers of water, of an ancient population that they conquered upon advancing into India. We {77} should not expect under the rule of an old patriarchal government to find religion and art divorced, nor a body of Masons, practising a system of religion as a separate organisation. Native Mysteries, which followed the Cabiric system of religion and art in union, would be rendered subject by caste laws to the Brahmins, and socially reduced to an inferior position, and new bodies would arise on this basis.

"Persia." The Magian system, as has already been observed, was not Persian

but proto-Median, and as their civilisation preceded the Aryan it argues strongly that a Mystery of the nature of the Cabiric, which combined Theosophy, Science and Art, was of greater antiquity than a Mystery founded upon caste laws, and that the latter system simply modified the former according to the doctrines of their incarnate deity with separate rites so arranged as to preserve caste distinctions. The pontificate of the Magi, as it had been received from the first Zaradust, was the instructor of the Persians, but reformed in the time of Cyrus by a second Zoroaster, and these Mysteries eventually spread over the world and into several counties of Britain. Art has a similar tradition to India.

"Mythraic Mysteries." It is believed that the Initiation of Mythras consisted of seven degrees. The first degree was "Soldier of Mythras," Porphyry says that the second was that of the "Lion" -- Lion of Mythras; then followed the "Child of the Sun," and we find Initiates termed "Eagles," and "Hawks." Herodotus asserts that Mythra is Urania; and Ouranos, the Hindu Varuna, was the highest god of Orpheus; Dionysius the Areopagite uses the term, "the threefold Mythras."

During the Initiatory ceremony the candidate passed, as is also said of the Brahminical, through seven caverns, the last of which was embellished with the signs of the Zodiac. Celsus mentions that there was a great ladder of steps, with gates or portals on each, coloured to represent the seven planets as in the turrets of the tower of Babel, {78} and the walls of Ecbatana, but Faber justly thinks that this ladder was a pyramid such as Babel itself. The Neophyte underwent 12 trials, the number of the Zodiacal signs, and during the reception was offered a crown on the point of a sword which he had to refuse, saying: "Mythras is my crown." He was then offered a wreath which he cast down, saying: "My crown is in my God." Justin Martyr says: "They take bread and a cup of water in the sacrifice of those that are Initiated and pronounce certain words over it."<<Faber i. p. 458.>> Augustine: "The candidate received an engraved stone as a token of admission to the Fraternity."<<2 "John," dis.

7.>> Tertullian: "Mythras marks the forehead of his soldiers, celebrates the oblation of bread, introduces the image of a resurrection, and under the sword wreathes a crown"; he also speaks of a baptism and the promise of absolution on the confession of sins.<<"De Proescriptione," c. 40.>> It is said that when Maxime the Ephesian Initiated the Emperor Julian, he used the following formula, on baptising him in blood: "By this blood I wash thee from thy sins. The word of the highest has entered unto thee, and his spirit henceforth will rest upon thee, "newly born." The newly begotten son of the highest god. Thou art the son of Mythras."

Bread and wine have been held to be the body and blood of Bacchus, and Mr. St. Chad Boscawen (1900) announces that he has just received from Egypt some old Gnostic papyri of the 2nd or 3rd century A.D. in which the names of Jesus, John, and Peter are said to be powerful. Over a cup or chalice these words appear in Greek: "This is not wine, this is the blood of Osiris," and over a piece of bread: "This is not bread, this is the very body of Osiris." It proves that the spirit of the Arcane Schools existed far into Christian times.

The European Temples of Mythras were an oblong square reached by a Pronas on the level, from which a few steps led to the actual temple. On each side of the entrance was a human figure, one of which holds a raised {79} torch, and the other a torch reversed. Benches occupied the two sides, and at the further end was the Altar, and beyond it a statue of Mythras Tauroticus with the sun at the god s left hand, and the moon at his right hand.

M. Caumont in his magnificent work on the Mythraic Mysteries gives an example of the Mythraic sculpture at Chesterholm. It is a bordered triangular structure on which is sculptured at the top a small circle, below that an equal- limbed cross, over a semi-circle or crescent. Below that a cock, and at the corner a double circle with cross in centre. The god often appears holding a pair of scales. He quotes a text of St. Jerome to prove that the Rite had seven degrees and that the Mystae (Sacratus) took successively the names of Crow, Occult, Soldier, Persian, Courier of the Sun (Heleodromus), and Father. There are representations of four small loaves marked with the cross, representing no doubt the bread and water which they consecrated. The lion, he says, is an emblem of fire, to which water is inimical.

From two of the passages quoted above it would seem that a simulation of death preceded baptism, thus making it a symbol of the new birth, and hence it follows that Christian baptism is a version of this mystic rite of the Mysteries. In a report of Fermecius Maternus, read before Constantine, it was said that at the celebration of the festival of the Sun, which took place at the same period of time as the Jewish passover, a young ram was slain. The priests of Mythras offered bread and water to the worshippers whilst whispering, "Be of good courage, ye initiated in the Mysteries of the redeemed god, for we shall find redemption from our afflictions."

There are Mythraic monuments which bear close resemblance to the symbolism of the "Apocalypse." In some the god is represented in the act of slaying a bull, and he is crowned with a tiara on which is seven stars; in others he appears with a torch in each hand, whilst a flaming sword issues out of his mouth. Most of the figures of this god have a man on each side of him, one

holding a torch {80} flaming upwards, and the other in a reversed position. Mr. Ernest de Bunsen compares the offering of bread to the Haoma sacrifices of the undivided Aryan family, where the priests offered in a cup a piece of the holy plant and some round flat cakes, or draona, corresponding with the Christian wafers, but mystically alluding to the solar disc, and he further says that these Hota priests correspond with the seven soma priests of the Hindus, and that the Avesta has this address for the Mysteries: "Eat, ye men, this mayazda, ye who are worthy of the same by your purity and piety."<<"Mis. Notes and Queries" (Gould), xii, p. 238.>>

After the revolt of the Persian tribe against the Brahmins, the former converted the Vedaic Ahriman into an evil being, or devil; and named other Vedaic gods as his followers; the Greek Ouranos is the Hindu Varuna and Mythras is associated with Ahura, as the Hindu sun-god is with Varuna.

"Arts." The invented arts have their legends. Hushang the son of their first King Kiumers accidentally discovered fire and the blacksmith s art, further developed by Tahumers; then weaving was invented; his slaves the demons taught him letters. The next king was the wise Jemschid, in whose time military accoutrements were fabricated; he built in brick and gave laws, but lost his life at the hands of Zohak, a monstrous usurper of Arabia, but was avenged by Feridun of the Kainian race, one of whose sons slew the other. According to the poet Ferdusi<<"Shah Namah.">>, who collected the annals of the Persian Kings close upon a thousand years ago, Jemschid erected the Artizans into a class by themselves, under a chief, that we should call Grand Master, giving them laws, which Jemschid himself interpreted: --

"Selecting one from each, the task to guide, By rules of art, himself the rules applied."

Brother C. P. Clarke informs us that the modern Persian Master-builder works out his ideas by a secret method, in {81} which a plan is divided into equal chequered squares, of which each square represents either one or four square bricks such as are used in Persia. It is a miniature of one which is transferred to the floor of the Master s workroom, where the patterns are incised in a plaster of Paris groundwork ready to serve as a "mould" from which slabs may be cast.<<"Ars Quat. Cor.", vi, p. 99.>> The system yet forms the floor-cloth of Free Masonry; it is still in secret practice in Persia and agrees with the square designs of old Egypt which served to fix a canon of proportion. The Guild Free Masonry says that Solomon s temple had squares of a cubit now represented on their carpet.

"Egypt." The worship of Osiris had its centre at Abydos, and was probably the system of an Aryan colony, even if the first King Menes was not of that race. Kaluka Bhatta mentions an Aryan king named Manu Vena, who was driven out of India after a five days battle and led his army into Egypt. Georgius Sincellus tells us that in the early times of Amenophis an Indian colony immigrated to Egypt, but the worship of Osiris is very much older than Amenophis. The historian Heeren demonstrates that certain skulls of mummies resemble those of Bengalese, though this rather connects them with a pre-Aryan race of Indians, and a modern Indian regiment found in the god-ruins of Egypt, the deities of their own country, and Philostratus shews that commercial intercourse existed. There is, however, a perfect resemblance of priestly governance in Egypt with the laws prescribed by Manu for the Aryan priests; moreover the social habits, creed, and even minute questions of costume, are resemblances between Egypt and India that cannot be explained away. As in minor so also in questions of religious sacrifice, the cow, bull, and crocodile were sacred animals, but equally the bull was sacrificed, and the doctrine of Metampsychosis was held, all equally by both nations. Flinders Petrie has sanctioned the belief that King Menes is the Mythical Manu of India. {82}

"The Mysteries." The Egyptian Mysteries were celebrated in honour of Isis and Osiris, the former symbolised by the Moon, and the latter by the Sun. We have few authentic details, but we know that Isis corresponds with the Grecian Demeter and Latin Ceres, and Osiris with the Grecian Dionysos and Latin Bacchus. Iamblichus says that Amen represents the hidden force which brings all things forth to light; he is Ptah when he accomplishes all things with skill and truth; and Osiris as the good and beneficent god. Damascius writes: "Of the first principles the Egyptians said nothing, but celebrated it as a darkness beyond all intellectual conception, a thrice unknown darkness." Jennings considers that the Mystic black and white banner of the Templars referred to this doctrine. Plutarch informs us that Isis was apparelled in clothing partly black and partly white to indicate a notion of the Deity, and that the dead were so clothed to shew that the idea remained with them. Dion Chrysostom says that the ceremonies of the Mysteries were an alternation of light and darkness. It is said that healing of the sick by sleeping in the temples was an actual fact, aided often by dreams, and was "not fable as amongst the Greeks, but actual fact."

The Mysteries of Isis required of the candidate a lengthy purification and
severe bodily trials. It was a representation of the trials of the soul in the future life, from which lessons for conduct in this life might be drawn. We shall see more of this in comparison with the Greek Mysteries, which were derived from the Egyptian.

In the drama of Osiris the legend relates how he was slain by his brother Typhon, in like manner as Bacchus was slain by the Titans, and his body thrown into the Nile. The river carried its burthen to Byblos and deposited it on a "tamarind" tree, which enclosed it in its growth. Isis travels about lamenting the loss of her husband, as did the Grecian Demeter and Latin Ceres lamenting the loss of her daughter Proserpine, and is at {83} length led to the place where the body rests and which she recovers. After this Typhon seizes again the body, dismembers it, and scatters the pieces over the 26 nomes into which Egypt was divided. The sorrowing Isis now wanders about to collect the various pieces, and at length recovers all but the generative part, for which a substitute is made. Eventually the son Horus overthrows Typhon, and reigns in the place of Osiris.

A curious analogy with Masonry may here be noted: the sacred word of the
Hebrews, JHVH, in that language signifies generation; in the Egyptian Mysteries it is the generative organ which is lost and a substitute made; in Masonry it is the word which is lost and a substitute which is given in its place. A level was recently found in the tomb of Semoteus, a King of the 20th dynasty. (Initiation, April, 1903, p. 39.)

In the natural aspect, followed by Plutarch, the allegory represents tropical heat and the fertilisation of the land by canals for the distribution of the Nile, which they represented by the sun, with a stream of water issuing from the mouth. In the second place Osiris is the sun, Isis the moon, Typhon is night, Nepthys twilight. Thus the sun sets in the west pursued by the moon, lost in the darkness of night, to rise again as Horus in the newborn sun. In another and higher aspect, Osiris and Isis symbolise spirit and matter, {Symbol: Venus}, or the two forces. Isis is usually represented as a mother nursing her son Horus, and this simile is used by Grecian philosophers, who were always less reticent than the Copt, to symbolise primal matter; thus Oscellus terms it "mother nurse"; Plato, "the reception of all generation as its nurse"; and Aristotle, "a mother." The "Aureus" attributed to Hermes makes use of this symbolism to reveal, and yet hide, the alchemical process. The true spiritual import, we must seek in the "Book of the Dead", for the "Books of Hermes" are lost to us. Brother Malapert professes to find the ceremony of Initiation in the jewels, rituals, and sculpture deposited in the Louvre, certain of which are considered {84} to shew that the approaching candidate, properly prepared, is taken charge of by his guide, and the purifications proceed, in regular order -- until the Neophyte is brought before the hierophant, who is seated upon his throne with the scales of justice before him. It is a Mystery of the cross as an emblem of eternal life, equally a Cabiric symbol, or still more ancient.

The Rev. Mr. C. W. Leadbeater has some very interesting remarks in regard to the ancient sacerdotal initiations, for the priests had their own Initiations to which they alone were admissible. He claims that the cross was the emblem of the descent into matter, and that, to represent this, the candidate was laid upon a cruciform bier, hollowed to suit the body of the candidate, wearied after a long preliminary ritual. His arms were loosely bound with cords, and he was then carried from the Hall of initiation into the Crypt, or lower vault of the temple, and placed upon a sarcophagus to represent actual burial. He remained thus for three entire days, whilst the tests of earth, water, air, and fire were applied to the divorced soul, as a practical experience of invulnerability. On the fourth day of the entombment he was brought forth and exposed to the first rays of the rising sun, and restored to natural life. He thus develops the Rubric of the hierophant: "Then shall the candidate be bound upon a wooden cross, he shall die, he shall be buried, and shall descend into the underworld; after the third day he shall be brought back from the dead, and shall be carried up into heaven to be the right hand of him from whom he came, having learned to guide (or rule) the living and the dead." There is a very ancient dirge, called the "Maneros", which is supposed to have been chanted over the Neophyte. There are said to be some ancient mystical MSS. which speak of this trial as "the hard couches of those who are in travail in the act of giving birth to themselves"; that is "crucified before the sun." Plutarch says that "when a man dies he goes through the same experiences as those who have their consciousness increased in the Mysteries. {85} Thus in the terms GR:tau-epsilon-lambda-epsilon-upsilon-tau-alpha-nu and GR:tau- epsilon-lambda-epsilon-iota-sigma-theta-alpha-iota we have an exact correspondence, word to word and fact to fact." It seems evident from this, and from other things that we shall mention in our next chapter, that Plutarch is alluding to the actual divorce of soul from the body, related to what may be an allegory which he recites, under the tale of a man named Aridaeus or Thespesius of Soli in Asia Minor, who apparently died from a fall, and after three days returned to his body, and detailed his experience of the exquisite sights which he beheld.<<"Theos. rev.," xxii, p. 232. Vide also "Secret Doctrine," ii. p. 359.>>

In the year 1898 an interesting discovery was made of the tomb of Amenophis

II. It is entered by a steep inclined gallery terminating in a 26ft. well, having passed which the tomb is reached. In the first chamber was found the body of a man bound to a rich boat-like structure, his arms and feet are tied with cords, and his mouth gagged with a cloth, the breast and head have marks of wounds. In the second chamber were found the bodies of a man, woman, and child. The third is the tomb of the king, the roof is supported by massive square columns painted deep blue and studded with golden stars, the walls covered with paintings. At one end is the sandstone Sarcophagus, rose coloured, which enclosed the mummy with chaplets of flowers round the neck and feet. To the right is a small chamber in which other mummies of later kings have been placed. The floors of all the chambers are covered with such articles as statues, vases, wooden models of animals, and boats. The Mysteries of the Latin Bacchus, who is Dionysos in Greece and Assyria,

and Osiris in Egypt, are thus spoken of by Macrobius: "The images or statues of Bacchus, represent him sometimes as a young man, at other times with the beard of a mature man, and lastly with the wrinkles of old age. The differences relate to the sun, a tender child at the winter solstice, such as the Egyptians represent him on a certain day, when they bring forth from an obscure nook of their Sanctuary his infantine {86} image, because the sun being then at the shortest, seems to be but a feeble infant gradually growing from this moment."

The learned French writer Christian considers that the 22 symbolical designs of the Tarot cards embody the synthesis of the Egyptian Mysteries, and that they formed the decoration of a double row of 11 pillars through which the candidate for Initiation was led, and that these designs further correspond with the 22 characters of all primitive alphabets.<<Vide "The Tarot," by Papus.>> Dr. Clarke finds the traditional characters of the ancient Mysteries in our modern pantomime.<<Vol. iv, p. 459, quoted in Disraeli s "Curiosities of Literature.">> He says that Harlequin is Mercury; Columbine is Psyche, or Soul; the old man is Charon, the ferryman over Styx; the clown is Momus, and he engraves the subject of an ancient vase, which, he says, represents Harlequin, Columbine, and Clown, as we see them on the stage. In further evidence of how such legends survive, in new dresses, Baring Gould has shown that the trials of St. George are but a transformation of the various martyrdoms and resurrections which were related to the weeping worshippers in the temples of Babylon and Assyria at the fate of Tammuz and Adonis; and that the dragon story in the life of St. George is but that of other dragon slayers in Semitic and Aryan Mythology. Maimonides mentions the work of Abn Washih as alluding to this. On the agricultural classes of the Mysteries there is a curious old Babylonian work translated by Chwolsohn about 35 years ago. Maimonides, who was physician of Saladin, "circa" 1200 A.D., speaks of it as "full of heathenish foolishness . . . preparation of talismans," etc. Its title "Nabatheans" is derived from the god Nebo, and the Persian Yezids say that the sect went from Busrah to Syria, and that they believe in seven archangels or stars. The book is a difficult esoteric one, by an amanuensis named Qu-tamy, and precedes the era of Nebuchadnezzar.

We now come to what is more interesting to Free {87} Masons, and to

Geometry which is one of the mystic or esoteric keys of most sacred books. Geometry, as applied to land-measuring, had its origin in Egypt, and we quoted the authority of Diodorus that the sacred alphabet represented some of the

implements of labour. In early times the superintendence of art was a priestly office. It is notewor-

thy that the tomb of the ancient King Osymandius has a ceiling of stars upon a blue ground the like of which is found in the Cathedrals of York, Canterbury, and Gloucester, truly there is nothing new under the sun. The tomb of an ancient Egyptian was recently opened by M. Maspero, and buried with the body were found the working tools of a Mason.   Herodotus informs us that they prohibited burial in wool for the reason of which he refers to the rites of Orphic and Pythagoric initiation, thus confirming their affinity with Egypt. Cleopatra s needle was a comparatively modern re-erection by that Queen, at a time when the Roman building fraternities may have influenced Egypt; but at its base was found, when taken down for removal to America, various stones designedly laid in accordance with Masonic Symbolism, and upon a block, in form of a square, was placed a cube, or Ashlar, also a stone wrought from the purest limestone symbolising purity.<<Vide "Egyptian Obelisks" (Weisse).>> In the Osirian temple at Philae, re-erected on the site of a   more   ancient   one,   about   300   B.C.,   are   found   many   interesting representations, such as the death and resurrection of Osiris, and also a cube opened out in the form of a Latin cross, with a man s head in the upper square. A writer in the Indian "Freemasons Friend" maintains that the Copts have preserved, from their ancestors to the present day, much information upon Masonry which may be gathered from the Hajjar, or stone cutters.   He also adds that Masons Marks are found upon the stones of buildings, as old even as the "well" of the great pyramid. There was a fine old stone in the possession of Consul John Green on which was the point within a circle, triple {88} tau, square, five-pointed star, crux ansata, level, triangle, {symbols: circle with point in center, Royal-Arch triple tau [like a "T" striking the cross-bar of an "H"], inverted "L", Pentagram, Ankh, upright sledge-hammer shape, triangle with dot in center}. Outside the Rosetta-gate are, or were, some old granite remains and two statues of Isis and Osiris, on the base of each of which, as well as on the many stones around, are found the first, second, and fourth of the characters before-mentioned, {symbols: circle with point in center, triple-tau, Pentagram}. On an old stone of red granite built into the Courthouse of Rosetta amongst those we have mentioned, and others, are the tau, sloping ladder of three steps, trowel, {symbols: "T", slanting elongate Roman numeral III, downward triangle with a handle on top}. At Heliopolis the above marks are found, as well as others of a different character, eye, crook, two concentric demicircles,
{symbols: oval on side with two horizontal lines issuing from ends, shape like a
vertical line with a little "u" at top right, open eye with eyelid, shape like a rainbow with only two colors}.<<F. M. Mag., 1861, v, p. 487.>> Amongst Masons Marks of the 12th dynasty, say 3,000-2,400 B.C., we find the svastica
{symbol: Swastika}, the equal-limbed cross {+}, both plain and in a circle
{Symbol: Circumscribed Greek cross}, our five-pointed star {Symbol: Pentagram}, open angles crossed like square and compasses, delta, letter H, &c., {symbols: +, circumscribed Greek cross, Pentagram, intersecting chevrons upright and inverted like the sigil of Saturn from the Kamia, Fire, "H"}.<<"A.Q.C.", iii.>> Guild Masonry tells us that semicircles denote an Arch Guild.
"Greece and Italy." The Dionysian and Bacchic rites, through which we may better comprehend the Egyptian, were of two classes. In the first Ceres goes in search of Proserpine to Hades, as did Ishter when she sought her lover

Isdhubar, Duzi, or Tamzi, these rites were in especial of an agricultural nature. In the higher Mysteries the Neophyte represented Bacchus. Plutarch says that Typhon revolted against Osiris, tore his body in pieces, mangled his limbs, scattered them abroad, and filled the earth with rage and violence. In like manner in those of Greece and Italy the rebel Titans tear in pieces the god Bacchus, and as these Titans were Cyclops it appears to mythologise the war of races. As we shall treat of these Mysteries more fully in our next chapter, we will only add here a few quotations as to their teaching. The Orphic verses apply these Mysteries to the sun, as known by many names: --
"The sun, whom men call Dionysos, is a surname, One Zeus, one Aides, one Helios, one Dionysos."
{89}

The Oracle of Apollo Clarius says: "Much it behoves that the wise should conceal the unsearchable orgies. But if thy judgment is weak, know that of gods who exist, the highest of all is Jao. He is Aides in winter; Zeus at the coming of spring-time; Helios in summer-heat; and in autumn graceful Jao."

Macrobius says that it was an inviolable secret that the sun in the upper hemisphere is called Apollo; also that the ancients perceived a resemblance between the sun and the wolf, for as flocks disappear at the sight of the latter, so stars disappear before the sun.

As the Chaldean technique was used in the Cabiric Mysteries, so in these we are said to have a trace of Sanscrit. The words Konx Oumpax, was a formal dismissal, or as we might say, "go in peace"; the original is said to be identical with the words "Kanska om Paksha," with which the Brahmins conclude some of their more important ceremonies. Le Plongeon finds the expression may be interpreted in Maya language, "go hence, scatter."

We equally find a Theosophical and Art fraternity in the Dionysiacs of Greece, and the Persians were near kindred of the Hellenic Greeks; but according to Herodotus the descent was Egyptian, for he says that the Creek Dionysos and the Latin Bacchus is Osiris, and that the same rites are practised in both countries, but though they are known to him he is compelled to be silent. Yet Dionysos is the Assyrian Dionisia, the Phoenician Melcarth, and the Akkadian Izdhubar.

The art of building in flat stone blocks in contradistinction to Cyclopean Masonry is mentioned in our last chapter, and seems to have been adopted about the period when Egypt colonised the country, and as we know the perfection masonry had reached in Egypt ages before the 16th century B.C., we may reasonably conclude that they introduced the improved art, with the Dionysian Mysteries. At any rate we find not only the State Mysteries of Dionysos, but as in other cases mentioned, where caste Hellenes or Aryans had invaded the native population, {90} an Art fraternity, under the same name, which above 3,000 years ago was designated the "Dionysian Artificers," and which superseded the style of the Cabiri by an improved system.

This body executed all level work in Greece and the Asia Minor at the period, and were an Incorporated Society; there are many inscriptions in reference to them, and their existence is placed beyond doubt. Their organisation was identical with the later Roman Colleges, which again have their counterpart in English Guild Free Masonry. They are said to have rebuilt the temple of Heracles at Tyre. Herodotus states that the priests told him that the temple

had existed for 2,300 years, and the old author enlarges upon two pillars which it contained, the one of gold, the other of emerald, which shone exceedingly at night, and which may emblemise the two pillars which Sanconiathon says were dedicated by men of the first ages to Fire and Wind.

In 1874 a peculiar discovery was made at Pompeii of a table in Mosaic work, which is now in the National Museum of Naples (No. 109,998). It is about a foot square and fixed in a strong wooden frame. The ground is of a greyish- green stone, in the centre is a human skull in white, grey, and black. Above the skull is a level, of coloured wood, the points of brass, and from the top point, by a white thread, is suspended a plumb-line. Below the skull is a wheel with six spokes, and on the upper rim of the wheel is a butterfly, the wings being edged with yellow and the eyes blue. Through the protraction of the plumb-line the skull, wings, and wheel, have the appearance of being halved. On the left is an upright spear, the bottom being of iron, and resting on the ground, from this there hangs, by a golden cord, a garment of scarlet and a purple robe. The symbol of a purple robe is worthy of note, as it corresponds with what Clemens said of the Cabiri, as quoted in our last chapter.

The Dionysian Mysteries passed into Phoenicia by way of Babylon, and thence entered Syria in dedication to the {91} god Adonis, from Adonai -- Lord, passing to Persia, Cyprus and Athens; they continued in Syria until the fourth century A.D. As Adonis was the sun who dies to rise again, as in the other Mysteries using other names, so the symbolic representation was conducted by acting the death of an individual for whom lamentation was made; Proserpine and Venus contend for the body of the handsome god, and the difficulty is settled by a six months residence with each. In the drama the priest, after an interval, signified the resuscitation of the hero by exclaiming: "thanks be to god for out of pains salvation is come unto us." The cries of grief were then changed for hymns and exclamations of joy. It is the ceremony of the weeping for Osiris by Isis, for Tammuz by Astarte, for Tamzi by Ishter, for Mahadeva by Sita, and that of which we read in the prophet Exekiel where he says: "behold I saw women weeping for Tammuz." The Phrygians, who were a very ancient Armenian colony, had a similar ceremony in honour of Anach, or Annoch (Enoch), for whom they mourned and rejoiced at the end of the old year. The Apamean medals of this race clearly refer to Noah and the Cabiri, and represent thereon a boat holding eight persons, and the word No. This Noachian legend appears to commingle the heavenly boat of Hea with the eight Cabiri, the deluge tradition, and that of Persia, which says that their first king sent out colonies in pairs of all created things. The Cabiric Mysteries of Phrygia were in honour of Atys and Cybele, and their priests denominated Corybantes.

Professor Louis, a Jew, who lectured recently before the Society of Biblical Archaeology, advanced that there were Guilds of Artizans and Craftsmen amongst his forefathers. This is not surprising when we remember that the exponents of the law made it incumbent upon themselves to follow some handicraft, and the "Mishna" advocates the dignity of labour, in numerous passages, such as the following: "He who derives his livelihood from the labour of his hands is as great as he who fears God." {92}

In all the countries, mentioned in this chapter, the religious and Masonic emblems, and the symbols of Initiation that have come down to us are of the same special type, in all time. Amongst these may be named, the pentagon,

the hexagon, the double triangles, the same in a circle and with a central point, the Jain cross of four squares, the equal-limbed cross, the lengthened cross, and crosses of other forms. At Chunar, near Benares, is found a triangle enclosing a rose. The 49 Hindu caste-marks are carved upon the stones of their ancient fanes; and we have the mystic picture of a god crucified in space.

In the case of Gautama Buddha who reformed the Buddha doctrine, or Jain religion, and sought to abolish caste, we have Masonic allegory in announcing to his disciples that he had obtained final beatitude, and the extinction of desire. He compares his body to a house, which the Great Architect will not re- erect: --

"Through various transmigrations I must travel, if I do not discover The Buddha that I seek.
Painful are repeated transmigrations! I have seen the Great Architect!
Thou shalt not build me another house. Thy rafters are broken,
Thy roof-timbers scattered; My mind is detached,
I have obtained extinction of desire."

The more humane worship and morality of the Aryans exercised an all- powerful influence upon the rest of the world. In the time of the elder Cyrus, or Khai-Khosru the Persian conqueror of Media, the State system was the Median Magism of the first Zaradust of Bactria. This Cyrus was the father of Cyaxarus or Ahashuerus, of Cambyses, and of Bardes. Cyaxarus on his father s death succeeded to the moiety of East Persia, and married Esther, or Atossa, so named after Ishter, the goddess who {93} descended into Hades. Cambyses or Lohrasp was a half brother by the daughter of Astyages or Afrasaib King of Media, and inherited the other moiety; he conquered Egypt about 520 B.C., and having first slain his brother Bardes, and then destroyed Cyaxarus, married his widow Atossa, and so again united Media and Persia. His son Cyrus II. favoured the Magi and liberated the Jews; he conquered Babylon 518 B.C., and died without issue 506 B.C. The way was thus paved for Darius Hystaspes, or the son of Gustasp, of the Achaemenion or Royal race of Persia, had been Viceroy of Egypt 520 B.C., and who, on the death of the crazy Cambyses 518 B.C., would seem to have married his widow, in which case she would have been the wife of three kings; and the pretensions of Darius might thus originate, as he was not, by birth, entitled to the throne. There is a legend which says that seven princes entered into a confederacy, and agreed, on their journey, that whosoever s horse first neighed, at sight of the rising sun, should be King, and the lot fell to Darius. This prince was everywhere successful, but the contest ended in the destruction of the Magi, whose growing power had long been offensive to the Persian Mazdeans. An Armenian of the name of Aracus, and a Babylonian of the name of Nadintabelus, set themselves forth as descendants of the Ancient Kings of Babylon, but were defeated in the year 493
B.C. Darius records his numerous victories in mild language, upon the
Behustan rock, and attributes his success to the grace of Ormuzd, in striking contrast to the bloodthirsty and fanatical boastings of the Kings of Assyria, and

we cannot doubt that when Ezra the Chaldean, re-edited the Jewish Scriptures, they gained in the direction of humanity by this contact with the Aryans.

The destruction of the Magi was commemorated by a festival termed the Magaphonia; eventually, by careful management, the brotherhood made their way again to power, and Plato speaks of the system as the most pure of all religious schools, and there is no doubt that as Gnostic {94} Christians and Islamites their succession has descended to our own times, and a form of the Magaphonia may be represented in the Mouharren, and similar festivals in honour of Houssein, or Ali. It would appear that after the successes of Darius his religious views as to Mazdeism may have undergone some change in favour of the Judeo-Magism of Media. He was succeeded by his son Cyaxarus III., or Xerxes, he and Darius his son were the first and second liberators of the Jews, and hence the originators of the second temple at Jerusalem.

In Egypt the Persians were succeeded by the Greek Ptolemies following upon the conquests of Alexander the Great, and these by the Roman Emperors and Consuls. Many sublime edifices were erected, including the building of Alexandria 332 B.C. The temple of Osiris at Philae was begun about 300 B.C., and building operations thereon continued for about two centuries, and here the Mysteries of Osiris were celebrated until late into Christian times. James Anderson, in his "Constitutions," says that Euclid the geometrician, and Straton the philosopher, superintended the erection of several great edifices.

With the foundation of Alexandria, and the introduction therein of the recondite doctrines of the Greek philosophers, which they had gathered by ransacking the Mysteries of all other nations, Ptolemy I. resolved to make it the seat of occult worship, by establishing there the Mysteries of Serapis, which united with the Egyptian rites of Isis and Osiris the learning of the Greeks. To inaugurate this scheme he brought from Sinope in Pontus a statue of the god. The representations of this deity often accompany him with the three-headed Cerberus, combining a lion, a wolf, and a dog, whilst his body is wound round with a serpent. He typifies Osiris not only as an earthly king, but as a judge of the world of spirits. In the work of Mr. C. W. King, who writes on Gnosticism, is a sard of about the reign of Hadrian, which represents the god as seen by Macrobius, Isis standing before him, with her sistrum in her hand as if in supplication, whilst {95} in her other hand is an ear of wheat: the legend is HE KURRA ISIS AGNE, immaculate is our Lady Isis. Erastosthenes, who lived 276-196 B.C., terms her the Celestial virgin.

Other inscriptions referring to Serapis are equally noteworthy; that on

Raspe s No. 1490 is -- EIS ZEUS SERAPIS AGION ONOMA SEBAS EOS

ANATOLE CHTHON, translated, The one only Lord Serapis, the holy name, glory, light, the dayspring, the earth, often abreviated to GR:Sigma-Omega- Sigma. He is also called EIS ZOOS THEOS, the only living God. The "holy name" may be the Arcane I-A-O, which Clemens says was worn upon the person by Initiates.

Apuleius comments upon these Mysteries but does so very reticently. He informs us that he had been initiated into those of the Great goddess Isis, as representing nature; and that though ceremonials of Serapis differed therefrom that the doctrine was the same. Damaskios asserts that the god appeared in a visible, but superhuman form, to his worshippers at Alexandria. The Rite, as in other Mysteries, required a nine days fast and purification. Apuleius hints

that the priests had other ceremonies, for he states that after Initiation into the Mysteries of Osiris he was made a Pastopheri of the temple and received into the College of Priests, exposing his bald head to the multitude, as a Catholic priest does his tonsure. In the "Virgin of tke World," by Hermes, Isis informs her son Horus that there was a triple set of Mysteries. (1) "Initiating them in the arts, sciences, and the benefits of civilised life." (2) "Religious representations and sacred Mysteries." (3) "Prophet Initiation, so that the prophet who lifts his hands to the gods should be instructed in all things." Hence it is necessary to keep in mind, both in antiquity and even in later and modern times, art, exoteric rites, and esoteric Initiation. Drummond expresses the opinion that the Chartomi, or superior priests of Egypt, alone possessed the full revelation, which they protected by a triple key of symbolic explanation. Bin Washih {96} says<<"Descent of Symb. Mas." John Amrstrong, Liverpool, 1896.>> that there were four classes of priests of Hermes (1) those of his male descendants, (2) the descendants of his brothers, (3) the descendants of his sisters or Easterns, (4) of the strangers who mingled with the family; and he gives a very interesting account of their alleged ceremonies.

The Eleusinian, Serapian, and Mythraic Mysteries were all very popular in
Rome, and spread into all countries, practising their rites side by side with the aboriginal Mysteries, for the utmost tolerance existed amongst all the priests. All are known to have existed in Britain, flourishing generally until the 4th century of Christianity, and practised long after in secret.

Besides the State Mysteries, Alexandria became the centre whence radiated the Mystic schools, the Cabala, Gnosticism, Neo-Platonism, and Arcane Christianity. The Emperor Hadrian when Consul reports that there were no bishops of Christ, Chiefs of Synagogues, Theurgists, Diviners, who were not also worshippers of Serapis, implying a general recognition of Serapis as the personal God of the world, and that the living God is the same under many names. The learned Cardinal Henry Newman asserts that the Arcane Discipline of the early Alexandrian Church was the introduction of Platonism into Christianity; it was, however, that Platonism formed by the union of Greek thought with Egyptian Osirianism in the Mysteries of Serapis. Mr. C. W. King in his "Gnostics" says "there can be no doubt that the head of Serapis, marked as the face is by a grave and pensive majesty, supplied the first idea for the conventional portraits of the Saviour." It is equally certain that the images of Isis and Horus continued to be manufactured, and were renamed as those of the Virgin and Child. Amongst the noted Christians of this period, who were Serapians and Christians or Members of the Arcane Discipline, were Origen and Ammonius Saccus, the catechists; the latter established a School in which he obligated his Disciples {97} to secrecy.<<Cardinal Newman.>> It is known also that the early Christians used the Tau cross on their tombs.<<"A.Q.C.", v.
p. 2.>> There seems even no doubt that the pre-Christian Rites had a Mystery
of the Cross, and there is said to be an ancient painting in Egypt of a candidate laid upon a cruciform bier. Justin Martyr observes that "the sign of the cross is impressed on all nature. There is scarcely a handicraftsman but uses the figure of it amongst the implements of his industry. It forms a part of man himself, as may be seen when he extends his arms in prayer." And, apart from this, the Spiritual and consolatory faith breathed in the "Ritual of the Dead" is so much in consonance with the beliefs of the Christian, that it must convince the most hardened sceptic of the antiquity of the doctrine, if he even discredit

them as articles of belief, and confirms the words of Augustine that Christianity existed from the beginning of the human race, until Christ came in the flesh.

It will form a fitting close to this chapter if we again point out that all ancient buildings contain a system of Masons Marks which were cut by the Masons to shew by whom the work was done. These are either symbols, emblems, or more or less the alphabet prevalent where the work was done. Of great antiquity in Egypt they are equally ancient in India. We find the symbols of these two ancient nations in use in Europe, side by side with Greek numerals, the Magical alphabet and Runic letters. That this custom has been handed down from remote ages to our own days as an organised form by which to ascertain the work of each member of an organised and united Fraternity, is one of the strongest arguments that can be used in favour of the equal antiquity, and faithful transmission of the organisation and ceremonies of modern Free Masonry which the reader will gather has so many points of resemblance to the ancient Mysteries; for there is ample evidence to shew that the Mark was a part of the acquisition of an accepted Mason {98} for centuries. But as there were various branches of the Mysteries, there must at one time have been various, varying Rites of Free Masonry. The origin of Tally (Taille -- Fr.) Sticks is very ancient and they are yet used

occasionally. The Celtic Ogham alphabet had a like origin. It consisted of notches cut at the corner of a square stone, or else from a stem-line. The letters B, L, F, S, N, are formed by cutting strokes at right angles to the stem- line on the right hand, and the letters H, D, T, C, Q, at right angles to the left. Thus a single stroke to the right is B, and to the left is H, two to the right is L, and the same number to the left is D. Three to one side is F, three to the other is T. Long strokes numbering from one to five, cutting the stem diagonally, expressed M, G, Ng, St, R, and short strokes, numbering from one to five, cutting across the stem at right angles give the vowels. The old Runic Staves for Calendars were somewhat similar. Strange symbols were used to mark the several festivals, but the days were indicated by notches. As Masons marks the Runic character is common. ("Chambers Journal," 1897, p. 285. S. Baring Gould.)

The evidence of this chapter goes to prove, with what has gone before, that

there was a system of Art Mysteries attached to the Sacerdotal Mysteries, and that they only became specifically operative by the introduction of caste laws, by Aryan invaders, and the necessities of the times.

CHAPTER IV. THE MYSTERIES IN RELATION

THE MYSTERIES IN RELATION TO PHILOSOPHY.
THE chief difficulty in the minds of writers who have written upon the Mysteries and Freemasonry is owing to the varieties of names by which the former have been known in different nations, and the comparatively modern

designation of the latter Society. But this difficulty disappears in a great measure when we recognise that the Rites are of great antiquity, derived from a primitive source, that they had all the same general principles and varied chiefly but in the technicalities and language of the country in which they were celebrated. We may safely admit that the general characteristics of the Mysteries were the same in all nations.

Thus in the course of ages, by national divergence in the mode of expressing thought, new names for the old Rites arose, and translations made into new tongues. The Assyrian Dionisu is the Greek Dionysos, the Latin Bacchus, and the Egyptian Osiris. In other cases the Mysteries were known by their place of conferment, or by the name of the Hierophant who introduced them. In other cases names varied according to the particular degree of the writer; thus it is said that Bacchus the Lord of the Cross and the pine-cone, becomes Iacchus in the mouth of an epoptae addressing him as Lord of the planet. Similarly we learn from Plutarch that Ishter, Demeter, Ceres, and Isis are all one, and represent living matter, or matter vivified by spirit, which is a doctrine of the Mystae, or first grade of Initiation. The higher spiritual birth of the twice-born is taught in the martyrdom of these gods. {101} Each nation, however, gave to the Mysteries a tinge of its own culture, precisely as Osiris, Isis, and Horus, are counterparts of the two deific principles, and created forms, equally with the Christian Trinity of Joseph, Mary and Jesus. Pausanius gives the name of Saotus or saviour to the Mystery-god, and he was designated Liberator, and GR:Upsilon-Eta-Sigma.

Varron, the most learned of the Latins, in his treatise "De Lingun Latina,"

says, iv. p. 17: "The principal gods are Heaven and Earth. They are the same gods which in Egypt are named Serapis, Isis, and Harpocrates, which with Phoenicians are Thoth and Astarte, the same in Latin as Saturn and Ops (the earth). In effect the earth and the heavens are the sacred instruction of Samothrace, treated as the Great Gods." That is they are the active and passive principles of nature, and belong to the earlier and less cultured life of the Greeks. Tertullian says that they raised three altars to the great gods -- that is the male and female principles became three in their progeny -- the oldest of trinities.

The ostensible hero of the Mysteries of Greece was the sun-god, and Martinus Capellus, in his hymn to the sun written in the fifth century, says: --

"Thee, the dwellers on the Nile, adore as Serapis, And Memphis worships thee as Osiris.

Thou art worshipped as Mithra, Dis, and cruel Typhon; In the sacred rites of Persia thou art Mythras,

In Phrygia the beautiful Atys;

And Lybia bows down to thee as Amon, Phoenician Byblos as Adonis;

Thus the whole world adores thee under different names."

Ausonius has verses to the like effect, adding Dionysos for India, and Liber for Italy: --

"Hail! true image of the gods and thy father s face, Thou whose sacred name, surname, and omen,

Three letters that agree with the number 608."<<Vide Pike s "Morals and Dogma," p. 587>> {101} YHS = 400 + 8 + 200 = 608. In Chaldee and Hebrew, Cham or Ham, heat, is also 608.

Although Cumberland, Bishop of Peterborough, in his "Origines Gentium Antiquissmae" has set himself the impossible task of deriving all mankind from Noah within the period of the Rabinical chronology, he has many valuable quotations which tend toe elucidate the Mysteries. He quotes Herodotus as affirming in his Euterpe, for a known truth, that Ceres or Demeter is also Isis; Clemens Alexandrinus also affirms it, and proves it out of a book of Leon, who wrote the history of the Egyptian gods. Diodorus Siculus is cited by Eusebius as saying that Osiris is Dionysus or Bacchus, and that Isis is Demeter or Ceres; Diodorus makes Prometheus the crucified Cabric God to be contemporary with Osiris. Plutarch quotes Anticlides to prove that Osiris is the same person as Dionysus or Bacchus. Prometheus is said to be son of Japhetus, or Japhet, and Isis the wife of Osiris his daughter, as is also asserted by Anticlides. Another son of Japhetus, according to Apollodorus, was Atlas. Pausanius affirms the Prometheus and his son Aetnaus planted the Cabiric Mysteries in Boetia, but that they received this sacred depositum from Ceres. Much of this is mystical, but it all goes to prove what we began by saying, namely, that the Mysteries were all one, and varied only in the language.

Herodotus speaks of the celebration at night, in Egypt, of the sufferings of a

god whose name is too sacred to be written. The Phoenician Mysteries, as we learn from Meursius, and Plutarch, exhibited the corpse of a young man strewn with flowers, for whom the women mourned, and for whom a tomb was erected. Macrobius says that in the Mysteries of Adonis there was a nine days fast and lamentation which was succeeded by hymns of joy in honour of the risen god. Fermecius informs us the similar rites were used in the Mythraic Mysteries. The Chevalier Ramsay affirms that this is the characteristic of all the Mysteries, and that of their traditional history, {102} and is a prophesy of the coming of a suffering Messiah, who is symbolised by the sun.<<"Nat. and Revd. Religion," ii,

p. 200.>>

According to Herodotus the Mysteries entered Greece from Egypt, and from Greece they entered Italy; and he informs us in positive language that the Rites of the Egyptian Osiris and Latin Bacchus are the same, and were carried into Greece about 2,000 years before his time (450 B.C.) by Melampus, who either took them direct, or derived them from Cadmus and his Tyrian companions. The system of these which Orpheus propagated taught a divine trinity in unity, which, according to Damaskios, was represented by a Dragon with three heads, that of a bull, a lion, and between a god with wings of gold; these Rites, if we may rely on tradition, were devoted to music. Dionysius Halicarnassus says that the priests of Serapis chanted a hymn of seven vowels: the same had place in Greece, and there are representations of these seven heads, over each of which is seen one of the vowels.

All the Mysteries had three principal trials or baptisms, namely, by water,
fire, and air; and there were three specially sacred emblems, the phallus, egg, and serpent, thus represented GR:Iota-Omicron-Phi. The two generative emblems were sacred in all the Mysteries.

The advantages gained by initiation into these Rites are thus set forth by various writers: They diffuse a spirit of unity and humanity wherever introduced; purify the soul from ignorance and pollution; secure the peculiar

aid of the gods; the means of arriving at the perfection of virtue; the serene happiness of a holy life; the hope of a peaceful death and endless felicity; also a distinguished place in the Elysian fields; whilst those who have not participated in Initiation shall dwell after death in places of darkness and horror.<<"Anacharsis" (Abbe Barthelemy, who gives the authors). v. p. 213.>>

Porphyry gives the following as the precepts of the Mysteries: (1) Honour parents; (2) Venerate the Gods; (6) be Humane to animals. Plutarch (Laconic Apothegms {103} of Lysander) to confess all wicked acts. The pre-Hebrew commandments termed the seven precepts of the Noachidae are: (1) Abstain from Idolatry; (2) Blaspheme not; (3) Do no murder; (4) Commit not Adultery; (5) Do not steal; (6) Administer justice; (7) Eat not flesh cut from the live animal.

The Rites of Eleusis in Greece are those of which we have the fullest particulars, and we shall therefore take them as the complement of all the others, and give as much as can be gathered from prejudiced and unprejudiced sources, poets, philosophers, and their bitter enemies the Christians. The Rite is said to have followed the Orphic doctrine, and to have been established about 1423 B.C., in the reign of Erectheus King of Athens, which city had previously been occupied by a colony from Egypt. Though best known, yet not the most ancient, the Eleusinia would seem to have constituted rather a democratic society than a Sacerdotal College, as if their intention was to absorb all the popularity of these institutions; to be followed, at a later period, by the appropriation, by minor schools of Philosophers, of all the knowledge to be gained in these Colleges. It is, however, noteworthy that the tradition of the ancient unity of King and Priest was preserved in the title of Basileus or King given to the Presiding officer; and Lysias says that it was his duty to offer up prayers, and to preserve morality. These Mysteries were at the same time essentially secret and sacred, embodying a scenic representation, in which all classes might participate except bastards and slaves, who were especially excluded by the action of Euclid, the Archon, or chief, in 402 B.C., and a different person from the later Geometrician. It is worthy of note that the old Constitutional Charges of Free Masons exclude the same persons.

Although the Cabiric Mysteries, like those of Egypt, preserved, at least in
name, an idea of the worldly sciences, the Eleusinia would seem to have abandoned the pretensions to these, and only required that the Neophyte should {104} in youth be liberally and appropriately

educated. The time had arrived when art in Greece could be learned outside the Mysteries which constituted a holy drama, influencing the ancient theatre, and the "Mystery plays" of Christians. Mr. James Christie in his work upon the "Greek Vases" holds that phantasmal scenes in the Mysteries were shewn by transparencies, such as are yet used by the Chinese, Javanese, and Hindus. In symbol, he says, a ball of wool represents the thread of life not yet spun; gutta, fecundity; sesame, fertility; water, the creation of beings from that element; wine, the life; an olive leaf at the top of a vase, spirit; and a wavy line, water on which spirit acts.

There were Nine Archons, of whom the Chief was properly so called as the word means Commander, he had jurisdiction over all ecclesiastical and civil affairs, with the title of Eponymus. The second was Basileus or King, who superintended religious ceremonies, festivals, and Mysteries. The third was the Polemarchos, who had care of strangers and conduct of war. The other six

were termed Thesmothetae, from two words -- "law," and "I establish" they formed a tribunal for judging minor offences. All were elected by lot, were free of taxes, and on their Induction took an oath to administer justice impartially.

Certain noted persons, of whom Pythagoras was one of the earliest and most remarkable, travelled over the whole known world, in order to obtain Initiation in the Mysteries of the countries that he visited. The society which Pythagoras established, as well as others of later date, was the result of an attempt to combine in one common society the knowledge to be gained in all the Mysteries; curiously enough the same principle has been followed in Freemasonry. The Pythagorean Society may thus be considered the forerunner of the various Arcane Schools which followed its decay; it has the closest analogy with the Masonic Society, and whether we look upon this Craft as a primitive system, an ancient imitation of the Mysteries, or a slightly altered branch of the Cabiri, we may {105} equally expect to find that there is the same doctrine, or the same wisdom religion which lay at the foundation of all the Arcane Mysteries; and this is what we shall find as we proceed; and at the same time it is one of the strongest proofs we can expect to have of the antiquity of Free-masonry.

We will now enquire into the general nature of the ceremonial of the Eleusinia as a fair representation of what was taught in these schools. They consisted of the Lesser and Greater Mysteries for which there was a general preparation or apprenticeship in the shape of "a preparation from youth in appropriate disciplines." Between the conferment of these two sections there was a probation extending from one to five years. The drama went on parallel lines with the Egyptian "Ritual of the Dead," which dwells upon the moral and spiritual qualities, which are necessary in this life, that the soul may obtain justification in a future state. The apocryphal book called the "Wisdom of Solomon" (c. 17) would seem to describe the Tartarean terrors of the Mysteries, applied to the plagues of Egypt.

The magnificent temple of Eleusis was lighted by a single window in the roof, and images of the sun, moon, and mercury were represented therein. Macrobius says that the temple of Bacchus at Thrace was also round and lighted also by a round window in the roof, by which to introduce the resplendent image of the sun. Proclus says that the proceedings were begun with a prayer in which "heaven" and "earth" were respectively invoked. In respect to the signs of the Zodiac the same writer

informs us that six were considered male, and six female signs; and Porphyry assimilates the journey of the sun through these signs with the twelve labours of Hercules.   The three chief hierophants of the Mysteries bore respectively the symbols of the sun, moon, and mercury; and as the Basileus represented the Demiurgos who fashions rude matter or chaos into created forms, so it was typified that the Basileus was to recreate the Neophyte or draw him {106} from imperfect nature to a more refined state, or as Masons equally would say, with the philosophers, work him from the rough to the perfect Ashlar.   The Stolistes, according to Clemens Alexandrinus regulated the education of the young, and bore as their emblem of authority the square rule; and the prophet had suspended at the neck an urn with the water of regeneration.<<Oliver s "Landmarks," i. p. 161.>> The ceremonial of Initiation began by a solemn proclamation<<"Origen Adv Celsus," iii. p. 59.>>: "Let no one enter here whose hands are not clean, and
whose tongue is not prudent."

The candidate was also, as a preliminary, desired to confess his sins, or at least the greatest crime he had ever committed. He was required to bathe in the pure sea in face of the sun, and pour water on his head three times. Certain fasts were enjoined, after which the sacrifice of an animal was made. After two days the shows began with a procession, then followed for three days and three nights the mourning of Demeter for her daughter. After which a sacramental meal of cakes and liquor was partaken.

Prior to the Initiation there was an opening catechism as follows: -- The Hierophant demands: "Who are fit to be present at this ceremony?" To which the answer was: "Honest, good, and holy men."

The Hierophant then ordered: "Holy things for holy persons."

The Herald proclaimed: "Far hence the profane, the impious, all those polluted by sin." For an uninitiated person to remain after this was death.

Stobaeus quotes an ancient writer who says, that the first stage of Initiation "is a rude and fearful march through night and darkness," but this over, "a divine light displays itself, and shining plains and flowery meads open on all hands before them. There they are entertained with hymns and dances, with the sublime doctrines of faithful knowledge, and with revered and holy visions."

{107} The first portion was emblematical of the wanderings of the soul in the paths of error and the punishments it would thereby bring upon itself; and the second part represented the dispersion of the shades of night, before the brilliant sun of the Mysteries.

Justin Martyr gives the oath of Initiation as follows: -- "So help me heaven, the work of God who is great and wise; so help me the Word of the Father which he spake when he established the whole universe in his wisdom." Dion Chrysostom speaks of Mystic sounds and alternations of light and darkness, and the performance of Mystic dances in imitation of the movements of the planets round the sun. Plato in "Euthydemus" speaks of Mystic dances in the Corybantic (or Cabiric) Mysteries where the cradle of the young Bacchus was guarded with Mystic dance and music.

The following remarks of a Naasene, or Ophite Gnostic, on these Mysteries are given by Hippolytus, Martyr 235 A.D., and confirms other quotations we shall give from Virgil. He says that: "The Lesser Mysteries are those of Proserpine below and the path which leads to them is wide and spacious to conduct those who are perishing." It is the truth which Chrishna the Hindu god taught to Arjuna, namely that those who give themselves up to worldly pleasures will be confined to the sphere of the earth and be reborn in such bodies as they have merited: "It is easier for a camel to go through the eye of a needle than for a rich man to enter the kingdom of heaven"; "Broad is the way that leadeth to destruction and many there be that go in thereat; but straight is the gate and narrow is the way which leadeth to life, and few there be that find it." Apuleius in his account of his reception into the Isisic Mysteries, after being relieved of his brutish nature by eating roses, which was a flower sacred to Isis, proceeds to say that he approached the confines of Hades, having been borne through the elements, and that he saw the sun at midnight.

The Latin Virgil, a poet, Platonist, astrologer, and {108} Geometrician, has
some noteworthy passages which bear upon these details. Priam of Troy sent away his son Polydorus into Thrace, with a large treasure, and in order to obtain this his attendants murdered him. Aeneas, a Trojan Initiate and therefore a Cabir, happening, on reaching that part, to pull up a myrtle growing

upon a hillock, discovered by the lamentations, which the plant is represented as magically making, the murdered body of Polydorus, upon which his remains are taken up and decently interred. The myrtle was a plant sacred in the Mysteries, and Virgil here speaks of the "secret rites of Cybele, mother of the gods"; and Cybele was the name for Ceres amongst the Phrygian Cabiri. Again when Queen Dido resorts to Magical arts to detain Aeneas from sailing: (Book iv.)
"A leavened cake in her devoted hands
She holds, and next the highest altar stands; One tender foot was shod, the other bare,
Girt was her gathered gown, and loose her hair."

A maxim of Pythagoras was: "Sacrifice and adore unshod." Ovid describes Medea as having arms, breast, and knees made bare; and Roman Postulants for religious and political offices, assumed an air of humility, with cloak and tunic ungirt, arm and breast bare, and feet slipshod. The "toga candida" is yet used in Masonry.

Another quotation from Pythagoras is this: "The path of vice and virtue resembles the letter "Y"; from the excellence of the sentiment it was termed the "Golden Branch," of which the broad, left-hand line, symbolised the easy road to Tartarus, whilst the narrow right line represented the path to Elysium. Decius Magnus Ausonius, a poet of the fourth century says: "The Bough represents the dubious Y, or two paths of Pythagoras." The sacred branch of the Mysteries varied in the different rites: the erica or heath was sacred to Osiris, the rose to Isis, the ivy to Dionysos, the myrtle to Ceres, the lettuce to Adonis, the lotus to Hindus, the mistletoe to Druids, the acacia to Jews, the palm to Christians. {109}

Turn we now to Virgil s interesting book, which contains the account of the descent of Aeneas into Tartarus, and which undoubtedly embodies the drama of the Eleusinian representation of Hades and Elysium.

A Sybil, or prophetess, requires for the purpose to be undertaken, that Aeneas shall seek a Golden Branch which shoots from a small tree. It is the mistletoe of the Druids who were of this school, and styled the plant "pren" "puraur" or the tree of pure gold: it could only be cut by a pure, white-robed

Druid with bare feet, and by using a golden sickle, it probably formed a part of the "brew of Cerid-wen," which was given to the Initiate to aid the gift of intuition; the Aryo-Celts were then in Italy. This Golden Branch was to serve Aeneas as a passport, but as the Sybil informs him of the death of a friend, a fact unknown to him, the body has first to be found; this done we have Lamentations: --
"With groans and cries Misenius they deplore, Old Coryanus compassed "thrice" the crew, And dipped an "olive branch" in holy dew,
Which thrice he sprinkled round, and thrice aloud Invoked the dead, and then dismissed the crowd."

Virgil is careful to inform us that these were ancient Rites to the manes of the dead, and "Ancient," or York, Masons of the last century, and even some in our day, used these Rites.
Aeneas now follows the Sybil to Tartarus, and Virgil describes the fearful scenes he witnessed by way of punishments inflicted upon those who left this life in an impure state. Arrived at the double path of the Branch:
"Before our further way the fates allow,
Here must we fix on high the Golden-bough."

and:

"These holy rites performed, they took their way, Where long extended plains of pleasure lay."

He now reaches the Elysian fields, where he finds his father Anchises, who proceeds to instruct him in divine things, with prophetic intimations as to his future. {110}
Such was the nature of the Lesser Mysteries; the Greater were intended to shew the felicity of the soul, when purified from mortal passions, it was reborn to the realities of its spiritual nature. They are again an exemplification of the further teaching of Crishna to Arjuna, that he who worships good angels will go amongst them, but that he, who in thought and deed, joins himself to the Supreme Deity will enjoy an eternity of happiness: "Thou must be born again." An Initiate to the Lesser Mysteries, or those of Ceres, had his place in the Vestibule of the Temple, beyond the sacred curtain was reserved for Initiates into the Greater Mysteries or those of Bacchus.
Preparation for the Greater Mysteries required a nine days fast and bathing in the river Ilyssus took place. The Mystic mundane egg of the Egyptians was a part of the symbolism, for Macrobius says: "Consult the Initiates of the Mysteries of Bacchus who honour with especial veneration the sacred egg." Seneca defines Bacchus as the universal life that supports nature. We have mentioned the Druid egg. Brother George Oliver, D.D., quotes the Orphic fragments as follows: -- "In these Mysteries af-ter the people had for a long time bewailed the loss of a particular person, he was at length supposed to be restored to life; upon this the priests used to address the people in these memorable words: Comfort yourselves all ye who have been partakers of the Mystery of the deity thus preserved; for we shall now enjoy some respite from our labours. To these were added the following remarkable words: I have escaped a great calamity and my lot is greatly mended. " Julius Fermecius gives this in

the lines following: --

"Courage, ye Mystae; lo! our god is safe, And all our troubles speedily have end."

But the same writer informs us that the Initiate "personated the God," for he says: "In the solemn celebrations of the Mysteries all things had to be done which the youth either did, or suffered in his death." The remarks of Hippolytus from the source previously mentioned, are more {111} curious, as

they seem to proceed from an Initiate who is comparing the ceremony with the Christian Mysteries. The Naasene Gnostic is made to say: --

"Those who are Initiated into the Lesser ought to pause and be admitted into the Greater and heavenly ones. Into these no unclean person shall enter. . . . . For this is the Virgin who carries in her womb, and conceives, and brings forth a son, not animal, not corporeal, but blessed for evermore." This Initiate, in the agricultural symbolism of Ceres, represents "an ear of corn reaped in silence." The re-birth of the Neophyte was represented pantomimically, for he says that the hierophant vociferates: "by night in Eleusis beneath a huge fire . . . . August Brimo hath brought forth a consecrated son Brimus, " words which no doubt typified both the sun and the initiate. The word Brimus signifies Powerful and was one of the designations of the Cabiric gods.

Yet after all the Lesser and Greater Mysteries were rather a popular version than a full revelation, we have hinted that there were three-fold interpretations of the Mysteries and what almost approached real death and not drama. Others existed of a more spiritual nature at various centres. Sopatius says that even the Epoptae had only a part of the secret. Theodoritos says that "all do not know what the hierophants know, the majority see only what is represented. " "The last term of the Epoptae" expressed high initiation. It may aid us to recall that these Mystics held all nature to emanate from two principles, of which Persephone and Dionysos, or Ceres and Bacchus, are the allegory. The first is soul, the second spirit. Lactantius,<<"Divine Institutions," vii.>> says: -- "Should anyone dare to deny the existence of souls after death, the Magician will soon convince him by making it appear." Irenaeus, Clemens, Tertullian, St. Cyprian, all affirm the same thing. The Mysteries knew equally well with the Christians, that if the purified soul remained attached {112} to spiritual things it would eventually purify itself, as the Alchemist purifies metals, and so attain immortal life.

We learn from various writers that the Mysteries had their secret signs of

recognition. Apuleius mentions in his "Metamorphosis" that it was pointed out to him "in a dream" that he would recognise a certain priest by his walking as if with a lame ankle; in the "Apologia" we read: -- "If anyone happens to be present who has been initiated into the same Rites as myself, if he will give me the sign, he shall then be at liberty to hear what it is that I keep with so much care." Plautus<<"Miles Gloriosus," iv, 3>> has -- "Give me the sign if you are one of the Bacchae." Iamblichus writes -- "Give not your right hand easily (that is, draw not towards you improper and uninitiated persons by giving them your right hand), for to such as have not been tried by repeated disciplines and doctrines, and have not proved themselves to participate in the Mysteries, by a quinquennial silence and other trials, the right hand ought not to be given." Homer makes Achilles to greet Priam thus -- "The old man s right hand at the wrist he grasped, lest he should be alarmed in mind."

Proclus advanced further and taught that there were Mystic passwords that could carry a person from one order of spiritual beings to another still higher, till reaching the absolutely divine. The Egyptians<<"Book of the Dead.">> and Gnostics held the same view. Origen<<"Contra Celsus.">> says: "There are names of a natural virtue, such as those used by the wise-men in Egypt, the Magi in Persia, and the Brachmans in India. Magic, as it is called, is no vain and chimerical art as the Stoics and Epicurians pretend; neither were the names of Sabaoth and Adonai, made for created beings, but appertain to a

mysterious theology concerning the Creator; hence comes the virtue of other names, when placed in order, and pronounced according to the rules."

The doctrine taught in regard to the nature of the soul in these Mysteries may be gathered from the Philosophers, but first we will see how they acquired the right to speak {113} upon the subject. The Chevalier Ramsay<<"Nat. and Revd. Religion.">> says that: "we may look upon the Pythagoric, the Platonic, and the Orphic theology as the same." Proklos, who was master of the School at Athens about 450 A.D., in his "Theology of Plato" says that: "Pythagoras was first taught the orgies of the gods by Aglophemus; Plato next received a perfect knowledge of them from the Pythagorean and Orphic schools." The last named Rites were those upon which the Eleusinia were established. Proklos, in speaking of matter says, "Plato was also of the same opinion concerning matter because he is supposed to have followed Hermes and the Egyptian philosophers." The philosophical schools, which followed the death of Plato, almost universally accepted him as their master, and he and Pythagoras had like veneration for the Chaldean and Magian teaching, and Ammanius Marcellenus<<xxviii, 6.>> teaches us that: "Platon, the greatest authority upon ancient doctrines, states that the Magian religion or Magia, known by the mystic name of MACH-AGISTIA, is the most uncorrupted form of worship in things divine, to the philosophy of which, in primitive times, Zoroastres made many additions, drawn from the Mysteries of the Chaldeans." The Emperor Julian<<"Oratio." >> seems to have been of a similar opinion and says: "Were I to touch upon the initiations and the secret Mysteries which the Chaldeans Bacchised respecting the seven rayed god, lighting up the soul through him, I should say things unknown to the rabble, very unknown, but well known to the blessed Theurgists."

We have, however, given such matters very fully in our previous chapters; the

Egyptian Initiation of Plato is specially affirmed by several writers; and we may add here that the more closely philosophy approaches Cabiric rites, the more does it resemble Free Masonry.

There was, however, a refinement of the coarser part of the dramatic. "Aphanism" and "Euresis" -- the "concealment and the finding of the slain god"

-- thus applied, in what follows. {114}

As to the nature of the recondite teaching of the Arcane Mysteries we will now quote various writers who have given us hints upon their doctrine. Plutarch says: "As to what thou hearest others say, who persuade the many that the soul, when once freed from the body, neither suffers . . . . evil, nor is conscious, I know that thou art better grounded in the doctrines received by us from our ancestors, and in the sacred orgies of Dionysos, than to believe them, for the Mystic symbols are well known to us who belong to the Brotherhood." Antoninus says: "Soul is all intelligence and a portion of the divinity." Proklos: "Know the divinity that is in you, that you may know, the divine One, of whom the soul is a ray." Heraclitus says of souls: "We live their death and die their life." That extraordinary man Apollonius of Tyana, who visited the Indians, entered the Mysteries of various nations, and reformed the Greeks, taught that both birth and death were equally an appearance, the first being the confinement of the "Real" in matter, and the second its release. Plotinus, who was a pupil of Ammonius Saccus, says: "for to be plunged into matter is to descend into Hades and there fall asleep," and of the doctrine itself he tells us that it is "what is taught in the Mysteries, and that liberation from the bonds of

the body is an ascent from the cavern, and a progression to the intellectual." Macrobius<<"Dream of Scipio.">> says that the first death is when the soul falls into the body "as a sepulchre," and that "the second is the natural death."<<A translation by Brother W. W. Westcott has been recently printed.>> Plato in his "Hippias" says: "The supreme Beauty consists in their resemblance to the divine sun, or light of all intelligence"; he also refers to Orpheus as terming our natural body GR:Sigma-iota-upsilon-mu-alpha (soma) or GR:Sigma-gamma-mu-alpha (sema), a sepulchre. Hierocles quotes the Chaldeans to the effect that, "the oracles called the etherial body, the thin and subtle vehicle or chariot of the soul," Suidas tells us, out of Isidorus, a Spanish bishop of the sixth century, what is interesting to {115} old Masons, especially as Isidore is quoted by the author of our old MSS. Constitutions called the "Cooke MS.," that, "according to some philosophers, the soul has a luminous vehicle, called "star-like," "sun-like," and immortal, which luciform body is shut up in this terrestrial (body) as light is in a dark lantern." Moderns would generally use the terms soul-body, and spirit, but Plato designates the former a "winged chariot." Here the reader may be reminded that a lantern in form of a five-pointed starlight, was formerly used by Masons, in the most solemn part of their ceremonies. There are portions of the "Divine Poemander" that must allude to Mystery-rites: "Hast thou not heard in the speeches, that from one soul of the universe are all those souls, which in all the world are tossed up and down and severally divided? Of these souls there are many changes, some into a more fortunate estate and some quite contrary; for they which are of creeping things are changed into those of watery things, living upon the land; and those of things living in the water to those of things living upon the land; and airy ones are changed into men; and human souls that lay hold of immortality are changed into daemons."<<"The Key," iv, 23.>> "The like also happeneth to them that go out of the body; for when the soul runs back into itself the spirit is contracted into the blood, and the soul into the spirit, but the mind being made pure and free from these cloathings, and being divine by nature, taking a fiery body rangeth abroad in every place, leaving the soul to judgment, and to the punishment it hath deserved."<<"Ibid," 56.>> Again, in the drama of the Mysteries: "Dost thou not see how many evils the wicked soul suffereth, roaring and crying out, I am burned, I am consumed, I know not what to say or do, I am devoured unhappy wretch, of the evils that compass and lay hold upon me, miserable that I am I neither see nor hear anything. "<<Ibid, 70. (Reprints by R. H. Fryar, Bath, also by Dr. W. W. Westcott.)>>
It necessarily follows that to be entombed symbolically {116} and raised
therefrom, as was done in these Mysteries, was emblematically, if not actually, to be spiritualised or exalted out of the body. Coupled with this recondite teaching as regards the soul was the theory of REMINISCENCE. According to this mystic doctrine which was advocated by Plato, Origen, and

some of the early Christian Bishops, as Synesius, all souls have pre-existence and have descended from the spiritual world into the earthly prison of the body, but some souls are more divinely advanced than others. Reminiscence is therefore that faculty of knowledge which the soul brings from its heavenly source, never entirely obscured, and when its faculties are stimulated, by discipline and a pious abandonment of the passions, is the cause of all civilising influences and discoveries. More than this, but we have said all that is necessary. Socrates,

at his trial by the Areopagus at Athens, and to the hour of his death by hemlock, asserted the guidance of his Daemon, or tutelary spirit, and has the following placed to his credit by Plato in his "Republic:" -- "The eye of the soul, which is blinded and buried by other studies, is alone naturally adapted to be resuscitated and excited by the mathematical disciplines." It is a repetition of the apothegm of the Persian Dervishes: "The man must die that the saint may be born"; it is the divinely illuminated eye of the Cabirian Cyclops, and the awakening or resuscitation of the consciousness of the divine image, implanted in the human soul.

As to the necessary Apprenticeship for even the Lesser Mysteries, we have some information in the writings of Theon of Smyrna, who was a disciple of Euclid, and an editor of his books. Theon is comparing the five liberal sciences as necessary for a mystically initiated philosopher with the five preparations for the Mysteries: --

"Again it may be said that Philosophy is the Initiation into, and tradition of, real and true Mysteries; but of Initiation there are five parts. That which has the precedency indeed, and is the first, is Purification. For the {117} Mysteries are not imparted to all who are willing to be initiated, but some persons are excluded by the voice of the Crier, such as those whose hands are not pure, and whose speech is inarticulate. It is also necessary that those who are not excluded from initiation should first undergo a certain purification; but the second thing, after purification, is the "Tradition" of the Mysteries. The third thing is denominated "Inspection." And the fourth which is the end of inspection, is binding the head and placing on it "Crowns;" so that he who is initiated is now able to deliver to others the Mysteries which he has received; whether it be the Mysteries of a Torchbearer, or the Interpreter of the sacred ceremonies, or of some other Priesthood. But the fifth thing which results from these is the "Felicity" arising from being dear to the divinity and the associate of the gods. Conformably to these things likewise is the tradition of the political doctrines, and in the first place a certain purification is requisite, such as the exercise from youth in appropriate disciplines, for Empedocles says, it is necessary to be purified from defilements by drawing from five fountains in a vessel of unmingled brass. But Platon says, that purification is to be derived from five disciplines, namely, Arithmetic, Geometry, Stereometry, Music, and Astronomy. The tradition, however, by philosophical, logical, political, and physical theories is similar to Initiation. But Platon denominates the occupation about intelligibles -- true beings; and ideas Epopteia or inspection; and the ability from what has been learned of leading others to the same theory must be considered analogous to binding the head, and being crowned; but the fifth, and most perfect thing, is the felicity produced from these, and, according to Platon, an assimilation as much as possible to God."

So far Theon, and his essay is a most important comparison between the

relative value of philosophy and the Mysteries; it might be worth while to ask ourselves, whether these "five" parts of Initiation, five sciences, and five fountains, have any relation to the mystic pentagon, {118} {Symbol: Pentagram} and the Masonic five points of Fellowship, in the ancient aspect; for in these old times the Liberal arts and sciences were not seven, but five. We are informed by Diodorus that the Egyptians had an especial veneration for the number five, as they considered it to represent the Universe, because there were five elements -- earth, water, air, fire, and ether or spirit; and it is

noteworthy that it was by these elements that the worthiness of the Neophyte was tested before Initiation. It is related that when the eminent Christian, Justin Martyr, applied for Initiation into the Society of Pythagoras, he was asked whether he had studied arithmetic, music, astronomy, and geometry, as these alone were capable of abstracting the soul from sensibles, and preparing it for intelligibles: as he could not reply affirmatively he was refused admission.<<Oliver s "Pythagorean Triangle." (John Hogg. London.>>

We see from these extracts that the requirement of the Liberal arts and sciences were common to Theosophy and Philosophy, as they were of old to Freemasonry, and is a proof, to be added to many others, that these three had one, and the same origin, and were rites of the same Fellowship. Discipline was made to precede Initiation into the Mysteries in the same way that Freemasonry, having abandoned the teaching of the arts, and especially Geometry, now requires a certain amount of education from its candidates. The Lesser Mysteries were intended to teach the sciences which the Art Mysteries transmitted. The Greater Mysteries were essentially spiritual, embracing man s origin, rebirth or regeneration, and his final felicity, and this passed to Gnostics, Mystics, the Church, and the later Rosicrucians.

In explanation of the terms Inspection, and Seeing, Epoptae, which are frequently used by writers who comment upon the Mysteries, we will give some quotations to shew that the claim was actual and not metaphorical. Though not necessary to our subject, we may say, that Iamblichus in his letter upon the Mysteries, has left us in {119} no doubt as to the significance of Epopteia or Inspection, and Autopsia or Seeing, for he repeats, over and over again in unmistakable language, paragraph after paragraph, the fact of the visible presence of supermundane beings at the celebration of the Theurgic rites.<<"On the Mysteries," par. ii, sec. iii to ix.>> These particulars, were it necessary, are too long for insertion here, but he proceeds to define with care, the appearance, functions, qualities and the good effects of beholding the gods, defining archangels, angels, daemons or tutelary spirits, potentates or demi- gods, hero-gods, and souls, with all the authority of one who had beheld and studied all their qualities. The means taken by these Philosophers for inducing the development of seership, was strict chastity and purity of life, accompanied by strict dietary, with fasts and prayer; principles adopted in all the sacerdotal Mysteries for superior Initiation. The following is recorded by Damaskios as to the appearance of the god in the Mysteries of Serapis: "In a manifestation which must not be revealed, there is seen on the walls of the temple a mass of light which appears at first at a very great distance. It is transformed, whilst unfolding itself, into a visage evidently divine and supernatural, by an aspect severe but with a touch of sweetness. Following the teachings of a mysterious religion, the Alexandrians honour it as Osiris or Adonis." This appearance corresponds, in its description, with what was said of Serapis in our last chapter.

Porphyrios, circa 270 A.D. records in his "Life of Plotinos," that that
Philosopher in order to satisfy the curiosity of an Egyptian priest, repaired with him to the Temple
of Isis in Rome, in order, as the most suitable place, to invoke his tutelary Daemon, which having
done, a divine being made his appearance, apparently so much above the rank of the ordinary daemons as to greatly astonish the Egyptian. The eminent Platonist, Thomas Taylor, translates a passage of the "Phaidros" thus: "Likewise in consequence of this

divine Initiation, we become spectators {120} of entire, simple, immovable, and blessed visions, resident in a pure light, and were ourselves pure and immaculate, and liberated from the surrounding
vestment which we denominate body, and to which we are bound, as an oyster to its shell." Proklos,
in his "Commentary" on the "Republic of Plato," has these words: "In all Initiations and Mysteries,
the gods exhibit many forms of themselves, and appear in a variety of shapes, sometimes a formless
light, shining from themselves, is thrown forth for contemplation, sometimes the luminosity is in a
human figure, and sometimes it takes a different shape," into all of which Iamblichus also particularly enters.

The wondrous works of Homer, "The blind old man of Scio s rocky isle," are as full of the appearance of gods and angels to man, as the Jewish Scriptures. In book iv. of the "Odyssey," in describing
the descent of Ulysses into the Cimmerian Cavern, leading to the abode of souls, he asserts that the
fumes of the blood of the victims offered in sacrifice, and slain for the purpose, were used by the
shades of the dead to reanimate and strengthen their corporeal faculties. Moses says, "the blood is
the life." Pope thus words it, on the appearance of the prophet or seer, Tiresias: --
"Eagre he quaft the gore, and then expres t
Dark things to come, the counsels of his breast."

Again, when Ulysses observes the wan and melancholy shade of his mother, Anticlea, standing
aloof, Tiresias the Seer thus informs him: --
"Know, to the spectre, that thy beverage s taste, The scenes of life renew, and actions past."
And when the mother approaches her son s sacrifice: --
"When near Anticlea moved, and drank the blood, Straight all the mother in her soul awakes,
And owning her Ulysses thus she speaks."

St. Basil instructs us in this, that "the blood being evaporated by fire, and so attenuated, is taken
into the substance of their body." It is said that in the Eleusinian Mysteries the Initiate took the
solemn oath required of {121} him, standing upon the skins of the animals slain in sacrifice. The
disgusting rites of the Taurobolium, said to have been practised in some of the Mysteries were of the
nature described; and it is alleged that when the Aspirant was to receive this baptism of blood, he
was put in a chamber, above which was another with the floor pierced with holes; in this a bull was
slain and the Aspirant received the crimson stream upon him in the lower chamber. Prudentius has
the following lines on the subject: --<<"Perieteranon," v. p. 146; "Fragments of Initiation," Bro. F. F.
Schnitger.>>
"All salute and adore him from afar
Who is touched with this uncleanliness, And sullied with such recent sin-offering, Because the vile
blood of the dead ox

Has washed him who was hid in filthy caverns."

The reader of these pages will no doubt remark that details of such matters have no reference to Freemasonry; that is so, but we were minded to shew of what the Mysteries consisted, and what they actually professed and practised. Nevertheless a large amount of affinity with Masonic rites, and its symbolism, will be found in this chapter by the attentive observer, and considerably more in the next.

The perfectly metaphysical mind of Plato eminently fitted him for an exponent of Mysteries which had reached him from remote ages, and it may be said that the Mysteries were Platonism, and that Platonism was the Mysteries, and in this sense we may aptly apply the words of Ralph Waldo Emerson, who says: -- "Out of Plato come all things that are still written and debated among men of thought." "Plato is philosophy and philosophy Plato; at once the glory and the shame of mankind; since neither Saxon nor Roman have availed to add any ideas to his categories." Plato himself holds that of the 5 orders of things (of which we have just written) only 4 can be taught to the generality of men.

CHAPTER V. PHILOSOPHY IN RELATION TO MASONIC RITE

WE mentioned in our last chapter the introduction into the State Mysteries of an intellectual class who, as laymen, were destined to exercise great influence upon succeeding generations. The most notable was Pythagoras, who was by birth a Samian of the period of 570 B.C. He obtained initiation into the Mysteries of various countries, and consolidated all that he had thus learned into a school of his own, which he opened at Crotono in Magna Graecia. He conferred upon himself and pupils the title of Philosophers, or lovers of Wisdom, and Philosophy began to lay claim to all the Wisdom possessed by the Mysteries. It was the first of the Arcane Schools that sprang out of the State Mysteries, in the same way that private Lodges of Masons sprang out of the General Assemblies; and in the language of Masons, the School of Pythagoras would be termed a new Rite of the Mysteries, but Pythagoras went beyond speculation, in a Masonic direction, by his practical views upon the necessity of studying the Liberal Arts and Sciences, and though he flourished nearly two centuries before Plato, and nearly three centuries before the time of Euclid, he made Geometry the basic plan of all creation.

The Rite of Pythagoras was divided into three classes or grades, and Dr.

George Oliver in his "History of Initiation," makes the School or Academy of Plato, to consist equally of three degrees with Initiatory rites, but it is doubtful whether he had any better authority than will be found in this section; it is full of Masonic doctrine {123} and symbolism which must be left for the reader to

apply. The Pythagorean Rite was Exoteric or public in its teaching, and Esoteric or private in things intended for his Disciples, and a like rule was followed by the Egyptian priests. The first step of the Esoteric teaching was an Apprenticeship of five years of silence, which Iamblichus informs us might be abridged in cases of merit; the Aspirants were termed "Mathematici," because the grade embodied instruction in the Liberal arts, and Hippolitus informs us that Deity was denominated "Grand Geometrician;" even as we saw that the Chinese termed Deity the "First Builder," and the Indian Art fraternity the "Great or Divine Builder." The brethren advanced to the second step were termed "Theorilici," and here they were instructed in the elements of divine wisdom. Then followed the very select class of "Electi," who were Perfect Masters. The School had a series of darkly-worded apothegms, as for instance, "Stir not the fire with a sword" -- be calm. "Abstain from beans" -- be chaste. It had also secret modes of recognition. Their brotherly-love was often exemplified in the most remarkable manner, and their devotion to the Society, and its laws, by the sacrifice of life itself. "The Master has said it," was an all- sufficient guide in their conduct.

Ovid in his "Metamorphosis" has an essay upon Pythagoras and his doctrines: -- "Why dread such mere visions as death and Hades? Souls cannot die; they only leave one body to enter another, as I (Pythagoras) know by experience who was once Eupherbus, and recognised the shield I, in his person bore. Death is mere change; the breath goes forth from one body to enter another (be it human or animal) but beneath different shapes the soul remains substantially the same. Hence the horror of killing creatures, it may be, tenanted by kindred souls. But one may go further and say, that not souls alone, but all things shift and pass -- night and day, the hues of the sky and sun, and the shapes of the moon. The seasons, the year, changes in correspondence with the ages of man, {124} Spring answering to youth, Summer to prime, Autumn to maturity, and Winter to old age."

Porphyrios, who was a Tyrian of the name of Melek, informs us that the numerals of Pythagoras are hieroglyphic symbols, by which he explained all ideas concerning the nature of things, and hence of the nature of the symbols to which we have previously alluded. It is said that he taught the true Astronomy, termed "Mesouranios," as typifying the sun in its relation to revolutions of the planetary bodies. Nor need we feel surprised at the knowledge which this implies, as the Vedas and Shastras of the Hindus indicate a conception that the earth was round and the planets in revolution, at least 2,000 B.C.<<Vide "Isis Unveiled," i, p. 10; also ii, p. 128.>> Pythagoras was Initiated in Egypt after severe trials, and Porphyrios states that he was initiated in Babylon by Zarades, but it is doubtful whether this person or even Zoroaster were names of persons. Zar-ades may be interpreted by Na-zar-ad, vowed or separated, and Zar-ades may be a chief or Rab-mag, whilst Zoroaster may have been a Zara of Ishter, and Zerubabel the Zoro or Nazar of Babylon, a Nazarene and recoloniser of Jerusalem.<<Vide "Isis Unveiled," i, p. 10; also ii,

p. 128.>>

Pythagoras claimed that all things were created by Geometry and numbers, or as his follower Plato expresses it, "God perpetually Geometrises." Censorinus thus develops his doctrine of the "Harmony of the spheres": "Pythagoras asserted that the whole world is made according to musical proportion, and that the seven planets between heaven and earth have an

harmonious motion and intervals, correspondent to the musical diastemes, and render various sounds according to their several heights, so consonant that they make the most sweet melody, but to us inaudible by reason of the greatness of the noise, which the narrow passage of our ear is not capable to receive." Our old Masonic MSS. allege that Jabal discovered the musical notes by listening to the sound of the hammers of Tubal Cain, and tradition {125} assigns the discovery to Pythagoras by the same chance.

The Greeks mention the visit of a man of the name of Abaris from the Hyperborean regions; he appeared at Athens carrying a bow and quiver, girt with a gilded belt, and a plaid round his body. He was a learned man, instructed in Greek, very judicious, and Toland shews him to have been a Druid from the Hebrides. Pythagoras had no reserve with him, nor the Druid with him, and they parted with mutual esteem. It is said metaphorically that Abaris shewed Pythagoras the sacred arrow which

Apollo used against the Cyclops by which we are to understand Druidical astronomy, and magic or in Celtic "dry," to which the Anglo-Saxons added craft, denominating Magic Drycraft.

Pythagorean Clubs or Schools were established at Crotona, Sybaris, Metapontum, Tarentum, and other places in Magna Graecia; and Cicero says that he died at Metapontum. The dates assigned to his birth vary from 608 and 570 B.C., and of his death 497 to 472 B.C.

The Philosopher Plato, who died at a great age in the year 347 B.C. was so much attached to Geometry, which the old Masonic Constitutions tell us was the original name of Masonry, that he wrote over his study: "Let none enter here who are ignorant of Geometry"; in his "Republic" he says that "Geometry rightly treated is the knowledge of the eternal"; and in "Timaeus" he says, that Pythagoras first brought Geometry to perfection; but Herodotus and Iamblichus say that Geometry was perfected in Egypt, owing to the necessity of surveying their lands after the overflow of the Nile; that is it had to be applied to the practical purpose of landmeasuring, and one of the probable derivations of the word Mason may be deduced from this use of Geometry.

The poet Chaucer, who was a Clerk of Works to the King and therefore in constant contact with Masons, uses the old word "Mase" to signify an artistic building, and "to mase" is to think out; and Krause observes that, in almost every tongue, m-t, m-s, metz, mess, masz, is used {126} to define the boundaries of an object, and in general, to invent, to measure, to work according to measure. In Latin we have mansio, a day s journey, and Macerieo, a boundary wall, hence our word mansion. The term Mase has now passed out of use, but at the period when the word Macon arose was well understood.

Our ancient MSS. distinctly state that in early Saxon times the word was not in use and the Craft was designated Geometry; we may therefore seek the origin of the word in the Teutonic. In the "Somneri Dictionarium Saxonico- Latino-Anglicum," Oxon. 1689, we have a word which covers what we seek -- Massa, or "Maca, par locius, censors, conjux, a peer, an equal, a companion, a mate." It is therefore a term equally applicable either to the Society or the trade. The builders were Masons because they were Sociates and Fellows of Craft, and the trade was the same because the Sociates made and mated the stones to form a building. The word Massa, a table, a mate, indicates fellowship.

Brother Wm. S. Rockville has hazarded a derivation from the Coptic "Mai" to love, and "Son" a brother, which is quite applicable philologically, and he points out that the hieroglyphic of the first word is a sickle, plough, or scythe, and of the second a chisel, or a seal is used.<<"Mis. Notes and Queries," xi, p. 2; also "Freemason s Mag." 1865.>>

Geometry was the chief qualification for the Arcane Schools, as well as for Masonry, and the following which Plato gives in the "Philebos," and perhaps derives from an older source, appears also in the Masonic MSS.: "All arts require Arithmetic, Mensuration, and Statics, all of which are comprehended in the Mathematical science, and are bounded by the principles which it contains, for the distribution of numbers, the variety of measures, and the difference of weights are known by this science." But Proklos makes Geometry to be also the basis of religion, and confirms what was stated in our last chapter, for he says: -- "The mathematical disciplines were invented by the Pythagoreans, in order to be a reminiscence of divine {127} concerns, at which through these, as SYMBOLS, they endeavour to arrive."

Even at the present day Geometry and its diagrams are the technical language of Architects by which they convey their ideas to each other, and which they have inherited with the Craft of the ancient Masonic Society. It follows that architecture is the best school in which to study speculative geometry, and there must always have existed a close relationship between operative Masonry and Speculative Philosophy, based as the latter is, to a great extent, upon geometrical science. There must be a good reason why old Masonic MSS. couple all the sciences which go to form a liberal education; and though it may seem incongruous to couple grammar and logic, with qualifications necessary to build houses, we can give very ancient Greek evidence to prove its necessity and bearing. Ammonius Saccus says: "For in general the end of theory is the beginning of practice; and so reciprocally the end of practice the beginning of theory. Thus, for instance, an Architect, being ordered to build a house, says to himself, I am ordered to build a house; that is to say a certain defence to protect against the rains and the heats. But this cannot be without a roof or covering. " From this point therefore he begins his theory. He proceeds and says, "But there can be no roof if there be no walls; and there can be no walls without some foundations; nor can there be laid foundations without opening the earth." At this point the theory is at an end. Hence, therefore, commences the practice or action. For, first, he opens the earth, then lays the foundation, then raises the walls, and lastly puts on the roof which is the end of the action or practice, as the beginning of the practice was the end of the theory. And thus also the philosopher does; being willing to form a demonstration he says to himself: "I am willing to speak concerning demonstration. But inasmuch as demonstration is a scientific syllogism, it is impossible to say anything concerning it without first saying what is a syllogism; nor can {128} we learn what is simply a syllogism without having first learned what is a proposition; for propositions are certain sentences; and it is a collection of such sentences that form a syllogism; so that without knowing propositions it is impossible to learn what is a syllogism, because it is out of these that a syllogism is compounded. Further than this, it is impossible to know a proposition without knowing nouns and verbs out of which is composed every species of sentence, or to know nouns and verbs without knowing sounds articulate or simple words, inasmuch as each of these is a

sound articulate having a meaning. " The same writer speaks of "the practical and the speculative part of Philosophy." Plato in his "Republic," makes Socrates to say: "It is indeed no contemptible matter, though a difficult one, to believe that through these particular sciences (arithmetic, music, geometry, and astronomy) the soul has an organ purified and enlightened, which is destroyed and blinded by studies of other kinds; an organ better worth saving than a thousand eyes; inasmuch as truth becomes visible through this alone."

An important part of the Mythologies of various peoples was founded upon TWO PILLARS, where the sciences were alleged to be written; and the old Masonic MSS. state that Hermes and Pythagoras respectively found the Pillars of stone and brick or "latres" upon which the antedeluvian sciences had been engraved. Iamblichus asserts that these two Pillars were preserved in the temple of Amen at Thebes, and Porphyrios, the Platonic philosopher, having addressed a letter of enquiry upon the Mysteries and their doctrine, to "Anebo the Egyptian Prophet," probably of a fifth order of priests established by the Ptolemies in a Synod, is thus answered by Iamblichus in a letter entitled, "The Reply of Ab-Ammon the Master, to the Letter of Porphyrios to Anebo": --

"Hermes, the patron of learning, in ancient times, was rightly considered to be a god in whom the whole sacerdotal Order participated. The One who presides over {129} true knowledge is one, and the same, everywhere. Our ancestors dedicated to him their wise discoveries, and named their respective treatises "Books of Hermes." . . . . It would not be becoming that Pythagoras, Platon, Demokritos, Eudoxes, and many other of the old Greeks, should have been able to receive instruction from the Sacred Scribes of their time when you, our own contemporary holding sentiments like theirs, are disappointed in your endeavour by those now living, and styled Public Teachers. . . . . But if you press an enquiry after the method of the Philosophers, we will adjudicate it according to the ancient "Pillars of Hermes," which Platon and Pythagoras have already recognised and combined with their own philosophical maxims. . . . . The knowledge of the gods is innate and pertains to the very substance of our being. . . . . From the beginning it was one with its own source, and was co- existent with the inherent impulse of the soul to the supreme goodness."

There is altogether much ambiguity and uncertainty as to the nature of these "Two Pillars," but it is evident from the foregoing, that they were much more than a mere record of the worldly arts. They probably stood for two very ancient traditional Pillars, used in the primitive Mysteries, which were copied in the "Petroma" of the temples of the various Mysteries of the world, from which the sacred laws were read to the Initiate, as in the two tablets of Moses in the Jewish law. There was an ancient Babylonian tradition that these Two Tablets were buried by Xisithrus, the Chaldean Noah, beneath the foundation stone of the tower of Borsippa, or Babel.<<A.Q.C., v, pt. 2 -- "Har-moad.">> Many kings sought for them in vain, until the time of Nabunahid, who professed, if we are to believe his inscription, to have discovered them. Josephus says that one of these Pillars existed in Syria, in his days. What he saw was probably a pillar recording some Egyptian conquest. Diodorus Siculus repeats a tradition that the Egyptians attributed to Thoth or Hermes the discovery {130} of geometry, arithmetic, astronomy, astrology, and the sciences; and as the "method of the philosophers," referred to by Iamblichus, was to employ geometrical symbols as a method of teaching Theosophy, the "Pillars of Hermes" would appear to cover such reference in the quotation.

Manetho, the Egyptian priest who compiled the annals of his order for the Ptolemies, says: "The second Hermes, called Trismegistus, translated, or rather transcribed into vulgar alphabetical characters, what the first Hermes had wrote in hieroglyphical characters upon pillars of stone." Hermes is the Greek name for the Egyptian Thoth, and this second of the name is believed to have been a Royal scribe of Menes the first King of Egypt, the first Thoth was a primitive traditional prophet, and the name, as Iamblichus has told us, of a god of Revelation.

The great Master of Geometry that followed Plato, after a lapse of about a century, was a Tyrian by birth of the name of Euclid, who opened an Academy of the Sciences at Alexandria under the Ptolemies. He was beyond doubt a Platonist, and described as such by Porphyrios in his "Life of Plotinos," a philosopher born at Lykopolis in Egypt, 205 A.D. The words of Porphyrios are thus translated: "In the first class of the Platonists there were Euklides, Demokritos, and Proklinos who lived near Troy. . . . . Of those philosophers, therefore, who were authors some produced nothing more than a collection and transcription of the remains of the ancients, as Euklides, Demokritos, and Proklinos." We see from this that Euclid did no more than reproduce what had existed from ancient times, and hence it is not without some show of authority that later scribes of the Masonic MSS. have substituted the name of Hermes for Euclid, as the author of the Constitutional Charges, and as a matter of fact Hermes was, in a sense, their remote originator. At this distant era there were only five liberal arts and sciences, and the assimilation of these to the five parts of the Mysteries was shewn in our last chapter. In the 11th century of our era these had been increased to {131} seven, in two divisions, designated the "Trivium" which comprised grammar, rhetoric, and logic, and the "Quadrivium" which included arithmetic, geometry, music, and astronomy.

In what has gone before we have various illustrations of the use of the cross

as a pre-Christian symbol in the religious Mysteries, and in these minor Arcane Schools of philosophy the symbolic cross is prominent. Aeschylus, the author of "Prometheus Bound," relegates this Cabiric god to a similar punishment on Caucasus for stealing the fire of the gods with which to endow mankind, and he himself narrowly escaped death under a suspicion that he had revealed some of the mystic doctrine. Plato advances that the Logos, or second person of his trinity, had impressed himself upon the world in the shape of an {"X"}, or St. Andrew s cross, as it is now termed; as this symbol is one of the forms used to express the union of two generative principles it may be Plato s secret way of expressing that.

The Indian Guilds say, as previously mentioned, that the Divine Builder crucified his son Surya (the Sun) upon his Lathe which is the Svastica {Symbol: Swastika} cross. All the Guilds, both ancient and modern, in one of the higher degrees, has a symbolic crucifixion at High XII. at noon, which is founded upon the laying of the Foundation stone of a Temple on the 5 Points, by 3, 4, 5, angle. But it goes far beyond this, as there was everywhere an actual sacrifice of human life to ensure safety to the building; and the assertion, traditional, of course, is that it occurred at the erection of Solomon s temple, and it certainly had place in our old English churches even. The temple of Solomon was a 3 to 1 structure, 60 x 20 cubits, the pyramids have a square basis, and therefore a Coptic Guild would lay down a perfect square. The Mysteries were no more than a Guild, and had equally the same rite. Vitruvius gives the {"X"} cross as a

canon of proportion of the human figure, the centre of the cross being the navel of the body. This was in Egypt "where also our Lord was crucified" {132} (Rev. xi. 8); a confession of Initiation, "crucified before the sun" as the Mystics say. Minucius Felix, a Christian, taunts the Romans themselves with the worship of wooden gods, and says: "Your victorious trophies not only represent a cross, but a cross with a man upon it."

Various writers of the Platonic school treat of the "Perfect Man" in the light of embracing all the virtues which lead to happiness, but which are never found combined in one individual. It is in this ideal of a perfectly virtuous man that we must look for such works as the Egypto-Greek life of Pythagoras, the Greco- Roman life of Apollonius; and exemplified to the full in the Greco-Jewish life of Jesus of Nazareth. The 2nd and 3rd Books of the "Republic" of Plato teach that goodness to be apparent must be stripped of all adventitious circumstances, and that a really good man will find so much opposition in the world that "he will be scourged, tormented, bound, his eyes put out, and die by crucifixion after he has endured all these evils." Again, "a good man will be tormented, furiously treated, have his hands cut off, his eyes put out, will be bound, condemned, and burnt."

Lactantius quotes Seneca as using similar language. Grotius, from whom we take our translation, considers that Plato writes prophetically, but, after the allusions made in previous chapters, we may be pardoned if we look upon them as applied to certain things in the Mysteries, which assigned a reason in the danger of making the Arcane doctrines too public.

The ancient Sybils, or inspired prophetesses of the Mysteries, have similar

language. Augustine<<De civ. Dei, lib. xviii, c. 23.>> thus quotes the Erythrean Sybil: "He will fall into the hostile hands of the wicked; with poisonous spittle will they spit upon him, on his sacred back they will strike him; they will crown him with a crown of thorns; they will give him gall for food, and vinegar to drink -- five forms of trial. The Veil of the temple will be rent, and at midday there will be a darkness of three hours, and he will die, {133} repose in sleep, and then in joyful light he will come again as at first." One of these Sybils had the following Oracle to deliver: --

"Then suddenly a sign for mortal men shall be,

When out of Egypt s land a stone most fair shall come safeguarded."

Celsus accuses the Christians of interpolating passages from these Oracles "without understanding their meaning," from which we gather that they had a mystical reference. The veil that is rent is that of the Sacred Curtain of Apollo, and Virgil has ascribed to his patron the coming glories of the age of gold. In the temple of Philae in Egypt there is an old-time painting of a man laid upon a cruciform bier asleep, over him stand two persons who are pouring upon his head water in which appears the sacred tau-cross, whilst the sun s rays strike upon him; and it is evident that such an Initiate is represented by a cube opened out as a Latin cross, the top square having a man s head, in the same temple. We mentioned this species of crucifixion in our last chapter, where the Initiate was carried into the lower crypt of the temple. Socrates Scholasticus in referring to crosses found in the temple of Serapis, when it was sacked by the Christians, says: "The Christians contended that the cross belonged to the Master, Jesus Christ, which they also which understood these rites maintained; the Gentiles on the contrary maintaining that the cross was common both to Jesus Christ and Serapis." An eminent Catholic divine says that the cross is "the hidden Mystery, a scandal to the Jews, and folly to the Gentiles, of which Paul writes." Foucart mentions a treatise by a disciple of Pythagoras entitled, "The passing into the invisible world, or the Descent into Hades."

In the ancient Mystery language of pre-Christian times, and with the Gnostics, and in the Arcane Discipline of the church, Chrestos meant a Disciple, whilst Christos was one anointed, purified, and accepted. Boeckhos, in "Corpus Inscriptionem," shews that it was an epithet applied {134} to the departed, or the saved and redeemed, of pre-Christian times, Aeschylus speaks of the Manteumata Pythocresta, or oracles of the Pythoness, in which Chrestos becomes the expounder of Oracles. Justin Martyr, in his Apology, speaks of Chrestians, and Lactantius (iv. c. 8) says that "it is only through ignorance that men call themselves Christians, instead of Chrestians."

As the Mysteries had a symbolic death so had the Minor Arcane Schools, but the language of the latter has a very realistic character, and we will see what has been said on this subject; first quoting Hermias in his "Commentary on the Phaidros:" "The word GR:tau-epsilon-lambda-epsilon-tau-upsilon (telete) or Initiation was so denominated from rendering the soul perfect; the soul was therefore once perfect. But here it is divided, and is not able to energise wholly by itself. But it is necessary to know that Telete, Muesis, and Epopteia, differ from each other. Telete therefore is analogous to that which is preparatory to purifications. But Muesis, which is so called from closing the eyes, is more divine. For to close the eyes in Initiation is no longer to receive by sense those divine Mysteries, but with the pure soul itself, and Epopteia is to be established and become a spectator of the Mysteries." Synesius in his treatise on "Providence," as translated by Thomas Taylor, says: "You also who have been initiated in those Mysteries in which there are two pairs of eyes, and it is requisite that the pair which are beneath should be closed, when the pair which are above them perceive, and when the pair above are closed, those which are below should be opened." This means that the spiritual eyes must be used for spiritual things.

Bishop Warburton, in his "Divine Legation," quotes an ancient writer, preserved by Stobaeus, as saying: "The mind is affected in death, just as it is in the Grand Mysteries, and word answers to word, as thing to thing, for GR:tau- epsilon-lambda-epsilon-upsilon-tau-epsilon-iota-upsilon (teleuteiu) is to die and GR:tau-epsilon-lambda-epsilon-iota-sigma-theta-alpha-iota (teleisthai) is to be initiated." By the word Grand is meant the Greater Mysteries which resemble the Master Mason. {135} Plutarch has some passages which strikingly illustrate the doctrines of the Mysteries and the relation of these to Ceres and Persephone. This writer says: "Now of the deaths we die one makes man two out of three, and the other one out of two. The former is in the region and jurisdiction of Demeter, whence the name given in the Mysteries GR:tau- epsilon-lambda-epsilon-iota-upsilon, resembling that given to death GR:tau- epsilon-lambda-epsilon-iota-tau-alpha-epsilon{?}.   The Athenians also heretofore called the deceased sacred to Demeter. As to the other death it is in the Moon or region of Persephone." The first separation is into what he terms "the Meadows of Hades," situate between the earth and the moon, where the soul wanders for a more or less period, where it plucks the soul violently from

the body, but Persephone mildly and in a long time disjoins the understanding from the soul"; that is separates the higher and lower self which is the second death, "as if they were returning from a wandering pilgrimage, or long exile, into their country, where they have a taste of joy, such as they principally receive who are initiated into sacred Mysteries, mixed with trouble, admiration, and each one s proper and peculiar hope." This of course refers to actual death, the "three" being body, soul, and spirit, and the "two" soul and spirit. These quotations all apply rather to the State Mysteries than the Arcane Schools of Philosophy, but we have other passages.

The following is found in the "Auxiliaries" of Porphyrios (printed by Ficinus the restorer of the Platonic Academy at Rome in the 15th century): "Hence there is a two-fold death, the one universally known, by which the body is liberated from the soul; the other peculiar to philosophers, by which the soul is liberated from the body; nor does the one at all follow the other." Celsus speaks of a Pagan priest who could voluntarily perform the separation of soul and body, "and lay like one dead void of life and sense."<<"Anatomy of Melancholy" (Burton).>> The "Phedon" of Plato has several similar passages, of which, in order not to tire the reader, we will take but one: "Now we have shewn that in {136} order to trace the truth or purity of anything, we should lay aside the body and only employ the soul to examine the objects we pursue."

Mr. Robert Brown, in his "Great Dionysiac Myth," says in allusion to the Hall of Arcane rites, or the "sekos," a word literally meaning sheep-fold but which came to signify the interior of a temple: "Here, deeply excited and agitated by all they had gone through, ready to believe anything, and every-thing, in that state of abstinence which is, or is supposed to be, most favourable to the reception of supernatural displays, and their minds more or less affected by drugs, and their whole being perme-ated with the impression and expectation of the more- than-mortal, they were allowed to SEE."

We have here to remember that the Mysteries required a long and protracted fast, and the passages that we have quoted state clearly enough that an ultra- natural state was produced. What in these times is called hypnotism, mesmerism, trance, was well known to the ancients. Proclos, quoting Clearchus "Treatise on Sleep," mentions a wand with which the operator, upon gently striking a boy, drew his soul a distance from his body, for the purpose of proving that the body is without sensation when the soul is taken away, and, by means of his rod, he again restored the soul to the body.<<Oliver s "Hist. Landmarks." ii, p. 614.>> The writings of the early Christian Fathers afford much testimony of the phenomena, and the Benedictine ceremony of covering the newly received Monk with a funereal pall, equally with a certain Masonic ceremony, is an exoteric reference to it. It is related by Hugh, a Monk of Saltery in Huntingdonshire, that a soldier of King Stephen of Eng-land visited "St. Patrick s Hole," in Donegal, and after a fast of nine days, as in the Mysteries, was laid in a kind of grave, where a view of Paradise was shewn to him, the whole of which account reads like a paraphrase of the descent of Aeneas into Tartarus and Elysium. It also resembles the relation in the Metamorphosis of Apuleius, {137} of his initiation into the Mysteries of Isis and Serapis, and as the latter Mystery was introduced into the Christian Church, as the Arcane Discipline, and equally claimed supernatural appearances as a part of the faith, we need be at no loss to account for these relations. The Druses of Lebanon, on the testimony of Professor A. L. Rawson, who is himself

an Initiate, require an interval of fasting, of more or less length according to circumstances, with a total fast on the day of Initiation, by which regimen a species of Epopteia is produced which the Professor terms mental illusion or sleep-waking<<Letter in "Isis Unveiled," ii, p. 313.>>. The same phenomena is found in the Yogi, or "twice born," and known in certain Rites of the Dervishes. It is almost certain that certain rites of the Egyptians have passed to the Africans, and Heckethorn, and other writers, have shewn that there exists on that Continent, and in other places where the race has carried the Initiation, a society called the Almuseri, with secret rites similar to those of the Orphic and Cabiric Mysteries. The reception takes place once a year in a wood, and the candidate is sup-posed to die; at the appointed hour the Initiates surround the Neophyte and chant funereal songs. He is then carried to a temple erected for the purpose, and anointed with palm-oil; after forty days of this probation he is supposed to have obtained a new soul; and is greeted with hymns of joy, and conducted home.<<"Secret Societies," ii, p. 283.>> We are informed that Freemasonic signs have been answered by the Kaffirs.

Galen<<"Dogm. Hipoc. et Platon," viii.>> may be quoted here as to the existence of this doctrine of a soul which may be separated from the body: "The soul is an immaterial substance, which has a luciform, etherial body, for its first vehicle, by which as a medium it com-municates with the gross etherial body." The Chevalier Ramsay says: "It appears that the Platonists, Pythagoreans, Egyptians, Chaldeans, and all Orientals believed that souls had an etherial, aerial, and

{138} terrestrial vestment, or tabernacle; that the last named was put off by natural death, the second by a supernatural death, and the other retained for ever."

The mathematical discipline, by aiding thought concentration, was intended to serve a similar purpose to that of the Hindu Yogism and of the Dervishes. Plutarch in his Symposiacs<<Vol. viii, 2.>> ascribes to Plato the words, "God is constantly a Geometer," hence to immerse oneself in Geometrical thought, is to think with the mind of God. All the Platonists taught that the gradations of the spiritual world were arranged in Geometrical order, hence it is, "a science that takes men off from sensible objects, and makes them apply themselves to the spiritual and eternal nature, as a view of epopteia of the Arcane of initiation into holy rites." Proklos makes this assertion of the Pythagoreans: "They perceived that the whole of what is called Muethsis is reminiscence, not externally inserted in souls, in the same manner as phantasms, from sensible objects, are impressed on the imagination; not adventitious like the knowledge resulting from opinion, but excited indeed from things apparent, and inwardly exerted from the reasoning power converted from itself. They likewise say that though reminiscence might be shewn from many particulars, yet it was evinced in a most eminent manner, as Platon also says, from the Mathematical discipline, for if any one, says he, is led to the diagrams he will, from them, easily prove that discipline is reminiscence."

The science of Geometry was also used in a symbolical sense, for Socrates in
the "Gorgias," accusing Kallicles of an intemperate life, says to him: "You neglect Geometry and Geometric equality." Zenocrates refused a candidate for Discipleship, saying to him: "Depart, for thou hast not the grip of philosophy."

Of the nature of the SYMBOLS used in the Arcane Schools there is almost as little to be gathered in its books as is to be found in old Masonry, and they were evidently {139} "close tyled." We may fairly seek what we do not know

respecting symbols, through what we do know of history, and to comprehend symbols we must study the old historical religions. The Masons, Rosicrucians, Templars, and Gnostics, all used the same class of symbols. The society of Druses in Syria, and the Sufi Dervishes of Persia and Turkey, admit themselves to follow the Platonic School, whether by inspiration from its writers or by descent from the old Mysteries, and from which each and all, in one form or another, derive their knowledge. We may also follow these religious symbols in the unchanged rites of India.

The basis of the Masonic Jewel of a Master in the Chair is an old Egyptian symbol, for Plutarch informs us that a triangle whose base is 4, perpendicular 3, and hypothenuse of 5 parts, the square of which is equal to the square of those sides containing the right angle, was an important emblem in Egypt, as a symbol of nature. The base figured Osiris, the perpendicular Isis, and the hypothenuse Horus; the originating and receptive principles, and the offspring of the two. It was the standard of their measures of extent, and was for modern centuries the traditional method by the application of which the stonemason tested the squareness of his plan (5 x 5 = 25; 4 x 4 and 3 x 3 = 25, the Guilds of both East and West employ the Rites to this day.)

Iamblichus (i. ix.) says: "Amongst those things which are everywhere set forth in the sacred dramas, some have a specific Arcane cause and higher meaning; others preserve the image of some idea beyond, as nature the genatrix develops certain specific formations from invisible principles; others are introduced from the sentiment of veneration, or for the purpose of illustrating something or rendering it familiar. Some enclose what is profitable to us, or in some way purify us, or set us free from our human frailties, or turn aside some other of the evils that are likely to befall us."

We have already referred to the Pythagorean sentiment {140} that "the path of vice and virtue resembles the letter Y," and though the apothegm has been forgotten in Masonry, yet the "Golden branch" by which it was represented is still remembered. The letter {"Y"} is equally a symbol which the Chinese consecrated to the Deity. It has been suggested that as an emblem it is a square {symbol: a chevron with a right angle} placed over a plumb-rule,

{symbol: vertical line}. Hermes Trismegistus, or the Thrice-greatest, describes God as "an intelligible sphere, whose centre is everywhere, and circumference nowhere," and this language tends to confirm the remarks we have ventured as to the Two Pillars. Pherekydes Syros, who had the early education of Pythagoras, in his Hymn to Zeus, cited by Kircher ("Oed. Egyptae") has the following noteworthy lines: --

"Jove is a circle, triangle, and square,
Centre, and line, and all things, -- before all."

Plato in his seventh "Epistle to Dion," says expressly that he never will write anything explicitly upon these sublime speculations, but that there are three things through which science, the fourth, is necessarily produced, the fifth establishes that which is known and true. "Now take each of these desiring to learn what we have lately asserted, and think as follows concerning them all -- a circle is called something whose name is so expressed. For that which everywhere is equally distant from the extremes to the centre is the definition of that which we signify by the name of a round or circumference and a circle.

But the third is the circle which may be blotted out. But the fourth is science, and intellect, and true opinion about these. And the whole of this again must be established as one thing, which neither subsists in voice, nor in corporeal figures, but is inherent in soul."

We have here an example of the way in which Plato employs Geometry to convey instruction, but in his second epistle to Dion, he employs concentric circles to discourse upon the divine triplicity of Agathos, Logos, and Psyche -- wisdom, mind, life -- Father, Word, Spirit. He says: "You inform me that the nature of the First has {141} not been sufficiently revealed to you. I must write to you in riddles, in order if my letter should miscarry, either by sea or land, the reader may not understand it. All things are round about the king of all things, all things exist for his sake, and that is the cause of all excellent things. Around the second are the things secondary. Around the third are the third class of things. The human souls endeavour to learn the nature of these, looking for what is homogeneous with itself, and consequently imperfect, but in the King, and in these others which I have mentioned, it is not such   The
greatest precaution is to be observed not to write, but to learn by word of
mouth, for it is hardly possible for what is written not to come abroad. For which reason I have written nothing upon such topics; no such books of mine exist, nor ever shall." Proklos in his Commentary upon this says: "The Demiurgos or creator is triple, and the three Intellects are the three Kings, He who exists, He who possesses, He who beholds." Several writers give the following appropriate

passage, on the authority of Suidas: "Thulis King of Egypt, thus went to the Oracle of Serapis: Thou who art the God of fire, and governest the course of the heavens, tell me the truth, was there ever, or will there ever be, one so powerful as myself? He was answered: first God, then the Word, and the Spirit, all united in one. Go hence, O! mortal, whose life is always uncertain. " In going thence the priests carried out the implied threat by cutting the throat of the egotistic Thulis.

In the "Ethical" Fragments of Hierocles, who wrote towards the end of the

second century and was a Pythagorean, the symbol of ten concentric circles is used to set forth our moral duties, and we have seen that the Chaldeans, Medes, and Persians, considered seven concentric circles as a sacred symbol, whilst still more ancient races that we have mentioned are said to have used three such. Hierocles says: "Each of us is, as it were circumscribed by many concentric circles, some of which are {142} less, but others larger, and some comprehend, but others are comprehended, according to the different and unequal habitudes with respect to each other. For the first and most proximate circle is that which everyone describes about his own mind as a centre, in which circle the body, and whatever is assumed for the sake of the body is comprehended. For this is nearly the smallest circle, and almost touches the centre itself. The second from this, and which is at a greater distance from the centre, but comprehends the first circle, is that in which parents, brothers, wife and children are arranged. The third circle from the centre is that which contains uncles, aunts, grandfathers, grandmothers, and the children of brothers and sisters." He then proceeds through six other circles: (4) relations, (5) the people, (6) tribes, (7) citizens, (8) villagers, (9) provincials, and concludes, (10) "But the outermost and greatest circle, and which comprehends all the other circles, is that of the whole human race." In sentiment nothing can be more Masonic than this, but Augustine has a very

apposite allusion to the symbolic point within a circle, and he had at one time been a Gnostic. He says: "As in a circle however large, there is a middle point, whither all converge, called by Geometricians the centre, and although the parts of the whole circumference may be divided innumerably, yet is there no other point, save that one, from which all measure equally, and which by a certain law of evenness hath the sovereignty over all. But if you leave this one point, whatever point you take, the greater number of lines you draw, the more everything is confused. So the soul is tossed to and fro by the very vastness of the things, and is crushed by a real destitution, in that its own nature compels it everywhere to seek one object, and the multiplication suffers it not."<<Oliver s "Symb. Dic." -- Art. Point. &c.>> The curious part of this is the involved verbiage, as if Augustine had in his mind, and sought to hide the secret method of finding a true square by the centre. {143}

Lucian makes Cato to say that, "God makes himself known to all the world;

He fills up the whole circle of the universe, but makes his particular abode in the centre, which is the soul of the just." Another mode of illustrating this is used by the Rosicrucian Paracelsus, who says: "All numbers are multiples of one, all sciences converge to a common point, all wisdom comes out of one centre, and the number of wisdom is one. . . . . Those who love the luminous circle will be attracted to it, and their knowledge comes from God."

Dionysius Thrax, an eminent grammarian, is quoted by Clemens Alexandrinus as saying, that some converse, "not only by speech but by symbols also." This implies that there was an understood signification attached to the symbols. The same writer informs us that it was a custom of the Egyptians to hold a branch in the hand whilst in the act of adoration.

Aristotle says that, "He who bears the shocks of fortune valiantly and demeans himself uprightly, is truly good, and of a square posture without reproof."<<"Old York Lectures.">> The Zoroastrian Oracle declares, "the mind of the father decreed that all things should be divided into three"; which Plato geometrises thus: "God resembles a triangle which has three equal sides." Xenocrates, the friend of Plato, assigned the equal triangle to gods, seeing that it is everywhere equal; the scalene to man seeing that it is unequal in its sides; the isosceles to daemons or tutelary spirits, because it is partly equal, and partly unequal in it properties, the daemons being placed between men and gods. Proklos says that, "Knowledge has three degrees -- opinion, science, and illumination. The means, or instrument, of the first is reception, of the second dialectus, and of the third-intuition." Diodorus of Sicily terms the "Sun" the architect of all nature, and thus we symbolise the Master Mason by that emblem. The square was one of the sacred emblems borne by the Stolistos of the ancient {144} Mysteries. In the real Guild Masonry Man is the living stone and the tools and emblems are used to bring him to due proportions as in the actual stone.

But a very important symbol, philosophic and Masonic, and one which has been common to the world in all time is the cube. Pythagoras is said to have taught that, "the number eight or the octad is the first cube, that is to say, squared in all cases as a die; proceeding from its base the even number two; so is man four square or perfect." Plato in his "Protagorus" causes that character to address Socrates in a quotation from Simonides, a man of Scio who flourished 556 B.C., "It is very difficult to become truly virtuous, and to be in

virtue as a cube; that is to say that neither our carriage, our actions, or our thoughts, shall shake us, or even draw us from that state of mind." It is the cubical stone of the Rosy Cross, which "sweats blood and water and suffers anguish of soul."

The passages that we have quoted are a fair example of the moral geometry of antiquity. Those from Plato, for example, indicate the use to be made of geometrical diagrams in teaching science and Theosophy; that from Hierocles the use made of them in teaching morals; and that from Augustine may explain why a Master Mason may find his secrets by the centre. The quotation from Aristotle ought to remind a Mason of the day when he stood at the north-east corner; and that from Simonides of what is required of him in order to become a perfect Ashlar, and the more especially as we have shewn that this cube had the same signification in Egypt, Chaldea, Persia, and America, and that it is, therefore, one of the most primitive symbols. A Persian proverb is thus: --

"O! square thyself for use; a stone that may Fit in the wall is not left in the way."

The "Regius" Masonic MS. tells us, in the Master s first Article, how he is to regulate his conduct as a judge of work: "And as a jugge stond upright, And then thou dost to bothe good ryght." Curiously enough the Egyptian {145} "Ritual of the Dead," quoted in our 2nd chapter, has a line symbolically identical.

There are numerous references to Symbols which are both Platonic and Masonic in the works of our learned Brother the late George Oliver, D.D., but unfortunately he does not often give references that will enable us to verify them. All the foregoing quotations have been taken from non-Masonic works, and may therefore be considered wholly unbiassed. The following are probably equally reliable, and are chiefly assigned by Oliver to the Pythagoreans, from which school Plato accepted much of his teachings. The "clasped hands" was a Pythagorean symbol. The divine essence was represented by a "quadrangle" or square, which implies order and regularity; it is found in Chinese books of great antiquity with the same meaning. The "right-angle" was the symbol of female deities, as Ceres, Vesta, Rhea. The "pyramid," a valued symbol, referred to the divine triplicity. The "cube" was considered by the Hermesians as the symbol of truth, as the appearance is the same in every point of view. The "double-triangles," "single triangles," "five-pointed star," "cross," etc., have been used by all nations, in all time, and in common with "square and compasses," "plumb," "square," "triangular-level," etc., have figured as alphabetical characters.

The triple-tau {symbol of Triple-tau, like a "T" striking the cross-bar of an "H" from above} is given as the monogram of Hermes; and the letter P crossed, {symbol: "P" with a short horizontal line across the lower vertical} as the staff of Osiris. But the most widely spread, and most ancient of all symbols is the Svastica, Filfot, or Jain cross {Symbol: Swastika}, formed of four squares joined at the ends, derived from the primaeval centre, and Cabiric. The five Platonic bodies are Masonic symbols, and in ancient Arcane Schools were held to teach that the world was made by God, "in thought and not in time," and of the elements thus evolved, "fire" is a pyramid; "earth" a cube; "air" an octohedron; "water" an icosahedron; the "sphere of the universe" a dodecahedron. The

"equilateral triangle," the "square," and the "equal hexagon" were considered the most perfect geometrical diagrams, {146} and it was pointed out by Pythagoras that there exist no other forms whose multiples are competent to occupy the whole space about a given centre; and which can only be effected by six equilateral triangles, four squares, and three equal hexagons.

There are certain ancient symbols some of which have the appearance of Roman letters but are not really so, which are found sculptured on stones in Egypt and elsewhere, and found, in later times, in this country as Masons marks. The letter {"Y"} may be found placed on a reversed triangle {symbol: inverted equilateral triangle with small "Y" hitting upper base}; we have the {X} cross; the reversed tau or level {"T" inverted}; and doubled it may form a cross {+}. There are the masculine and feminine symbols {"V"} and {"V" inverted}, which united may form the {N} symbol, so often found as a Mason s mark, the same symbol is found on pre-Christian coins of Persia, in various angles; the {"V" inverted} and {W}, the latter a double symbol; the {I} is phallic; the {"V" inverted} and {V} crossed or interlaced, as in the Masonic square and compasses. Another very ancient symbolic mark is two triangles {symbol: Two equilateral triangles, top inverted, lower upright and joined at vertices in center like an "X" with closed top an bottom} joined at the apex, which is still a sacred symbol in Thibet, Turkey, and India.

Our readers, who have carefully noted the symbols mentioned in our previous chapters, will have perceived that whilst many of the Arcane emblems have been continued in Free Masonry, throughout the centuries, others have been lost in the speculative system, but were preserved by the Guild and also as Masons marks; they must at one time have enclosed a recondite doctrine, which was common to both the sacerdotal, and art Colleges; and marks of this class, which go beyond mere monograms, admit of a mystic interpretation, which indicates a culte common to Theosophia and philosophic Geometry or Masonry; it happens that some of these symbols may be interpreted to contain the doctrine of the pre-existence of souls; the union of the spiritual and material nature in man, which enables him to live two lives -- the sensual and the spiritual, the Fall of Man as the Cabalists pretend being figured in the predominance {147} of the former over the latter. Other emblems have reference to the divinity, and an example of the Masonic manner in which these may be made to convey instruction may be illustrated by the equilateral triangle. It has three points; a point has position only; a line has length only and terminates in two points; three lines of equal length at equal angles form an equilateral triangle, or the primary figure in geometry, and represents the trinity in unity, or Deity pervading all space, creator of all things animate and inanimate; doubled it represents the perfect godhead, and the male and female energies of nature. Or again, a "point" is the beginning of any active duty, the flowing of which point generates a "line;" a line is therefore either reward, duty, pleasure, or profit. A "right line" is a duty performed and pursued with constancy. The extension of a right line to generate a "surface" is therefore perfect duty. Better still is a passage from Macrobius in his "Commentary on Scipio s Dream": "And as a line is generated from a point, and proceeds into length from an indivisable, so the soul, from its own point which is a monad, passes into the duad, which is its final extension."

But the most remarkable of all the Arcane and architectural symbols is the vesica-pisces {symbol: an ellipse with major axis vertical, two vertical lines

issuing at top and bottom}, it was in use until our days, and Brother Conder (a member of the Masons Company) says that its formation was the diagram by which old operative Masons tested their squares. Proklos repeatedly refers to this figure, which he had seen in Egypt, and heard interpreted there; it often appears on temples, as well as modern churches, and is found especially on the throne of Osiris. In the Platonic system it is said to have constituted the sign of Epopts, the open hand being united at the finger-ends and the wrists touching each other. We mentioned in our third chapter the affinity of Philosophy with the Mysteries of Serapis, and the Arcane Discipline of the Christians. The Ptolemies, who had the Jewish Scriptures translated in the Septuagint, seem to have found a mode, or thought {149} they had, in the establishment of a fifth order of prophets, of harmonising all faiths in the mysteries of Serapis, and Clement, of Alexandria, informs us that the initiates of these Mysteries wore on their persons the mystic name I-ha-ho, the original of which appears to be IAO, which embodies the symbols of the two generative principles. It is further asserted that the before-mentioned sign of Epopts constituted that of the Arcane Discipline, coupled with the lettering of the word ICHTHUS, a fish, and the Pope s ring is that of the Fisherman. Oliver, quoting Kerrich, says that the vesica-pisces is the great secret of church architecture, and the determinator of all dimensions.<<"Pythagorean Triangle" (Hogg).>> It continues an equally important symbol amongst the Dervish sects.

We will now pass on to the use in the Platonic system of other symbols in which Masons are interested. Plato in his Philebos has a triad under the names of Bound, Infinite, and Mixed, and likewise a triad still more Masonic of Symmetry, Truth, and Beauty, which, he says, "are seated in the Vestibule of the good." The Masonic pillars of Wisdom, Strength, and Beauty, are an analogy, and the divine triad of Agathos, Logos, and Psyche, if literally translated are a close approximation. He likewise prescribes the following moral qualities as essential in a student of Philosophy: -- "He must have a good memory, learn with facility, be magnificent, magnanimous, and be the friend and ally of Truth, Justice, Fortitude, and Temperance; qualities which are equally made the essential points in a Freemason. Again, in the Phedon, which is a dialogue on the immortality of the soul, we find the following important passage, which he adduces on the authority of the most ancient Mysteries: -- "Wisdom is the only true and unalloyed coin, for which all others must be given in exchange, with that piece of money we purchase. . . . Temperance, Justice, Fortitude, and Prudence, or wisdom itself, are not exchanged for passions but cleanse us of them. And it is pretty evident {149} that those who instituted the Purifications called by us Teletes, i.e., perfect expiations, were persons of no contemptible rank, but men of great genius, who, in the first ages, meant by such riddles to give us to know, that whoever enters the other world, without being Initiated and Purified, shall be hurled headlong into the vast abyss; and that whoever arrives there after due purgation and expiation shall be lodged in the apartments of the gods. For as the dispensors of these expiations say -- There are many who bear the Thyrsus, but few that are possessed of the spirit of God. Now those who are possessed, as I take it, are the true Philosophers." So far Plato, and he may be put into other words -- "Many are called but few are chosen." The Thyrsus here alluded to, as a badge of office in these Mysteries, was carried by the soldiers of Bacchus, Sabazios, or Dionysos; the Chevalier Ramsay says that it was twined with ivy, and very often had upon it a

cross, and he compares the Greek conception of Bacchus, as god of the vintage, with the description of Messiah as given in Isaiah and the Apocalypse.

Porphyrios has a long description of the advantage of the four Cardinal virtues, but after the illustration of the Master Plato we may omit this. Stobaeus says of them pretty much what Masonry tells us.<<"Eccl. Ethio," p. 167.>> The pagan Emperor Aurelius Antoninus, "circa" 145 A.D., has several passages on these virtues; in one he says: "If any man should conceive certain things as being really good, such as Prudence, Temperance, Justice, Fortitude, he would not after endure to listen to anything which was not in harmony with what is really good." We wonder how many Masons have this feeling.

The doctrine of equality and brotherly love, which forms the base of the Masonic Institution, may be paralleled in the Arcane Schools with such passages as the following: -- "Alypios," "Tell me, O! Philosopher, is the rich man unjust, or the heir of the unjust! "Iamblichus," "That is not our method of disputing, O! illustrious man; no one is considered rich by us, even if he does possess external riches, unless he likewise has the virtues characteristic of a true philosopher." That is the virtues which have been already mentioned; and brotherly-love is often enforced, but in the "Regius MS." of the old Masonic Constitutions there is a passage which states that the Stewards of the Hall are to serve one another, "like sister and brother," for which sentiment Platon s "Symposiom," or Banquet of Life, may be consulted. Demokritus expresses the gist of this work in a few admirable words: "He who loves the goods of the soul will love things more divine, but he who loves the goods of its transient habitation will love things human."

We may close this chapter with a few hints as to the changes which
Christianity forced upon the ancient schools. Iamblichus phrases a Pythagorean dogma thus: "As
the Lesser Mysteries are to be delivered before the Greater, thus also must discipline precede philosophy." If the Lesser gave the title of Mystae, the Greater gave that of Epoptae, and if the passage
means anything it must be this, that science and art, represented by Geometry, is the counterpart
of the former, whilst philosophy is in relationship with Epoptae. Hence after the break-up of the
State-Mysteries, we see a succession of two schools, closely related to each other -- the Craftsmen,
or art school, and the Gnostics who know. Ragon<<"Orthodoxie Maconique," p. 44.>> says: "Do
we not know that the ancient Initiated Poets, when speaking of the foundation of a "City" meant
thereby the establishment of a doctrine? Thus Neptune the god of reasoning, and Apollo the god
of hidden things, presented themselves before Laomedon the father of Priam to help him to build
the city of Troy, that is to say, to establish the Trojan religion." In other words to "build a city" is to
establish a public culte, to "build a temple" is to found an Arcane School. The Mystae, or veiled, are
they who see things as they appear; the Epoptae, or set apart, see things as they really are, that is they
are Gnostics or knowing

ones. There is a passage in the "Prometheus" of Aeschylus, which seems to correspond with the ad-
ventures of Aeneas that we have related; and to advise the god that he was to look for an Initiate
who would give peace to humanity: "To such labours look thou for no termination to thy pangs till
a god shall appear, as thy substitute, willing to go down to gloomy Hades and to the murky depths
around Tartarus." Blavatsky observes, and we see no reason to disagree with her views, that when
the Hierophants of the Mysteries saw that it was necessary to rebuild the sinking speculative edifice,
the "Mystae" had

committed to them the rebuilding of the "Upper-temple," or exoteric part; whilst the "Epoptae" had
the "Lower-temple," the crypt or the esoteric portion; "for such were their respective appellations
in antiquity, and are to this day." Initiation was spoken of as a "walking into the temple," and the
"cleaning" or rebuilding of it referred to the body of an Initiate on his supreme trial.
The misfortunes which befell the establishment of Pythagoras at Crotono may possibly have had
their origin in the jealousy of the State Mysteries, though the destruction of its building and its
members is usually attributed to the anger of one Cylon who had been refused admittance. It is evident, however, that two centuries later the State Mysteries must have lost much of their exclusive
power over the mind, when the Arcane Schools of Philosophy were permitted without check to assume the entire role of their doctrines.
The Emperor Galen, at a still later period, gave permission to Plotinos, to build a city by the name
of Platonopolis, where the Philosophical system was to be taught, but this does not appear to have
been carried out. It is, however, quite clear that the State Mysteries and the Arcane Schools taught
the same truths, if in somewhat varied forms, and that these truths are equally represented in Masonry, which is as far as we desire to go in this chapter. It is quite possible that there are some trifling
resemblances between Platonism and Masonry, which may have been introduced at a modern date,
but it is utterly impossible that this can apply to the great mass of things which are in common, and
we shall see more of this affinity, and in the ancient times of Masonry, as we proceed.

Before the reader advances to the next chapter he will be pleased to note, and to remember in regard to all which follows, that these five chapters afford ample evidence that the original "Mysteries" had now culminated in "three" classes, but varying only in profession and technique, in the several systems viz.: 1, "The Sacerdotal." The drama refined into a temporary trance death. 2, "The Military." The original drama of a murdered god. These two classes were suppressed by the Christian Emperors of Rome, but continued to be secretly practised by what one writer terms "strolling priests." The third class learned to "close the lips," which in the Greek is the equivalent of Mystery, and as Art was necessary to the Church they received protection. 3, "The Artizan." A version of the last-named; entering India, China, and Babylon from the North, and Greece, Phoenicia, and Palestine by way of Egypt, at times, in India, imparting the Yogism of the first class. Our Saxon ancestors for these adopted the term Guild, which implies contribution of money

CHAPTER VI. THE MYSTIC AND HERMETIC SCHOOLS

THE MYSTIC AND HERMETIC SCHOOLS IN CHRISTIAN TIMES.
WITH the close of our last chapter Philosophy had begun to play an important part upon the stage of ancient Mystery, and the old spiritual faith of Isis, Osiris and Horus, was becoming still more subtilised by the restless Greek at Alexandria, under the rule of the Ptolemies. Here was established a new, or fifth order of priests with the title of Prophets, and the Mysteries of Isis, Serapis, and Anubis became the favourite Arcani.

Ptolemy Philadelphus assembled a Council of Jews, alleged to be 70 in number, for the purpose of translating their scriptures into Greek, which

version is yet known as the Septuagint. He also treated with Asoka in regard to the doctrine and progress of Buddhism.<<Erest de Bunsen.>> A wide eclectic school was to be established, under which the existing faiths might be assimilated, and the secret and sublime Mysteries of the School were those of Serapis. How this succeeded may be gathered from a letter of Hadrian, Emperor 118 A.D., to the Consul Servianus, preserved by Vopiscus<<"Vita Saturnine.">>, in which we find the following, of the Egyptians: "They who worship Serapis are Christians, and such as are devoted to Serapis call themselves Bishops of Christ" .... ("another translation has it"): "those who call themselves Bishops of Christ are vowed to Serapis; there is no ruler of the Jewish Synagogue, no Samaritan, no priest of Christians, who is not an astrologer, a diviner, and a charlatan. Their Patriarch himself when he comes to Egypt is by some forced to adore {154} Serapis, and by others Christ.... . They have all but one God, Him the Christians worship, Him the Jews, Him all the Egyptians, and those of all other nations."<<"Herodian s History" (J. Hart, 1749). p. 184.>>

Between the years 300 B.C. and 300 A.D. Alexandria was the seething cauldron whence mystic learning spread over the world: -- Mysteries, Cabala, Theurgy, Gnosticism, Alchemy, Astrology, and even Christianity, for it is said that "out of Egypt I have called my son." The philosophers termed themselves Philalethians, or Lovers of Truth; and the numerous societies which we shall mention in this chapter have much interest, but we must mention them in the briefest possible manner: in many cases successions exist to this day.

CABALISM. It is quite probable that this system of interpreting the Jewish Scriptures was a part of the instruction of the Beni-Hanabiim, or sons of the Prophets, alluded to in "Samuel." According to Clemens Alexandrinus these Colleges consisted of classes designated Sons and Masters, and he observes that there were Novices amongst the Levites, and that Converts were divided into Exotericii or proselytes of the gate, and Trinisecti or proselytes of the covenant -- Perfecti. We are informed by the "Book of Esdras,"<<"Esdras ii," c. xiv, 8>> that Ezra the Scribe dictated to five men, during a period of forty days, books to the number of 204, of which 70 last written, were to be hidden, or Apocryphal, and confined to the "wise amongst the people." The gist of the Cabala is expressed in the words of Philo, who says that: "The law of Moses is like to a living creature whose body is the literal sense, but the soul is the more inward and hidden meaning, covered under the sense of the letter." The Mystery is divided into "three veils," and is said to have been delivered by Moses orally to the Levites and Elders, from whom it descended to the Rabbis. The two grand Pillars of the temple of Solomon were important symbols, and Franck says that upon entering the first veil we are in the Vestibule; in the second the Holy-place; and in the {155} third the Sanctum Sanctorum. The ten Sephiroths, which represent the descent of creation from the Divine, are also divided into three classes which remain an indivisible trinity. The first three express the intelligible first manifestations; the second triad the virtues or sensible world; the third, nature in its essence and active principles. As a system it admits of a perfect assimilation with the wisdom-religion of the old nations. It was prescribed in the "Mercaba," and the Chaldean "Book of Numbers," that the Neophyte was to be led to a secluded spot by an Ancient who whispered in his ear the great secret. The "Sepher Jezirah," which it is argued from astrological allusions therein to be as old as Abraham, says: "Close

thy mouth lest thou should speak of this, and thy heart lest thou should think aloud; and if thy heart has escaped thee bring it back to its place, for such is the object of our alliance." The European Jews had an association called the "Order of Elijah," which is said to be mentioned in the "Mishna" and "Gemara," it had passwords, signs, and countersigns, and is believed to have been in existence in Poland and Saxony at a very early period.<<"The Kneph" (Mackenzie), i, p. 28.>> The Masonic Royal Arch Degree has drawn on the Cabala and Talmud, but periodical revisions have taken place. ESSENES. This important mystic sect amongst the Jews has puzzled historians. It may have struck out a new path from the Cabalistic road, but the extreme veneration of its members for the sun is more characteristic of Chaldea, and of the existing Yezids. Jewish critics believe that they are the Assideans, Chasdim, or old believers allied with the Maccabees; they afterwards divided into two sects, or the practical, and contemplative members. Other writers consider that they were Egyptian priests, driven into Syria by the conquests of Cambyses of Persia, and Alexander the Great, and it is very probable that this may be partly correct, and that they may have included Jesus ben Panther, a nephew of Queen Salome, who after studying Egyptian Theurgy, and preaching to the people, {156} was proclaimed for 40 days, and then stoned to death, and hung on a tree at Lyda, about the year 100 B.C.

The Essenes are said to have recognised eight (some say ten) spiritual stages of ascent to beatitude; and they had, like the Pythagoreans, a system of degrees with a probationary period between each. Their doctrines were delivered orally and they took an oath of Secrecy, Chastity, and Justice in all their dealings. When addressing their Chiefs they stood with their right hand below their chin, and the left let down by the side. As the Pythagoreans assembled in companies of ten, so also the Essenes considered that ten made a lawful assembly for divine worship, but this resemblance may derive from still older societies. The Roman Collegia and English Guild Masonry were ruled by tens and hundreds. Ernest de Bunsen, whom we mentioned in our second chapter, holds that amongst the Egyptian and Jewish Gnostics there was a twofold tradition which passed into Christianity, and that it had the doctrine of a spiritual development which transformed them into "living stones," hence denominated "Banaim," or builders, that is of a bodily temple, and therefore they neglected the material temple of Jerusalem.

A select class of the Essenes were termed "Therapeutae" who were healers, and dwelt in small cottages wherein was an inner shrine used for contemplative purposes. They kept the Sabbath, and, every seventh time seven, they had a special service with Mystic dances, such as we have referred to in the Mysteries. Philo says: "They have impulses of heavenly love by which they kindle, in all, the enthusiasm of the Corybantes, and the Bacchanalians, and are raised to that state of contemplation after which they aspire. This sect had its rise in Alexandria, before the Jews were very numerous, and spread exceedingly throughout Egypt."

Eusebius, the Christian historian, has some curious remarks on the sect. He says: "Their doctrines are to be found among none but in the religion of Christians, according to the Gospel. Their meetings and the separate {157} places of the men and women at their meetings, and the exercises performed by them, are still in use amongst us at the present day, equally at the festival of our Saviour s passion . . . . it is highly probable that the ancient

Commentaries which they have are the very writings of the Apostles, and probably some expositions of the ancient Prophets, such as are contained in the Epistle to the Hebrews, and many others of St. Paul s Epistles." Josephus had personal knowledge of the sect, and makes mention of Books which were kept secret, referring to the "names of the Angels," which may mean powers or attributes, and reappearing in the Arcane Discipline. We must remember also in connection with Eusebius mention of the Saviour s passion that the weeping for Adonis continued in Syria down to the fourth century A.D.

There can be no doubt that a Christianised form of the Mysteries was continued by the Monks, and we have the testimony of the Fathers to this effect, but we might expect that these would vary in the country where they were practised; thus we might expect to find the influence of Adonis in Syria, of Serapis in Egypt, Dionysos and Bacchus in Greece and Rome, and throughout the Roman Empire the influence of the rites of Mythras with the before named.

It would appear, however, that there were branches of the Essenes, and Therapeutae, who became actual Christians -- as Nazarenes, Ebionites, and Nabatheans, and the first term is yet in use in the East to designate Christians, who first took that name at Antioch. Theodoret says: "The Nazareens are Jews, honouring the anointed as a just man," and using the Evangel according to Peter, portions of which were discovered a short time ago in Egypt, and a litle later fragments of the "Logia of the Lord." The Ebionites were a portion of the sect, and had amongst them relatives of Jesus, and used the Gospel of Matthew, derived, it is believed, from the "Logia;" they dwelt in a region near the seat of the Adonisian Mysteries; they looked upon Jesus as assuming his apostleship at the {158} descent of the Holy Spirit, and that his Messiahship would begin with his second coming. The Nabatheans were followers of the Baptist in Lebanon, and the Books of this Sect yet exist in Syria. Marcion, who left Rome, about 140 A.D., would seem to have followed the Gospel of Luke. Eusebius, St. Jerome, and Epiphanius have asserted that these sects were branches of the Essenes, and there is no doubt that several of the sects, which were eventually classed as Gnostic by the Church of Rome, proceeded from them.<<Jones "Ecc. History.">> We will, for convenience, before proceeding with the Gnostics, take the secret system of Platonists who Christianised themselves.

ARCANE DISCIPLINE.   This system was in vogue in the church of Christ between the first and fourth centuries of our era. For a clearer comprehension of the subject we must consider what has already been written in regard to the assimilation of Philosophy and the Mysteries, more especially the Serapian, and these to esoteric Christianity; that there is a great identity between these cannot be doubted; nor that Arcane Christianity was the essential adoption of Serapian rites. Tertullian, Origen, Cyril, Theodoret, Gregory, Chrysostom, and others, all allude to these Arcane things, in the precise terms in which the Philosophers spoke of the Mysteries. Basileus says that they kept their doctrines secret, their preaching was public; that is, it was esoteric, and exoteric, as the Philosophers held the Mysteries to be. Cardinal J. H. Newman holds that the Arcanum was the introduction of Platonism into the church of Egypt, and he mentions that Ammonius Saccus and Origen were Catechists of the Discipline, and that when the former established an eclectic school of his own he swore his disciples to secrecy. The historians are in doubt whether

Ammonius forsook Christianity, or not, upon founding his School; but, in any case, such a man would give more than he received.

The grades of the System are given by some writers as follows: -- Catecomonoi or learners; Pistoi or faithful; {159} Photozomenoi, illuminated or baptised; Memuemenoi or initiated; and Teleioumenoi or perfected. But Bishop Warburton, quoting Casaubon in his 16th exercise on the Annals of Baronius, gives the degrees as follows: -- Catharsis or purified; Myestis or initiated; and Teleosis or the end; but remember the relationship of "telete" to death. Casaubon says, "that which is called a symbol of faith is various in its kinds, and they serve as tokens or tests, by which the faithful may recognise each other." Minucius Felix says that the Christians were known to each other by signs and tokens, which were a ready pass-port to friendship.<<"Morals and Dogma" (Pike), p. 547.>> Rufinus compared the use of pass-words to those given by a general to his army. Clemens says: "Let the engraving upon your ring be either a dove, emblem of the Holy-spirit; a palm-branch, peace; an anchor, hope; or a ship running, the church; or a fish." A French writer on Masonry, stated last century that a copy of the Secret Constitutions was in the possession of some Monks on Mount Athos, as late as 1751, and that they were as old as 327 A.D.<<"Mac. Adoniramite," i, p. 69.>> The church itself was divided into three portions; the Nave for the Catechumens, as was the Vestibule for initiates of the Lesser Mysteries; the Aisles for the Faithful; the Chancel for the Perfected.

When the Catechumen had completed his probation, which was usually of two years, he was apparently a Pistos or probationer, and had to fast for 21 days, as usual in the Mysteries; his shoes were removed and all his clothing with the exception of an undergarment, and with a lighted taper in his hand he was led into a room adjoining the church. Prior to Baptism, the aspirant, with his hand raised aloft, and face to the west, or place of darkness, thrice renounced the devil and all his works; then with his face to the east, or place of light, he thrice declared his belief in the

doctrines he had been taught, and his intention to remain a soldier of Christ. The Exorcist thrice breathed upon him, in the name of Father, {160} Son, and Holy-spirit, requiring all unclean spirits to depart from him. A prayer was offered that the element of water might be sanctified; and the operator breathed upon him, in expression of the Holy- spirit. After this he was anointed with oil as a wrestler in the faith; his forehead was signed with the cross, and salt tendered as emblem of divine wisdom; his ears were touched with the word Ephphatha -- "be opened," his eyes anointed with clay. He was plunged three times in the water, in the name of each person of the Trinity. He assumed a new name, and was clothed in a pure white garment, and led amongst the Faithful; from whom he received the kiss of peace; but for seven days he had to go veiled. He could now attend service in the aisles as one of the Photozomenoi and was instructed in the full mystical meaning of the Lord s prayer, which he was enjoined to repeat thrice every night, as well he was instructed in the esoteric doctrines; this probably made him one of the Memuemenoi, that is those who are in the light.
The High-mass of the Eucharist was usually celebrated at Easter, or the
festival of darkness and resurrection. In the Jewish equivalent whilst the fully initiated pronounced mentally the sacred name with the priest, the masses knew only the substituted word Adonai, chanted by the assistants. In the Church, the Deacons brought water for the Ministers to wash their hands, and

the kiss of peace was passed round from the priest, the men and women to each other respectively. The priest offered thanks for the love represented by the death, resurrection, and ascension of Christ. Before entering the chancel the priest exclaimed: "Holy things for holy persons, ye Catechumens go forth." Bread and wine were presented. Pliny states that in the Agapae, or Love feasts, all took a sacred oath to be faithful, reveal no secrets, do no wrong, nor steal, rob, violate a trust, nor commit any act of unchastity. The communicant was now one of the Teleioumenoi or Perfected. There are several points in {161} this account that we have already related as ancient customs of the Mysteries.
No explanation is given of the reason for a long fast, and as this account is but a mystic form of the present exoteric ceremony, we may feel a strong doubt whether it covers all that was done, in the various grades of becoming a Christian. The New Testament repeatedly admits that Jesus had a secret or Mystical teaching, and something may be gathered from the Fathers. Clemens Alexandrinus, who wrote a century after Apostolic times, says: "But it will be an image to recall the architype of him who was struck with the Thyrsus . . . but we profess not to explain secret things sufficiently; far from it, but only to recall them to memory." Again he says: "And was it not this which the prophet meant, when he ordered unleavened cakes to be made, intimating that the truly sacred mystic word, respecting the unbegotten and his powers, ought to be concealed." Origen, whom Socrates in his "Ecclesiastical History" terms the "Expositor of the mystical tradition of the Church," and flourished 185-252 A.D., taught the pre-existence of souls, and on the evolution of man in his ascent to the divine source, he says:<<"Contra Celsus," B. i, ch. 7.>> "But that there should be certain doctrines not made known to the multitude, which are (revealed) after the exoteric ones have been taught, is not a peculiarity of Christianity alone, but also of philosophic systems, in which certain truths are exoteric and others esoteric. Some of the hearers of Pythagoras were content with his "ipse dixit," whilst oth-

ers were taught in secret those doctrines which were not deemed fit to be communicated to profane and insufficiently prepared ears. Moreover all the Mysteries that are celebrated everywhere, throughout Greece, and barbarous countries, although held in secret, have no discredit thrown upon them, so that it is in vain that he endeavours to calumniate the secret doctrine of Christianity, seeing he does not correctly understand its nature." Again<<"Ibid." B. viii, c. 8.>> "He would have us believe that we and the {162} interpreters of the Mysteries equally teach the doctrine of eternal punishments." Again,<<"Ibid," B. iii, c. 60.>> "Whoever is pure   let him be
boldly initiated into the Mysteries of Jesus, which properly are made known
only to the holy and pure. . . . . He who acts as Initiator according to the precepts of Jesus, will say to those who have been purified in heart, he whose soul has for a long time been conscious of no evil, and especially since he yielded himself to the healing of the Word, let such an one hear the doctrines which were spoken in private to his genuine Disciples. " Again,<<"Pref. Gos. John.">> "To the literal minded we teach the Gospel in the historic way, preaching Christ Jesus and him crucified; but to the proficient, fired with love of the divine wisdom we impart the Logos." Synesius, Bishop of Ptolemais, says that: "the truth must be kept secret, and the masses need a teaching proportioned to their imperfect reason." Both the Mysteries and Arcane Christianity were clearly of opinion that more should not be given than the intellect could understand.

It is a moot point how far architectural symbolism was in use by this School, some writers maintain that all these sects used building symbolism, and Christianity was strong in the Roman Colleges of Artificers. Oliver asserts that in the Catacombs of Rome, a cross was constructed of a square, level, and plumb-rule, in such manner that, if touched, it fell to pieces, and the detected fraternity were supposed to be studying architecture. A representation of the temple of Solomon was found in these subterraneans. That the learned of these times did not ignore the use of Masonic symbolism is very certain, and St. Paul terms himself a "Master Builder," who was engaged in erecting the new church, numerous passages of the same character occur, hints at initiation, which would lead us to believe that there was a Masonic character in the secret system of the Church. The apocryphal book called "The Vision of Hermas" compares the faithful to Perfect ashlars, "of a true die or square," and the less
{163} holy to imperfect stones, and rough ashlars. In the so-called Apostolical
Constitution, the church is compared to a ship, as it is in the Egyptian "Ritual of the Dead," -- the Minister is Captain, the Deacons Mariners, the congregation are passengers. The Nave of the church is equally an allusion to the ark of the Mysteries.
We have some information upon the organisation of the Arcane Church in the "Stromata" of Clemens, in "Degrees of Glory in Heaven corresponding with the dignities of the church below"; but which is more fully explained by Dionysius the Areopagite; equally based upon heavenly and ecclesiastical hierarchies. In each it is 3 x 3 = 9 classes. In the first division we have Seraphim, Cherubim, and Thrones; in the second, Dominions, Virtues, and Powers; in the third, Principalities, Archangels, and Angels. In the earthly counterpart Jesus stands in relation to it as does the heavenly Father to the celestial Hierarchy. The first triplet is baptism, communion, and consecration of the chrism, representing purification, enlightening, and perfecting. Second, the orders of Deacon,

Priest, and Bishop. Third, Monks, Members, and Catechumens. Here we have the Exoteric, Esoteric, and Divine church. The Lectures of the Order of Harodim -- Rosy Cross, which claim a Culdee Masonic origin, speak of these matters; and the Christian Mysteries, equally with the Platonists, speak of hylics, sepulchres, and the dead, as applying to those who are buried in worldly matters and things of sense. We have been more diffuse on this subject, for the reason that Christian churches could only have been built by Masons who possessed its arcanum.

There are two accounts which indicate in this country that either the history of the Arcane Discipline is not fully known, or in the other case that the Culdees had inherited a special Rite from their Druidical ancestors, a Rite which resembled that of the Mysteries of the Philosophers, and they should be considered together. The first Culdees had been Druids and St. Patrick is said to {164} have been born at Dumbarton, and to have gone to Ireland in 432 A.D. St. Columba left Ireland with 12 companions in the 6th century, intending to found a Monastery at Icolmkil on an Island in the Hebrides. It was thought necessary, the legend says, following a widely-spread belief, that the structure should be sanctified by a living sacrifice, and Odrian offered himself for that purpose, and was buried alive; after a lapse of "three days" Columba thought he would like to have a look at his old friend, and uncovered him; upon which Odrian started up alive, and began his experience: he had learned the truth in the other world, there was no fall of man, no personal Christ, no personal devil,

and no hell. The scandalised Columba ordered his friend to be covered up again, "that he blab no more." This tale enshrines some of the alleged heresies of the Culdees for there were many others. It is further explained by the following account which we copy from Froissart, and Gough s additions to Camden.<<"Britannia," iii, p. 641.>> One Owen, or Tindal, a soldier of Stephen, King of England, repaired to the old Monastery of St. Patrick in Donegal, where was his "Purgatory." He was prepared for his initiation by a nine days fast on bread and water, but which Matthew Paris says was originally a fast of 21 days, and as this fast is reported both of the Mysteries and the Arcane Discipline, it serves to connect the three accounts. Each day a procession was made round the place, three times the first seven days, and six times on the eighth, bathing each night in the lake, such processions and bathings being also a part of the ancient Mysteries. On the ninth day he observes a complete fast of 24 hours, with the exception of a little water, and was then conducted to the Chapel, "out of which all who enter do not return;" there was a deep well at one end. He then laid down in a sort of grave large enough to hold the body; the only light being from a single window of small dimensions, which looked out upon a field and a {165} hall. Here Owen was visited during the night by 15 persons, clothed in white, who warned him of the trials he would undergo. To these succeeded a troop of demons, who seemed to place him upon a burning pile, which he extinguished in the name of Christ. They then dragged him through scenes of torment, where the wicked suffer a variety of tortures, such as Virgil gives as common to Tartarus. Standing proof against these horrors Owen is taken in hand by two venerable persons, who favour him with a full view and description of Paradise, corresponding with that shown to Aeneas. After this Owen proceeds on a pilgrimage to Jerusalem, and after visiting the Holy Sepulchre, returns to Ireland and labours at erecting the Abbey of Besmagoveisth. Trials were made of this cavern as late as the 15th century, as Froissart records that he had interviewed two soldiers, who had spent a night in the cave, but forgot their visions after leaving the place.

GNOSTICS. These sects are ancient, and Christian Gnosticism sprang out of

sects more ancient than themselves. The word means "to know," in opposition to mere theory, and has deep significance, equally with Veda, Wizard, Witch, all meaning a class "who know." An extraordinary man, of the first ages of the Church, was Apollonius of Tyana; Theurgic powers, and many wonderful things are recorded of him: he was an initiate of various Rites, and visited the Indian Gymnosophists, after which he went about Greece reforming the Mysteries. As the Catholic Church uses the term Gnostic he can scarcely be considered one of them, but he was born about the same date as the Gospel Jesus and lived to be 100 years of age. The first Gnostic "of the Church" was Simon Magus, a contemporary of the Christian Apostles, who passed at Rome as "a great power of God," that is an Aeon or Sephiroth, in the language of the Gnosis and Cabala. He was born at Gitta, in Samaria, and his Gnosis is couched in the symbolical language of the period. He was personally known to the Apostles, who {166} clearly considered him a person to be reckoned with, although he would seem to have looked upon them favourably, and mildly asked Cephas -- "Pray for me." Some of his enemies admit his honesty and single-mindedness. He had numerous disciples, and was deeply learned in Oriental, Greek, and Jewish culture, as well as Theurgy. As an anatomist, he wrote upon the circulation of the blood, and the physical system of the female. The handle

which he gave to his enemies consisted chiefly in this, that he reformed and married a beautiful harlot, who repaid him with her devotion, and whom he believed, whether rightly or wrongly, to be a reincarnation of Helen of Troy, doomed to such rebirth for her ancient sin with Priam. Irenaeus, who flourished in the second century, and was born 116 A.D., says that the Simonians had a priesthood of the Mysteries, and that such "Initiated priests" practised magic arts, and exorcisms. Simon had as disciples Menander, and Cerinthus, a Jewish Cabalist, and Dositheus was a contemporary; they looked upon the Creation in Genesis as consonant to the gestation of the foetus, and the temptation of Eve had a like characer, as well as the Garden of Eden. After this followed Saturninus of Antioch; Prodicus, 120 A.D.; Valentinian, an Egyptian, 130 A.D.; Ptolemy, and Marcion, 136 A.D. A few details follow.

"Carpocratians." The founder of this Sect was Carpocrates of Alexandria. He

would seem to have been a Disciple of Jehoshua ben Panther, previously mentioned, rather than the Gospel Jesus. It is not improbable that the older portions of the Jewish "Sepher Toldoth Jeshu" was a Gospel of Cabalistic Sects, and that Jesus ben Panther was an Essenian leader. The system of Carpocrates taught that Jesus derived the Mysteries of his religion from the temple of Isis in Egypt, where he had studied for six years, and that he taught them to his Apostles, who transmitted them to Carpocrates. The sect used Theurgic incantations, and had grips, signs, and words; symbols and degrees. His son Epiphanes wrote {167} a work on his father s system, but died young. The sect is believed to have endured for some centuries. The Comte de Tromelin, in the Paris "Initiation" (Oct., 1902), says: -- "Hermes has as seat a cross between the four branches of which are written the four letters I.N.R.I., in that order. Is it not the grand Hermetic prediction of the Mages attendant on the Messiah?"

"Cerenthians." These were apparently Essenian Gnostics, and made a
distinction between the earthly Jesus and the Angel Messiah that united with the mortal man. Some
leading German Savants are now agreed that the Apocalypse, from the 4th to 21st chapter, was the
Gospel of the Sect, the remainder being of later date; in this they agree with the Presbyter Cajus
of Rome, and Bishop Dionysius of Alexandria, who, according to Eusebius, attributed the book to
Cerinthus.

"Marcians." Irenaeus gives an account of their ceremony of Initiation, but which the sect repudiated,
but the nature of these details have some agreement with the modern Dervish sects; there is first
a baptismal Invocation, a second to light, spirit, and life; followed by one to "angelic redemption,"
by which the Neophyte became united to his Angel, finally a formula of "restitution," or unity to
the super-celestial power, to which the Neophyte responds in declaring his redemption by the name
IAO. They gave numbers to the Aeons.

"Basilideans." This sect was founded by Basilides of Alexandria, who was a disciple of Menander, a
pupil of Simon Magus; but Clemens says that he claimed to have received his esoteric doctrines from
Glaucus, a disciple of the Apostle Peter. The system had three grades -- the material, intellectual, and
spiritual; and they had two allegorical statues, the one male and the other female. A quinquennial
silence, as in the Mysteries, was exacted from the Disciples; and the doctrine seems to have many
points of resemblance to that of the Ophites. It ran on the lines of Jewish Cabalism with a succession of Aeons, Emanations, and Sephiroth, over which an {168} Archon, or Angelic-

prince presided. They taught that Simon of Cyrene took the place of Jesus at the Crucifixion.
Basilides was succeeded by his son Isidorus, and they say that Matthias communicated to them secret
discourse, which being specially instructed, he heard from the Saviour.<<Hippolytus, Refutation
of all Heresies.">>

"Ophites." The Ophites were an organised fraternity early in the 2nd century as it is said to have
numbered Valentinian amongst its supporters, but Clemens attributes its foundation to Eucrates at
the beginning of our era. It was very Osirian or Serapian, with Semitic names for the Coptic ones.
In the "Ritual of the Dead," which is of incalculable antiquity, there are certain chapters which refer to secrets of Initiation, which the translators have not mastered, and which have reference to the
passwords required by the Guards of the heavenly temple or Amenti, from the aspiring soul, these
are illustrated in the Ophite Ritual. To some extent the doctrine corresponds with that of the Men-
daens, or followers of John the Baptist. Symbols to represent purity, life, spirit, fire have to be shewn
to the Guards. We may imagine such to be the cube, tau-cross, pentagon, or other symbols. "The
soul greets the first power saying: I come from thence pure, a portion of the light of the son and
father. To prove this, the sign must be shewn, as well to every Archon, that the soul passes. To the
principal Archon, Ildabaoth, is said, Greatest and seventh Archon of the Logos, sub-Archon of the
Spirit, the through-father-and son, I offer to thee perfect work in this figure, the sign of life. The
address to Jao is, -

- To thee I now offer just the same sign figured in the spirit. Then going to the
Sabaoth, Archon of the fifth permission, Lord Sabaoth, proclaimer of the law of the creation, perfected by thy kindness, by the power of the most mighty fifth number, let me pass. See here the

crime-clear sign of thy art, which has been passed by all the previous Archons, in the form of this sign, a body absolved by fire. After the soul has {169} shewn this figure thrice it needs no further sign for the succeeding Archon, Aristophanes, but addresses him confidently, Let me pass, thou seest one Initiated. "<<"Originis Opera" -- de la Rue, i, p. 54.>> These Seven Archons were represented in this System by animals -- Michael by a lion; Suriel by a bull; Raphael by a serpent; Gabriel by an eagle; Thoutabaoth by a bear; Eratsaoth by a dog; Ouriel by an ass; these names being Cabalistic equivalents of the Archons, Origen names the rulers thus: Adonai (sun); Jao (moon); Eloi; (Jupiter); Sabao (Mars); Orai (Venus); Astapohi (Mercury); Ildabaoth (Saturn). Ophite, or serpent symbolism, is ancient as the world, and one of the sacred alphabets represented the writhing curves of serpents.

"Naasene." The Naasene were a branch of the Ophites, the name being

derived from the Hebrew Naas, a serpent, and we have quoted the words of one of the sect in the last chapter.<<Vide "A.Q.C.," iii, p. 60.>>

"Valentinians." The five Gnostic words GR:Zeta-Alpha-Mu-Alpha Omega Zeta-Zeta-Alpha Rho-Alpha-Chi Alpha-Mu-Alpha Omega Zeta-Alpha-Iota, are translated: "The robe, the glorious robe of my strength," and are said to have been on the shining garment of Jesus at his glorification; they are said to represent the five mystic powers of the reborn which become seven upon bodily death. Heraclian was a follower of this school, and wrote about 170 A.D. a Commentary upon the gospel of St. John s opening words.

"Bardisanians." The founder of this sect was Bardaisan, a man of noble descent born at Edessa 155 A.D., and died 233 A.D. He was author of an Armenian history; a book on the Indian religions; a book of Hymns; another on

the Marcionites; Book of laws of the Countries, concerning fate, freewill, and nature. A most beautiful hymn of his symbolises the Gnostic Initiation. Professor A. Bevan terms it a "Hymn of the Soul," but the "Theosophical Review," to which we are indebted for many hints on Gnosticism, terms it the "Hymn of the Robe of Glory." His antagonists brought these charges against him: -- (1) he denied the resurrection of the body; (2) he {170} held the theory of a "divine Mother," and a "Father of life," as the origin of the "Son of the living"; in other words the Gnostic doctrine of the concealed Logoi; (4) he believed in a number of lesser gods, such as the seven who are said to surround the throne. The subjects appear in the poem mentioned as the "King of Kings," the "Queen of the East," and the "Brother next in rank"; finally the lesser gods are the "Kings who obey the King of Kings."

"Manicheans." The most noted of the Gnostic sects was the Manichees,

whom Herder ranks as a sect of the Persian Magi. The founder is said to have been a pupil of Scythianus, an Arab of the purest morality, who was contemporary with the Christian Apostles; he studied the Egyptian Philosophy and composed four books designated Chapters, Mysteries, Treasures, and Gospel. A disciple of this man, named Ferbulio, assumed the name of Buddha, it may be to imply reincarnation, and dying by accident, a widow with whom Ferbulio lodged, had a slave of the name of Cubricus educated, and gave him the four books, which he took into Persia, where he asumed the name of Mani, which means conversation; it is said that the King of Persia had him flayed alive with reeds.<<Vide "Memoirs of Jacobinism" -- Barruel.>> The entire tale looks like a fable of the enemies of the sect.

In addition to the class of Disciples, the sect had that of Auditors, who were permitted to hear the writings of Mani read and interpreted in a mystical form; a custom we saw followed by the Brahmins in dealing with the Warriors. The third grade was the Perfect, or Elect, who were the priestly order of the sect. From these last were chosen the Magistri, or Council, who were 12 in number, as in the Culdee system, with a 13th as President. When a Manichee passed over to orthodoxy in Rome, he was required to curse his late associates in the following terms, which implies a reference to the Sun-god of the Mysteries: "I curse those persons who say that Zarades, and Budas, {171} and Christ, and Manichaes, and the Sun are all one and the same." The Sun, Urim, and Mani, being the saviour symbol, and the old Mystery-god, under various names, a Sunday festival was observed in March, when funereal rites were celebrated. On this occasion the altar was adorned with great magnificence, and a splendidly decorated pulpit, ascended by five steps, was erected, before which all prostrated themselves.

This sect, in common with all the other Gnostics, had secret forms of

recognition; Augustin says: "signa, oris, manum et finus," which Barruel translates: "three, that of the word, the gripe, and of the breast." Epiphanius, who had been a member, professes to give the mode by which they tested strangers -- tickling the palm of the hand with the finger. Augustine was at one time of his life a Manichee, but failing, for some reason, to obtain advancement, withdrew from the sect.

Synesius, Bishop of Cyrene, and a pupil and life-long friend of the unfortunate Hypatia, who was torn to pieces by a Christian mob before the very altar, continued a Platonist to the last; and he bitterly reproaches one of his friends for having lightly betrayed to uninitiated Auditors a part of the Secret

doctrines of the Philosophers. The contest between the Roman Church and the Gnostics, broadly speaking, resolves itself into this: first, the historical Jesus, the Christ of the Church; and second, the ancient Crestos of the Serapian Culte, the good god, with a Spiritual Cristos to be developed within each Perfected Gnostic. The former view was that of Peter and the Judaising Christians; the latter that of Paul, Origen, and the British Culdees. The Arcane Discipline was the union of the two, in which the literal history was taught Exoterically, and the spiritual version Esoterically; in the end the Church sought to teach both Exoterically.

"Arcane Symbols." A number of the peculiar symbols of the various sects have come down to us, but have not yet been properly classified by any writer.

1. Those with {172} a cock s head upon the top, and the name Abraxas upon some of them: these may be Mythraic and Basilidean, as the cock was a Mythraic symbol; Abraxas is Basilidean. 2. Those with the head, or body of a lion, commonly inscribed "Mythras." 3. Those with the figure or name of the Egyptian "Serapis." 4. Those which have figures of sphynx, ape, scarib, asp, ibis, goat, crocodile, vulture, etc., all Egyptian symbols. 5. Those which have human figures and the names Jao, Sabaoth, Adonai, Eloi, Basilidean, Ophite, and Jewish sects. 6. Those with a costly monument, and the word "Abraxas," Basilidean and perhaps Manichean. 7. One represented in the work of Chiffalet, which has upon it 7 stars, and a larger one above them, together with a pair of compasses, a square, and

other geometrical emblems, perhaps Cabiric. 8. One in the British Museum engraved by Brother Wm. Hutchinson in his "Spirit of Masonry;" it is in the shape of an egg; on one side is a head which he interprets as the Ancient of Days or Great-workman; on the other side, sun, moon, five-pointed star, and a serpent; it has an inscription which he interprets: "The earth shall praise Thee, 1305." 9. Representations of the eternal Father, with arms crossed on breast. 10. To these may be added numerous emblems from ancient gems, chiefly of Greek workmanship, some of which embrace Masonic signs, some with Pelicans, crosses of all shapes, squares, triangles, circles, point within a circle, etc. The Gnostics had great respect for the number seven {symbol, upright equilateral triangle floating above square} because it results from adding the side view of a square to those of a triangle, or the three principles and four elements, applied spiritually. In regard to the number seven we may quote Mr. T. Subba Row,<<"Five Years of Theosophy.">> who says: -- "Algebraically the number of entities evolved from three primary causes is 2 cubed -1 is 8-1=7. Thus the seven rays are evolved out of three primary coloured rays, and the three primary colours exist with the four secondary colours. Similarly the three primary entities, which brought man into existence, {173} exist in him with the four secondary arising from different combinations of the three primary entities."

The real cause of the veneration of the Manichees for the reed, upon mats of which they affected to lie, is not very apparent, but it was everywhere a sacred symbol. In the ancient Finnish poem of the "Kalevala" the "virgin Mother of the north-land" conceives a heavenly child who is "hidden in the reeds and rushes." The Hindu goddess Kartikeya was nourished amid reeds. Moses was saved in an ark of bulrushes; and a reed was put into the hand of Jesus, as a sceptre. As the plant grows upright out of water it may symbolise truth springing from sacred doctrine; but as the virgin mother is primal matter, that requires another key of interpretation.

The Gnostics adopted the Apostle John as their Patron; his symbol was the Eagle, or bird of the sun, which was the Sectarians sacred emblem; it is found in Egypt at the foot of the tau cross, and now on the jewel of a Rosy-cross Mason. The Gnostic tokens were a sectarian version of the older pagan "Tesserae hospitalis," on which was the head of Zeus, and under the Roman Empire there was the "tesserae frumentaria," which entitled to a public distribution of grain.<<"Notes and Queries" (London, 14 Mch., 1874).>> There was the white stone presented on Mythraic Initiation; and Clemens in his "Hortatory Address to the Heathen," appears to allude to both sign and pass, and material token -- "nam equidem nullo unquam periculo compellar, "quae reticenda accepi hac ad profanos enuntiare." Again, "Vel unius Liberi patris symmystae qui adestis, "scitis quid dani conditum celetis et . . ." tacite veneramini." There can be no doubt that the Arcane Discipline had them as tokens of preparation for the Supper of the Lord; many, if not all, the Catholic confraternities present a token which is generally worn under the clothes from a ribbon. Some of the tokens yet preserved belonged to the Templars, and there are a quantity of Abbey tokens, which are struck in lead or {174} pewter with the cross on one side, and on the obverse a variety of designs.

"Esoteric Budhism." This living system has every appearance of great antiquity; its symbols are ideographs, interpretable in any language, and touch the Mysteries. It has two divisions, theory and practice, or the active and contemplative of the Essenes. The doctrine of the "heart," as opposed to the "eye"; the secret path as opposed to the "open," and is the seal of truth," which leads to the growth of "the tree of knowledge," or the "dragon tree," which is the development of the "higher self." The "Secret heart" has three halls, from which lead two Paths for the "Listener" and the "Exerciser." The first is the four-fold Dhyana; the second is the seven noble gates of virtue opened by the "golden keys" of charity, harmony, patience, worldly indifference, persistence, until finally the initiate arrives at the attainment of supreme wisdom, by travelling the paths of hearing and seeing.

These paths may be compared with the seven Halls and Staircases of the Egyptian "Ritual of the Dead." Similarly we have the "seven stepped Ladder" of the "Golden Precepts," each step being an advance towards union with the divine, its rungs are of suffering and pain, its sides of love. To hear and see reaches the second stage of ascent, when the four senses blend, and pass into the inner sense; the fifth and sixth carry perfect renunciation and concentration of the "higher self"; on the seventh, "thyself and mind are like twins upon a line," the "star" which is thy goal burns over head.<<"Voice of the Silence," transl. by H. P. Blavatsky.>> Thibet like Thebes denotes Sacred Ark, and points to the high table-land of Thibet as a centre of the Mysteries.

"Arcane Schools." The Gnostic Sects, Neo-Platonists, and the Mysteries, descended down the stream of time, with mutual forbearance and goodwill, until late on in the fourth century, when evil times come upon them. The Church was becoming powerful and intolerant, and there was no room left for the Mysteries of Mythras, {175} Serapis, Bacchus, the Cabirs, Hirtha, Druids, or Gnostics; and the Church considered itself capable to absorb their teachings. The Emperors Valentinian, 372; Theodosius, 381; Theodosius II., 450, all forbade the assemblies of Gnostics, Platonists, and all other religious Mysteries, but this but led to greater secrecy and disguise, for Psellus tells us

that the Eleusinian Mysteries continued to be practised at Athens in the 8th century, and were never entirely suppressed.

In the sixth century the Gnostics were put to the sword in Persia, but some embraced Islam, and transmitted their system amongst the Dervish sects. In 657 the Manichees had assumed the name of "Paulicians," and it is said that in the course of three centuries one hundred thousand were put to death by the Romish Church, or at its instigation.

The name of "Cathari" succeeded and implies, as in the Discipline, purity. Some took the name of "Euckites," others "Bogomiles," "Albigensis," and later "Lollards," travelled over Europe, seeking proselytes, and continuing, either openly or secretly, until modern times. There was nothing offensive in the word Gnostic, it means knowing as opposed to believing. Clemens, in his "Stromata," uses the word in orthodxy thus: "Happy are they who have entered into Gnostic holiness." Heckethorn says that in 1022 the Canons of Orleans were burnt for Manichaeism by King Robert; as Cathari they were persecuted in Italy 1150-1224, and were compelled to perform their Rites in woods and forests, like the Carbonari, and it is not improbable that the latter whose Mysteries represent the passion of Christ, is one of their branches.

"A further impregnable evidence of the derivation of Catharism from Manichaeism is furnished by the sacred thread and the garment which was worn by all the "Perfect" among the Cathari. This custom is too peculiar to have had an independent origin, and is manifestly the "Kosti" and "Saddarah," the sacred thread and shirt the wearing of which was essential to all believers, and the use of which by both Zends and Brahmins shows that its origin is to

{176} be traced to the prehistoric period, anterior to the separation of those branches of the Aryan family. Among Cathari the wearing of the thread and vestment, was what was known amongst the Inquisitors as the "haereticus indutus" or "vestitus," initiated into all the mysteries of the heresy."<<H. C. Lea, "Hist. of Inquisition of the Middle Ages" (i, p. 92). London, 1888.>> This may be the origin of that consecrated Girdle, which was one of the charges brought against the Templars during their trials, 1311-13.

"Metempsychosis, and the pre-existence of the Soul was an integral part of the system."<<J. H. Blunt, "Dict. of Sects and Heresies," London, 1891.>> This statement is confirmed in numerous ways, and is even mystically stated in the Graal Poem of Wolfram von Eisenbach. The French writer Aroux quotes Pierre Cardinal the Troubadour, as to the veiled language of the Graal legend, which was of a nature of the Culdee secret symbolism. He says: "The ungent which heals all kinds of wounds, even the bites of the "venemous reptiles," is in fact none other but the word of the gospel, so also the "golden vessel" in which it (the graal) is contained, adorned with most precious stones, is none other than the holy grail itself, or the book of the Gospels, as the Albigensis had adopted and translated it; the Golden book, the vessel containing the true light, visible only to the Initiated, to the Professors of the Gay Science." We shall add later some account of these sects.

Early in the 12th century the celebrated St. Bernard, Abbot of Clairvaux says

of the Gnostics: "If you ask them of their faith nothing can be more Christian like; if you observe their conversation nothing can be more blameless, and what they speak they make good by their actions   As to life and manners,

he circumvents no man, overreaches no man, does violence to no man, he fasts much, eats not the bread of idleness, but works with his hands." Another

Roman writer says that the "Perfected" were divided into Bishops, Major, and Minor brothers, and Deacons, and that these abstained from {177} animal food, and from women. It is related of the Waldenses, who were a branch of the Albigensis who may have preserved the Arcane Mysteries from their first reception of Christianity, that the Initiated assumed new names, and that when the Believer was on the point of death he was perfected thus: "They assembled in a dark room, closed on all sides, but illuminated by a great number of lights affixed to the walls; then the new Candidate was placed in the centre, when the presiding officer of the sect laid a book (probably St. John s Gospel) on his head, and gave him the imposition of hands, at the same time reciting the Lord s prayer; saying also: Have pity on this imprisoned spirit. " The last a very Platonic formula. Saccho says, in speaking of the 13th century: "In many of the sects their secrets are by no means revealed." Limborchi says: "They had also a peculiar manner of saluting each other, by embracing, putting their hands to both sides, and turning their heads three times to each shoulder, saying every time, Praise the Lord. " Of the Waldenses, who followed Peter Waldo, who was probably a Waldense, it is said that "those who are Perfect put in the upper part of the shoe, a Zabbata, a sort of escutcheon, as a sign, from which they are called Inzabbata." This statement, referring as it does to the 13th century, seems to amount only to this, that they wore sandals or wooden shoes. The Rev. Henry Stebbing (1834) says that in the 14th century Pope Honorius III. "condemned to perpetual infamy the Cathari, Patarines, the

Leonists, the Speronists, and the Arnoldists."

VEHM GERICHTE. According to Abbe Trithemius, who wrote his
"Polagraphia" about the year 1500, the Emperor Charlemagne instituted in 770 for Saxons of Westphalia, or the red earth, a Secret Tribunal, for the suppression of paganism and bad morals, "with
secret laws, private signs, and a form of oath.   using amongst themselves certain cyphers and alphabets

which are now lost." The original society was no doubt attached to the old pagan worship. A society
very similar to the Holy Vehme was {178} established at Castile and Leon, in Spain, in the year 1245,
and designated the HERMANDAD. In the 1906 volume of Ars Quat. Cor. (page 31) I printed a
paper on the Ritual of the Vehm Court of the year 1490. In this Ritual the Free Count is supposed
to occupy the throne of Charlemagne, in the same way that the Master Mason is supposed to occupy the throne of Solomon, but the curious point is that, with a quite different object in view, it
has all the formula of Guild Masonry. Bro. F. F. Schnitger informs me that the three sides of his
father s house overlooked five of the old Friestules, or places of judgment, and that he has known
people who participated in some of the last meetings of the Vehm; and his opinion is that Charlemagne, of whom hereafter we will say something as a builder, adapted the existing tribal jurisdiction
to his ends, and that the Secret Tribunal is the jurisdiction of the ancient priests. The Association
possesed two Courts -- an open one (offenes ding) and a secret one (Geheines Gerichte), and to the
latter the Free or Initiated were only admitted. Their laws and signs are partially known, their words
absolutely, and their Oath exists in a dozen documents.

ALCHEMISTS. The Alchemical Art is doubtless as old as other branches of
science and is traceable in Egypt, China, and India, in the earliest times. Modern writers on Chem-
istry assert that it was practised by the Essenes and Cabalistic Jews. When it was suppressed in Egypt
it still lived on in China,

where the terms used correspond with those of the European Alchemists. In all countries it had
three interpretations and three objects: the "Alkahest" or universal solvent; the "Lapis," or stone or
powder of transmutation; and the "Elixir," or universal medicine. As a secret Mystery in which art
and religion are combined it no doubt originated amongst a metallurgic people. Thus it is "physical," as we have said; and "psychological" in its interpretation and as such allied to Gnosticism; and it
is "moral" in its relation to humanity. It aimed, in this sense, at converting the "lead" of the body, and
the "silver" {179} of the soul, into the "gold" of the spirit, and it is this meaning that Aristotle employs it when he says that all men have the Stone within them, and that its conversion is the labour
of wise men. The Mystic Marriage of the Sun and Moon, in its spiritual and inoperative sense, is
the Union of Soul and Spirit to form the Gnostic Crestos. The Hermetic system united all nature
inasmuch as "that which is above is the same as that which is below." When it descends to the min-
eral kingdom, and the vegetable, it finds in these the same three principles as in man, namely a visible body, a virtue or soul, and a spark of the spirit, termed salt, sulphur, and mercury, a divine triad
{Symbol: Fire}; whilst the four lower principles are earth, air, fire, water, {symbol: a square}, but
which in another phase represents the physical, psychic, mental, and spiritual plains of existence;
which are again the fixed, unstable, and volatile. Professor Roberts Austin, C.B., F.R.S., in a Lecture

on Metals, says that the Alchemists "recognised in metals the possession of attributes which closely resemble those of organisms . . ." and that, "the first Alchemists were Gnostics, and the old beliefs of Egypt are blended with those of Chaldea in the second and third centuries." Alchemy and Masonry were early subsidiary schools of the Mysteries.

In its operations the Society held that as "all things proceed from the Will of one," so all were again resolveable to first principles, and that metals might be separated, refined, and reunited; and they claimed that Moses was an Adept because he possessed the difficult process of reducing the golden calf to a powder. The "Aurea," attributed to Hermes Trismegistus, is one of the oldest Arcane works on the subject, and couched in Egyptian Symbolism. The writings of Athenagoras have tracers of Alchemy and the Emperor Caligula is said to have experimented with red arsenick. Thoelden says: "Our ancestors united themselves again in the time of Valerius Diocletian in the year 284 A.D." However that may be, this worthy in the year 296 was engaged in burning Christians, {180} Gnostics and Alchemists with zealous indiscrimination, and equally all works on Alchemy and the Secret Sciences on which he could lay his vile hands. Colin MacKenzie<<"Processes in Manufactures," London, 1825.>> says that, we find Alchemists amongst the Essenes, Cabalists, Manichaeans, the Hermits of Thebes, and the Gymnosophists of India. The Emperor Julian, who, though termed the apostate, was one of the purest Emperors Rome ever had, and apostate from the vices of men like Constantine, restored these Sciences. Zosimus the Panopolite has an express treatise on the "divine art of making gold and silver." Cedrinus, 491, gives an example of a Magician who professed Alchemy. Morienus, who was a Hermit at Rome, learned the art of Transmutation and the Elixir, from Adsar, who was an Alexandrian and a Christian, and afterwards taught it to Calid, the son of Gezid the Second, who was Sultan of Egypt about the year 725 A.D.; the works of Morienus were translated from Arabic into Latin in 1182 A.D. Successors

continued the Science; Geber, whose real name was Abou Moussa Djafar qualified as "al Sofi" the Wise, devoted his life, about 730 to Alchemy; he was born at Houran in Mesopotamia; and we owe to him the first mention of corrosive sublimate, red-oxide of mercury, nitric acid, and nitrate of silver. A Marcus Graecus is mentioned in the 13th century, nothing is known of him, though erroneously asserted, he is mentioned by the Arabian physician Mesue, and his M.S. contains the secret of gunpowder.<<"Eph. Chambers nc.">> Alfarabi flourished later, at the beginning of the tenth century, and was considered the most learned man of the age. Avicenna, whose real name was Abu Cenna, another great Alchemist, was born at Bokara in 984 and died in 1036. After this time but few philosophers of note are mentioned by name in Arabia, and it now began to attract attention in Spain, into which country the Moors and Jews had introduced it. Schools of the Arts, Sciences, and Magic were established at Toledo, Salamanca, Barcelona, and elsewhere, and to these drew Gerhard of {181} Cremona, circa 1130; Arnold de Villanova, 1243; Roger Bacon, 1215; Albertus Magnus, 1270; Raymond Lulli, 1320, etc.<<"Aureus," preface (Fryar, Bath).>> We will divide this notice for convenience, and continue it under the head of "Rosicrucianism," it is an appropriate division because we have better and fuller evidence of its symbolism, much of it being identical with Masonry and Gnosticism, and doubtless derived, through Spain, from the House of Wisdom at Cairo. During the dominion of the Moors in Spain, the Jews enjoyed consideration, and numbered many of the most learned men of the time amongst their race; and proportionately held in estimation. After the fall of the Moorish power the Jews were persecuted, and in the 14th and 15th centuries under the name of "Maranos," they met in great secrecy at Inns, disguised, using grips, signs, and passwords; the temple of Solomon was bound to have its prominent place, but it is unlikely unless in the Arch ritual that the Society could have any connection with Masonry whose broad and liberal platform is opposed to the exclusive nature of Judaism.<<Vide "Freem. Mag.", 1860, iii, p. 416.>>

ISLAMITE MYSTICS.   We have mentioned that Islamite Gnostics arose in Persia at an early period; and they claim to be as old as the time of the Prophet. It is said that their origin is the "Alli Allahis," a continuation of the old sect of Medo-Persian Magi. The Sects are termed "Tariks" or Paths, for they are Pilgrims or travellers on the "urug" Or ascent, in which there are three "ourouens" -- the road, the stages, the goal.

At this time we have numerous sects of these Mystics, and it is claimed that Ali, who according to the Persian sect was the lawful successor of Mohamed, founded them by bestowing some article of his clothing when he established their orders; thus one sect claims to have received his "Tailji" or cap; another his "Khirka" or Mantle; another his "Kemei" or girdle; thus fixing a succession.

"Benai Ibraham." Every reading Mason is aware that {182} from the time of the original of the "Cooke" MS. Constitutions, say A.D. 1400, it has been handed down that the hunter King, Nimrod, was a Grand Master, and that Abraham, who is said to have fled from him, taught the Egyptians geometry. It is not worth while to attempt to refute the latter statement, as according to Biblical chronology Abraham was not in Egypt until about 1925 B.C., but it would be worth while to ascertain, if we could, what ancient writer, probably Oriental, is responsible for the Abrahamic origin of geometry in Egypt. I am aware, of what I have never yet seen mentioned by any Masonic writer, that

amongst the Moslems, throughout the world, there is a very ancient Secret Society which claims to derive from the Koreish, or Guardians of the Kaaba, who were a superior Arab race and the descendants of Ishmael, and of which Mohammed was a scion. In the 1st and 2nd degrees of this system precisely the same assertions are made as in the MS. Constitutions of Masonry, whilst the 3rd degree is devoted to the erection of the Kaaba by Ibraham, Ismael, and Isaque, as the three presiding G.M.M. Sale, in his "Preliminary Observations" to his translation of "Al Koran" gives a full account of the legend as to Abraham s erection of a square temple similar to one destroyed in the deluge, the plans of which were etherially let down from Heaven on the prayer of Adam. I am inclined to give credit to the alleged great antiquity of these three degrees of the Sons of Ibraham, for two reasons, or rather three. In the first place Mohammed himself confirms the basis of the legend in treating of Abraham; in the second place the thirteenth century account of the erection on "Salvation Mount" of the square temple of San Graal, the plans being similarly heaven designed, is admittedly, by the writer himself, taken from Moslem sources; and, in the third place, I believe, with Ashmole, that the present system of Masonry was a thirteenth century reform of an older system. In 1872 the late Bro. Mackenzie organised the "Order of Ishmael," of 36th Degree, the basis of which, he informed me, {183} he had from an Arab in Paris, and in 1884 I was myself in relation with Prince Moustafa ben Ismael, ex-Prime Minister of Tunis, then in Paris. But Mackenzie s idea seems to have been that our Biblical legends were the transmission of the "Order of Ishmael," of which the "Sons of Ibraham" were a very ancient branch, or, as he terms it, the oldest secret society in the world.

M. Edmond Demoulins in his work "Anglo-Saxon Superiority," which has

created an immense sensation in France, says that in all the Oases, or Deserts, under Moslem rule Secret Brotherhoods (Zalouahs) exist, and he quotes, in confirmation, M. L. Ponsard on ancient Egypt and Chaldea in prehistoric times. He says: "They have their passwords, their signs of recognition, and are ruled by an official hierarchy which starts from the Grand Master, or Khalif, and ends with such subaltern agents as the messengers, banner-bearers, guards, etc. There are general assemblies for the purpose of receiving instructions from the Khalif, or for the initiation of fresh members, or again to promote the rising of the population against some interior, or exterior foe. This variety of patriotism inspired the societies which formerly occupied the two large Oases of Assyria and Egypt, at least, during the first part of their history, which extends over the time when, recently issued from the Desert, they still were under the more or less domination of the Brotherhoods and priests of Ammon. Mahomet and his votaries also partook of this species of patriotism, and so did all the Societies started under the inspiration of Islam, whether in the Arabian Desert and the Sahara, or at their two extremities from Asia Minor to Spain."

"Brothers of Purity." This was an association of Arab philosophers seated at

Bosra in the 10th century. They had forms of Initiation, and they wrote many works, which were afterwards much studied by the Spanish Jews.<<"Royal Mas. Cyclo.," K. R. H. Mackenzie.>>

"House of Wisdom." The Tarik of the House of Wisdom was founded at Cairo and had seven Initiatory {184} degrees. According to von Hammer, who gives his Arabian authorities, Abdallah a Persian, living in the 9th century of the Christian era, accepted, what was the Gnostic doctrine, of the Aeons, or Sephiroths, or emanations of divinity, and applied the system to the successors

of the Prophet of Arabia, upholding Ismael as the founder of his "Path," and one of his descendants as the Seventh Imaum. This man created "Dais," or Missionaries, for the propagation of the system, and was succeeded by his son and grandson. One of the name of Karmath brought the "Path" into repute. The Secret Institution was now seated at Cairo and termed the "Dar-al-hicmet," translated Tent of Skill, or House of Wisdom, and Assemblies were held twice a week, when all the members appeared clothed in white. The members were advanced gradually through a series of Seven degrees, over which presided a "Dai-al-doat," or Missionary of Missionaries. Their then Chief, Hakem-bi-emir- Illah increased these degrees to nine and erected, in 1004 A.D., a stately building which he abundantly furnished with mathematical instruments. In 1123 the Vizier Afdhal destroyed this building, but meetings continued elsewhere. Corresponding with the seven (or nine) grades of the Society was a seven-fold gradation of officers: -- Sheik, or Grand Master; Dai-el-Keber, or Deputy; Dai, or Master; Refik, or Fellow; Fedavie, or Agent; Lassik, or Aspirant; Muemini, or Believer. The Initiate was successively taught that there had been 7 holy Imaums; that God had sent 7 Lawgivers, who in the interval of their appearance had each 7 Helpers, and that each of these had 12 Apostles. It would appear that in 1150 the Sultan of Egypt recognised the grades of the Society, for when a special rank was created for the learned Jewish physician Maimonides, it is added that "the enlightened men of the kingdom were divided into seven grades, each occupying a corresponding position near the throne";<<"The Talmud," Polani, p. 226.>> it is also a slight confirmation of what we have said respecting the Spanish affinity with the Egyptian. {185} Sir John Maundeville, of St. Albans, served with the Sultan about 1320 and would seem to have been half converted to Islam; he relates that they denied the crucifixion of Jesus, and asserted that Judas was substituted in his place.

"Assassins." Before the year 1090, one of the Dais of the House of Wisdom

admitted an Aspirant of the name of Hassan Sabah, who thus details his conversion: "I had been reared, like my fathers, in the doctrine of the 12 Imaums, but I made the acquaintance of an Ishmaelite Rafeek named Emir Dhareb, with whom I knit fast the bonds of friendship. My opinion was that the tenets of the Ishmaelites resembled those of the Philosophers and that the Ruler of Egypt was a man who had been initiated into them." Hassan goes on to relate that he finally gave his fealty to a Dai named Moomen, set out for Egypt, and was met on the frontier by the Dai-al-Doat. Hassan saw that the failure of the "House" as a political Society arose from the lack of a fortress, and set about to remedy this defect. He obtained by a cunning strategical purchase in the year 1090 the Castle of Alamoot. Here he founded the Society of "Assassins" in seven degrees, the Class of Fedavees being those devoted to the main object, the killing of the enemies of the order. At a later period the Society was dispersed, but yet exists in its seven degrees in India and other countries, under its old designation of "Ishmaelites."

DRUZES. About the same period as the foundation of the "Assassins" a Dai

of the name of Hamsa prevailed upon the Druzes of Lebanon to accept the Initiatory System of the House of Wisdom. These Syrian Mountaineers are a peculiar race who are probably of Phoenician descent; it is known that before the time of Hamsa they possessed secret Rites, Degrees, and modes of recognition.<<"Vide Ars Quat. Cor.," iv, Smith.>> It was probably a phase of the Assyrian culte, such as is possessed by the Yezids, who worship sun,

moon, and bull, and have signs of recognition.<<Ibid, iv, Yarker.>> From the time of {186} Hamsa they have remained faithful conservators of the organisation received from him. The Sect recognises six degrees of which the three first are typified by the "three feet of the candlestick of the Inner Sanctuary which holds the five elements," and these "three feet" are "the holy application, the opening, the phantom," referring to man s inner and outer soul, and the body of matter. The Ignorant are presided over by the Akkals or wise, and these are of three higher grades, which represent more advanced principles and developments. The members are sworn to absolute secrecy, and strictly observe their oath. They are known to have signs of recognition which are common to Freemasonry.<<Ibid, iii.>> They also profess to have some tradition relative to assistance rendered at the building of Solomon s temple, but this may only be one of their modes of hoodwinking the Cowan. Blavatsky, who was an Initiate of the Sect, informs us that the fundamental principles of Hamsa are chastity, honesty, meekness, and mercy; and that its basis is the old Ophite Gnosticism, which, in the most ancient times, claimed immense antiquity as the builders of the Draconian stone enclosures, scattered over the old world, and even America. The Society admits, like other Ishmaelite Mystics, an affinity with the Platonic philosophy, and festivals are held at which raisins and figs are eaten; which it is thought is one of the tests of membership; it reminds us that priest Cyril of Jerusalem<<"Catech. Lec.," vi, 23.>> speaks of the "detestable ceremony of the fig." The Aspirant before admission has to undergo a long fast, which is entire on the last day, and a species of trance vision is induced before the ceremony closes.

"Ainsarii." The Ishmaelite Sect continued to exist after the destruction of the stronghold of the Old Man of the Mountain, as the Chief of the Assassins was termed. The most prominent of these is named the Ainsarii; they hold secret meetings for receptions and have signs, words, and a Catechism. Lyde, who has investigated this Sect, {187} classes them with ancient Templars, and Modern Freemasons.<<"The Asian Mystery," Rev. C. L. Lyde.>>

"Dervishes." The various "Paths" of the Dervishes are very ancient and spread from branches in Persia and Egypt. Though their rites and doctrines vary from one another, the object of all is similar to each other and to Magian and Indian Yogism, namely, Union with the Deity. We will take the "Bektash" as typical of the others. In the 15th century, Bektash of Bokhara, received his "Mantle" from Ahmed Yesevee, who claimed descent from the father-in-law of Mohamed. On this he proceeded to establish a "Path," consisting of seven nominal, but four essential degrees. These are magical in their nature, inasmuch as they aim at establishing an affinity between the Aspirant and the Sheik, from whom he is led, through the founder, and the Prophet, to Allah. Their Initiatory ceremony is shortly as follows. After a year s probation, during which the Aspirant is tested with false secrets a lamb is killed from which a cord is made for his neck, and a girdle of Initiation for his loins; he is led into a square chamber, and between two armed attendants, who present him as a slave who desires to know truth. He is led by the cord round his neck, and one of the axes used, or carried by these godfathers is in the writer s possession, bearing on one side the name of Ali and the other that of Mohamed. He is then placed before a stone altar on which are twelve escallops. The Sheik, who is attended by eleven others, grips the hand of the Aspirant in a peculiar way, and administers the oath of the order, which is equivalent to the Monkish vow

of poverty, chastity, and obedience. He is then informed that death awaits him if he betrays his order; and he makes his profession in.the following formula: "Mohamed is my Rheper (guide); Ali is my Murchid (director)." The Sheik then asks: "Do you accept me as your Murchid?" and upon an affirmative reply adds: "Then I accept you as my son." {188} He is invested with a girdle, on which are three knots, and receives an alabaster stone as token. The sign of recognition is that of the first degree in Masonry. Their grace is called the "Gulbend," or "rose of fraternal love." Amongst their important symbols are the double triangles {Symbol: Hexagram} and two triangles joined at the apex {symbol, like an "X" but with the top and bottom chevrons closed to equilateral triangles}. One of their maxims is, "the man must die that the saint may be born."<<"The Dervishes," J. P. Brown.>> As a Jewel they make use of a small marble cube with red spots to typify the blood of the martyred Ali. The Sects are not popular with the orthodox Turkish Mussulmans, but all branches swear to devote themselves to the interests of their order or Path with body and soul. The Jewel of another branch, in possession of the writer, has at the top a small green stone, and suspended from this by three silver chains, is a large sized bloodstone, oval; and from this again is suspended three other chains: the first three chains has two small silver discs, the second three has each a silver disc and two are double, in all making seven. The Mantle of the order has on each shoulder a representation of the Sword of Ali.

Amongst the immense number of operative Masons employed by the

Saracens, there must have been a large number of such Initiates, but it is not intended by these details to absolutely identify Freemasonry with the Societies using the formula; but to shew the existence of certain ancient features in common with the Arcane Schools in various channels. Yet it is quite possible that the original Roman ritual of the Guild may have been modified by the addition of Solomonic legends preserved in the East, or on the other hand taken "en bloc" from the Jewish Guilds of Syria and Egypt, and the probability is that the Jews of Spain were in a position to hand on the Guild system, but we shall enter into this later.

TEMPLARS. The rule of the Templars resembled that of the Benedictines and Cistercians, and was drawn up by {189} Bernard, Abbot of Clairvaux, some short time after their establishment in 1118. In it the prelate terms them "Valiant Maccabees"; they were to wear on their clothing and horses neither gold nor silver; not to have more than three horses each, because, as he says, they could not rival "the world renowned temple of Solomon," on the site of which they had acquired a residence. The reception was a strictly secret one, which gave rise in 1310 to a shameful persecution. Before admission to the Chapter the Aspirant was thrice cautioned as to the rigorous trials that he would have in becoming a member, and asked if he firmly persisted in his demands to proceed, and if he responded in the affirmative he was admitted to the Reception.

In an old number of "Blackwood s Magazine" appears what professes to be the burial service of a Templar, no authority is given, but we know no reasons to deny its authenticity. It is a highly symbolical ceremony, at which the classes of Preceptors, Knights, and Servitors were present; and the Grand Master presided with an iron hammer in his hand, with which three knocks were struck upon an iron cross. The three classes had each an active part in the ceremony; and in answer to a question of the Grand Master: "Know ye for a

truth that our brother is dead, and ripe for the long sleep of the grave?" A Serving-brother takes the hand of the corpse and answers: "The flesh cleaves not to the bone, nor the skin unto the flesh, he is dead." After other questions seven knights advance to the corpse, and place their hands upon the head, eyes, face, mouth, heart, hand, and feet with a fervent blessing, and the corpse is then lowered into the grave.<<"Vide Fre. Mag.," 1864 p. 205; "Rosicrucian," 1876. p. 75; A. Q. C., vi. The late Bro. Albert Pike revised the ceremony for the Kadosh burial service of the A. & A. Rite.>>

It has been maintained by von Hammer, that the members of the Order were Initiates of the Cairo House of Wisdom, and the resemblance is peculiar, both had {190} secret receptions, a similar government, and both used white and red in their clothing. That they had a secret reception is beyond doubt, and one of their maxims was that "secrecy is the soul of the order." Authorities differ very much as to this secret reception; those who believe in the Gnostic heresy of the order, assert that such Initiation was adopted from the Saracens about years 1250-70, and which added to their old Reception, a degree of Professed wherein the cross was trodden underfoot; a girdle was given to the Initiated; he was taught an Enlightened Deism, and made a disciple of John the Baptist. If there was such a ceremony as indicated it would be as a test of obedience. The third grade, it is said, was for high Officers; a symbolic Gnostic cord was consecrated by the head of Baphometis, and presented to be worn under the clothes. Blavatsky says that the Nazarians of Persia have a tradition that they initiated the Templars.<<"Isis Unveiled," p. 232.>> The head here mentioned may allude to two words -- Baphe metios, or Baptism of Wisdom, and represent the head of John the Baptist; but de Quincey suggests that it is cabalistically composed in substituting B for P to refer to the Pope and Mahomet, whose tenets the later Rosicrucians designated "blasphemies of the East and West." On the other hand the Secret Mysteries of the Templars are said to have been the Arcane Discipline, and to have referred to the faith of Christ. Philip le Bel, King of France, and Pope Clement V. combined in 1309 to suppress them, and in 1313 the latter dissolved them on the plea of Gnosticism, which would apply to any of these suppositions.

There was in the time of the plenitude of the Templars a peculiar Culdee
legend travelling around termed the "Quest of the Sangrael;" it was supposed that there was a lost cup, which had contained the blood of the Saviour, that could only be found by a chaste Knight who journeyed in search of it. It had, if found, various magical properties, oracular answers to enquiries could be {191} read thereon. Von Hammer professes to read the "Graal" upon certain old offertory dishes which he considers to have been Templar property, but his views have not been generally credited. There are yet certain ceremonies practised alluding to Joseph, Jesus, and Mary, said to have been of Culdee origin, that have a sober resemblance to the Quest. The Mystic tradition may hide the old blood baptism of the Mysteries. Eugene Aroux speaks very positively of an Albigensian and Templar connection with the legend, which is supposed to have some basis in the Gospel of Nicodemus. San Marte takes the same view and lays stress upon the use by the Templars, at the Lord s Supper of the opening words of St. John s Gospel. The Rev. Baring Gould gives credit to a Templar connection with the Mythos. Von Hammer says the poem of Titurel is nothing but an allegory of the Society of Templars and its doctrine

and one with the Gnostic and Ophite symbols. This legend is a lengthy subject to write upon, but it is necessary to say something upon it.

The origin of the Graal legend is curious, romantic, and ancient. The Persians have a legend of a golden cup discovered in making the foundations of Persepolis which they named the "Goblet of the Sun"; we have also the Hermesian cup in the Poemander. There is also the Welsh legend of Peridur, which means "Companion of the Bowl." Peridur enters a castle, and two young men enter a room, where he is seated, with a lance from which falls three gouts of blood, which the company seeing set up a lamentation; then enter two damsels, with a charger in which is a head swimming in blood, and the company utter a piercing wail. The bowl here is the Cauldron of Ceridwen, and the blood is the three drops of her brew that conferred intuition. In Hanover there is some Templar connection with a charger and the head of John the Baptist, to be mentioned later. Taliesen s poem of Bran the blessed mentions the bowl of Pheredur, which could restore the dead to life, "but those who were restored to life by it were not to speak lest they should {192} divulge the mysteries of the vessel." Bran sails to the "Island of Joy," with 39 Companions.

M. Pauline de Paris mentions the "Liber Gradalis" of a British priest about 30
years after the death of Cadwallader. About the year 717 the priest had a vision of Christ, and of Joseph of Arimethea, who brought the cup to this country, with the blood of Christ.

These legends admit their indebtedness to the Moslem legends, and there can be no doubt as to what that legend is; it refers to the erection by Abraham of the Temple of Seth, which we refer to elsewhere, in which on the petition of Adam an etherial temple was let down in appearance to which Adam could direct his prayers.

The more modern version of the legend was compiled about 1189, under the title of "Sir Coules del Grail," by Chretien de Troies. Saniber, prince of Cappadocia in the days of Vespasian, had three sons, who went eventually to Rome; and his great-great grandson Titur-el was the Graal King, and the pure and noble Knight. When dying the Graal King instructed his children in the mystery, and the Knights had explained to them the symbols, ceremonies, and the powers of the 12 precious stones. Shortly after we have the version of Guyot de Provens, who had been a monk with Bernard of Clairvaux, and visited Jerusalem about the year 1170; it was an elaborated version of the preceding, which the author as well as Guy de Provens attributed to the Arabian astrologer and philosopher Flegantan. This was translated into German about the year 1207 by Wolfram von Eschenbach, and would be known in 1248 when Conrad von Hochstetten laid the foundation stone of Cologne Cathedral. Later on another version was completed by Alfred von Scharfenberg. In the oldest account Titurel builds the Graal temple, but in this last version it is Parsifal, grandson of Titurel, who is selected to build a magnificent temple upon a design miraculously shown on curtains of light, and upon a mount called "Saviour s Mount" placed in the midst of a "square" wood, the temple {193} itself was to be "round," as are the Templar churches. The plan appears miraculously upon a stone, and indicated an inner Sanctuary to hold the Graal, which was to be guarded by chaste Temple, or Templar Knights, for both these forms are used in different MSS. The groining of the roof was to shew a lamb holding a red cross banner in its claws (a Templar standard). The Lecterns were to have carved Apostles, Martyrs, Prophets, and their "wise

saws"; and in one of these MSS. England is named in connection with four crowns, four virgin martyrs, and their legends.<<"Freem. Quart. Mag.," 1853; also "Canadian Craftsman," 1892.>> Besides the Glastonbury legend of this cup and the account of the Romances of King Arthur, another claim is made for a Sapphire cup in the monastery of Richeneau, Lake Constance, founded by Charles Martel in 725; there is also a third claim for a cup said to have been brought from the East by the Crusaders, and lodged at Genoa; it is now believed to be made of green glass.

A Benedictine Monk of St. Werburgh in Chester, where the Polychronicon was compiled, often quoted in Guild MSS., Hy. Bradshaw, who died in 1513, has some very similar ideas wherein he is describing the feast of King Ulpha given at the Abbey of Ely, when his daughter Werburge took the veil. The tale also runs on the line of the old Masonic Constitutions. The tapestry of cloth of gold and arras. The story of Adam, of his wife Eve, and how they were deceived was "goodly wrought." Cain and Abel making their offering. Tubal and Tubal Cain were pourtrayed, "the inventours of Musike and Crafte."

"Noe and his shyppe was made there curyously, Sendying forthe a raven which never came again, And how the dove returned with a branch hastily."

Abraham was there on a mount to offer up Isaac. The 12 Sons of Jacob; Joseph sold into Egypt. Moses "wyse and bolde." Our Lorde appearing in a bush on fire. The 10 plagues of Egypt embossed. The two tables given to Moses. Dathan and Abyrom "full youre." Duke Josue leading the Israelites to the land of promise. {194} Pharaoh and the Red Sea. King Saul and David and prudent Solomon.

Rehobom, Hezekiah, and his generacion. "And so to the Machabees and dyvers other nacyons." But over the highest dais, where three kings sat crowned, was represented the IX Angelical orders divided into III hierarchies. Holy! Holy! Lord God of Sabaoth. Three persons in one deity.

Then followed representatives of the Virgin, the 12 Apostles, and the 4 Evangelists teaching and preaching "the faythe of holy chyrche." Martyrs followed, the Innocents, St. Stephen, St. Laurence, St. Vincent.

Virgins crowned, some with the lily, others with roses for their great victory. On the other side of the Hall were noble, ancient stories, Sampson, Hector of Troy, Noble Anthony, with many others. At the feast which followed each spake freely: --

"Knyghtes of theyr chivalry, of Crafts the common."

The evidence of Titurel speaks well for the Templars, yet it is possible that some of the Preceptories may have introduced Oriental Rites and Symbols. Von Hammer, confirmed by Hallam and other writers, states that in various Preceptories their most secret place (crypt) contains indecent emblems sculptured, without particularly describing these. It may be said that one of these is a female figure holding in each hand a staff, at the head of one of which is the sun, and on the other the moon, whilst at her feet is the five- pointed star and other symbols. This is Basilidean in its character and there are references to the Templars confirming a statement "by Sun and Moon." Addison mentions a copper medallion, intended to be worn around the neck by

a chain, and which was found in France; it consists of the double equilateral triangles interlaced, and enclosed within two circles, and in the centre is the lamb and banner of the Temple. Clavel, quoted by Oliver,<<"Hist. Land.," ii, p. 355.>> says that in the 17th century there was discovered in the grave of a Templar in Germany, who died before the dissolution of the order, {195} "a stone cube inscribed with the square and compasses, the pentalpha, the celestial sphere, a star of five points, and several other stars." Eliphas Levi says that, "a box was found in the ruins of an old Commandery in which was a Baphometic figure. It had a bearded face with a woman s body. In one hand it held the sun, in the other the moon, by chains." (Gould s N. & Q. xi. p. 188.) Von Hammer mentions Templar churches at Erfurt, Schoengraben, and Prague, as containing such emblems -- the square, level, triangle, compasses, compasses with quadrant, interlaced triangles, the flaming star, the Tau cross of Egypt. All such matter confirms the charge of Gnosticism, but such decoration may be due to the Masons who erected the Churches; and the symbolism equally with the Reception of a Templar have points of affinity. The Templars were large builders, and Jacques de Molay alleged the zeal of his order in decorating churches on the process against him, 1310, hence the alleged connection of Templary and Freemasonry is bound to have a substratum of truth. A French version of the Compagnnonage asserts that, during a dispute, a section placed themselves under the patronage of Jacques de Molay, the Master who was roasted to death on an island in the Seine in 1314 by the vicious scoundrel Philip le Bel. Nicolai, quoted in "Acta Latamorum," asserts that in Italy are several churches formerly belonging to the Templars, which have preserved the name "l eglise de la Mason," as derived from the table Masa, a club, that is tyled by a Mace or club; but Paciandi considers the derivation to be from Magione, as the places were used for residences; there are some such in France as well as Italy. Besides the symbols already mentioned an old writer of the name of Assemani mentions a shield, on which is the lamb, the cup, and two crossed torches. The last was a Mythraic symbol, and the chalice or cup was a common symbol of the order. They used the cross patee, the equilimbed cross, the Latin cross, the patriarchal cross; in later times they adopted the Eagle as a symbol. Recently a Lecture by Brother F. F. Schnitger has shown that most {196} of the Charges of 1310 are explicable, by an evil construction being placed on ceremonies in use by the Masonic branch of the order last century. There is a body in France of which Philip of Orleans was the Grand Master in 1705, which claims to have continued the order;<<Vide Ars Quat. Cor., iv, Yarker.>> in Portugal it changed its name to Knights of Christ; in Scotland it preserved its name, owing to the wars that Bruce was conducting against England, and in Hungary it continued to exist in name. Frater Ladislas de Malczovich, of Budapesth, has made a study of Templar

history, tracing them in their Standards, Badges, and Seals, and divides these into three periods: --

1. The "Beauseant," of black and white, was the standard of the Hospitallers of St. John before the institution of the Temple Order, and are moreover their colours. But on the grant of a Red Cross they assumed the "Vexillum Belli," a white standard charged with a red cross; and they then attached a secret Mystery to the old black and white standard, with a plain cross. In the third period they used the cross "patee," in place of the plain cross.

There were also three periods in the Seals. The first was two Knights on one horse. This is super-seded by the head of Christ crowned with thorns, and it has three stars placed triangularwise. The last Seal is found near the Order s dissolution, and is a single-headed eagle with wings expanded, upon a high rock, and looking heaven-wards; at the top is a small cross "patee" and two stars.

Of their crosses we find the following in use: -- the "patee;" the elongated cross; the patriarchal cross; also a plain equal-limbed cross with a lamb in the centre holding the red cross banner.

Armorially, they used the crossed torches, a chalice, and the Agnus Dei upon a shield. There are various instances in Sculpture which prove the importance of the Chalice symbol; in some cases Knights are represented as holding it aloft, and there is also a representation of two serving {197} brethren with one arm round each other, whilst the right hand, in one figure, holds the chalice, and the other has a book under the arm, which is considered to allude to it, and to be one with the Chalice of the Graal.

1st Period: "Beauseant," Black and White. "Seal": Two Knights on one horse.

Implying, death to infidels, friendship to Christians.

2nd Period: "Vexillum Belli," White with plain red cross. "Seal": Head of Christ. Implying, Soldiers of Christ fighting for the cross.

3rd Period: Standard, White with red cross patee. "Seal": An Eagle. The independent and high flying policy of the Order.

The French Templars adopted a Gospel called the "Leviticon," which they alleged was discovered in the Temple at Paris, with other things; and Heckethorn states that it was composed in the 15th century by a Greek Monk Nicephorus, who sought to combine Moslem tenets with Christianity.

POETICAL GNOSTICISM, TROUBADOURS, GAY SCIENCE.

The persecution of the enlightened by the Church of Rome necessitated various disguises by the Sectarians -- Poetical, Artistic, Theosophic and Hermetic --and it could not be otherwise; humanity, in the abstract, seldom abandons that which it "knows" to be true and takes steps to transmit it through the centuries: truth never dies. One of the modes employed was to speak, or write, in a language that will bear a double interpretation, the one intended for the ordinary hearer, and the other for the Initiate who had the Key of interpretation. Masonic MSS. term it the arts of Logic and Rhetoric. This custom was undoubtedly prevalent in the most ancient times and Mythology, Cabalism, etc., are examples of it. Heckethorn mentions certain "Knights of the Swan," who sang in this speech in the early part of the 12th century, and the same writer observes that the Minstrels and Troubadours of France were divided into four degrees. It is {198} very probable that many of our own northern minstrels transmitted from the time of the Culdees, who existed until the Templar persecutions, an anti-papal programme, and were in the secrets of the Continental Minstrels in the time of Wycliffe, and later. The artistic participation in this propaganda is shewn in the way that the vices of clerics and monks are satirised by stone and wood carvers; as in the representation of an ape carrying the Host; a nun in the lewd embrace of a monk; or a pope amongst the damned.<<Findel, "Hist. Freem." >>

Gabriel Rossetti<<"Disq. on the anti-papal spirit which produced the Reformation.">> shews that the species of writing which we have named was introduced from the East by the Manichees, who passed it on to the Cathari, Albigensis, Ghibellines, and Templars, through whom it spread over Europe. Logic was considered by them the science of expressing thought in a subtle manner. Many persecutions arose from this species of writing, but the Papal Conclave at length determined to close its eyes, rather than make the allegory apparent to all the world. The reformation liberated to the world various Mystic Societies. With the object of proving his views he quotes largely from Dante, Petrarch, Boccacio, and other poets and writers of the middle ages, and arrives at the conclusion that there existed three principle branches of Sectaries, which indoctrinated their Disciples by a secret Initiation of seven or nine degrees, according to the Rite or Sect. The allegory used was often that of a journey, and to go on a Pilgrimage to the temple of St. John signified to become a proselyte of the Templars; to go to St. James in Galicia was to be of the Albigensis; and St. Peter s at Rome of the Ghibellines; the Albigensis, in alluding to the first named, expressed Faith; to the second Hope, and to the last Charity. We have an Oriental pilgrimage in Boccacio s "Filocopo," which means a young workman; seven Companions figure in this account; the names of four are already known to the Pilgrim and represent the Cardinal {199} virtues; the other three are unknown until he has accomplished his journey, or initiation, upon which it appears that they are Faith, Hope, and Charity; in allusion thus to the ancient ladder of the Mysteries of 3, 7, or 12 steps. The object was to found a Christian Jerusalem to rival Rome; and the allegory frequently alludes to the rebuilding of Jerusalem and the return of its people; the later Reformers drew upon the same idea as we will show. The writer has, however, gone over this more at length in an earlier book, and space does not admit of it here.<<"Notes on Sc. and Relg. Mysteries," 1872.>> An acute and learned historian<<"Philosophy of History," Fredk. von Schlegel, p. 456>> takes a similar view, on the spirit of the age, and has the following, in which he is alluding to Freemasonry: "As to the origin of this esoteric influence, the impartial historical enquirer cannot doubt, whatever motives or views some may have to deny the fact, or throw doubt on its authenticity, that the Order of Templars was the channel by which this society, in its ancient and long preserved form, was introduced into the West. The religious Masonic symbols may be accounted for by the Solomonian traditions connected with the very foundation of the Templars, and indeed the occasion of these symbols may be traced in other passages of holy writ, and in other parts of sacred history, and they may very well admit of a Christian interpretation. Traces of these symbols may be found in the monuments of the old German architecture of the middle ages."<<"Philosophy of History," Fredk. von Schlegel, p. 456>>

Rossetti holds also that Barbarossa, Henry VII. and Frederick II., are the leading characters referred to in the double language of Dante s works. The latter was the grandson of Frederick Barbarosso (Red Beard) who died in Syria at the head of 150,000 Crusaders. The Popes thrice excommunicated the grandson, whom Matthew Paris terms the "wonder of the world" ("Stupor Mundi et immutator Mirabalis"), and truly he was -- he was suspected as a heretic even a Moslem, hereditary King of Sicily, he was the last Christian King of Jerusalem, the last who ruled {200} the holy land, or wore a crown in the holy city; the most successful of the Crusaders since Godfrey de Bouillon, and

gained Jerusalem by policy; was excommunicated for going there; excommunicated for coming back; excommunicated as a Sectarian, of which the Pope distinctly accuses him, and there is a fable of 1378 by John of Florence, in which he is named as a man "fond of the gentle language. " There is no doubt it is this man whom in 1767 Morin mistook for Frederick II. of Prussia in the Rite of Heredom, which see later.

We have said that the art of expressing things to bear a double meaning was taught as part of the "Trivium," and Dante, who is thought to have been a lay Brother of the Templars himself tells Con Grande that the "Divine Comedy" admits of four keys of interpretation -- literal, allegorical, moral, and mystical. He speaks of Christ as "Him our Pelican," an Egyptian Symbol of the Sothic cycle, the bird being mystically said to fly every 1260 years to the altar of the Sun at Heliopolis, where it was consumed by fire, and out of its own ashes restored to life. Ozanam, a Roman Catholic, considers the "Divine Comedy" to follow the same lines as an Initiation into the Mysteries of Egypt. Vecchioni, president of the Supreme Court at Naples, took the same view, and sought unsuccessfully, to print a book thereon, to prove that such Initiation had been handed down by philosophers and poets, and that the "Divine Comedy" was arranged after the plan of a "Teletes," ending in an "Eposis," or divine vision. Loiseleur, a French writer, considers the teachings of the Sects as closely connected with the Euchites, and both Cathari and Templars girdled themselves with a white thread like the Hindu and Persian Mystics. They made use also of Symbolic ages, as is done to define degrees. Reghellini of Scio treats Dante as a Cabalist and Rosicrucian. King<<"The Gnostics and their Remains.">> quotes the 18th canto of the "Purgatory" as "replete with the profoundest symbolism which the Freemasons claim for their own," to wit, the imperial {201} eagle; the mystic ladder; the rose and cross; pelican; supper of the lamb; pillars of Faith, Hope, and Charity; symbolic colours; letters and geometric figures, as point, circle, triangle, square; the trampling of crown and mitre under foot; the "Vito Nuovo," and the "Convito" or Banquet being equally mystical. To these may be added the Invocation of Divine vengeance upon the destroyers of the Templars, and the choice of St. Bernard as the High priest.<<Vide "Theos. Rev.," viii, Cath. Hillard.>> It is not, however, the

Masonry of the Guild, but that which has been added thereto.

Mrs. Cooper-Oakley has some pregnant remarks upon the TROUBADOURS, who were the undoubted poets of the Albigensian heresy; and quotes Baret s Paris work of 1867 as to the following Schools, all of which were again subdivided into groups: -- That of Aquitaine; of Auvergne; of Rodez; of Languedoc; of Provence. Again classified as: -- The Gallant; the Historical; the Didactic; the Satirical; and the purely Theological. Again of the Mystical; the Hermetic. Aroux demonstrates that their "Celestial Chivalry" was derived from the "Albigensian Gospel," whose Evangel was again derived from the Manichaean-Marcion tradition. These Albigensis were identical with the Cathari, and the Troubadours were the links bearing the secret teaching from one body to another. "Thus one sees them taking every form by turns, artizans, colporteurs, pilgrims, weavers, colliers . . . . deprived of the right to speak they took to singing."

Amongst the most illustrious of the Troubadours was Alphonso the Second, King of Arragon, 1162-96. Peter the Second of Arragon was the principal ally of the Albigensis and Troubadours, and in 1213 perished nobly in their cause at

the Battle of Muret. Escaping from their burnt and bloody homes, not a few of them hastened to the Court of Arragon, where they were sure of protection. Says Ticknor, in his "Hist. Spanish Literature," London, 1849: "Religious romances were written....in the {202} form of Allegories, like the Celestial Chivalry, the Christian Chivalry, the night of the Bright Star ; and the Celestial Chivalry, of Hieronimo de San Pedro (Valencia, 1554) uses such titles as (1) The Root of the fragrant Rose, and (2) The Leaves of the Rose. " In the paths of the Dervishes the candidate is said to "take the rose" of the path.

The basis of the Christian legend of the Graal is said to be found in apocryphal gospel of Nicodemus, which was translated into Provencal verse, "a Mystical Gospel" in every sense, says Paulin Paris, who in referring to the MS. in the Vatican (of the Graal), further writes: "This latter text was of great antiquity and evidently mystical, showing a profound knowledge of the Apocryphal Gospel concerning the secret teachings of the Eucharist."

Eugene Aroux thus speaks of the grades of the Troubadours: "Like the other Aspirants to the Sectarian priesthood they went into seminaries or lodges to receive instruction; then having become deacons or squires, having undergone tests and given required pledges, they were admitted to the rank of Perfect Knights, or Perfect Troubadours. Having thus graduated they started in the character of Missionaries or of Pilgrims of Love, as Dante says, sometimes undertaking long and dangerous journeys " -- "i.e.," as Wild or Errant Knights. (Aroux).

ROSICRUCIANISM. In the 13th century we have traces of an organised body of men professedly Christian, who had organised themselves after the manner of the Oriental Societies. The name with which we head this article had not then become prominent, but at a later period it became the generic title by which everything of the nature of Cabalism, Theosophy, Alchemy, Astrology, and Mysticism was designated.

It is stated in a Rosicrucian MS., lying at Cologne under the nom-de-plume of Omnis Moriar, that a Society termed the Magical Union was established at this city in the year 1115. F. C. E. Weise mentions it<<"Rosenkreutzer in seiner Blosse," -- Amdsterdam, 1786.>> and gives {203} the conditions for entering this body of "Wise Men," the last and youngest possessors of the secrets of the ancients; the Initiates wore a triangle as symbolising power, wisdom, and love. They had secret sciences, known only to the highest among them, called Mu- alpha-gamma-omicron-sigma, Mage, or Wise Masters, able to do things that seemed supernatural. Traces of an organised body are to be found in the "Rosary" of Arnold de Villanova, "circa" 1230, inasmuch as the Cabalistic term of "Sons of the Order" is used. In the "Theoria" of Raymond Lulli "circa" 1322 there is a passage in which mention is made of a "Societas Physicorum," and also of a "Rex Physicorum." Also in the "Theatrum Chemicum Argentoratum," 1628, a Count von Falkenstein, Prince Bishop of Treves in the 14th century, is termed "Most Illustrious and Serene Prince and father of Philosophers." Hence it would seem that besides the Moorish Schools which existed in Spain, there were similar associations amongst Christians. It is not difficult to account for the transmission of such Brotherhoods from ancient times, since the Cabalists and Gnostics studied the secret arts, and it is quite probable that the persecutions to which these were subjected were prompted rather by alarm than any real abhorrence of their pretended heretical doctrine. A few of the more curious and important works may be mentioned here.

The "Romance of the Rose" is an Initiative system in the Allegory of the Gay Science, in which the term Love is used Theosophically. Eliphas Levi says: "It is the most curious literary and scientific work of the middle ages, it carries on the chain of the tradition of Initiation." Heckethorn holds that, "it divides the degrees into four and three, producing again the Mystic number seven   it describes a castle surrounded by a sevenfold wall, which is covered with emblematical figures, and no one was admitted into the castle who could not explain their mysterious meaning." Amant is admitted into this beautiful garden, which is surrounded by walls on which is painted figures of 9 vices, such as hatred, envy, avarice, {204} etc. Discourses take place between the ladies and gentles assembled, and at the close Amant appears as an armed Pilgrim, wearing a scarf and bearing on his shoulders the usual burthen, with description of how he succeeded in introducing it through the wicket of the Tower, and "gathers the roses," upon which he returns thanks to Venus, her son, and the nobles assembled. The work was begun by William de Lorris, about 1282, as the Templars and other Orders are mentioned, and the early use of the word Macon appears in it. It was completed by Jean de Meung, and Geoffrey Chaucer translated it. Meung wrote also, "The Treasure" or seven articles of the faith, "The Testament, the Codical," on life and Morals, also two poems, entitled, "The Remonstrance of Nature to the wandering Alchemist," and "The Reply of the Alchemist to Nature." Other Societies would seem to have abandoned art, and confined themselves,
like the Dervish sects, to a Mysticism which aimed at "uniting its members to God." Brother R. F. Gould relates that the famous Dominican John Tauler, who was born in 1290 and died in 1361, established a Fraternity the members of which concealed their place of burial and recognised each other by secret signs. He was followed by Nicholas of Basle, who had four companions, styling themselves "Friends of God," in whom they sought to be "wrapped up"; these also had secret signs of recognition.
The most noted Alchemist of this century was Nicholas Flamel, a poor scrivener of Paris, who, by the art, became enormously rich. He purchased for 2 florins in 1357 an ancient book bound in brass,

which appeared to be written on leaves made from the bark of trees, perhaps the papyrus; it was subscribed by "Abraham the Jew, Prince, Priest, Levite, Astrologer, and Philosopher." It had thrice 7 leaves, and every seventh leaf was a picture, symbolising the Great Work. Flamel travelled about in search of some one who could aid him in interpreting the contents, and after much loss of time, trouble, and {205} experiments, he succeeded in making gold. According to his own account he bestowed the riches thus acquired in erecting and endowing 10 churches, 3 chapels, and 14 hospitals in Paris alone, and others in two other cities, besides aiding indigent families. He relates how in the Church of the Innocents, Rue St. Denis, Paris, he caused to be erected "Hieroglyphical Couvertures," of the art of transmutation, under veils of the "Mysteries of our Salvation." We learn from a recent reprint that the Count de Cabrines told Borel, that the actual book of Abraham the Jew passed into the possession of the celebrated Cardinal Richelieu.<<"Nic. Flamel," Pref. Dr. W. W. Westcott (Fryar, Bath).>>

In the possession of a German gentleman, to whom we will refer later, there

is a copy of an old MS. which claims to be of the year 1374, that mentions the "Fraternitas Rosae Crucis," and it was in the year 1378 that the beginning of the Fraternity was attributed to Christian Rosenkreutz. Up to this period there

is a lack of the nature of Alchemical Symbolism, but the following is beyond doubt. Borel describes the house erected at Montpelier, about the year 1450 by the celebrated French traveller and financier Jacques Cuer or Coeur. It was named "La Loge," and Coeur is represented on the frieze with a "trowel in his hand." "Three porches may there be seen in the form of a furnace; similar to those of Nicholas Flamel. On one there is, on one side, a "sun" all over fleur- de-lis, and on the other a full "moon" also covered with fleur-de-lis, and surrounded by a hedge or crown as it were of thorns, which seem to denote the solar and lunar stone arrived at perfection. On another portal is seen, on one side, a fruit-tree with branches of roses at its foot, and on the tree the arms of Jacques Coeur. On the other is an escutcheon, and within it what would appear to represent the chemic character of the sun. On the third portal, which is in the midst, there is on one side a stag bearing a banner, and having a collar of fleur-de-lis environed with a branch of a tree, to represent Mercury,

{206} or the philosophical matter, which at the commencement is volatile and

light as in the stag; on the other side is a shield of France supported by two griffins."

This symbolism has nothing in common with that of Flamel, who does not profess to have been an Initiate, but one who having acquired some oral information of the first agent of the work, acquired the art by experiments conducted by himself with the aid of his wife; but on the other hand it is much in keeping with that of Abraham the Jew, and therefore argues a great antiquity. The whole symbolism is so equally Masonic and Alchemical that it would be difficult to say definitely to which Society it belongs; both Societies seem to have a common transmission, the one as a building, the other as a Mystic Fraternity; the natural inference here, on this evidence, is that Coeur was a member of both Societies, and that he combined the symbols. Alchemically the Sun and Moon signify gold and silver; the chemic character of the sun is a point within a circle; the branch of a tree, said to represent Mercury, has nothing to define the species. It may be mentioned here that the Syrian Mysteries of Adonis represented the slain God as changed by Venus into a red rose; and Theodoratus, Bishop of Cyrus in Syria, asserts that the Gnostics deemed "Ros" to be a symbol of the Saviour; the Egyptians considered the rose as a symbol of regeneration and love, and as the Latin word Rosa is derived from Ros, the dew, it has a relation with baptism; hence the rose-tree in Christian symbolism is the image of the regenerated, whilst dew is the symbol of regeneration. In the Crypt of St. Sibald s in Nuremberg, is a double triangle, interlaced with a circle, within which is a rose.

Basil Valentine, who flourished at the same time as Jacques Coeur, in his "Azoth Philosophorum," has a figure which is thus described: it represents a winged-globe on which is a triangle inside a square, upon which reposes a dragon; on the latter stands a human figure with two heads, and two hands; surrounding the heads, one of {207} which is male and the other female, are the sun, moon; and five stars; the hand on the male side holds a compass, that on the other a square. The symbolism here clearly alludes to the dual sexual nature of all metals. In "The Triumphant Chariot of Antimony" it is asserted that the Adept should be capable of building his own furnaces.

The most noted of the Alchemists after this date was Philippus Aureolus Theophrastus Bombast of Hohenheim, who was born in 1493, and died in 1541, and there is a strong suspicion that it was from injuries inflicted by his

enemies. Whilst travelling in the East he was taken prisoner by the Tartars, who treated him kindly, and the Khan sent him with his son to Constantinople; it is probable that he studied Magic in these regions. He had studied Magnetism and initiated medical treatment by mercury and opium. Franz Hartman, M.D., has shewn the identity of his teaching with the Eastern Adepts of the Secret Doctrine. His philosophy divides man into seven principles of the outer and inner body; (1) the visible body; (2) the mumia, archaeus, or vital force; (3) the sideral body, which gradually dissolves; (4) the animal soul, common to all things; (5) the rational soul; (6) the aluech, or spiritual soul; (7) new olympus, or divine spirit, which must be caught and bound to the other principles if man is to become immortal. He fills the elements with spirits of many kinds, and mentions the Flagae, who act as our guides and familiars, and instruct us in the sciences. He designates himself "Monarch of Philosophers," and the "Comte de Gabalis," a work of 1675-80 definitely states that he was elected "Monarch" of the Rosicrucian Society.

We will now refer to a few Societies which seem to have been Cabalistic or Speculative rather than Alchemical, but with a tinge of the Sciences. Between the years 1400 to "circa" 1790 there existed at Lubeck a Guild called the "Compass Brothers" which met twice a year; their badge was a compass and sector suspended from a crowned letter "C," over which was a radiated triangular plate; in {208} 1485 they adopted chains composed of these emblems united by eagles tails.<<"Ars Quat. Cor., iii, p. 120.>> About the year 1480 a Society was established at Rome under the name of the "Platonic Academy;" it was a revival of the School of Plato, and the Hall in which they met is said to contain Masonic emblems. Another Society, which may have sprung out of it, was the "Brotherhood of the Trowel," at Florence. It was composed of eminent architects, sculptors, and painters, and continued until last century. There are some old drawings in Paris which represent its members as Labourers, Assistants, and Masters; the latter appear with a trowel in their hands and a hammer in their girdle; to the Labourers are assigned pails, hods of mortar, the windlass, mallet, chisel, and rough ashlar. Their patron was St. Andrew, whose festival was commemorated annually by peculiar ceremonies allied to the old Mysteries, such as the descent into Hades through the jaws of a serpent.<<"Freem. Mag.," 1868, xvii, p. 131.>> The celebrated Inigo Jones, to whom Anderson attributes quarterly meetings on the model of the Italian Schools, may possibly have known something of this Society. Pico de Mirandola and Reuchlin gave themselves to the study of Cabalism and Theurgy, as did the Abbe Trithemius who was the friend, instructor, and co-labourer of Cornelius Agrippa. Use was made at this period of a form of the Masonic cypher in 9 chambers, with a Key which being dissected and triply dotted gave 27 letters. Trithemius attributes this to the ancients, and he gives numerous cyphers.<<Vide Barrett s "Magus.">> Agrippa established in Paris and elsewhere a secret "Theosophical Society" with peculiar Rites of admission, and signs of recognition, and when he was in London in 1510 as the guest of Dean Collet he established a branch in that city. There is a letter of Landulph s to Agrippa introducing a native of Nuremberg who was dwelling at Lyons, and whom he "hopes may be found worthy to become one of the Brotherhood." Agrippa says, as to Alchemy, that he {209} could tell many things were he not "as one Initiated sworn to secrecy." Eirenaes Philalethes, whose real name is not certainly known, and who was author of several Rosicrucian works, 1667-

78, terms Agrippa "Imperator" of the Order. Agrippa distinctly states that outside operative Alchemy, which is vain and fictitious when practised literally, there is another to be sought within man s own self in the operation of the internal spirit.<<Vide Barrett s "Magus," p. 179.>> There is a possibility that the well-known "Charter of Cologne" may have reference to these Brotherhoods; it professes to be signed in 1535, by the representatives of 19 lodges, assembled at Cologne on the Rhine, and amongst these signatories are those of Coligny and Melancthon; these somewhat doubtful Lodges do not profess in the document to be operative, but to have sprung out of the Masonry dedicated to John, about the year 1440. An American writer attributes to John Bunyan the allegory of Initiation in his "Pilgrim s Progress;"<<"American Freemn.," 1865.>> it is not very satisfactory but Bunyan s "Solomon s Temple Spiritualised" was probably used in the 18th century, for Craft and Arch Lectures.

"Rosy Cross." There are traces in 1484 of a Rosicrucian Order at Sleswick, in
Denmark: "Fraternitatus Rosarii Sleswicii condito, anno, 1484."<<"A.Q.C.," v, p.
67.>> Early in the 17th century there are traces that the King was head of such an order.<<Private Letter.>> Again, last century, such an order unconnected with Freemasonry was patronised by the King and seems to have consisted of seven degrees, according to the statement of an aged Danish physician to Colonel W. J. B. M Leod Moore, who connects it with the Arcane Discipline; though its immediate source will be the Order of Rosy Cross; and it will be sometime found that the peculiar aspect of Swedish Masonry is due to this old Danish System.

A Society termed "Militia Crucifera Evangelica" held a meeting at Lunenberg in 1571; and one Simon Studion {210} wrote a book in 1604 entitled "Naometria," or Temple Measuring, or the Temple opened by the key of David, referring mystically to the inner and outer man carried to the temple of the New Jerusalem; the MS. refers to the Rose and Cross, and to the "Militia Crucifera." A Society called the "Friends of the Cross," existing in Holland, is said to have joined an operative Lodge

of Freemasons before the year 1726, when Count Spork, who had been initiated therein, according to Brother Malczovich, established a Lodge in Austria in that year, and a medal was struck, of which one side represents the New Jerusalem.<<Vide "A.Q.C.">>
In the year 1614 appeared anonymously a work entitled the "Fame and Confession of the Rosy Cross." It relates the Eastern travels of a certain Christian Rosenkreutz, at the end of the 14th century, who was Initiated at Damascus into the Secret Wisdom of the Arabians, Chaldeans, and Gymnosophists; then after visiting Egypt and Morocco, he returned to Germany, where he established a small fraternity, which was to be continued secretly for 120 years, each brother, before he died, to appoint his successor. At the close of 120 years, that is about 1604, some alterations were made in their temple of the Holy Spirit, when his remains were found intact with the book T in his hand. All the paraphernalia and instruments were there necessary to constitute the Order. The work informs us that they had received the Order
"from the Arabians. . . . The Eastern countries have been always famous for
Magical and Secret Societies." Here the founder translated the book M (Marginal, "Liber Mundi") into good Latin. The "Fame" was to be translated into five languages, that even the unlearned might hope to belong to the Fraternity, "the which should be divided and parted into certain degrees."
 They exacted

"vows of silence and secrecy," and "though they held out the Rose as a remote prize, they imposed the Cross on those who are entering." The mention of a book which contains all that has yet been written in other books is supposed
{211} by some writers (perhaps unnecessarily) to refer to the Tarot.
Another work, entitled, "The Echo of the Divinely Illuminated Fraternity of the R.C.," 1615, asks the question whether the Gospel put an end to the secret tradition and answers it thus: "By no means; Christ established a new College of Magic amongst his disciples, and the Greater Mysteries were revealed to St. John and St. Paul." This, Brother Findel points out, was a claim of the Carpocratian Gnostics. There exists in the library of the University of Leyden a MS. by Michael Maier which sets forth that in 1570 the Society of the old Magical brethren or Wise Men was revived under the name of the Brethren of the Golden Rosy Cross. The "Fame and Confession" is usually attributed to J.
V. Andrea, but Brother Dr. W. Wynn Westcott points out that though the two tracts may have been edited by this author they are apparently of different eras. The "Fame" shews no evidence of a divided Christianity, but ranks only against Mohammedanism, whilst the "Confession" is Lutheran, and implies a post-reformation date.
Andrea is admittedly author of "Christian Mythology," Strasburg, 1619; and "Ehrenreich Hohenfelder von Aister Haimb," 1623, in which are the following lines, translated by Brother F. F. Schnitger: --
"And if we here below would learn,
By compass, needle, square, and plumb. We never must o erlook the meet, Wherewith our God has measured us."

Andrea employed himself in spreading a Society called the "Christian Fraternity," no doubt a branch of the older Societies of the Cross, and lists of members are preserved beyond the date of his death in 1654.<<de Quincey.>> The Universities had their Scholastic oaths, Luther and Fludd mentions them, and they would seem to have had formal Rites, for the latter in his "Mosaicall Philosophy," 1659 (p. 31) {212} repudiates "any allegiance which I have by a ceremonial rite vowed unto Aristotle in my youth." Michael Maier, who published his "Silentia post Clamores," 1617, says, "Like the Pythagoreans and Egyptians the Rosicrucians exact vows of silence and secrecy. Ignorant men have treated the whole as a fiction; but this has arisen from the five years probation to which they subject even well qualified Novices before they are admitted to the higher Mysteries; within this period they are to learn how to govern their tongues." Maier published in the same year as this the "de Vita Morte et Resurectione" of his friend Robert Fludd.

There existed at the Hague in 1622 a Rosicrucian Society with branches in Amsterdam, Nuremberg, Hamburg, Danzig, Mantua, Venice, and Erfurt. "The Brothers wore a black silk cord in the top button hole; a MS. of last century says that this cord was given to them after they had promised, under oath, to be strangled with such a cord rather than break the silence imposed upon them. Their other sign is, that when they go into company they all wear a blue ribbon, to which is attached a golden cross with a rose on it, and this they are given on being received into the Society. This they wear round their necks under their coats, so that not much of it is visible; the golden cross hangs

down on the left side. The third sign is that on the top of the head they have a shaven place, about the size of a louis d or, as you may see on myself; hence most of them wear a wig in order not to be recognised; they are moreover very devout and live very quietly. The fourth sign is that on all high festivals, very early at sunrise, they leave their residence by the same door ("i.e.," the East), and wave a small green flag. When another of them appears at a place where one lives, he goes to this same place, and there they enter into conversation, in order to recognise one another; for at the beginning they do not trust one another. Thus they have a certain "Greeting," among themselves, which is as follows. The Stranger says to the man he is visiting, {213} Ave frater ! to which the other answers, osae et Aureae ! Then the first says, Crucis ! They then, both together, say Benedictus Deus Dominus Noster, qui Nobis dedit signum. Then they have a large document to which the Imperator has affixed the secret seal." The M.S. from which this is taken is a part of the documents in possession of Mr. Karl "Kisewetter," who is a grandson of the last Imperator and who says that the seal which the last Imperator used in office between 1764- 1802 is of brass about the size of a mark. It consisted of a shield within a circle, on which was a cross, at the base of which was a conventional rose with five petals; at the top, bottom, and sides was the letter "C" signifying, Crux Christi Corona Christianorum (the cross of Christ is the Christian s Crown).<<"The Sphynx," Leipzig.>>

The English leader of the Rosicrucians was Dr. Robert Fludd, a deep student of the Cabala, Astrology, Alchemy, and Magic. He published at Leyden, in 1616, his Rosicrucian "Apologia," after a visit that Maier paid to England. In 1629 appeared his "Summum Bonum," and "Sophia Cum Moria Certamen," in which, in answer to Father Mersenne as to where the Rosicrucians resided, he replies, -- "In the house of God, where Christ is the Corner stone," a spiritual work, in which men are the "living stones." He speaks in 1633 "of the formerly so-called Rosicrucians who are now known as Sapientes, Sophoi, or Wise men," and impresses on the reader that it is "under the type of an Architect they erect their House of Wisdom." There was a Mr. Flood who presented a copy of the Masonic MS. Charges to the Masons Company of London, and as Robert Fludd died 8th September, 1637, and resided for a long time near Masons Hall he was probably a Mason<<Vide "Ars Quat. Cor.," viii, p. 40-43.>> Maier (as quoted in Initiation) says that numerous societies of Rosicrucians had arisen by the various interpretations placed upon their ancient symbols, and that the Society consisted of an outer and inner circle to which last the most {214} esoteric part was confined, and there is much which would cause us to think that Fludd s Society of the name was the Masonic Masters Fraternity, known as the Harodim, and all Continental tradition of the High-grades, or Masters grades, support this.

Dr. John Dee, John Booker, William Lilly, and Father Backhouse are well known Occultists, but as Masons we are more interested in two men who were not only given to those pursuits, but were also well known Masons, Sir Robert Moray, who was made a Mason at Newcastle-on-Tyne in 1641; and Elias Ashmole, who was made at Warrington in 1646. It is conjectured that Thomas Vaughan, the author of many Rosicrucian works under the assumed name of Eugenius Philalethes, may have been accepted in 1641, or thereabouts; he was a friend of Ashmole, and the language of some parts of his works corresponds with our Ritual; Moray also patronised him.

Elias Ashmole in his Diary makes several mentions of the "Feasts of the Mathematicians and Astrologers," and under 1653 says that Father Backhouse, when at the point of death, "instructed him in syllables of the matter of the Philosopher s Stone." In "Theatrum Chemicum Britannicum," 1652, he gives from the "Breviary of Philosophy," the Oath of the Alchemists, which Society he says was divided into Sons, and Fathers:

"Will you with me to-morrow be content, Faithfully to receive the Blessed Sacrament, Upon the Oath that I ball heere you give, For ne gold, ne silver, so long as you live;

Neither for love you beare towards your kinne, Nor yet to no great man, preferment to wynne, That you disclose the seacret I shall you teach, Neither by writing, nor by swift speech,

But only to him, which you be sure,

Hath ever searched after the seacrets of nature, To him you may reveal the seacrets of this art, Under the cover of Philosophie, before the world you depart."

The symbolic tracing of the Rosicrucians was a Square {215} Temple approached by seven steps, of which the four first represented the four elements, and the remaining three salt, sulphur, and mercury, the three great principles; here also we find the two Pillars of Hermes, the five-pointed star, sun and moon, compasses, square, and triangle.

ILLUMINATI. This Society was founded 1st May, 1776, by Professor Weishaupt, of Ingoldstadt with the object of arriving at political power, and revolutionise religion and governments. It is only related to other Societies in so far as this that Weishaupt, Knigge, and Bode drew upon ancient mysticism for their Ritual, and induced their own members to spread themselves into the Masonic Lodges to influence the Society. Its grades were: -- 1st Degree Novice; 2nd Degree, Minerval; 3rd

Degree, Minor Illuminee; 4th Degree, Major Illuminee; 5th Degree, Directing Illuminee -- Scottish Knight; 6th Degree, Epopt, or Priest. These were entitled the Lesser Mysteries, and had their "Insinuators," and "Scrutators," whose duties were to collect information from the members. 7th Degree, Regent; 8th Degree, Mage, or Philosopher; 9th Degree, King Man. These were the Greater Mysteries. The order used the Persian era of 620 A.D. Each Initiate had a characteristic name assigned, usually taken from classical literature; and very much of their Ritual appears in the Abbe Barruel s "Memoirs of Jacobinism." Some of their Chapters studied Alchemy, and the Masonic Lodges equally dabbled in this Art, but we shall allude to it in our Chapter on the High Grades. Innumerable Societies of Mystics exist in America, but we have no space even

for their names, and must therefore refer the reader to Vol. II. of "The Rosicrucian," 1908, by S. C. Gould, Manchester, N.H., U.S.A., under the head of "Arcane Societies."

SOCIETIES OF CHINA. There exists amongst the Chinese certain Secret Societies which profess, in some measure, to continue a system of Brotherhood derived from ancient customs, and which may have arisen out of their ancient Guild life. The members are sworn to support {216} each other; to be of good

morals, and they have secret signs of recognition. The Initiation is couched in Symbolic Mystery and divided into degrees; its aim corresponds with other Societies of which we have already given particulars.

"The Thian-ti-Hwii," or Heaven-earth-league is ancient, and said to be traceable in 1674. The Candidate before reception has to answer 333 questions.

"The Triad Society." The Candidate, scantily clothed, is introduced into a darkened room, between two members, who lead him to the President, before whom he kneels. A knife is placed in his right hand, and a living cock in his left. In this position he takes a very lengthy oath to aid his brethren even at the risk of his life; he is then directed to cut off the head of the cock; the blood being collected in a bowl, by a slight puncture it is mingled with his own blood, and that of the three chiefs who officiate at the ceremony. He is then warned that death will be his own fate if he should betray the Order. After this he is intrusted with the signs and tokens of recognition, which run in threes; as, to take up anything with three fingers. Generally speaking these Societies aim to continue an ancient Symbolical System, but have added political aims, and are therefore discouraged.

Scattered over the world are numerous societies which are believed to

continue the Mysteries of the Ancients, but we need not burthen our pages further with them. Heckethorne s "Secret Societies of all Ages and Countries" may be consulted; and the subject will be partially referred to in our later chapters.

"Conclusion." In closing this chapter we may point out that there was an undoubted connection between the Hermetic Societies and Freemasonry, apart from the similarity of the symbols employed by both. Basil Valentine is quoted as saying that a man cannot be called an Adept unless he can build his own reverberatory furnaces, in which is required the skill of a Mason and {217} an expert geometrician.<<"Briscoe s Constitution," 1715.>> Thomas Norton, 1477, states that Masons were students of the Hermetic art; Paracelsus terms himself a Grand Master of Mechanical Secrets; "The Wise Man s Crown," of 1664, equally asserts that the Masons were students of the Secret Sciences, but we shall have to allude to these again.

On the whole it would rather seem that Masons who desired to extend their learning sought Hermetic Initiations, but at a later period these latter made use of the Guild system of the former, as a convenient basis for their own views, and wants. But the main issue of this chapter is that whilst Masonry is a synonym of the Art branch of the Mysteries, the Arcane, Mystic, and Hermetic Schools transmitted the rites and doctrines of the Greater Mysteries though shorn of old splendour, until such times as Freemasonry reunited the two divisions, in what was technically termed Ancient Masonry though itself of modern organisation.

CHAPTER VII. RECAPITULATED PROOFS

RECAPITULATED PROOFS OF ANCIENT MASONRY.
THE information embodied in the foregoing pages might have been extended to a great length; and in giving so condensed an account the tastes of the general reader have been consulted. Some recapitulation of the salient points may be advisable as a short preparation for the chapters upon Masonry which follow; by way of laying the foundation for the introduction of the Association of Geometry, Craft and Art, or what is now called Freemasonry, into England.

Though Free Masonry, using this term to indicate a Brotherhood embracing religion, morality, symbols, and art, has passed under various names according to the language of the country in which it has existed, yet the most casual reader must have observed that the various Schools which we have described, as derived from a primitive system, had all the same essential Rites, and are in agreement with the Masonic System. The mere fact of the use of an organised system of esoteric Marks in architecture, in all time and in all countries, is itself proof of equal continuance of degrees, and ceremonial rites, in affinity with them; but we are not solely dependent upon this, and though the proofs of a continuation of a secret Society is naturally less prominent than in the case of a Church or a Sect, they are strong enough to remove all reasonable doubt on the subject. {219}

The evidence which we have already adduced goes to shew that the first

Great Mysteries were, at the very least, a union of the traditions of religion and art. The various phenomena of life, the revolutions of the heavenly bodies, their effect on vegetable and animal life were carefully studied; astronomy and all those arts which are so largely indebted to mathematics and geometry, were combined with Theosophia in the ancient Mysteries; and all the facts of physical science and art were embraced in their instruction.

A widespread Ugro-Finnic, or proto-Aryan, civilisation preceded the Aryan and Semitic developments, and it is even amongst the earliest of these people that we can trace a system which combined tuition in religion and science and which corresponds in its essential features with Freemasonry. The Mongolian races of Thibet and China afford us proof of this, equally with the "Masters of Secrets," who left us above 8,000 years ago the ruins of Erech, Serpal, Eridu, and Babel on the plains of Shinar.

"China." The primitive Indian Manu, whose era is so remote that no date can be assigned, speaks of a written character composed of geometrical Symbols. We find in China amongst a people who spread from Thibet at a remote period, and were contemporary with primitive Babylon, a system of operative and speculative Masonry of which the Kings, as was the case upon the plains of Shinar, were the Grand Masters. One of the oldest words in the Chinese language is literally "square and compasses;" and the "Skirret" is an hieroglyphic; the altar was a "cube." "Aprons" with "emblems" of office were worn; and one of the most ancient books contains the "square" and "plumb" as jewels of office, which had to be returned on the death of a Monarch-ruler, whose emblem was the "hammer." The Diety was designated "First Builder,"

and the Magistrates Level men. At a later period, but still 3,000 years ago, the then Emperor has the "circle" and "rule" as his attributes, as the Egyptian Osiris had the "Cubit." Coupled with this we have the doctrine of Universal

{220} Brotherhood, and the use of North-east, and South-west to indicate the beginning and end of any object in view. Confucius, Mencius, and other philosophers, equally apply the use of Masonic tools in their writings. In every sense of the word this system is Freemasonry without its name, and traditional Jewish legend. Sir John Mandeville, in 1356, mentions a coincidence with the Societies of the Essenes, Pythagoreans, and Ancient Masons. He says that the Khan of all Tartary before the eruption into China, decreed that all men should be governed by Masters of tens, hundreds, and thousands. Moorcraft<<Quoted by Dr. Kenealy.>> says that when he entered Thibet he was met by an officer of the Government named the "Nerba" and "on the back of his habit, and on the right shoulder were sewn the saw, adze, chisel, rule, and all the insignia of Freemasonry in Iron, the Symbols of a fraternity of which he said he was a member." Japan 2,500 years ago had the Chinese Guilds introduced by way of Korea.

"Egypt." The most ancient Memphis of Egypt has traces of this system; in the use according to Diodorus of tools in the hieratic writing; in the use of the cubit-rule as an emblem of truth; in the building symbolism of the "Ritual of the Dead," a book so old that 4,500 years ago, it could not be understood without a commentary added to an older commentary, that had become unintelligible. The architect at this period, and 6,000 years ago, was a "Royal Companion," and some of them mated with Princesses. The Very Rev. C. W. Barnett, Dean of Capetown, says in a recent address, that he had himself seen, on buildings 3,000 years old, the square, triangle, circle, sun, moon, pentacle, and that the evidences of Masonry are found at Thebes Luxor, Philae, Abu Simbel, Osioot, Dendera, Carnac, and on other noted archaic ruins, as well as in the pitch dark recesses of the great pyramid; and that the Sphynx holds in its colossal paws an exquisite small temple, which has Masons marks indented into the solid walls, roof, and monolithic columns. {221}

"Babylon." Ancient Babylon was allied in blood and religion with the two races that we have just mentioned. What we have not yet to record in Symbols we find represented in their language. The earliest Monarchs were termed Pat- te-shi, which is interpreted literally to strike or anoint the foundation stone, and with the addition of tsi-ri is translated Sublime Master. Again the seven Cabiric gods, or eight with one slain by his brother-gods, are named Patecei, from Patasso, a hammer, and though we need not go to Asgard, which is believed to be near the Caspian, the God Thor has the hammer for his weapon and the Svastica {Symbol: Swastika} for his emblem. There is similar proof that the first Kings and Viceroys were Masters of the builders, and probably the designers, or at least superintended the erection; and such edifices were consecrated with the Rites of Modern Masonry. The Kings are represented with a Maltese Cross worn from the neck. We seem to lose the Akkadian Symbols of the Mason in the conquests of the Tent-dwelling Semites. The highest chamber of the tower of Borsippa or Babel was a perfect cube. Brother G. W. Speth, the late eminent Secretary of Lodge 2076, has pointed out some interesting bearings which Cabiric emblems have upon modern Freemasonry. We have shewn that the most ancient style of building was termed Cyclopean, of which the Cabiric Initiates were the Masters, and that it is a prehistoric style existing

in all countries, running in later times into level work and often cruciform in its plan. The Cabiri recognised seven ancient gods, of which three were Chiefs, and an eighth was slain by the others. In Masonry whilst three rule a lodge, seven make it perfect, and the eighth, or Initiated Candidate, is represented by the slain god. There is also the common symbolism of a cube with 8 corners, which the Greek Cabiri termed Eshmon, and the Phoenicians applied to Ouranos, or heaven, and as Esh is eight it equally represents the Ashlar.<<"Ars Quat. Cor.," v, pt. 2.>> These Cabiri laid claim to be the inventors of {222} all the arts of life, including the smelting of metals, and were termed Technites or Artificers. Aeschylus introduces Prometheus as a Cabiric god, inasmuch as amongst the arts that he taught mankind are the erection of houses of brick, the construction of ships, the invention of letters, and the art of digging gold and silver from the prolific earth, and of fabricating instruments for ornament and use; he is the Tubal-Cain of the Semites, and Greek Mythology condemns him to a cruel punishment on Caucasus, for stealing the fire of heaven to aid mankind.

"Greece." Primitive Greece was allied in its culte with the races already

mentioned; and its early gods were those of the Cabiri, and their buildings Cyclopean; early Greek culture is found in tombs and palaces 3,000 B.C. excavated by Dr. Schliemann, and the contents of these tombs appear to ally the occupants with the Scythians. A long period of barbarous wars succeeded, attendant upon the invasion of the country by the Hellenes, an Aryan or Celto- Iranian people, spreading general devastation. In Hellenic Mythology it is figured to us in wars with a race of giants, Titans whom Jupiter at length conquered and condemned to servile employment in the forges of Vulcan. Reduced to plain matter of fact, it is the war between the Aryan invaders, who invented the mythology, and the primitive inhabitants who worshipped the Cabiric gods, and were reduced to artistic labour for their conquerors. By this invasion the Cabiric Mythology became Hellenised; in one direction the conquerors Aryanised the old myths that had grown up in the country, and in another direction they appear to have Grecianised the legends of Egypt and Phoenicia.<<Vide "Origin of the Aryans," Isaac Taylor, M.A., LL.D.>>

For some centuries Greece sank into semi-barbarous desolation; its true

civilisation was that of Egypt, whence culture passed through the Romans to Europe. Egyptian colonists with their religious mysteries settled at Argolis, the ancient seat of those Cyclops or Cabiri who built the enormous walls of Tyrenes, and Mycenae, at a period too {223} remote to be defined; their chief Inachas it is said lived 1976 B.C., and was succeeded by his son Phoroneus, whilst the deluge of Ogyges, in Boetia, occurred 1796 B.C., but it is probable that little reliance can be placed on these dates. To the new race is attributed the destruction of the older Cyclopean towns. At dates from three to four centuries later there entered Greece fresh colonies of Egyptians and Phoenicians: Cecrops arrived in Attica from Sais, in Egypt, 1687 B.C.; assembled the well-disposed inhabitants, laid the foundation of Athens, and of that peculiar tribunal termed the Areopagus. Cadmus settled with his colonies in Boetia 1594 B.C., and founded Thebes; he brought with him into Greece the

Phoenician alphabet, which, originating in Egypt, forms the basis of our own alphabet. Danaus settled a new colony in Argolis 1586 B.C., which had previously been settled by Egyptians, and to this year is also credited the deluge of Deucalion.

"India and Media." Primitive India and Proto-Media shared the same fate as ancient Greece; Aryans equally invaded these countries and reduced the ancient inhabitants. Egypt also received Colonies of the same race, and the great pyramid is constructed upon the Mystic design of the temple of the realms of Osiris. The Aryan invaders of India established bounds beyond which the artizan, as a third caste, was not allowed to proceed. Accordingly this third class, which was largely the prehistoric inhabitants of the country, continued Rites of their own, in which as we have seen, they used art Symbols and measurements to typify the truths of a religion, which differed only from that of the Brahmins and Maharajahs in the use of art instead of nature Symbols. The priests of Benares say that this Fraternity constructed all the marvellous works that are spread over the land. As in China, it was a Society of the Level and Plumb.

"Persia." The ancient Persians say that their ruler Jemschid erected the Artizans into a class, though the country never accepted strict caste laws. This ideal king {224} gave them laws which he superintended, and allowed them to appoint a Chief or Grand Master to oversee them. Hence in strictly Aryan countries, governed by firm caste laws, we have a triple set of Mysteries, those of the Brahmins, or Priests, with an intangible Diety; in the warrior Caste such Mysteries as those of Mythras, Bacchus and Serapis; and amongst the Artizans the Art, or Cabiric gods.

When an apprentice has completed his time he applies to his Guild for his Freedom and makes the customary payment. A priest is called in and after prayers he receives the "acolade" from the Master of the Guild. The Rev. P. J. Oliver Minos says that he has traced 20 Masonic Landmarks to Hindu Rites; and that in Persian Mazan is a Sorcerer, -- a Scientist, and that "Free" may be the Sanscrit "Pri" to love as brethren, as distinct from slaves, the root "vri" or "var" to choose. Mazandun is land of sorcerers, scientists.

As the caste system extended itself in India to different trades, a Guild system arose, such as we had in old times in England. In India at this day, each caste forms such a Guild, embracing the whole of that class, exercising an influence for the general advantage. Some of these lay claim to the "twice born thread" of the Brahmins. The deserving members are rewarded by titles and offices, the undeserving are punished by fines, or condemned to furnish a feast; the refractory suffer by temporary or permanent caste deprivation.

"Aryan Greece." The origin of Classical Greek is Aryan, and was first introduced into Thessaly by the followers of the Mythical Deucalion, in three great tribes designated Hellenes. The Dorians are said to take their name from Doris, son of Helen; the Aeolians from another son Aeolus; and Ionians from a grandson Ion. It is noteworthy that it is after the recivilisation of Greece and the introduction of the Egyptian Mysteries that the method of building edifices of squared and level blocks in contradistinction to the polygonal and irregular style {225} of the Cyclops, arises in that country; hence it would appear that either the Dionysian artificers must have superseded the Cabiri or instructed them. There are traces in India, Greece, Palestine, and other countries, of a gradual improvement, as exemplified by the use of both styles in the same building, and there can scarcely be a doubt that the improvement came from the Aryan race. Ancient Greek writers identify the Pelasgi with the older style and attribute it to Assyrian introduction. The Etrurians were of the Pelasgic race, and their buildings are of the Cyclopean style, and from them we derive

the Tuscan style of column; Varro mentions a tradition that they conquered North Italy 1044 B.C. To the Aryan Greeks the solidity of Cyclopean Masonry, which went beyond their early Kings Inachides and the Oenostratus, could only be the work of giants, and similar views were held in other countries. It is from the tribes of Dorians and Ionians that we derive the Doric and Ionic styles, after follow the Corinthian and the Composite, as the developments of the three original Greek styles, with the Tuscan. But Isocrates justly says that the Greeks borrowed their ideas, and the forms of their temples, from the Egyptians. It is known that the Phoenicians often employed Egyptian architects; and it was from the former that Solomon obtained his chief workmen for the erection of the temple of Jerusalem, and the style had points in common with that of Etruria, from which Rome derived much of its art.

"The Dionysiacs." There are three questions to be considered in reference to the application of the name Dionysius to the slain and resurrected sun-god of Greece. In the first place, Herodotus positively asserts that these Mysteries were derived from Egypt, it is certainly not the Cabiric version. But Assyria had its God Dionisu, and the Aryan Greeks in some cases Hellenised the older Mythology. It therefore seems to be pretty evident that the Hierophants, who first organised the system, found it politic and expedient to use the Assyrian name in place of the {226} Egyptian. It is somewhat doubtful whether the Great Mysteries of Dionysos were practical Masons, as well as teachers of secret truths of a spiritual nature. The usually accepted statement is that the builders were Initiates into the Mysteries of Dionysos; but as these Mysteries, according to the savant Heeren, were allied with those of the warrior class of Persia and India, it is possible that there was a separate class of builders, as in India, under the designation of "Dionysian Artificers," for though neither Egypt nor Greece were caste ridden, and the latter left the Aryan home before caste laws were promulgated, yet both in Egypt and Greece there was a custom of hereditary transmission of Art, as honourable in itself.

The probability of the evidence is that the Dionysiacs were an operative body who had their Initiated Masters or Chiefs appointed by the Hierophants of the Mysteries, and who taught them and superintended their labours; and that they developed in Greece the method of building with flat, squared blocks. As the priests of the Mysteries in early times had the superintendence of the erection of their temples, they may have reserved the right of Initiating Masters; and the echo of this may be found in the old MSS., which caused King Athelstan to grant a Master s Charter in Witenagemote, which new body then proceeded to add "points" for the governance of subordinate workmen.

We read that in the year 1263 B.C. the Council of Amphictyons built the temple of Apollo, a combination of Architects two centuries before the time of Solomon. These Dionysiacs existed in Greece above 3,000 years ago; hence Cabiric art fell into abeyance, and became a tradition. On the Ionic emigration they carried their art into Asia, and the erection of the Temple of Heracles at Tyre has been attributed to them, and which had two Pillars, one of gold, the other of emerald. They were divided into Lodges under Masters, had emblematical Jewels, degrees, ceremonies, and tokens of recognition; {227} they also admitted amateurs as Honorary members. They became a powerful body which exercised much political influence, and were incorporated as a Society of Architects by the Kings of Pergamos. At one time they were termed Daedalidae, from Dedalus, the architect of Crete, and the Labyrinth, respecting

whom there is a myth which has some analogy to Masonic legend; he is often represented with the square and compasses in his hand, hence the Greeks fabled that he invented these working tools and that he was father of architecture in general; and was banished for murdering a Fellow out of jealousy. Lord Bacon, in his "Wisdom of the Ancients," allegorises the legend as to Daedalus, coupled with the death of his son Icarus by falling from a flying machine which his father had invented; by the Labyrinth, he says, is typified Art in general. It is admitted that the Dionysiacs were attached to the Osirian legend; and one of the walls of Thebes has a representation of the Ark of Osiris, with a sprig of five branches, and the legend "Osiris sprouts forth," being an analogue of the Jewish Ark, and the Rod which budded. A symbolic ladder had its place in the Greek Temples, and Aelian says that Pittacus of Mitylene introduced a ladder into the temples of his country to imply "the rise and fall in the vicissitudes of fortune, according to which the prosperous might be said to climb upwards; the unfortunate to descend." This is but the exoteric explanation of an esoteric spiritual Mystery. We mentioned in our third chapter a Mosaic table of a Masonic character found at Pompeii. There can be no doubt that we have in the "Book of Chronicles" the Hebrew equivalents of the divisions of labour in the great building operations of other nations, these cannot be a Hebrew invention, but equally represent the organisations of Chaldea, Egypt, and India. We read (1) of Ish Chotzeb, or men who hew at the quarries; (2) Ghiblim, stone cutters or artists; (3) Ish Sabbal, or men of burdens; (4) Bonai, the builders or setters; (5) Menatzchim, the comforters or foremen; (6) Harodim, rulers or princes, who {228} superintended the whole levy. It may be noted that Gebal, where Solomon s Masons wrought, was a seat of the Adonisian Mysteries, and that he was said to have been slain in Lebanon. Even the more ancient Job, according to our modern translators, though said to be incorrect, may have had a knowledge of Masons Marks, for he says: "In the hands of all men he (God) putteth a Mark, that every man may know His work." Solomon s Temple was completed in the year 1004 B.C. and the old York lectures taught that its erection occupied 7 years, 7 months and 7 days. Josephus, in his treatise against Apion informs us on the testimony of Menander, that Hiram rebuilt the temple of Melcart -- the City King, which, if Herodotus is correct in his data, must then have existed for over seventeen centuries. Hiram then abandoned old Tyre and took up his residence on the adjacent island, and encompassed the City square with high walls of cut stone. Hence the temple which Herodotus saw was that of Hiram then near six centuries old. The Talmud has a legend that Hiram was granted 600 years of Paradise for reward, for the Cedars of Lebanon which he supplied to the builders of the temple of Jerusalem, and the book "Yalkutt" which is a compilation from the "Midrash," a word which means "to gather together," says that Hiram built himself, in the midst of the sea, a paradise of seven heavens (as was Babel), and that, for his great pride, Yod sent Nebuchadnezzer against him who destroyed his Paradise and cut him to pieces when he was about 600 years old.

"Roman Collegia." In Rome the Arts were erected into Colleges by charter of

Numa Pompilius, 703 B.C. The early architecture of Italy was Pelasgic, but Greece contributed much to its advance, and their Colleges of Artizans have such a close resemblance to the Dionysic system that the rule of one must have been the rule of the other. In point of fact Latin historians assert

distinctly that the founders of Numa s Colleges were Greeks, which {229} would lead us to suppose that Dionysian artificers were brought to reconstitute older schools.

Zosimus informs us that Numa was created Pontifex Maximus, and all his successors, and he derives the origin of the title, which may be translated Bridge-Master-General, from Thessalian Greeks who, before statues and temples began to be built by them, had images placed on a Bridge over the Peneus from which the Sacrificers were termed Bridge-priests. It is curious that the civil government had a similar constitution to the Masonic Colleges. At the birth of the republic there were 3 tribes -- Sabines, Albines, and Strangers. Each was divided into ten Curies, these into Decuries, at the head of which were placed Curions, or Decurions, and above these 100 Centurie. Gradually, however, this gave way to an enlargement, the Umbrians were the most ancient population and the Dacians, Thracians, and Italian Celts were Aryans, but not closely related to the Hellenes of Greece. It is believed that Numa was an Initiate of the Etruscan priests, and Salverte holds that he was acquainted with electricity and used it in his rites. Herodian says that the Romans obtained from the Phrygians a statue of the "Mother goddess," by representing that they were of the same blood through the colonies of Aeneas, 1270 B.C., when Troy was destroyed by the confederate Greeks.

The Roman formula was that "three form a College," but when formed one

might continue it. According to the Laws of the "Twelve Tables," the Collegia had the right to make their own laws, and were also permitted to form alliances amongst themselves. They were divided into "Communities"; had a common Arca or chest; elected their officers annually; accepted Honorary members as "Patrons"; had priests, as there is mention of a "Priest of the builders or artificers." They had emblems of office; signs of recognition; many of the symbols used by Freemasons, as, says Schauberg, the rough and perfect cube, and they could distinguish a {232} brother by day as well as by night. Their Wardens ruled ten men, a custom which Sir C. Wren says was in use amongst the old Free-masons. The Communities or "Maceriae" were held secretly and in secluded rooms; generally met monthly; each member was bound by oath to assist another; some of the Registers of Members are yet extant. Their officers were, a Magister, who presided over a hundred men and was elected for five years; Decurions or Wardens, each of whom presided over 10; Seniores or Elders; Scribe or Secretaries; Sacerdotes or priests; Tabularii or archivists; Erratoris or Messengers; Viatores or Serving brethren; Signiferi or Flagbearers. One inscription informs us that the Collegium held a yearly feast in anniversary of its foundation. Throughout the whole Roman Empire the Collegia were in active operation, and the "Corpus Juris" mentions amongst the Arts legally existing, and free from taxation, the architects, masons, stone cutters, painters, sculptors, carpenters, and ship and machine builders. We know the Collegia were established in Britain, as last century an inscription was found in Chichester which says that the "Collegium Fabrorum" had erected a temple to Neptune and Minerva and the safety of the family of Claudius Caesar, "circa" 52 A.D. The great architect Vitruvius defined the art of Masonry, 2,000 years ago, as "a science arising out of many other sciences, and adorned with much and varied learning"; he also shews us that the Romans had a canon of proportion, which being a secret goes far to shew that he was an Initiated temple architect, and which canon is still represented in

our Masonic Lodges by a tessellated pavement.<<"Ars Quat Cor.," viii, p. 99.>> Aristophanes, in one of his Comedies, introduces Meton, the astronomer, with rule and compasses in his hands, preparing to lay out the plan of a new city. Upon the tombs of Roman members of these Colleges are found emblems identical with those of modern Freemasonry, and we find upon tessellated floors, and mural paintings, the {231} triangle, double triangles, square and compasses, gavel, plumbrule, five-pointed star, the branch. There has recently been dug up at Rome, near the Triano, a glass bowl, upon which, on one side, is a square and above that the blazing star or sun, and the letters J. N. Underneath the square are two pillars, standing upon a Mosaic pavement.<<"Liberal Freemnson," 1888.>>

Mr. Toulmain Smith points out that contemporary with the Roman Collegia were the Greek "Eranoi," or "Thiasoi," numerous at Rhodes and Piraeus, and other parts. Their organisations had even a closer resemblance to Freemasonry than the Collegia.

Although the Celtic races of Britain had in early times many fine cities, and though the York Lectures state that Ebrank, Bladud, and Croseus were eminent as Masons, yet it is considered that the Latin term "Marus" indicates that we had stone building from the Latins. This Ebrank is Ebroc, the great founder of York; Bladud founded Bath, and brought from Athens four philosophers whom he located at Stamford; he is said to have been a great Mathematician, and having invented a flying machine fell from the temple of Apollo on the site of St. Paul s, London, and was killed; Croseus will be Carausieus, once Emperor of Britain, and Patron of the Collegia.

We mentioned in our last chapter the Benedictine Monk Henry Bradshaw, of St. Werberg Monastery, Chester, before 1513. Speaking of that city he has the following lines: --

"The founder of this citie, as saith Polychronicon, Was Leon Gaur, a myghte strong gyaunt,

Which builded caves and dongeons many a one, No goodlie buildyng, ne proper, ne pleasant, But King Leir a Britain fine and valiaunt,

Was founder of Chester by pleausant buildyng, And was named Guar Leir by the King."

"Syria." It is not improbable that a Masonic School {232} continued to exist in Palestine during the centuries: the Macabees were considerable builders. Recent discoveries in Jerusalem shew that stones of a remote, but uncertain, antiquity bear Masonic Marks, some of which are cut in the stone and others painted thereon in red; some of these marks are assumed to be Phoenician characters.

In the Talmud, in "Sabbath," 114, it is said that "the wise-men are called builders because they are always engaged in the upbuilding of the world." The Essenes were called Bonaim or builders because it was their duty to edify or build up the spiritual temple in the body. Chief Rabbi Henry Adler says that the Jewish Sages followed all professions, including Masoning, and that Shammai is, on one occasion, represented with the cubit rule in his hand. The Sages were termed Chaberim, associates, friends, brethren. There is found represented the triangle, square, and circle, as constructive rules, as, for

instance, in the erection of the Succuth, or Booths, at the feast of Tabernacles.<<"Vide Ars Quat. Cor.," 1898, Yarker.>> In the Book of Maccabees<<2nd ch. ii, 29-34.>> there is a very interesting paragraph which says: "For as the Master Builder of a new house must care for the whole building; but he that undertaketh to set it out and paint it, must seek out fit things for the adorning of it, even so I think it is with us. To stand upon every point, and go over things at large, and to be curious in particulars, belongeth to the first authors of the story; but to use brevity, and avoid much labouring of the work, is to be granted to him who will make an abridgement." Now although such passages as these, which are fairly common amongst Jewish and Christian writers, may not prove that the authors were Masons, as the term is now understood, it confirms the belief of those writers who assert that the Arcane Schools of Christians did make use of building symbolism; and indicates moreover that the art of building, or masoning, was one which the learned thought to be symbolically useful, and how much more then by the {233} builders themselves, to whom it would recommend itself so aptly.

There exists to-day a Jewish Guild at Assuan in Egypt which claims great antiquity, and practises Jewish Rites connected with the building of the two first temples, and for that purpose meet annually at sunrise and labour till sunset. An Architect who is now out there, and received initiation in Derbyshire, 1866-75, says that they practise the very same ceremonies which he there received. Of course in a Jewish Guild circumcision is necessary for reception. The native Copts have similar Guilds, but their ground diagrams are designed for the square pyramid and not for a 3 to I temple like that at Jerusalem, but they assert that Solomon had his initiation from Pharaoh, to whom he paid a great price. The triplicity of a pyramid is one of their symbols, as it is equally in the ancient Guilds of this country and in the modern Royal Arch degree of Freemasonry. Of course in the building of the 1st temple Yah was the God of Jedediah; Baal of the King of Tyre; and On (which is both Egyptian and Greek, if not also Hindu) the god of Hiram the Abiv. Plato has a line which says "Tell me of the God On, which was, is, and shall be," it is therefore the equivalent of the tetragrammaton. Oliver quotes in the like sense, Rev. i. 4: GR:Omicron Omicron Omega Ka-alpha-iota Omicron eta nu, Kappa- alpha-iota Omicron epsilon-rho-kappa-omicron-mu-xi-upsilon-omicron-sigma -
- ("God (On) is, and was, and is to come.")

We are told that Herod, King of Judea, employed 10,000 Masons besides Labourers, in rebuilding the temple of Zerrubabel; and it is quite certain that recollections of the temple of Solomon had not died out. It is even believed that, from the time of Alexander the Great, large numbers of Jews emigrated into Spain and were the founders and builders of Toledo, Seville, and Barcelona, besides other buildings in Bohemia; and the best time of their race was during the Moorish rule, when Oriental and Secret Societies were prevalent.

The Journal "Israelite" of 1860 contained a paper in reference to the existence in Spain of certain old legends {234} in proof that the Jews emigrated thither in the days of the tyrannical Rheoboam and of Adoniram s journey thither to gather taxes and was slain. The writer says: "It is a fact that there are numerous tombstones with old Hebrew or Samaritan inscriptions in Seville or Toledo -- we cannot positively say which of these two places -- and among them is one which bears the name of Adoniram the Collector of Solomon and his son

Rheoboam. . . . The Jews were the founders and builders of most of the ancient cities of Spain -- Toledo, Seville, Barcelona, and others; and also that the Jews were the inhabitants of these places at the time when the Ostragoths invaded the peninsula. Al Tanai Synagogue is of great antiquity, neither Greek or Gothic. The most ancient chronicle of Bohemia says that this building was found there when the founder of the city of Prague laid the first corner stone of it." There is an ancient Hebrew book, certainly 1,500 years old, entitled the "Testament of Solomon," which gives a full account of the legions of daemons employed by Solomon in the construction of the Temple, and the positions assigned them, but it is more than probable that these Talmudic legends originally referred to the 72 Suliemen of pre-human times, and were engrafted in Babylon upon the personality of the Israelite King. Sir Charles Lemon informed his P.G. Lodge in 1846, that when visiting Poland he saw an ancient Jewish Synagogue which was built 600 years B.C., where he found Masonic emblems now used by the Fraternity. (See "Freemason," 1814 page 176.)

The "Mishna," or oldest portion of the Jewish "Talmud," preserves the measurements, and details, of the first temple, with its utensils, and, very recently, a representation of it was found in the Roman Catacombs. According to Josephus, Clemens, and Eusebius, each and all its details, were symbolical of the Universe.

The third temple, or that of Herod, was destroyed in the year 70, and the Emperor Hadrian erected in 136 a fourth temple upon its site which he dedicated to Jupiter {235} Capitolinus, and compelled the Jews to pay taxes for its maintenance. It is said in Hadrian s time that there was a temple erected to Astarte which was destroyed at the instigation of Helena, the mother of Constantine. In the 4th century many churches were erected in Palestine, and the Emperor Justinian built a great number in that country.

The Emperor Julian attempted to rebuild on the site of Solomon s temple, and there is a very curious account, which confirms in a remarkable manner the Rites of the Guild of Free Masons, namely -- that a Reed below the floor (about 10 feet) there was a vault which contained a pedestal, with the plans, and the centre diagrams, and which is drawn upon to form the Arch degree in modern Freemasonry, and that this centre had to be discovered on the erection of the 2nd temple. An old writer relates that when the Emperor s labourers were set to clear away the rubbish they came upon a vaulted chamber into which one of the workmen was let down with a rope; he returned and reported that in the centre was a square pedestal surrounded with water, and produced a scroll which Nicephorus relates was a verse of the Bible. The Guilds say that this was and is the first lines of Genesis, and that it was carved over the Eastern entrance of the 1st temple. Julian was obliged to desist from his intentions as Nicephorus says that fire broke out which destroyed his workmen. An older writer Philostorgius circa 853 A.D. has the same account.

It may be convenient to mention here the Holy-sepulchre at Jerusalem which led to the introduction of round churches into England; though the temples of the Greeks and Romans were often circular, as was that of Venus in Cyprus mentioned by Homer; that of Vesta and the Parthenon. The Christian Church of the Holy Sepulchre was consecrated in 335. Its round part represents the Sepulchre of Christ, and leading from it is a broad aisle, at the end of which is a rec-

tangular church on the site of Golgotha. This was partially destroyed by
{236} Chosroes, King of Persia, in 614, and restored 14 years later by Bishop

Heraclius, to fall in 636 into the hands of the Islamite Caliph Omar. On the death of Haroun al Raschid his three sons contended for the throne, and the churches were burnt, but shortly after restored by Bishop Thomas. In 1010 the Caliph Hakem destroyed them, but they were again rebuilt next year. In 1048 the three churches were reconstructed by Constantine Monomachus; the original rectangular church would seem to have perished by the year 1102, and many changes were made in the remaining portions<<"The Holy Sepulchre," Northampton, 1897. Wm. Mark.>> During all the period of their occupation the Saracens erected numerous buildings, and the building art was not extinguished down to the time of the Crusaders, who added largely to the structures existing. "Greco-Egyptian." Although we do not know much about the remote organisation of the building fraternities in Egypt, yet M. Maspero opened the tomb of an architect, builder, and carver of inscriptions at Thebes, and with the mummy was found a square, level, compasses, and other implements. At Tel- el-Amarna, 1500 B.C., Bek the hereditary successor of a line of Architects, terms himself the teacher of the King; and, as we have seen, the symbols and representations, however ancient, are more Masonic than in any other country. It is not, however, an unreasonable supposition to suppose that from 500 B.C. when the Persians had conquered the country, to be succeeded by the Greeks and Romans, gradual changes took place, under this foreign influence, in the more ancient Corporations of Masons.

The Roman Collegia may have modified Guild life of the more ancient native fraternity, and it is this explanation which must be placed upon the English tradition of the "Charges of Euclid." Draper mentions the conquests of Alexander the Great as leading to the establishment of "the mathematical and practical Schools of Alexandria, the true origin of science." When the "Needle"
{237} which Cleopatra had re-erected 22 B.C. came to be removed in 1880, there was found at the base a peculiar arrangement of stones, which was held to symbolise a Masonic Lodge as now known; thus a portion was laid so as to form a square, on which rested a rough Ashlar, and a perfect Cube, also an oblong of the purest limestone carefully polished and without spot or flaw.

We have expressed a decided opinion that the origin of Free Masonry is to be found in the primitive system of a secret School which developed a Mystery in which natural religion was taught in union with science and art, and that, before the divorce of the two, the great State Mysteries organised a better style of building with squared blocks, in other words the Osirian, Dionysian, or Bacchic Mysteries, which were a highly spiritualised faith, still more subtilised and spread by Greek philosophers as the Mysteries of Serapis, a Gnostic pre- Christian system, which used the cross, and had all the characteristics essential for the faith "before Christ came in the flesh." It is idle to suppose that the Ceremonial Rites of Masons were then absolutely uniform; those of a Cabiric or Pelasgian civilisation could not be entirely uniform with those of the Aryanised Dionysiacs, yet such ceremonial rites existed beyond doubt, and each had their slain-god if the mode of his death was not quite uniform, and Initiates only had acted a part in the ceremony, nor need we have any doubt of the possibility of the transmission of such Rites, from the earliest period, though we cannot produce yearly minutes for it. What right have we to expect this? It means the violation of solemn oaths, perhaps death. Take the universality of laying a foundation stone, and we see that the modern ceremony

was exactly paralleled in ancient Babylon and Egypt. Even Job must have known something of it in his desert home, for he says: "Where was t thou when I laid the foundation of the earth? Who laid the corner stone thereof: when the morning stars sang together and all the Sons of God shouted for joy." If a Rite which professed to date {238} from Solomon s temple existed in early times, as it probably did, it would be amongst a small number of Jewish Masons, and a modification of the Phoenician Cabiric Mysteries, but we can leave this for the present.

The Legend of the Origin of English Masonry which has been handed down to us from the times of Edwin and Athelstan repeats a tradition which traces the Society to Egypt, and particularises its derivation and organisation. It is clearly a legend which existed at the time, and there is no probable basis which would justify us in expressing a doubt that, as a legend, it had actual existence in Athelstan s time, nor in going beyond it to invent a theory that the forerunners of the Society were at the building of Solomon s temple, an assertion which is not there, and never intended to be there; and the absence of which is a good proof of the antiquity of the account related.

The Legend to which we refer may be inaccurate in some of its details; the name of Euclid, the eminent Geometrician, may have been inserted for Thoth or Hermes as the Greeks termed the god of art; and we may be sure, that in the centuries through which the legend had passed, before it reached the form of our oldest MSS., it would be modified in minor particulars; but we may be well persuaded that it contains a basis of truth, as it would be a likely Legend to be handed down by Romans and Romanised Britons who worked by Euclid s traditions, and onward through Culdee monks who taught the rules of handicraft to the people at York, and other places, practised the teaching of the Mysteries of Serapis in the Arcane Discipline of the Church, and even superintended, built, and laboured with their own hands at the erection of their churches and monasteries.

This tradition alleges that Egypt finding her people to be generating a too
numerous population of well-born youths, for whom it was difficult to find suitable employment, sought anxiously for a remedy. A proclamation was made, and Euclid an Initiate of Serapis, of the Platonic Academy, and it may even be of the Colleges {239} of Builders, undertook to provide a remedy. For this purpose he accepted these Lords sons, and taught them Geometry "as the most honest art of all," and when they were capable proceeded to organise them into a Brotherhood, and give them a "Charge," which examination will shew to agree in all essential points with the Roman Collegia. There may be something in the alleged Grand Mastership of Euclid, who is said in Anderson s "Constitutions" of Masonry to have acted as the architect of some noble edifices in Egypt, but it is more probable that he owes the rank assigned to him from his eminence as a Geometrician, about 276 B.C., and it is noteworthy that in the old Masonic MSS. it is not claimed for Masonry that it was exclusively a society of Sculptors and Stone-cutters but embraced all arts that work by the rules of Geometry. There is good reason to accept judiciously this alleged Alexandrian descent of Masonry into England. We are told that the original builders of St. Mark s at Venice were Alexandrian refugees, and, it may be, the style of the palace of the Doge, which is called Moorish but is not so. The Byzantine style was probably Alexandrian, and when the Saracens took Egypt the Artists were dispersed over Persia, Greece, and Europe.

In the light of what has preceded, the traditional legend resolves itself broadly into this: that besides the great State Mysteries, but derived from them, there were minor schools of Philosophers, and Colleges of the Arts and Sciences, all with special, but similar, ceremonies of their own, and that Euclid held a prominent position in all these. Further that the Masonic association was of Greco-Roman introduction into England, a genealogy which attaches itself to the divine Father, Mother, and Son of old Egypt.

Nor was Art itself in Egypt confined, in its practice to mere Artisans, for there were sacred images which could only be wrought by the priests of the Mysteries. Synesius, Bishop of Ptolemais, has a peculiar passage ("Calvit."), in which he writes: "The prophets or hierophants, {240} who had been Initiated into the Mysteries, did not permit the common workmen to form idols or images of the gods, but they descended themselves into the sacred caves, where they have concealed coffers, containing certain spheres, upon which they construct their image secretly, and without the knowledge of the people, who despise simple and natural things, and wish for prodigies and fables." We see from-this that there was a Craft secret and symbolism known only to the priests, and that like the "Four crowned Martyrs," of Christian Masonry, they were capable of practical sculpture. The "sacred caves" were the Crypts of their temples; and the word translated "sphere" is indefinite, for there are yet drawings to be found in Egypt which shew that the "Canon of proportion" was a chequered tracing even from the time of the very ancient 5th dynasty. The primitive canon divided the human figure into 19 squares, of which the head occupied 3 squares, the pubis began at 9 1/2, and the knee-joint at 6th square from the bottom one. A seated figure occupied 15 squares; but the proportions varied in the course of ages.<<"Ars Quat. Cor." (W. H. Rylands). vi.>> The learned Dr. Stukeley was of opinion that the Isaic Tablet of Cardinal Bembo<<Pub. by Dr. W. W. Westcott.>> was a tracing-board of the Egyptian Mysteries, a temple spread out in plane, and that it could be divided into Porch, Sanctum, and Sanctorum.

In the time of Euclid one of the most beautiful buildings in all Egypt was in progress and dedicated to the divine Triad, namely, the re-erection, on its ancient site, of the temple of Philae, which was begun about 300 B.C. and continued for two centuries. Mr. James Ferguson thus eulogises it: "No Gothic architect, in his wildest moments, ever played so freely with his lines and dimensions, and none, it must be added, ever produced anything so beautifully picturesque as this. It combines all the variety of Gothic art, with the massiveness and grandeur of the Egyptian style." In it are nine sculptured tablets {241} on the wall which pourtray the death, resurrection, ascension, and deification of the god to whose honour it was erected. The most sacred oath a Copt could swear was, "By Him that sleeps at Philae, and by Him that sitteth upon the throne." The Mysteries of the god continued to be celebrated in this temple until about 450 A.D., after which it was probably used for Christian worship.<<"Egypt," Wm. Oxley.>>

Another building of great extent was erected by Ptolemy Philadelphus as a temple of Serapis, the Greco-Egyptian triad in an Eclectic form. It was the most magnificent temple then in existence, and had numerous subterraneous passages and caverns, artificially constructed for the Rites of the Mysteries. It contained a library said to consist of all known books in 700,000 volumes; a library destroyed by the Moslems in 638 A.D. It was partially destroyed previously by the Christians when emblems of a cruciform character were exposed. The steady advance of Christianity, developing into a ferocious intolerance, necessitated even greater secrecy in the celebration of the Mysteries, followed by persecutions of the Initiates by the later Emperors, made it essential to reorganise them under other names, with the assumption of a humble disguise. It is in this way that we renew our acquaintance with them in the Colleges of Art, and in the Gnostic and Occult fraternities.

So far as this country is concerned we know nothing from documents of a Masonry dating from Solomon s temple until after the Crusades, when the Constitution believed to have been sanctioned by King Athelstan gradually underwent a change. To advance an opinion amongst well read people, that all Craft Masonry must necessarily date from Solomon s temple, can only raise a smile. The building was erected by Phoenicians and partly of wood, and its magnificence is no doubt greatly exaggerated in the Talmud; and the Jews, with a special God for their own race, were unpopular with all other nations; and far more extensive and magnificent buildings, {242} of which the ruins exist to this day, are found in Egypt, India, and the Americas. It is, however, a curious thing, in regard to Solomonian legends, that there seems to have existed amongst the oldest proto-Aryan races, we have knowledge of, a dynasty of Solymi, or Sulieman, entitled Kings; and it has also been discovered amongst the ruins of Babylon as the name of a God of these ancient people, whilst the real name of King Solomon was Jedediah, or the beloved of Jah. It is therefore possible that the title may have been prehistorically known in some Cabiric Rites, and that Ouranos, Ur, Urim, has been corrupted to Hurim, or Hiram Abif, and perpetuated from the building of the 2nd Temple; for we may assume that the graphic form of the legend has been the gradual growth of centuries, though perpetuated as a drama in the Mediaeval Guilds, and when the Talmud and the Koran tells us that Solomon employed troops of daemons to erect the temple we may feel sure that the Talmud is drawing upon the pre-human Suliemen, or Kings of the Jins or Afreets.

There can be no doubt that the early Christian Monks found amongst their
skilled Masons certain forms of reception, or Mysteries, similar to, if not identical, with those which had descended to themselves as heirs of the Epoptia of these Mysteries. It suited some of these Monks to transform the Serapian Sun-god into Jesus, in obedience to the prevailing policy of the church; whilst it pleased others, whether Jews, Christians, or Moslems, matters little, to substitute Hiram; these Rites would also vary in different countries, and at different eras; hence sects of Masons arose, and, as we shall see later, have come down to our own days.

When we first began to examine the ancient MSS. of the Masonic Craft, of which the result will be found in these pages, we scarcely expected to find more than chance coincidence between Masonry and the Arcane Colleges, but the resemblances which we have before us in Rites, Symbols, and Organisation, will admit of no such general {243} explanation. It must be clear to the most superficial thinker that there is far more in the Masonic MSS. and the Rites than they have yet been credited with, for their whole tenor proves the intimate affinity which existed, even in the most ancient times, between all the Arcane Schools of knowledge. This is equally apparent whether we seek it in the Egyptian Constitution of Athelstan, which informs us it was originally a Craft for the study of Geometry, and which therefore implies a Society equally speculative and operative; or in the Semitic Constitution which came into England later; for such a distinction only shews the transmission of certain rites, with the same aim, through two different channels; the one a continuous type of that Speculative Masonry which erected the great Pyramid to represent the Egyptian s faith in the soul s future destiny; the other of that Chaldean faith symbolised in the tower of Borsippa; somewhat opposed as Rites, but one in general aim; two systems pointing respectively to Egypt and Babylon. In this chapter we have leant rather to the Greco-Egyptian than the Semitic view, but when we reach Anglo-Norman times of the Masonic Guilds we shall see much change in this respect and that a close connection with Palestine introduced new legends and their concomitant Rites.

CHAPTER VIII. MASONRY IN SAXON ENGLAND.

DURING the period embraced in this heading, which includes British times, all the manual arts were Clerical professions in so far as this, that the Monks acted as teachers and directors of lay associations, more or less attached to the Monasteries. Architecture was exercised under the shadow of the church, and

M. Blanqui in writing of the French Monasteries observes that "they were the true origin of industrial Corporations; their birth confounds itself with the Convents where the work was arranged; it is thence that serving with the Franks liberty and industry, long enslaved by the Romans, goes out free to establish itself in the bosom of the towns of the middle ages." Nor is this all, from the earliest times of Christianity a community of interests, and of knowledge and art, was maintained by means of Couriers journeying to and fro throughout the world, amongst the whole Christian Fraternity, which may account for the sudden and widespread adoption, of particular styles, in countries distant from each other.

There is no doubt that, even in Druidical times, the Romans organised in the chief cities of this country Colleges of Artificers on the Latin model, although the Britons were themselves, at the time, noble architects. These Colleges were continued by Romanised Britons after the withdrawal of the Roman troops near the middle period of the fifth century, and though the wars with the Saxons must have greatly retarded the labours of the societies, the Saxons interfered but little with city life, {245} contenting themselves with rural affairs. We may therefore conclude that the Art-fraternities were continued, even if influenced by the Clergy and by such Guild life as the Saxons may have brought over with them.

Arranmore has some ancient fortresses. One of these, built 2,000 years ago, had walls 220 feet long, 20 feet high, and 18 to 20 feet thick, and is built on a cliff hundreds of feet sheer to the sea; three sets of massive walls surround the largest fort.

As we have remarked the "Articles and Points" of the Masonic MSS. are in agreement with the "Corpus Juris" of the Collegia, which again are found in an Egypto-Greek source.

As the Clergy were the builders of their Churches, the chief Monks and Bishops figure in the Constitutions of the Grand Lodge, prepared in 1723, as Grand Masters of the Fraternity; and it must at least be admitted that Anderson was half correct, and there is little of any other mode by which the matter can be treated in this chapter; for Art was an Oath-bound Society the property of those who had learned Art by an Apprenticeship.

There are numerous Roman remains in this country of buildings which were erected during the occupation of the island by the Latin troops; and amongst these are to be found many interesting particulars in York, London, Chichester, St. Albans, but scattered over the whole island. Newcastle was in ancient times a place of great importance, and the Romans had a military station in the place by A.D. 78, and a bridge was built over the river to connect it and Gateshead and named the "Pons" Aelii. The Roman foundations were eventually occupied by Monks, for we learn that when Aldwin, with two Monks, travelled from Gloucester in 1194 to restore the religious foundations, the place was known as Monkchester; and the mother church of St. Nicholas is said to have been erected upon a Roman temple; and St. Mary s Church at Gateshead is said to be as old, if not older. {246} Pandon, now a part of Newcastle, was peopled by Saxons, and was a Royal residence before 654 A.D. Didron<<"Ichnography," i, p. 456.>> gives a Latin sculpture, of the first ages,

on which is represented a pair of callipers, compasses, square, skirret, level, maul, chisel, and pen or stylus; an ordinary set-square is often found as an amulet on Egyptian mummies. With the exception of the first and last these comprise the symbolic tools of a Free-mason, and though the plumb rule, 24 inch gauge, which is an old Egyptian emblem of Truth and of Thoth, the perfect Ashlar, a symbol everywhere as ancient as Man, are lacking, these are found on other Roman remains, with many other emblems, and Masons Marks of which mention has already been made.

In Masonic history special mention is made of Verulam, out of the Roman remains of which St. Albans was built, and, it is said that the town was walled round by Alban the Martyr. It is a legend which may have been taken from some Monastic history by a Masonic lodge of the 13th century in that place. Chichester had a College of Roman Artisans that erected a temple circa 46-52 A.D., and Masons Marks are found in the remains of the city. In the year 114 Marius the British Pendragon, so named as the military chief of the great golden Dragon-standard of Britain, executed a treaty with Tacitus by which Roman law was to be recognised in such towns as might become Municipia or colonies; and the garrisons of York, Chester, and Bangor were to be recruited from British Volunteers; as Rome strengthened herself Christianity was tolerated, but Druidism was prohibited. A quantity of Roman coins was found in the South-basin at Chichester in 1819, and three with the following emblems: Nerva 96 A,D., two joined hands, and "concordia execretus," encircling. Hadrian, 117 A.D., moon and seven stars. Antonius Pius, 138 A.D., two joined hands, two ears of corn, "Cos III."<<"Freemasonry in Havant," 892a, Thos. Francis.>> We might assume that {247} Chichester in Sussex was the centre of the Roman fraternity, and Verulam a branch. Upon St. Rook s hill is the remains of an ancient building with entrenchments which during the last

and the previous century was used as a place of Masonic Assembly, and near this, at Lavant, are caves with a series of chambers where a very curious copper level, intended to be worn, was discovered.<<"A.Q.C.," 1898, W. H. Rylands.>>

York has a multitude of Roman remains dating from the time of Adrian and Severus, 134-211 A.D., and later under Constantius. There was discovered at Toft Green in 1770 beneath the foundation of a Roman temple of brickwork a stone with this inscription, "Deo sancto Serapi Templvm asolo fecit Cl. Hieronymianus leg. vi. vic." -- "This temple, sacred to the god Serapis, was erected, from the

ground, by Claudius Hieronymianus, Lieutenant of the sixth conquering legion." On each side of the inscription are two identical ornaments which it is difficult to describe, each is of three circles with a rod, or straight line drawn through them; the other is a peculiar trisula having in its centre a star of six points; at the bottom is a circle with an eight-pointed star in the centre, and in that a point. There was also found in Micklegate in 1747 a piece of sculpture said to represent Mythras sacrificing a bull; and in 1638 was found an altar erected to Jupiter by the Prefect Marcianus. A semi- subterranean temple of Mythras was discovered in 1822 at Housesteads in Northumberland, containing an Altar dedicated in 235 A.D., and there are other remains in Chesterholm and Rutchester in the same county; at the latter place is a recess hewn out of the solid rock, called the giant s grave, measuring 12 X 4 1/2 by 2 feet deep. At one end is a hole; this seems to resemble "St. Patrick s hole," in Donegal. Several altars have been found in Cumberland and Westmorland dedicated to Baalcadris. "Acta Latamorum" and Rebold give a very probable explanation of the Masonic Legend of Verulam. Carausius caused himself to be elected and proclaimed Emperor of Britain by the {248} Channel Fleet in 284 A.D., and braved all the efforts of Diocletian to dethrone him. He renewed the privileges of the Collegia in their entirety as these had been much curtailed in the course of centuries, and is therefore supposed to have appointed Albanus as his Inspector. An inscription to Carausius was found at Carlisle in 1894, and his coins are numerous. He was assassinated at York in 295 A.D., and Constantius Chlorus took up his residence there, and confirmed the privileges of the Guilds or Collegia. Brother Giles F. Yates states that an old MS. of the life of St. Alban, the proto-martyr, in British characters was found in the tenth century,
and Matthew Paris refers to a book of great antiquity as existing in the
Monastery of St. Albans.
Britain had clearly attained architectural distinction in the time of Carausius and was able to send competent men to instruct the Gauls, for Eumenius, the panegyrist of Maximium, congratulates the Emperor on behalf of the city of Autin, which he informs us was renovated by architects from this country, in the following words: "It has been well stored with Artificers since your victories over the Britains, "whose provinces abound with them," and now by their workmanship the city of Autin rises in splendour by rebuilding their ancient houses, the erection of public works, and the instauration of temples. The ancient name of a Roman brotherhood which they long since enjoyed is again restored by having your Imperial Majesty as their second founder."<<"Paneg. Maximian Aug. dict." -- Oliver s "Remains," iii, and v; also "Masonic Mirror," 1855, p. 32.>>

Christian architecture, however, is not much in evidence until Saxon times, though the "new superstition," as the Romans termed it, is said to have entered Glastonbury in the Apostleship of Joseph of Arimathea. Welsh historians assert that Christianity was accepted in a National Council held by King Lucius
A.D. 155, when the Archdruids of Evroc, Lud, and Leon, became Archbishops and the Chief Druids of 28 cities became bishops. It is {249} further asserted that of the British captives carried to Rome, Claudia and Pudens are addressed by name in the Gospel. King Lucius is said to have been educated at Rome by St. Timotheus, the son of Claudia, to have been proclaimed King in the year 125, and to have been baptised by Timotheus 155 A.D.; after which he proceeded to erect churches

at Winchester; Llandaff; St. Peter s, London; and St. Martin s, Canterbury; the faith was then styled Regius Domus, or Royal house. British history says that at this time there were in existence 59 magnificent cities, and numberless handsome residences. Of Monasteries the Triads say: There are three perpetual Choirs in the Isle of Britain -- Great Bangor, Caer-Salog (Salisbury), Avillon (Glastonbury); the first named was munificently endowed by King Lucius; it covered a square of five miles, had 10,000 teachers, and every graduate had to learn some profession, art, or business. Minucius Felix comments upon the absence of temples and altars amongst the Christians of the 3rd century, and of the uselessness of such works in honour of an all embracing Deity, and then says: "Is it not far better to consecrate to the Deity a temple in our heart and spirit?" It was not until about the year 270 that Christians were allowed to assemble in buildings of their own at Rome, and these appear to have been first erected in imitation of the "Scholae" or Lodge rooms, of the artizans, but in Britain there was but one year s persecution of the Christians, when Socrates, Archbishop of York, the Bishop of St. Albans, and others lost their lives. About the year 300 church was erected at Verulam over the martyred body of St. Alban, which Bede says was a handsome structure; and Tanner says that there was a church at Winchester, dedicated to Amphibalus who converted him. There was an Archbishop of York at this time, for Eborius in the year 314 attended the Council of Arles in Gaul and is described as "Episcopus de civitate Eboracum Provincia Brit." The same Council was attended by Restitus of {250} London, and Adifius of Caerleon on Usk, which is Lincoln.

These Christian Britains -- monks, priests, and bishops, were known as

Culdees, servants of God; they established Monasteries and Churches in various parts of England, Wales, Scotland, and Ireland, and there is no doubt that many of them were converts from the Druidical faith; in these countries they opened Colleges, and Schools where handicrafts, arts, sciences, and religion were taught to the people. Their faith was heretical according to the standard which the Church of Rome had adopted after the succession of Constantine, and they were what Cardinal J. H. Newman terms Platonising Christians, or of the esoteric Arcane Discipline. They believed in the immortality of the soul, but not in the Jewish doctrine of a resurrection of the material body, which was the teaching of Judaising Christians. They are also accused of denying the existence of a personal devil, and the personality of Jesus, in which case they were Gnostics, but the reader may refer back to the subject in Chapter VI. St. Patrick is said to have been born a Druid and to have left Dumbarton for Ireland in the year 432. Both ancients and moderns charge them with possessing a secret doctrine, and when in 589 Columban

went to Burgundy with 12 companions from Ireland (as Columba had previously done in 561 to Icolmkili, the Arcane Mystery gave offence; the King demanded of him, why, as in his own country, "access to their secret enclosures was not granted to all Christians," upon which the Culdee sternly replied, that if he sought to destroy the Cenobia of God his kingdom would assuredly perish. This mission founded the Abbey of Luxeville, and others in France and Italy. In England their principal seat was York, in Wales Bangor, in Ireland Donegal, in Scotland the Hebrides. Those Masons who possess intuition, and the faculty of reading between the lines of such writers as we have quoted, will perceive that Philosophy found it essential, and safe, to openly embrace Christianity, whilst secretly conforming {251} to their old ideals, had it been necessary we could have given plain proof of this. Even Eusebius says: "In order to render Christianity more acceptable to the Gentiles, the priests adopted the exterior vestments and ornaments used in the Pagan culte." Philosophy thus secured the survival of its secrets, hence we find the

12 sons of Jacob assimilated to the Zodiacal signs; and much Gnostic

symbolism is found in church architecture -- lions, serpents, and things to be named in due course. The Rev. W. L. Alexander in writing upon "Iona" says that whilst the Roman armies were harrying the Druids at Anglesea there was a College of them in the Scottish islands situated 56 Degrees 59 N.L. designated "Innis-nan-Druid- neach" -- the Isle of the Druids -- and that that priesthood prevailed over all the other islands until the year 563-4 when Colum or Columba arrived with 12 companions who were continued in that number till after ages. It is said that there existed there certain Druidical priests who professed to be Christians in the hope of inducing Columb to withdraw, and after the settlement of Columb and his friends, the island began to he known as "li-cholum-chille" -- the island of Columbus Cell, corrupted to Icolmkill, and we have also "li-shona" -- the holy island, corrupted to Iona.

We may now say something in reference to the construction of their churches. Prior to the 5th century, all Christian churches were after the model of the ancient temples of Egypt divided into three parts, and which corresponded with the secret or esoteric doctrine; and we need have no doubt that the emblematical significance of the architecture was a "close tyled" Mystery of the Initiated builders, and that as in the ancient temples, they were built to symbolise a spiritual doctrine, which ordinary Christians were unacquainted with. The first part, or "Ante-temple," was for the Catechumens, disciples, and penitents; the second part or Nave was for the lay members and the faithful; the third part or "Sanctuary" was a semi-circular recess with an arched roof, raised above {252} the floor by steps; it represents the Sanctuary of the ancient gods, open only to the priests; within it was the throne of the Bishop which was usually veiled, and placed besides it were smaller thrones for the Clergy; in the centre of this most holy place was the altar. In Gothic buildings, of a later date, this part is called the "Chancel" and was separated by a "Rood-screen" of carved wood or other material; and it is remarkable that the carvers, at times, took great liberties with the Monks and priests, in the representation of their vices. There is even much recondite symbolism to be found on the outer walls of such buildings. The Secret Discipline, at these early dates, regulated the symbology of the edifices, and the "Vesica-piscis," so often found on ancient temples, and churches of all eras, is held to be the great

secret of constructive measurements, and, as has been stated, the Sign of the Epopts both in Philosophy and Christianity.

In regard to early erections, a small church of rough stone was raised at Peranzabulae in Cornwall about the year 400 by the Culdee Pirau an Irish saint, over whose tomb was found an equilimbed cross of the Greek form, when the building was disinterred in 1835, after having been covered over for ten centuries. Thong Castle in Lincolnshire was erected for the Saxons about the year 450, it must have been a British labour. A church of stone was erected at Candida Casa, by the Culdee bishop Ninian 488 A.D.; and Matthew of Westminster tells us that the British King Aurelius Ambrosius, who slew the Saxon Hengist at Conisborough in 466, repaired the churches, travelling to and fro for that purpose, and sent for Cementarii or Masons, and Lignarii, or Carpenters. Legends state that he erected Stonehenge with blocks brought from Ireland by the engineering skill of Merlin, and that both himself and his brother Uther the Pendragon were buried within its circle (but Norman Lockyer examining it as a Planetarium, dates it, by the Sun, at 1680 B.C.); he defeated Hengist s sons at York in 490. In 524 Arthur son of Uther, defeated the Saxons, and at {253} Christmas of that year he held a Council at York to consider ecclesiastical affairs, and methods were taken to restore the churches and the ruined places at York, which had been occasioned by his wars to expel the Saxons. Though Arthur the Pendragon is alleged to have been buried at Glastonbury the legends of the Prince seem to belong chiefly to Cumberland and the adjacent parts, which formed the Kingdom of the Strathclyde Britains; the names used in the Romances of his Round Table and in the connected tales, are Cambrian, and Blase of Northumberland is said to have registered his doings. Denton says that near St. Cuthbert s Church, Carlisle, in Cumberland, "stood an ancient building called Arthur s chamber, taken to be part of the mansion house of Arthur, the son of Uter Pendragon, of memorable note for his worthiness in the time of antient Kings."<<Quoted in "Hist. Cumb." by Wm. Hutchinson, 1794. ii, p. 606.>> The Prince was no doubt a Romanised Briton, though his name does not belong to the Celtic language, and that he was a real person who strove to unite the British Christians against the Saxons is beyond serious question. The allegorical history of the Round-table, and the Knights "Quest of the Sangrael," or cup of the blood of Christ, is supposed to refer, in mystic terms, to Culdee rites; and in spite of the efforts of Rome the Culdee culte continued to exist in England, Wales, Scotland, and Ireland down to the Norman conquest, and, in places, until long afterwards. At Caerleon on Usk were two churches, and an important Culdee "College of two hundred Philosophers learned in Astronomy, and in all the sciences and the arts."

It is more than probable that the peculiarities of the Culdee system arose from the engraftation of Druidical beliefs upon the Christian faith. Many learned writers have sought to derive Free Masonry both from a Druidical and Culdee establishment. The latter is not at all improbable for one of the branches. The following may be pointed out at random: -- The custom of symbolising Craft officers by the sun and moon; for the Arch {254} Druid bore the sun and crescent moon on his head dress, whilst the Bard was designated by the crescent moon, equally the tonsure of a Culdee Monk went from ear to ear, in crescent, as opposed to the coronial tonsure of the Romans. A Culdee origin has also been claimed for the Templars, and the modern ceremonies of that body commemorate the 13 of Iona.

St. Cibi s, as asserted by Sir John Stanley, was founded in 550 on a Roman temple at Holyhead. It was, however, rebuilt "temp." Edward III., and again in the reign of Henry VII.

Toland says that the Druidical College of Derry was converted into a Culdee Monastery. About the year 561 Columba and twelve companions left Ireland to build the Monastery of Icolmkill, and Masonic legend assigns the lectures of the Mastership of Harodim to this Monastery; they founded Colleges at Govan and Kilwinning; and Aidan, one of the twelve, established the original Abbey of Melrose. The fraternity had other establishments in Scotland; at Abernethy; St. Serf in Lochleven; Dunkeld; St. Andrews; Moneymusk in Aberdeenshire; Dunblane; Dunfermline; and Aberdeen. Their establishment at Brechin has left a cylinder or Round Tower of unknown date. At each side of the western entrance, near an ancient gateway, is carved in relief an elephant having the feet of a lion and a horse. Brother R. Tytler, M.D., in a paper read before the Antiquarian Society of Scotland,<<Vide "Freem. Quart.," 1834.>> makes a precise comparison between this and an astronomical allegory, in like situation, in various Hindu temples. Above this carving is an apparently later crucifixion scene with two Monks. It is said that during the life of Columba 100 monasteries were erected, and the Irish claim to have sent architects to Britain some centuries before this time.

The voyage of Bran, son of Febal (a MS. of 1100), to the Island of Joy, or the

Land of the Living, is attributed to Adamnan, Abbot of Ionia, who died in 703; it mentions {255} nine grades of heaven in three steps, and that a fiery circle surrounds the land of the blessed. The throne is a canopied chair with four columns of precious stones, and beneath it are seven glassen walls. The sect in England had seats at Lindisfarne, York, and Ripon.

Mr. Grant Allen in his Anglo-Saxon Britain (1884) says: "It is possible that the families of Craftsmen may at first have been Romanised Welsh inhabitants of the cities, for all the older towns -- London, Canterbury, York, Lincoln, and Rochester -- were almost certainly inhabited without interruption from the Roman period onward."

The Roman law, and therefore the Guilds or Collegia, never became extinct in any place where the Romans had once had a footing. They entered Germany with the sack of Rome by the Goths, a country unconquered by arms. Alaric II. of the Wisegoths, 484-507, commissioned Roman Jurists to compile a code on the basis of the Lex Theodosii which was adopted by all Gaul. Theodrich the Ostragoth in the year 500 promulgated a similar code, which aimed at fusing Roman and Goth into one people. A third compilation of Roman law called the Burgundian "Lex Romano" was promulgated about the year 520 by Sigmund.<<"Arminius," Thos. Smith, F.S.A.. London, 1861.>> It follows from this that, so far from the Roman Collegia being extinguished with the Empire, they spread throughout Germany. Smith further says: "These Colleges are evidently the Guilds of the Middle ages; in the Roman Disciple we may detect the modern Apprentice, and in the hereditary obligation to follow a particular trade, we may discern the origin of freedom by birth, or by servitude, in Corporate towns. The leading idea in Roman institutions was Municipal. Every franchise was the result of belonging to some College, and we thus infer that the franchise of Cities owe their origin to Rome. Thus to the Municipia of Rome, not to German institutions, are to be ascribed the origin and form of the

Municipal Corporations of the middle ages."<<"Arminius," Thos. Smith, F.S.A.. London, 1861.>> Apropos of this quotation is the existence of the Magistri {256} Comacenes, settled near the lake of Como, who hired themselves out to build for the Lombards and are mentioned by the Rev. Charles Kingsley.<<"Roman and Teuton," 1891, Lec. x. p. 253.>> They are supposed to have fled to a small island on Lake Como, on the sack of Rome by the Goths, where they kept alive the ancient rules of their art, whence was developed the various Italian Styles, the Norman, and the Saxon. Not only was their organisation that of the Collegia but the ornamentation of their architectural work. They venerated the Four crowned Martyrs, and were divided into Scolia or Apprentices; Laborerium, operii or those who did the actual work; the Opera or Fabbrica, or the Magistri who designed and taught the others. Leader Scott quotes an Edict of the Lombard King Rotharis, dated 22nd Nov., 643, conferring privileges on the Magistri Comacini, and the Colligantes, and this when they had been long established. She also quotes an inscribed stone of 712 to shew that they had then Magistri and Discipula under a Gastaldo or Grand Master and that the same terms were kept up in Lombardy, amongst Free Masons, until the 15th century, and it is known that St. William, Abbot of Benigne in Dijon, a Lombard by birth, brought in his countrymen to build his monastery, and that Richard II., Duke of Normandy, employed this architect for 20 years in like work.<<The "Cathedral Builders," Leader Scott, 1899, London.>> It is not so difficult to connect Freemasonry with the Collegia, the difficulty lies in attributing Jewish traditions to the Collegia, and we say on the evidence of the oldest charges that such traditions had no existence in Saxon times.

"In this darkness which extended over all Italy, only one small lamp remained alight, making a bright spark in the vast Italian Necropolis. It was from the "Magistri Comacini." Their respective names are unknown, their individual works unspecialised, but the breath of their spirit might be felt all through those centuries, and their name collectively is legion. We may safely say that of all the {257} works of art between 800 and 1000, the greater and better part are due to that brotherhood -- always faithful and often secret -- of the Magistri Comacini. " (J. A. Llorente, "Hist. of the Inquisition;" London 1826. "I. Maestri Comacini;" Milano 1893.)

The conquest of Rome, by the Teutonic nations, led to a great extension of the Christian Monasteries, during the 5th and 6th centuries, and these were usually placed in quiet or inaccessible situations, the better to escape from the tumults of the times. Here libraries were established and the ancient learning found a resting place. This led to the cultivation of the Mystical and the spiritual in man, and it may be observed that the term Mystic is derived from the rank of Mystae in the Mysteries, even as the term "Mystery" was adopted by trade Guilds to mean their art, and "closed lips."

Stowe says that in the 7th or 8th century the walls of London were rebuilt by Benedictine Monks brought from Birkenhead. The founder of this brotherhood was St. Benedict, born at Nursia in Umbria about A.D. 480; he went to Monte Cassino, 530, afterwards the centre of his order, and there composed his rule, which entered England between the 6th and 7th century. Archdeacon Prescott says: "The finest Abbeys, and nearly all the Cathedrals, belonged to the order."

About the year 597 Augustine came over to England from the Church of the Quatuor Coronati at Rome. His instruction from Pope Gregory was: "Destroy

the idols, never the temples; sprinkle them with holy water, place in them relics, and let the nations worship in the places accustomed." He is said to have brought over Roman Masons, and a further number in the year 601; he died in 605. It has been supposed that he built the Church of the Four crowned Martyrs at Canterbury, which is mentioned casually by Bede in 619. This introduction of Masons from Rome is usually taken to prove that the building fraternities had become extinct in this country, but it does no such thing. There was no doubt a scarcity {258} of capable men amongst the Saxons for the work which the Romish Saint had in view, but we cannot altogether rely upon the good faith of their historians, nor are we at all justified in assuming that the native British Masons, Carpenters, and the building fraternities derived from the Romano-heathen population were extinct, and we have proofs to the contrary in the Culdee erections of St. Peter at York in 626, and in the Culdee establishment at Lindisfarne in the year 634 by Aidan, a Monk of Icolmkill in Iona; and in the "Holy Island" St. Cuthbert was interred before the City of Durham existed. There lies, behind, the fact that Rome considered all British Christianity as heretical, and all the successors of Augustine followed his role, with the unsuccessful object of wholly destroying Culdee influence. Bede informs us that the British Christians refused either to live, or eat, with the Augustinians, and they replied to a demand for obedience: "We owe obedience only to God, and after God to our venerable head, the Bishop of Caerleon-on-Uske." Bede complains also that Monasteries had been established by laymen with themselves as Abbots, whilst still continuing married relations with their wives, a Culdee custom, sanctioned by example of Bishop Synesius. He says also that a Martyrium of the "four blessed Coronati" existed at Canterbury 619-24.

The British Pendragons seem to have kept the Saxons in check, but they were able to destroy Bangor in the year 607. Deira was strongly reinforced by Angles from the Saxon coast, and King Edwin solicited from his friend Caswallon, the British Pendragon, that he might assume the regal crown as Bretwalda, but Caswallon refused his sanction, on the ground that there was "one sole crown of Britain." Kemble says that, "The Saxons neither took possession of the towns, nor gave themselves the trouble of destroying them." The Heptarchial princelings and their villagers were Pagans, and exercised but small influence. Pope Boniface IV. is credited with the grant {259} of privileges in 614 to those architects who had the erection of sacred buildings.

In 616 Ethelbert King of Kent built the Church of St. Peter, and St. Paul, at Canterbury, upon the site of a small church erected by the early Britains; also the church of St. Andrew in Rochester; and he is thought to have restored St. Paul s in London, erected on the site of a temple to Diana, though other writers suppose it to have been built within the area of what was the Roman Pretorian Camp in the time of Constantine. Siebert King of the West Saxons, in 630, built the Monastery of Westminster, on the site of a Temple to Apollo, and it was repaired in the next century by Offa King of Mercia. About the middle of this century, say 650, an Irish saint of the name of Bega established a small Nunnery at the place now called St. Bees in Cumberland, then a British port, and a church was erected afterwards in her honour.

The Romans had a temple at Teignmouth, and here an important Priory was erected. In the reign of Edwin over Yorkshire, Durham, and Northumbria, circa 626, a wooden edifice was erected here, similar to Aidan s Church at

Lindisfarne, and was followed by a church of stone erected by his successor St. Oswald, circa 663. After it had been destroyed by the Danes, it was restored by Ecgfrid, in the 15th year of whose reign the neighbouring church at Jarrow was dedicated, and which, with that of Wearmouth, is in the diocese of Hexham.

In the year 675, Benedict Biscop is said to have brought over from France skilled Masons to erect the Monastery at Jarrow. At the same date Wilfrid founded Ripon, Hexham, and Ely, bringing Masons from Rome or Italy and France. King Ina also rebuilt Glastonbury; and William of Malmesbury informs us that it possessed a sapphire of inestimable value, perhaps the origin of the legend of the Graal cup. The same writer says: "In the pavement are stones designedly laid in triangles and squares, and fixed with lead, under which if I believe some sacred enigma to be enshrined I do no injustice to {260} religion"; he also alludes to two pyramidical structures in the churchyard.

Anglo-Saxon building, sometimes of wood, and then of stone, continued upon their gradual conversion to Christianity. In 643 Kenweath of Wessex "bade timber the old Minster of Winchester." In 654 "Botulf began to build a Monastery at Icambo" (Boston). In 657, Penda of Mercia and Oswin of Northumbria built a Monastery at Medeshamstede (Peterborough). Oswin built six in Deira. In 669 Echbert of Kent gave "Reculver to Bass, the Mass-priest, to build a Monastery." In 669 St. Ethelreda "began the Monastery at Ely." Before 735, religious houses existed at Lastringham, Melrose, Lindisfarne, Whithern, Bardney, Gilling, Bury, Ripon, Chertsey, Barking, Abercorn, Selsey, Redbridge, Aldingham, Towcester, Hackness, and several other places. The Irish Monks were active abroad; in 582 St. Peter s Convent at Salzburg was erected by Rudbert. About 610, convents at Costnitz and Augsburg erected by Edumban. About 606, convents at Regenburg under Rudbert. About 740, convents at Eichstadt under the Irish monk Wildwald. As to military architecture we read that Edward, the father of Athelstan, had twenty fortresses between Colchester, Manchester, and Chester. Why then should we dispute the existence of such Guilds as are shadowed in our ancient Masonic MSS.? Professor Freeman says that St. Mary le Wigford Church was built by Coleswegan.

Aelfred, brother of Ecfrid King of Northumberland, sojourned in Ireland to

acquire from the Monks the learning of the period, and on the death of Ecfrid, in 685, he was recalled to succeed him, but it is very doubtful whether the Britons recognised these Saxons as Kings, until Egbert became Bretwalda in the year 824. In 690 Theodore, Bishop of Canterbury, erected King s School in that city.   In 716 Ethelbald built Croyland in Lincolnshire.   Of this period a series of drawings exist amongst the Cottonian MSS. in the British Museum, and have been engraved for the "Freemasons Magazine," scenes in the {261} life of St. Guthlac; one of these represents him in the act of building his chapel. The Saint is hoisting up material to a Mason who is laying a stone at the top of the building; near the Saint is a stone-cutter who is hewing the stone into shape with an axe. We shall see later that a chisel was used in Norman times, and soon after a claw-adze. Although the Arch had its origin in high antiquity, and is said to have been found in Babylonian remains near 10,000 years old, preference was given in early English church architecture to the straight lintel of the Pagan temples, then Arches followed, but it was not until the 10th century that vaulted roofs came into use, and soon spread over the whole of Europe.   As early as the 8th century the English Monk, St. Boniface or Winifrid, established in Germany a special class of Monks for the practice of

building, with the grades of Operarii or Craftsmen, and Magistri operum or Masters of Work. Some of these acted as designers, others as painters or sculptors, others wrought in gold and silver embroidery, and others were Cementarii or Stone Masons: occasionally it was necessary to employ laymen under their superintendence.<<"Ludwig Steiglitz," quoted by Mackey.>>

The church of York, erected in 626, was damaged by fire in 741, and Archbishop Egbert began a new church. About the year 793 Offa King of Mercia erected the Monastery of St. Albans near the old Roman Verulam, and in the Cottonian Library is a picture, also engraved for the "Freemasons Magazine," shewing him in the act of giving instructions to his Master Mason, who has the square and compasses in hand; a Mason on the top is using a plumb-rule, whilst another is setting a stone; below are two Masons squaring stones with an axe. These drawings are by Matthew of Paris about the year 1250. Offa before beginning this work made a journey to Rome by way of France, and Brother

C. C. Howard, of Picton, supposes that he brought Masons thence for his work. At Lyminge in Kent there is an old church built upon a

{262} Roman Basilica by Saxon Masons; it is noteworthy as having an old Roman sun-dial built into the south wall of the Nave by St. Dunstan circa 965. It may be noted here that in recent times a bronze square and compasses were dug up at Corfu, along with coins and vessels of the 8th and 9th centuries.

The Romans seem not to have had a settlement at Durham, and we do not hear of the place during the time of the Saxon Heptarchy. The Bishop s See was founded at Lindisfarne as early as 635. In 883 the Bishop and his clergy took up their abode at the Roman Chester-le-Street, where they remained with the body of St. Cuthbert until 995, when the Danes caused them to take up their wanderings with the body of that Saint. In 999 Aldune the Bishop caused the Cathedral to be erected, and ere 90 years had passed this small edifice gave place to the present stately fabric.

During all this period the Saxons had a Guild system in full operation; and the old laws of Alfred, Ina, and Athelstan reproduce still older laws acknowledging the Guilds. The old Brito-Roman cities must have continued their Guilds during these centuries, even whilst the Saxons were making laws on the subject, and establishing new ones on the old lines. The laws of Ina, 688-725, touch upon the liability of a Guild, in the case of killing a thief. In 824 England had absorbed Britain and Saxon under Egbert, and the latter had become the ruling element. These Guilds exacted an Oath of secrecy for the preservation of trade "Mysteries," and obedience to the laws. The Judicia Civitatis were ordinances to preserve the social life of Guilds, of the time of Athelstan. A law of Edgar, 959-75, ordains that "every priest for increase of knowledge shall diligently learn some handicraft," but this was only enforcing old Culdee customs. There is said to be a letter of the 9th century, written by Eric of Auxerre to Charles the Bald of France, in praise of certain Irish philosophers, who, as "servants of the wise Solomon," were visiting France under the King s protection, who "for {263} the instruction of his countrymen," attracted thither Greeks and Irishmen. This probably refers to the erection of Aixe-la-Chapelle by his grandfather Charlemagne. It was introduced into the Irish Masonic Calendar by the late Brother Michael Furnivall, and has created an impression that there existed in Ireland at this period some Society analogous to the Sons of Solomon in France, which we shall mention shortly.

St. Werberg at Chester is said to be erected on the site of a Saxon Church as old as 845.

About the year 850 Ethelwolf, King and Bretwalda, is said to have employed St. Swithin to repair the pious houses. The Danes burnt Croyland Monastery in 874 and slew Abbot Theodore at the altar steps. Alfred the Great, about 872, fortified and rebuilt many towns, and founded the University of Oxford. In 865, and again in 870, the Priory of Teignmouth, where the Nuns of Hartlepool had taken refuge, was destroyed by the Danes and again rebuilt.

It is certain that in these times, a large number of timber structures were erected; it was a style of building which admitted of rough stone and rubble work, and was equally common both in England and France. This is probably the reason why our ancient "Constitutions" state, as they do, that the original designation of the Fraternity was Geometry, which was as necessary in buildings of wood as of stone, and is some evidence of the antiquity of these ancient MSS. An authority maintains that later erections of stone, by the Saxons, were influenced by this style, as in the use of stone buttresses in imitation of timber beams, and in window balustres or pillars made to imitate work turned in a lathe.<<"Freems. Mag.," J. F. Parker, F.S.A., 1861. iv, p. 183.>> Doubtless many of the churches burnt by the Danes were of wood, and rebuilt of stone. In Constantinople, and the East generally, wooden structures continue, and are preferred to stone.

In the year 915 Sigebert, King of the East Angles, began the erection of the University of Cambridge, which was completed by Ethelward the brother of King Edward {264} the elder. This latter erected many considerable works and fortifications, repairing, says Holinshed, in 920, the city of Manchester, defaced by the wars of the Danes. He was succeeded by his elder, but illegitimate, son, Athelstan, who is said in the oldest MS. Constitution to have "built himself churches of great honour, wherein to worship his God with all his might." Anderson says that Athelstan rebuilt Exeter, repaired the old Culdee church at York, and also built many castles in the old Northumbrian Kingdom to check the Danes; also the Abbey of St. John at Beverley; and Melton Abbey in Dorsetshire. If for the advancement and improvement of architecture this King granted an actual charter to York, he would naturally do the same to Winchester, in which city he fixed his royal residence; and there we find architecture flourishing. Few Saxon specimens of architecture now exist; there is the tower of Earl s Barton Church, Lincolnshire; Sempling in Sussex; St. Michael s in Oxford.

A fine specimen of military architecture of the period is Castle Rushen in Man. It is believed to have been begun by King Orry and completed by his son Guthred, circa 960; it resembles so closely one at Elsinore in Denmark that they are both supposed to be by the same architect. The one in Man is built of the limestone of the district, and is in a state of perfect preservation; the elements have had no effect upon the stone, owing to a hard, glass-like glaze, admitting of a high polish, from which it may be inferred that the military architects were acquainted with some chemical secrets that remain a secret to this day.

In 942 Odo, Archbishop of Canterbury began the restoration of his Cathedral; it was afterwards much injured by the Danes in 1011, and King Canute ordered its restoration; again it suffered by fire in 1043. In the time of Ethelworth and St. Dunstan, who was a Benedictine Monk, Anderson says, 26

pious houses were erected, and under Edgar 48 pious houses. Between 963- 84, {265} Ethelwold, Bishop of Winchester, erected 40 Monasteries, and is styled the "Constructor," of his Cathedral church. Edgar, in 969, at the instance of Dunstan, repaired Westminster Abbey church. In 974, Ednoth, a Monk of Winchester, superintended the erection of Romsay Abbey church. From 977-81, Aelfric, Abbot of Malmesbury, is said to have been skilful in architecture.

There is a charter of King Aethelred of the year 994 which describes the Deity in Masonic terms as "Governor of the bright pole and Architect of the great ethereal design . . . .of the world, unexpressibly placing in order the Fabric." Another of King Canute uses the same preface.<<Thorpe s "English Charters," 1865.>> The paucity of Anglo-Saxon remains prevents our dealing largely with their Masonic Symbolism. There is, however, a bronze seal of Aelfric Duke of Mercia, 992, with the legend "{+} Zigillum Aelfrici {symbol, a "T" above two " s" abutted to form a crossed-pair of chevrons, one chevron inverted.}," thus placing the cross, and the square and compasses in juxta-position.<<"Freem. Mag.," 1855, p. 509.>> De Caumont mentions a sarcophagus, of this period, which bears a cross within a circle, and two levels placed sideways.

With the close of the year 1000 A.D. a great impulse was given to church building, as a feeling pre-vailed that this year would see the end of the world. When the panic had passed the Christian nations in thankfulness began building. The Danes had caused great havoc in this country, and especially at York, and had even revived heathen rites, which Canute proclaimed in the year 1030. There is no reason to suppose that these wars extinguished the building fraternities, and Canute in 1020 erected a stone Minster at Assingdon, and also repaired the Minsters throughout England, as we are informed by William of Malmesbury. Leofric Earl of Coventry, circa 1050, built the Abbey of that City and 12 pious houses. King Edward the Confessor rebuilt Westminster Abbey, devoting to the work a tenth of all his substance. Of this reign there was a curious inscription at Kirkdale, W.R. Yorkshire, which says that Orin, son of Gemel, rebuilt the {266} church; Chelittle was archi-tect, assisted by Howard and Brand the Priest. Yorkshire being strong in the Danish element, Mason s Marks are often Runic letters.

Remains of Saxon architecture yet exist in the churches of Jarrow; Monkwearmouth (both Biscop s 681); at Repton, Co. Derby (875); Ripon, Hexham, York (in Crypts); Earls Barton, and Barnick, Co. Northampton; Barton on Humber; Sompting, Co. Sussex; Caversfield; Deerhurst, Brixworth, etc. It is well known that the Tower of Babel was one of the most ancient traditions of Masonry, and there is an old Saxon MS. which represents it in course of erec-tion with the Saxon pick, and on the top step of a very tall ladder is the Master Mason giving the hailing sign of a Craftsman yet used, whilst behind him, on the same level, is the angel with drawn sword; a copy of it in Cassells History of England, of the year 1901, can readily be examined. It is said that the keep of Arundel Castle dates from Saxon times, but the chief entrance is a fine Norman doorway.

Mr. James Ferguson says that in these times the working bands of Masons served under Bishop, Ab-bot, or Priest, and this continued down to the 13th century. In travelling from one place to another their costume was a short black, or grey, tunic open at the sides, to which a gorget, or cowl or hood was attached; round the waist was a leathern girdle from which depended a short,

heavy sword, and a leathern satchel. Over the tunic they wore a black scapulary, similar to that worn by the priests, which they tucked up under the girdle when working. They had large straw or felt hats; tight leather breeches, and long boots. Attached to the Monasteries were "Oblali," who were usually received as Monks, acted as serving brothers of the Masons, and whose costume was similar to the travelling Masons, but without the cowl.

Owing to the fact that modern Free Masonry has always looked to the North of England as its Mecca, inasmuch so that last century its system was denominated "Ancient" York Masonry in op-position to the Grand {267} Lodge of England organised in 1717, which was termed "Modern," we will retrace a little in respect to this division of the old Saxon Heptarchy, which bore the name of Deira, and extended from Humber to Forth, save the Western half which was the Kingdom of the Stratchclyde Britons. It was these two portions which continued to form the centre of Culdee influence, the capital of Deira being York, and the centre of Ancient Masonry.

The city of York possesses numerous remains of the Roman occupation, which the early Christians converted to the use of the Church. The Monastery of the Begging Friars is known to have been a temple dedicated to the Egyptian Serapis, and we have already mentioned the inscription to Serapis discovered at Toft Green in 1770. In this City the British Legionaries, on the death of Constantius Chlorus, raised his son Constantine, surnamed the Great, on their shields, and proclaimed him Emperor 25th July, 306. The Culdee King Arthur is believed to have occupied and repaired it in 522.

It is considered that the Crypt of York Minster affords evidence of the progress of Masonry from Brito-Roman times to Saxon occupation. The Crypt has a Mosaic pavement of blue and white tiles, laid after the form used in the 1st Degree of Masonry; it shews the sites of three stone altars and such triplication was of Egyptian derivation; but these stone altars are also said to have had seats which were used by the Master and his Wardens who met here, after the manner related by Synesius of the Priests of Egypt, as a sacred and secret place, during the construction of the edifice. It is known that the Craft occasionally met in this Crypt during last century, and the alleged Masonic custom of meeting in Crypts elsewhere is no doubt founded in fact.

As the Christian worship at York was of Culdee origin, so the veneration paid to Mistletoe was derived from the Druids. The learned Brother Dr. Wm. Stukeley has this passage in his "Medallic History of Carducius": "The {268} custom is still preserved, and lately at York on the eve of Christmas Day they carry mistletoe to the high altar of the Cathedral and proclaim a public and universal liberty, pardon, and freedom to all sorts of inferior and even wicked people at the gates of the city towards the four quarters of heaven."

It follows from what we have seen that the Roman Collegia and the Mysteries of Serapis existed side by side at York, and amongst the members of these it is no improbable thing to suppose -- after the close connection which we have shewn to have existed in Egypt -- that there were Brito-Romish Christians who established the Culdee fraternities at York, before the days of Constantius Chlorus, about 2 1/2 centuries before King Arthur was in possession of the city, and that these Culdees influenced the Masonic Collegia, and the same remark equally applies to other cities of the time; and though there is no absolute proof that York was the first centre of Culdee influence in the North, yet everything lends itself to that supposition. Every circumstance gives weight

to the statements of the old Northern Constitutions of Masonry, that, as Associates in Geometry, it was of Greco-Roman derivation from Egypt; and that when it was thought fit to reorganise the Fraternity of Artisans, the Craft produced MSS. in Greek, Latin, and British, which it is said were "found to be all one "; and through this descent we reach those Sodalites which studied in Symbols, Geometry, Science, and Theosophy in their home at Alexandria.

When we examine the MSS. which embody the ancient Laws of Freemasonry we find that their historical statements and organisation are as much in agreement as their ceremonies were, with the Arcane and Mystic schools. Nor is this to be wondered at since the Culdee Monks were equally Serapians, Christians, and the Schoolmasters who taught science and religion to the people. As the Colleges of Artisans, which were introduced by the Romans as early as 46 A.D., ceased to exist in the lapse {269} of years, if ever they did cease to exist, which is very improbable, the members became attached to the Culdee Monasteries and transmitted, through this alliance, their traditional art secrets, and as the priests had their own version of the ancient Mysteries, they understood that which the Masonic MSS. imply.

It is an historical fact that the early Culdee priests were sometimes educated in Rome, and that they were converted Druidical Initiates; generally speaking it must have been so. Toland says that in Ireland, Columba, the follower of St. Patrick, converted the Druidical Sanctuaries into Christian Monasteries.<<Toland, i, 1726, p. 8.>> He also provides us with a theory to explain the preservation of the Masonic Constitutions in rhyme in this, that with the absorption of Druidism, which was prohibited by Rome, into Christianity, it was found necessary to frame new Regulations for the Bards and Minstrels. Accordingly in 537 an assembly was held at Drumcat in modern Londonderry, at which was present the King Ammerius, Aidus King of Scotland, and the Culdee Columba, when it was resolved that, for the preservation of learning, the Kings and every Lord of a Cantred or Hundred, should have a Bard, and that schools should be endowed under the supervision of the Archpoet of the King.<<"Ibid," p. 4.>> Thierry<<"Norman Conquest.">> states that

when Northumberland, Cumberland, and Westmorland, circa 1138, formed part of Scotland, the Anglo-Saxon traditions were preserved by the Minstrels, and that from thence the old English poetry, although obsolete in places inhabited by the Normans, again made itself heard in a later age.

The oldest version of the Constitutional Charges is in poetical form, and was first printed by Mr. James Orchard Halliwell, who considers it to be a copy written in the latter part of the 14th century. Recently a copy has been printed in fine facsimile, with a most valuable Commentary by Brother Robert Freke Gould, P.M. 2076, who conferred upon it its present name of "Regius MS." He {270} adduces strong evidence for our belief that this version of Masonry may have been patronised by the Culdee Monks of York, and that the system actually dates from the time of Edwin King of Deira, who was converted to Christianity in the year 626 and for whose baptism a small church or Oratory was constructed of wood, completed by St. Oswald in 642, and repaired by Bishop Wilfrid in 669.

The Culdee Alcuin, surnamed Flaccus and also Albinus, was engaged with Eanbald under Aldbhert, who became Archbishop, in the rebuilding of York Minster of stone between the years 760 and 780. Alcuin and Eanbald made

some journeys to the continent together, and on one occasion at least to Rome, between the years 762 and 766, in search of books and other knowledge, and it was in the year 766-7 that Aldbhert became Archbishop, and converted Alcuin from a Layman into an ordained Deacon. Two years before his death in 788 the Archbishop created Eanbald Coadjutor Bishop, and gave to Alcuin the charge of his schools, and the now renowned library.

When Alcuin went to France and became the friend and tutor of Charlemagne it would seem that French Masonry would interlace with that of the North of England. Charlemagne was crowned a King in the year 754, hut his father King Pepin lived until 768; and when Alcuin speaks, as he does, "of the temple at Aachen which is being constructed by the art of the most wise Solomon," he is paying a compliment to his friend Charlemagne; and again in his treatise "De animae ratione" for the King s cousin Gundrede he also compares him for wisdom to Solomon. Hence it seems to be possible that Alcuin might have some knowledge of a Solomonian Masonry, and the Moslems then were, or had been, occupying the South of France. It is a curious fact that the receptions into the Vehm, founded by Charlemagne, embraces all the salient points of Masonic reception, though the aims of the two Societies were so dissimilar;

{271} and this must be considered in estimating German Masonic receptions.

The ancient Monasteries possessed a "book of gestures," by which they could converse by signs. The Trappists in Africa use it at this day. The Masons of old seem to have had a knowledge of this.

We have every just reason to believe that a Masonic organisation was thus early in existence, and that it was ratified and sanctioned by King Athelstan, who now ruled all England from Winchester to Edwinsburg, now called Edinburgh; and who visited York in the year 933, and again in 937, conferring great privileges upon Beverley and Ripon of which Saxon charters, in rhyme, are produced; he also enriched the Coldei, as they are then termed at York, where they were acting as the priests of St. Peter s, and where they continued until they were relegated to St. Leonard s Hospital by the Bastard to make room for Norman clerics at St. Peter s. According to this poetical Constitution, Athelstan, in order to remedy divers defects which existed in the organisation of Craft Geometry or Masonry, invited all the Men of Craft to come to him with their Council: --

"Asemble thenne he cowthe let make, Of dyvers lordes yn here state, Dukys, Erlys, and barnes also, Knyzthys, squyers, and mony mo, And the grete burges of that syte, They were there alle yn here degree."

The details of this poetical MS. is confirmed by a prose copy attached to a more modern historical version in a MS. written before the year 1450, and which is known to have been in possession of Grand Master Payne in 1721, and which was first printed in 1868 by Brother Matthew Cooke and is hence termed the "Cooke MS." A very precise examination of this MS. has been made by Brother G. W. Speth in a Commentary which he has issued with a facsimile, as well as the MS. itself, in book form bound in oak-boards, which Brother W.

J. Hughan {272} has justly described as a "gem." Brother Speth has clearly

demonstrated that this MS. is a copy made about 1450 by a later writer than the original compiler. The first part is a Preface drawn by the author from various histories, Masonic traditions and charges, and is of a later period than the Saxon Charges. To this Preface has been attached an actual copy of the most ancient "Book of the Charges." With some slight differences; which we will note from time to time, the poetical "Regius MS.," and the closing "Book of Charges" of the "Cooke MS." are in substantial agreement, and either might well be the original of the other. The prose version of the composition of Athelstan s Assembly is not so ornate as that of the poetical, but informs us that "for grete defaut founde amongst Masons" he ordained "bi his counsellers and other greter lordys of the londe, bi comyn assent," a certain rule. A number of such old MSS. tells us that Athelstan granted a charter to hold such Assembly to his son Edwin, and although Athelstan had no son of the name, he had a younger brother Edwin, whom he is accused, on very insufficient evidence, of having caused to be drowned in 933; Mabillon says, on equally doubtful evidence, that this Edwin was received into the Benedictine Monastery of Bath in 944<<"Annals of the Order of St. Benedict," Paris, 1703.>>

It has been recently held by Brother R. F. Gould, in a paper of 1892 upon the
nature of the Masonic General Assemblies that it may refer, not to a grant of their own Masonic
right of Assembly by Athelstan, but to the Saxon Court- leets, Shire-motes, Folc-motes, or Hundred
Courts of the Sheriffs. The author of this theory grounds it chiefly upon that part of the MSS.,
which we have already quoted, in regard to the great Lords forming part of the Masonic Assembly.
But such argument can amount to no more than this, that the writers of these documents attribute
the grant of the right of Masonic Assembly by Athelstan at a meeting of the Witenagemote; and that
the Masonic Assemblies were held, or supposed to be held, {273} in similar form to the Folcomtes,
and they were in fact, a Court of this nature, confined strictly to Masonic affairs. Probably Athelstan sanctioned the Masters "Articles" in a Council of Nobles, and the Masonic Council added the
"Points" to govern Craftsmen. The nature of the Constitutions, thus alleged to be sanctioned, describe an organisation which is out of harmony with what we might expect to find in Norman times,
or at any period to which we might assign it after the 12th century. The Athelstan grant of Masonic
Assembly was held for admitting Fellows, and Passing Masters, whilst, on the other hand, the French
Masons had their "Masters Fraternities" to which none were admitted without much difficulty. It has
also been suggested by Brothers Speth, Rylands, and Begemann that the Masonic Assemblies may
have been held on the same day as the Witenagemote to assure an appeal to the Sheriff if necessary.
In regard to the origin of the poetical Constitution which is termed the
"Regius MS.," there is good reason for believing that it was handed down in rhyme in the Kingdom
of Northumbria until it was committed to writing in some other part of England; and that it was
intended for a Guild or Assembly of Speculative brethren consisting of Artisans of all descriptions
connected with buildings, and admitting Clerics and Esquires; for moral addresses suited to all these
classes are strung together in the same MS. Dr. Begemann considers from the language that the copy
was made in North Chester, Hereford, or Worcestershire. In other words, it is addressed to, and for,
an Assembly similar to the imitation made by our present Grand Lodges. Charters of privileges were
given by the Norman Bishops of Durham, to a class of people, who must have

long existed, called "Hali-werkfolc"; for the name being Saxon they were clearly pre-Norman work
folk. The late Brother William Hutchinson, of Barnard Castle, tells us that, in 1775, he had several
Charters alluding to these people, and gives the preamble of one, granted about 1100 by the then
Bishop of Durham, {274} which is addressed to both "Franci et Hali-werk folc." This writer believes
that the class were Speculative Masons, and he instances a branch connected with the old Culdee
Shrine of St. Cuthbert, and if his views were accepted, it would give good grounds on which to as-
sume the connection of this fraternity with the poem.
It is worthy of note that the Culdee system existed in Scotland for some centuries after the Norman
Conquest, nor does it then seem to have been extinct in Ireland. The continuation of the name of
the Templars in Scotland ages after its suppression in France, is probably owing to the continuance
of Culdee heresy. The Monastery of Brechin, as Mr. Cosmo Innes points out, existed in the time of
David I., the promoter of Royal Burghs, 1123-53, and that after the erection of the Episcopal See,
the old Culdee Convent became the electoral chapter of the new Bishopric; the Abbot of Brechin
was secularised, and transmitted to his children the lands which his predecessors had held for the

church; and one of these, in the time of William the Lion, made a grant of lands to the monks at Arbroath.<<Quoted in Abbott s "Eccl. Surnames," 1871.>> Now the seal of Arbroath has a design which has been taken to refer to the secret Initiation of the Culdees: a priest stands before an altar with a long staff in his right hand, upon the upper part of which is "IO," the top forming a cross; before the altar kneels a scantily clothed man with something in his hand, he might be swearing upon a relic; three other persons are present, of whom two are brandishing swords. An antagonistic theory is that the seal represents the murder of Thomas a Beckett. All we will say here is that it is a very fair representation of the former view, and a very poor one of the latter; and that, in consonance with the times, it may have a double meaning. Sir James Dalrymple says that the Culdees kept themselves together in Scotland until the beginning of the 14th century, and resisted the whole power of the primacy.

"Constitutional Charges." We will now make a slight {275} examination of what we will call the Athelstan Constitution, as it appears in the Regius MS., at times quoting the version of the Cooke MS. The former includes much ornate comment, which is given more soberly in the latter, but essentially the two documents are one. Both consist of two series of Charges for "two Classes," and a final ordinance. These, in both MSS., are preceded by a simple history of the mode in which Euclid organised the fraternity in Egypt, and the regulations by which Athelstan ensured a more perfect system. The first series of Charges in the Regius MS. are 15, called ARTICLES, and concern the duties of a MASTER to his Prentices, Fellows, and their Lords or employers. The second series of Charges are called POINTS, and arrange the duties of CRAFTSMEN to their Master and to each other. In the Cooke MS. these "Articles and Points" have exactly the same bearing but are each divided into 9 in place of 15. The closing part of the Regius MS. is headed "Other Ordinances," and refers to the grant of a right of Assembly by Athelstan and the duties it had to discharge; but a comparison with the Cooke MS. might suggest that this portion is misplaced and should precede the Articles and Points, though in another point of view it might be taken to be a later addition, and to prove the much greater

antiquity of the "Regius," as having a history settled before the grant of the Assembly. In the Cooke MS. the last thing is Charges to "New Men that never were charged before," which looks like a more ancient form of the Points, but in the Regius MS. this part constitutes the closing Points of a Craftsman, and is concluded in a very characteristic way. It personates Athelstan himself, and is held to have the very ring of the original grant; and is a record of that King s assent to.all that has been related: --

"These Statutes that y have hyr y fonde,
Y chulle they ben holde throuzh my londe, For the worshe of my rygolte
That y have by my dygnyte." {276}

Athelstan built several castles in Northumberland, and there yet exists a family of the name of Roddam of Roddam who claim their lands under the following Charter, and there is actually no greater improbability in the one than in the other: --<<Burke s "Landed Gentry," 1848.>>
"I Konig Athelstane, giffe heir to Paulane, Oddiam and Roddam, als gude and als fair, als ever ye

mine ware,

ann yair to witness Maud my wife."

Following the Regius Constitution we have a later section devoted to moral duties and etiquette. It begins with the legend of the "Quatuor Coronati," four "holy martyrs that in this Craft were of great honour," Masons and sculptors of the best. The church legend relates that they were Christians who were employed in sculpture, and always wrought with prayer in the name of the Lord Jesus Christ, after signing with the cross, and their skill was so great that the Philosophers attributed it to the mysterious words of art magic. Diocletian gave them the option of worshipping the Pagan gods, which they refused to do, and were put to death circa 290, and the Catholic Church canonised them as the "Four Crowned Martyrs." After this they came to be acknowledged as Patrons of the building trades, and as such are found in the Strasburg, English, Lombard, and other Constitutions. They are respectively represented with axe, hammer, mallet, compasses and square; sometimes wearing crowns; at times a dog is represented with them.

Attached to the Regius Constitutions are two other documents intended to

complete the instruction in moral duties, begun in the legend just related; the first of them is equally found in a MS. entitled "Instruction to Parish Priests," and concerns behaviour at church; the closing part of this portion is found in another MS. termed "Urbanitatis," and refers to the general behaviour of {277} young persons, whether Artisans or Esquires; MSS. of these two latter portions, as old as 1450 are found separately, but their actual origin is unknown, and it is supposed that they may have had Norman originals. The motto of William of Wykeham was "Manners makyth man," and line 726 has "Gode maneres maken a mon." Between the legend of the Four Martyrs and the other documents is a portion which has the appearance of being imperfect, but which

refers to the building of Babylon and Euclid s tuition in the seven liberal arts and sciences; it is a part of the matter forming the Preface to the "Book of Charges" in the Cooke MS., so that it is possible there was a MS., now lost, from which the writers of these two documents respectively copied additions. In any case both these MSS. are but copies of older documents, both have many imperfections attributable to the copyists, and which prove that they were but copyists.

In both MSS. again, these Constitutions clearly prove that there was a recognised Euclid Charge, who is termed "Englet" in the prose copy; that these Charges were ratified by Athelstan; and the value which the ancient Masons attached to these Charges is proved by the general agreement which exists between two diverse documents, treated in a dissimilar manner, and no doubt used in parts distant from each other. Both documents equally allude to Masters as a degree of the General or Heptarchial, or provincial Assembly, both assert that a Congregation might be made every year or third year, as they would; there is mention also of Elders, and the "principal of the gathering "; and both equally profess to give the Laws as transmitted from Egypt, and sanctioned by Athelstan.

The Regius MS., 12th Point, says that at these Assemblies: --

"Ther schul be maystrys and felows also, And other grete lordes many mo;

Ther schal be the Scheref of that contre And also the meyer of that syte, Knyztes and sqwyres ther schul be,

And other aldermen, as ye schul se." {278}

The prose MS. has it, "if need be, the Scheriffe of the countie, or the Mayer of the Cyte, or Alderman of the towne in which the congregacon is holden schall be felaw and sociat of the Master of the congregacon in helpe of him agenst rebelles." That is the Sheriff and Mayor were to be called to support the Master s authority. This prose version also mentions the "Maister who is principal of the gadering." Also, that "Congregacons scholde be maide by "Maisters" of all "Maisters Masons" and "Felaus" in the foresaide art. And so at such congregacons thei that be mad Masters schall be examined of the Articuls after written and be ransakyed whether thei be abull and kunnynge to the profyte of the lordys them to serue and to the honour of the forsaide art."

From this it is clear, and we shall see it more plainly as we proceed, that after the accepted Fellow had developed his architectural knowledge it was the province of the Congregation, Assembly, or Chapter, to examine into his competency for Mastership, to swear him to his special "Articles," and, according to traditional custom, to Pass him by a ceremony which gave him certain signs, tokens, and words, which enabled him to prove his capacity wherever his travels might carry him. That is to say, not actually to Install him a Master of Work, but to enable him, as was the main object of such Tokens, to shew that he was a Passed Master; for the Assembly considered it to be its duty to see that the Craft and Art of Masonry was not dishonoured by ignorant pretenders. In actual practice, both in this country and on the continent, the Master had to execute an approved task, or piece of work, or "Master piece," as evidence of his ability. In London in 1356 there was a dispute of such nature

between two classes of Masons, when the very authorities cited in these Constitutions, namely, the Aldermen, Sheriffs, &c., arranged the difficulty by a law that any Mason taking work in contract should bring "Six or four ancient men of his trade," to testify to his ability to complete it. In the laws of the Haupt Hutte of Strasburg, {279) which though of the 15th century must reproduce much older laws, and which resemble our own, it is enacted that they might be altered by "three or four" masters of work, when met together in Chapter; and we find that a Craftsman or Fellow, who served but five years in place of the English seven, could not be made a Parlirer or Foreman until as a Journeyman he had made one year s tour of the country, in order to increase his proficiency. Such duties the Regius MS. gives in Norman-French as "Cure," and later they are designated Wardens duties; in Guild Rites sworn officers.

It would seem from what has passed that originally the Fellows and Masters met together in Assembly, but the time came when the Masters met by themselves quarterly, as Findel shows in regard to Germany, whilst the Fellows met monthly. There the Masters Fraternities were presided over by an "Old Master," and the Fellows by an "Old Fellow."

In addition to what has been described it was in the power of the General Assembly to overlook the Liberal Art of Masonry, regulate it, reward merit, and punish irregularities. It would also appoint officers until the next "Gathering," and fix contributions. Brother R. F. Gould has disinterred an old 16th century reference to the Guild of Minstrels, which alleges that they had met annually at Beverley, for that purpose, from the day s of King Athelstan; the similar claims of Masons may be valid, though we have access at present to no records, to prove that the Masonic Assembly met annually at York, or elsewhere, beyond what we find in the Laws of the government, and the assertions of old Masonic MSS.

In the Regius MS. we have the following account of the divisions of the Society by Euclid: --
"Mayster y-called so schulde he be."

For: --

Again: --

"To hym that was herre yn this degre
That he schulde teche the symplyst of wytte."
"Uchon schulle calle others felows by cuthe, For cause they come of ladyes burthe." {280}

Now the Cooke MS. had not to accommodate itself to the metre, and may be supposed to give the same thing in closer conformity to the original document. Speaking of the Constitution granted by Enclid to Egyptians it says: "Bi a serteyn time they were not all ilike abull to take of the forseyd art. Wherefore the foresayde Maister Englet ordeynet thei (that) were passing of conynge scholde be passing honoured. And ded to call the conynge Maister for to enforme the lesse of counynge Maisters of the wiche were called Masters of nobilitie of wytte and conynge of that art. Nevertheless thei commanded that thei that were lass of witte scholde not be called seruantes nor sozette but felaus ffor nobilite of their gentylle blode."
We learn at least from this that a "dual" system was instituted, which finds its equivalent in the lesser and greater Mysteries, for what we find similar in

Rites, between these bodies, extends to organisation, and we see it composed of the noble or Knowing Masters, and the less knowing. Fellows -- craftsmen, or journeymen -- and we begin to see why the Masters Articles make mention only of that rank, and the Craftsmens Points apply only to those subordinate to the Masters. The two MSS. distinctly tell us that both the Masters and the Prentices were to term the Craftsmen their Fellows. It is evident that the Apprentices had no call to the Assembly, but we shall soon see what their status actually was. They may possibly have been sworn in private Lodges of journeymen, and certainly for about 2 1/2 centuries it has been considered that the Charge of the prose MS. to "New Men that never were sworn before," referred to them.
The two MSS. are again in entire conformity in the following Regius extract.
The first Article of the Masters orders says: --
"The Mayster Mason must be ful securly, Both steadfast, trusty, and trewe,
Hyt schal him never then arewe,
And pay thy felows after the coste." {281}
But the 6th Article distinctly specifies "three" grades of payment: --
"That the Mayster do the lord no pregedysse, To take of the lord for his "prenfysse,"
Als much as hys "felows" don in all vysse, For yn that Craft they ben ful perfyt,
So ys not he ze mowe sen hyt."
The Article, however, goes on to enact that the Master may give a "deserving Apprentice" higher wages than a less perfect one. Such an one was no doubt at times accepted in the Assembly before the

expiry of his seven years; and there was a similar custom in the Arcane Schools, for Iamblichus (ci., vi., p. 22) tells us it was a custom of the Pythagoreans that "the Novitiate of five years was abridged to those who attained sooner to perfection." It is yet a custom in some countries that when an Apprentice applies to be made a Fellow Freemason, he requests "augmentation of salary."

We will now follow on to that class of Masons who had not been passed as Masters, or who were employed under a Master of Work. These rules are called "Points" and here also the poetical and prose MSS. are in perfect accord. They enforce Brotherly-love as fully as did the ancient Society of Pythagoras. The first Point says: --

"That whoso wol conne thys craft and come to astate, He must love wel God, and holy church algate,

And his Master also, that he hys wythe, Whether it be in field or frythe,

And thy felows thou love also."

The third Point enjoins secrecy in regard to all he may see or hear: -- "The prevyste of the Chamber tell he no mon,

Ny yn the logge whatsoever they done, Whatsever thou heryst, or syste him do, Tell it no mon, whersever thou go,

The cownsel of halle, and zeke of bowre, Kepe hyt wel to gret honoure." {282}

The fourth Point is as conclusive as to degrees as was the Masters Articles: --

"Ny no pregedysse he schal not do,

To hys "Mayster," ny his "fellosw" also, And thazth the "prentis" be under awe."

The seventh Point is a law against unchaste conduct with a Master s wife, daughter, sister, or concubine, which we mention here because it assigns a penalty, which confirms what we have said, that a deserving Apprentice might be made free of his craft before the expiry of seven years, and in this case it implies a secret or traditional regulation; for the crime specified the penalty is: --

"The payne thereof let hyt be ser, That he be prentes full seven zer."

The eighth Point alludes to the duty of a Cure or Warden: --

"A true medyater thou most nede be, To thy Mayster and thy felows fre."

The ninth Point concerns Stewards of "our halle," and has evident reference to the Charges of Euclid with which the MS. commences: --

"Lovelyche to serven uchon othur,

As thawgh they were syster and brother."

The later Points are not numbered as such in the prose MS., but follow its ninth Point as unnumbered laws. The 12th is of "gret Royalte," and at the Assembly: --

"Ther schul be Maystrys and felows also, And other grete lordes many mo."

The fourteenth Point tells us that the Fellow had to be sworn. As the Assembly had two series of laws for Masters and Fellows, it is quite evident that they had authority over two ranks, besides the Apprentice; and hence the Grand Lodge of England from its revival in 1717, down to 1725, claimed like power over the degrees of Masters and Fellows, thus treating the majority of the subordinate bodies as if Apprentice Lodges. This 14th Point says: --

"A good trewe oathe he must there swere,
To hys Mayster and hys felows that ben there." {283}

The fifteenth Point is a Penal law made against the rebellious and these Statutes close with a confirmation, claiming to be that of Athelstan.

Now although it must be admitted that these ancient Constitutions are exoteric in character, and do not make it a part of their business to settle the work of degrees, in their esoteric aspect, which it left to the ancient traditional mode; yet what does appear is in perfect affinity to a similar system of degrees such as we possess, and with oaths, ceremonials, and secrets for these. As there was an examination, ending in an Oath, there must of necessity have been some ceremony, and in its proper place we will give evidence much older than this copy, that the Craft had its secrets, signs, and watchwords and a president whom they swore to obey. Certificates were not in use at this early date, and in common with the Arcane Schools these secrets did duty for a certificate, and proved as well the degree of skill a Mason possessed; in more ancient times such Rites and symbolic instruction had a higher value than a mere formula by which to recognise each other. Apart from trade secrets there was another reason for great secrecy as to Masonic Rites in the fact that whilst the Christian Emperors of Rome were destroying the Arcane Schools and hounding them to death, the protection of the Masonic art was necessary to the glorification of the Church -- and each sought to protect themselves. There is no doubt that these ancient traditional Rites, which were originally

the type of an ancient religion, would vary with circumstances, the convenience of time and place, and the members of the Lodge. In the very early times of the Society, the Apprentice had no ceremony, until, with time, he merited to become a Fellow. The esoteric Ritual of the Assembly was then dual, but there is evidence in modern times that the Apprentice was sworn to a Charge. In very extensive buildings where the Lodge was numerous, -- and we read of some embracing from hundreds to thousands of workmen; the {284} Apprentice would be sworn, and the chief Master s Fellows would come to include two divisions: Some who had been Passed as "Noble Masters" would take employment on such works as Journeymen, and we should thus find in the same Lodge, sworn Fellows, and Masters, under a sole Worshipful Master of Work, or the system we have to-day in our Lodges, but without the ancient technical knowledge.

Though these Constitutions had other legends tacked on to them in Norman

times, and to which we shall refer in our next chapter, the Anglo-Saxon Masons must have considered them as the time-immemorial Charter of their privileges, even down to the 14th century. They were the authority under which they continued to hold Assemblies, the existence of which is vouched by the laws which the State made to suppress them. We have seen that the meetings were held under a president, who had power to swear Freed- Apprentices or Passed Fellows, and in due course to examine and pass these as Masters if fully competent. Besides the tokens by which they could prove their rank, they had a system of Marks to indicate their property and workmanship; it is alleged there was even a double system, evidenced in this, that as a Stone Cutter possessed a Mark for his work, and the Master one for his approval; traces are claimed to exist where, at a later period, the stone-cutter s Mark comes to be used as the Master s symbol of approbation. Brother Chetwode Crawley, LL.D., draws attention to this, that during the centuries when the Masonic Association was in full operation, Arabic numerals and therefore modern arithmetic was unknown, and calculations could only be made by aid

of the Roman notation; hence the traditions and secret rules of geometry were all important to the Craft, and made it essential that Masons should be geometers. Mr. Cox finds that the design or tracing-boards of various old buildings are grounded upon the five-pointed Star of Freemasonry, and on the Pythagorean problem of a modern past-Master, with its ratio of 3, 4, {285} 5, or the multiples thereof as 6, 8, IO, and this was especially a Guild secret of construction.

The MSS. upon which we have been commenting represent the best days of the Saxon Craft; with the Norman Conquest came over French Masons in large numbers; and we may see between the lines, a subtle struggle between antagonistic systems, and possibly much of the secrecy of Masonry that existed throughout the centuries down to 1717, may be owing to this; and to the fact that the Saxon Mason was assigned a subordinate position. There can be no doubt that at the comparative late date when these two MSS. were written there were Masons in various parts who still clung to the Athelstan constitution. On the other hand the Anglo-Norman Kings, 1350-60, were passing Ordinances and laws, against "all alliances, covines, congregations, chapters, ordinances and oaths," amongst Masons and other artisans. These laws were endorsed by others in 1368, 1378, 1414, and 1423. They seem, however, to have affected very little the Masonic Assemblies, and in 1425 a law was passed to specially prohibit Masons from assembling in Chapters; even this law remained a dead letter on the Statute book; but it is from about this period that the Saxon system passes entirely into disuse. In this contest between the alleged Saxon right of Assembly, and the objections of the Anglo-Norman rulers to meetings held without a Charter, we see the necessity that existed for the Masons to submit their Constitutional Charges to the reigning Sovereigns, as they had been commanded by Athelstan to do, from King to King; indeed Acts were passed in 1389 and 1439 ordering the officers of Guilds and Fraternities to show their Patents to the neighbouring Justices for their approval, but it does not seem clear whether other is meant than the Chartered Livery Companies.

It has been previously mentioned that in these two priceless documents which have all the marks of a genuine Saxon transmission, there is not one word which leads us to suppose that the members of the Society thus {286} formed had an idea that their forefathers had wrought at the building of Solomon s temple; and it is impossible to suppose that if the ceremonies then in use had referred to such a circumstance all reference thereto would have been omitted from the Constitution.

The language in which these documents are couched is Christian, of a liberal but perfectly orthodox cast. Christian churches could only be symbolically constructed, with Christian symbolism, by Masons practising Christian Rites, and the priests would have been ready enough to burn any Mason that supported the Talmud; we have an instance of this intolerance in the destruction of the Templars in the year 1310-13. This is a question of simple historical fact in which we need have no bias either one way or the other. All Masonic tradition is opposed to uniformity of Rites, and in France, from the earliest times, we find three opposing schools whose ceremonies may be broadly classed as Trinitarian and Monotheistic rites.

When we consider that the Masons of pre-conquest times were not subordinated to those of France, we should not expect uniform Rites in the two

countries and when we examine the MSS. of the former and the latter it is clear that such did not exist.   In France itself no such uniformity existed; coming down side by side, shrouded in secrecy for centuries, there existed three sections denominated the "Compagnonage" formed of artizans generally and not confined to Masons, and it is altogether an error to suppose that the most ancient Saxon fraternity was confined to workers in stone, they included all men who used Geometry in their trade, as the MSS. themselves inform us. Besides these, at an early period, probably much earlier but at least co-eval with the Norman conquest of England, there existed in France Master s fraternities of an essentially Christian character attached to some church, and to the support of which Fellows and Apprentices had to contribute.   As a Sodality the Council of Rouen in 1189, and of Avignon {287} 1326, recorded their disapprobation, against their signs, their oaths, and their obedience to a President.   The English laws of the Norman Kings followed this prohibition, Scotland followed suit, and it is not improbable that this circumstance led to the chartering of Livery Companies in England, and Incorporations in Scotland. "The French Sects."   The three divisions of the French Compagnonage became chiefly journeymen, and for a period of over 500 years were in mutual dissension, and at times even at actual war, when many lives were lost. These are, were, and still are, -- (1) the "Children of Master Jacques," which is represented in Anglo-Saxon Christian Masonry; (2) the "Sons of Solomon," classed with our present system; and it is quite possible they may derive a Semitic system from Spain in very early times for the Moslems were in possession in the South until Martel expelled them; (3) the "Children of Father Sonbise "who were chiefly Carpenters, as many of the most early builders must have been, and whose name is supposed to have some affinity with Sabazios, one of the names of Bacchus or Dionysos.   Each of these Sections had their own peculiar ceremonies in which is the drama of an assassination, all somewhat similar but apparently arranged in such manner as to cast odium on their opponents.   One peculiarity is that the Members assume the name of some animal, and branches are known as wolves, werewolves, dogs, foxes, which reminds us of the masks of criminals worn in the religious Mysteries of Greece and Egypt, and we saw that the sun was compared to a wolf in the Mysteries of Bacchus.   Brother Gould has expressed an opinion that the Carpenters were the oldest association, the followers of Jacques the town association, and the Sons of Solomon the privileged corporations that set out from the Monasteries, after the crusades, when architecture became a lay occupation. It is perhaps as probable, though not irreconcilable with thls view, that the sects arose out of the successive developments of civil, sacred, and military architecture. Brother {288} F. F. Schnitger expresses an opinion that the Masons belonging to a "Domus" (civil) were unfree; those attached to the Castle of a Lord would be "glebae proscripti" (military); and that it would only be the travelling church Masons (sacred), free to work anywhere that would be actual Free Masons, and that these would be likely to have different
ceremonies, even if the two first-named were allowed any.
The probabilities are exceeding strong in France for the transmission of old Roman Rites, and the Fraternities would seem to possess traditions or customs common to the Gnostics and Saracens. Like the Manichees they reverence the reed and like the Dervish sects they allege the receipt of a

Charge by the act of receiving some particular garment of the Master; thus one received his Cap,

another his Mantle, and a third his girdle; the same is alleged in the Moslem sects. It is a rite or claim that has the appearance of derivation, though possibly from an ancient common source, and would scarcely arise accidentally.

In the legend of Master Jacques, that personage is slain by the followers of Soubise. The "Sons of Solomon" have a relation in regard to the death of Hiram, or Adoniram the collector of tribute to Solomon and Rheoboam, who was slain by the incensed people, and the account relates that his body was found by a dog; this sect claims a direct Charge from King Solomon and admits all religions without question in contradistinction to the other sects which require their members to be orthodox. Perdiguer says of its Initiation, that "in it are crimes and punishments."

In reference to the cause of the ill feeling between the sects the legends vary. One account carries back this hostility to a period when a section placed themselves under the patronage of Jacques de Molay, Grand Master of Templars 1308-1310, and immediately before the destruction of that Order by Philip le Bel. Another account attributes these dissensions to the time of a Jacques Molar, who is said to be the builder in 1402 of {289} the towers of Orleans Cathedral; the Sons of Solomon refused to labour with the children of Jacques, struck work and fled, and the strong arm of the law had to be requisitioned. It looks like the quarrels of an ordinary trade-union whether occurring in 1308 or 1402. If the Jacques Molar version is historical it is possible that some of the Sons of Solomon may have left that Society and joined an already existing fraternity of Jacques, thus adding a building programme to the many already represented in that fraternity. The traditions would seem to possess the same reliability as our own Masonic legends; and the one tends to prove the antiquity of the other; for as the Compagnonage and English Masonry, have each their ceremonies, degrees, oaths, and tokens of recognition, they have had a derivation in common, for there has been no alliance between the two at any period.

In regard to Rites the "Children of Master Jacques" admit only Roman

Catholics, and say that they "accept Jacques as their mortal father and Christ as their spiritual father," and adopt the sensible maxim that "whilst Solomon founded them, other men modified them and that they live under the laws of these last." We have endeavoured, however imperfectly, to shew what Anglo- Saxon Masonry was, and consider this system to assimilate with it; and we must bear in mind that the Continent was much indebted to this country at one time, thus Diocletian sent Artists from Britain to Gaul, Columban journeyed to Burgundy, Alcuin of York to the Court of Charlemagne, St. Boniface to Germany.

The "first step" is termed Attendant or Affiliate, and corresponds to our Apprentice, he is a young workman, protected and looked after, but considered to be outside any Mystic Rites as was the Saxon Apprentice. The "second step" is termed Received Companion; which is equivalent to the term accepted and the Fellow of the Saxon Assemblies, he has certain secrets and takes part in a dramatic ceremony of the assassination and burial with lamentations as in the old Mysteries, of Master {290} Jacques, whose corpse was discovered supported by reeds. It is practically a disguised drama of the betrayal of Christ. The "third step" probably points to a time prior to the establishment of Masters Fraternities, and corresponds with the Passed Masters and Harodim of the

Guilds; it is termed Finished Companion, in which the Aspirant passes through a dramatic representation of the passion of Christ, and this ceremony, as was doubtless the case in old times in England, rendered and still renders, its possessor eligible for offices of dignity and honour; and may be classed with the Noble, Knowing, or Worshipful Master which formed the chief rank of the Saxon congregations, save those who had been the "Maister who is principal of the gadering." It is curious that the names should agree so closely with those of the Persian Magi, in the time of Cyrus, which were in translation, -- Disciple, Master, Complete Master. Two other circumstances point in the same direction for the descent of this branch of the Society, namely the use of the reed, and of some article of clothing to confirm a "Charge;" both the Manichees and the Dervish sects are descendants of the Persian Magi. This ceremony in the grade of Accepted Companion represents the heroic and pre-Christian anti-type; and as such is parallel with the Pedestal point of Harodim-Rosy Cross, where the Candidate is led up a pinnacle and sees a word that is prophetical of what is given in the degree of Finished Companion which is the explanation and complement of the anti-type. English Masonry has lost much by the refinements of the learned, or by those who "imagined themselves to be learned," and in any case it is easy for such to influence the ignorant. The French have lacked this in the several sects, and have therefore transmitted what they received without understanding it. So have English Stone Masons. There is a peculiar system of salutation called the Guilbrette, two meet, cross their wands and embrace; it has its analogue in all Guilds both East and West.

{291}

The legends as to the schism, though old and in writing now, are of course traditional, and cannot be unconditionally accepted. We learn something of what their ceremonies consisted 250 years ago, as the Doctors of the Sorbonne examined some traitorous members between 1648-50, and accused the Compagnonage of profaning the Mystery of Christ s passion and death, of baptising in derision, of taking new names, using secret watchwords, obligating to mutual assistance "with other accursed ceremonies."<<Vide Gould s "Hist. Freemasonry.">> Much of thls we have seen was common to the Arcane Discipline of the church, and the Charges read very similar to those made by the Fathers when they desired to have the Ancient Mysteries suppressed; in the same spirit they have destroyed all literature that made against themselves and their acts. Almost the same thing might be said by a fanatic and fool against the old Ancient degrees of Harodim-Rosy Cross in this country: and it is very noteworthy and "very suggestive" that the ancient oath of the English Rosy Cross has a penalty, alluding to the Saviour s death which is absolutely identical with the highest grade of this French fraternity of Jacques. The French "Fendeurs," or Charcoal burners, resemble so closely those described by the priests in 1650, that there can be no doubt both have the same common origin; the Fendeur Initiation carry their legends back to remote times, and claim a Scottish origin; possibly it points to a Culdee or other sectarian derivation thence.

"The Salute." Most of the Mystic Sects which derive from what we term the Arcane Schools, seem to have a "Salute" by way of recognition, that is, a phrase by way of "Salutation," and this is probably what Brito-Saxon Masonry possessed, before Semitic legends and Hebrew words were introduced in Norman times. This "Greeting" went with the "Word" until it was abandoned last century. A Christian system that had no allusion to Solomon s temple would have the "Greeting," and is therefore probably one of the most ancient parts of our Rites. {292}

Brother J. G. Findel in his "History of Freemasonry" professes to give the Catechism in use amongst the Masons of the Haupt Hutte of Strasburg, which termed their Assemblies Chapters, after the usage of the Benedictines. In the strict sense of the term what is called "Words" in this ritual is a Greeting. The questioner asks: -- "How many words has a Mason? Seven. Q. What are they? God bless all honourable conduct; God bless all honourable knowledge; God bless the honourable Craft of Masonry; God bless the honourable Master; God bless the honourable foreman; God bless the honourable Fraternity; God grant honourable preferment to all Masons here, and in all places by sea and land." We have here seven prayers easily remembered; and the following passwords were elicited by the Questioner: -- "Kaiser Carl II.; Anton Hieronymus; Walkan." The two last are supposed to be corrupted from Adoniram, and Tubal Cain, the last named, it may be, through Vulcan. Professor Robison, who wrote upon German Masonry last century, expresses an opinion that an Apprentice received an additional word with each year of his labour. During last century there still remained old members of the Strasburg Constitution, though it had then lost all its influence, and there is an interesting statement recorded on the authority of Mr. Vogel, an old operative Mason, who is reported to have said, in 1785, that the German Masons consisted of three classes: -- "The Letter Masons," or those made by Certificate; "The Salute Masons," or those who used a form of Salutation similar to that just quoted; and "the Freemasons," who he says, "are the richest, but they work by our word and we by theirs;"<<Gould s "Hist. Freemasonry," ii, p. 312; also Findel s "Hist. Freem.">> which implies that he was a "Salute" Mason, and that the "Greeting," and the "Word" were originally the marks of two distinct sects but had come to be united. Another writer states, on the authority of a newly received Freemason, who was a member of the Haupt Hutte systems, that the grip was the same in both societies. {293}

We may dismiss the "Certificate" Mason in a few words; in England it corresponds with trade Freedom granted by Municipal bodies from the time of Queen Elizabeth to our own days. Our oldest Catechisms not only include a triplicate "Greeting" but the "Word" system, but we need not give this until its proper date, and on the evidence we have given it may be assumed, that in the ancient Masonry of this country the "Salute" was the "Word," and that upon it was engrafted certain Hebrew words. As the Saxon system was a Christian one, no doubt its chief grade, or Master s Fraternity, has descended to us in the degrees of Harod and the Harodim-Rosy Cross, translated by the French Rose- croix of Heredom, Templar, etc., for all these grades are very similar; and its transmission is equally probable with the known transmission for centuries, of the Christ-like ceremonies of the French fraternity of Jacques, but this we will again refer to in a chapter on the high-grades.

"Conclusion." As we have observed several times, but may again repeat, the drama of the Mysteries was of a spiritual nature designed to teach how man might so conduct his earthly pilgrimage as to arrive at immortal life, and the Initiate during the instruction personated a god who was slain and rose again from the dead. It is not difficult to comprehend how such a symbolic death and rebirth was transformed into the drama of the career of the Saviour of fallen man. Such a Rite is in entire accord with what we know of the Culdee Monks and Masons, who were at York when King Athelstan granted them a Charter, whilst Hiramism is in discord thereto. We may summarise the details of this chapter in a few words; they point to the derivation of a system of trade Mysteries introduced by Greco-Romans into Britain from an Egyptian source; modified into orthodox Christianity by Culdees who had similar recondite Mysteries of a spiritual type, and who taught and directed the Guilds of Artizans during the whole Saxon period; our next Chapter will indicate a system in consonance with the French "Sons of Solomon."

CHAPTER IX. MASONRY IN NORMAN ENGLAND

WE made mention in our last Chapter of a series of Masonic legends which are, in some measure, historically opposed to the old Saxon Constitutions. These first appear in written documents of about 1450 A.D., but as these are copies of still older MSS., may well date into the 12th century in this country. There are two old MSS. the laws of which differ in essential points: in the elder or "Cooke MS." those legends which imply a Semitic origin and actually represent our present Craft Rites, form the Preface, or Commentary, to an actual Saxon Charge; whilst the later, or "Wm. Watson MS," is a copy of a much older document, and itself over two centuries old, is complete in itself, with a modified series of charges: the second part might belong to a "Guild" which had a traditional preference to a Saxon Constitution, and the first to a later compiler, one who had accepted the Norman system, and its Rites. We will endeavour in this Chapter to supply such reliable information, as can be gathered, to account for the legends superimposed upon the older.

It is in Norman times, adding French details, that this matter shews itself,

and as there is yet no established view on the subject, it may be examined in various aspects. In the first place these legends may have been fixed in France by the conquests which the Saracens made in that country; or 2ndly, they may have reached that country through the Moorish conquests in Spain; or 3rdly, and a probable view, they might have been brought {295} from the East, by those Masons who returned in the train of the Crusaders; lastly, but upon this we place small credence, some of our able critics have held that the Oriental legends are collected from books of general history by the first compiler of this version of the Charges, though admitting that the author had old Masonic Charges to guide him.

A very elaborate paper, which may be classed with the first of these views, has been written by Brother C. C. Howard, of Picton, New Zealand, and he relies upon the fact that this new Charge draws its inspiration from Roman Verulam and the erection of St. Albans by Offa, King of Mercia, circa 793, and that one Namas Graecus, under various spellings, is given as the teacher of

Masonry in France. Offa is supposed, by Brother Howard, to have brought Masons from Nismes, or Nimes, in Southern France, for the purpose in view, hence the derivation of Namas Graecus.

A theory such as that of Brother Howard would well account for all that is peculiar in this Constitution. The present Nimes is a very ancient Greco- Roman town, and has perfect remains of the work of their architects; moreover it was for two centuries in the hands of the Saracens, until Charles

Martel, who was the traditional patron of French Masons and the Hammer of the Saracens, drove them out of that town, and may then have appointed a Duke or prince to rule it. The "Cooke MS" like the Strasburg Statutes speak of Charles II., but this is an error, and it is noteworthy that the "Charges of David and Solomon," are invariably united with the French patronage, proving that we derive these Masonic views from French sources. At whatever date these Constitutions first appeared in this country they eventually superseded the English version.

The Saracens were large builders in the East, and even the Mausoleum of Theodric of Ravenna, erected in the 6th century, is considered by de Vogue to be the work of Syrian Masons brought forward by Byzantines. It is {296} said that about the year 693 they assembled 12,000 stonecutters to build the great Alamya at Damascus.<<Condes "Arabs in Spain.">> The Tulun Mosque at Cairo which was built in the 9th century, has all the main features of Gothic styles, and the same race erected numerous magnificent works in Spain. Gibbon informs us that between 813-33 the Moors brought into Spain all the literature which they could obtain in Constantinople, and that between 912-61 the most celebrated architects were invited from thence. We learn from a catalogue of the Escuriel library that they possessed 70 public libraries, and that the MSS. handed down includes translations from Greek and Latin and Arabic writers on philosophy, philology, jurisprudence, theology, mysticism, talismans, divination, agriculture, and other arts. They gave us astronomy, alchemy, arithmetic, algebra, Greek philosophy, paper-making, the pendulum, the mariners compass, and our first notions of chivalry, and armed- fraternities. Whether they gave us Gothic architecture may be doubtful but the durability of their own buildings is astounding, and Cordova, the seat of empire, covered a space 24 miles by 6 miles, even in the 8th and 9th centuries, and was filled with magnificent palaces and public edifices. Roger Bacon probably derived gunpowder through their intermediary. It is possible that Syrian fraternities of Masons continued to exist until its

invasion by the Saracens, and they themselves, as we have seen, had secret fraternities analogous to Freemasonry, and as the Koran accepts the history of the Jewish Patriarchs such a system as we now possess is in accord with their feelings, and might possibly be acceptable to a French fraternity who were Christians and had derived building instructions from a Moslem race. If the Saracenic theory in regard to Nismes is inadmissable, or the derivation of the French Charges under Norman introduction, when the system had consolidated under the "Sons of Solomon;" there are two other views we may notice. The possibility of a derivation from the {297} Spanish Moors; or through the Crusaders who returned from Palestine after erecting endless works with the assistance of the native Masons. Neither of these two views will account fully for the fact that the "Constitutions" of the period of this Chapter connect the Charges of David and Solomon with the Namas Graecus "who had been at the building of Solomon s temple," with Charles Martel, or even Charles II. But

this is not a great difficulty, for Namas does not appear until circa 1525, and was always a trouble to the Copyists, sometimes he is Namas, at others he is Aymon, or the man with a Greek name, and on one occasion he is Grenaeus. Again building, in Europe, was a clerical art down to the 12th century and laymen were subject to them; but the religion of the Saracens was of a different cast, and admitted from the very first, of the continuance of independent schools of Architecture attached to no Sheik-ul-Islam, Mollah, or Dervish. On the whole we seem to be led by these considerations to the Norman-French introduction into this country of a species of Masonic rules, rites, and legends which existed in Southern France, and which were still further influenced in the 13th century by Masons from the East; but the reader can judge of this upon reading all the facts.

When Abdur-Rahman built the great Mosque of Cordova in the short space of ten years, he said, -- "Let us raise to Allah a Jamma Musjid which shall surpass the temple raised by Sulieman himself at Jerusalem." This is the oldest comparison which we have of Solomon s erection as compared with mediaeval erections, and coming from a Moslem is eminently suggestive. Some 30 years ago Bro. Viner Bedolphe brought forward some cogent arguments to prove that though our Craft Masonry had been derived from the Roman Colleges the 3rd Degree of Modern Masonry had been added, in its second half, by Moslems. But as a matter of fact the existing Jewish Guilds have a ceremony from which our Modern 3rd Degree is derived through the ancient Guilds, and it is quite possible that the work {298} men of Abdur-Rahman found it of old date in Spain, as we shall see later; and that a Guild of them was employed at Cordova. Mecca has had for ages a semi-Masonic Society which claims its derivation from the Koreish who were Guardians of the Kaaba; namely, the Benai Ibraham. For some hundreds of years our Constitutions have asserted that Nimrod was a Grand Master and gave the Masons a Charge which we still follow. Its first degree is the "Builders of Babylon," and is directed against Nimrod and his idols, and against idolatry in general. Its second degree is the "Brothers of the Pyramids," and teaches, as do our own Constitutions, that Abraham taught the Egyptians geometry, and the mode of building the pyramids. The third degree is "Builders of the Kaaba," in which the three Grand Master Masons Ibrahim, Ishmael, and Isaque, erect the first Kaaba, on the foundations of the temple erected by Seth on the plans of his father Adam. At the completion of the Kaaba, the twelve chiefs or Assistants of the "three" Grand Masters are created Princes of Arabia. The Society was clearly ancient in A.D. 600 as al Koran alludes to the legendary basis on which it is formed.

There is a very interesting French romance of the 12th century by Huon de Villeneuve which seems to have a bearing upon the names of our old Masonic MSS., or at least on a corrupt version of them; and which moreover commemorates the Masonic death of a person who is supposed to have battled with the Saracens in France and Palestine. Either the work may veil legends of the Compagnonage, or, with less probability, these latter may have drawn something from it. This romance is entitled "Les Qualre Fils Aymon." Charlemagne returns victorious from a long and bloody war against the Saracens in Easter, 768, and has to listen to accusations against Prince Aymon of the Ardennes, for failing to perform his fealty in not warring against the Saracens. Charlemagne has as colleagues Solomon of Bretagne, and his trusty

friend the Duke of Naismes. Renaud, Allard, Guichard, and {299} Richard, the "four sons of Aymon," depart from the Court in quest of adventure. They defeat Bourgons the Saracen chief before Bordeaux, cause him to become a Christian, and after that restore Yon, King of Aquitaine, to his throne; Renaud marries his daughter Laura and erects the Castle of Montauban. Yon fears the anger of Charlemagne, persuades the four Aymons to solicit his grace, and they set out "with olive branches in their hands," but are treacherously waylaid by their enemies, and would have been slain but for the arrival of their cousin Maugis, and the "cyprus was changed for the palm." Richard is taken prisoner, and condemned to death, but Maugis disguises himself as a Pilgrim, hangs the executioner, carries off Richard, and also the golden crown and sceptre of Charlemagne, who thereupon resolves to attack Montauban. After a due amount of battles, peace is restored on condition that Renaud departs on a pilgrimage to Palestine. On arrival there he is surprised to meet Maugis, and between them they restore the old Christian King of Jerusalem to the throne. After an interval Renaud is recalled to France and on his arrival finds his wife dead of grief, as well as his aged father Aymon and his mother. His old antagonists -- Naismes, Oger, and Roland have been slain at Ronciveux. Five years later Charlemagne visits Aix-la-Chapel, with the three brothers Aymon and their two nephews, and the following is a literal translation of what occurred: " Hollo! says the Emperor, to a good woman, what means this crowd? The peasant answered, -- I come from the village of Crosne, where died two days ago a holy hermit who was tall and strong as a giant. He proposed to assist the Masons to construct at Cologne the Church of St. Peter; he manoeuvred so well that the others who were jealous of his ability, killed him in the night time whilst he slept, and threw his body into the Rhine, but it floated, covered with light. On the arrival of the bishop the body was exposed in the Nave, with uncovered face that it might be recognised. Behold what it is that draws the {300} crowd. " The Emperor approached and beheld Renaud of Montauban, and the three Aymons, and two sons of Renaud, mingled their tears over the corpse. Then the bishop said: -- Console yourselves! He for whom you grieve has conquered the immortal palm." The Emperor ordered "a magnificent funeral and a rich tomb." In the translation of Caxton it is the bishop who does this and also Canonises him as "St. Renaude the Marter." In the time of Charlemagne, and even much later, there existed a great number of pre-Christian and Gnostic rites, and the Emperor is credited with reforming, or establishing, in Saxony, the country of Aymon, whose memory was held in great veneration even down to the 19th century, a secret fraternity for the suppression of Paganism, which has most of the forms of Modern Freemasonry. Hargrave Jennings holds that the fleur-de-lis may be traced through the bees of Charlemagne to the Scarab of Egypt, and is again found on the Tiaras of the gods of Egypt and Chaldea. After the Culdee Alcuin had assisted in building the Church of St. Peter at York, he went over to France, and became a great favourite at Court, having the instruction of the Emperor himself whom he terms a builder "by the Art of the Most Wise Solomon," who made him an Abbot. Apart from the significance of this romance in a Masonic sense, which appears to have drawn on existing Masonry, there are some peculiar correspondences. The body of Osiris was thrown into the Nile, that of Renaud into the Rhine. The address of the bishop to the mourners is almost identical with that of the old Hierophants to the mourners for the slain sun-god. As

before stated the "branch" varied in the Mysteries, as the erica, the ivy, the palm, the laurel, the golden-bough. As in the case of the substituted victim for Richard the Moslems held that a substitute was made for Jesus. The romance confuses the time of Charlemagne, if we accept it literally, with that of a Christian King of Jerusalem, as the Masonic MSS. confuse the date of Charles of France with an apocryphal Aymon who was at the building {301} of Solomon s temple. Possibly the Masons confused the Temple of Solomon with that existing one which Cardinal Vitry and Maundeville inform us was "called the Temple of Solomon to distinguish the temple of the Chivalry from that of Christ;" they allude of course to the house of the Knights Templars. These legends may well represent some ancient tradition, and we know not what MSS. have perished during the centuries. A curiously veiled pagan Mythology may be traced in Paris; comparing St. Denis to Dionysos. The death of St. Denis takes place on Montmartre, that of Dionysos on Mount Parnassus; the remains of Denis are collected by holy women who consign them with lamentations to a tomb over which the beautiful Abbey was erected; but he rises from his tomb like Dionysos, and replacing his severed head walks away. Over the southern gate of the Abbey is also sculptured a sprig of the vine laden with grapes which was a Dionysian symbol, and at the feet of the Saint, in other parts, the panther is represented, whose skin was in use in the Rites of the Mysteries.

Other attempts to identify Namas Graecus may be given. Brother Robert H.

Murdock, Major R.A., considers that this person is the Marcus Graecus from whose MS. Bacon admits in "De Nullitate Magiae," 1216, that he derived the composition of gunpowder. There is one old MS. in the early days of the Grand Lodge that has adopted this view. Here again we run against the Saracens, for Duten shews that the Brahmins were acquainted with powder from whom it passed to the Lulli or Gypsies of Babylon, the Greeks and Saracens, and it is thought to have been used by the Arabs at the siege of Mecca in 690; again Peter Mexia shews that in 1343 the Moors used explosive shells against Alphonso XII. of Castile, and a little later the Gypsies were expert in making the heavy guns. Very little is known of Marcus Graecus but early in the 9th century his writings are, erroneously, supposed to be mentioned by the Arabian physician Mesue.<<The "Cyclo. of" Eph. Chambers, art. "Gunpowder.">> {302} The acceptance of Marcus of gunpowder notoriety as identical with Namas or Marcus of Masonic notoriety, necessitates one of two suppositions: (1) either he was the instructor, or believed to be so, of Charles Martel in Military erections; or (2) the fraternity of Masons had a branch devoted to the study of Alchemy and the hidden things of nature and science: much might he said in its favor, but unless there was some MS. of a much earlier date that mentions Namas or Marcus, and is missing, the introduction is probably only of the 16th century when Masons were actually Students of Masonry and the secret sciences. Another theory has been propounded by Brother Klein, F.R.S., the eminent P.M. of the Quatuor Coronati Lodge, namely that Haroun al Raschid s son the Caliph al Mamun is "the man with a Greek name." He shews that in the time of this Caliph the books of Euclid were translated into Arabic for the Colleges of Cordova, and it was not until the 12th century that Abelard of Bath rendered them into Latin. The original Greek MS. was lost for 700 years when it was found by Simon Grynaeus, a Suabian and co-labourer of Melancthon and Luther. In 1530 he gave the MS. to the world,

and we actually find that in some of our MSS. Graecus is transformed into Green, Grenenois, Grenus, Graneus. Caxton printed the "Four Sons of Aymon" in the 15th century, and we find some scribes transforming Namas into Aymon. Here we have a later attempt to identify the personality mentioned; he was a man of whom nobody knew anything, and each scribe sought to develop his own idea, if he had any.

Charlemagne was a contemporary of the Haroun al Raschid here mentioned who sent him a sapphire ornament and chain by his ambassador.

Green in his "Short History of the English People" (London, 1876) says: -- "A Jewish medical school seems to have existed at Oxford; Abelard of Bath brought back a knowledge of Mathematics from

Cordova; Roger Bacon himself studied under the English Rabbis" (page {303} 83). Bacon himself writes: "I have caused youths to be instructed in languages, geometry, arithmetic, the construction of tables and instruments, and many needful things besides." The great work of this mendicant Friar of the Order of St. Francis, the "Opus Majus," is a reform of the methods of philosophy: "But from grammar he passes to mathematics, from mathematics to experimental philosophy. Under the name of Mathematics was enclosed all the physical science of the time."

It is beyond doubt that after the Norman conquest in 1066 the predominant genius of Masonry was French; the oversight and the design were French, the labour Anglo-Saxon; but the latter were strong enough as shewn, by an eminent architect, to transmit their own style in combination with that of the French. It must also be borne in mind that if the English towns have some claims to Roman succession, that feature is doubly strong in France, even to the language. Long after the conquest of the country by the Franks, and even until modern times, the people were allowed to continue Roman laws, privileges, colleges, and Guilds; pure Roman architecture exists to this day, and notably at Nimes. Lodges, though not perhaps under that name, must have existed from the earliest times, for we find that in the 12th century, the Craft was divided into three divisions; we may even say four, for besides the Passed Masters Associations, there were Apprentices, Companions or Journeymen, and perpetual Companions, or a class who were neither allowed to take an Apprentice, or to begin business as Masters; that is they could employ themselves only on inferior work. The eminent historian of Masonry, Brother R. F. Gould, shews this, and also that the so-called "Fraternities" of France were the Masters Associations, but that the Companions and Apprentices had to contribute to the funds that were necessary for their maintenance. The qualification necessary to obtain Membership of this Association was the execution of a Master-piece, which was made as expensive as possible, {304} in order to keep down the number of Masters. It will be seen at once that this is a very different organisation to the Constitution of the Assemblies of our last Chapter, and the reader must keep this distinction in mind, as well as the fact that there came over to this country a class of men impressed with these discordant views.

It would extend far beyond the scope of this book to give more than a very slight account of the numerous Abbeys, Monasteries, Churches and Castles which were erected after the Norman conquest; it is, however, necessary, in our inquiry after the Speculative element, to say something of these, and of the persons who erected them. Doctor James Anderson states that King William the Bastard employed Gundulf, bishop of Rochester, and Earl Roger de

Montgomery in building, or extending, the Tower of London, Castles of Dover, Exeter, Winchester, Warwick, Hereford, Stafford, York, Durham, Newcastle, also Battle Abbey, St. Saviour s in Southwark, and ninety other pious houses; whilst others built forty two such, and five cathedrals. Battle Abbey was in building 1067-90, the architect being a Norman Monk who was a noted arrow- head maker and therefore named William the Faber, or Smith. Between 1070- 1130 Canterbury Cathedral was in course of erection. In 1076 Archbishop Thomas began the re-erection of the Cathedral of York, which had previously been burnt in contest with the Normans. Between 1079-93, Winchester Cathedral was in progress. The White or Square tower on the Thames is of this period and Jennings mentions one of the main pillars which has a valute on one side, and a horn on the other, which he considers to have the same significance as the two pillars of Solomon s temple, that is symbolising male and female. It is evident that Masons must have now been in great demand and that whether Saxon or Norman were sure of employment; the following are of interest, and as we meet with any particulars, which have a distinct bearing upon the Masonic organisation, we will give them. {305}

The New Castle, whence the name of that town is taken, was built by a son of the Bastard, and thenceforth became, as in Roman times, a place of great strength, and also the chief home of the Monastic Orders, for Benedictines, Augustinians, Carmelites, Franciscans, Hospitallers of St. John, and Nuns all built houses here, and their conventual buildings within its walls, and many an Hospitium for wayfarers, many Guilds, and many a chapel of black, white and grey Friars were founded. The Percys had a town residence here in the narrow street called the Close.

In 1074 Lincoln Cathedral was begun by Remgius Foschamp, the Norman Bishop, who had it ready for consecration in 8 years. It was destroyed by fire in 1141, but Bishop Alexander restored it to more than its former beauty. Where the Castle now stands existed an ancient fortress which the Bastard converted into a Norman stronghold.

In 1077 Robert the Cementarius, or Mason, had a grant of lands in reward for his skill in restoring St. Albans; and we may find in this circumstance the origin of the St. Alban Charge combined with that of Charles Martel and David and Solomon; including the Norman fiction that St. Alban had for his Masonic instructor St. Amphabel out of France. We say fiction because Britain at that day sent Masons to Gaul.

In Yorkshire a Godifried the Master-builder witnesses the Whitby Charter of Uchtred, the son of Gospatric. These are Danish names and the Marks of Yorkshire Masons, in this and the following century, are strong in the use of letters of the Runic or Scandinavian alphabet.

Baldwin, Abbot of St. Edmund s began a church in 1066 which was consecrated in 1095. Hermannus the Monk, compares it in magnificence to Solomon s temple, which is the first Masonic reference we have to that structure, and in Norman times.

Paine Peverell, a bastard son of the King, built a small round church at Cambridge which was consecrated in {306} 1101, this form being a model of the Holy Sepulchre at Jerusalem. He also began a castle in Derbyshire, on a peak inaccessible on three sides one of which overlooks the Peak Cavern, which Faber supposes was used in the Druidical Mysteries.

A round church was erected at this period in Northampton, probably by Simon de St. Luz. An ancient sun-dial is built into its walls; the tooling of the building is Saxon chevron style, in contradistinction from the Norman diagonal axe work.

There is a curiously mystic monument at Brent Pelham to Piers Shonke, who died in 1086. Weever calls it "a stone whereon is figured a man, and about him an eagle, a lion, and a bull, having all wings, and an angell as if they would represent the four evangelists; under the feet of the man is a cross fleuree." We must not hastily confound these emblems with the present quartering in the Arms of Freemasons.

During the reign of Rufus the great palace of Westminster was built, and thirty pious houses. In 1089 the King laid the foundation of St. Mary s Abbey at York. In the same year the Bishop of Hereford laid the foundation of the Gothic cathedral at Gloucester, and it was consecrated in 1100. In 1093 William of Karilipho, Bishop of Durham, laid the foundation of his cathedral, in the presence of Malcolm King of Scots and Prior Turgot. Surtees says that it "was on a plan which he had brought with him from France." In the same year the church of the old Culdee settlement of Lindisfarne was erected, and Edward, a monk of Durham, acted as architect.

In 1093 Hugh Lupus, Earl of Chester, sent for Anselme, Abbot of Bec, "by his conseile to build the Abbey of St. Werberg at Chester." It contains an old pulpit of black oak which is full of heraldic carving which has been mistaken for Masonic emblems.<<Past Grand blaster Smith, U.S.A.>> It was in this Monastery {307} that Ralph Higden compiled the Polychronicon, a history often referred to in the "Cooke MS."

The work of Durham Cathedral was continued by Bishop Ranulf de Flambard from 1104 and completed before the year 1129. Under Bishop William de Carilofe the grant which Waltheof, Earl of Northumberland, had made to the See of Durham was confirmed, of the Priory of Teignmouth to the Church of Jarrow, which was built by Benedict Biscop in 689 and of Wearmouth 8 years later. Also Robert de Mowbray brought monks from St. Albans to rebuild the Priory Church, which was completed in 1110. Anything connected with these Northern provinces is Masonically important, for Northumberland and Durham had many Operative Lodges long prior to the G.L. of 1717, and any legitimacy which that body can have it owes to those Northern Lodges, which eventually joined its ranks.

Northumberland is studded with fortified piles or towers and fortified vicarages which must have given much employment to Masons. Elsden possessed one of these and also two folc-mote hills, where in old time, justice was administered in the open air, as in the Vehm of Westphalia, dating back one thousand years.

Oswold the good Bishop of Salisbury built the Church of St. Nicholas at Newcastle about the year 1004. In 1115 Henry I. made grants to the Canons regular of Carlisle. Many parts of the Church of St. Andrew are earlier than St. Nicholas, but its erection is of later date.

The Church of St. Mary, Beverley, is supposed to have had upon its site, a Chapel of Ease dedicated to St. Martin by Archbishop Thurston, of York, between 1114-42; it is certain, however, that it was constituted a Vicarage of St. Mary in 1325. The Nave was built about 1450, and consists of six bays and seven clerestory windows, but in 1530 the upper part of the central tower fell

upon the Nave with much loss of life. Its pillar was erected by the Guild of Minstrels, which like that of the Masons, claimed to date from Saxon times; it has upon the fluted {308} cornishes five figures of the Minstrels with their instruments, of which only two respectively with guitar and pipe are intact; and stands on the north side facing the pulpit. The "Misere" stalls in the chancel are of the 15th century, with carved bas reliefs under the seats; one of these represents a "fox" shot through the body with a woodman s arrow, and a "monkey" approaching with a bottle of physic.

In regard to symbolism Brother George Oliver, D.D., mentions an old church at Chester, which he does not name, containing the double equilateral triangles; also the same in the window of Lichfield Cathedral. Mr. Goodwin states that the triple triangles interlaced may be seen in the tower of a church in Sussex. We are now approaching the period of the Crusades, and it may be noticed that Cluny and other great French Abbeys are usually considered the centres of action whence proceeded the builders that accompanied the armies of the cross to Palestine. Here an enormous number of buildings were erected, between 1148-89, in which Europeans directed native workmen, and in which the former learned a lighter style of architecture which resulted in pointed Gothic; a style which had early existence in the East, for Professor T. Hayter Lewis points out that the 9th century Mosque at Tulun in Cairo has every arch pointed, every pier squared, and every capital enriched with leaf ornament; this style the returned Masons began to construct and superintend in the West. Mr. Wyatt Papworth mentions that a Bishop of Utrecht in 1199 obtained the

"Arcanum Magisterium" in laying the foundation of a church, and that he was slain by a Master Mason whose son had betrayed the secret to the Bishop. About this time was begun the old church at Brownsover, near Rugby; when it was restored in 1876 two skeletons were found under the north and south walls, in spaces cut out of the solid clay, and covered over with the oakblocks of two carpenters benches. A similar discovery was made in Holsworthy parish church in 1885; {309} in this case the skeleton had a mass of mortar over the mouth, and the stones were huddled about the corpse as if to hastily cover it over.   There is no doubt that in this and many other cases the victims were buried alive as a sacrifice.<<"Builders   ites and Ceremonies," G. W Speth, 1894.>>   They are instances in proof of a widespread and ancient belief of a living sacrifice being necessary.

King Henry I., 1100-35, built the palaces of Woodstock and Oxford, and

fourteen pious houses, whilst others built one hundred such, besides castles and mansions. The Bishop of Durham confirmed and granted privileges to the Hali-werk-folc who would be Saxon artificers.

In 1113 Joffred, Abbot of Croyland, laid the foundation of that Abbey; about 22 stones were laid by Patrons, who gave money or lands. Arnold is described as "a lay brother, of the art of Masonry a most scientific Master." About this time, or a little earlier, the seven Liberal Arts and Sciences are designated the "Trivium" and "Quadrivium," and the Chronicler gives us the following illustration of the first division: -- "During this time Odo read lessons in "Grammar" to the younger sort, Terrick Logic to the elder students at noon; and William "Rhetoric" in the afternoon; whilst Gilbert preached every Sunday, in different churches, in French and Latin against the Jews, and on holiday evenings explained the Scriptures to the learned and clergy." In Essex s Bibliotheca Topographia, 1783 (vol. iv.) we find it stated that the builders of

this portion cut rudely at the west end of the south aisle, a pair of compasses, a lewis, and two circular figures, which, he supposes, are intended for sun and moon; in 1427, however, there were repairs in progress, not of this part, but in the west and north aisles. This Abbey possessed a library of 900 books, and save that Joffrid, or Gilbert, exhibited so much animosity against the Jews, is so consonant with the first part of the "Cooke MS." that we might have taken it as a proof that the Semitic Rites existed in 1113. They probably did in France and parts of Spain. The bronze candelabrum of {310} Gloucester was made in 1115, and has the double triangles and much other Masonic symbolism; it is of Byzantine design and approximates to old Egyptian work and symbolism.

King Stephen, 1135-54, employed Gilbert de Clare to build four Abbeys, two Nunneries, and the Church of St. Stephen at Westminster, whilst others built about ninety pious houses. Jesus College at Cambridge was founded in this reign, and a very remarkable church was erected at Adel near Leeds. It is recorded of a soldier of King Stephen, named Owen or Tyndal, that he received a species of religious Initiation at the Culdee Monastery in Donegal, placed in a "pastos" of the cell; he then went on a pilgrimage to the Holy-land, and on his return, as has been recorded of Renaud of Montauban, assisted in building the Abbey of Bosmagovsich. The Marks of Birkenhead Priory of this date have been collected and printed by Brother W. H. Rylands, also those of St. John s Church in Chester, the Cathedral, Chester, and the walls, some of which are Roman work.<<"Ars Quat. Cor.," 1894.>>

In 1147 Henry de Lacy laid the foundation of Kirkstall Abbey in Yorkshire; it
is of pointed Gothic. Roche Abbey was built between this date and 1186, and these two are believed to be by the same architect. Rivaulx and Fountains Abbey were begun in 1199 and 1200. At this time Adam, a Monk of Fountains Abbey, and previously of Whitby, was celebrated for his knowledge of Gothic architecture, and officiated at the building of the Abbeys of Meux, Woburn, and Kirkstede; it is not said whether he was lay or cleric. York Cathedral was again destroyed by fire in 1137, and Archbishop Roger began to re-erect it in 1154.

In Normandy the Guilds were travelling about like those of England and were of importance in 1145, and had a Guild union when they went to Chartres. At this time Huges, Archbishop of Rouen, wrote to Theodric of Amiens informing him that numerous organised companies {311} of Masons resorted thither under the headship of a Chief designated Prince, and that the same companies on their return are reported by Haimon, Abbe of St. Pierre sur Dive, to have restored a great number of churches in Rouen.

The Priory of St. Mary in Furness was commenced by Benedictines from Savigney. In 1179 the Priory of Lannercost was founded by Robert de Vallibus, Baron of Gillesland. Bishop Hugh de Pudsey rebuilt the Norman Castle of Durham, dating from 1092 to 1174. Between 1153-94 this Prelate was the great Transitional Builder of the north, and he began the erection of a new church at Darlington in 1180 on the site of an old Saxon one. The great Hall of the Castle of Durham was the work of Bishop Hadfield in the reign of Richard
III. on an older Norman one.

Henry II. between 1154-89 built ten pious houses, whilst others built one hundred such. It is the era of the advent of the "transitional Gothic." In the first year of this King s reign, 1155, the "Poor Fellow Soldiers of Jesus Christ, and of the Temple of Solomon," began to build their Temple in Fleet Street, London, and continued at work till 1190. It is a round church in pointed

Gothic to which a rectangular one was added later. By Papal Bull of 1162 these Knights were declared free of all tithes and imposts in respect of their movables and immovables, and their serving brethren had like favours, indulgences, and Apostolic blessings. James of Vitry says that they had a very spacious house in Jerusalem, which was known as the Temple of Solomon to distinguish the Temple of the Chivalry from the Temple of the Lord. In the Rule which Bernard, Abbot of Clairvaux, drew up for them, he speaks of the poverty of the Knights, and says of their house that it could not rival the "world renowned temple of Solomon"; in chapter xxx., he again speaks of the poverty of the house of God, and of the temple of Solomon." As a fraternity he designates them "valiant Maccabees." Sir John Maundeville visited the house, and {312} speaks of it in 1356 thus: "Near the temple [of Christ] on the south is the Temple of Solomon, which is very fair and well polished, and in that temple dwell the Knights of the Temple, called Templars, and that was the foundation of their order, so that Knights dwelt there, and Canons Regular in the temple of our Lord." As Masonic symbolism is found in their Preceptories, this would be a channel from which to deduce both our Solomonic legends, and the alleged Papal bulls, which Sir William Dugdale asserted were granted to travelling Freemasons; but this view has never met with favour from Masonic historians, who aim chiefly at writing things agreeable to their patrons and rulers. Brother Oliver states that the high altar has the double triangles, at any rate these appear on the modern embroidered cover; there is the anchor of the Virgin, also the Beauseant of black and white, which Vitry interprets that they are fair to their friends but black to their enemies, but Jennings says: "This grandly mystic banner is Gnostic, and refers to the mystic Egyptian apothegm that light proceeded from darkness." He further mentions these symbols in the spandrels of the arches of the long church -- the Beauseant; paschal lamb on a red cross; the lamb with the red cross standard triple cloven; a prolonged cross issuing out of a crescent moon, having a star on each side. The arches abound with stars, from which issue wavy or crooked flames; the winged horse, white, on a red field, is one of their badges. He adds that there is a wealth of meaning in every curve of the tombs, which appear in the circular portion.

Ireland has many works erected during this period, and Mr. Street says of them: "I find in these buildings the most unmistakable traces of their having been erected by the same men, who were engaged at the same time, in England and Wales." The same remark will apply to Scotland.

The ancient Preceptory of the Temple at Paris contained (says "Atlanta" xi. p. 337) "24 columns of silver {313} which supported the audience chamber of the Grand Master, and the Chapel hall paved in Mosaic and enriched by woodwork of cedar of Lebanon, contained sixty huge vauses of gold." The fortress was partially destroyed in 1779.

Batissier in his Elements of Archaeology (Paris, 1843), says that the name "Magister de Lapidibus vivis" was given in the middle ages to the Chief artist of a confraternity -- Master of living stones. Or the person was simply termed "Magister Lapidum," and he refers on both these points to some statutes of the Corporation of Sculptors quoted by Father de la Valle. For the origin of the first of these terms consult the Apocryphal books of Hermas, but the term has more in it than appears on the surface, for in Guild ceremonial the candidate had to undergo the same treatment as the stone, wrought from the rough to the perfect. Amateurs were received, for the 1260 "Charte Octroyie" is quoted by

the Bishop of Bale thus: "The same conditions apply to those who do not belong the "Metier," and who desire to enter the Fraternity."

A Priory of the Clunic order of Monks was founded in 1161 at Dudley by Gervase Pagnel, and they had others at Lewes, Castleacre, and Bermondsey.

A fire having occurred at Canterbury, Gervasius, a Benedictine Monk, in 1174, consulted "French and English Artificers," who disagreed in regard to the repair of the structure. The account which Gervaise gives is highly interesting and instructing. The work was given to William of Sens, "a man active, ready, and skillfull both in wood and stone. " "He delivered models for shaping the stones, to the sculptors"; he reconstructed the choir and made two rows, of five pillars on each side; but in the fifth year he was so injured by the fall of his scaffold that he had to appoint as deputy a young Monk "as Overseer of the Masons." When he found it necessary to return to France the Masons were left to the oversight of William the Englishman, a man "small in body, but in workmanship of many kinds acute and {314} honest." The Nave was completed in 1180, and Gervaise informs us that in the old structure everything was plain and wrought "with an axe," but in the new exquisitely "sculptured with a chisel."

We gather two points of information from this account of 1160; first we have the information that William of Sens issued "Models" to the workmen, which explains a law of the Masonic MSS. that no Master should give "mould" or rule to one not a member of the Society; we see, in the second place, that the chisel was superseding the axe. We will also mention here that there is Charter evidence of this century, that Christian the Mason, and Lambert the Marble Mason had lands from the Bishop of Durham for services rendered. The fall of Jerusalem in 1187 brought back from the East many artisans to the West, whose influence is traceable in the early pointed style, or as it is termed the "Lancet," or "Early English."

A noteworthy movement, which extended to other countries had place in France at this period. A shepherd of the name of Benezet conceived the idea of building a bridge over the Rhone at Avignon; the bishop supported his scheme and superintended its erection between 1171-88. Upon Benezet s death, in 1184, Pope Clement III. canonised him, and sanctioned a new Fraternity of Freres Pontives -- bridge builders.

In 1189, Fitz Alwine, Mayor of London, held his first assize, from which we learn that the Master Carpenters and Masons of the City were to be sworn not to prejudice the ancient rights ordained of the estates of the City.

Between 1189-1204 Bishop Lacey was engaged in adding to Winchester Cathedral.

There are references worthy of note in Scotland at this time. In 1190 Bishop Jocelyne obtained a Charter from William the Lion to establish a "Fraternity" to assist in raising funds wherewith to erect the Cathedral of Glasgow; it is supposed to imply the existence of a band of travelling Masons. The same bishop undertook the erection of the Abbey of Kilwinning. The Templar {315} Precep-tory of Redd-Abbey Stead was erected at the same time, and an ancient Lodge of Masons existed here last century.

In the reign of John, 1200-16, about forty pious houses were erected. Hugh, Bishop of Lincoln, about 1200, wrought with his own hands at the choir and transept of the Cathedral, the designs being by Gaufrids de Noires, "constructor ecclesiae." The Masons Marks are numerous; and it is as-serted

by Brother Emra Holmes that, from the central tower, may be seen three large figures of a monk, a nun, and an angel, each displaying one of the signs of the three degrees of Masonry. The Cathedral has also an ancient stained glass window, which has the double triangles in four out of six spaces, an engraving of which appears in the "Historical Landmarks" of Brother George Oliver. Brother Fort asserts that the Masons of the middle ages must have received their technical education from the

Priories, and that a tendency continually reveals itself to use the abstruse problems of Geometry as the basis of philosophical speculations, thus blending the visible theorems with unseen operations of the spirit. He considers that the building operations of the Masons were canvassed in the Lodge and worked out mathematically, the plan of the building serving as the basis of instruction. These views mean in two words that Masonry in all times was Operative and Speculative, but the identical system prevails to-day in some still existing Stone Masons Guilds.

In 1202 Godfrey de Lucy, Bishop of Winchester, formed a "Fraternity" for repairing his church during the five years ensuing. There is nothing to disclose the nature of these Fraternities; it may mean no more than a committee for collecting the means, possibly the Masters Fraternities of the French may have given the idea. At this period Gilbert de Eversolde was labouring at St. Albans Abbey, as the architect, and Hugh de Goldcliffe is called a deceitful workman. In 1204 the Abbey of Beaulieu in Hants was founded by King John, and {316} Durandus, a Master employed on the Cathedral of Rouen, came over to it by request. In 1209 London Bridge, which was begun by Peter de Colchurch, was completed. There is a slab, of this period, in the transept of Marton Church,

W.R. Yorkshire, which has upon it a Calvary cross, a cross-hilted sword, and a Mason s square and level, pointing to the union of arms, religion, and art.

In 1212 a. second Assize was held in London by Mayor Fitz Alwyne, when owing to a great fire it was thought necessary to fix the wages. At this time a horse or cow could be bought for four shillings. Masons were granted 3d. per day with food, or 4 1/2d. without; Labourers had 1 1/2d. or 3d.; cutters of free- stone 2 1/2d. or 4d.; the terms used are "Cementarii," and "Sculptores lapidam Liberorum." John died in 1216, and Matthew of Paris, and others, write his epitaph: "Who mourns, or shall ever mourn, the death of King John "; "Hell, with all its pollutions, is polluted by the soul of John." (i. 288)

In the reign of Henry III., 1216-72, thirty-two pious houses were erected, and the Templars built their Domus Dei at Dover. The beginning of this King s reign is the period when Laymen, emancipating themselves from the Monasteries, come to the front as builders, and leaders of working Masons. It is also the commencement of a more highly finished style of pointed Gothic introduced by the Masons who returned from Palestine. During this reign flourished the celebrated Friar Roger Bacon, who, as member of a sworn fraternity, gave himself to the investigation of the hidden things of nature and science.

In the reign of Henry III. the Monks of Teignmouth raised a masterpiece of architecture in their new conventual church, which they completed by 1220, and were engaged in constant contention with the claims to jurisdiction of the Bishops of Durham; and then followed disputes with the burgesses of Newcastle, owing to the Monks fostering the trade of North Shields. The Prior s officers were in the habit of meeting those of the common {317} law on the hill

of Gateshead, or beneath a spreading oak in Northumberland, when they came to hold assizes in Newcastle.

In 1220 the foundation of Salisbury Cathedral was laid by Bishop Poore; Robert was Master Mason, and Helias de Berham, one of the Canons, employed himself on the structure. Its base is the Patriarchal cross, its erection occupied 38 years, and it is the only Gothic cathedral in England built in one style of architecture. The five-pointed star is found in the tracery of the arcades, and heads of 32 windows, and the equilateral triangle is the basic design of the parapet. In 1220 Peter, Bishop of Winchester, levelled the footstone of Solomon s porch in Westminster Abbey. He is the same person as Peter de Rupibus, a native of Poictiers, who served with Coeur de Lion in Palestine, and was knighted by him, created Bishop of Winchester in 1204, Chief Justice in 1214, went on a Pilgrimage to Palestine and returned in 1231. Amongst his architectural labours is a Dominican convent in Winchester; the Abbey of Pitchfield; part of Netley Abbey; a pious house at Joppa; and the Domus Dei in Portsmouth. He died in 1238, and his effigy, which is a recumbent figure in Winchester Cathedral, has the right hand on the left breast, and his left hand clasping a book.<<Ars Quat. Cor.>>

From 1233-57 the "Close Rolls" give numerous details of the King s Masons who were employed at Guildford, Woodstock, and Westminster. In 1253 the King had consultations with Masons, "Franci et Angli." It is also the period of origin of the "Geometrical" style.

There is a document of 1258 which, though French, has an important bearing on English Masonic legends, referring amongst other things to Charles Martel, and which, though traditional, was accepted as sufficient to secure important freedoms. In this year Stephen Boileau, Provost of the Corporation of Paris, compiled a code of "Regulations concerning the arts and trades of Paris, {318} based upon the Statements of the Masters of Guilds," and amongst these we find the following in regard to the Masons, which gives them a double title to the term "Free," for they were free-stone cutters and free of certain duties: xxi. The Masons ("Macons") and plasterers are obliged to do guard duty, and pay taxes, and render such other services as the other citizens of Paris owe to their King. xxii. The Mortar-Makers are free of guard duty, as also every stone-cutter since the time of Charles Martel, as the ancients ("Prudolmes" or wise men) have heard, from father to son." The question arises here whether Masons and setters, who, were not free of duty, though cutters and sculptors were, use the term Carolus Secundus in England as a claim for the Masons and Setters. The Prudomes were the Wardens under the "Master who rules the Craft," and we are further told that this Master had taken his oath of service at the Palace, and afterwards before the Provost of Paris. It is also said that, after six years service the Apprentice appeared before "the Master who keeps the Craft," in order to swear "by the Saints," to conform to Craft usage. He thus became a Journeyman, or Companion, but could not become a Master, and undertake the entire erection of a building, until he had completed such a "Master-Piece" as was appointed him, and which entailed much outlay; but if this was Passed he became a member of the "Masters Fraternity." The difference between the Saxon and the French custom appears to be this: that whilst in the former case the acceptance of a Master rested with the same Assembly as that to which the Journeyman belonged, in the latter case the Masters Fraternity was now a separate body, with independent laws.

The custom of Montpelier, according to documents printed by Brother R. F. Gould, would seem to have developed somewhat differently. Here, after an Apprentice had served three years, he was placed for another four years to serve as a Journeyman, under a Master. At the end of this period he might present his Master-piece, and if it was approved he took the oath to {319} the Provosts and only such sworn Master was permitted to erect a building from the basement; but it was allowable for a Journeyman to undertake small repairs. Thus as city customs varied confusion must at times have arisen in journeying abroad. There is mention in 1287, when the Cathedral of Upsala in Sweden was begun, that Etienne de Bonneuill took with him from Paris "ten Master Masons and ten Apprentices"; possibly some of the Masters or some of the Apprentices, were what we call Fellows, but there is nothing to warrant any classification. It is important to shew the secret nature and the import of the French organisation, and Fraternities, and we quote the following from Brother J. G. Findel s "History of Freemasonry": -- "The "Fraternities" existing as early as the year 1189 were prohibited by the Council of Rouen ("cap." 25); and the same was most clearly expressed at the Council of Avignon in the year 1326, where ("cap." 37) it is said that the members of the Fraternity met annually, bound themselves by oath mutually to love and assist each other, wore a costume, had certain well known and characteristic signs and countersigns, and chose a president ("Majorem") whom they promised to obey." Nothing very vile in this.

In 1242 Prior Melsonby made additions to Durham Cathedral, and others were made by Bishop Farnham before 1247, and by Prior Hoghton about 1290. At Newcastle the church of All Saints was founded before 1296, and that of St. John in the same century. The church of St. Nicholas was rebuilt in the 14th century, but the present tower only dates from the time of Henry VI. Clavel says that the seal of Erwin de Steinbach, Chief Master of Cologne, 1275, bears the square and compasses with the letter G.

Turning to the North of England we find that at York in 1171, 1127, 1241, and 1291, the choir, south transept, and nave of the Minster were either completed or in course of erection, and the workmanship is infinitely superior to later portions of the building. In 1270 the new church of {320} the Abbey of St. Mary in York was begun by the Abbot Simon de Warwick, who was seated in a chair with a trowel in his hand and the whole convent standing around him. There is also a Deed of 1277 with the seal of Walter Dixi, Cementarius, de Bernewelle, which conveys lands to his son Lawrence; the legend is "S. Walter le Masun," surrounding a hammer between a half-moon and a five-pointed star. In this same year, 1277, Pope Nicholas II. is credited with letters patent to the Masons confirming the freedoms and privileges, said to have been granted by Boniface IV. in 614; if such a Bull was issued, it has escaped discovery in recent times.

In these somewhat dry building details it will have been noticed that references are made to French designers, and to consultation with French and English Masons, and with this enormous amount of building there must necessarily have been a constant importation of French Masons, with the introduction of French customs.

On the symbolism of this period there are some interesting particulars in the "Rationale" of Bishop Durandus, who died in 1296. The "tiles" signify the protectors of the church; the "winding-staircase" "imitated from Solomon s

temple" the hidden knowledge; the "stones" are the faithful, those at the corners being most holy; the "cement" is charity; the "squared stones" holy and pure have unequal burdens to bear; the "foundation" is faith; the "roof" charity; the "door" obedience; the "pavement" humility; the four "side walls" justice, fortitude, temperance, prudence; hence the Apocalypse saith "the city lieth four square."<<"Ars Quat. Cor.," x, p. 60.>> The custom is Hindu, French, British.

In a paper recently read before one of the learned Societies Professor T. Hayter Lewis has shewn that the builders of the early "Pointed Gothic "of the 13th century were of a different school to those who preceded them in the 12th century; he shews that the Masons marks, the style, and the methods of tooling the stones, differ from the older work, and whilst the older was wrought with diagonal tooling, the later was upright {321} with a claw adze. He traces these changes in methods and marks through Palestine to Phoenicia. This new style, he considers, was brought into this country by Masons who had learned it amongst the Saracens, and though Masons marks were in use in this country long before they were now further developed on the Eastern system.<<"Ibid," iii, also v, p. 296>> There is as well tangible evidence of the presence of Oriental Masons in this country; two wooden effigies, said to be of the time of the Crusades, were formerly in the Manor house of Wooburn in Buckinghamshire, of which drawings were shewn to the Society of Antiquaries in 1814, and have recently been engraved in "Ars Quatuor Coronatorum."<<"Ibid," viii. 1895.>> These effigies are life size, one represents an old man with quadrant and staff, the other a young man with square and compasses, and "the attire, headdress, and even features, indicate Asiatic originals." It has been thought that the Moorish Alhambra at Grenada indicates the presence of Persian Masons, and we find the translator of Tasso s "Jerusalem Delivered" in every case substitutes the word Macon for Mohammed, but this is only a provincial abbreviation for Maometto.

Though supported in a superior manner, the theory of Professor Hayter Lewis
is not new to Freemasonry, as in the 17th century Sir Wm. Dugdale, Sir Chris. Wren, and others fix upon the reign of King Henry III. as the period when the Society of Freemasons was introduced into England by Travelling Masons, protected by Papal Bulls, and Wren is said to have added his belief that pointed Gothic was of Saracenic origin, and that the bands resided in Huts near the erection upon which they were working, and had a Warden over every ten men. But Elias Ashmole held that whilst such a reorganisation actually took place, it was upon a Roman foundation. Dugdale probably derived his views from some monastic document, or tradition, whilst Ashmole as a Mason, with better information followed the old MS. Constitutions, as we {322} have done in these chapters. Brother Gould is of opinion that the alleged Bulls were given to the Benedictines and other monkish fraternities who were builders, and that they only apply to Masons as members, or lay brothers of the Monasteries; and, we may add, Templars.

It must be clear to all who have eyes to see, that with this importation into
England of the foreign element a new series of legends were engrafted upon.the original simple account of the old English Masons. Such are the Charges of Nimrod, of David and Solomon, and of Charles Martel, and though we have no MSS. of this period to confirm us, there is no doubt that they are of this period; equally we have no contemporary text of the Charges by which the newly imported Masons were ruled. The information already given enables us to see

that there was a difference both in legends and laws between the two elements and that it was a sectarian difference.

English MSS., of more modern date, refer to "Books of Charges," where those of Nimrod, of Solomon, of St. Alban, and of Athelstan are included, and if they actually existed, as we see no reason to doubt, they were of this century. Moreover the references to Carolus Secundus, or to Charles Martel, must be of this period (though there can be no doubt that this refers to Carolus Magnus or Charlemagne) as small importations of French Masons in Saxon times would not have influenced the older legends, nor stood a chance of adoption by the English. In regard to the laws by which the French Masons were governed, we are, however, informed in the more modem MSS. that they differed but little, or "were found all one" with the Roman, British, and Saxon Charges. It is very evident that the early foreign element had a Charge of their own referring to Nimrod, David, Solomon, and Charles of France, applicable to their own ceremonies, and that in England, they united therewith the "Charges" of Euclid, St. Alban, and Athelstan in a heterogeneous manner; and these are found in two, or more, MSS. to which we refer {323} later, as having been approved by King Henry VI., and afterwards made the general law.

There is one piece of evidence which might enable us to settle certain difficult

points if we could rely upon it. Professor Marks, a learned Jew, has stated that he saw in one of the public libraries of this country a Commentary upon the Koran of the 14th century, written in the Arabic language, with Hebrew characters, referring according to his view, to Free Masonry, and which contained an anagrammatical sentence of which each line has one of the letters

M. O. C. H., and which he reads: "We have found our Lord Hiram" (Chiram); but the Dervish Sects have a similar phrase, which would read: "We have found in our Lord rest" (Kerim, or Cherim). We must therefore hold our minds in reserve until the book has been re-found and examined. In any case it seems to add a link to the chain of evidence as to the Oriental origin of "our present Rites." We may feel assured that the Masons who returned from the Holy-land were of a class calculated to make a marked impression on the Society. The word to which the foregoing alludes, in modern Arabic, might be translated "Child of the Strong one." Several modern writers, both Masons and non-Masons, hold to the opinion that there were two Artists at the building of Solomon s temple: Huram the Abiv, who began the work, and Hiram the son, who completed what his father had to leave undone. Succoth, where the brass ornaments for the Temple were cast, signifies Booths or Lodges, and Isaradatha means sorrow or trouble.<<Vide "Light from the Lebanon Lodge." Joel Nash.>> Josephus says that Hiram was son of a woman of the tribe of Napthali, and that his father was Ur of the Israelites. The account that we have of him, in the Bible, is that he was expert in dyeing, and in working in gold, and in brass; which makes him a chemist and metallurgist, rather than a Mason. There were many Arts in which the ancients were our superiors. A very important {324} lecture on this point has recently appeared from the pen of the Rev. Bro. M. Rosenbaum.

After this long digression we will return to architecture in general. Mr. Wyatt Papworth points out the use of the term Ingeniator, in various documents, between 1160-1300 referring to castles repaired or constructed. Some of these were undoubtedly Architects and not Engineers, whose duties were the construction of warlike machines; and though gunpowder had not yet come

into use in this country, the connection with Masoning might, at a later period, lead to the introduction of Marcus Graecus into our MSS.

In the reign of Edward I., 1272-1307, Merton College in Oxford, the cathedral of Norwich and twenty pious houses were founded; the noble Gothic style had reached its climax. Between 1291-4 several crosses were erected; and there are mentions of Masons who were employed by the King, some items of expense refer to timber, "to make a Lodge for Master Michael and his Masons." Peter de Cavalini designed the "Eleanor Crosses;" the one in Cheapside was begun by Richard de Crumble, and completed by Roger de Crumble; it was of three stories, decorated with Niches having Statues executed by Alexander le Imaginator. A still more beautiful one was the Charing Cross. From 1290- 1300 West Kirkby Church was building, and the Marks are recorded by Brother Rylands, as well as those of Eastham, and Sefton Churches.<<"Ars Quat. Cor." vii.>> In 1300 Henry the Monk, surnamed Lathom, Latomus, -- Mason or Stone-cutter, rebuilt part of the Abbey of Evesham. In 1303 the Mayor and 24 Aldermen of London, made ordinances for the regulation of the Carpenters, Masons and labourers; the Mayor was Gregory de Rokeslie, and the Mazounes Mestres, or Master Masons, and Master Carpenters are mentioned, in conjunction with their servants. From 1308-26 William Boyden was employed in erecting The Chapel of the Virgin at the Abbey of St. Albans. {325}

In the reign of Edward II., 1307-27, Exeter and Oriel Colleges in Oxford, Clare

Hall in Cambridge, and eight pious houses were built. During this King s reign we have the advent of the "Curvilinear," or "Decorated" style, which held its ground for near a century. In 1313 the Knights Templars were suppressed with great brutality in France; in England their property was confiscated to the Knights of St. John, their leading Preceptories being at London, Warwick, Walsden, Lincoln, Lindsey, Bollingbroke, Widine, Agerstone, York, Temple- Sowerby, Cambridge, etc.; they were distributed throughout the Monasteries, or joined the Knights of St. John; those of York had lenient treatment by Archbishop Greenfield, and were relegated to St. Mary s adjacent to the Culdee hospital of St. Leonard. Their Lay brethren, amongst whom would be a numerous body of Masons, were liberated; a circumstance from which might spring more than a traditional connection. Some of the Knights returned to Lay occupations, and even married to the great annoyance of the Pope. In Scotland the Knights, aided in their aims by the wars between that country and England, retained their Preceptories and though they seem to have united with the Order of St. John in 1465 they were as often distinguished by one name as the other. The Burg-laws of Stirling have the following in 1405, -- "Na Templar sall intromet with any merchandise or gudes pertaining to the gilde, be buying and selling, within or without their awn lands, but giff he be ane gilde brother."<<"Freem. Mag." xvi, p. 31.>> Thus implying that the Knights had actual membership with the Guilds. The Templars, at the like date (1460) are mentioned in Hungary.<<Malczovich -- "Ars Quat, Cor." Yarker. Also 1904, p. 240.>> In Portugal their innocence of the charges brought against them was accepted, but to please the Pope their name was changed to Knights of Christ. In an old Hungarian town, where the Templars once were, the Arms are a wheel on which is the Baptist s head on a charger. {326}

A bishop of Durham, circa 1295-1300 named Beke had required more than the accustomed military service from the tenants of St. Cuthbert, who pleaded the privileges of "Haly-werk folc, not to march beyond the Tees or Tyne," and Surtees explains that "Halywerk folc or holywork people, whose business, to wit, was to defend the holy body of St. Cuthbert, in lieu of all other service"<<"Hist. Durham, Genl." xxxiii.>>, are here alluded to, but of Culdee original the term implied an art origin. Sir James Dalrymple, speaking of Scotland, says, -- "The Culdees continued till the beginning of the 14th century, up to which time they contended for their ancient rights, not only in opposition to the whole power of the primacy, but the additional support of papal authority." Noted Lodges exist from old times at Culdee seats, such as Kilwinning, Melrose, Aberdeen, and as the period when this was shewn was that of the suppression of the Templars, and the Scotch generally never allowed themselves to be Pope-ridden, we have one reason why the name of Templar was continued in that country. There was everywhere a growing discontent against the Church of Rome secretly indicated, even in the art of the Masonic Sodalities. Isaac Disraeli alludes to it in his "Curiosities of Literature." In his Chapter entitled, "Expression of Suppressed Opinion," he states that sculptors, and illuminators, shared these opinions, which the multitude dare not express, but which the designers embodied in their work. Wolfius, in 1300 mentions, as in the Abbey of Fulda, the picture of a wolf in a Monk s cowl preaching to a flock of sheep, and the legend, "God is my witness, how I long for you all in my bowels." A cushion was found in an old Abbey, on which was embroidered a fox preaching to a flock of geese, each with a rosary in its mouth. On the stone work and columns of the great church at Argentine, as old as 1300, were sculptured wolves, bears, foxes, and other animals carrying holy-water, crucifixes, and tapers, and other things more indelicate. In a magnificent {327} illuminated Chronicle of Froissart is inscribed several similar subjects, -- a wolf in a Monk s cowl stretching out its paw to bless a cock; a fox dropping beads which a cock is picking up. In other cases a Pope (we hope Clement V.) is being thrust by devils into a cauldron, and Cardinals are roasting on spits. He adds that, at a later period, the Reformation produced numerous pictures of the same class in which each party satirised the other.

Over the entrance to the Church of St. Genevieve, says James Grant in "Captain of the Guard" (ch. xxxiii.), at Bommel is the sculpture of mitred cat preaching to twelve little mice. There is a somewhat indecent carving at Stratford upon Avon. The Incorporated Society of Science, Letters, and Art, in its Journal of January, 1902, contains a paper by Mr. T. Tindall Wildbridge upon the ideographic ornamentation of Gothic buildings. He observes that there were Masons who possessed the tradition of ancient symbolic formula, and that whilst the Olympic Mythology is almost ignored, the "Subject being (by them) derived from the Zodiacal system," and it is, he observes, that this symbolisation, often satirical, holds place on equal terms with the acknowledged church emblems. He instances some of these at Oxford and elsewhere, one of which is the symbol of Horus in his shell, and in a second instance reproduced as a "fox" with a bottle of holy water. The altar of the Church of Doberan in Mecklenburg exhibits the priests grinding dogmas out of a mill.

In 1322 Alan de Walsingham restored Ely, himself planning and working at the building. The 1322 Will of Magister Simon le Masoun of York is printed in the Surtees Society s collection. Of 1325 is the tomb of Sir John Croke and Lady Alyne his wife at Westley Wanterleys in Cambridgeshire; upon it is the letter N, with a hammer above it, and a half-moon and six-pointed star on each side; the N is an old Mason s mark, and also a pre-Christian Persian Symbol. Of this period there is a stone-coffin lid at Thornton Abbey in Lincolnshire, which

{328} has upon it a shafted floriated Greek cross, and besides the shaft a square -- religion and art united; a similar one occurs at Blidworth in Northamptonshire having upon it a square and axe. At Halsall in Lancashire is a three-step cross on one side of which is a square, and on the other an ordinary set-square. There is also in Lincoln Cathedral a gravestone of this century representing Ricardus de Gaynisburg, Cementarius, or Mason, on each side of whom is a trowel, and a square. Chartres Cathedral in France has a window containing the working tools of masons. Mr. Wyatt Papworth observes that at the end of the 13th century, and beginning of the 14th, there is mention of the "Magister Cementarii" and his Socii, or Fellows. There is documentary evidence of the term Freemason in 1376, and it may have been in use at an earlier date. Brother F. F. Schnitger argues, on the evidence of a Nuremberg work of 1558, that the prefix indicates a free art, as sculpture, which the ancients say that handicraft is not, but that the former is, "the use of the square and compasses artistically."<<Vide "Ars Quat. Cor." ii., p.141.>> Brother G. W. Speth advocated, with a little hesitancy, that as the travelling Masons moved about they adopted the term "Free" to indicate that they were outside, or free "from," any Guild but that established under their own "Constitution." It does not, necessarily follow, however, that the term "Free" had everywhere the same import.<<"Ibid" vii.>>

"Scotland" has many important documents. The Chevalier Ramsay, in his
Paris Oration of 1737, states that James, Lord Steward of Scotland, in 1286 held a Lodge at Kilwinning and initiated the Earls of Gloucester and Ulster into Freemasonry. What authority there is for this statement no one now knows, but Tytler in his History of Scotland shows that these two Earls were present at a meeting of the adherents of Robert Bruce at Turnbury Castle, which is about 30 miles west of Kilwinning Abbey, and were concerting plans for the vindication of his claims to the Scottish throne. {329}

The rebuilding of Melrose Abbey in Scotland was begun in 1326 under King Robert the Bruce, who seems to have been a protector of the Templars. There is a legend in regard to a window which is said to have been wrought by an Apprentice who was slain by his Master out of jealousy, and the same myth applies to similar work in other countries. The structure is full of recondite symbolism both within and without; the Chapel is interpreted to represent the human body in all its parts; in Symbols there is a pelican feeding its young, and the phoenix rising from its ashes. It contains a later inscription on the lintel of the turret stairs, as follows, and there are others of like import: --

"Sa gays ye compass royn aboute, Truith and laute do but doute, Behold to ye hende q. Johne Morvo."

   A second on the west wall of the south transept is a shield inscribed to the next John Moray, or Murray, who was son of Patrick, bearing two pairs of compasses laid across each other between three fleur-de-lis, though his own

arms were three mullets, in chief, and a fleur-de-lis in base. The older of the two inscriptions refers to a John Moray who died 1476, a Mason but also Keeper of Newark Castle in 1467; and whose son Patrick had the same status until 1490. The epitaph of the second of the name is thus read: --
<<"Ibid" v, p. 227; also ix, p. 172>>
"John Morow sum tym callit   -gu Melros and Paslay of was I and born in Parysse   Nyddysdayll

and of Galway, certainly an had in kepyng   Pray to God, and Mari baith.

all Mason work of Sant An-   And sweet Sant Tohn to keep this droys ye hye Kyrk, of Glas-   haly

kirk fra Skailh."

This John Moray had grants of lands from James IV. in 1490 and 1497, was Sheriff of Selkirk 1501, and assassinated on his way to the Sheriff s Court in 1510.

In the reign of Edward III., 1327-77, we are told by Anderson that Lodges were many and frequent, and that great men were Masons, the King patronising the arts {330} and sciences. He says that it is implicitly implied, in an old record, "that in the glorious reign of King Edward III., when Lodges were many and frequent, the Grand Master with his Wardens, at the head of Grand Lodge, with consent of the Lords of the Realm, then generally Free-masons, ordained -- That for the future, at the making or admission of a brother, the Constitutions shall be read and the Charges hereunto annexed." Such specific statement is not at present known and is doubtless a paraphrase of the existing MSS. The King founded the Abbey of Eastminster, and others built many stately mansions and about thirty pious houses, in spite of all the expensive wars of this reign.

The south transept of Gloucester Cathedral was begun about the year 1330,

and is traditionally said to be by "John Goure, who built Camden Church and Gloster Towre." He is believed to be represented in a monument, of which an engraving appears in "Ars Quatuor" (vol. ii.); it is in form of a Mason s square, and the builder is represented as if supporting it; his arm is in the position of hailing his Fellows; below the man s effigy is a budget of tools. Until a recent restoration of the ancient Church of the Dominicans in Limerick, there was, on the gable end, the half length figure of a person in Monkish dress; the right hand was clutching the heart, and the left arm, kept close to the side, was raised with the palm outward, index and second finger raised.<<"The Kneph." C. M. Wilson, J.P.>>

In 1330, Thomas of Canterbury, a Master Mason, began work at St. Stephen s Chapel, Westminster. The Abbey-gate of Bury St. Edmund s contains the double triangles, and is of this period. On the carved bosses of a Gothic church at Linlithgow are these emblems: -- (1) a double circle within which is a book upon which are square and compasses; (2) a double square within which are two circles, and in these a double lozenge in the centre of which is the letter G.<<"Freem. Mag.," May 1853.>> The brass of John de Bereford at Allhallows, Mayor 1356-7 of Oxford, contains a shield {331} on which are square and compasses. At Dryburgh Abbey there is a tomb, late this century, on which is a cross-hilted sword, surrounded by a wreath of ivy, and on each side of the sword, the square and compasses; this, and others of like nature, might imply the Initiation of a person of Knightly rank.

The condemnation of the 1326 Council of Avignon would seem to have had its influence in England, for upon the "black death" of 1348, when near half the population died, an Ordinance of 1350 confirmed by Statute law in 1360, forbade "all alliances, covines, congregations, chapters, ordinances, and oaths," amongst Masons, Carpenters, and artisans, and this Statute was endorsed by others of a like nature in 1368, 1378, 1414, and 1423. These laws are, however, rather directed against Journeymen, Apprentices, and labourers, and, in any case, from their repetition at long intervals, had little effect upon the Masonic Assemblies.

A much more important bearing upon the Masonic organisation is a record of 1356. At this period there was a dispute in existence between the "Layer Masons or Setters," and the "Mason squarers." Six members of each class appeared before the Mayor, Sheriff, and Aldermen of the city of London, to have their organisation defined in order that the disputes, which had arisen between them might be adjusted, "because that their trades had not been regulated by the folks of their trade in such form as other trades are." That is, they had not yet been so regulated in the city of London. Amongst these representatives of the Mason squarers was Henry Yeveley; the "Free-masons" as opposed to the "Layer Masons," who were perhaps derived from the ancient body of the Kingdom, who would suffer in status by French importations, and would prefer, elsewhere, the Saxon Constitution. The Mayor, after consultation with these two sections, drew up a code of ten rules, which appears in full in "Gould s History of Freemasonry," and which virtually allowed the two bodies identical privileges, {332} and rules, mutually with a seven years Apprenticeship. In either case a Master, taking any work in gross, was to bring 6 or 4 "sworn" men of the "Ancients" of his trade, to prove his ability and to act as his sureties; and they were to be ruled by sworn Overseers. Twelve Masters were sworn, which virtually united both bodies, and made a uniform rule for both, thus establishing the London Company of Masons. Such a union of the Christian Masonry of York and the Semitic Masonry of the Normans, coupled with the grant of Royal Charters to the Masters, might lead to the recognition of the Rites of the Harodim-Rosy Cross as the unification of the two, which it actually is. It is quite probable that this judicious action of the Mayor saved London a repetition of the disturbances which occurred in France amongst the sects of the Compagnonage.

In the middle of the 14th century Ranulf Higden had compiled his "Polychronicon" in the Benedictine Monastery of St. Werberg, Chester, which is here noted as it constituted the authority for all the Masonic Charges as to Jabal, Jubal, Tubal, and Naamah; Nimrod and his cousin Ashur, the two pillars of Enoch, the origin of Geometry, etc., and which introduced into the Saxon Charge by the author of the "Cooke MS.," whoever that may have been, became the basis of all the later Charges which have come down to us.

It is quite probable that the old 17th century Lodge, of which Randle Holmes was a member, dates from the earliest period of Norman architecture in Chester, if not beyond; its prior antiquity is proved by the fact that it had in the 17th century ceased to have any practical object in relation to architecture. The ancient Scotch Lodges in most cases advance such claims.

This era was the beginning of the "Rectilinear" or "Perpendicular" style of architecture, which continued in vogue down to 1550 From 1349 works were in progress at Windsor, and John de Spoulee, Master stone-cutter to whom

Anderson has given the title of "Master of the {333} Ghiblim," though in Ashmole s "Order of the Garter" the term used is Stone-cutter, had power given him to impress Masons; he rebuilt St. George s Chapel where the King instituted the Order of the Garter in 1350. In 1356 William of Wykeham, who was made Bishop of Winchester in 1367, was appointed Surveyor, and in 1359 Chief Warden and Surveyor of various castles, and employed 400 Free-Masons at Windsor. In 1360 the King impressed 360 Masons at his own wages, and attempts were made to punish those who left work, and this is the year in which the Statute law was passed against all alliances, covines, and oaths, so that the one may have influenced the other. About this year William Edington, Bishop of Winchester, erected a very beautiful church at Edington. In 1362 writs were issued for the King s works to impress 302 Masons and delvers of stone, and the counties of York, Devon, and Salop were to furnish 60 men each. These arbitrary proceedings of the King have an explanatory bearing upon both the Statute laws and the Masonic Charges. In 1365 Henry Yeveley, already referred to as a Mason-cutter, was director of the work of St. Stephen s Chapel, now the House of Parliament, and according to Anderson is "called at first, in the old Records, the King s Free Mason"; he built for the King the London Charter-house, King s Hall in Cambridge, and Queensborough Castle. In 1370 William de Wynnesford, Cementarius, was sent beyond sea to retain divers Masons for the service of the King. In 1375, Robert a Barnham at the head of 250 Free Masons completed St George s great Hall; and Simon Langham, Abbot of Westminster, repaired the body of that cathedral.

In Prior Fossour s time, 1341-74, the great West window of Durham
Cathedral was placed, and the Altar-screen finished in 1380 to which Lord Neville of Raby contributed 600 marks.

Green, in his "History of the English People," has some remarks on the English Guilds which we may run over here. He says that "Frank-Pledge," and the "Frith-Guild" {334} sprang out of kinship and were recognised both by Alfred and Athelstan. The Merchant Guild of London sprang out of various Guilds in the city which were united into one by Athelstan. But this led to a Craft Guild struggle, for their Wardens had the Inspection of all work done, all tools used and everything necessary for the good of their several trades. Apart from the Masons who had their own records, not mentioned by Green, the first to secure royal sanction was the weavers who had their charter from Henry I., though the contest went on during the reign of John, for the control of trade in the 11th century had begun to pass from the Merchant Guild to those of the Craft. It may also be added that the Masons had begun to pass from Monastic control and were becoming secularised. A constant struggle was taking place between the "Prudhommes," or Wise, and the Commune; those Craftsmen who were unenfranchised united in secret Frith-guilds and Mobs arose, but the open contest did not begin until 1261, when the Craftsmen invaded the Town- mote, set aside the Aldermen and chose Thomas Fitz Thomas for their Mayor. The contest continued until the time of Edward III., who himself joined the Guild of Armourers. Charters had now been granted to every trade, and their ordinances duly enrolled in the Mayor s Court, and distinctive Liveries assumed. Green adds that the wealthier citizens now finding their power broken sought to regain their old influence by enrolling themselves as members of the Trade-guilds (p. 189-95).

With the exception of the Masons Guild at York, which was continuously employed on the Minster, and other churches in York, and as these sent Guilds to other distant parts which ceased to exist when their work was done, it is impossible to trace old Guilds in permanency. When they had completed their labours they would report to York, and as workmen were required elsewhere, a Guild with the proper complement of Apprentices, Fellows, and Passed Masters would be sent there. In some cases, in small towns, a remnant would remain in permanence, and {335} it is to such as these that we owe a special Charge distinct from that of the General Assembly.

In 1377 the Guilds of London were reconstituted and became known as "Livery Companies," from their special Livery or dress. In place of "Guild," we now have "Crafts and Mysteries," and for "Alder-men," the Masters or Wardens. The Masons had sent 4 members and the Free Masons 2 members to the Municipal Council, but an old list shews that this distinction had been done away with and an erasure is made to credit the delegates as "Masons." The oath of the Wardens is preserved; they swore, well and truly to Oversee the Craft of Masonry, to observe its rules, and to bring all defaulters before the Chamberlain of the City; to spare no man for favour, nor grieve any man for hate; to commit neither extortion nor wrong, nor in anything to be against the peace of the King or city. The Oath concludes, as in the French formula before mentioned, "So help you God and all Syntes." The title of the London Company of Masons, at this time, was "The Craft and Fellowship of Masons." The "Court Rolls" of the Manor of Long Benynton, county of Lincoln, the lord being Thomas of Wood-stock, the youngest son of Edward III., has John Playster and John Freemason in this year.<<"Cole-man s Catalogue," 1882, xviii, No. 150.>> The Charters of City Companies of Masons was clearly a legalised usurpation of the Saxon right of Assembly, and modelled upon the older "Fraternities" of France; where such City Companies were chartered the result might be the withdrawal of the Mas-ters into the Livery, leading to the continuation of the Assembly by journeymen and amateurs. To put the question in other words, some Assemblies may have become Livery Companies, whilst York, and other northern towns, continued the ancient right of Masonic Assembly; and in regard to this the views of Brother Speth that the Masonic Assembly, and the Charges belonging thereto, is a claim that they were free "from" the Guilds is worthy of close consideration. Brother Gould {336} has mentioned several instances where Journeymen attempted to establish Guilds for their own enjoy-ment and protection, but were speedily suppressed by the Masters; in 1387 three Cordwainers had been promised a Papal brief for this purpose, but only obtained the privilege of the London prison of Newgate; a similar attempt of the Journeymen Saddlers was suppressed in 1396; the same befel the Journeymen Tailors in 1415; also the Journeymen Guild of St. George at Coventry in 1427. Un-fortunately all the documents of the London Company of Masons prior to 1620 have been lost, or we should have had valuable information as to the working of that Guild. Brother Edward Conder has shewn that the Company at the earliest period of its records had a speculative Lodge meeting at its hall, which was not confined to Masons by profession; and that a Master s grade such as is spoken of in the "Regius" and "Cooke" MSS. was the appanage of the Fellowship, by which "accepted" or non-operatives became qualified for the rank of Liverymen and Assistants who composed the

governing Council, and thus the esoteric or symbolic branch was allied with the exoteric one on the Council.

We will now return, in a few notes, to works in progress at this period. In the reign of Richard II., 1377-99, about fifteen pious houses were built. Between 1380-86 the building of the new College, in Oxford, was accomplished by William of Wykeham; the Wardens and Fellows, 14th April, 1386, made solemn entrance, marching in procession with the cross borne before them and chanting Lita-nies. Between 1387-93 the same architect founded Winchester College; it contains the arms of the Architect, which have a peculiarity worthy of notice; they are -- two chevronels or carpenters cou-ples between three roses; motto, Manners makyth man. It is probably but a coincidence that if we reverse a Master Mason s apron, it is a copy of the arms of Wykeham, whilst the motto, as previously noted, is found in the "Regius" MS., and in a book on etiquette styled "Urbanitatis," of which it is {337} possible he may have been author. His Master Mason was William de Wynnesford, mentioned here in 1370, and his portrait as William Wynfor, "lathomus," appears in stained glass, with that of the Master Carpenter, and Dominus Simon Membury, Supervisor or Clerk of the Works. In the old Masonic Charges there is a law that no Fellow shall go into the town at night, without a Fellow to bear him company, as witness of his good conduct; and Brother F. Compton Price, who has executed the beautiful facsimiles of Masonic MSS., points out that Wykeham had the same law for the Monks and Canons, who were prohibited from going abroad without leave of the Prior, and without a Companion.

From 1389-91 the celebrated poet Geoffrey Chaucer, was Clerk of the Works over the King s Masons, and it is possible that our old Charges may have had some influence upon his poetical works. Romsey Abbey has a pillar in the south aisle, upon the capital of which is sculptured certain figures supposed to represent the Dedicators of the Church; it has a trowel and a large square said to contain the words: "Rohert me fecit." Between the years 1389-91 two very beautiful churches were erected, one at the village of Shottesbrook in Berkshire, and the other at Winnington in Beds, but the "Perpendicular "style had not reached these places. St. Michael s Church in Coventry was completed in 1395; St. Nicholas in Lynn, 1400; the Collegiate Church in Manchester was in progress, and it has been supposed the builders met at the adjacent "Seven Stars," a very ancient hostelry.

Works were in constant progress at York from 1349-99, and even down to 1520. In the year 1352, the Chapter of the Minster issued regulations for the Masons employed, which are interesting in themselves, and indicate to us various particulars which shew how carefully old Masonic customs have been handed down to us. It would be an error to suppose that such Lodges as are described herein were the York Assembly; that body was an annual Assembly drawn from all the Masons within a wide circle. {338} Such Lodges might possibly receive Apprentices. The document from which we quote the following particulars is part of the "Fabric Rolls," printed by the Surtees Society: 1352, "The first and second Masons, who are Masters of the same, and the Carpenters," took an oath to carry out these regulations. After work, between May and August, breakfast was to last half an hour, "and then the aforesaid Masters, or one of them, shall knock upon the door of the lodge, and forthwith all shall go to their work." After dinner they shall sleep within their lodge, and when the Vicars have come from the Canons dinner table, the Master Mason,

or his substitute, shall cause them to rise and come to their work. Then they were to work from the first bell for Vespers, and then drink within the lodge until the third bell of St. Mary s Abbey called le longe bell. "The aforesaid two Master Masons and Carpenters of the Fabric shall be present at each drinking time, and these shall notify to the Keeper of the Fabric, and to the Controller thereof, all failures and absences."

In 1370 the Dean and Chapter issued another Code of regulations under which none were allowed to go away above a mile, under penalty of a fine. A new workman was to be tested for a week, and if "he is foundyn conisant of his werke, be recayde ye commune assent of ye Mayster, and ye Keper of ye werke and of ye Mastyr Masoun, shall swere upon ye boke yet he shall trewle ande bysili at his poure, for out anye manner gylary, fayntis, outher desayte, hald, and kepe holy, all ye poyntes of ys forsayde ordinance in all thynges yt him touches or may touche, fra tyme yt he be recavyde." In this same year Master Robert de Patryngton, and 12 Masons appeared and received Articles to this tenor: - "Lords, if it be your wyles, we grant for to stand at our workes trewly, and at our power." In the following year we find that this Master had under him 35 Masons and Apprentices, 18 labourers, and the church found them Livery of tunics, aprons, gloves, and clogs. {339}

In 1389 the Masters and Wardens of Guilds were ordered by the Crown to make a return of their laws, oaths, feasts, meetings, and if they possessed charters to produce them, and the existence of both social and Craft Guilds is admitted by issue of separate writs. A body such as the London Fellowship of Masons, says Bro. R. F. Gould, would not be affected by such writs, for it had the governance of the London Craft, and Anderson expresses an opinion, in 1723, that its members had first been received according to well-known Masonic forms. Masons in many parts, who had no Charters, would no doubt be affected by the Writs of 1389, and it is very probable that the order may have led to the compilation of a series of Constitutional Charges, which were, again and again, recopied and handed down to us in later MSS.; but it is clear that such scribes did not hesitate, at any time, to introduce supposed improvements of their own. Whether or not such a recompilation originated thus, the laws of the country shew that Assemblies continued to be held down to the 15th century, and Masonic documents prove their later continuance, and the variations in the MSS. lead us to believe that if there were Masons who preferred a Norman French Charge, there were others who preferred their ancient Saxon privilege of a right of Assembly to obligate Fellows, and pass Masters, and we will give particulars of two such documents shortly, both of which embrace legends of this date.

We will now say a little upon the Symbolism of the time both English and Foreign. Dr. Inman, of Liverpool<<"Ancient Faiths in Ancient Names.", has the following: -- "The ancient parish church of Bebington, Cheshire, has not only the solar wheel, the spikes of which terminate in the phallic triad, as one of the adornments of the reredos, but abounds with deltas, acorns, Maltese crosses, enfolding triangles, and Virgins who, like the ancient Isis, are crowned with the inverted crescent, the chaplet being still further adorned with the {340} seven planets." A very interesting series of Marks, cut between 1120-1534 has been collected by Brother Rylands.<<"Ars Quat. Cor." 1894.>> At Great Waltham there are some well carved panel heads of open seats, the tops of which in triplicated form contain the five-pointed star, with a ball in the centre. The

pavement of Westminster Abbey contains the double triangle, each angle containing a small one, whilst three triangles separated appear in the centre. During last century certain leaden medals designated "Moralli" were disinterred at Dover, and believed to be travelling tokens from one Monastery to another, ensuring welcome, some bore a five-pointed star, others had a dot at each angle, and the letter G in the centre.<<"Feem. Mag.," 1863, viii, p. 86.>> Masons as a necessity were travellers, and could not carry work to their shop. The Rev. Bro. A. F. A. Woodford, whose ability as a Masonic authority is unquestioned, has several times stated in print that there was found in the Minster Yard in York an ancient token or seal, undoubtedly of the 14th century, which had upon it words only known to Masons and Hiramites.

By a Statute of Henry VI. (1406) the Liverymen of Guilds were permitted to wear girdles of silk, embroidered with silver and gold. The date to the Will of John Cadeby is indecipherable, but earlier than 1451, as one of the persons mentioned in it died in that year. Bro. G. F. Fort in his treatise on builders marks quotes Matthew of Arras and Peter Arler, whose images in the Cathedral of Prague, of the end of the 14th century, wear in the former case his mark on a keystone "set in a semi-circle," depending from a broad band of blue, and Peter Arler s is a perfect square. A Guild Mason would say that the Mark of Matthew of Arras proves him to have belonged to an "Arch" Guild, though blue is a Craft colour.

The inventory of the Will here named of John Cadeby, of Beverley, Mason, has mention of several Zonas, which though literally girdles, may be interpreted Aprons: -- {341}

One silk zona, green and red, silver mounted, weight 17 oz., 32s. 8d.

One silk zona, silver mounted, with leaves and ivy, weighs 7 1/4 oz., 40s. 8d. One silk zona, silver mounted, with Roses, weighs 9 3/4 oz., 16s. 3d

One damaged silk zona, silver mounted, with letters B and I in the middle, weight . . . .

One zona, of mixture, silvered, ornamented with stars, 3s One zona, of black and green silk, weight 3 oz., 3s

The Girdle, then an article of clothing in general use, was appropriate to a Master.

The foreign churches of the 14th century are equally suggestive in Symbolism common to Masonry. The dome of Wurtzburg, in front of the chamber of the dead, has two columns, which are supposed to date from 104o but may be later; on one is the letters IAC-HION, and BOO-Z. There is an old church in Hanover which was building from 1284-1350, and which contains the circle, double triangles, and pentagon; in this church is also a statue of St. George with the red cross, and one of St. James the Pilgrim; at one time it possessed a charger with the Baptist s head; an inscription says: "The fire was a sore thorn to Stoics and Hebrews," which a Chronicle of 1695 refers to the fact of the burning of the Templars, 1310-3, a remark which would seem to imply a belief that these Knights were guilty of Monotheistic heresy. Hargrave Jennings says that in old representations of the Cathedral of Notre Dame in Paris, the sun and moon, with other emblems, are placed respectively on the two porches.

The Church of Doberan has many double triangles, placed in a significant manner; three vine-leaves united by a cord, and symbolic cyphers; there is also a painting in the same church, in which the Apostles are represented in

Masonic attitudes.<<"Hist. Freem." J. G. Findel.>> Fort asserts that in one of the churches of Florence are life size figures in Masonic attitudes. Many paintings of the old Masters are said to {342} exhibit similar characteristics. The Church of Santa Croce, Florence, over the main portal has a figure of Christ, holding in the hand a perfect square; he it was who told Peter that "upon this stone ("petra") I will build my church, and the gates of hell shall not prevail against it." Clavel states that the figure of Christ in the Church of St. Denis has the hand placed in a position well known to Freemasons; at the beginning of this chapter we gave other information hereon. The Abbey Church of St. Owen in Rouen begun in 1318, and completed by Alexander Berneval, who died in 1440 and was buried in the church, has a legend in regard to a very fine Rose-window which is identical with that of Melrose; the five-pointed star appears in the stone tracery, and Murray says that there is a tradition that it was made by an Apprentice whom Berneval, the Master mason, slew out of jealousy because he had surpassed himself. Other edifices at Rouen contain the pentagon. This general identity of Symbolism in various countries tends to prove a secret understanding amongst all Masons as to its meaning, and a similar Initiation of the builders everywhere, which as they travelled about ensured a brotherly welcome.

Victor Hugo in his novel of "Notre Dame" says that "there is an intimate connection between architecture and the Hermetic philosophy." He further alleges an alchemical symbolism in the sculpture attributed to Bishop William of Parys in the great Portal; he also instances the Virgins with their lamps turned down, and those turned up; the opening of the book (of philosophy); some naked figures at the foot of Mary; one with wings on the heels (Mercury); the Sower; Job (the philosopher s stone, tortured to become perfect); a dragon with its tail in a bath from which rises smoke and a king s head, demons and dragon s head; and Abraham offering his son Isaac.

In the reign of Henry IV., 1399-1413, six pious houses were built; the Londoners erected their Guild Hall, and the King founded Battle Abbey in Shrewsbury, and afterwards that of Fotheringay. In 1399 Hugh de Hedon {343} had employed at York 28 Masons; but fuller information will be found in the "Fabric Rolls."

In the reign of Henry V., 1413-22, eight pious houses were built, and the King rebuilt the palace, and the Abbey of Sheen, under the direction of Henry Chichley, Archbishop of Canterbury. At York, "our dred lord the King" had, in 1416, given them William de Colchester from Westminster Abbey; the appointment must have been an unpopular one, for, in the third year of his Mastership, certain stone-cutters assaulted and did grievously injure him and his assistant; the work continued here down to 1520. Cattrick Bridge was constructed in 1413, and the three Masons were to have a gown "according to their degree," but this will mean employment rank. Cattrick Church was begun in 1421, and the Masons were to have "a Luge of tre," with four rooms of "syelles," and of two "henforkes."

The reign of Henry VI. lasted from 1422-61, and he was an infant upon his succession. It is tolerably certain that in his reign the Masons were dabblers in the Hermetic sciences. During the time of Henry IV. Alchemy was made felony, by an act of 1404, which continued in force during the reign of Henry V. Henry VI. took the art under his protection and obtained the consent of Parliament, empowering three Lancashire gentlemen, "lovers of truth and

haters of deception," to practise the art.<<"Vide Scientific and Relig. Mysteries." Yarker. 1872. p. 62.>> An Act of Parliament was passed in 1425 alleging that by the "yearly congregations and confederacies of the Masons in their general Chapters assembled," the good effect of the Statutes of labourers was violated and prohibited all such meetings; no effect was given to this act, and it remained a dead letter on the Statute book until the reign of Queen Elizabeth, when it passed into oblivion, being annulled by other Acts.

In 1424 Prior Wessington repaired the tower of Durham Cathedral, and spent 1,454 Pounds of the money of the time.

In 1426 the Masons erecting Walberswick steeple were {344} to be provided with a house to work in, to eat and drink, and to lie in and to make "mete" in, to be built near the place of working. In 1427, William of Warmington began the rebuilding of the western tower of Croyland Abbey, and the vaulting with stone of the north aisle; his memorial stone, which has been engraved in "Ars Quatuor"<<"A.Q.C." v, p. 146.>>, represents him as holding a square in his right hand, and a pair of compasses in his left; there are other Masonic symbols carved here, for which consult the reference under the date 1113. There was a Lodge of Masons attached to the Priory of Canterbury at this time; as the Register of William Molash, in 1429, mentions Thomas Stapylton, the Master, John Morys the Custos, or Warden, both of whom rank as Esquires; and 16 Masons; all receive their livery, or clothing. Chichley also had livery, and these extracts prove that Christ Church Convent had a considerable body of Masons working at the building. St. Mary s Church, Bury, was begun 1424. In the contract with Horwood for building the Nave of Fotheringay Church in

1434 it is enacted, "that if the two said letters, or any of them, be noght profitable ne suffisant workmen for the lordys availle, then by oversight of Master Masons of the countie, they shall be denyd." If Horwood did not fulfill his engagements, "he shall yielde his body to prison at my lordy s will (Duke of York), and all his moveable goods and heritages be at my said lordy s disposition and ordinance." In 1439 the Abbot of St. Edmundsbury contracts with John Wood for the restoration of the great bell tower, "in all manere of things that longe to Free-masonry, and to have borde for himself as a gentleman, and his servant as a yeoman, and thereby two robys, one for himselfe after a gentleman s livery."<<"Archaelogia," xxiii, p. 331.>> Southwold Church was begun 1440.

In 1436 an Act was passed which required the Masters, Wardens, people of the Guilds, fraternities, and other companies incorporate, to produce their letters Patent to the Justices and others, where such Guilds and fraternities

{345} be, for their approval. This Act is directed against such bodies making their own laws, and it mentions the Chief Master as distinct from the Masons under him. It is a very valid supposition that it was this circumstance which led to the production of the Masonic Constitution for the sanction of the King, as several old copies known last century assert that it was. It has been suggested that the King s Master Mason of our large cities might be the head of the Masonic Assemblies to whom the rest were responsible.

There is a Catechism purporting to be the examination of a Freemason by Henry VI., which admits Occult studies; it was given to the world last century under the name of the antiquaries Leland and John Locke, and though possibly a forgery, in its present shape may have been the actual Catechism of some lodge given to these studies. There, is, however, ancient and genuine

testimony to the practice of Alchemy by the Masons. We instanced in our Chapter (VI.) on the Hermetic Schools, the nature of the Symbolism of Jacques Coeur, 1450 and that of Basil Valentine. Whatever uncertainty there may be about this there is none in the fact that Thomas Norton classes the Free Masons by name as giving themselves to Alchemical studies. One Richard Carter in this year 1476, had granted him a license to practise Alchemy.

During this reign Wainfleet, Bishop of Winchester, and Archbishop Chichley superintended the erection of various buildings in Oxford, Cambridge, and others built twelve pious houses. Fuller says of King s College in Cambridge, founded by Henry VI., in 1441, that it is "one of the rarest fabrics in Christendom." Churches begun, St. Mary s Redcliffe, 1440; Tattershall 1455.

In Scotland William St. Clair built Roslyn Chapel in 1445, and Mr. James Ferguson considers that the builders were from North Spain. Within it is a very beautiful Pillar called the Prentice s Pillar, to which a legend is attached which says that whilst the Master went to Rome for instruction, an Apprentice completed the work in his {346} absence and that out of envy at seeing the beauty of the workmanship he slew the Apprentice by a blow on the forehead. Three heads are shewn in the Chapel as representing those of the Master, the Apprentice, and the widowed Mother, but it has been suggested that they may equally represent Joseph, Jesus, and Mary, in their application to the Rites of Harodim-Rosy Cross. A similar Apprentice legend is attached to Cologne, Strasburg, Rouen, Melrose, Lincoln, and to other places, and though it has a distinct esoteric reference easily understood by all Masons, may possibly be carried forward to an Asiatic superstition that a building intended to endure must be cemented by the sacrifice of life. Brother Speth is of opinion that in addition to a foundation-sacrifice, previously mentioned, there was a completion-sacrifice made at the crowning of the edifice, and that it was a custom obtaining amongst the Teutonic and other races, of which he gives many examples.

Two documents, actually copied at this period, deserve ample reference here;

one is the "Cooke MS.," written about 1450; and of the other there are several duplicates, the "Wm. Watson MS.," which we shall take as our reference; the duplicates being the "Heade MS.," dated 1675; another is quoted by Dr. Plot in 1686, and Dr. James Anderson, between 1723-38 had seen a copy. Bro. Dr. W.

W. Begemann has investigated the "Cooke MS.," and considers that it is copied from one about the year 1410, whilst the second part or book of Charges is much earlier, by at least a century; the Preface being compiled in a west Midland County. Upon the "Watson MS., a valuable Commentary by Brother C.

C. Howard, of Picton, has been printed, with a facsimile, and he shews very forcibly that it is a more complete and unabridged version than the Preface to the "Cooke MS.," but this also has been taken from a copy at least three removes from the original compilation, which served both for the "Cooke" and the "Watson" MSS., which again might be amplified copies of still older MSS. It is probable that {347} modifications may have been made to adapt it for presentation to Henry VI., and the "Lords of his honourable Council," about the year 1442; and it may have been slightly modified in the next reign, when again copied, as little changes are made in all copies, no two being verbally alike. It will be convenient to place the two copies side by side, and to distinguish where the variations occur, to suit them to two different Masonic schools.

These MSS. begin with a description of the Seven Liberal Arts and Sciences, upon which all Crafts in the world were founded, and especially Geometry, which is the basis of all other arts, for there is "no handicraft but it is wrought by Geometry." The author s legendary origin of the Craft begins with Adam, -- before Noah s flood there was a man called Lamech who had two wives, -- "one hight Adah, and another Zillah, by the first wife, that hight Adah he begat two sons, that hight Jabal, and the other hight Jubal." Jabal was "Cain s Master Mason and governor of all his works, when he made the city of Enoch, that was the first city." Jubal was the founder of Music. "Lamech begat upon his other wife, that hight Zillah. . . . Tubal Cain . . . and his daughter Naamah   This son Tubal Cain was the founder of Smith s Craft   Naamah was the founder of weaver s Craft." Being forewarned of the deluge they wrote the sciences upon two manner of stones, marble and latres, one of which would not burn, nor the other sink. "A great clerk that was called Putugoras found that one, and Hermes the philosopher, found the other." Nimrod began to build the tower of Babel and taught the workmen Craft of measures, and had 40 thousand Masons whom he loved and cherished well. Nimrod sent to his cousin Asur 30 hundred of Masons, and gave them a Charge. Abraham "a wise man and a great clerk" taught Geometry to the Egyptians, and had a worthy clerk called Euclid as his pupil. A relation, varied in terms, from the more ancient form, is given as to Euclid s governance. The author then tells us that the Children {348} of Israel learned Masonry when they were in Egypt, that "King David loved well Masons, and he grave them (Charges) right nigh as they be now" and "Solomon confirmed the Charges that David his father had given to Masons." Thence the worthy Science passed into France where was a worthy King called Charles the Second; "he was a Mason before he was a King and gave them Charges." Up to this point the two MSS. are in perfect agreement, allowing for copyist s errors, but they now diverge in a remarkable manner, and we give a summary, side by side, the "Watson" MS. complete in itself, the "Cooke" having an older part attached: --

WATSON MS.   COOKE MS.

In the Watson MS. the account   In the Cook MS. the Charge given of a charge by St. Alban   and
account of St. Alban is
is very full. It gives Athelstan   much abridged. It says "soon
for authority that "Amphabell   after that came St. Adhabell into   came out of France," and con-
England, and converted St. verted St. Alban to Christendom,   Alban to Christianity, who gave
he was Steward of the King and   them Charges," "And
built the walls of Verulam;   after that there was a worthy   cherished Masons, and "made
    King in England that was called them good pay," and gave   Athelstan, and his youngest son
Charges "as Amphabell had   loved well the Science of Geo- brought them out of France."
    metry,   wherefore he
Edwin (son of Athelstan)   drew him to Council and learned purchased from his father the
    the practice of that Science to right of Assembly and "correc-   his speculative, for of specula-
tion within themselves," and   tive he was a Master, and he held an Assembly "at York."   loved
well Masonry and Masons."
The style of Cbarges differ   It is an abridgement of the

from the "Cooke MS.," and yet   "Watson MS.," and goes on to allusions are made in these   say
that this unnamed son pur- legends to "Books of Charges,"   chased a free Patent of the King as if
existing, which embrace   "that they should make
Nimrod, Solomon, Euclid, St.   Assembly when they saw a   Alban, Athelstan.   reasonable time."
 This omission
A general series of Charges   of the son s name, partially avoids {349} has been collected out of these,

a difficulty, as Athelstan had no   which do not differ so much in   son, but he had a younger
substance from the Saxon   brother Edwin, who went to sea
Charge, as they are differently   in a leaky boat and was drowned,   arranged.
Certain of the "Points,"   and in later times attempts were
such as duty to King, and   made to fix his death upon King   Church, and Employers, are
Athelstan. The MS. concludes   Charges to "Masons in general."   with the remark that as to the
There is also no distinction   manner of Assembly "as it is   between Masters ARTICLES, and
written and taught in the Book   Fellows POINTS, but this might   of our Charges wherefore I
be work of a later Scribe.   leave it at this time."
Stewards of the Lodge,   The author attaches an actual   Chamber, or Hall, are men-   "Book of
Charges," which is   tioned as in the "Regius MS."   admittedly of an older date than   The "Cooke
MS." may have an   the Preface of the MS. to the   imperfection, as the duties   point at which
it leaves off. appear but not the word Steward,
to which evidently the duties are intended to apply.

The closing lines, which precede the Charges of the "Watson MS." are as follows: -- "These Charges have been seen and perused by "our late" Soveraigne Lord King Henry ye Sixth, and ye Lords of ye Honourable Councell, and they have allowed them well, and said they were right good and reasonable to be holden; and these Charges have been drawn and gathered out of divers ancient books, both of ye old Law, and new Law, as they were confirmed and made in Egypt, by ye King, and ye great Clerk Euclidus, and at ye making of Solomon s temple by King David and Salom his sonn, and in England by St. Alban, who was ye King s Steward yt was at yt time, and afterwards by King Ethelstone yt was King of England, and his son Edwin yt was King after his father, as it is rehearsed in many and diverse histories and stories and Chapters."

To some extent the false chronology of these MSS. might be reconciled if we substitute Hermes for Euclid, {350} and Chaldeans for Abraham, but this latter would only be correct at a certain period of Egyptian history, when the Shepherd Kings were in power, and scarcely historically accurate. The chronology has been disarranged apparently by adding the Euclid Charge in a document to which it does not belong. The introduction into the Albanus legend of Amphibulus with Charges from France, betrays the work of an Anglo- Norman, for Britain supplied France with Artisans at that remote period. The whole basis of the "Watson MS." and the first part of the "Cooke MS.," point to a French original, and the laws might be considered more applicable, as given in the "Watson MS.," to a Chartered Company which had the supervision of

Lodges of the Craft; we consider, as we have before stated, that the "Watson MS.," may represent the union of two Sects, and the amalgamation of their Constitutional Charges. Our learned Brother the late W. H. Upton, Past Grand Master of Washington, U.S.A., thinks that Hermes may have been first described as "Lucis Pater," and that Euclid may have been described as pupil of Hermes, until some one destroyed the context by interpolating Abraham. In reference to the Alban legend he supposes that Amphibalus may be a later gloss; and that the Saxon text might be accommodated thus, -- "the good rule of Masonry was destroyed until the time of Knight Athelstan (a worthy son of King Edward), and he brought the land into good rest and peace, and he (Athelstan) loved Masons more than his father." The Edwin legend thus arising by substitution of the short Edwd. of the father. He would restore the Saxon thus, -- or tid cnihte aedlstanes daegs hwele weorthfull sunne cyninge Eadwearde waes, ond se sunu brohte . . . ond he lufode Craeftinga mare d oune his faedr (Eddwd.). Other emendations will be found noticed in the Appendix, with which we close this book.

Architecture is said to have been much neglected during the 17 years of the

Wars of the Roses, but in the reign of {351} Edward IV., 1461-83, the walls of London were rebuilt, and seven pious houses erected. Wakefield Church, Yorkshire, was begun in 1470; St. Stephen s, Bristol, same year; Blithborough Church, Suffolk, was completed in 1472,; St. Laurence, Norwich, in the same year; Swaffham, Norfolk, 1474; St. Mary s, Oxford, and St. Mary s, Cambridge, in 1478; Long Melford, Suffolk, 1481. Heswell Church tower, Cheshire, was in course of erection, and its Masons Marks were printed in 1894 by Brother Rylands. The King in 1475 expresses general dis-approbation against "the giving of livries, signs, tokens, retainers of indenture, promises, oaths, and writings," and this is about the date when the "original" of the "Watson MS." was made. John Islip, Abbot of Westminster, finished the repair of the Abbey in 1483. In 1472 "the hole Craft and Felaw-ship of Masons" had coat armour granted, -- "sable, a chevron argent engrailed, between three castles, garnished with doors and windows of the field, on the chevron a compass, sable. Crest, -- A castle triple towered as in the arms." The oldest motto, -- God is our guide, which later gave place to this, -- In the Lord is all our trust. With slight differences the Lodges generally adopted these arms. Brother Conder informs us that the Company, at one time, possessed the Constitutions of the Fellowship, presented to them in the Mayorality of John Brown in 1481; these were the laws of their own body as a Company, but are now lost.

"Germany." It is known that the Emperor Rudolph I. even in the year 1275,

authorised an Order of Masons, whilst Pope Nicholas III. in the year 1278 granted to the Brother-hood of Stonemasons at Strasburg, a letter of Indulgence which was renewed by all his successors down to Benedict XII. in 1340. The oldest order of German Masons arises in 1397, next follow the so-called Vienna witnesses of 1412, 1434, 1435. Then the Strasburg Order of Lodges in 1464; that of Torgau 1462, and finally 16 different orders on to 1500, and the following centuries, for Spiers, Regensburg, Saxony, Altenburg, Strassburg,

{352} Oesterrich, and Ungarn. ("Geschichte der Freimaurerei in Oesterreich und Ungarn," Ludwig Abafi, Budapest, 1890-1). The German statutes of Ratisbon 1459 and of Strasburg 1464, confirmed by the Emperor Maximilian I. on the 1st May, 1498, are but a more ornate version of those of Eng-land. They were to be kept secret by the Master upon his Oath, and were his authority, as

he had Charge of the (Contribution) book, and they were to be read yearly to the Fellows in the Lodge, and the "Brotherhood book" of 1563 mentions 22 towns where copies were kept. This book contains the following: -- LIV. . . . . .

   "Every Apprentice when he has served his time, and is "declared free, shall promise the Craft, on his troth and "honor, in lieu of oath, under pain of losing his right "to practise Masonry, that he will disclose or communi- "cate the Masons greeting and grip to no one, except
"to him to whom he may justly communicate it, and also "that he will write nothing whatever." LVI
   "And

"every Master having aforesaid Apprentices, shall "earnestly enjoin and invite each one when he has thus "completed the above written five years to become a "Brother by the Oath which such one has taken to the "Craft, and is offered to each."

Vicentius in the "Mirrour of the World." printed by Caxton in 1480, contains short descriptions of the Seven Liberal Arts and Sciences, similar to the description in the Masonic Charges, but adding to each an explanatory woodcut. A book was published by Veldener in Holland in 1486 which is said to contain symbolism of Craft and Egyptian Initiation.

The book of Ludwig Abafi says of Bohemia and Hungary that they had other Mystic Brotherhoods "Die Bruder von Reif und Hammer" -- Brothers of the Circle and Hammer. "Die Hackbruder-schaft" -- Brotherhood of the Hatchett. "Die Freund vom Kreuz" -- Friends of the Cross, which spread to Netherlands and were still holding meetings in 1785 in Wallachia, Transylvania, and other places. {353}

The Torgau Ordinances of 1462 indicate clearly the German qualification for granting a Mark, enacting, in Article 94, that no Fellow shall qualify if he "has not served his time or has bought his Mark, and not honestly earned it." By Article 25, at his Freedom he demanded a Mark from his Workmaster, and had to make a payment for the service of God. Article 12 enacts that if any one communed with a harlot he should retire from the Lodge, "so far as one may cast a gavel."

Of the reign of Richard III., 1483-5, nothing noteworthy is recorded.

In the reign of Henry VII., 1485-1509, various royal works were in progress, and about six pious houses were built. Reginald Bray, raised the middle chapel of Windsor, and rebuilt the palace of Richmond. The Savoy was converted into a hospital, and in 1500 the Knights of St. John elected the King as Protector.

In 1495 the law forbade the giving of liveries, signs, tokens, etc., being an official enforcement of the Complaint made to the Star Chamber in 1475. Various minor works were in progress which we need not particularise here; we may mention that John Hylmer and William Virtue contracted, in 1507 for the groined roofing of St. George s Chapel at Windsor; and in 1509 Robert Jenyns, Robert Virtue, and John Lobins, are styled "Ye King s III Mr. Masons."

The palace of Sheen was rebuilt after the fire of 1500 in the Burgundian style. Additions were made to Windsor, also to Hundsden, Bridewell, and Newhall or Beaulieu in Essex.

Edward Stafford, Duke of Buckingham, began the palace of Thornbury, in Gloucestershire, but went to the scaffold before completion. The King in 1544 gave a Patent to John of Padua as "designer of his Majesty s buildings," and a noted engineer, and Gothic architect, -- Sir Richard Lea, was employed as a Master Mason, and had a grant of the Manor of Topwell in Hertfordshire. The Church of St. Mary at Beverley -- already mentioned {354} -- was rebuilt, in the reign of Henry VIII. It has upon the 6th Pillar: "This pillar made the Minstrels." The city usually had five officials of this character; the Chief Minstrel had a long loose coat trimmed with fur, and the costume of the others was a yellow jacket, long brown hose, blue belts, and a heavy gold chain round the neck.

A new style in domestic architecture termed the Tudor had arisen and is said to be Burgundian. The Rev. Wm. Benham says that Richard III. left an illegitimate son, 16 years of age at his father s death, who got his living as a Mason, and was buried in Eastwell, Kent, thus recorded: -- "Richard Plantagenet was buried the 22nd day of December ut Supra" (1650), so that he must have been 81 years of age. Drake (Eboracum p. 117) states that he was knighted by his father at York.

The reign of Henry VIII., 1509-47, was more remarkable for other things than Masonry, Charles Dickens disposes of the King as a blot of blood and grease on the page of English history. Cardinal Wolsey and Thomas Cromwell built several great works, -- Hampton Court, Whitehall, Trinity College in Oxford, the College of Ipswich, St James Palace, Christ s Hospital in London, Esher in Surrey, and Greenwich Castle. Lord Audley built Magdalen College, and Audley-end. In 1512 the "Master of Works" at Christ s Church College in Oxford was Nicholas Townley, a priest. In 1520 York Minster was completed, and at the erection of St. Michael le Belfry, 1526, the Master Mason was John Freeman with 13 Masons, 2 Apprentices, 1 Intailer, and 17 labourers. In 1530 the London "Craft and Fellowship of Masons," adopted the title of "Company of Freemasons." There was in building at this date, and at the period of the Reformation: -- St. James Church, Bury; Lavenham, Suffolk, Bidston Church tower, the Marks of which were collected in 1894<<"Ars Quat. Cor." 1894.>>, St. Stephen s, Norwich; Whiston, Northamptonshire, 1534; Bath Abbey Church, 1539; Trinity College Chapel, Cambridge, 1539. Of this {355} century there is in Winchester Cathedral, a carved stone of the Freemasons Arms, and containing also the square, level, and compasses.<<"Ibid," i.>>

Brother H. R. Shaw points out in the "Banner," some interesting symbolism in the pavement of Printing-house Square, London, which would be of value, had it been shewn to be ancient. The manager of the "Times" told him the site was that of old Blackfriars Monastery, and, after the Reformation, of the King s printing-house. The square is slightly oblong and divided with granite cubes, by diagonally crossed lines, so as to form four triangles, each of which has a circle of cubes and in the centre an emblem: in the east is a "cross," or it may be a pair of diagonals; in the west is a five-pointed star.<<"Freemason." 7 Sep., 1594.>> An interesting find was made in digging a drain, near Arreton, in the Isle of Wight, in 1856, -- a basin of a species of bell-metal, which has on the outside of the base the double triangles, a tau cross within three circles, and at each of the six outer angles a star, and a seventh in the Centre, near the Cross.<<"Freem. Mag.," 1856, p. 845.>>

The German Rivius, in his "Steinmetzen Grund," 1548, terms the circle and triangle "the two most distinguished principles of stone Masons," and he also

adds that "the dimensions of the equilateral triangle are the primitive and most distinguishing marks of ancient cathedrals," of the period treated in this Chapter. As practical symbols they typified arithmetic and geometry, and were treated as the standpoints of all created matter. It is somewhat remarkable that an ancient emblem of the theological trinity of Egypt, the triangle with an eye in it, passed into the Christian Church, and is yet used as an emblem in the Oriental churches. It was carved in 1173 on the Sarcophagus of Bishop Eusebius who was interred at Mount Athos, we have also seen it upon an old Armenian sword.

The regulations of the Masons and other Crafts for {356} the City of Norwich are given in the 1903 volume of "Ars Quatuor Coronatorum." The Corporation possessed a "Book of Customs" from the 13th or 14th century. The Bailiff and some 12 to 24 members of each Craft had the examination, with power to levy fines, of the Craft guilds. All apprentices were to be indentured for seven years, and some of the 15th century are preserved. The Smith s Craft was at this period united with the Masons, and some regulations were made in 1469 because of faults "used by the Masons to the dishonour of their Craft," and it is stated in 1491 that no Masters or Wardens had been sworn to make search for defective work. An Apprentice roll from 1512 is preserved and there are lists of Wardens until the middle of the 18th century. In the Mystery plays they had to perform the part of "Abel and Cain." Each member paid an annual penny to the priest of the Chapel of St. John who "sang for the prosperity of the brethren who are alive, and the souls of those departed." Some changes took place at the dissolution of Guilds in 1548 but the "feasts" and "fellowships," and the priest s salary, were continued. In 1572 rules for the Masons are drawn in the "Assembly Book," and the Limeburners are included, with the fines each had to pay for various faults. The Masons were to assemble every year with their two Wardens and headmen, and were to elect 12, 11, 10, 9, or 8 of the members, and these had to elect new Wardens, headman, a beadall, annually, and fines are imposed for not attending meetings, when summoned by the latter. If necessary the fines were recoverable by distress, half of which went to the town and half to the Society. These regulations do not differ very materially either from the London Livery Companies, or the Scottish Incorporated Masters, nor from the trade Incorporations granted by the Bishop of Durham. There is no doubt such bodies had usually a Speculative Lodge held of them, as at London and as at Newcastle in 1581. In other cases such assemblies granted an annual commission, say of five, to Initiate. {357}

"Scotland." We will now hark back a little to examine the system which

prevailed in Scotland; it embraces the features of the English Livery Companies and the French Fraternities of Masters, with a much stricter control over its members than the English Companies found it convenient to enforce; and probably, at a later period, and even to this day through the Grand Lodge, may have had an influence upon the English Society of Free Masons, though the term Mason is always used in Scotland. There is no doubt that at an early period Scotland had its Masonic Assemblies,but early in the 15th century, a cause was at work which modified the Assemblies, by withdrawing the Masters into bodies, similarly to the English Companies. A Statute was passed in the reign of James I., 1424, empowering handicraftsmen to elect a "Wise Man of the Craft" as "Dekyn or Kirk Master;" and it was found necessary to bring Craftsmen from France, Flanders, Spain, Holland, and England; the reason

assigned being that all Scottish Men of Craft had been slain in the wars. The powers granted were obnoxious and abolished 2 years later. There followed upon this the constitution of Masters Incorporations granted by "Seal of Cause," upon a petition to the Lord provost and town Council. The Masons, Wrights, and Weavers received their Charter in 1475, which would confirm their older self-made regulations; the Hammermen in 1475; Butchers, 1488; Cordwainers, 1489. The members of these Incorporations had to contribute "a weekly penny," to support the altar and priest, equally a custom of the French Masters Fraternities. Trial-pieces, "essays," or examinations, equally with France, were exacted upon application for admission to the Masters Incorporations. On opening and closing the meeting prayer was offered up by the Deacon, as the Master was termed. An oath was required which embraced secrecy, obedience to their own and the Burgh laws, and to the Deacon of their own trade, and also to a higher Officer that began to be constituted in various towns, namely the {358} Deacon Convener, loyalty to the King and the whole Craft.

The "Convenery" was established somewhat later than the "Incorporations,"
the object being to unite the whole of the trades or Arts of a town under one head and Assembly,
composed of the Deacons or Masters of the various "Incorporations;" these elected their own president or "Convener" thus providing a supreme central authority.

We thus see the gradual transformation of the primitive Assemblies into "Lodges" of Apprentices and Journeymen; "Incorporations" of Masters; "Conveneries" of all trades; which were recruited by an accepted trial-piece; the private Lodges being held in subjection to the Masters-Fraternity initiated by "Seal of Cause." These various bodies never lost their legal status, and the Incorporations of the Masons and Wrights exist to this day; but many of the private Lodges, which were subject, or subordinate to them, went under the Grand Lodge of Scotland when it was established in 1736.<<"Vide Ars Quat. Cor." ii, p. 160; also v, p. 126.>> It forms no part of our labours to give a history of Scottish Masonry, but some information is necessary in regard to countries other than England.

The Burgh records of Aberdeen afford evidence from 1483-1555, that the Craft dealings with their employers, without reference to esoteric Lodge work, resembled that of the 14th century Freemasons employed in York Minster. In 1483 the Masons at work are "obligated be the faith of thare bodies," and there is mention of the Luge. In 1484 it was ordered that the Craftsmen "bear their tokens" on their breasts on Candlemas day; in 1496 that every Craft have their standard. In 1498 Matheu Wricht agreed "be his hand ophaldin to make good service in the luge," also "that Nicol Masone and Dauid Wricht oblist thame be the fathis of thar bodies, the gret aith sworne to remain at Sand Nicholes werk in the luge. . . . . to be leil and truve in all points." In 1532 a "Seal {359} of Cause," established a Masters Incorporation; and in 1555 it was ordered that "thair be na craftsman made fre man to use his craft except he haf seruit a Prentis under one maister three yeiris, and he found sufficient and qualified in his Craft to be one Maister." How are we to read this? After serving an apprenticeship he had to be made free of his Lodge, and could only become a Master and a Member of the "Incorporation," after an "essay." It is an instance of the loose language so often found in Masonic documents, by which we are necessarily led away in reasoning upon Masonic rites and laws. A law of the

Incorporation was in force in 1587 that Journeymen and Prentices, though not members of the Society, were to be entered in the books of their Craft, whilst apprentices were to be entered in the books of the Town, to enable them to obtain the rights of Freedom of Craft, as free Burgesses. It seems like a side blow at the Lodges, and the same custom was in force in the chief towns of England. In 1599 a Convenery of all the trades was established, and their rules of 1641 enact that all Indentures between Masters and Prentices shall be presented to the Town Clerk, within 21 days, for registry. Of course all this legislation, and the foundation of special bodies for the Masters, must have affected the status and position of the Scottish Lodges materially, and the same in England where Lodges were established in towns in which there was a Chartered Livery Company.

Powers which had been granted 1424 were restored 1555. A Dicreet Arbitral was issued by James VI. in 1580 by which the Council consists of: "The auld Pro-

"vost, four auld Baillies, the Dean of Guild, and Treasurer "of the next year preceding, and three other Merchants "to be chosen to them, and also to consist of eight "Craftsmen thereof, six Deacons, and the other Crafts-

"men, mak, and in the hail, the said Council eighteen persons."

Regulations follow as to the form of Apprenticeship. In 1590 the same King, 25 Septr., appointed Patrick Copeland of Udaucht "Warden and Justice" of {360} the Masons, but in 1601-2 the Freemen Maisons request the St. Clairs to procure from the King the office of Patron and Judge, and the document having perished by fire, the Lodges confirm it in 1628. In 1598 and 1599 William Schaw, "Maister of Wark" to King James, granted Constitutions to Edinburgh and Kilwinning districts, and perhaps also to Stirling and others at these dates; these have already been mentioned.

There is a tomb in the Chapel Royal of Holyrood of the year 1543 upon which is a stepped-cross; on one side of it is a compass and some other emblem beneath, on the other side a square and below that a square-headed gavel. In Glasgow Cathedral, on the inside of a stone window-sill of the south side of the choir and carved over the date 1556, is an eye, crescent moon, three stars, hand pointing a finger, ladder of five steps, square and compasses; these were pointed out by Brother W. P. Buchan who casts doubt, we think unnecessarily, upon the date given.<<"Freem. Mag.," 1869 (engraved).>> It may be noticed here, that the Lodge of Mary s Chapel, Edinburgh, has minutes from 1599, and was old then, and that these minutes, those of the Incorporation, and those of the Convenery are independent of each other, and confirm what we have stated, and which we shall refer to more fully. In the year 1543 the Castle of Wark in Northumberland, was repaired by an Italian of the name of Archan. Soon after 1549 the Wark Lodge sent a contingent Guild to Haddington, which afterwards went on to Aitchinson s Haven, and St. John s Kilwinning Lodge, at Haddington, claims to be an offshoot of the Wark Lodge.<<"Some old Scot. Lodges," 1899, Liverpool, Bro. Jobn Armstrong.>> The Belgian Masons, Tilers, etc., had a Guild-house of the "Four Crowned,"

erected at Antwerp in 1531, the walls of which were decorated with the 4 Statues, and with seven large pictures representing their martyrdom; the Guild is mentioned in 1423, and their Incorporation by the Magistrates dates from 1458. At Brussels at this {361} date the ranks alluded to are Apprentices,

Fellows, and Masters, but the Antwerp laws of 1458, allows an Apprentice, at 18 years of age, who has served 4 years, to make his trial-piece and become a Master.<<"Ars Quat. Cor." 1900. pt. 2. Bro. Count d Alviella. P.G.M.>>

A recent history of Spanish Freemasonry, by Brother Nicholas Diaz y Perez states that in 1514 Mosen Rubi established a Masonic temple in Avila, and that the celebrated Admiral Coligny initiated a large number of Spanish personages in Catalonia, and later in the army. We give this last with reserve. In Danver s "Portugese in India" is an engraved portrait, of which there is a copy in the British Museum, representing Prince Henrique, surnamed the Navigator, in the upper left hand corner of which is the level, square, plumb-line and weight, and open compasses: it was printed about 1620 by Simon van de Paes.

In Sebastian Munster s "Cosmography," printed in 1554, is the square and compasses in which is the letter G as a marginal ornament. "The Enemie of Idleness," by W. F. (Wm. Fleetwood), London,

1578, mentions a work on architecture and the science of building by Baptista Leo, a Florentine, and his "Secrete and hid discipline."

The compilation of this Chapter is much indebted to the collections of the late E. W. Shaw, and Mr. Wyatt Papworth, also to the Histories of Anderson and Gould, and the various papers of "Ars Quatuor Coronatorum." The particulars, though interesting in themselves, relate rather to the Craft in its operative and exoteric aspect; but they also shew the nature of the speculative and esoteric Symbolism, the plan of the Societies organisation, the nature of an esoteric ritual, the fact that Assemblies continued to be held; and that all things of the period of this Chapter point to a perfect conformity with what is known of Guild Masonry, and its imitation in the Free Masonry of to-day. The Statute law and the chartering of Livery Companies or Masters Fraternities, seems to have gradually shorn the Assemblies of much of {362} their prestige and privileges, and contributed to make the more extensive Assemblies stationary town Lodges, with a modified Constitution. The abandonment of Gothic Art about 1550, and the death of the operative Masters of that Art about 1580 accomplished the rest and left Free Masonry what it was in 1700. The Gothic "arcanum" had died out; its Lodges had become mere social clubs; but a counter movement was in progress under Inigo Jones to restore the "arcanum" of the Classical architecture of Italy.

We cannot conclude better than with the following quotation from Robert

Fabian s "Concordance of Histories," which appeared in 1516 (Pynson). The writer was Sheriff and Alderman of London, 1493-1502; and died about 1511, but his book was not printed until 1516 by Pynson. The following is from his prologue of 28 Stanzas of which this is the 5th and 6th. He may have been a member of the Mason s Company: --

"And I, like the Prentice that heweth the rought stone, And bringeth it to square, with hard strokes and many, That the Master after, may it oeur gone

And prynte therein his figures and his story, And so to work after his propornary

That it may appear, to all that shall it see,

A thynge right parfyte, and well in eche degree; So have I now sette oute this rude worke,

As rough as the stone that comen to the square,

That the learnede and the studyed Clerke, May it oeur polysshe, and clene do it pare,

Flowyrsshe it with eloquence, whereof it is bare, And frame it to ordre that yt is out of joynt,

That it with old authors may gree in every poynt."

We will only add that we think that this Chapter clearly proves that there was engrafted upon the simple Anglo-Saxon Constitution of Masonry a series of Semitic legends, and their compliment in the Free-Masonic ceremonies, which entered this country from the East in {363} Anglo-Norman times, with an improved style of building, of Saracenic origin.

Whence England derived its Semitic ceremonies of Free Masonry is not very definite but circumstances point very clearly to a direct importation from Palestine, extended by French Masons who came over from time to time and it is in that country that we find the earliest allusion to the Solomonic legends, and it is evidenced in this Chapter that these legends were introduced into the older Saxon Charges from that country.

CHAPTER X. FREE-MASONRY IN MODERN TIMES.

THE pretensions that Dr. James Anderson has made for the Grand Masterships of numerous Bishops, Priests, and Monks, should not be passed over with a shrug of contempt. Ages after architecture had been relieved from Monkish trammels the great architects were mainly Clerics, who have left their marks upon the soil of England. We have mentioned many such in our last Chapter, and these stand out prominently: -- Peter Bishop of Winchester, 1220; Edington and Wykeham, both Bishops 1364; the work of the latter, some author observes, is stamped with a genius, almost a style in itself; Prior Bolton, in conjunction with Sir Reginald Bray, 1503; and Cardinal Wolsey was a most accomplished architect, as is proved by all the buildings with which he was connected. It has been aptly said that, "the Classic styles are the prose of architecture, Gothic its poetry; the Classic its speech, and Gothic its song." The period of this Chapter is the "Renaissance Style," which arose in Rome, and spread to this country. The change of style was in part a matter of taste, and in part a matter of vanity as with the affectation of classical learning it became the fashion to treat the brilliant Gothic as a barbarous style. The Gothic fraternity laboured in bands or guilds, travelling about, and disappearing when their work was accomplished, and each man left his individual stamp upon the work: as each part of a Gothic edifice supports both itself and some other part, so the Free Masonic bands supported each other. Under the Renaissance {365} each building bears the stamp of one man, and

the architect came into being with the loss of the old Sodalities. With the Reformation we have the decay of Catholic symbolism, and the loss of it to the modern Freemason. With the Renaissance we find this symbolism, as a part of Catholic doctrine in the old times, carried into the erection of private buildings, and we have castles and mansions built on a cruciform basis; or in the form of variously shaped triangles; and in the shape of letters of the Roman Alphabet. It is said that John Thorpe, who erected many mansions in the Elizabethan style was a pupil of John of Padua. But it is to the Italian masters of the 17th century that we owe the preservation of the Rites of Guild Masonry.

The period which we have now reached in Freemasonry exhibits an organisation which somewhat diverges from its ancient Constitution; for reasons assigned in our last Chapter. The ARTICLES and POINTS of a Master and Fellow have become combined in one code, in a new series of Constitutional Charges dating from about the Reformation. York was now universally recognised as the primary seat of Masonic Assembly and London may have acquiesced in this from the fact that the Oversight of Masonry rested with the Company of Freemasons known to date from the time of Edward III., though it had a Speculative Lodge attached to which amateurs, and others for the Livery, were admitted.

Authorities are not quite agreed as to the original date to which we may carry back the numerous copies of Masonic MSS. that we possess, but there seems not the slightest reason to doubt that all our modern Guild Charges are derived from an abridgement of the "Cooke and Watson MSS.," which had become too lengthy for general use in the Lodges, and with its reduction in length was associated other changes brought about by the circumstances of the times. Of this new Constitution some 70 copied have come down to us dating between 1560-1700, and most of them no doubt have been the {366} Official Copies of Masters of Lodges. They are all verbal departures from some one abridged copy, made perhaps about the years 1535-45, but in what locality there is nothing to shew. They usually begin with an invocation to the Trinity, and are addressed to the "Good Brethren and Fellows." The Euclid Charge which is the sole feature of the primitive Saxon Charge, is condensed as in the "Watson MS.," to ordain a duly Passed Master or a Master of Work, and which, in the esoteric work of a Lodge, is somewhat equivalent to the Installation of a Master; but which would be inapplicable to a large Provincial Assembly, met to receive Fellows, and pass Masters, as arranged for in the Athelstan Constitution. The new MS. also agrees with the present ritualistic system, as it brings into prominence the Charges of David and Solomon, and the assistance of Hiram of Tyre. The Laws begin with a "General Charge to all Masons," collected out of the oldest Articles and Points, and then follows a "Charge to Masters and Fellows." Where an "Article" of the Master has been copied out of the oldest MSS. the word Fellow usually follows it, as if with the intention of claiming that a Fellow in a Lodge was equally a Master. Usually the distance assigned, within which attendance at the Assembly is compulsory is 50 miles, which gives 100 miles diameter in a circle round a common centre. All these later Charges are the basis of the esoteric receptions then, and still in use.

These later Constitutions are in main agreement with the "Watson MS." and the Preface to the "Cooke MS.," which state that the great Patron of Masonry in France was Charles II., the Karl II. of the German Catechism, and the grandson

of Charlemagne, respecting which we volunteered some remarks in our last chapter. But in the later MSS., however the correction has been reached, a return has been made to Charles Martel, who, though only Regent of France, was the accepted Patron of stonecutters in France before the 13th century. Possibly {367} "secundus" was a German error either for Magnus or for Martel and obtained credence in England. The instructor of Martel has a name that has puzzled most Masonic scribes, as he appears in endless forms, amongst others, Naymus Grecus, Manus Graecus, Mamongetus, Namus Grenaeus, etc., and he had wrought at the building of Solomon s temple with Ammon, Aymon, Anon, etc. It is possible that the origin of the name was from Nimes in Southern France, then from Namus to Marcus Graecus, a philosopher of the 8th or 9th century it is supposed, though not heard of till the 13th century, and when in the 16th century the name was disfigured beyond recognition, and Caxton had printed the "Four Sons of Aymon," which contains a Masonic legend, that Aymon was adopted. The name Aymon was used in baptism as Cornelius Agrippa gave it to his firstborn son. Simon Greynaeus also obtained countenance from his eminence as a Geome-trician. Brother Schnitger, in his Commentary upon the MS. Charges printed by the Newcastle College of Rosicrucians in 1893, suggests that the difficulty in regard to Namus labouring at Solomon s temple and then instructing Charles Martel may be got over by reading it that he was one "who had been at the buildings of Solomon s temple," that is had visited the site. All these later Constitutions preserve the relations as to Hermes, Pythagoras, and Euclid, and we cannot admit that the Masons who recognised these personages as, in some sort, their predecessors, were ignorant of the sublime spiritual geometry which underlaid their ancient philosophy.

It is probable that in time we may adopt a theory developed in a paper before the Quatuor Coronati Lodge 2076 by Bro. Dring that Carolus Secundus of the Cooke MS. is an error for Carolus Magnus or Charlemagne, and that Manus, Namus, or the man with the Greek name, was Alcuin Flaccus of York, also called Albines, who it was suggested might be the St. Alban therein mentioned, and who terms Charlemagne "the wise Solomon" and speaks of the erection of the Church at Aixe-la-Chapelle as the {368} work of this wise Solomon. The theory has the merit of rectifying the chronology, which is erroneous as it stands.

The importance of York as a Masonic centre would decline from various causes. In 1538 the Monasteries were dissolved, and building requirements ceased for a time; this was emphasised by the suppression of the Minor Fraternities, Brotherhoods, and Guilds. One of the Guilds thus suppressed at York had endured exactly for a century, and was named the Guild of "Corpus Christi" and consisted of a Master and six priests, who annually on Trinity Sunday regulated the "Mystery-play" of Corpus Christi when every trade in the city was bound to furnish a Pageant; this sacred drama existed at York in 1220

A.D. Another reason is that with the abolition of Guilds, the existing Livery Companies lost even the lax hold which they had possessed over the trades; and the Municipality of York, and other cities, had adopted a form of City Freedom, as early as the 14th century, which was granted by the Lord Mayor and Common Council to the Apprentice who had served his term of seven years. It was an Exoteric mode resembling the Esoteric reception of a Mason. An Apprentice was bound by an Indenture, in which he took upon himself

rules of conduct, which are practically the same as those to which, as a Mason, he would have been sworn in Lodge; this Indenture was taken to the City Clerk, who endorsed it "Entered." At the end of his seven years Apprenticeship he repaired to the Guild Hall, and took an oath addressed "to the Lord Mayor and Good Men," that he would keep the privities and maintain with his body the Freedom of the City. The Clerk then "Charged" him to protect the tolls and dues of the City, and conferred the "Freedom." We have not the precise date when this form began at York, though there are lists of Freemen from early in the 14th century; the same usage was in force at Boston in Lincolnshire, and lists of the Apprentices "Freed" are preserved there from 1559; it existed at Leicester, {369} Norwich, Appleby, etc., etc.<<"Ars Quat. Cor." iv.>> A like custom was adopted in Scotland, and ordered at Aberdeen in 1641.<<"Ibid." ii, p. 161.>> Smith, in his learned Essay on the Romano-German laws, which we have previously quoted, considers that the Roman Collegia were the foundations of our Municipal corporations, and says: "In England the Guilds appear to have been the immediate foundation of the old Municipal corporations. Many of the exclusive privileges, which are scarcely yet forgotten, and many of the customs derived from the Guilds, with regard to the exercise of a Craft, have passed into common law, though now disconnected with the immunities derived from the Municipalities." At this period, and for long afterwards, the Crown had ample cause for uneasiness in regard to the Assembly of any large body of Men in the North of England; and no other portion of the kingdom so strongly resented the suppression of Monasteries and Guilds as did Northumberland, Durham, and Yorkshire. Brother Francis Drake, the historian, says that their dissolution inflicted a terrible blow upon the grandeur of York, the sick, the infirm, and all sorts of religious persons were turned out of house and home to starve or beg. A formidable rebellion was organised in 1537 under the name of the "Pilgrimage of Grace," in which the leading men of the country, with the Abbots of Fountains, Jervaux, and Rivalx, took part. These Pilgrims took an oath of their good intentions to church and King, and at their head marched a body of priests, habited in their vestments, and with crosses in their hands. The leaders assumed characteristics such as Charity, Faith, Poverty, Pity. Their banner was embroidered with a crucifix, a chalice, and emblems of the 5 wounds of Christ, and the last mentioned emblems were placed on the sleeves of their robes, with the name of Jesus in the centre. The rising was suppressed in Henry s usual brutal manner, but the dissatisfaction continued to slumber on, and must have caused the government to look {370} with suspicion upon any considerable gathering of men, however innocent their intentions might be. This dissatisfied element was also very strong in South Durham as well as North Yorkshire, and extended into Northumberland. A second and final rising occurred in 1569, under Elizabeth, but was as disastrous as the first, but though these "Recusants" were often persecuted, and large numbers hanged, they made no further attempt to regain their lost position; it is however, known that they adopted secret modes of recognition, such as passwords, by which to recognise friends; one of these was Gibb, and Gibbs in a continental system was one of the 3 Ruffians.

We find nothing worthy of mention in the reigns of Edward VI., 1547-53, or

that of Mary, 1553-8, but the long reign of Elizabeth, 1558-1603, has much to record. The "old tradition," recorded by Anderson, that Queen Elizabeth sent

an armed force in 1561 to break up the annual Assembly at York is probably of an authentic character. He states that it was held under Sir Thomas Sackville, as President, and that by his friendly management the Assembly was allowed to continue its labours. There is an ancient song in reference to this which may be almost contemporary.<<"Rosicrucian," 1878, p. 464>>

The Law complained querulously, in 1548, that "artificers made confederacies not to meddle with another s work"; which is exactly what the Masonic Charges had insisted upon from ancient times. In 1562 all previous laws are superseded by Statute empowering Justices to rate the wages of journeymen and forbidding the exercise of trades without an Apprenticeship to such trades, which requirement is what Masons always contended for as a necessity of their trade. Anderson quotes the view of Judge Coke, as to the Statute of 1425, which he said was now abrogated, and adds that it confirms the opinions of old Masons that "he was a faithful brother."

It is asserted in Masonic histories that, up to 1561, York was paramount in Masonic Government, but that North {371} and South were now divided, and the existing remnants of the old Guild system teaches that the Trent was the division line; it is, therefore, probably a true statement.

In the feeble rule of the Masons Company and the existence of independent Guilds there is traditional basis for the foregoing statement, which seems to be represented by a Southern version of the old Charges. These MSS., for there are several copies, do not differ materially from the others except but in one or two points; they omit the Euclid Charge, but that seems to be an accident of the scribe. Edwin is said to have been the son of a worthy King of England in the time of Knight Athelstan, thus referring to their father, Edward the elder, and this Edwin was made a Mason "at Windsor." Hebrew MSS. are now said to have been produced at the Assembly which Athelstan held at York, and there is actually a Jewish profession of Faith before Solomon in use by the French "Sons of Solomon." The oath in these MSS. is confirmed by the Invocation of Almighty God, or as a copy of 1686, which is believed to have been prepared for the London Guild whence sprang the Lodge of Antiquity, has it "Almighty God of Jacob," in place of "by my Halidame." The most important script of this version is the "Landsdowne MS.," reproduced in facsimile by the "Quatuor Coronati Lodge," and supposed to have been in the possession of Lord Burghley, who died in 1598. There is some doubt of its alleged antiquity, and the changes made savour of Commonwealth times, 1649-60 when the Jews were readmitted. A critical examination of the several copies has been made by Brother Dr. W. W. Begemann, with the conclusion that there was an older version than any of the three versions examined, such might have been Burgley s.

If Queen Elizabeth did contemplate the suppression of the Assembly at York,

it would go before the law officers of the Crown, and the Secretary of State at that time was Sir William Cecil, a Lincolnshire man, who was created Baron Burghley, and is alleged to have possessed this {372} Constitution. He began the building of Burghley House about 1556, and it was continued down to 1578, and all details of the work were submitted to him. One of the Free- Masons employed was Roger Ward, Peter Kempe was Clerk of Works, and Richard Shute Surveyor. We read 10th January, 1562, Of "one freemason yt was hyred by ye yere working upon ye ij wyndows of ye courte" in the letter of Kempe to Sir William Cecil.<<Trans. Ro. Inst. of Brit. Arch. 1890.>> Burghley

and Sir Nicholas Bacon, who was Lord Keeper, married two sisters, and Bacon died in 1578, leaving a son Francis born in 1561, and created Baron Verulam and Viscount St. Albans in 1618-19. Now the following curious coincidences occur in regard to these three closely related persons of rank and ability: --

1. This peculiar Charge is supposed to have belonged to Lord Burghley.
2. The house of Sir Nicholas Bacon, called Gorhambury House in St. Albans, built about 1565, contains portraits of persons distinguished in the seven Liberal Arts and Sciences, and beneath each of these two Latin lines, expressive of benefits to be derived from the study of each: --

"Grammar" -- Donatus, Lilly, Servius, Priscan. "Arithmetic" -- Stifelius, Budaeus, Pythagoras. "Logic" -- Aristotle, Rodolp; Porphyry, Seton. "Music" -- Aryan, Terpander, Orpheus. "Rhetoric" -- Cicero, Isocrates, Demosthenes, Quintilian. "Geometry" -- Archimedes, Euclid, Strabo, Apollonius.

"Astronomy" -- Regiomontanus, Haly, Copernicus, Ptolomey.<<Vide "Royal Mas. Cyclo." -- Mackenzie.>>

3.   Francis, son of Sir Nicholas Bacon, wrote in 1624 the unfinished fragment called "New Atlantis, or the House of Solomon, or of the Six Days Work." Many foreign writers of note have erroneously thought that it led to the establishment of Freemasonry; but it is likely that the writer had the Masonic Society in his mind and desired to {373} shew how its value might be enhanced. The 1620 edition of his "Instauratio Magna" (John Bell, London) has as engraved title a ship between two columns.

In 1570 Sir Thomas Gresham built the Royal Exchange in London, and the movement to revive "the Augustan style" and depreciate the Gothic was general. The facsimile of a map of Portsmouth, of this period, shews the position of a "Masons Lodge," probably a body was at work on some building at the port.<<"A.Q.C." vi.>> In 1584 Sir Walter Mildmay founded Emanuel College at Cambridge. A colony of Spaniards settled at Galway in 1584, and many of their buildings yet exist, and are said to resemble the older Moorish architecture.

The north is in evidence in the year 1581: "The Ordinary of the Company of Masons of Newcastle upon Tyne, dated the first of September of this year, constituted a body Incorporated of themselves, with perpetual succession, enjoyned them to meet yearly to choose Wardens, &c. That whenever the general plays of the town called Corpus Christi should be played they should play the burial of our Lady St. Mary the Virgin, every absent brother to pay 2s. 6d., and that at all the marriages and burials of the brethren and their wives, the Company should attend to the church such persons to be married or buried." The Arms attached to this paragraph are -- On a chevron between three towers a pair of compasses extended. "Crest" -- A tower. "Motto" -- In the Lord is all our trust.<<Richardson s "Border Table Talk," i, p. 219.>> It would seem that the intention of the Newcastle Council was to constitute a body held of themselves; at the same time the Lodge may have long existed, and have sought a Municipal Charter to legalise their meetings. In reference to the "Corpus Christi" Mystery-plays, they are mentioned at Newcastle in 1426, but would seem from the "Ordinary" to have been on the decline in 1548, the house-carpenters, whose "Ordinary" dates 1579, played the Burial of Christ, and the Masons that of St. Mary. The Lodge may have been privy to the

Initiation {374} of Sir Robert Moray in 1641 by a Scotch deputation, and had late meetings of their own. The "Watson MS." was discovered in the town, and is signed by Edward Thompson in 1687, who was doubtless a member of that Lodge, the Arms attached to it are identical with those assigned to the body of 1581. It is now known to have come through the hands of Dalziel, a member of Lodge 24. We shall allude to these Masons again in later notices.

The position of this "Ordinary" of Newcastle needs a better explanation than that here given. Durham and Northumberland were a County Palatine under the Bishop, but Newcastle as an important military station was a county in itself. Previously to 1215 Newcastle was governed by Bailiffs, but Henry III. in this year ordered a Mayor and 4 Bailiffs to appoint a trusty Moneyer and Assayist. But it was in 1400 that Henry IV. chartered the town as a separate county with a Sheriff, a Mayor, and 6 Aldermen. The Newcastle "Ordinaries" begin in 1426 with the Coopers. The Skinners "Ordinary" of 1437 contains the names of the Mayor, Sheriff, and the 6 Aldermen. In 1527 the Weavers met in Carliel tower, and in 1532 the Tanners had the Black Friary. The "Ordinary" of the Goldsmiths in 1536 included Braziers, Plumbers, &c., and they had to play the Three Kings of Cologne (the 3 Magi who visited the infant Jesus), at the Corpus Christi. It would seem therefore that an old Masters Guild of Masons existed here which accepted its "Ordinary" from the Mayor, Sheriff, and Bailiffs in 1581.

Whoever examines an old Cathedral cannot fail to see that two classes of

Masons were employed on them, a class which did the level and square work, and a class which did the curved and arched work, yet their separate duties was one of their trade secrets. Surprise has often been expressed that amongst these Mystery plays there are none recorded as specially Masonic. Mackenzie states in his "Cyclopaedia" that an "Arch Confraternity" of builders existed in 1540 and enacted Mystery Plays in the Colosseum of Vespasian and expresses belief that it {375} still exists. There is some evidence that in 1561 Masonry at York was in a declining state, as the Records say that their share of the Corpus Christi plays was given to the Minstrels.

Incorporations also continued to be granted by the Bishops as Count Palatines. The Cordwainers of Durham in 1436. In 1559 Bishop Tunstall re-incorporated the Barkers and Tanners of Gateshead. Up to 1565 the City of Durham had been governed by Bailiffs, but in that year Bishop Pilkington Incorporated the Aldermen. In 1638 a charter was granted to the Free Maysons, Rough Maysons, etc., etc., of the Cittie of Durham.

We gather from the Schaw Statutes of 1598, the Warden General of James VI., that Edinburgh was a district governed by "Six men of Ancient Memory," who had to "tak tryall of the offensis," and these "six of the maist parfyte and worthiest of memorie" had to "tak tryall of the haill Maisons within the boundis foresaid." They appear to be the "Deacon Maisters," and Wardens of the old Lodges, and they were authorised to Pass Fellows of Craft, after serving a seven years Apprenticeship, and another seven years as Journeymen unless the latter was reduced by the Assembly, and after making a trial-piece. We see from this that to become a Passed Master a Freed Apprentice had to serve seven years as a Passed Fellow. A similar Constitution was given to Kilwinning in 1599, and their Six Quarter Masters were to appoint a famous notary as Clerk. King James sanction was awaited this Constitution, and possibly there were other districts that may have had similar grants by the Lord Warden

General. Thus we learn from a Kilwinning Minute that the Six Quarter Masters of Cunning, Carrick, and Barrowthrow in 1659 continued to meet once a year at Ayr to "tak order with the transgressors of the Acts of Court." There can be no question that these six in every case were duly Passed Masters and that they correspond with what we shall hear of as "Harods" in Durham.

For want of contemporary MS. ceremonials we will {376} occasionally refer to Masonic symbolism in several countries; for identity of symbols and the mode of their application, press on towards the proofs that Initiatory ceremonies were identical in all times. In Ireland a Mason s square was deposited in the "east" corner of the northern landpier of Baal s Bridge in Limerick. It bears date 1517, and was dug out in 1830. There is a heart at the angle on each side, and this inscription in one line at each side: --

I will strive to live with love and care, 1517,

Upon the level, by the square.<<Freem. Quart., engd., 1850, p. 330>>

In Coverdale s translation of Wermylierus "Spirituall and Most Precyousse Pearle," 1550, is the following:" -- The Free Mason hewyth the harde stones, hewyth of here one pece, there another, tyll the stones be fytte and apte for the place where he wyll lay them. Even so God the heavenly Free Mason buildeth a Christian churche, and he frameth and polysheth us which are the costlye and precyous stone with the cosse and affliction that all abbomynacon and wickedness which do not agree unto this gloryus buyldynge mighte be removed and taken out of the waye." (Cowderie s "Treasurie of Similies," 1609.)

In the old church in Hanover of which we made mention in our last chapter there is a sun-dial with the date 1555, and the letters H.B.A.S., which a chronicle of 1695 says alludes to Hans Buntingsen, "who loved his art, and was well acquainted with the compasses and square and the great secret thereof."

In the parish register of Much Wenlock in Shropshire is an entry of value, as it shews the meaning then attached to the word "Speculative," as theory; it refers to dates between 1546-76: "Burd. out of tenmts. in Madfold Street, next St. Owen s well, Sir William Corvehill priest of the service of or. Lady in this ch., which 2 tents. belonged to the sd. service; he had them in his occupacon in pt. of his wages, wch. was viii. marks, and the said houses in an ov plus. He was well skilled in geometry, "not by speculation" {377} but by experience, could make organs, clocks, and chimes, in kerving, in Masonry, in silk weaving, or painting, and could make all instruments of music, etc., etc. All this country had a great loss of Sir William, he was a good bell-founder and maker of frames." The same Register records in 1599 that "Walter Hancox, free mason, was buried 16 September. This man was a very skilfull man in the art of Masonry."

A Melrose MS. of 1581 alludes to "Loses or Cowans," and contains a caution

that "he ought not to let you know ye privilege of ye compass, square, levell, and ye plum-rule." The Master Wincestre who gives the Charge as a Certificate to his freed Apprentice, was evidently an Englishman, as he dates it in the 12th year of the reign of Queen Elizabeth.<<"Ars Quat. Cor." v, p. 129.>> "Be it known to all men to whom these presents shall come, that Robert Wincester hath lawfully done his dutie to the science of Masonrie, as witness whereof, I, John Wincester, his Master Free Mason, have subscribed my name, and sett to my Mark, in the year of our Lord 1581, and in the raing of our Most Sovereign

Lady Elizabeth the (22) year." Probably Robert Wincester was an English Mason settling at Melrose, and the Constitution is further endorsed thus: "extracted by me A. M. [in margin Andrew Main] upon the 1, 2, 3, and 4 dayes of December Anno MDCLXXIII."

Brother W. H. Rylands has contributed much information, at various times, upon Masons Marks, and amongst these we have those of Stoneyhurst, 1585; Bidston old Hall, 1590; Bromborough Manor-house,etc. At Ayton Church, near Nantwich, is a monument of 21 April, 1596, to Peter and Elizabeth Ashton; it has two shields of arms, one containing a five-pointed star, and the other a square from which hangs a pair of compasses.<<"Ibid," viii, p. 88.>>

The reign of James I., 1603-25, is Masonically important. When he came to this country, he had at his own request, been accepted a Mason, by his Master Mason John Mylne, who was Deacon, or Master, of the Scoon and Perth {378} Lodge. This is related in positive terms in the 1658 records of that Lodge, and the King accepted membership in it.<<A copy in "Scottish Freemason," Aug. 1894.>> He claimed to be a patron of the learned who designated him the "Scottish Solomon." A rising artist who had professionally made the tour of Italy under the patronage of Thomas Earl of Pembroke, named Inigo Jones, was employed by the King in 1607 to build a new banqueting hall at Whitehall, and Anderson asserts that at this time many wealthy and learned men were received into the Craft. In 1649 he and Stone were engaged to repair St. Paul s. Part of Wigan Church was rebuilt in 1620, the Rector having a Charter from Richard III. as Lord of the Manor. It is the seat of irregular Lodges in recent times.

In the reign of Charles I., 1625-49, whom Anderson claims as an Initiate,

many erections were made under the superintendence of Inigo Jones, who died in 1652 aged 80 years. Anderson (1738) cites a MS. by Nicholas Stone which was burnt in 1720, to shew that Jones "remodelled the Lodges" after the manner of the "Schools," or "Academies of designers in Italy," of which we gave a specimen in the "Cuchiari" of Florence (ch. vi.); he is said to have held Quarterly Communications of the Masters and Wardens of Lodges, and Nicholas Stone was a Warden of these Assemblies. Possibly the system of the Guild which built St. Paul s was the system "remodelled" by Jones.

The Stone family was actively employed at this time, and were no doubt members of the Masonic Society. Nicholas was born in 1586 at Woodbury, near Exeter, and buried at St. Martin s-in-the-Fields in 1647, and the records of the Masons Company prove that he was a member of the Speculative Lodge there before 1639; he had several sons; it is recorded upon the monument of his son Henry at Long-acre, that he "spent the greater part of thirty-seven years in Holland, France, and Italy," and died in 1653; therefore he may have been known to Jehtudi Leon mentioned later; he also seems to have been {379} a member of Masons Company Lodge in 1649. A somewhat interesting inscription appears on a tablet in the Chancel of Sidbury Church in Devonshire,<<"The" "Critic," 15 June. 1861.>> to the memory of John Stone, Free-Mason, who died 1 January, 1617: --
"On our great Corner-Stone, this Stone relied, For blessing to his building, loving most
To build God s temples, in works he died,

And lived the temple of the Holy Ghost,
In whom hard life is proved, and honest fame, God can of Stones raise seed to Abraham."

Mackey quotes a sentence of 1607: "Yet all this forme of formless deity drewe by the square and compasse of our creed."
In the year 1619 two books were printed in London, one having the title, "Keep within compasse"; the other, "Live within compasse." An old black-letter book on Bees, printed at London by H. B., 1608, is dedicated "To the Worshipful Master M. gentleman," and although the patron s name and profession is not given it proves the use of a certain title at that date. In Speed s "Description of Britain," 1611, we have some characteristic language of a Masonic cast, worth reference: "Applying myself wholly to this most goodley building, has as a poore labourer, carried the carved stones and polished pillars, from the hands of the more skilfull architects, to be set in their fit places, which I

offer upon the altar of love to my country."

Dating from 1620, Bother Edward Conder, junr., has given us some valuable information in regard to the Speculative Lodge of the London Company of Masons, which met, from time to time, in their own Hall, accepted Master Masons, and had a framed list of such, now unfortunately lost. The fees, 1622, are thus recorded: "As a gratuity to the Company, 1.Pounds 0s. 0d.; for being made a Master, 3s. 4d.; fee for entrance, 6d." The Company preserved "the names of the Accepted Masons in a fair enclosed frame with a lock and key." The Inventory (of {380} 1660 and 1675) mentions, "one book of the Constitutions that Mr. fflood gave." In 1629-33 the celebrated Dr. Fludd has various symbolic allusions to his wise brethren who are labouring as architects. The Lodge had also a set of 1481 laws for the governance of the Livery. In 1649 certain persons were admitted on the "Livery," after "Accepting Masonry," or in other words after Initiation and Passing as Masters. This proves that Anderson had grounds for expressing a belief that in former times members of the Masons Company had first to be admitted in a private Lodge; and also that Continental writers had slight grounds for their belief that Freemasonry arose at Masons Hall.

Brother J. Ross Robertson, P.G.M. of Canada, alludes to a boulder stone,

with square and compasses, and the date 1606 indented upon it, which was discovered in 1827 on the shore of Annapolis Basin in Nova Scotia.<<"Canadian Craftsman," xxvii, p. 206.>> Brother Hosier mentions in the "Bauhutte" of 1889 that amongst the portraits of his ancestors is one of 1624 of Jacob Hosier, which represents him decorated with Masonic emblems and using the Master s sign. In Derrykeighan, County Antrim, is a tombstone of Robert Kar, who died 1617; it appears to have Masonic application to family arms; the top is a species of shield: Quarterly, 1st and 4th, a sun, or star of eleven points; 2nd and 3rd, a deer s head upon which is a square.

A Lodge at Berwick upon Tweed has an old armchair of 1641,<<"Ars Quat. Cor." Plate, iv.>> which may be described as a carved shield of arms; a chevron between various Masonic emblems; in the lower division a circular body, apparently an armilliary sphere, and "1641" above the chevron a pair of compasses and square, and reversed, back to back, with the others, square and compasses; in chief a scallop shell between two circular or floral emblems, with a raised point in the centre.

Of Commonwealth times, 1649-60 there is nothing that need be specifically named. Speculative Masons have no {381} Lodge minutes of any antiquity in England, such as they have in Scotland, and though these are rather a puzzle to us than of serious value, our want of such is regrettable. Besides the paucity of the material to be found in such minutes, there is the fact of their dependence upon the Masters Incorporations, and a doubt whether the rituals of Scotland and England were identical though no doubt they had in ancient times been so. The Jews were readmitted in Cromwell s time, and Catholic attacks in France alleged that he founded Masonry. In 1655 the London Company dropped the title of "Free," presumably because there existed independent Guilds of Free Masons, and Robt. Padgett who signed the MS. of 1686, now in possession of Lodge "Antiquity," was not a member of the Company.

The Kilwinning records shew between 1642-56 that the Lodge consisted of

Fellow Crafts or Masters and Apprentices. Prentices on entering paid 20s. and Fellow Crafts at Passing 40s. Scots, with 5s. additional for their Mark. This incidentally confirms certain old Catechisms which make the Fellow Craft degree to consist of two parts -- the Master s part being the second portion. Scotland certainly had, in some sort, two degrees in their Lodges, whilst the Chair and Work Masters were in the Incorporations and had their trials upon admission; opening and closing prayers, with oaths as in the English Companies. In neither company, at any time in their history, does the Society seem to have confined the Lodge receptions to operative Masons, and certainly, in the 17th century, amateurs and gentlemen were accepted in both countries; in Scotland the non-operatives were termed "Geomatic" and the operative "Domatic"; thus distinguishing Geometers and house builders. Nor can we form any other opinion of the Constitutions during a thousand years, when they tell us that it was a Society for all trades using Geometry, and we see Clerics as leading members. A Lodge was held at Newcastle, by deputation, on behalf of the Lodge of Mary s Chapel, the 20th May, 1641, under {382} commission to Robert Mackey, General Quartermaster of the Armies of Scotland, to receive Sir Robert Moray; amongst those present were General Hamilton and John Mylne. This latter family were Master Masons to the Kings of Scotland for many generations, and for five they were members of the Lodge of Mary s Chapel; the last of them was buried in St. Paul s Cathedral in 1811, having been surveyor of that edifice for fifty years.<<Gould s "Hist. Freem." i, p. 151.>>

In 1646 Elias Ashmole was made a Mason in a Lodge at Warrington, and it is

now ascertained that the majority of the members present were not operative Masons. Amongst the Sloane MSS. is a copy of the Masonic Charges, endorsed by Robert Sankey in 1646; the name is a place name, and that of an old Warrington family.

The reign of Charles II. extended from 1660-85. Anderson asserts that he was made a Mason abroad during his exile, which is not improbable, and may have been traditional. In a proclamation of 1661 he advocates the building in brick and stone in place of timber, for the safety and beauty of London, the former being equally cheap. Early last century the clerical enemies of Masonry in France attributed a Cromwellian use to Masonry, but on the other hand, and with more probability, there has existed a Masonic belief that the Lodges were used by the Stuarts to further the return of Charles II., and Brother Charles

Purton Cooper, past P.G.M., has given us a note to the effect that "G" (Geusau 1741), who was acquainted with the Chevalier Ramsay and often conversed with him on Masonry, had learned from him that the restoration was prepared by the Freemasons, and that General Monck belonged to the Lodges.<<"Freem. Mag.," xii, p. 301; vide also Bonneville s "Jesuits Chasse," 1788.>> "The Wise Man s Crown," 1664, alludes to the "late years of tyranny," in which Masons, who are mixed with other trades in the notice, were allowed to write and teach Astrology; the affinity between the two must lie in the {383} abstruse geometrical and mathematical calculations required in both professions.

Brother George E. Turner some short time ago bought from a widow a quantity of Masonic scraps, amongst which are 27 plates, apparently torn out of various books, and referring chiefly to the ancient gods and Mysteries. These he printed in 1896 at Blandford, and, from the mode in which they were acquired we give them with reserve. One of these is a readable "set off," from an alleged work entitled: -- "Treatise on Phremazeonry," with dedication to the Earl of St. Albans, 1670. A fragment of printed matter on one of the plates, mentions a 12 mo. tome of 1539 entitled "Solis Adoraio," which alludes to Phre- Mazonry, and says Lord Danby (died 1643), Sir Gilbert Gerherd (named in sister s Will 1637), Sir John Brooke (created Baron Cobham 1645), "and many others; noted members of the Order," were of this opinion, whatever that may be.

The Scottish Kirk was tainted with the narrow-mindedness of the times of the Commonwealth, as is proved by an attack upon one of their own Ministers: -- Extracted from the MS. records of the Presbytery of Jedburg, parish of Minto, by the Rev. J. Thompson Grant. "1652. James Ainslie, A.M....called 11th January and admitted and instituted (after being sustained by the General Assembly). December 9th, 1652, objection having been taken because he was a Freemason, and the neighbouring Presbytery consulted previous to entering him on trial, the Presbytery of Kelso, 24th February, 1653, shewed that, to their judgement, there is neither sinne nor scandal in that Word, because in the purest tymes of this Kirke, Maisons having that Word have been, and are daylie in our sessions, and many professors having that Word are daylie admitted to the ordinances, " Two other references, 1678 and 1691, as to the nature of this Word, have recently come to light. The first is from the letters of the Rev. George Hickes, D.D., Dean of Worcester, amongst the MSS. of the Duke of Portland. He says: -- "The {384} Lairds of Roslyn have been great Architects and Patrons of building for many generations. They are obliged to receive the Masons Word, which is a secret signall Masons have throughout the world to know one another by. They allege it is as old as since Babel when they could not understand one another and conversed by signs. Others would have it no older than Solomon. However it is he that hath it will bring his brother Mason to him without calling to him, or you perceiving the signe."<<Vide "Ars Quat. Cor." vii, pp. 55-8.>> The other notice is from a MS. in the advocate s Library entitled the "Secret Commonwealth," by Mr. Robert Kirk, Minister of Aberfoil, 1691. It contains the following:" -- The Masons Word which tho some make a misterie of it, I will not conceal a little of what I know. It is like a Rabbinical Tradition in way of comment on Jachin and Boaz, the two Pillars erected in Solomon s temple (I. Kings 7, 21) with ane addition of some secret signe, delivered from Hand to Hand, by which they know and become familiar one with another."<<Vide "Ars Quat. Cor." vii, pp. 55-8.>> Much nonsense has

been written by Modern Masons by way of proving that Scottish Masonry consisted in a Single Word, but there is no doubt that well informed Initiates meant more by it than four letters, in the same way that Plato and St. John meant more than the five letters in "Logos." An Oath must have had some ceremonial.

The traditions of the ancient Masonic Guilds are not to be altogether despised. The actual Guild of York is said to have claimed to date from A.D. 79 in the time of Agricola, and there was a Carpenters Guild which claimed to date from A.D. 626. The former built a Roman temple at that time, and the latter a church of wood on the model of the Tabernacle of Moses. Like the old operative Lodge of which the Duke of Richmond was Master which claimed to date from the time of Julius Caesar it would seem to have been the fashion of the Guilds to claim from some great ancient work, thus there was an operative Lodge {385} at Berwick which claimed to date from the erection of the great wall to keep out the Picts.

The detached printed notices which we have of Free-Masonry in England during the reign of

Charles II, shew that small Lodges were scattered over the country, independent of each other, but with a copy of the old Constitutions as its right of Assembly, and with a formal ceremony of reception. All Trades are admissable, and gentlemen affect their company. Here and there, as we might expect, one Lodge seems more faithful to the old traditions than another. It is evident that in the 17th century the Speculative, or Geomatic, element was becoming predominant, and that an attempt was made to retain the Society in its old groove, and to keep on foot the general Assembly. This is indicated in the existence of several Copies of the old MSS. which contain a Code headed "New Regulations." It is quite probable that there was an earlier and a later formal adoption of this Code. Two of these MSS., the "Harleian" and "Grand Lodge No. 2," have been printed in facsimile. Yet we have no record, either of the date of these, or the place where the Assembly was held. They are supposed to be early 17th century, but Anderson says that they were adopted, though it may be readopted with the addition of an article limiting the reception to persons of full age, at an Assembly held on the 27th December, 1663, under the Earl of St. Albans. Critics admit that none of the existing MSS. are copied from each other and that there was an older copy not now extant. A version was printed by J. Roberts in 1722. which states that the "New Laws" were adopted at a General Assembly held at (13 dashes -- which may read "the city of York ") on the 8th day of December 1663. The New Laws, of this latest Charge, enact that in future the Craft shall be ruled by "one Master and Assembly," and that there shall be present a Master and Warden of the trade of operative Free-Masonry, and that certificates were to be given and

{386} required. The "Grand Lodge, No. 2;" "Roberts; "and the MSS. seen by

Anderson contain a Clause which is not in the "Harleian MS.," that no one shall be accepted if under 21 years of age; possibly this indicates the 1663 revision of an older form. Attached to these "New Regulations" is, for the first time, a separate Apprentice Charge, which closes with an oath of Secrecy, and indicates that Apprentices and Fellows had a ceremony of reception. A York origin for this form may be thought to be indicated by the fact that most of the Copies in which the Apprentice Charge appears are found in the North of England; the form was used at Bradford and elsewhere 1680-93; at Alnwick

1701; and is minuted in 1725 at Swalwell. Brother Conder, however, considers that it originated with the London Company of Masons.

There are no minutes now preserved at York of the 16th and 17th centuries, but there are other proofs that Assemblies continued to be held. There is a copy of the Charges which was discovered at the demolition of Pontefract Castle, where persons sent their documents for safety during the civil wars; it is supposed to date about the year 1600, and contains: --

"An annagraime upon the name of Masonrie: Willm. Kay to his friend Robt.

Preston upon his Artt of masonrie as followeth: --

   M Much might be said of the noble Artt,   . A A craft that s worth estieming in every part,   :
S Sundry Nations, Noables, and Kings also,   :
O Oh how they sought its worth to know.   : Masonrie." N Nimrod and Solomon, the wisest of all men,   :
R Reason saw to love this science then   :

I I ll say no more, lest by my shallow verses I, :
E Endeavouring to praise should blemish Masonrie .

    Another MS. was found at York circa 1630. There is also a mahogany flat rule of 15 inches containing the following names. It is considered that John Drake was cousin of the Rev. Francis Drake who was collated to the {387} Prebendal Stall of Donnington in 1663, and father of the historian of same name: --

. .

:   WILLIAM {Symbol: Hexagram} BARON   :
:   OF YORK, 1663.   :
:   :
:   JOHN DRAKE.   JOHN {Symbol: Hexagram} BARON. :

. .

    Before 1660 there existed a Lodge at Chester of which Randle Holme was a member. A Copy of the Charges, written by himself, is No. 2054 of the Harleian MSS., which contains the ordinary information and two fragments: -- "There is severall words and signes of a free Mason to be reveiled to you, which as you will answer before God at the great and terrible day of judgement you keep secret, and not to revaile the same in the heares of any person, or to any but the Masters and Fellows of the said Society of free Masons, so helpe me God." The second fragment is a list of fees, and no doubt a Lodge list, beginning: -- "William Wade wt. give for to be a Free Mason," twenty-five names follow paying sums from 5s. to 20s. Brother W. R. Rylands has shewn that it was a Speculative Lodge, embracing many who did not follow operative Masonry. In his "Academie of Armorie," 1688, Randle Holme, a member of above Lodge, says: -- "I cannot but honour the Fellowship of the Masons because of its antiquity; and the more as being a member of that Society called Free Masons. In being conversant amongst them I have observed the use of their several tools following, some whereof I have seen borne in coats of armour." Lord Egerton held a special P.G.L. at Chester 18 April 1892 to erect a memorial to this old Brother, and quoted the following words of his, as written

above 200 years ago: -- "By the help of Masonry the most glorious structures in the world have been set up, as if their art had endeavoured to imitate the handiwork of God, in making little worlds in the great fabric of the universe." The tomb of the third Randle at Chester, erected by his son, has the skull and cross bones.<<Vide "Ars Quat. Cor." 1897. But see full arguments in the History of F.M. in Cheshire, by Bro. John Armstrong. London, 1902.>> {388}
There is an interesting document at Gateshead dated 24 April 1671, which the Bishop of Durham, granted as a Charter of Incorporation of a "Communitie. ffelowship, and Company," to make freemen and brethren; amongst the Charter members are Myles Stapylton, Esquire (son of Brian Stapleton of Myton, co. York); Henry Fresall, gentleman; Robert Trollop; Henry Trollop; and others, Masons, Carvers, Stone-cutters, and various trades mentioned therein. It would seem to represent an ordinary Masters Incorporated Lodge of the time. They were to assemble yearly on St. John the Baptist s day, and to elect four to be Wardens, and a fit person to be Clerk; each Warden was to have a key of the Chest. On the dexter margin of the Charter are various trade arms, those of the

Masons, Azure, on a chevron between three Single towers a pair of compasses; "Crest," -- A tower; "Motto," -- In the Lord is all our trust. On the sinister side are the arms of the sculptors.<<Vide "Hist. Freem.," R. F. Gould.>> The Masons arms are the same as those in the MS. of 1687 written by Edward Thompson, and termed "Watson MS."
As a Masters fraternity it would hold Craft Lodges, and as Harodim would
rule them.
There is an early grave cover in St. Nicholas church, now the Cathedral, with a floriated Greek Cross lengthened, on the left side is a fish, and on the right a key. It is said to have had an inscription to the Architect of the Newcastle town Court, built in 1659. The two Trollopes who are mentioned in the Bishop s charter were Masons of the City of York.
The inscription to Robert Trollope is said to have been as follows: --
   Here lies Robert Trollope, Who made yon stones roll up, When death took his soul up, His body filled this hole up.
It may be mentioned here that Brother Horace Swete, M.D., described in 1872, a tobacco box, which he says {389} formerly belonged to the Jacobite John Drummond, created Earl of Melfort in 1685, and which with the date and initials "J.D. 1670." contains emblems identical with those of the catechisms of 1723.<<"Spec. Mas." -- Yarker; also "Ars Quat. Cor." 1901.>>
It is not probable that Christopher Wren was a Mason accepted at this period, though it is said there is an Arch Guild minute of his reception in 1649, but no doubt his colleagues the Strongs were such. Valentine Strong, son of Timothy of Little Berrington, is termed Free-Mason and was buried Novr. 1662, at Fairford, Oxfordshire. He was father of Thomas Strong of London; and of Edward Strong, senior, who with his son laboured at St. Paul s. Thomas laid the first stone 11th June, 1677, and brought from Oxford a Lodge of Masons for whom a special Act was passed to make them free of London for seven years; he died in 1681, and his brother Edward laid the last stone 26th October 1708.

Hayden in his "Dictionary of Dates" (p.51) mentions the Court of Arches is so called from its having been held at the Church of St. Mary le Bow, London, whose top is built on stone pillars erected archwise. An old record says that it was built by "Companions of the Arch Guild," and was designed by its Master, and was considered a Master piece. The "Bow-Makers Guild" included "Bow Carpenters," who had the construction of the wooden centres to build Arches. It is said that Strong was a member of the Arch Guild and that they received Chris. Wren in 1649. They reckoned seven degrees as in the Craft, but where the latter held, as symbols three straight rods to form a "square," the Arch-i- tectus, of whom there were three, had curved rods with which to form a "circle." They, only, used compasses and employed themselves in curved, and in Assemblies they sat in circular and not in square fashion.
Elias Ashmole records his own presence at a Lodge in London in 1682, and
Brother Conder makes no doubt that it was the Speculative Lodge held at Masons Hall {390} by the Company, 10th March 1682. Ashmole says that he was the Senior Fellow present amongst a number whose names he gives, and that there was admitted into the Fellowship of Free Masons, Sir William Wilson, Knight; Captain Richard Borthwick; Mr. William Woodman; Mr. William Grey;

Mr. Samuel Taylour; and Mr. William Wise. These notices, and those which follow, have been so often printed verbatim, that we give only a summary of them.<<Vide "Kneph;" also Gould s "Hist. Mas."; also a "West Yorks reprint.">>

The next printed notice is one of 1686, by Robert Plot, LLD., in his "Natural History of Staffordshire," wherein he says: -- "To these add the "customs" relating to the "County" whereof they have one of admitting men into the Society of Free-Masons, that in the Moorelands of this County seems to be of greater request than anywhere else; though I find the custom spread more or less over all the nation." "For here I found persons of the most eminent quality that did not disdain to be of this "Fellowship." Nor indeed need they, were it of that "antiquity" and "honour" that is pretended in a large "parchment volume" that they have amongst them containing the History and Rules of the Craft of Masonry." He then goes on to give an account from the old Masonic MSS., and the nature of the copy which he had seen is indicated by his stating that "these Charges and manners were after perused and approved by King Henry VI. and his Council." He then describes the mode of admission, with signs whereby they are known to each other, and the obligations of mutual assistance. He then comments in an abusive manner upon the Society, and thinks the old Acts against the Society ought to be revived.<<Vide "Kneph;" also Gould s "Hist. Mas."; also a "West Yorks reprint.">> The names of Ashmole, Boyle, and Wren, appear amongst the subscribers to the work.

Aubrey next mentions the Society in his "Natural History of Wiltshire" (page 277): -- "Sir William Dugdale told me many years since, that about Henry, the Third s time, the Pope gave a Bull or Patent to a company of Italian Free- Masons to travel up and down over all Europe to {391} build churches. . . . . The manner of their adoption is very formall, and with an oath of secrecy."<<Vide "Kneph;" also Gould s "Hist. Mas."; also a "West Yorks reprint.">> "Memorandum, -- This day, May the 18th being Monday 1691, after Rogation Sunday, is a great convention at St. Paul s Church of the Fraternity of Adopted Masons, when Sir C. Wren is to be Adopted a Brother, and Sir Henry Gooderic of the Tower, and divers others. There have been Kings that have been of this Sodality."

There is no doubt these three interesting accounts give an accurate view of the state of Freemasonry in England at the time.

Both an "Arch" and "Square" Guild existed at St. Paul s in 1675 and minutes have been preserved with extreme care. Its ceremonies are known to the writer and it sent a branch into Derbyshire to build Chatsworth, though in the jurisdiction of York. Some 30 or 40 years ago, an Assembly of about 400 could be expected annually and it is not yet extinct. The St. Paul s Guild was quite independent of the Masons Company which in 1677 obtained a Charter from the King. One of their Initiates is now at Assuan, and affirms that an ancient Jewish Guild exists there, and that they practise Solomonian ceremonies with exactly the same rites as he received in 1866-76. They have a plan of a quarry, of three rooms through which the stone is perfected, and near thereto are other three for the officers, and a "site" for the building. Egypt has a "Slant Masons Guild" unknown here.

A properly constructed Lodge room in these several offices or yards would

have double folding doors, forming a porch to each, where the preparation takes place. Solomon s temple is said to have had only a single door in the East. The 1st Officer sits in the West, the 2nd in the East, and the 3rd in the North; and this applies to all the six sections; in the Modern Freemasonry of 1717 they sit East, South, and West, or with their backs to their assigned duties. Their carpet has squares of one {392} cubit and the border is a lozenge 8 x 6 inches, a figure which includes the 3-4-5 angle four times repeated.

All Stones are sent from the Quarry to the 1st yard and dressed 1/16th larger than required; in the 2nd yard they are trued to their required size; and in the 3rd are marked and fitted for the site. The 5th, 6th, 7th Offices are Overseers.

Now as to the ceremony continued to our own day; the Candidate passes through the same process, and as a "living stone," is first taken as a boy rough dressed, then polished, and advanced.

Ist Degree "Apprentice," received by a ceremony similar to the Ist Degree in Speculative Freemasonry. Three officers are sent out to prepare him in the Porch. He bathes as in the ancient Mysteries, is refreshed with food, clothed in the white Roman Cloak, examined by the doctor, and finally admitted on the report of the three officers sent out. He remains a brother 7 years, but is not a Free-Mason as in the speculative system.

2nd Degree "Fellow," at about 21 years of age the Brother applies to be relieved of his Bond; is accepted as a square Fellow by a ceremony similar to the 2nd Degree of modern Freemasonry.

3rd Degree "Super-Fellow," after 12 months is "Marked" as a "living stone," and sent to the "site." He is instructed in marking and fitting the actual stone.

4th Degree "Super-Fellow, Erector," knowing the system of Marking he knows how to join the stones and is himself erected in that position. If it has any connection with Modern Masonry it is the 1st part of 3rd Degree. The two sections, however, are found in the degree of Mark Man and Master.

5th Degree "Superintendent." These represent the 3,300 Menatzchim of Solomon. They are foremen, and were of old termed "cures" or Wardens under the Master. Receives technical instruction. Has 10 men under him as Intendant.

6th Degree Passed Masters. These are the ancient Harods or Chiefs of whom there were 15. The qualification, absolutely {393} required, is that of a modern

Architect. The ceremony of reception is of a most solemn character, and cannot be given publicly.

7th Degree "Grand Master." There are three of these, co-equal, received in private. The degree has no analogy in Modern Freemasonry, except in the three Principals of a Royal Arch Chapter, which seems to have restored a portion of the old Guild ceremonial.

"Annual Commemorations," given 2nd and 30th October. (1) Laying Foundation and fixing the centre by 3, 4, 5, and by the 5 Points; there is a portion referring to the 2nd temple which has originated the Modern Royal Arch degree. (2) A tragedy, and Solomon appoints Adoniram the 3rd G.M.M.; the 2nd part of the Modern 3rd Degree is taken from this. (3) The Dedication. There is a symbolical sacrifice in the 1st or Foundation. These Rites should be performed by the Grand Master, acting in the 6th Degree and transferred to the site of the Temple or 4th Degree. -- All these commemorative ceremonies are Semitic, the rest might equally appertain to any nation. When first I heard of these ceremonies in 1856 the Guild could number 400 members at the annual Drama.

There is a curious analogy between the seven "degrees" of the Guild and the seven "ranks" of the

London Company of Masons, which had a Charter of Incorporation, granted, in 1677, with a 7 mile radius: Conder gives these ranks as follows (p. 139): -- (1) Apprentice, bound for 7 years to a member, and paid 2s 6d; (2) Freedom or Yeomandry; (3) the Livery or robes; (4) the Court of Assistants; (5) Renter Warden; (6) Upper Warden; (7) Master in the Chair; these would have to be sworn though no ceremony is mentioned. They had however the Guild Society s branch, and Conder considers that they were termed "Accepted," because they were received as amateurs to qualify them for acceptance into the Livery of the Company.

The Guild Masons say that before the advent of Modern Freemasonry they had four Head Guild Houses {394} which ruled different parts of the country and are those given by Anderson. As I read Anderson, who wrote in 1738, guided by what we actually know before 1738, he can only mean that when, in 1716, Anthony Sayer was elected Grand Master, by "some old brothers," he had one or more of some, or of all these Guilds, or is supposed to have had them. It seems an attempt to hoodwink the reader. No. 1, the Antiquity, certainly continued to meet for some years at the Goose and Gridiron, the House of St. Paul s Guild, but Modern Nos. 2, 3 and 4, seem never to have "met" at the other three Guild houses.

The reign of James II., 1685-8, was too short to leave its influence upon Free- Masonry but much of importance must have occurred in that of William III., 1689-1702, had the particulars been preserved. We do not doubt that 16 May 1691 is the actual date of the Initiation of Sir C. Wren as an Accepted Mason; even though a Master of the Arch Guild 1649; and with the Convention of St. Paul s it may be conjectured that the connection of the Accepted Masons with the Livery Company ceased to exist, if any existed, which the Arch Guilds deny. The notorious Prichard, who wrote in 1730 makes 1691 to be the actual beginning of the "Quarterly Communications," which ended in the formation of the Grand Lodge of 1717 by the dissidents who had been members of a real Guild. Dr Anderson in his Constitutions (1738) writes that a Lodge met at St. Thomas Hospital in 1691 at the instance of Sir Thomas Clayton; and, on the

authority of "some brothers living in 1730" that six other Lodges then assembled in London; and besides the old Lodge of St. Paul s (whose bastard offspring, according to the Guild, was the Lodge of Antiquity), which possesses a copy of the Masonic Charges written by "Robert Padgett, Clearke to the Worshipful Society of Free-Masons for the City of London," he mentions one in Piccadilly opposite St. James Church; one near Westminster Abbey, which may be represented in a printed catechism of {395} 1723 alluding to the "Lodge of St. Stephens"; one in Covent Garden; one in Holborn; another on Tower Hill; and some others that assembled at stated times, these were probably no more than meetings at Inns frequented by Masons. No doubt the great fire of London, and the efforts of Sir C. Wren in restoring the city after that calamity, would attract people from all parts of England, Scotland, and Ireland, and lead to the Assemblies of Masons.

In the North there is a copy of the old MSS. at York, of 1680, which concludes "that at every meeting or Assembly they pray heartily for all Christians." Another copy of 1693, includes the Apprentice Charge, and has a peculiar reading which is doubtless ill translated Latin, it reads, -- "Then one of the Elders takeing the Booke, and that hee or "shee" that is to be made Mason, shall lay their hands thereon, and the Charge shall be given." It concludes, -- "These be the constitucions of the Noble and famous History, called Masonry, made and now in practise by the best Masters and Fellowes, for directing and guiding all that use the said Craft. Scripted p. me, vicesimo tertio die Octobris, Anno Regni Regis et Regina Gulielmy et Marie quinto annoque domini 1693. Mark Kypling. The names of the Lodg, -- William Simpson, Anthony Horsman, Christopher Thompson, Christopher Gill, Mr. Isaac Brent, Lodg. Ward."

The Duke of Richmond seems to have been Master of a Lodge at Chichester in 1696. The Minutes of Grand Lodge of 2 March 1732 contain an entry that Edward Hall was "Made a Mason by the late Duke of Richmond six and thirty years ago." Hall s petition was recommended by the Duke s son, who was then Grand Master, and the Chichester Lodge was registered by Grand Lodge as dating from the time of Julius Caesar.<<"Freemasonry in Havant." -- Thos. Francis. 1892.>>

A Lodge met at Alnwick, Northumberland, in 1701; it was an operative Craft Lodge, and may have kept more {396} closely to old customs from its nearness to Scotland, where the ceremonial work was practically extinct though the legal basis of Masonic Guilds was still in force. We give two of the regulations of 1701 in regard to Entering Apprentices, and Accepting Fellows,, -- "5th item. That no Mason shall take an Apprentice and give him his Charge within one whole year after. Not so doing the Master shall pay for any such offence 0Pounds 3 4." "9th item. There shall noe Apprentice, after he has served his seven years, be admitted or Accepted but on the Feast of Michaell the Archangel, paying to the Master and Wardens 0Pounds 6 8." A minute of 21 January 1708, decrees, "that for the future no Master, Warden, or Fellow shall appear on St. John s day, or attend the church service at Alnwick, without his apron, and common square fixt in the belt thereof."

We must carefully guard ourselves from the supposition that these (Passed)

Wardens and Masters, are those now termed such; they were the Menatzchim and Harods, or Superintendents and Passed Masters of the old Guild ceremonies. In the County of Durham up to 1813, Wardens, as well as other

officers, took the same O.B. as the Master. The Guilds O.B. the Master in the 6th Degree and the Minor officers in the 5th Degree Lodge.

A similar operative Lodge existed in Durham, and is supposed to have been first established at Winlaton circa 1690, by a German iron Master, which art had been established at Solingen from early centuries, from Damascus, thence it removed to Swalwell in 1725. This last date is later than the period with which we intended to close this Chapter, but as it is considered to date from 1690, and as its Lodge customs were similar to those at Alnwick, and were maintained to the last unaltered, it is not inappropriate here. Its regulations are minuted in 1725. The "Penal Laws," that when a youth was taken as Apprentice by a member of the Lodge, his Master was required to "Enter" him within 40 days, in contrast to the one year at Alnwick, and a small fee was charged. {397} The form by which the Apprentice was "Entered" is given in the Minute Book, and is an abridgement of the history given in our Charge. Of course the Apprentice Charges, known to date between 1600-63, are those he would be sworn to keep. Nothing is said about Secrets, but the 8th Penal Laws imposes a fine of 10 Pounds, "not faithfully to keep the 3 fraternal signs, and all points of fellowship." When the Apprenticeship expired the youth was made free of his Craft by the full ceremony. On the 21 March 1735 the Lodge went under the Grand Lodge of London, but retained its old customs intact for over 30 years afterwards. But we now read of two Masters grades, the one termed Harodim, spelled in the minutes Highrodiam, given in a "Grand Lodge," and the other termed "English Master," and the presumption is very strong, and especially as a mutual recognition of fees are made, that Harodim was their old Passed Master s Ceremony, but we shall again refer to the nature of these Rites in our next Chapter, as operative Masons. There was also an independent Lodge at Hexham, but nothing is known of its history.

In the Minute Book of the Haughfoot Lodge, Scotland, there is an entry under

date 22 Decr. 1701, after a missing leaf, which clearly alludes to Fellow Craft work, as it says, -- "Of entrie as the Apprentice did leaving out the common Juge (Gudge? Luge); they then whisper the word as before, and the Master Mason grips his hand after the ordinary way." As we understand it, the "common," or Apprentice part, who is a rough dresser, was omitted from the ceremony, and the Fellowcraft word was given in a manner similar to the former degree. But the Scottish system seems to have been so loose that very little reliance can be placed upon what we meet with in their minutes, as a general custom, and it would appear that, at times, Apprentices were present when a higher ceremony was conferred, and that the signs, tokens, and words, were communicated privately, whispered, shewn in the Bible, or given in a separate room. The regulations {398} of the old Dumfries Lodge, 20th May, 1687, enact that on Entering Apprentices a fee of 10 Pounds Scots had to be paid, and when afterwards passed as Fellow Craft a fee of 5 Pounds Scots, in each case besides gloves and entertainment. (A Scots Pound is 1 shilling.)

If Professor Robison is correct in his conclusions as to the operative Masonry

of Germany, and he seems to have carefully studied the subject, the instruction and therefore the ceremonies varied in that country. . He says that there were "Wort Maurers," and "Schrift Maurers;" and that there were Borough Laws enjoining the Masters to give employment to Journeymen who had the proper words and signs; that some Cities had more.extensive privileges in this respect than others; that the Word given at Wetzler entitled the possessor to

work over the whole empire; and that we may infer from some Municipal decisions that the Master gave a Word and Token, for each year s progress of the Apprentice, the Word of the City upon which he depended, and another by which all his pupils recognised each other. The Word and Token were abolished in 1731 in favour of the Script Masons. At Halberstadt there is a copy of the German Statutes of 2 December 1713, from which we gather that there were still four Overmasters at Koln, Strasburg, Wien, and Zurich. These are designated Old-Masters, as distinct from the Old-Fellows who governed the Craft. The first were a Chief or Arch-fraternity, the second were Masters of Lodges. A Master who made his Apprentice Free of the Craft had to bind him to keep the Word concealed in his heart, under the pain of his soul s salvation.

There is an old Arm chair at Lincoln of the date of 1681.<<"Ars. Quat. Cor," v,

-- Plate.>> In a semi-circular top is carved a hand holding a balance in equilibrium, and under it PIERI--1681--POYNT. Below this are two stalks with leaves, each bearing what appears to be a passion-flower. Beneath are two panels, one of which contains the double triangles, {399} and the plumb-rule; the other panel has the square and compasses. A member of the family deems the chair to have belonged to William, 4th Earl of Kingston, Lord Chief Justice in Eyre beyond Trent. In the grave-yard of Slane Castle, Ireland, there is a tomb-stone to John Frow, who died in 1687, in the up-per arc are compasses, Greek cross, and square. The "Freemasons Chronicle" (2 March 1909) says that in the Leicester Corporation Museum there is an old chair which, 250 years ago, belonged to a Free Masons Guild which met at the White Lion down to 1790. Upon the back is a design to mark a square building and the letter B, and it is thought there may have been another with J. A second chair is said to have belonged the Arch Guild.

Until very recent times our knowledge of what transpired in Ireland has been
almost nil, but Brother Chetwode Crawley has recently shown that in 1688 a Lodge of Free-masons, "consisting of gentlemen, mechanics, porters, parsons, ragmen, divines, tinkers, freshmen, doc-tors, butchers, and tailors," thus heterogeneously denominated, in the 1688 Tripos of John Jones, as connected with the University of Dublin. It is further mentioned by Jones that a collection was made for a new brother, "who received from Sir Warren, being Free-Masonised this new way, five shillings." This new way may mean by some new regulation, or simply in reference to the collec-tion,<<"Ars Quat. Cor.," 1898, p. 192; also Oliver s "Rev. of a Square.">> but that was old Guild custom. The tomb of John Abell of Sarsfield, Herts, 1694, has a representation of himself and his two wives; between a circular hoop at the bottom is a square,
and above that a plumb, over which is a pair of compasses.

It is said<<"Voice of Masonry." 1887.>> that one John Moore settled in South Carolina in 1680 from England, thence removed to Philadelphia, and in a letter which he writes in 1715, he speaks of having "spent a few evenings in festivity with my Masonic brethren." The celebrated Jonathan {400} Belcher, Governor of Massachusetts, was made a Mason in the year 1704, for he writes to a Boston Lodge, in 1741, "It is now thirty-seven years since I was admitted in the Ancient and Hon-ourable Society of Free and Accepted Masons." There is a record at Newport, U.S.A., "That ye day and date (1686 or 1688) We mett at ye House of Mordecai Campunall and after synagog We gave Abm. Moses the degrees of Masonrie." If this took place it would be Operative Masonry, and I see no reason to express a doubt.

We have alluded in the foregoing, and shall again, to Scottish customs, the more fully because there are traces, to be read between the lines, that the Advent of the Stuarts, and later introductions of Scottish Masons into the South, was instrumental in somewhat modifying the Free-masonry of London, and that what is taken for English is sometimes Scottish.

Yorkshire is notably rich in the old Charges, as besides those which formerly belonged to the York Grand Lodge, and are in possession of a modern Lodge there, there are others in private hands, and in the "West Yorkshire, Masonic Library." It is stated in a Manifesto of the Lodge of Antiquity (1778) that there was one old MS. in the hands of Mr. Wilson, of Broomhead, near Sheffield, writ-ten in the reign of Henry VIII., which is now missing, and there appears to have been one dated 1560. The Lodge of Hope, Bradford, has a copy of circa 1680. It forms no part of our plan to give an account of these old MSS., but students of them are greatly indebted to the late Brother Thomas W. Tew,
P.G.M. of the West Riding, who had eight of these, in possession of his Provincial Library, printed and distributed at his sole cost. Amongst them are the "Thomes W. Tew MS." circa 1680; the "Wais-

tell MS.," circa 1693; and the "Clapham MS.," circa 1700. The Rolls in possession of the Lodge at York have also been printed by subscription; one of these, dated 1704, is headed with the same Anagram on "Masonrie" as that of 1600, but addressed by Robert {401} Preston to Daniel Moult. It also appears in a Newcastle Roll, addressed by Richard Stead to his friend Joseph Claughton.

There are other documents at York, but none older than the reign of Anne, 1702-14. It seems that George Benson was President in 1705, and that he was followed by other gentlemen at each annual election. We learn also from an old copy of the Charges which has passed into the possession of the Grand Lodge of Canada, that a "Private Lodge" was held at Scarborough, Yorkshire, 10th July, 1705, with Wm. Thompson, Esq., as President, when six members were received whose names will be found in the facsimiles executed for the West Yorkshire Masons. Last century the Grand Lodge of All England at York had minutes from the year 1704, but they are not now to be found, they have, however, at the York Lodge some later parchment Rolls, which to some extent take the place of minutes. The probability is that such information as we have prior to 1726 belongs to the Operative Guild.

On the 19th March, 1712, we read that several members were "sworne and admitted into the honourable Society and fraternity of free Masons by George Bowes, Esq., Deputy President." In 1713 the Ancient Lodge held a meeting at Bradford, "when 18 gentlemen of the first families were made Free-Masons." Meetings were held each succeeding year at York, those on St. John the Baptist s Day, in June, being termed a "General Lodge on St. John s Day," whilst the others are designated "Private Lodges." This was four years before any movement was made in London, and the meetings at Scarborough and at Bradford are in agreement with the ancient Constitutions which state that the Masons were to hold an Assembly "in what place they would"; and it seems very apparent that where the term "General Lodge" is used, as distinct from a "Private Lodge," it is the tradition of the ancient Assembly continued. {402}

Again in 1716 it is minuted on this parchment roll as follows: -- "At St. John s Lodge in Christmas, 1716. At the house of Mr. James Boreham, situate Stone-gate in York, being a general Lodge held then by the Honoble. Society and Company of Free-Masons in the City of York, John Turner, Esqre., was

sworne and admitted into the Said Honoble. Society and Fraternity of Free- Masons." "Charles Fairfax, Esqre., Dep. President." Lists of the Grand Masters are found in any Modern Masonic Cyclopaedia, but Brother Whitehead recently discovered in an old Armorial MS. that the name of Sir Wm. Milner, Bart., 1728, has been omitted, "being the 798th Successor from Edwin the Great," apparently claiming an annual election of Grand Masters from the year 930.

However much we may regret it, yet we cannot blame the York Brothers for the strict respect shewn to the obligations. In such written documents as we have the terms used are simply well known Guild terms. We can draw no inference on such slight grounds as to the nature of their ceremonies, we do not know from contemporary documents what they were, and we have no right to expect that we should know. We can only judge of them by what they were when publicity began to be given to Masonic Rites in the 18th century. We have not the least warrant for thinking that, on the one hand, they took up new inventions and palmed them off as old Rites, nor on the other hand can we hope that they were very much better than the Grand Lodge of London, and shut their eyes to all improvement of the Ritual; they would be guided in this by old tradition and landmarks. We note that in the facsimile of the "Stanley MS.," 1677, it is closed with the tail-piece of a chequered pavement.

The "Tatler" for 9 June 1709, has an article upon a class of Londoners termed

"Pretty Fellows"; the paper is believed to be by Sir Richard Steele, and alludes to matters with which he seems to be acquainted, for he says: "they have signs and words like Free-Masons," and a similar reference is found in the same journal for 1710. There is {403} no record of Steele being a Mason, but there evidently was an impression that such was the case, for Picart, in his "Ceremonies and Costumes," gives a medallion portrait of "Sir Richard Steele," on a screen which gives a copy of the engraved list of Lodges in 1735.

As illustrating the state of things in Scotland at this date we may instance a dispute which occurred with the Mary s Chapel Lodge in 1707. A portion of these withdrew and established without permission the Lodge "Journeymen." Lodge Mary s Chapel objected to their meeting to take fees and give the "Mason s Word," and the dispute ran on for some years. The Masters Incorporation was the legal head of such bodies, and the Journeymen obtained leave to sue Mary s Chapel for such Masonic rights as the latter possessed. The Incorporation agreed in 1715 that the Journeymen should have an "Act of Allowance" to give the Mason s Word. From this circumstance Bro. R. F. Gould is inclined to think that the custodians of this privilege were the Incorporations, and that this case is the old survival of a claim that the private Lodges were Agencies or Deputations of the Incorporations for that purpose. It is a reasonable and just conclusion, and however loose the Lodges may have been in their working, we may feel sure that the Incorporations were Custodians of ritualistic Catechisms, probably of a Christian nature, of all known grades in Masonry, whether the same were conferred or had lapsed.

Brother Clement E. Stretton, who is eminent as a writer of books on his own

line as a C.E., has stated in the journals of the day and confirmed to me by letters that Dr. James Anderson was made chaplain of the St. Paul s Guild in 1710, in succession to Dr. Compton, who had been in the habit of holding a daily service. In September, 1714, Anderson proposed that men of position should be admitted to a species of honorary membership, which was carried by one vote, and the accounts, in that and the following year, show seven fees of 5

guineas each. All the time St. Paul s work was in operation the Guilds met

{404} at High XII. on a Saturday, but Anderson changed the period of meeting to 7 o clock on a Wednesday evening, at the Goose and Gridiron, and in September, 1715, the Operatives found that their old pass would not admit them, and they complained to Wren and Strong and the dissidents were struck off the Rolls; and this is probably why Anderson complained that Wren "neglected the Lodges." Now, under such circumstances, no honourable man can say that Anderson acted a creditable part. But we can see what he actually "digested." He made the Apprentice in a month, in place of seven years, struck out everything technical, including the ceremonies of conferring the Mark Mason; and left a fine moral institution on the lines of the Mystic Societies of the Ancients, but it is not Free Masonry, but an imitation of it; he retained as much of the Old Rites as suited his purpose, and

could be worked into the modern system, but it lacked the explanation the Guild Rites afforded. In the Stanley MS. of 1697, facsimiled for the West Yorkshire P.G. Lodge, there is a peculiar addition which is of later date. A very precise investigation of the allusions therein was made by Brother Gould in 1888, and he has come to the conclusion that the lines are applicable to 1714. It is supposed to have been a North Country MS., and we give the endorsement: --
"The prophecy of Brother Roger Bacon, Disciple of Balaam, Wch Hee Writt on ye N.E. Square of ye Pyramids of Egypt In capital, Letters.
"When a Martyr s Grand Daughter In ye Throne of Great Brittain,   [Mary.] Makes Capet s Proud Son look you d think him beshitten,   [Louis XIV.] When ye Medway and Mais Piss together In a Quill,   [Kent and Holland.] And Tagus and Rhine of ye Seine have their will,   [Germanic Confedn.] When ye Thames has ye Tay taen for better, for worse,   [Act of Union, 1707.] {406}
An to purchase ye Doxy has well drained his purse,   [Scotland.] When by roasting a Priest ye Church has her wishes,   [Dr. Sacheverell.] Loyal Tory s in places, Whiggs silent as fishes,   [Anne s reign.]
When Europe grows Quiet and a man yts right wily,   [Peace of Utrecht, 1713.] Setts up a wood bridge from ye Land s End to Chili,   [South-sea. Co.] Free Masons, beware, Brother Bacon advises,   . [Old members
Interlopers break in and spoil your Devices,   :   are being Your Giblin and Squares are all out of Door,   :   swamped.] And Jachin and Booz shall be secrets no more." .
It is evident that York was more advanced than London in the practice of a system of Speculative Freemasonry, because it had a more close operative derivation and was less reduced, and whether the lines above given originated North or South, they indicate the views of some old operative Brother, who saw changes which did not please him.

Brother Edward Conder has recently shewn that Viscount Doneraile must have held a Lodge at his mansion, Cork, about the year 1710. At one of these Assemblies some repairs were in progress in the library when his daughter Elizabeth secreted herself to watch the ceremonies, but was detected and forced to undergo the Rites of Making and Passing. As she was born in 1693,

and married to Richard Aldworth in 1713, we may reasonably fix 1710 as about the date of the reception. Brother W. J. C. Crawley, LL.D., has gone also into this matter in "Coementaria Hibernica," and expresses his opinion that similar Lodges may have existed at the Eagle Tavern under Lord Rosse, and at Mitchelstown under Lord Kingstown.

There is an Irish MS. amongst the Molyneux papers endorsed "Feb., 1711," which clearly indicates a 3-Degree system, and is headed with a {symbol: This is like an elongated "H" with a vertical line down to the center of the cross bar. Above, across the vertical line, are two horizontal cross lines, upper shorter and just below top.}

All the serious works which refer, in print, to the Society of Free-Masons make no question of its antiquity, {406} either during the 17th century or after it had passed into an entirely Speculative System. The "Antiquities of Berkskire" by Elias Ashmole (London 1719) has a paragraph which includes the information given by Plot and Aubrey that we have before referred to; and we add some interesting particulars from the letters of Dr. Thomas Knipe, who flourished between 1660 and 1711, in which year he died, and which were used by the compilers of Ashmole s Biography in 1748. This writer repeats the statement in regard to the Papal Bull of the time of Henry III., and goes on to say: "But this Bull, in the opinion of the learned Mr. Ashmole, was confirmative only and did not by any means create our fraternity, nor even to establish them in this kingdom." He then proceeds to give an account of the statements gathered from the old Charges from St. Alban to the ratification of the Constitution by Henry VI., and closes with a statement that in the Civil Wars the Free-Masons were generally Yorkists, and abuses Plot for his injurious comments.<<"The Kneph;" Gould s "Hist. Freem.," etc.>>

In Scotland technically it would seem that a Scottish Master was Work

Master of the Domatic Lodge, and the Chair Master of the Geomatic Lodge, but who had to be examined and Passed as a Master; for it is to be presumed that non-operatives might be ritualistically dispensed from the 7 years probation required for a Fellow of Craft. Melrose had a very old Lodge which kept to the ancient system until a few years ago, when it joined Grand Lodge. There is a Melrose minute of 1764 of which an unwise use is made; it enacts that the Apprentice and Fellow Craft ceremonies -- for that is what is meant -- shall be "administered in a simple way and manner free of anything sinful and superstitious," at this date it had two degrees and the Praeses was Master Mason. It only proves the presence of a puritanical spirit in the Lodge. That there was a Fellow Craft degree in Scotland worked in Lodges is proved by the Charge of St. Mary s, Edinburgh, against the Journeymen in 1713 {407} that they "presumed at their own hand to enter Apprentices and Pass Fellow Crafts in a public change house."

From the middle of the 17th century the Scottish minute books show

numerous admissions of military men, and of Lairds who are designated by their lands. The Kelso Lodge, to which Sir John Pringle s name appears in 1701, in 1705 imposes a fine for absence upon "Cornet Drummond and Lovetenant Benett." The Haughfoot Lodge, opened in 1702 by John Pringle of Torsonce, leave us in no doubt that it then conferred and "Passed" Apprentice and Fellow Craft, the Master Mason occupying the chair. Sometimes both degrees were given at one meeting, at others after an interval. The annual meeting was held for business, and a "Commission" given each year to 5

members to Initiate others. The Lodge at Aberdeen had two classes, Geomatic and Domatic Masons, and the admissions differently worded for each. The Master was Geomatic, and the Senior Warden Domatic, and this latter class had to make a trial-piece for each degree.

"Old Catechisms." The most important question with Freemasons will be by what sort of Rites were these 17th century Masons received into the Brotherhood? and the answer must depend on the nature of the Lodge which acted. It does not seem very difficult to form an approximate idea of this. There are various old Catechisms which, though of doubtful authority, and not wholly written in this century, but yet are clearly of it, and moreover are in general unison with the reduced 16th and 17th century Constitutional Charges. There is one copy of these Catechisms which the late Rev. Bro. A. F.

A. Woodford, who further quotes competent authority, considers from its archaisms to date 1650 if not earlier, and there are versions of 1723, 1724, 1729, 1730 and onwards. A copy was printed in the "Scots Magazine" of 1755, and is said to reveal an actual reception at Dundee in 1727. Although the general {408} character of these Catechisms are similar they differ in detail, but the Dundee specimen is in close agreement with the one that Brother Woodford has attributed to 1650, or earlier, and which is found amongst the Sloane MSS., and has been printed by him; it raises the question whether it is not actually a Scottish version brought South.

All these documents besides the recognition of some Apprentice ceremony, of an operative appearance, divide the Fellow s part into two portions; "first" the Catechism of that degree which we now term Fellow-craft, and "second" the degree now termed Master, and this last clearly defined in every copy that we have, and quite as clearly in the "Sloane MS." as any other. They are all a debased version of the original system prevailing when it took some years to become an operative Fellow or Master. Equally some sort of mark or ceremony is in evidence. In Scottish Lodges such a system might arise from a desire to continue to confer a Master s degree after the actual Masters had Incorporated, and in parts of England where the Fraternity ceased to be practical, from a desire to shorten the reception of Fellow and Master; in other words, to make an amateur into an Apprentice, Fellow, and Master in one evening; in any case all give 5 points of Fellowship as applicable to Craftsmen, but in the ancient Guilds they had a technical reference.

Sometimes a Passed Apprentice would appear to mean a Fellow, and a

Passed Fellow a Master, so loose is the wording. In all cases, however, the Catechisms give certain secrets of the modern 3rd Degree, from which we may justly infer that they had knowledge of a certain annual Rite, or drama, and that if it should have passed out of practice it was owing to the changed position of the Lodge. Precisely the same thing has occurred amongst the Guilds claiming mediaeval descent, of which many yet exist, and Passed Masters have to be called in from a distance; one of the most expert workers is a York Mason. {409}

It is unnecessary to particularise much of these Catechisms, but in our chapter viii. we advocated on the evidence to be obtained from the Saxon Charge, old operatives, and the usages of Societies similarly constituted, that the most ancient form of recognition was a "Salutation," and this is found in every Catechism that has come down to us, until it was expunged in 1813. If this is correct the most ancient Masons were "Salute Masons," the Freemasons

were Hebrew "Word Masons"; no doubt when this union took place, whether in the 13th century or any other date, it would be followed from time to time with revisions, to correct inaccurate oral transmission. The "Salutation" varies in these old MSS., but the following from the "Sloane," and the printed 1723, are given as specimens; those of Germany were more elaborate as they contained seven prayers or "Words": -- "The Right Worshipful, the Masters and Fellows, in that Worshipful Lodge from whence we last come, Greet you, Greet you, Greet you well." The Warden replies: "God s Greeting be at this meeting, and with the Right Worshipful the Master, and the Worshipful Fellows who keeps the keys of the Lodge from whence you come, and you also are welcome, Worshipful Brother, into this Worshipful Society."

In the "Sloane MS." there is found "a Jerusalem word," Giblin, as well as a two-syllabled word, Maharhyn, and doubts thrown on a sign, said to be given in France and Turkey, which may be considered in relation, to what was said at the opening of chapter ix.

The Catechism of 1723 has the following lines: --<<Gould s "Hist. Frem." -- Appendix.>>

"An Entered Mason I have been, Boaz and Jachin I have seen,

A Fellow I was sworn most rare,

And know the Ashlar, Diamond and Square; I know the Master s part full well,

As honest Maughbin will you tell." {410} Then the Master says: --

"If a Master Mason you would be, Observe you well the "rule of three," And what you want in Masonry,

Thy "Mark" and "Maughbin" makes thee Free."

   The printed catechism of 1724 represents a body qualified as a St. John s Lodge, a term we saw used in the oldest York minutes, and it is in altogether better form than some of the others. We find in it a "version" of an old Rosicrucian and Gnostic symbol, an equal cross with a triangle over it {Symbol: as described}; it has also the word "Irah," which no one has ventured to explain, but it occurs in the Lectures of HRDM-RSYCSS. Symbolism couched in rhyme is found in the Scottish and north England Catechisms, to a late period. In a MS. of the old Charges belonging to the Dumfries Lodge, of date early 18th century, is the following, but we have no space to quote the Christian Catechism of the old Temple Symbolism found therein.<<Vide "Ars Quat. Cor." vi, p. 42.>>: --

"Q. Where ought a Lodge to be keapt?

A. On the top of a mountain or in ye middle of a boge,

Without the hearing of ye crowing of a cock or ye bark of a doge.

Q. What was the greatest wonder yt was seen or heard about the Temple?

A. God was man and man was God, Mary was a mother and yet a maid."

There can be little doubt that one of the customs here referred to originated in the British and Teutonic customs of holding a Council, Folcmote, or Thing, Friestuhl or Vehme, either on the top of a mountain, or in the open, in the middle of a field, and every Free-Man had a voice in such Courts. According to a MS. of the learned Mr. Jones in the Cottonian library, the early British Kings when they held a Council either personally or by deputy, --"went to a certain private house or tower on the top {411} of a hill, or some solitary place of counsel, far distant from any dwelling, and there advised unknown to any man, but the Counsellors themselves."

The following lines, of much interest, appear in the "Dumfries MS." just quoted: --

"A caput mortem {symbol: circle with face: two dots with eyebrows, a curve for a nose and a small dash for a mouth} here you see,

To mind you of mortality."

"Behold great strength {symbol of two vertical, parallel lines} by Herod fell, But stablishment in heaven doeth dwell."

"Let all your acts {symbol: vertical line with horizontal line at top to right} be just and true,

Which after death gives life to you,"

"Keep round within {symbol: small circle over inverted "V"} of your appointed sphere,

Be ready for your latter end draws near."<<Vide "Ars Quat. Cor." vi, p. 42.>>

A formula of old transmission has the following: --

"By letters four and science five, This G aright doth stand."

Brother J. A. Cockburn of Adelaide thinks they are of very great antiquity. He holds that originally the G was the Hebrew "gimel," and the Greek "gamma," which is a Mason s square, held sacred by the Pythagoreans, and the Cabiric Initiates of the earth-goddess "Ge" or "Gai," and he further suggests that the primitive emblem may have been the Svastica {Symbol: Swastika} which embraces "four" gammas, and again represents the sacred tetragrammaton of the Jews, -- Plutarch says "The number four is a square"; and Philo says, -- "Four is the most ancient of all square numbers, it is found to exist in right angles, as a square in Geometry Shows." Brother Sydney T. Klein, P.M. 2076, in a lecture upon the ancient Geometry<<"Ars Quat. Cor." x.>> says, that the Greek "gamma" was actually the etymon or name designating the square in the earliest times. The same Brother considers that the great secret of prehistoric geometry was, "how to make a perfect right angle, in any desired position without possibility of error," and gives as illustration an Egyptian deed of 2,000 B.C., and later papyrus of 1,500 B.C. Both English and Coptic Guilds still give it, and the old York Lectures also. He shews that the {412} ancient geometers had this secret, and that it could be made by means of the centre, from any straight line, or by taking any triangular line drawn from the circumference of a circle, by the rope or skirret. On the formation of Grand Lodge, he says, in 1717, every gentleman desired to be a Master Mason, and as the property of

the square was assigned to one W.M., whilst the ritual retained the original wording, the symbolic allusion was lost, and the Euclidean problem was given to the W.M. in place of the simple square. The Ancient Guilds have possessed this as a secret for ages and based much ceremony upon it.

Malvern old church, is said to have a curious window, but no information is afforded as to its date; -- "In the left hand division of the last window, at the east end of the south aisle (the subject alluding to paradise); in the top section, is a figure before a dial column (the dial gone) holding in his right hand a square and a huge pair of compasses. In the next section of the same window, westward, is a figure kneeling, having a globe on a stand, on a pedestal behind him, with the moon, the sun, and seven stars before him; a root of corn is at the foot near a stream of water, with a branch of acacia on raised ground. And in the third section is a figure prostrate, on a piece of square pavement; the latter is, however, only a compilation of odd pieces of ancient coloured glass."

Brother Ker of Scotland has written something in reference to an examination of the Master s grade by two astronomers who decided it was some very ancient system.

The celestial and terrestrial globes were rectified to the time of the foundation of Solomon s temple, and "the signs and words were obtained, and the reason of the implements being used; the legend of the third degree; also the name being thrice repeated; why the ear of corn and the waterfall are depicted; and the direction in which the procession moves." A lecture similar to this, but not covering all these points, embracing chiefly the temple of {413} Solomon as a type of the Universe, is in the Library of the Grand Chapter of Scotland and attributed to Dr. Walker Arnott, an eminent Scottish Mason. The late Brother Albert Pike seems to have entertained a similar opinion, and argues for the identification of Hiram with the Sun-god.<<"Morals and Dogma; Vide also Liverpool Mas. Jol.," Dec. 1901.>> In Egypt, Horus is represented as seated upon lions, the same word meaning both sun and lion. Again Hari is a Hindu name of the sun, and Khurum or Hiram is the Egyptian Her-ra, Hermes, Hercules. He thinks certain assassins may possibly be recognised in the Arabic names of certain stars; when, by the precession of the equinoxes, the sun was in Libra, in autumn, he met in the east, where the reign of Typhon commenced, three stars forming a triangle, they are thus designated Zuben-es- chamali in the west, Zuben-hak-rabi in the east, Zuben-el-gabi in the south; of these the corrupt forms, he thinks, may be found in Jubela-Gravelot, Jubelo- Akirop; and Jubulum-Gibbs.<<"Ibid," pp. 79, 488.>> The theory of Brother Ker s two celebrated astronomers might imply the arrangement of the Rites by old astrologers.

A similar theory is embodied in the Swedenborgian Rite, which upholds the

Masonic symbols as those of the "most" ancient races, allied to the doctrine of correspondences. Thus the Masters degree is an astrological, or astronomical allegory, based upon the position of the stars 5873 B.C. The Lodge is a symbol of the Universe (also Dr. Arnott s contention), and the Rites represent the building of God s temple in nature, and the building up of humanity; it has a further reference to the erection of the Succuth, Booths, or Lodges erected at the feast of Tabernacles. Brother Samuel Beswick, in his work on the Rite, asserts that Emanuel Swedenborg was made a Mason at the University of Lunden in 1706, and that this date appears upon a minute of 1787 when King Gustavus III. presided, but that it is erroneously entered London. He {414} also

asserts that Charles XII., who was assassinated in 1718, had Lodges, and Chapters or Encampments in his army. The ancient Guilds may have been continued in Sweden, and with reference to higher degrees we have already mentioned the existence of Rosy Cross in the 15th century and there was a similar non-Masonic Society in the 18th with the King as Chief.

It is not supposed that any quarrel occurred at York to separate the Operatives and the Speculatives; the former continued to hold their meetings at High XII., and the latter withdrew to meet in the evening; and their Ritual retained much of the Operative customs not now found in the modern ritual of 1813.

In the 1st Degree the Candidate took a short O.B. before preparation, in order that if he was rejected or withdrew, he might be pledged to secrecy, and the same system exists in the Guild, as the boy is O.B. in the porch before admission. On a York reception he was invested with the Operative Mason s leather apron up to the neck; and as in the Operative Guild he was shewn how to hew the rough Ashlar.

In the 2nd Degree he was thrice tested by the J.W., S.W., and W.M. in the use of the plumb, level, and square. At the 1st and 2nd rounds he had to test the columns of the Wardens, and the W.M. required him to prove the perfect Ashlar with the square; there is this difference however that the Guild used the hollow square of the nature of a picture frame as a guage both for the stone and the Fellow. The 3rd Degree begins as Fellow, and ends as "Casual" Master. The old Masters ceremony of York, and the north of England, contained much that is now omitted, and had many points of resemblance to the ancient Mysteries. The names of the criminals are given, and after the death of Hiram the Superintendent Adoniram succeeds him, and is ruler of Perfect Masters. The details would read thus, on the lines of the ancient Mysteries: Hiram the Abiv or father of Craftsmen is lamented for twice 7 days, {415} when the fraternity is gladdened by a reappearance in the person of Adoniram the prince

of the people. In real history Adoniram was slain, whilst according to Oliver, who quotes Dius and Menander, Hiram returned to Tyre, where he is known as Abdemonos. The York ceremony was a good representation of the "Aphenism" and "Euresis" of the Mysteries; respecting which Diodorus informs us that Egypt lamented the violent death of Osiris for fourteen days at his tomb, referring to the lunation of the moon, after which they rejoiced on a proclaimed
rising.

In regard to the Masonic symbols it is tolerably certain that the more recondite of these have been received by the Free-Masons from the most ancient times, yet that their actual signification became lost, to the society which ceased its connection with architecture, and in many cases as we know new meanings were assigned by the Grand Lodge in 1717.

In reference to what has already been said of the perpetuation of a Mark for tools and work, it may be pointed out that the custom was continued in Scotland when an Apprentice was Entered, and Fellows had it in England according to the Catechism quoted and the remnants of Guild life still have it. By the 1670 Laws of the Aberdeen Lodge the Apprentice, besides other fees, had to pay one Mark for his Mark. The Laws of this date enact that Apprentices were to be "Entered," in their "Out-field Lodge," in the parish of Ness, save in ill weather when, -- "We ordain lykwise that no lodge be holden within a dwelling house, where there is people living in it, but in the open

fields, except it be ill weather, and let there be a house closed, that no person shall heir or see us." In the old Dumfries Lodge, No. 53, by the Laws of 1687 Apprentices had to pay, "a mark Scots money assignt mark." The "Scots Magazine" gives a Dundee Initiation of 1727 and has, -- "How got you that Mark?" Answer, -- "I took up one Mark, and laid down another." {416}
In the Catechism, printed in England, we quoted the lines: --

    And what you want in Masonry,
Thy "Mark" and "Maughbin" makes thee Free."

    All the evidence which these documents afford us, -- rudimentary, aid- memory, or fragmentary though they may be, point to this, that in some parts, and especially in Scotland, the ancient Fellow and Master of the General Assembly had become the Apprentice and Fellow of the Lodge, first by swearing the Apprentice to a Charge, and then by reducing the seven years qualification for Fellow-ship, until finally there was little or no interval, but customs were not uniform, for there was no general central authority.

In other cases, where a stricter tradition was followed, the Apprentice was sworn to a Charge by some ceremonial and at the end of his seven years Apprenticeship was accepted a Fellow by a formal ceremony and then, or afterwards, received the more ancient secrets of a Master Mason; or, as in certain Northern Lodges was created a Harod or ruling Chief; for as the Lodges ceased to be schools of architecture there was no call to continue a strict examination for the title of a Passed Master. This apparently was the view of Grand Lodge in 1717, adopted with some changes to suit a new state of things.

It is quite open to belief, as modern critics contend, that when an unindentured man, or a gentleman, was made a Mason in a Lodge, such as that of York, he would receive the whole degrees at once, in a running ceremony. The Guild received amateurs in the 6th Degree only. It must therefore be true, in a modified sense, that Fellow and Master were convertible terms. It is all but certain that the Speculative, so-called revivalists of 1717 had oral or written Catechisms of Guild ceremonies, and we are told by Anderson, that the 1721 meetings of Grand Lodge were made very interesting by the Lectures of old Masons. At any rate, we are required to believe in their good faith, {417} and that the men who formed the Grand Lodge of London in 1717, transmitted us what they had or could remember from the ancients; revised, subtracted, added a little, it may be, but their chief alteration was eventually to make three ceremonies the rule of Speculative Masons, and to contain, in one form or another, all which they had obtained from the Ancient Guild Masons; who when they received an Amateur swore him only in the 6th Degree. As they had now no use for an Indentured Apprentice, they divided the degree of Reception into two portions, in our present Apprentice and Fellow- Craft degrees, revising somewhat the Passed Fellow and adding a second part to their Master s degree.

At least they knew, however badly instructed they may have been, better of
what genuine Masonry consisted than the iconocalistic critics of near two centuries later; and we must bear in mind that we are dealing with a Society that was established for secret and oral transmission of its Mysteries, and which bound its members to absolute secrecy on every point under the most binding penalties. The whole allegory of a Master, it has been observed,

enforces the lesson that it is a danger, even to allow it to be suspected that he possessed certain Rites, that were a certificate of his proficiency in the Craft. Nor must we forget that speculative Masonry was constituted as a Triad Society governed by threes, after the manner of the Druids. Shakespere says, "that a rose by any other name would smell as sweet;" and the Grand Lodge established in 1717 is the same thing whether we call it by that name, or term it Assembly, Congregation, or Chapter, as the ancient designations ran. Practically 1717 was the revival of a previous attempt to continue a ruling body without its Rites and ceremonies, and from this period Freemasons can have little doubt as to the nature of the Society and its degrees so far as the ordinary Craft Mason is concerned. The supposed claim of the Modern Grand Lodge to a full possession of the entire {418} system of Masonry was not universally acknowledged but denied, and led to York, and other centres of Masons, being termed ANCIENTS, whilst the Grand Lodge of London was designated MODERN. The guiding principle of the founders of the Grand Lodge Rites was Universality, and with antiquarian tastes, and logical views, nothing was accepted as Masonry but what concerned Solomon s Temple, and in adopting Guild ceremonies they did so without reference to the 2nd temple. The question arises here whether or no they were fully informed Initiates, and that is very dubious.

After a full consideration of all the facts produced in previous chapters can
we arrive at any other conclusion than this, that though Freemasonry of the present day, may have undergone modifications in its ceremonies, and changed with the manners of Society, yet that the general tone of its ritual has descended to us from the most remote antiquity. As to the 2nd part of the Master s ceremony, on which so much criticism has been wasted, there can be no doubt that it has been taken from the yearly celebration of the Guilds of what is supposed to have occurred at the building of the Temple.

Throughout these pages we have followed the ordinary histories which treat Modern Freemasonry as a succession of the Operative Guilds; it is one of the descendants of these bodies, but lacking their technical instruction, and the abridgement which it has undergone can only be fully understood by placing the two Rites in juxtaposition. It is, -- what else can we say? a moral and speculative imitation of the more ancient Rites of the Guilds, socially of a higher status, but separated from them, and with the next Chapter we enter entirely upon a Speculative Freemasonry.

Much confusion has arisen owing to writers attempting to trace Masonry from a special class of what were termed "Mysteries." We have seen that the early Mysteries were Guilds, and that even after Caste influenced them, and divided them into three sections {419} they were still all one, varying only in the names, &c. There were then (1) those of the Priests; (2) those of Warriors and agriculturists; (3) those of the Artisans. All three were equally Mysteries; all were equally Guilds; equally one Mystery; with like ceremonies varying mainly in the object and technical part of their Rituals. Masonry is the only one of these that has come down to us unchanged at the date we close this Chapter. They were a necessity to the priestly builders of Temples and Churches, and therefore encouraged. It must be admitted, however, that the modern rites have a remarkable reference to those of the Cabiri. It had "seven" anthropomorphised Gods of Art, the number of a "perfect Lodge"; of these, three were "Chief" Gods, and one was

slain by the others and buried in the roots of Olympus. It is said that the Roman Emperor Commodius in initiating a candidate was so energetic that he sent him to join his prototype.

CHAPTER XI. THE SYSTEM TERMED HIGH-GRADE

THE SYSTEM TERMED HIGH-GRADE. SPECULATIVE FREEMASONRY.
God bless the King! I mean our Faith s Defender, God bless -- no harm in blessing -- the Pretender, But who Pretender is, or who is King,
God bless us all! that s quite another thing.
JOHN BYROM, Manchester.

THE general opinion of Freemasons will be that this Chapter should conclude the next on the establishment of a Grand Lodge in 1717. The reason for placing it before that event is a reasonable belief in the assertions of the ANCIENTS, as opposed to the MODERNS, who admitted themselves the characteristic by which the former distinguished the latter. The subject of these degrees is a very intricate one and I am rather puzzled how to put it clearly to the reader without much repetition.

With Chapter IX. the Gothic Builders died out and their Lodges relaxed into small social gatherings, but in the North of England where there were Lodges in the jurisdiction of York, the Lodges continued the "Harodim," or Masters Fraternity, of which Gould in his large history affords ancient proofs. What became of these bodies, for Grand Lodge has no knowledge of them? But on the death of the Gothic Builders and the attenuation of their Lodges there arose, temp. Jas. I., a young Englishman of the name of Inigo Jones, whom the Earl of Pembroke took into Italy. He studied with much interest, amongst the disciples of Palladio and the Comicini, the classic works of Italy, and on his return reorganised such bodies as existed on the model of the {421} Italian academies, and brought over Italians to instruct the Guilds in the classical Masonry of old Rome, and it became a fashion to term the magnificent Gothic erections a barbarous style? Our principal authority for this statement is Anderson who says that the account was recorded in a MS. by Nicholas Stone which was burnt in 1720, in order, we may suggest, that it might not fall into his hands. He further states that Jones held Quarterly Meetings, and Lodges of Instruction; now there is no reason why Anderson should have falsified history on this matter, and his statements are accepted by Preston, and by so careful a writer as the German Findel; but the known ceremonies of the Guild is a confirmation strong enough in itself, for they certainly represent a Guild of the classical style. They had also the old Jewish Menatzchim or Intendents,

and Harods, termed Passed Masters, of which rank Grand Lodge has no knowledge.

The best work on the Comicini is by "Leader Scott," she shows that on the sack of Rome by the Goths they settled at Como, and spread their Guilds over the whole of Italy and even to France; and retained the same style of architecture and ornamentation for centuries. Her impression seems to be that they had added to the Collegia a reference to Solomon s temple, and this is not improbable when we remember that the Roman Emperor Justinian after he had completed "Agia Sofia" in Constantinople exclaimed: "I have surpassed thee, O! Solomon." These Italian Academies had their " Caput Magistrum, " and their " Arch Magister, " who according to Leader Scott had to be a grandee. The head-master was no doubt the Master of the Level Men, the Arch-Master of the Guild working curved work. At the same time any authority that had central jurisdiction was termed an "Arch Fraternity," and M. H. Shuttleworth mentions a reprint of 1776 at Paris, of the 13th century Statutes of the Knights of St. John which mentions their "Archiconfrere Royale. . . de Jerusalem." {422}

Every country had a special class to "Pass" Masters; Scotland had its "Six

Men of Ancient Memory"; Saxon England its "Elders"; France its "Masters Fraternities"; Germany its "Old Masters"; who assembled "Chapter-wise." The establishment of the Grand Lodge of England and its depletion of the technical parts of the Guild, in time destroyed the power of these Harods, Rulers, or Passed Masters, and sought to occupy their place in a very perfunctory manner. The dissatisfaction against the Grand Lodge was everywhere great and England, Ireland, and Scotland had its Arch Masons in or about 1740, France had its Menatzchim, its Harods, its Provosts and Judges, its Architects, and its Royal Arch. They were the real Grand Lodge, with secret Rites and tokens, they formed a Court of Award, as they united the Geomatic and Domatic Sections, until the law and the Grand Lodge rendered their functions obsolete; chiefly held in cathedral towns, we may find the sacred name over its gates.

Besides the feeling, engendered by members of the old Operative Guilds, that

Modern Masonry was an imperfect system, various other ideas operated in the development of a system of "Masters degrees," at a later period termed High- grade Masonry. English Masonry, in the course of ages had gathered much Christian Symbolism upon its Semitic ceremonies, which, in certain parts, would intensify the dislike to the Modern system.

1.   On this question of teaching it may be noted that whilst the Jacobite Masonic faction sought to strengthen the Christianity of our Rites, the Southern Masons, had sought from the time when Cromwell readmitted the Jews, to broaden its lines

2.   In politics again there existed great, but suppressed, antagonism between North and South; the Grand Lodge of all England at York was essentially Jacobite, that of London, Hanoverian.

3.   There was an Hermetic element, from early times in the Guilds, and we shall see that this was well understood {423} in 1721; for there was, as we have indicated in previous Chapters, a very early quasi-connection.

4.   There were in existence from the time of the Reformation in the 16th century, many mystical societies, and as these passed along the ages, they influenced the Masonic Lodges, and in some instances were drawn upon to

establish high-degrees; and we will preface the information we can give upon some of these.

England seems to have first began an innovation upon the system of the Modern Grand Lodge, but the hot-bed of the high-grades was France. From 1688 when a quantity of English, Irish, and Scottish Masons emigrated with James II. there was an ancient Masonry in France of which Hector MacLean was Grand Master, and who was succeeded in 1725 by the Earl of Derwentwater who held that position until the Elector of Hanover decapitated him in 1745. But a little earlier, namely in 1737, the Duke of Richmond, who had been G.M. of England, opened a Lodge in which he initiated the Duc d Antin who in 1743 became Grand Master of the English Grand Lodge of Paris; we will leave him there for the present and take a survey of earlier matters. There is a Carbonari Certificate of 1707, printed by St. Edme (Paris, 1821) as authentic, which says that a Count Theodore born at Naples in 1685 had already obtained the High Grades of Free Masonry in France.

We cannot doubt, upon the evidence afforded in Chapter VI. that the

Epoptae, or higher Initiates, of the first ages of Christianity, transmitted their Mystical Rites; these were taken up and carried forward by Monks, Dervishes, Manichees, Catharoi, Templars, Albigensis, Ghibellines, Friends of God, Militia of the Cross, Rosicrucians, and sects too numerous to mention; and that such secret Schools were in existence long prior to the Reformation in the church, as witness the labours of such men as Fiscini, Pico de Mirandolo, Reuchlin, Erasmus, Agrippa, Rudolphus Agricolo, and many more, and that educated Free Masons, in their Masters Fraternities and Fellow {424} craft Lodges, were more or less conversant with Pythagoreanism, Platonism, Cabalism, Rosicrucianism, and that these Societies interested themselves in Germany and elsewhere in the spread of the doctrines of the Culdees, of Wycliffe, Huss, Luther, and other Reformers, and the Secret Society established by Cornelius Agrippa in London, in 1510, may have been of this nature. How far these adapted the Craft guild ceremonies, or at what date if they did so, can only be plausible conjecture.

These Secret schools, which the Church of Rome would term Gnostic, must

have permeated the whole of Europe and entered into the Guild life of the traders and artizans, and we cannot, well otherwise, account for the friendliness shewn to Luther, when in 1517 he began his fearless crusade against the overwhelming force of Rome. It is supposed that Luther himself was a Guild member and he actually uses Guild terms in 1527, when he says that he is "already passed-Master in clock-making." It is stated that about 15 days after the holocaust which he had the temerity to make of the Pope s Bull, he was waited upon by a member of some Guild holding a meeting at Wiittemberg, and induced to go to an Assembly at the Guild Hall, where after Reception "by ancient ceremonies," he received a medal bearing Mystic characters, and was then placed under the protection of the Brotherhood.<<"National Freem.," Washingtorn, 1863; Row s "Masonic Biographs," 1868; "Canadian Craftsman," 1893.>> It is quite certain that Secret Societies of Mystics, united by ceremonies with signs, then existed; and it may be that the Reformers strengthened themselves by such Societies, intended for mutual protection, and the Charter of Cologne, 1535, if genuine, may represent such Assemblies. The early Secret Societies of the Albigensis and the Ghibellines usually represented their position under the symbol of an Egyptian

or Babylonish captivity, for both forms are used, and Luther himself adopts this in his book entitled the "Babylonish Captivity." He says, -- "The Christian

{425} people are God s true people, carried away captives into Babylon, where they have been robbed of that which they received at their baptism." Salandronius the Swiss, thus writes to Vadian, -- "Oh! saw you how the inhabitants of the mountains of Rhetia, cast away from them, the Yoke of the Babylonish Captivity." Melancthon, in 1520, says, -- "the finger of God is to be seen in what Luther is doing, even as the King of the Egyptians refused to acknowledge what was done by Moses." We can even find language amongst them, which forms the most secret part of certain Masonic high-grades, but which we cannot repeat. Luther in 1520 thus writes to the Elector. -- "With one hand I hold the sword, and with the other I build the walls of Zion"; similar language was used in Paris and Toussaint Farrel, 1525, says, -- "The 70th year will come at last, the year of deliverance, and then we shall have freedom of mind and conscience." Nor is this symbolic language absent from the works of the English Rosicrucians for John Heyden, writing in 1663, has an allusion to it, particularly forced; speaking of Christian Rosenkreutz, circa 1400 he says (p. 18), -- "After five years came into his mind, the wished return of the Children of Israel out of Egypt, how God would bring them out of bondage. Then he went to his Cloyster, to which he bare affection, and desired three of his brethren to go with him to Moses." These he explains were Brothers G.V., I.A., and E.O., who constructed a "Magical language." This may be traditional or found in MSS. to which Heyden had access, if history, it indicates a company of four working in a like direction to Luther a century and a half before his days.

We find this symbolic language reduced to emblems, two of these brought from Nuremberg are engraved in the "Transactions" of the Newcastle College of Rosicrucians. One of these has, on one side, the figure of a Pontiff in the act of blessing, also the figure of a Monk with a lighted taper in his hand, and between the two an Altar with an open Bible upon it, around the {426} border is the inscription VERBUM DOMINI HB:YHYH (irradiated) MANETINAETER (nitate); the obverse has an armed man, with a drawn sword, holding the scales of justice, in the heavier pan is a human figure, and in the lighter pan a writhing serpent; several inscriptions appear in the centre but are indistinct, the legend is JOSUA CONFIDE NON DIRELINQUAMTE. In the Peasants league against the Nobles, 1524-5, the motto of Munzer was "we must like Joshua destroy all the nations of Canaan with the sword," and in one of his letters he signs himself, "Munzer, armed with the sword of Gideon," possibly this medal is Anabaptist. The Roman Catholic clergy are very fond of making Faustus Socinius the founder of Freemasonry, this, of course, is false, but Socinius seems to have established a secret Society by which he spread his views in Poland. The second medal we have named is a Jubilee one of 1617, the obverse being precisely the same as that just described; on the reverse we find a bee-hive, the HB:YHYH (irradiated), a serpent twined round a cross, three other indistinct emblems, at the top EGYPTUS ET ISRAEL; at the bottom ANNO JUBILAEI OM; around the border, in two lines is the legend DEMSCHWERN EGYPTISCHEN DIENSTH AUS WIE MOYSES GEUHRTAUS VNS CFURTAVS DESBAEST FINIS TEKNU, ALSOHATT MARTIN LUTHERUS. The Jubilee date of 1617 is about the period when the Rosicrucian Societies began to supersede the Mystic Schools mentioned in Chapter VI., of which, to a slight extent, this

is a continuation. Although the Clerical enemies of Masonry in France pointed out last century the bearing of all this upon the Masonic Rites then practised, it is not in the province of a Mason to do so, but those who have the Red Cross and its analogous grades will comprehend.

We have alluded to the Harodim, which in France became the nucleus of the high grades, and the secret Societies from which these latter drew some of their material. There is, however, another Order, which the Romish Church associates with a Secret Discipline, and {427} an enlightened purpose, which they suppose has been embodied in Freemasonry -- we allude to the Order of the Temple. The Templar origin of Masonry, or at least one of its Rites, was quite a cardinal doctrine abroad last century; and we have already given the facts leading to this view. Philip le Bel before he undertook the suppression of the Templars in 1310, had, two years before this, interdicted the trade Fraternities. Two branches of the Templars escaped destruction, the one in Scotland the other in Portugal, and a third is mentioned in Hungary down to 1460, these would correspond with each other, and they could not feel any friendship for Rome. The difficulty of a widespread continuation would arise from the vigilance, after 1313, of the priesthood, but the Order may have been continued in spirit under other names; and we must ask what became of the numerous bodies of Artisans expelled by this action from the Preceptories of the Templars. Starck in his reply to Dr. Beister<<"Anti Saint Nicasse," 1786, ii,

pp. 181-202.>> says: "Had he been somewhat better acquainted with ecclesiastical history he would have found, not only one, but several religious bodies which under far more violent oppression than those endured by the Knights Templar, have secretly continued to exist for a far longer period." In Scotland there was a strong leaven of Culdee opinion to preserve the Templars, and Papal opinion was always more lightly considered by the independent Scot than his English neighbour. Hence Scotland preserved the name of the Templars even after the dissolution of the Chivalric Orders in that country in 1560. These Knights were often addicted to Hermetic studies, and may have become amalgamated with some of these. Thory points out, in writing of the times of Lord Bacon, what he calls the singular fact that here and there in works of the time are found allusions to the Templars, and that Alchemical works have references to their red-cross banner.

Mere denial of some such connection does not admit {428} of being loosely made, and Aberdeen had its share of support as a seat of Masonic Templary. Baron Hunde inherited some such traditionary belief and sent emissaries to investigate the belief. When the lands of Maryculter were surrendered in 1548 the Knights took up their residence in the city, where an old Lodge existed which embraced the noble and gentle; and we find this Lodge meeting in Tents, or Encampments under canvas, designated "Outfield Lodge," or held in the Bay of Nigg, "where no one could see or hear," and hence believed to have included Templar rites. It is also alleged that certain Templars, before 1600, united with the ancient Stirling Lodge. For some time after the Reformation the orthodox party would seem to have recruited themselves secretly with the sanction of the Grand Master at Malta, and it is very probable that the same thing had place in England when James I. was the "Mason King" and the craft included men of learning and gentlemen. The first assimilation of Chivalry and Freemasonry would arise within the Domus or Preceptory, amongst the Artisans and Lay- brothers there employed; and when they were expelled together in the 16th

century, there would be a desire amongst both parties to continue the connection, and still stronger amongst the Protestant parties; gradually, in the course of a century, the Temple began to be looked upon as a Masonic appanage, owing to the chief members belonging to both orders. Finally, in order to make the Orders homogeneous, the craft and other degrees were treated as the necessary gradation by which to become a Templar. There was undoubtedly an ancient traditionary connection besides this, even if the Templars, as seems most probable, did not in the 12th and 13th centuries, introduce the Rites of Freemasonry now practised.

We will now consider the participation of the Freemasons themselves in the aims of the old Hermetic Schools of "Sons and Masters." We must all admit that the builders of our ancient religious houses were men {429} of great intelligence, who would seek to increase their knowledge from all available sources, and amongst these sources from the Societies of Alchemists and Rosicrucians, including Astrologers and Mathematicians. We have given instances in 1450 where Hermetic Symbolism was identical with that of Freemasonry; but the "Ordinall of Alchemy" compiled by Thomas Norton of Bristol, "In the yeare of Christ, 1477" (83 pp. of MS.), commences as follows: --
"To the honour of God, one in persons three, This Boke is made that laie men shouldn t see."

He undertakes, "To teach by Alkimy great riches to winn," and enumerates the great personages who have worked in the Mysteries of Hermes, Popes, Cardinals, Byshopes, Priests, Kings, Lords, Merchants, and adds: --

"And goldsmithes whome we should lest repreve, For sights in their Craft move them to beleeve."

He styles Alchemy a "Noble Craft," and says (page 2) in allusion to the Freemasons: --

"But wonder is it that Weivers deale with such worke, Free-Masons, and Tanners, and poore P issh Clarkes, Stayners, and Glasiers will not thereof cease,
And yet seely Tinkers will put them in prease." He closes his instruction in the Noble Art thus: --
"All that hath pleasure in this Boke to reade,
Pray for my soule, and for all both quick and dedde;
In this yeare of Christ, one thousand four hundred seaventy seaven, This warke was begun, honour to God in heaven."

This participation may have gone on for centuries, and we may feel sure that it did; various Societies of Oriental origin then existed using symbols by which Masons would be attracted to them, and it is in evidence that the early Rosicrucians were Initiated by the Moslem sectaries. In 1630 we find Fludd, the chief of the Rosicrucians, using architectural language, and there is proof that his Society was divided into degrees, and from the fact that the Masons

Company of London had a copy {430} of the Masonic Charges "presented by Mr. fflood," we may suppose he was a Free-Mason before 1620. From the language of Eugenius Philalethes or Thomas Vaughan we may assume that he also was a Mason. Sir Robert Moray and Elias Ashmole, who were received Masons in 1641 and 1646 respectively, were both of them diligent students of Occult matters, and it is within the bounds of probability that the Rosicrucians may have organised a system of the Craft degrees, upon which they superadded their own Harodim receptions long before Free-Masonry passed to the Grand Lodge in 1717.

"The Wise Man s Crown," 1664, has the following: "The late years of tirany admitted stocking weavers, shoemakers, millers, masons, carpenters, bricklayers, gunsmiths, hatters, etc., to write and teach Astrology." This latter Society Ashmole terms the Mathematicians; it held an annual festival, which was active in London in 1648 and again in 1682. Even Wren was, more or less, a student of Hermeticism, and if we had a full list of Freemasons and Rosicrucians we should probably be surprised at the numbers who belonged to both systems. It included a study of the Jewish Cabala, and a Dutch Jew was exhibiting a model of Solomon s temple in 1675, and he would be likely to draw upon the Talmud and Cabala in his explanatory lectures; for the Cabala has a branch which possesses a semi-Masonic character in "Architectonic Gematria," which refers to the construction of words from the numbers given in the Bible when describing the measurements of the Temple, and the Ark of the Covenant, in relation to man himself. Brother W. W. Westcott, M.B., has translated a very curious passage entitled "The Secrets of Initiation, by J. J. Casanova, born 1725, Fr. R.C. circa 1757," in which he says: "The secrets of Initiation are by their very nature inviolable; for the Frater who knows them, can only have discovered them by himself. He has found them whilst frequenting well-instructed Lodges, by observing, comparing and judging the doctrines and symbols. Rest assured then, {431} that once he has arrived at this result, he will preserve it with the utmost care, and will not communicate it, even to those of his Fraters in whom he has confidence, for since any Frater has been unable to discover the secret for himself, he would be equally unable to grasp their real meaning, if he received them only by word of mouth."

There can be no reasonable doubt from the evidence of numerous degrees of
high-grade Masonry, and their symbolism, that what we have here described has contributed to the development of the systems now worked, though it must always be difficult to trace the development seriatim. These Mystical Societies had survived in various centres of Europe down to the period when Craft Masonry underwent a revival, and such traditional and mystical ceremonies were revised in many cases to adapt them to a new basis in new Rites. This is proved by identity of aims and emblems, but the system has such scant influence on the general work of the Craft that few consider these things worthy of notice; and moreover their ancient value as a means of uniting the forces of sectarian Brotherhoods, ceased to exist in their new form, with the general acceptance of freedom of conscience. The enquiry is of interest, but the secrecy of the old Mystic Societies will ever be an obstacle to full elucidation. Thus amongst Masons meeting together in Lodge, there were members of other Societies which had similar Rites to themselves, and therefore every probability that one would influence the other. The "Modern" historians, the word is used in its double sense, have always conceded scant justice to this section of

Freemasonry, and it has been their effort to assign all degrees, above the three first, of which the Grand Lodge, at its start, adopted two, to a foreign origin; and although French and German systems were introduced into this country in the 18th century; the evidence goes to show that with our Craft system went the nucleus of all the high-grades which were carried from England as early as 1688 and afterwards {432} manipulated abroad. There is far more probability for the continuous transmission of secret societies of mystics in this country than on foreign soil, and nothing is gained by the contention. We cannot be a party to the insinuations that truth is found only amongst English Masons, who are usually more ignorant than those abroad, nor concede an allseeing infallibility to the conceited critic who imagines that he knows everything.

In affinity with this subject of the high-grades must further be noticed, in one section at least, the essentially Christian character of its ancient ritual. Thus in a printed Catechism we find after a question of "How many lights?" the farther question, "What do they represent? A. The three persons; Father, Son, and Holy Ghost. Q. How many pillars? A. Two, Jachin and Boaz. Q. What do they represent? A. A strength and stability of the Church in all ages. Q. Who is greater than a Freemason! A. He who was carried to the highest pinnacle of the Temple of Jerusalem." This Christian character is found, in its strength, in the "Dumfries MS." from which we have had quotations, and was probably the system of such bodies as possessed the old Christian Masters Grade of Harodim-Rosy Cross.

The earliest printed evidence of something beyond the then new speculative Craft is a work by Robert Samber, written in 1721 under the nom-de-plume of Eugenius Philalethes, Junior, and which he dedicated to the Grand Lodge of London in 1722; and there is no doubt that much has passed out of existence that would have enlightened us upon the writer s views, inasmuch as he claims, as did the Carpocratian Gnostics, that Jesus established an esoteric doctrine which he communicated to his disciples, and the possibility of such views implies a much broader field to survey than most writers wish to concede.

This Preface of "Long Livers" clearly refers to certain high-grades then known, and is written in the easiest of three keys used by the Hermetic Societies, namely, the operative, philosophic, and religious; it bears entirely {433} upon the latter, and has no reference to operative Alchemy but uses the terms of this Craft, after the mode of Fludd, to convey Theosophic and Masonic truths. Almost whilst we write Brother Edward Armitage has discovered in the Bodleian Library, Oxford, fragments of a Ritualistic nature which bear upon the printed Preface, and is admitted to be in the handwriting of Samber. It is the preparatory application of a Rosicrucian formula to something missing. It embraces a trial by "water", in washing; of "fire" in purification; of "light" as a symbol carried to its extinguishment; of giving the "coal" and "chalk;" the "cord," or girdle, binding the recipient to the brotherhood; the "incense," the symbolism of "knocking" at a door; of "entrance;" and the "Oath" which is that of secrecy, extending even to the persons acting, and treats of the Aspirant s duties in general.<<Vide"Ars Quat. Cor.">> As a Preparation, which it says that it is, it may bear some relation to that which follows, as there is verbiage in common.

In the Preface of 1721, Samber alludes to the grades of the Arcane Discipline of the early Christians as comparable with Masonry; to a spiritual cube, and he

associates Masons spiritually with the three principles of the Hermetic Adepts, namely, salt, sulphur, and mercury, and there are other comparisons which agree with three Masonic grades. He claims that in all time there was a Brotherhood which preserved true religion, essentially what Dermott claims for the Royal Arch, and he goes on to demonstrate the doctrine of the Unity, passing from Moses through the Schools of the Prophets, and the Rabbis. He has also three traitors who correspond with the Cain, Achan, and Enni (Annas) of Harodim-Rosy Cross who slew the "Beauty" of the world. He ends by making Christ the reorganiser of a Masonic Brotherhood, and "holy brother St. Paul," is alluded to with a marked emphasis which shews that he had a Masonic theory respecting him. He thus leads us through the natural law exemplified in the Craft, the Jewish law in the Arch {434} or Red Cross, to the law of grace in Christian Masonry; for these things are fully implied though no such grades are alluded to by name. He says that he is addressing "a higher class who are but few," and this is done in Hermetic language, which shows that he perfectly understood the mystic language of that body. He speaks of those who ought to be "erased from the Book M.," which implies here Masonry, but remotely that mentioned in Chapter VI. We are rather concerned in defending Samber against his critics of the last 20 years, who represent him as little better than an idiot; the fault is theirs, for they "have eyes but see not." We will now follow with some extracts which shew that it was a well understood thing that there were certain degrees above the Craft system.

The learned Dr. Stukeley states in his "Autobiography," "7 Novr. 1722. The Order of the Book instituted," he terms it also "Roman Knighthood," and says, 28th December that he admitted to it Lords Hertford and Winchelsea. There is nothing to shew the nature of it, and it is not probable that it survived as a Masonic degree.

Bro. R. F. Gould has stated, in one of his papers, that there is an advertisement in the "Daily Mail" of 1724 announcing that a new Lodge is to be opened at St. Alban s Tavern for regulating the modern abuses which had crept into the fraternity, and "all the old real Masons are invited to attend." It is evidently the beginning of the agitation which led to "Ancient" Masonry, and the role of the Royal Arch.

In the years 1724 and 1725 there appeared two editions of a pamphlet entitled "Two Letters to a Friend," in which are allusions to Dr. Thomas Rawlinson, a leading Freemason, who left the Craft some documents referring to this period. In this print it is stated that the Brother styles himself R.S.S. and LL.D., and "he makes wonderful Brags of being of the Fifth Order The Doctor pretends that he has found out a mysterious "hocus pocus" {435} Word .

. . that against whomsoever he (as a member of the Fifth Order) shall pronounce the terrible word the person shall instantly drop down dead." To whatever degree Rawlinson really belonged it is certain that the allusion is to the Jewish tetragrammaton, and that the worthy doctor had been incautiously airing his knowledge of the "Essays" of Reuchlin and Agrippa upon the "Cabala," and the Mirific Word. There is no reason why the "fifth order," should not mean the 5th Degree which it is known the Arch was a little later. The nom-de-plume of the writer of the pamphlet is "Verus Commodus," and he mentions that some of the Masons "write themselves STP," after their names, which in his blatant fashion he tries to make a profanation of the Trinity; from this it may be inferred that a civil reference was not to be understood by him

but that it represented something Masonic, and we know, later on in the Century, that the Templar grade was abbreviated T.P. either as here, or with the crossed {symbol: "P" with vertical extended below and crossed as a Greek cross} and is so found on the 1791 Seal of Grand Conclave. The writer also says: "they tell strange foppish stories of a tree that grew out of Hiram s tomb."

In Ireland there seems an incipient reference to the Christian grades in the newspaper report of the Installation at Dublin of Lord Rosse as Grand Master, 24th June, 1725. The representatives of six Lodges of "Gentlemen Masons" were present, and it is said: "The Brothers of one Lodge wore fine Badges painted full of crosses and squares, with this Motto "Spes meo in Deo est," which was no doubt very significant, for the Master of it wore a yellow jacket and Blue Britches."<<"Caementaria

Hibernica," fasc. II.>> It was well known that the clothing refers to the brass handle and steel legs of a pair of compasses. The reporter also speaks of the "Mystical table" being in form of a Mason s square.

There is a burlesque advertisement of the tailors, 24 Dec. 1725, which accuses their "whimsical kinsmen of {436} the hod and trowel," with having changed their day of meeting and Patron, "on new light received from some worthy Rosicrucians."

On the 31st Dec. 1728, Brother Edward Oakley delivered an address at London, in which he quotes largely from Samber s Preface to "Long Livers," so that it must have had some Masonic importance given to it, and its references understood. Also, in 1729, Ephraim Chambers mentions in his "Cyclopoedia" that there are certain Free-Masons who "have all the characters of Rosicrucians," or "as retainers to the art of building."

There is a still more precise statement signed A.Z. in the "Daily Journal" of 5th Septr., 1730, from which we extract a small portion: -- "It must be confessed that there is a society abroad, from which the English Freemasons have copied a few ceremonies, and take pains to persuade the world, that they are derived from them. These are called Rosicrucians from their Prime Officers (such as our Brethren call Grand Masters, Wardens, etc.), being distinguished on their High days by Red Crosses."

The "Gentlemans Magazine," April 1737, contains a long attack upon Masonry signed JACHIN, in which he says: -- "They make no scruple to acknowledge that there is a distinction between "Prentices" and "Master Masons," and who knows whether they have not a higher Order of "Cabalists" who keep the "grand secret" of all entirely to themselves." It looks very like an intimation of the Royal Arch degree.

All this points out that prior even to 1717 the mixed Lodges possessed a higher section, whether known to the Grand Lodge or not, which could be spoken of in Rosicrucian Jargon, thus raising the question whether there was not then a Freemasonry that had been passing as Rosicrucian during the previous century; even the Chapter of Clermont, a Templar system, asserted that the system of Solomon, contained 7 degrees, and other books asserted that they had received a 7 degree system "from the very heart of Albion, the sanctuary of the high degrees." {437}

One of the earliest bodies of which we know something was the following: THE GORMOGONS.

It is possible that the Gormogons had some relations with the Jacobite Lodges of Harodim, as they used pseudonyms like the latter, and were equally attached to the Stuarts. Prichard, who wrote in 1730 hints that they had pre- 1717 or Ancient Masons in their ranks. Particulars of the body is found in the 1724 pamphlet entitled "Two Letters to a Friend," from which it appears that they had an Emissary at Rome, and Samber the author of "Long Livers," is identifiable under the designation of a "Renegade Papist." Ramsay was with the Pretender at Rome in 1724, and the Duke of Wharton, P.G.M. of England is evidently alluded to as a Peer who had suffered himself "to be degraded" by having his apron burnt in order that he might join the Gormogons, was with the Pretender at Parma in 1728, and had received the title of Duke of Northumberland from him about fourteen years previously. They had a secret reception and cypher of their own, and Kloss considers, no doubt rightly, that in their jargon "China" meant Rome.

Brother R. F. Gould has been at great pains to disentangle the history of the

Gormogons, and has made it clear that not only was Wharton a member, but probably founded the Society on an older Jacobite plan; and he shows that the dates of its activity syncronises with the events of Wharton s life; and the lampoon may very probably be Wharton s own composition, in which case it throws added light upon the matter in reference to Dr. Rawlinson. The "two un- happy busy persons" who obtained their idle notions . . . "about Adam, Solomon, and Hiram be- ing Craftsmen," and who abused, "a venerable old gentlewoman under the pretence of making her a European Hiramite," is interpreted to signify Anderson and Desaguliers in the new Constitution, whilst the venerable old gentlewoman is the old Operative {438} Charges. The whole satire was em- bodied by William Hogarth in a plate designated "The Mystery of Masonry brought to light by ye Gormogons." which went through three editions, the last about 1742; in this plate the old woman upon an ass who is about to be saluted by a man with his head in a ladder is thus explicable. As to Duke Philip, his father Thomas was somewhat to blame, Dr. Johnston flings the most opprobrious epithets at him.

THE NORTHERN HARODIM.

This degree was at one time very popular in the County of Durham, and may be supposed to be a part of the work of the Gateshead body to whom the Count Bishop granted a Charter in 1681. Bro. F. F. Schnitger was well acquainted with the last surviving Harod Bro. R. R. Read, a D.P.G.M. of the Mark, who received the degree from his father at Gateshead, where his grandfather also con- ferred it, and he had been received in the Lodge in youth as an Apprentice and it is said that the Lodge possessed his operative Indentures. Bro. Read made over all his privileges "free from Haro- dim," to the Newcastle high grades.

Bro. Robert Whitfield first mentioned the Swalwell Minutes of the degree in the "Freemason" of 11th Decr., 1880, and says that the Lodges claimed important privileges from former ages; the ap- pointment of the P.G.M., and the wearing of hats at the P.G.L. meetings.

The first mention of it, if it can be called so, is the quotation by Bro. Joseph Laycock, who brought the Swalwell, and the Gateshead Lodges under the G.L. in 1735, and was appointed P.G. Master of the Co. of Durham in that year. On these occasions he gave a quotation, in an Oration he then made, and which is

printed in the "Book M., or Masonry Triumphant," in 1736 at Newcastle. He terms these "old verses," and they are yet a part of the 4th section of the Jacobite Harodim-Rosy-Cross.

The next reference is a minute of the Swalwell Lodge {439} as follows: "July 1st 1746. Enacted at a Grand Lodge

"held this evening that no brother mason shall be "admitted into the dignity of a Highrodiam under less "than a charge of 2s. 6d.; or as Domaskin or Forin as "John Thomson of Gateside paid at the same night 5s. "Memorandum: Highrodiams to pay for making in that "order only 1s. 6d." (8 names follow and 9th line closes) "Paid 2s 6d. English, William Ogden. N.B. The "English Masters to pay for entering into the said "Master-ship 2s. 6d., per Majority."

Of course the "English Masters" refers to the Master Mason of the Grand Lodge of London, intro- duced by Laycock, and as they style themselves a Grand Lodge, and as the name of Joseph Laycock does not appear as a Harod at any time, it seems very clear that the object was a semi-rebellion of the old operative Masons against the innovations of 1735. A man who spells Harodim as Highrodiam may be excused for spelling Domatic as Domaskin, but Bro. Schnitger seems to think it may mean Damascus. The Lodge was mostly composed of the men employed at Cowley s foundry, and he brought over from Solingen, steel workers who claimed that they had inherited their method of working the metal from Damascus, as the Markgrave had brought instructions thence in the time of the Crusades.

The Ceremonial was a system of secret receptions in points, similar to the Jacobite Harodim-Rosy-Cross to which we will shortly refer. They were the custodians of the Ritual of all Masonry, which was what Oliver invariably termed the "Old York Ritual," and which certainly contains Harodim points, and no doubt York at one time had the ceremony. The two Trollopes who were part of the Gateshead foundation of 1681 were Stone-Masons of the city of York. Its position in Masonry is precisely that which we have described as Passed Masters, in the old pre-1717 London Guild. In operative times the Ritual, of which they claimed to have been the custodians, was doubtless the yearly Drama; it is the key {442} to all York Masonry after 1725, and begins with the 7th Degree and goes down even to the Apprentice.

They had oversight of all the Lodges of their jurisdiction, there were 9 of them, and they travelled in groups of 3 to punish irregularities, and reconcile differences. At receptions there were to be 9 present, but 6 and 3 candidates would suffice in emergencies.

At Sunderland Bro. Hudson states that the Harodim was conferred from the first establishment of the Phoenix Lodge, and that between 1755 and 1811 they received 150 members. In 1787 R. Markham "Passed the Bridge," and a month later was made a Royal Arch Mason. Bro. Logan has shown that Palatine Lodge, 97, had the Harodim. In each case members visited from neighbouring towns.

HARODIM-ROSY-CROSS.

This was a London version, clearly of Jacobite derivation, which in 1743 claimed a time immemorial origin; we would suggest that it might have been carried to France from the North by Derwentwater who belonged to this part of the country. It is clearly the grade which Baron Scheffer had from him, in two sections, when he gave him authority to establish Lodges in Sweden 25 Nov. 1737. Ramsay in his speech of 1737 alludes to the old Arcane Discipline of the Alexandrian Church when he says: "We have amongst us three classes of confreres, the "Novice or Apprentice; the Companion or Professed;

"the Master or the Perfected. We explain to the first the "moral virtues; to the second the heroic virtues, and to "the last the Christian virtues. . . the fourth quality is "a taste for the useful sciences and the liberal arts. . . .

"Religious discords caused us to change and to disguise, "and to suppress, some of our Rites and usages, which

"were opposed to the prejudices of the times." He also alludes to the Jews working with the sword in one hand and the trowel in the other, which are the lines quoted by Laycock in 1735. Dean Swift must have had some {441} knowledge of this, and he was acquainted with Ramsay in 1728; and he thus writes in 1731, -- "the famous old Lodge of Kilwinin, of which all the Kings of Scotland have been, from time to time, Grand Masters without interruption," and he speaks of the adornment of "Ancient Jewish and Pagan Masonry, with many religious and Christian Rites," by the Knights of St. John and of Malta.

It is quite possible that Scotland may have had the Rite of Harodim-Rosy- Cross at an early date. There is a curious passage in the "Muses Threnody," a metrical account of Perth, published in 1638 for Henry Adamson, M.A. The extract may mean much or little in the argument, according to the idea in the mind of the student, for he says:<<"Ars Quat. Cor.," 1898, p. 196. Vide also the writer s paper in A.Q.C., 1903.>>

"For we be brethren of the Rosie Cross,
We have the Masons word and second sight,"

The claim is made for this Metrical system of Lectures that it is of Culdee origin, and had I-colm-Kill for its birth place.

The following list of London Chapters has been carefully preserved at Edinburgh, and does not come down later than 1744:

1.   Grand Lodge at the Thistle and Crown in Chandos Street,
Immemorial.
2.   Grand Chapter   "   "   "   "
3.   Coach and Horses in Welbeck St.   Immemorial.
4.   Blue Boar s Head, Exeter St.   "
5.   Golden Horse Shoe, Cannon St., Southwark, December 11th, 1743.
6.   The Griffin, Deptford, in Kent, December 20th, 1744.

In 1750 there is a petition of Sir William Mitchell, FDLTY to Sir Robert RLF, Provincial Grand Master of the Most Ancient and Honourable Order of the HRDM of KLWNNG in South Britain; Sir Henry Broomont, FRDM, Deputy Grand Master; Sir William {442} PRPRTN; and Sir Richard, TCTY Grand

Wardens; and the rest of the Right Worshipful Grand Officers of the said orders."

It is said that the Grand Master had held his office since 1741, so that is probably the date when the Rite was reconstituted as here given. A Charter was granted to the Hague in 1751, and this was carried to Edinburgh in 1763, since which period the Rite has handed down the Lectures intact. It is likely however that some revision may have been made about 1740 say in the last section and the title. It has since 1767 been termed the "Royal Order of Scotland." In 1786 they Chartered a body at Rouen, when an interesting correspondence ensued between Wm. Mason the Grand Deputy Master, and Murdoch the Grand Secretary, in which the latter speaks of the dormancy of the Order for some time in Scotland, in a light that scarcely agrees with the facts of the case. Rebold says that the ceremonies of the Royal Order were revived on the formation of the Grand Lodge of St. John s Masonry the Mastership of the Jacobite Lodge Canongate Kilwinning, and it is a fact that in 1735 that Lodge had, as is proved by the Minutes, a "Masters Lodge" quite distinct from the Craft, and which in its work and organisation, was identical with the London Lodge, No. 115, designated in 1733 a "Scotts Masons Lodge," and Brother John Lane holds that this was identical in Constitu-

tion with certain Lodges established as "Master Masons Lodges" conferring that degree only of the English Ritual, that therefore the so called Scotts Lodges differed only in this that their members were Scottishmen. But though this be so it is no proof that the Rituals were the same, and it may well be that the actual Scots Lodges had a special ceremony such as the Mastership of Harodim. It is probable therefore that there is truth in Rebold s statement that the Cannongate Kilwinning Lodge, which was a Jacobite Lodge, was the Christian Harodim which expired, as the Scotch Rite contends with the ruin which befel that political sect. Thory who was {443} "Atharsata," or Most Wise, of the French Branch in 1807 makes the Mason of Heredom; the Knight of the Tower; and the Rosy Cross to correspond. -- as they clearly do, -- with the degrees of Scotch Master; Knight of the East; and the Prince Rose Croix; the fourth and last step termed the Sanhedrin he considers "the figurative banquet of the Pascal lamb," we rather consider it was converted into the Templar Kadosh.
RED AND ROSY CROSS.

In the absence of any old Minutes of these two degrees, it may perhaps be thought idle to express an opinion that they may have had an existence amongst Hermetic Masons long prior to the establishment of Modern Freemasonry. Ramsay told to Geusau, when occasionally visiting him at Paris in 1741, that General Monck had used the Lodges as meetings at which to promote the return of Charles II. Geusau s Diary passed into the keeping of the Prince of Reuss, and it is held that at this period it was sought to further ally the Hermetic associations of London with the Craft for the same purpose. There is this further to be said on the matter that the quaint old rhyming ritual of Heredom-Rosy Cross would seem to be a system of Lectures referring to these two degrees, which constituted with the Craft a Rite of themselves, the only qualification for the Rosy Cross being the Red Cross, -- sometimes termed the "Mysterious Red Cross of Babylon." When Harodim-Rosy Cross was carried to France by the followers of James II. the title was translated into "Rose Croix

of Heredom," and the Red Cross was designated Knight of the East, and in 1744, Knight of the Sword, whilst the Rosy Cross is the Rose Croix. In the Red Cross there are three points, namely: -- (1) The Obligation of the 3 Sojourners, Shadrach, Mesech, and Abadnigo, who have escaped the "fiery furnace of affliction"; (2) the Arch Chapter of Jerusalem, which includes the Passing of the Bridge on the way to and from Darius; (3) the Council of the Persian Monarch. There are many points {444} in the degree which have reference to the Harodim Lectures; such as passing the Bridge; the dungeon of the Tower; the journey of Zerrubabel, and the essays on the respective strength of Wine, Women, and the King, when Truth is said to be mighty above all things. Would that it applied to Masonry and Masons! There is one curious thing in this portion, in which it is said that the Lord will provide a victim, and it probably alludes to the ancient Guild Rite of a human sacrifice. Whilst the Red Cross is a mystery of the second temple added to that of Solomon, the Rosy Cross of Harodim is the erection of a spiritual temple not made with hands, the Mystery of the ancient Gnostics -- "God with us" in the bodily temple. There is an ancient alphabet given in Barrett s "Magus" called "Passing the River," having much similarity to Masons Marks, which may be allied with "Passing of the Bridge."
It is, to say the least, somewhat singular that so favourite a symbol, in all
time, as the Rose has been, in both religious and civil architecture, should have been neglected by the

modern Freemasons, and proves that it must have lost much of its symbolism. We have mentioned that Bishop Theodoratus connects mystically "Ros" with the Rose, which was a Gnostic emblem of the Saviour; and applies equally to the Arcane Discipline and the Rosy Cross -- "Ros," or dew, implying regeneration, and the Rose the thing regenerated. Shall I say it? The writer has seen an old Rosy Cross ritual, where the Adonisian fable that a drop of blood from the slain god, sprang up a rose, is applied to the Christian Saviour. In Egypt the Rose was consecrated to Isis or Mother Nature, and Apuleius fables himself as drawn from brute nature, or an Ass, by eating roses. Chaucer translated the Romance of the Rose, wherein a pilgrim is represented as going in search of roses. We have mentioned the Girdles of the Guild Mason, John Cadeby, of Beverley: a much worn one contains the letters J and B, whilst another is embroidered with roses, in the manner of modern Rose {445} Croix clothing. The Arms of William of Wykeham were two carpenters -- couples between three roses. The emblem was often carved in the centre of the ceilings of mansions to symbolise that what passed at the table was "under the rose." One other example we will mention: the Chapter House of York Minster, which is octagonal, and therefore based on the eight pointed Cross of the Temple, has upon the lintel of the entrance door the following Latin couplet, which, though it looks modern, is said to be ancient, but renewed when necessary: --

"Ut Rosa flos florum
Sic est domus ista domorum."

As the Rose is the flower of flowers, so this house is the house of houses.

Under the name of Macons Ecossois, Harodim, the "Parfait Macon," 1743, gives the degree of Knight of the Sword, or of the East, our Red Cross, as of the time of Darius and Zerrubabel, but in 1766 "Le Plus Secrets des Hauts Grades," omits Darius and adopts Cyrus, and terms the degree a military

ceremony, which goes to prove that the Army was employed to spread these degrees. Out of these two versions arose the Royal Arch, and other degrees.

The 4th point of Harodim-Rosy Cross was made Scottish by claiming Bruce as founder of it as a Knighthood, but Gould has shown that in ancient times, in the primitive Guilds of Paris, the Masters and Wardens were Esquires, and the Provosts (our Harods) Chevaliers. They also elected a Chief who had the title of Prince or King.

HOLY ROYAL ARCH, KNIGHT TEMPLAR, PRIEST.

This Rite is that of the Ancient Masons of York and London; yet although we have information that in or about 1740, it was known in London, Dublin, York, Stirling, very little that is reliable has appeared to show its actual origin. It is usually held that it originated with the dissident Ancients; yet as there was no Ancient Grand Lodge at the time when it had some prominence, it could {446} only have been established by the numerous Lodges of Masons which then existed, and which did not recognise the Grand Lodge of London. When Rawlinson brags of a 5th Order in 1724 it is just possible he may have belonged to such degree whether then termed the Red Cross or the Royal Arch. Only one thing is historically certain, sometime between 1723 and 1740 there were ancient pre-1717 Guild Masons, who were dissatisfied with the "digestive" faculties of Anderson and Desaguliers, and made up their minds to restore to Modern Masonry some part of what it had lost. There are so many features in common between the Red Cross of Babylon and the modern Royal Arch degree, that we are quite safe in assuming that there was a primitive Ritual from which both were evolved, and we can easily prove what that primitive ritual was. The term Red Cross seems to be far the most appropriate name for the degree, and for this reason that the term Royal Arch refers to a special Guild which members of this degree are not, they are essentially Craft Masons.

Both York and Dermott practised the Templar degree, but it seems never to

have assumed the rank of Masonry, but was occasionally, in all parts, at times, conferred on non-Masons; whilst the Priest was essentially a Protestant ceremonial.

THE ARCH. We have previously alluded to the ancient drama, or annual Commemorative Ceremonies, of the primitive Guilds. We have also mentioned that in laying the Foundation Stone of the temple of Solomon, a vault was constructed 1 Reed, or 6 cubits, below the floor, where, over the centre, was erected a Pedestal, in which were the plans and a scroll with the first lines of Genesis. This Foundation is laid on the "Five point method," and the instant the centre is fixed it is guarded by four men armed with swords in one hand and building tools in the other. When the fugitives returned from Babylon the centre of Solomon had to be found, and the labourers were set to find the vault and report to the duly Passed Masters {447} who had to report to the three Grand Masters. The vault being found, three Passed Masters descended and brought away the plans and the scroll which every modern Arch man brings away also. Nor did these revisers end here; they could not understand why modern Masons had only one Grand Master, whilst the Guilds had three, and they therefore gave the three Principals all the attributes of the original builders of the first temple; these held as their attributes three Rods by which to form a square building, or oblong as the 3 to 1 temple; the Arch Principals

instead of rods have sceptres; the private receptions of these principals, and their secrets, are all but identical with those possessed by the representatives of S.K.J., H.K.T., and H.A.B. Masons are so utterly careless about historical truth, that we might safely have left them to puzzle out the origin of the Arch degree for themselves, but what we have written, we have written.

There is no doubt that the old northern Harodim gave much of this information owing to their having been of Operative origin before they joined the Grand Lodge of London. The author of "The Illustrations of Masonry," William Preston, who was sometimes a Modern and sometimes an Ancient, reorganised the system of the Lectures in 1786 under the designation of the "Grand Chapter of Harodim," and established them in London 4th January, 1787; he claims that "it is of ancient date in different parts of Europe   The

Mysteries are peculiar to the Institution, and the Lectures of a Chapter include every branch of the Masonic System." The Rulers were a General Director and a Grand Harod, of which Harodim is the plural. The members were divided into Clause-holders, Sectionists and Lecturers. Thus the 5 first sections would carry a member to the Royal Arch; and four more sections conducted to the "Ne plus ultra," in a total of 81 points.

The Arch of the Ancients represents the Sanhedrin, composed of 72

members, as a Supreme Court of Judicature amongst the ancient Jews, so also does the Red Cross, {448} Knight of the Sword, and Prince of Jerusalem. Hence it is supposed to have a standing superior to that of a Grand Lodge which has irregularly usurped its functions. Although the ritual has undergone many changes, since none of its tinkers seem to have understood what it was, there is no doubt that it had developed into a stately reception before the year 1750. Brother A. J. Cooper Oakley has gone so far as to suggest a more ancient origin for the Arch Pedestal than any previous writer, namely, that it is the "Yantram" or symbol of the Temple of Jehovah, for the temple of every Hindu deity is bound to have a Yantram composed of a geometrical or monogrammatic emblem upon which the god is placed.

An old catechism printed in 1723 asks the question, "Whence comes the pattern of an Arch?" and the answer is, "From the rainbow." Another printed Catechism of 1730 but grounded on the modern system of 1717, speaks of a word "which was lost, is now found," and there are French tracing boards of the Craft for 1743, which contain the word "Jehovah," and the Rituals of that period say that a word was substituted out of fear lest Hiram should have been induced to reveal the genuine one. We must bear in mind that the work of the Grand Lodge was not that of the Harods, though Anderson s Constitutions of 1723 has the representation of an Arch.

Oliver in his "Discrepancies" embodies the excellent authority of the late Peter Gilkes that the lost secrets of the Moderns, for the Guild had no lost secrets, were anciently given to the newly received Master after an interval of 15 days, and the old French ritual, before quoted, gives them at the close of the ceremony. There is a symbolism at York and Stirling which seems to make the Arch and the Rainbow synonymous. The minutes of Dermott s Grand Lodge in 1752 mentions the "absurdities" of Dr. Macky, of London, "one of the leg of mutton Masons," so called because they made Masons for that useful joint, "who gave a long story about twelve marble stones, &c., and that the rainbow was the Royal {449} Arch." Yet Oliver in confirmation of this quotes "an old Masonic work," in which the Royal Arch is carried up from the building of the

second temple to Moses, Aholiab, and Bezaleel, and from thence to the Altar and Sacrifice of Noah, under the Rainbow as an Arch, and with the Altar as a Pedestal, thence to the expulsion of our first parents from the Garden of Eden.<<"Landmarks," ii, p. 350.>> Similar matter is referred to in the Old York Lectures, and its 2nd Degree has a legend of 12 stones erected in the river Jordan.

Dr. Crawley thinks that an incipient form of the Arch degree can be traced in Anderson s Constitutions of 1723,<<"Cem. Hib.">> and that this is hinted at in two parts of the ceremony of Installation of Master, sanctioned by the Duke of Wharton in 1722, where he speaks of the "cement of the Brotherhood," and of the "cement of the Lodge," when the "well built" Arch was formed, and the word may have been then given. It is a very plausible theory and the only thing against it is that the oldest rituals we have give no hint of it. The Arch degree, by written evidence, first consisted of three steps or Veils, entitled the Excellent, Super-Excellent, and the Royal Arch itself.

In the "Impartial Enquiry" of Dr. D Assigny, printed at Dublin in 1744, he makes allusions to the Arch degree as composed of a body of men who had passed the Chair of Master, and alludes to some propagator of degrees in Dublin who claimed to have the York system "a few years before" (1744), and that his want of knowledge was exposed by some brother who was acquainted with the Royal Arch degree as it was practised in London, which is "prima facia" evidence that it was widely spread. He adds in a note: "I am told in that city (York) is held an assembly of Master Masons, under the title of Royal Arch Masons, who as their qualifications and excellencies are superior to others, they receive a larger pay than working Masons, of which more hereafter." This seems to allude to an Operative Arch Guild at York, as it is doing violence to his language to read it that whilst the Craft was the {450} initiation of working Masons, the Arch was intended for Initiates and Rulers of a higher standing.

At the "General Assembly on St. John s day," there may have been practised ceremonies of which we are allowed to have no written knowledge, and which may have been discontinued in the sleep into which it fell between 1740 and 1760; their old Lectures ask the question: "Who amongst Masons are entitled to knowledge?" A. "Those who are justly considered Free and Accepted, and have been Exalted to the Royal Arch Degree, and Knighted in a Masonic Encampment."

D Assigny goes on to say that there had "lately" arrived in Dublin some itinerant Mason, evidently a different person to those he had mentioned, who offered to add three more degrees to the Craft, of some "Italic" Order, and he warns his brethren against foreign schemers. When Lord Sandwich asked a definition of "Orthodoxy" from Bishop Warburton, the latter wittily replied, "Well, my Lord, Orthodoxy is my doxy, but Heterodoxy is another man s doxy." Hence we need not worship D Assigny s doxy; what we learn from his remarks is that about 1740 there had entered Dublin two systems of working the Arch, one of York, and a London one which D Assigny favoured, and that these were, in some respects, opposed to each other. The three grades of an "Italic" system may have been Clermont Templary, Jacobite and Romish.

For some 15 or 20 years the Grand Lodge of all England at York was dormant, but was revived in 1762 by one of its old Grand Masters., Francis Drake, Jacobite in his leanings. The Grand Lodge formally recognised the Arch, and there are minutes which show that in 1778 the Templar was a

ceremony equally recognised. It would seem, however, that the officers named, 7th Feb., 1762, are H.Z.J., so that the Arch degree related to the 2nd temple as with Dermott, but that in 1776 it referred to Solomon s temple, and would therefore be the "Arch of Enoch," and Oliver says that he saw an old {451} ritual of 1778 in which this ceremony appears as introductory to the Arch of the 2nd temple, and that after his own Exaltation in 1813 he saw another ritual in which the portion relating to Enoch s Arch was struck out. At a later period, however, the officers are those of the 2nd temple as in Dermott s System.

The actual earliest mention of the Royal Arch in print is at Youghall in 1743, where there was a procession of Lodge 21, with display, amongst these particulars we have: "Fourthly, the Royal Arch, carried by two Excellent Masons."<<"Faulkner s Dublin Journal," 10-14, Jany. 1743 (1744) quoted by Dr. Crawley.>>

If these grades were given at York before 1740, it is curious to note that degrees, or systems, called "Scotch Masters," are alluded to in minutes. Thus in Royal Cumberland Lodge, 41, Bath, appears the following, 8th January 1746: "Brothers Thomas Naish and John Berge were this day, made Scotch Masters, and paid for makeing 2s. 6d."; five others were received 27th Novr., 1754. In the minutes of the Salisbury Lodge, 19th October, 1746, we find this: "At this Lodge were made Scotts Masons, five brethren of the Lodge," one of them being the W.M. The Lodge of Longnor, Co.

Derby, claim that they received the method of the secrets from the rebel Army whilst in Derby. Kloss quotes J. F. Pollett as saying, 25th April, 1763, that the Scotts degree was the same as that known as the Royal Arch of France, where it dates from the raising of the Scottish Regiment Ogilvy in 1746, and he gives the clothing as green and red, which is that of the Red Cross, and the two, crossed, of Harodim-Rosy Cross. This would render it probable that "Scotts" in England went with the rebellion of 1745. The old Scottish Minute books show Initiations of military men, many of whom joined James II., and established these degrees in the Army and on the Continent.

Lawrence Dermott, to whose labours London was indebted for the establishment of the Grand Lodge of the "Ancients," who termed themselves York Masons also, {452} had no doubt received the London version of the Royal Arch in Dublin apparently in 1746. In his "Ahiman Rezon" of 1764 is a note, not found in any earlier or later edition<<Reprinted "Ars Quat. Cor." vi.>> in reference to the Arms, quarterly, a lion, ox, man, and eagle, which he says were found in the collection of the Architect and Brother, Rabbi Jacob Jehudah Leon, who had constructed in 1641 a model of Solomon s temple, for the States of Holland, which he exhibited in Paris, Vienna, and in London under the great seal and the signature of Killigrew. At the same time Leon published a description of his labours entitled "A relation of the most memorable things in the Tabernacle of Moses, and the temple of Solomon, 1675," and dedicated it to King Charles II., and Dermott adds that in 1759 and 1760 he had examined and perused such curiosities, and he concludes, "As these were the Arms of the Masons who had built the Tabernacle and Temple, there is not the least doubt of their being the proper Arms of the most Ancient and Honourable Fraternity of Free and Accepted Masons, and the continual practice and formalities, and tradition, in all regular Lodges, from the lowest degree to the most high, "i.e.," THE HOLY ROYAL ARCH, confirms the practice thereof."

Dermott in his "Constitutions" seems to follow the lines indicated by Samber in 1721, and he informs us that the Arch degree possessed (circa 1740) the peculiar square alphabet, which he says that he had known for over 30 years. A similar alphabet was in use amongst the Occultists, who termed it the "Aiq Bekar," or Cabala of nine chambers; it is found in Barrett s "Magus," and when dissected gives an alphabet of 9 characters increased to 27 by adding to the first series one and two dots respectively; Trithemius, the friend of Cornelius Agrippa, is known to have possessed it.

In reference to Dermott s claim to the Arms used by Rabbi Leon, it is easy to prove that they were not used by Craft Lodges, unless it might have been by some unknown {453} Speculative branch. All the ancient Guild MSS., which add Arms, use those granted to the London Company of Masons in 1472, or a variation of them. Randal Holme gives these in his "Acadamie of Armorie," with triple towers, according to the original grant, but he adds as supporters, which are not in the Grant, two pillars of the Corinthian Order, "or," or gold. But we cannot hastily dismiss Dermott s contention, for Leon s Arms of the Masons were used by the Grand Chapter of York, and Bro. W. H. Rylands posesses an old panel brought from St. Albans, of date circa 1675-80 which gives these Arms over the interlaced square, level, and plumb of the Masons. There are moreover Rosicrucian and Cabalistic works which treat of these symbols, and it is probable, as they represent the banners of the four leading Hebrew tribes, that Leon might derive them from the Cabala or Talmud, or he might have been a member of the ancient Jewish Guild. In Masonry peculiar systems are taken up by small bodies, then die out, to be revived in another part of the country. The "Book of Razael," alluded to by Cornelius Agrippa in his book on "Magic," affords evidence of the signs used in the Arch degree, and the "Exagogue" of the Jew Ezekiel, written, so Wharton thinks, after the destruction of Jerusalem, and translated into Latin by Fr. Morellus at Paris in 1580, gives details which have reference to the Signs of the Veils, omitted from the modern ceremony, but which gave the titles of Excellent and Super-excellent. Clemens and Eusebius give portions of the drama, so its great antiquity is unquestionable. The following seems to have been the general practice before the modern revision; Masons under the G.L. of the Ancients prefaced the Arch ceremony by the Mosaical Veils; those under the G.L. of the Moderns prefaced it with the Arch of Enoch. France at the same period had a degree said to refer to the time of Vespasian which they termed the Royal Arch of York.

A London Lodge of 1754 practised degrees to which the ordinary Mason was not admitted; Dermott terms it {454} Ancient Masonry held every third Lodge night, on account of extraordinary benefits its members had received abroad. The Lodge met at the Ben Johnson s Head in Spitalfields, and Grand Lodge censured them. Moderns, however, became members of both the Royal Arch and Templar, but without the sanction of their Grand Lodge. They sought and obtained from Lord Blaney, 22nd July, 1767, a Charter of Institution and Protection, formulated a "Charter of Compact" in 1778, and printed an "Abstract of Laws for the Society of Royal Arch Masons in London," 1778, and followed by a 2nd edition in 1782. Bristol had a Lodge founded in 1757 and erased in 1769, in which the Arch degree was worked. A Charter was granted in 1769 to Manchester under the title of "The Euphrates Lodge, or Chapter of the Garden of Eden, No. 2"; the writer tried to save it from erasure in 1854, but the old members were indifferent to its fate. At Bristol on 7th August, 1758.

Bro. Henry Wright gave a "Crafts Lecture," and on the 13th of the same month "Brothers Gordon and John Thompson were raised to the degree of Royal Arch Masons"; on the 31st of the same month, "Brother Peter Fooks requested to be raised to the degree of Royal Arch and accepted," and this was done on the 3rd Septr., 1758, along with two others, "and a Lecture on the degree was given by Brother James Barnes"; the minutes are headed "A Royal Arch Lodge,"<<W. J. Hughan, "Freemason," 17 Dec. 1898.>> and there are other receptions down to 1759.

From recent discoveries it appears that Brother Thos. Dunckerley, a scion of royalty on the wrong side of the blanket, was Exalted to the Royal Arch degree at Portsmouth in 1754, as he states in a letter of 14th January, 1792. Bro. Alexr. Howell discovered at Portsmouth, in recent years, an old Minute book in cypher of the Chapter of Friendship, No. 3, chartered 11th August, 1769. We read: 1st Septr., 1769 -- "The Bro. G.M. Thomas Dunckerley bro t the Warrant of the Chapter, and having lately received {455} the Mark, he made the Bre n Mark Masons and Mark Masters, and each chuse their Mark, &c. He also told us of this mann r of writing which is to be used in the degree, which we may give to others, so that they be F.C. for Mark Masons, and Master M. for Mark Masters." In Novr. 1770, the degrees of Excellent and Super Excellent Masons are mentioned, to pay 10s. for two steps and two guineas for the Arch as before. In Octr. 1778, the term Companion is used, and Dunckerley gives the Chapter permission to make Knights Templars.

In 1769 the Arch was known at Darlington, Co. of Durham. as the
"Hierarchal Lodge"; and Lodge 124, Durham possessed the Mark as we read 21st Decr., 1773,
"Brother Barwick was also made a Mark d Mason, and Bro. James MacKinlay raised to the degree,
of a Master Mason, and also made a Mark Mason, and paid accordingly."
In Scotland the Mark was usually recognised by the Arch authority, and Stirling has a very old Chapter named the "Stirling Rock Chapter" which possesses two old and rudely engraved brass plates
which alludes to the REDD-CROSS or ARK. The Chapter has been admitted to date from 1743,
and they had minutes from that period, but we will allude to this when we reach the Templar.
At Dumfries some interesting matter has been discovered by Bro. James Smith. The Register of Passings to the Royal Arch degree begin in 1756, with a form of Certificate after a Minute of "Passing
the Chair," and the "Sublime degrees of Excellent, Super-Excellent, and Royal Arch Mason" of the
8th October 1770, in which the degree of Mark Mason is mentioned.<<"Freemason," 17th March,
1894.>> There was also a Royal Arch Chapter at Montrose in 1765. In the "Pocket Companion"
of Joseph Galbraith, printed at Glasgow in 1765, is a song of which a verse follows; it also contains
a letter on the Acts of the Associated Synod, which first appeared in the "Edinburgh Magazine" for
October, 1757, under the signature of "R.A., M.T.L., Edin. {456} Oct. 25th, 1757." The Chapter
mentioned in this verse would be the "Enoch": --
"May every loving Brother, Employ his thoughts, and search,
How to improve, in peace and love, The GLASGOW ROYAL ARCH."

A Glasgow Templar was "remade" in the Manchester Royal Encampment in 1786, the year chartered by the G.L. of All E. at York.<<Notes on the Temple and St. John, 1869 - Yarker.>> There are
minutes at Banff, 1765-78, of the Arch and of the Mark, when the two steps of the latter were conferred on F.C. and M.M. The Scoon and Perth Lodge, which claims our "British Solomon," James
I. of England, as one of its members, had these degrees, as we learn from the Minutes of the Edinburgh Chapter, No. 1, 2nd Decr. 1778, when they were conferred on members of the St. Stephen
s Lodge. Certain brethren were made Passed Masters, and 4th Decr. 1778, the Officers received --
"Ex. and Sup. Ex. Mason, Arch and Royal Arch Masons," and lastly Knights of Malta.<<"Scoltish
Freem.," Aug. 1894.>>
In Ireland it has hitherto been difficult to obtain information as to Lodge work, but we have already
mentioned allusions to it, in Dublin, circa 1740, and elsewhere four years later. It was generally
worked under the Craft Charter, as was equally the case, under authorisation of Dermott s G.L.,
from 1751. The Red Cross was required, but it has now been divided into three sections since they
accepted the Scottish Rite of 33 degrees, and they professed to claim it from the 1515 Order of Kt.
of the Sword of Gustavus Vasa.
In America the Arch degree was practised early. At Virginia, U.S.A., there is a record that, 22nd
Dec., 1753, a "Royall Arch Lodge" was held, when "three brethren were raised to the degree of
Royal Arch Mason." Philadelphia has had a Chapter since 1758. At Boston. U.S.A., the "St. Andrews" has a Minute that Wm. Davies was {457} "made by receiving the four steps, that of an Excellt., Sup.-Excellt., Royal Arch, and Kt. Templar," and it is afterwards said these are "the four steps
of a Royal Arch Mason."<<Hughan s "Englsh Rite.">> Brother Benjamin Deane, Past Gd. Master

of Templars, has lithographed a certificate which says that, 1st Augt., 1783, a brother was "pass d, been raised to the Sublime Degrees of an Excellent, Super-Excellent, Royal Arch Mason, Red Cross, Knight Templar." Bro. G. W. Bain, of Sunderland, has printed the copy of a certificate issued by the Dominica Lodge, No. 229, of the Ancients. It was given by the High Priest of an Arch Chapter, 22nd Decr., 1785, and records that John Lucas was appointed to constitute the Lodge and proved himself -- "Past Master in the Chair, Grand Alarm, Signs and Summons, Ark, Excellent, and Super-Excellent, Arch, and Royal Arch, Super-Excellent Mason in the Royal Art . . . a Sir Knight of the Red Cross."<<"Freemason," 31st Jany. 1891.>> These notices might have been very greatly extended from English Minutes of bodies that worked these degrees under Craft Warrants, but we have said enough to show the nature of the system, which had not "one" central organisation. The Ancient Masons of the 1751 Grand Lodge of London, printed Royal Arch Regulations in 1771, which they again revised in 1789 and 1791. The members frequenting the Modern body of 1717, issued a 3rd edition in

1796, and a 4th in 1807.

There is a peculiar duplication of Rites, alluded to in these last pages which we may point out before proceeding further. We have two separate and distinct rites as follows: --

I. 1. Craft Masonry in 3 degrees.   II. 1. Craft Masonry in 3 degrees.

2.   Red Cross (passage of the Bridge).   2. Royal Arch (Enoch etc.)

3.   Rosy Cross (Harodim, etc.).   3. Templar.

If to the first we add the Kadosh, and to the second the Templar Priest, we have (including the required Past Master) a double Rite each of seven degrees, practically {458} distinct, yet all through identical in ceremony, or almost so, and yet no evidence that either Rite is derived from the other.

TEMPLAR PRIEST.

All the Templar bodies of the 18th century in England, Ireland, and Scotland, possessed this degree, which was at one time in esteem; it is now entirely abandoned; in Ireland because the Orangemen obtained it, at a time when there was a close alliance between that body and Freemasonry. The ceremony is an embodiment of Fludd s idea that: "It is under the type of an Architect that the prophet warns us -- Let us go up to the mountain of reason and there build the Temple of Wisdom. " Again, its laws have: "Wisdom hath builded her house, she hath hewn out the seven pillars thereof." The rite had seven steps, or journeys, with seven passwords, and seven species of refreshment, seven seals, and seven emblems. Its certificates sometimes gave the era as "the year of revival 1686." In the French Ordre du Temple the Profession of Knight exacted the tonsure, and conferred clerical functions; and it is a reasonable conjecture that conscientious convictions led to the establishment of the degree, in or about the date named. The Early Grand Lodge of Ireland dated its Era from 32 A.D. York Templars did the same.

KNIGHT TEMPLAR.

The early history of this degree, or Order, is shrouded in much mystery, and all that we can do in the elucidation of it in this country is to give such views as have some probability.

The writer suggested in "Notes on the Order of the Temple, etc," 1869, that it entered England with the followers of James I., after 1603. Bro. F. F. Schnitger, in a Lecture given at Newcastle, sought to show, and with some force, that all the charges brought against the actual {459} Knights of the Temple in 1311 can be explained by a forced and false view of certain Rites in the modern ceremony, which proves an actual descent of the ritual from the ancient body.

In a lecture by the late Bro. T. B. Whitehead, of York, some years ago, he advocated the probable connection of the Templars, whom Archbishop Greenfield placed in the Monastery of St. Mary s Abbey, and the York Guild Masons. Through the Knights of St. John and the Temple some such connection is feasible, as Masonic history asserts that in 1500 the Knights in London and the Guild Masons were under the protection of Henry VII. Lessing advocates the chivalric union through a certain house at which Wren assembled, with his Masons, during the erection of St. Paul s. Bro. Henry Sadler<<"Facts and Fictions.">> shows that numerous independent Lodges existed termed "ye Holy Lodge of St John," and the Grand Lodge list of 1723, contains a Lodge held at St. John s Gate, Clerkenwell, the old property of the Knights, and the Lodge must have withdrawn itself at once, as it is not mentioned in later lists. Hogarth in his burlesque of the "Scalde Miserable Masons," has the Tyler of "His Grace of Wattin, Grand Master of the Holy Lodge

of St. John of Jerusalem at Clerkenwell." By Whattin does he allude to the Duke of Wharton? It would seem so. During the 18th and 19th century the "Gate" was a favourite meeting place for conferring the high grades and was much frequented by the adjacent Lodges. The Grand Master at Malta in 1740 expelled six of his Knights for being Freemasons.

The late Bro. Col. W. J. B. McLeod Moore, of Canada, a Past G.M. of Templars, had a theory, which he had received from an aged Danish Physician, and which included Templars and Masons. He asserts that the Benedictines, who date circa 600 A.D., practised the sacred mysteries of the "Arcane Discipline" of the Alexandrian Church. The aged Dane informed him that the King of {460} Denmark was head of a secret non-Masonic Society in the 18th century, of which he himself was a member in 1785. It had seven degrees. When the United Orders of St. John and the Temple were suppressed in the 16th century, and Torphican and its Knights dissolved, these fugitives carried their mysteries to Denmark, and that he belonged to the body at Copenhagen 60 years previously. These sacred Mysteries represented the Fall of Man; his Redemption by sacrifice; and the Resurrection.<<"Canadian Craftsman," vol. 19- 22, 1885-8.>> They saw Christ by Faith and represented his doctrine by symbols; they taught that none can claim the right of eternal life beyond the grave, but those that "believe on Him that liveth, and was dead, and is now alive for evermore." The object, the end, the result of the great speculations of antiquity, was the ultimate annihilation of evil, and the restoration of man to his first state by a Redeemer, a Master, a Christus, the Incarnate Word.

Of course this view as to the Mystery of the Templars has been advocated by many writers, and has been equally applied to Masonry by Samber in 1721, by Ramsay in 1737, and is the same thing as the claim to a Culdee origin by the Harodim-Rosy-Cross. There were, as we have indicated, many similar Societies and the following may be noted. On 6th Dec., 1623, John Chamberlain wrote to Sir Dudley Carlton, a letter which appears in the "Court and Times of James the First" (London, 1848), from which it appears that Lord Vaux s regiment had brought from the Low Countries a Society the members of which had become numerous in London, and "under colour of good fellowship have taken certain oaths and Orders, to be true and faithful to the Society, and conceal one another s secrets . . . having a Prince . . . wearing blue or yellow ribbons, having certain nicknames for their several Fraternities." Apparently all the formula of Freemasonry.

The Stuarts in the 17th century made an effort to revive the Order of St. John

and the Temple, then of Malta, and {461} a North Convent seems to have existed about Montrose, and it is alleged, on the authority of Dom Calmet, that Viscount Dundee was Grand Master of "the Order of Templars in Scotland," and that when he fell at Killiekrankie he wore the Grand Cross which was given to Dom Calmet by his brother. It is also asserted that Mar and Athol succeeded him, and that Prince Charles Edward Stuart was installed Grand Master at Holyrood in 1745, and that John Olivant of Bachilton succeeded him, and held the office until his death, 15th Oct., 1795.<<"Scottish Statutes of the Temple.">> After this the remnant of the Order is said to have united with some Scoto-Irish Templars, of whom Alexander Deuchar, Lyon Herald, was Grand Master, and who said, no doubt truthfully, that he could trace the Order back in Scotland to 1740, by means of living members.

It is quite certain that there was at this period in France an "Ordre du Temple," with a charter from John Mark Larmenius who claimed appointment from Jacques de Molay. Philip of Orleans accepted the Grand Mastership in 1705 and signed the Statutes. Its enemies, in recent years, have asserted that these Statutes were forged by the Jesuit Father Bonani, and that it was actually the re-suscitation of a 1681 Society entitled the "Little resurrection of Templars," and that it had as one of its members the learned Fenelon who converted Ramsay to Orthodoxy. In any case, if of 1705, the Charter proves the existence of a branch of Scottish Templars, because it was considered necessary to place them, with the Knights of St. John, "outside the bounds of the Temple, now and for ever." In 1766, de Tschoudy speaks well of these French Knights as the "Fraternity of Jerusalem," nicknamed "Freres de Aloya" from the compositon of their suppers.

At Stirling a system of Masonic Templary prevailed which they attributed,

rightly or wrongly, to certain Knights of St. John and the Temple who became protestants, and joined the Masonic Lodge at that place, {462} whence an order of "cross-legged masons" arose. We should put it that the Knights continued the superintendence of the Masons of their Domus. In confirmation of this they show two rudely-cut brass plates about 9 x 3 inches, which they believe to date into the 17th century. The first of these has on one side, the words STIRLING ANTIENT LODGE, and the Apprentice Symbols; -- the obverse having the Fellow Craft emblems. The 2nd contains on one side the Masters symbols,

-- two pillars, sun, moon, figures 1 to 12 in a circle (a clock); obverse, at top the words REDD-CROSS OR ARK, with a cross, a dove, and an ark; at bottom, a series of concentric arches, like a rainbow, but with a Key-stone in place, within a border of three equal divisions the inscription SEPULCHRE, with an adze, stone, and sarcophagus. KNIGHTS OF MALTA, with lamb, &c., and three tapers joined, KNIGHT TEMPLAR, with what appears to be a serpent, and 12 tapers in 7 and 5. Name of Lodge as 1st plate.<<Vide Plates. "Ars Quat. Cor." xiii, p. 34>>

Allusions to the bye-laws appear in the Lodge Minutes in 1745, and a copy appears of 14th May, 1745, signed by Jo. Callender M. The 8th bye-law reads:

--

"Entered Apprentice 10s.   To Grand Lodge 2s. 9d.

Passing Fellow-Craft 2s. 6d.   Passing Master 7s. 6d.

Excellent and super excellent 5s. Knight of Malta 5s.<<Hughan s "Pref."

to D Assigny, Leeds 1898.>>

And that each Entered Apprentice shall treat the Lodge to the extent of 5s. if demanded."

It is possible the plates may date about 1743. There is a minute of 1784 that Alexr. Craig then conferred on certain brethren the Order of Malta, and that about 10 years previously he had conferred the degrees of Excellent, super Excellent.

The objection is sometimes made that as Masonry was an Operative Guild they were not a likely body to have continued difficult Rites and ceremonies, or to have appreciated anything but simple tokens of recognition. But this is a very shallow view to take as will be apparent {463} when we remember that Masons, and other trade Guilds, were engaged for ages in the spectacular dramas entitled the Mystery plays, and they were therefore, from ancient times,

the very men who were most likely to appreciate such Rites in their own secret Assemblies. With the Reformation the sacred drama came to an end in this country, and it is to the feeling thus engendered that we owe such a Minute as that at Melrose, enacting that the Rites were to be administered "free from superstition."

Dublin seems to have the most steady continuation of the Templar of St. John, though we have no written proof of the accuracy of its claims. There is a valuable paper on this subject by Bro. C. A. Cameron.<<A.Q.C., 1900.>> It appears that the Early Grand Encampment of Ireland on the 29th Augt. 1805, issued a document contesting a proposal of the Grand Lodge to take over the control of that body, in which it is said, -- "Our Early Grand Encampment of Ireland has subsisted in the City of Dublin for above a century," and additional currency was given to this by Caesar Gautier, who says, -- "its age was above a century, as appears by its books." Some of its Warrants established bodies of non-Masonic Templars of St. John, and the like is known to have been the case, from time to time, in England, Ireland, Scotland, and in America as says Dr. Folger; and although all the Ancient Masons in these countries gave the Templar in succession to the Arch degree, there seems equally a feeling everywhere, that it was not looked upon as a Masonic degree.

There was formerly an Early Grand body at Carisbrooke, I. of Wight; they also

existed in Lancashire, and I have supplied to enquirers copies of a Ritual of 1800. The body ceased to meet about 1836. The "Freemasons Quarterly" (1846 p. 176) gives information in regard to an Early Grand Encampment of England, the minutes of which passed into the hands of the Duke of Sussex,

G.M. It contained a curious document of 1312 in the shape of a Prayer, or supplication {464} of the ancient Knights, at the time of their trial, at the hands of the two scoundrels Bertrand de Goth, and Philip le Bel, a coiner of false money. This ancient document is said to have been deposited under the high- altar of the Temple Church London, where it was discovered in 1540. Then it passed, -- how is not stated, -- into the hands of Jacob Ulric St. Clair of Roslyn, in whose family it was handed down, until it came to William St. Clair, the Scottish Grand Master of 1736, who gave it to his nephew John St. Clair, M.D., of Old Castle, Co. of Meath, who translated it, with assistance, and forwarded this copy to the said E. C. E. of England.

There was however a second body of Templars in Ireland termed the "High Knights Templar," who conferred the Rite under their Craft Charter. These men applied in 1770 to the Kilwinning Lodge of Scotland for a Charter under the designation of the "High Knights Templar Kilwinning Lodge," who granted the same without any enquiry. It is said that Baron Donoughmore was their G.M. in 1770, and that these said H.K.T. of Ireland s Kilwinning Lodge in 1779 conferred the degrees of E., S.E., H.R.A. The Knights Templar are mentioned in 1786, 1792; and the Rose Croix, is said to have been carried to Dublin by the Chevalier St. Laurent.

The Early Grand has been extinct for half a century but at the present moment is represented in Scotland by an independent body working the degrees of Red Cross of Rome and Constantine; Kt. of St. John; Knt. of the Holy Sepulchre; the Christian Mark; the T. I. O. of the Cross; Pilgrim, Templar, Mediterranean Pass, and Knight of Malta. Besides which they recognise other side degrees formerly practised in Scotland. It appears that after the Early Grand Encampment of Ireland had issued some 30 Charters to Britain they

gave to Brother Robert Martin as Grand Master, in 1822, a Charter of renunciation of rights and of Erection under which this body works to the present time quite unattached to the ordinary history of Templary in Scotland.

{465} At York the Templar was formally recognised by the Grand Lodge, and they chartered several subordinate "Royal Encampments" before 1780, when a Charter was granted, 6th July, to Rotherham.

We have mentioned that the "Modern" members of the Royal Arch had established themselves under a so-called Charter of Compact, and the Templars of Bristol executed a similar Charter, 20th Decr., 1780, with Joshua Springer as G.M. Its 20 rules will be found in W. J. Hughan s "English Rite;" in which they style themselves, -- "The Supreme Grand and Royal Encampment of the Order of Knights Templars of St. John of Jerusalem, Knights Hospitallers, and Knights of Malta, &c.;" these Regulations settle the question of Costume, &c., but we have not the "Charter of Compact" itself, nor the bodies thus compacted.

About the year 1790 Thomas Dunckerley, who had long taken a very important part, in every degree of Freemasonry, and was Grand Superintendent of the Royal Arch for Bristol &c., and he himself writes to the York Encampment of Redemption, 24th July, 1791, that the Bristol Knights had requested him to take the Grand Mastership of their Order, which of course would include all the bodies which had "Compacted," no doubt Bath and Salisbury. There was an Encampment termed the "Observance" of London, which had evidently a Foreign origin, as Lambert de Lintot, who was a P.M. of Lodge "St. George of Observance," and who had been initiated in 1743, had for many years been working the seven degree system of the French Templary of Clermont, ostensibly as "Agent of Prince Charles Edward Stuart." A Rose Croix ritual in French was printed at London which says that a member of the degree had "power to assemble Masons, and perfect them up to the 6th degree of Ecossaise Knight of the East;" qualifying for the 7th Degree of R.C.

Bath, it has already been noted, had the practice of "Scotts Masonry" in 1746, nor was it then abandoned, {466} for there are other minutes of 1754. But whatever degrees

Bath had, with Bristol, under the Charter of Compact, Dunckerley commissions in 1791 Charles Phillpott, a Banker of Bath, to confer his system, and in 1793 he writes to T. West, who had been present at Phillpott s initiation in 1784, -- that he expects he will have conferred upon him "the 1st section of the 5th degree, viz.: Rosae Crucis"; and there is a 1790 Minute at Bath with an evident Dunckerley reference, -- "William Boyce took all the degrees of the Red Cross, also Royal Ark Mariners, and many other sections and degrees, having first a Dispensation afterwards a Warrant thereby to act." Dunckerley had at once under his Grand Conclave, of which Prince Edward was Patron, at least four subordinate bodies to which he assigned "time immemorial" rank, the Observance of London; the Redemption of York; the Eminent of the seven degrees at Bristol; and the Antiquity of Bath. His order was styled "Royal, Exalted, Religious, and Military Orders of HRDM-KODSH, Grand Elected Knights Templar of St. John of Jerusalem, &c." His history of the "Seven Steps of Chivalry" is crude, but his views are shown to be after the minor series of the Arch; 4th Degree, Rosae Crucis; 5th Degree, Templar of St. John; 6th Degree, K. of the E. & W. -- T.P.; 7th Degree Kadosh-Palestine. There was also a Grand Inspector, but the whole series was often conferred in one ceremony, and the titles combined in the K.H. Varying fortunes followed this

G.C. Dunckerley died in 1795, and was succeeded by Thomas, Baron Rancliffe, 3rd Feby., in 1796; he by Judge Waller Rodwell Wright, 10th April, 1800; he by Edward Duke of Kent 2nd Janry., 1805; and he by the Duke of Sussex 6th Augt., 1812. Judge Wright gave prominence to a degree termed "Red Cross of Rome and Constantine" which has been revived as a special Rite in recent years.
It also appears that French Masons had introduced into London various degrees, of which the members belonged to a Lodge chartered by the G. L. of London {467} in 1754. On the death of Lambert de Lintot, about 1775, an Inventory was taken of his effects in which numerous references are found to French high-grades, which are not now practised.<<Vide "Knept," viii, p. 22.>> The Initiation of Lintot must have taken place about 1743, when the Jacobites were very active, and meditating a descent on England, to enforce the rights of the Stuarts. In circularising a plate dedicated to the foundation of the Girls School in 1788, he states that he had been made a Mason 45 years previously, and that he was Past Master of the Lodge "St. George de l Observance," No. 53, and he speaks mystically of the "Seventh and Ninth heavens." One of his plates also has reference to the Rose Croix, and Kadosh.
CONTINENTAL ECOSSAISISME.
We have already alluded to the existence in France of two species of Masonry the earlier of which was that of the Jacobites and termed Ecossaisme, the ritual of Modern Masonry was later by a generation.
Two works published in France in 1727 and 1731 had some influence upon the high-grades; the first was the "Travels of Cyrus" by the Chevalier Andrew Michael Ramsay; and the other was the "Life of Sethos" by the Abbe Terasson; but they founded no degrees.
There need be no mystery in regard to Ramsay s degrees, but there is much as to where he received them. Born in 1680 it is pretty clear that the system to which he belonged was not that of the Grand Lodge of London and though he was in England and Scotland, 1728-36, there is no record to show that he mixed with the Modern Lodges, but we have given a quotation from a work of Dean Swift s

that has some affinity.

French writers seem to be of the opinion that the earliest additions to the Craft degrees were three, termed "Irlandais," and included a Potent, or Powerful Irish Master. Then succeeded "Ecossais" degrees; usually assumed to be {468} a 4th Degree voted by the Craft Lodge, to which Professor Robison, who was a member, assigns the date 1690; but if, at an early date, it had reference to one degree only, it ended in being applied to all degrees of the "Ancient" system.

The first step in the increase of the degrees was this: In old pre-1717 Guild Masonry there was a trial of three traitors, and this system applies it in the best form; and as old Jacobite Masonry was that of the old Scottish Operative Lodges, and as the portion was omitted by the "Moderns," though adopted by the Ancient-Moderns, so, as the Modern Rituals became known, three degrees of Elect -- of 9; of 15; and of Sublime, were established. The Heredom-Rosy Cross was the old Guild Passed Master or Harodim. Out of these sprang the high-grade system, but most of these degrees were soon permeated by Hermetic influence -- and I will therefore first speak of it.

ROSICRUCIANISM.

One of the first Societies to make use of the Craft as a basis for their own operations was the Rosicrucian, and it may even date from the time of Agrippa, and Fludd. Abroad the same view was adopted by the "Golden Rosy Cross," and, once inaugurated, the Hermetic culte expanded. In 1714 a German pastor of the name of S. Richter published a book entitled "Sincerus Renatus," which contains the basis of the order of the "Golden Rosicrucians," and which, itself, contains many points which resemble Modern Freemasonry. About the year 1730, when the two Societies had been associated publicly, some of the former joined the latter. In 1716 Richter published at Breslau, -- "The true and complete preparation of the Philosopher s Stone of the Brotherhood of the Golden Rosy Cross for the benefit of the Sons of the Doctrine." In this he says that "some years ago the Masters of the Rosicrucians went to India, and since that time none of them have remained in Europe." {469} Mr. "Karl Kisewetter," to whom we referred in a previous chapter, has stated

that his grandfather was Imperator of the Order between 1764 and 1802, and that amongst his papers is mentioned, under the Cypher of F.R.C. an Adept who lived in honourable imprisonment at Dresden, and who made four quintals of gold for the Prince of Saxony, and that he vanished, in a mysterious way, leaving some "tincture of health." His serving brother Johann Gotleib Fried, was afterwards employed at Taucha, near Leipzig, and had some of the tincture which "was of lead and quicksilver and found to give true results." The last mentioned Imperator of the operative craft was admitted at Amsterdam by Tobias Tschultze. In religious matters the then members seemed to have sympathised with Boehme, and were in touch with the "Emanation" theory of the Cabala, and therefore with the ancient Gnostics. Then arose an amalgamation with the Masonic Rite founded by Martines Pasqually in 1754, and that of his pupil the Marquis de St. Martin, and which was instituted after a journey which the former made to the East. Schrepper, St. Germain, and Cagliostro, are said to have been connected with this Order of the Golden Rosy Cross; but the Masonic element, and a connection with the Illuminati of Germany, would seem, says "Keiswetter," to have forced it out of its grooves, and in 1792 it was decided to relieve the members from their vows, and to destroy their archives.

THEURGIC.

Martines Pasqually was making proselytes between 1754 and 1762 under a Jacobite authority of 20th May, 1738, which describes Charles Stuart as King of Scotland, Ireland, and England, and Grand Master of All Lodges on the face of the earth. According to the book "Martinesisme," (Paris, 1899) which seems to be written on the evidence afforded by contemporary writers, he added three degrees of Apprentice Coen, Companion Coen, and {470} Master Coen. A letter says, -- "I have been received Master Coen, in passing from the triangle to the circles." The seventh degree was that of Rose Croix. His work was Theurgic and sought union with deity, as in Oriental Societies. He traced the Initiatory Circles, and the Sacred Words himself; and prayed with great humility and fervour in the name of Christ. Then the super-human beings appeared in full light to bless the labours. After these had departed Martines instructed his

Disciples how to obtain like results, and it was to these only to whom he gave the 7th Degree of Rose Croix. Females were not refused admission. Jean Baptist Willermoz organised the Rite at Lyons about 1760 and the Marquis de St. Martin was a member between 1785 and 1790, when he resigned, having first made a system of his own by extending the degrees.

The Rite of Cagliostro was clearly that of Pasqually, as evidenced by his complete ritual which has recently been printed in the Paris Monthly -- "Initiation;" it follows so closely the Theurgy above noted, that it need leave no doubt as to whence Cagliostro derived his system; and as he stated himself that it was founded on the MS. of a George Cofton, which he had acquired in London, it is pretty certain that Pasqually had Disciples in the Metropolis. Chastannier was at one time acting with Cagliostro, and left a Rite termed Swedenborg in London.

Amongst the Masonic Rites which dabbled more or less in Hermeticism and Theurgy may be mentioned the Beneficent Knights of the Holy City; the Philalethes; the Philadelphes; the Unknown Philosophers; the Philosophic Scotch rite; the True Mason; the Hermetic Rose Croix; the Cabalistic Rite; the Illuminees of Avignon, founded by Dom Pernetti; a system of Masonic Rosicrucianism and Alchemy was worked in Hungary by the Knights of St. Andrew in 1773. There was also the Fratres Lucis, or Brothers of Light, of which an {471} interesting ritual appears in the "Theosophical Review" of 1899.

THE HOMUNCULI.

Some of the Lodges appear to have gone in for the creation of the "Homunculi" of Paracelsus, and Dr. Hartmann in his "Life of Paracelsus," gives a very lengthy and curious account from a MS. diary printed in the "Sphinx" of Dr. Emiel Besetzay published at Vienna in 1873, and which is shortly as follows. The Count Joh. Ferd. Von Keuffstein, in Tyrol 1775, carried these bodies in bottles to the Lodge of which he was Master, where they were seen by Count Max. Lemberg, Count Franz Josef Von Thurn and others. These Homunculi were created by Keuffstein, and the Abbe Geloni, or Schiloni. Owing to the bottle being overturned one of the objects died, and the Count attempted to make another, but in the absence of the Abbe he only succeeded in making something of the nature of a leech, which soon died.

It is however impossible to dwell at length upon the numerous Rites which sprang out of the Hermetic and Mystic culte, and we must return to the basis upon which the existing and popular Rites are founded, and which we have already pointed out is to be found in the "Elect" degrees, and in the "Harodim," and, as well, in the legends of the old operative Guilds.

CUMULATION OF RITES.

Although Rites were being established with feverish haste, their cumulation into one Rite of numerous degrees was gradual. Though Derwentwater was considered, as we have shown, to be Grand Master of the Scottish system, yet the real claim to rule was in the hands of the Masters Fraternity. There is little truth to be gathered from the pretended history of Modern Masonry, and when Past G. M. Richmond had brought the Duc d Antin into the Modern system in 1737, and made him G.M. until his death 11th Decr. 1743, the Venerables

assembled and {472} elected the Comte de Clermont as G.M. of a new Grand Lodge "Anglais," and a law was passed that the claims of the Ecossaise had recently arisen and were not to be recognised. Kloss gives an extract from an address published in the "Franc Maconne" of 1744, thus translated.<<"Frem. Quart." 1853. K. R. H. Mackenzie.>> -- "Ignorance is so common that the Masters and Wardens do not know that Masonry consists of seven degrees and the "Loge Generale," in its blindness, resolved, on the 11th Dec. 1743, to regard the Masons of the fourth degree, that is to say the Scotch Masters, only as common Apprentices and Fellow Crafts." This refers to the law of the English Grand Lodge just mentioned, and if, it has any meaning it is, that the Modern Masons were ignorant legislators who considered the Scots degrees as the equivalent of the Modern Craft, and some historians of to day fall into the same error.

The French Heredom-Rosy-Cross consisted of three steps: -- (1) Lectures on the Craft; (2) the temple of Zerubbabel; (3) the Rosy Cross; (4) the Knighthood which is attributed to Bruce, and which it was sought to tack on to the Order of the Thistle. Out of these an Order of Templars, of which Bruce had assumed the protection in 1314 was established at Clermont, and with which Ramsay, a disciple of Fenelon, who belonged to the Temple, is supposed to have had some connection about the year 1740

CHAPTER OF CLERMONT.

The original degrees of this Chapter were Scotch Master Elect; Knight of the Eagle; Illustrious Templar; and a little later a 4th degree was added viz.: that of Sublime Knight. Graf von Schmettau introduced these claims into Hamburg in 1742. In 1741 Field Marshal Von Marshall was admitted a Knight; the Baron Von Hunde followed in 1743. The Baron Von Weiler claimed to have received the degrees in 1743 at Rome, by some one whom he terms Lord Raleigh, the reception being {473} made in a church of the Benedictines with two Monks in attendance. Out of this sprang the German Rite of "Strict Observance," worked jointly by Marshall and Hunde, the latter of whom said that he had been created by Lord Kilmarnock, the Grand Master of Scotland, and that Lord George Clifford acted as Prior, that he was then introduced to the "Knight of the Red Feather," whom he believed to be Prince Charles Edward Stuart, and the Supreme Grand Master. At a later period he sent two members to England and Scotland, who returned with a charter in cypher, creating him the head of the Seventh Province.

Between the years 1743-7 Sir Samuel Lockhart constituted Lodges of a Rite called the Vielle Bru, or Faithful Scots, at Toulouse, at Montpelier, and at Marseilles in 1751. The Rite, if we know it, drew on the legends of the old operative Guilds and did not proceed in its instruction beyond the 2nd temple. It consisted of 9 degrees of which the last was Menatzchim, or Prefects. In 1751 a similar Rite, and evidently derived from it, existed at Paris under the designation of "Knights of the East," and ruled by a de Valois. It was democratic in its nature, whilst the Clermont Chapter was aristocratic. This Clermont Chapter in 1754 had added, to its degrees, under an unknown de "Bonneville" some of those of the Vielle Bru, as well as others of an Apocalyptic character, that we may find amongst the Friends of the Cross, the Militia Crucifera, and the Christian Fraternity of Andrea, previously referred to.

Brunswick received the degrees of the Clermont Chapter before any great change was made, and the following account has recently appeared from the pen of Archivist and Librarian F. Kistner.<<A.Q.C., 1904, p. 233.>>
"According to the legend of the Order it is said to have passed through five periods of time, and to have been founded by Adam. The 2nd period deals with the time of Nimrod. The 3rd period with Moses, who {474} brings the knowledge from Egypt. The 4th period begins with Solomon, and contains the division into "seven grades," and the distribution of the arts and sciences among them. The 5th period begins with the Order of Templars." The Chapter concerned itself with the 4th and 5th periods. The 1754 version of the degrees in Brunswick was as follows; after the three Craft degrees: --
4th Degree, Maitre Ecossais. (Scotch Master).
5th Degree, Maitre Eleu. (Master Elect, or Knight of the Eagle).
6th Degree, Maitre Illustre. (Illustrious Master, or Knight of the Holy Sepulchre).
7th Degree, Maitre Sublime. (Sublime Master, and Knight of God).
"A legend of Solomon s revenge was omitted from the Masters degree and woven into the high-grades. The Maitre Illustre had to take vengeance on the murderers." (Jewel a dagger struck into a skull, a white black edged apron, a black sash worn from left to right with a dagger at the end. In the 7th Degree, a hexagonal star of mother of pearl, suspended from the neck by a black ribbon).
Bro. Kistner goes on to say that the Jesuits created clerical grades for the Jerusalem ones; and that in 1758 certain French Officers, prisoners of war, introduced the degrees into Berlin, with some changes, the organisation consisted of three grades, -- "Capitulum Electum;" Illustrious; Sublime. Pastor Philip Samuel Rosa introduced it into Brunswick, where he received "seven members" into it.
I.
It cannot be denied that between 1725-47 the Irish, English and Scottish Jacobites were making political capital out of Masonry, and the eventual changes may be thus summarised. Their first essay, though the evidence is slight, would seem to have been, after the Craft degrees, -- 4th Degree, Irish Master; 5th Degree, Perfect Master; 6th Degree, {475} Powerful Master. The system then became divided into two branches: --
II.
"The Vielle Bru, 1743-7."   "The System of Clermont, 1740."
1-3rd Degree, Jacobite Lodges.   1-4th Degree, St. John s Lodges. 4-7th Degree, Four "Elects"

5th Degree, Knight of the Eagle,

8th Degree, Ecossaise.   Elect.

9th Degree, Menatzchim.   6th Degree, Illustrious Templar.

7th Degree, Sublime Illus. Knight.

III.

In 1751-5, College de Valois,   In 1754 a certain Chev. de

Kts. ofthe East, de Tschoudy a   Bonneville devised the Grades Member. Statutes signed 15
of the Chapter of Clermont and Janry. 1758, in 15 articles. . .   increased them.

1-3rd Degree, M. Grand Lodge.   1-3rd Degree, M. Grand St. John s 4th Degree, Perfect Irish Master.   Lodge.

5th Degree, Master Elect.   4-5-7-9th Degrees, Ecoss. of Valois 6-8th Degrees, Scotch App., Fellow and   College.

Mr.   10th Degree, Knight of the Eagle, Elect.

9th Degree, Knight of the Orient.   11th Degree, Illustrious Templar.

12th Degree Sublime Illus. Knight.

In 1761 a Ritual was printed in France entitled, -- " Les Plus Secrets   ou
le vrai Rose Croix Traduit de l Anglais; suivi du Noachite traduit de l Allemande." The grades given resemble those of the College de Valois and are:

-- I-3rd Degree, Craft; 4th Degree, Perfect Mason Elect; 5th Degree, Elect of Perignian; 6th Degree, Elect of 15; 7th Degree, Little Architect; 8th Degree, Gd. Architect; 9th Degree, Knight of the Sword and Rose Croix, really the Red Cross; 10th Degree, Noachite, which is thought to be the Alitophilote of the German Rite of "African Architects." The true Rose Croix is not given, yet its Jewel of a Pelican feeding its young is engraved therein. The true Rose Croix appeared in French at London in 1770, and is distinct from the English Ritual of Rosy-cross, and the present Rose Croix is a translation of it. It speaks of seven degrees, or 4 besides the Craft. The 6th Degree is Ecossaise Chevalier d Orient (East or Red Cross); 7th Degree, Knight of the Eagle, Perfect Prince Mason, Free {476} from Heredom, Sovereign of the Rose Croix. The dedication is "on behalf of a Lodge of the Royal Art."

Nicolai in 1783, and N. de Bonneville in 1788, London, repeat a general, but
an old tradition, that the Rosicrucian Society in London and Craft Masonry were united by General Monk for the purpose of aiding the return of Charles II., and as rallying signs they added 5 symbols to be found in "Typotii Emblematii," 1601, which were abandoned in England, after they had served their purpose. The Abbe Barruel says that they were used by the Chapter of Clermont, and we know that in 1764 they designated the Seven Templar Provinces in Germany. They are engraved for the "Francs-Macons Ecrasse," 1747, 1772. 1778, &c, -- placed crosswise, with a crouching lion in the centre, a fox, an ape, a dove, and a pelican feeding its young, de Bonneville also gives a Kadosh circular of England 1788.

A certain Lord de Berkley granted to Arras on the 13th Feby. 1747, in the name of Prince Charles Edward, to the Lodge "Jacobite Scots" at Arras, a charter for the Rose croix, in which he speaks of the degree having first been named -- Chapter of H, (Harodim), then the Eagle and Pelican, (which was the standard of his father James III. in 1715), and "since our misfortunes (of 1745) Rose Croix." The Charter is signed Berkley and is not unassailable, for we know of no authenticated copy. Some writers say that Charles Edward is termed King Pretendant, his father James III. being then alive; Ragon in his "Orthodoxie Maconnique," gives a copy which omits the word Pretendant, and uses the term "substitue G.M."

Considerable change must have taken place in the feelings of the Grand Lodge of France since 1743, for they abandoned the English title, and in the

1755 Statutes testified by Louis de Bourbon, G.M. the following appears as the 42nd Article: "The Scot s Masters shall

"be Censors of the labours, they only may correct faults. "They shall at all times have liberty of speech, and that

"of carrying arms, and remaining covered, and can only {477} "be called to order, if they fall into error, by Scot s

"Masters."

There is some analogy between the Culdee legend of the Quest of the Sangrael, and the Rose Croix Masons search for the Word. In the old Harodim- Rosy-Cross it ends in the discovery of J.M. and J., in the modern Rose Croix in the discovery of the word I.N.R.I., and has drawn upon the Catholic "Miserere," which is thus described by Lord Beaconsfield in his "Lothair." He says: "The altar was desolate, the choir dumb; the service proceeded in hushed tones of sorrow and even of suppressed anguish. As the psalm and canticle proceeded all lights were gradually extinguished. A sound as of a distant and rising wind was heard and a crash as it were of the fall of trees in a storm. The earth is covered with darkness, and the veil of the Temple is rent. But just at the moment of extreme woe, when all human voices were silent, and it was forbidden even to breathe Amen ; when everything is symbolical of the confusion and despair of the church at the loss of the expiring Lord, a priest brings forth a concealed light of silvery flame, from a corner of the Altar. This is the Light of the World, and announces the Resurrection, and then all rise up and depart in peace." In former times the degree of Rose Croix, or Rosy Cross, was considered and practised as the Easter celebration of the Templars of England.

IV.

In 1758 we have the "Emperors of the East and West;" about 1760 entered the Grand Lodge of France as the Chapter of Clermont, now 25 Degrees. We need not repeat the names as they are found in any Cyclopaedia. In 1761 the Count of Clermont, G.M. appointed as his Deputy an objectionable character of the name of Lacorne. {478} The Grand Lodge refused him

The system of the "Emperors," a Council which practised a revised version of the degrees of the Chapter of Clermont, increased to 25 degrees of which the original Grades were the two last, 24th Degree-25th Degree.

Grand

"Rite of Perfection of Heredom,"

1-18th Degree Ineffable to Rose Croix.

19th Degree Grand Pontiff.

20th Degree Grand Patriarch.

21st Degree G.M. of the Key of

Masonry.   a seat and he, and Challon de
22nd Degree Prince of Libanus.   Joinville, who was Venerable of 23rd Degree Sov. Prince Adept.
   the Lodge founded by the Duke 24th Degree Kadosh, Black & White   of Richmond, assembled their
Eagle.   adherents, and 25th Augt. 1761,
25th Degree Sublime Prince of the   conferred the 25th Degree by Patent
R.S.   upon Stephen Morin who was Though the Grand Lodge of   proceeding to San Domingo. France claimed possession of   In the course of a year the Count these degrees, the "Emperors"   of Clermont restored peace, by

remained a separate Council for   the withdrawal of Lacorne, and 28 years, when they united with
 the substitution of de Joinville. the G.L., as did the Knights of
the East.

   V.

The primitive Scottish Rite of 33 degrees was established at Namur in 1770, of which Oliver gives a list of its degrees in his "Historical Landmarks." (ii p. 89). It was constituted by a Brother of the name of Marchot, and it is necessary to mention it here, because several of its degrees went to swell the "Ancient and Accepted Scottish Rite" of 33 Degrees, which was known at Geneva before 1797, as Chemin Dupontes gives a certificate of it at that date, granted to Villard Espinasse, an officer of the Grand Orient of France: the 33rd Degree title of Grand Inspector General was acquired by the G.L. of France from the dignatory Officers of the "Emperors" when, together with the "Knights of the East," the remains of these Orders united with the Grand Orient in 1786, and into which de Tschoudy had introduced the "Noachite."<<Thory.>>

Between 1762 and 1780, this de Tschoudy was working a Rite of his own termed "Adoniramite Masonry," of which the last is the 13th degree or Noachite; but it is not a Rite of any importance in this enquiry.

THE MORINITE RITE OF PERFECTION, 25 DEGREES.

We are now approaching a subject which in every way is discreditable to Freemasonry. Stephen Morin {479} proceeded to San Domingo, as we have said, with a patent of the 25th Degree as Grand Inspector of Lodges, but there is no evidence of what he did until later. On the 17th August, 1766, he was accused in Grand Lodge of "propagating strange and monstrous doctrines," and his patent of a Grand Inspector was withdrawn; and the rank conferred on Henry Martin, who was proceeding to San Domingo. Upon this Morin, no doubt with revenge in his heart, proceeded to Kingston, Jamaica, where in 1767 he established a Grand Consistory of the 25th Degree, off his own bat. We know quite well, on the evidence of his own rituals what the changes which he made were.

The "Freemasons Magazine" for 1885 (p. 506-7) gives a full description of his ritual of 1767. He had with him, or they were sent after him, certain statutes of 1762, enacted and agreed to at the East of "Paris and Bordeaux," and are so designated, even in the reprint of them which the late Bro. Albert Pike made. In 1767 Morin terms them of "Berlin and Paris," and says they were of the "Grand East of France and Prussia." To give a colour to this lie he introduced the degree of Prussian Noachite, which had been translated, from the German, at Paris in 1757. This he ranked as 21st Degree, and added the degree of "Key of Masonry" which he had on his patent of 1761, to the 23rd Degree "Knight of the Sun." He shows his ignorance of Prussian heraldry by using the double headed Eagle of the "Emperors," and retaining the mantling of the French Royal Arms. He probably -- ignorant charlatan as he was -- mistook Frederick II., Grandson of Barbarossa, an actual King of Jerusalem, for his contemporary Frederick II. of Prussia.

He seems to have shown ability in selecting energetic and pugnacious individuals as his disciples. He first conferred the degrees of his irregular Consistory at Kingston upon Henry Andrew Franken in 1767, who admitted M.

M. Hayes, of Boston, who conferred the {480} same on Spitzer of Charleston, who received others until we find them in possession of Mitchell and Dalcho. In 1802, when these latter issued to the world their Manifesto, they had certainly heard of the increase of the rite by 8 degrees, though they would seem to have been ignorant of their very names. In this Manifesto all the falsities of Morin are accepted without question, and others are added to them, as for instance, Challon de Joinville is termed "Deputy of the King of Prussia," instead of what he actually was, Deputy of the Count of Clermont. When they forged the name of Frederick of Prussia to a charter they had discovered that several of the 8 added degrees were taken from the "Primaeval Rite," or that of Namur 1770. On the 21st February, 1802, Mitchell and Dalcho signed a patent of the 33rd Degree on behalf of de Grasse Tilly, and also for Pierre Delorne of San Domingo.

Franken also conferred the 25th Degree upon Augustin Prevost, as Deputy Inspector of the Windward Islands and the British Army; and this Brother in 1776 conferred the degrees upon J. P. Rochet of Scotland, who is understood to have established them there. Prevost also conferred the degrees upon Major Charles Sherriff of Whitchurch, who was propagating them between 1783-8, and who gave Laws and a Charter for the Ineffable degrees to Grand Treasurer Haseltine, and Grand Secretary White, through whom they entered the Templar Conclaves. One important fact is little known. When de Grasse Tilly was a prisoner of war in England, one or two French Lodges were established by him and his confreres, and in 1811 Ben Plummer and six other "Noble Knights" -- the requisite seven -- were received members of the Conclave at Bath. Plummer had been member of a Lodge held at Wincanton in Somersetshire, and on the 20th, 5th month, 1813, Tilly certificated him as a member of Lodge "Les Mars et de Neptune" of which he was Master at Abergavenny, and terms him "a Royal {481} Grand Commander of Templars," which he had attained before his membership at Bath, where he was regularised.

THE MARTIN RITE OF THE GRAND LODGE, 25 DEGREES.

In the meanwhile the Grand Lodge of France was asserting itself, and as Henry Martin was proceeding to the West Indies he was appointed a Grand Inspector to supersede Morin, and Rituals, stamped, signed, and sealed, were ordered 17th August, 1766, to be prepared and handed to him. He laboured at the Consistory previously established by Morin, though little is recorded. He was succeeded in his office by Matthew Dupotet, with whom was the Frenchman Joseph Cerneau. In 1801 it is believed that Dupotet and German Hacquet had converted the Consistory of San Domingo into a S. G. C. of the 33rd Degree of the Scottish Rite. Towards the end of 1802 a second insurrection of the blacks occurred, and Cerneau fled to Cuba, and Hacquet to France by way of New

York. Dupotet would seem to have appointed, 1st July, 1806, Joseph Cerneau, as Grand Inspector for Cuba. Hacquet revived the Rite in the Grand Orient of France in 1803, and Cerneau established a S.G.C. 33rd Degree in New York 22nd October, 1807, yet flourishing. Emanuel de la Motta,

of Charleston, in 1813 gave him trouble by establishing his S.G.C. there; Folger treats him as a crazy lunatic; he acted it well.

It may be mentioned that the Lacornites continued to give trouble to the G.L. of France, and in 1766 a dozen of them were expelled. The Count of Clermont died 16th June, 1771, and with the aid of the Duke of Luxemburg, and the recognition of the Grand Lodge of London, Philip Egalite was elected G.M. of a new Grand Orient, which in 1786 reduced the degrees to seven, or 8 with the Kadosh.

Now we have the "Martinites," the "Morinites," and the "French Rite;" and the chief distinction between the two former is this: in the Rite of Morin the 33rd Degree claims to govern all Masonry under the pretended charter of {482} Frederick of Prussia; with the Rite of Martin the bodies are governed chiefly by the 32nd Degree, the 33rd Degree forming a Supreme Court of Appeal.

CHANGES ON THE CRAFT UNION OF 1813.

Considerable changes arose in the Constitution of the High grades on the Union of the two rival bodies denominated "Ancient" and "Modern" Masons. The Duke of Sussex had been received into the Royal Arch degree in 1810. In the Templar Order -- HRDM -- KDSH -- His Royal Highness was proposed as Grand Master 5th May, 1812, and duly installed 6th August of the same year, but he seems at no time to have shown interest in aught but the Craft.

In 1813 the Modern Grand Chapter had issued to its members 183 separate Charters for the Royal Arch, whilst on the other hand the Ancient-Modern Grand Lodge of 1751 empowered the working of the Arch under their Craft Charters, and it was now stipulated in the Articles of Union that the Royal Arch should be considered as the completion of the degree of Master Mason, and the members allowed to join the Chivalric Orders under separate governance. As a completion of the 3rd Degree, however, the statement is more imaginary than real. Up to 1813 if a Mason had not been a Chair Master the Past Master s degree was conferred upon him, as is yet done in America.

Accordingly it was resolved by the United Grand Lodge, 30th November, 1813, that a United Grand Chapter should be constituted with the Craft Grand Officers as its Rulers; and unlimited powers were given for this purpose. An Assembly was held on the 18th August, 1817, with the Duke of Sussex as First Principal. There is no doubt that many old Chapters, previously held under Craft Warrant, neglected to renew their privileges by applying for Charters, as they were required to do; and that such bodies gradually passed out of working. In August, 1826, it was decreed that none but Past Masters were eligible as Principals. The ceremonial of the {483} degree was revised, and reduced to its present form in the year 1835 by the Duke s Chaplain, the Rev. Bro. Adam Brown, under a Committee of nine, appointed 5th February, 1834.<<"Freem. Mag." ii, 1860, p. 471.>> A Chapter of Promulgation, consisting of 27 members was chartered May 1835. Also a new edition of Regulations of the United Grand Chapter, was published in 1817, and was followed by one with plates of Jewels, and a list of Chapters, in 1823; since which there have been editions printed in 1843, 1852, 1864, 1869, 1875, 1879.<<Hughan s "English Rite," 1884.>>

The death of the Duke of Sussex, in 1843, caused further changes in the rule of the High-grades; he had held the Supreme power of the Orders of Knight

Templars, HRDM-KDSH, since 1812, though he gave scant countenance to the High-grades. At one time he accepted a Patent as Grand Prior of the French Ordre du Temple, and it is said that Paul of Russia made him Grand Prior of the Order of Malta; he had also the degrees of the Rite of Mizraim conferred upon him. Ragon gives a ritual of the early time of the Duke s rule granted to a subordinate body at Porte-au-Prince, from which it appears that the ceremony was assimilated to the Templar Kadosh. The Jerusalem Conclave at Manchester, which had originally been chartered by the Grand Encampment of All England at York in 1786, and had gone under Gd. Master Dunckerley in 1795, issued its own certificates during the neglect of the Duke. It installed certain brethren from Liverpool in 1813 who constituted the St. Patrick Conclave; and there was also in 1830 a Conclave entitled the Jacques de Molay emanating from Scotland and which in that year went under the banner of the French Ordre du Temple, at the instance of Brother W. H. Stewart, a Grand Cross of the Scottish Conclave who sought recognition at Paris, and was made Commander, Bailly, and Grand Cross for the Liverpool Convent,<<"Letters" of Dr. Morison to Bro. Michael Furnivall, 33rd Degree.>> and printed, in 1830, a full {484} translation of the French Statutes.<<"Manual of the Knights of the O. of the Temp.," by Frater H. Lucas of the Jacques de Molay, Liverpool. 12mo. Printed by D. Marples, 71 Lord St., Liverpool, 1830.>> Brother Dr. Robert Bigsby was a member of the Metropolitan Convent of the Order, and nominally received a few members into the Order, after it had ceased to exist.

THE ANCIENT AND ACCEPTED RITE.

Certain members of the Templar Order and of the Rite of Perfection of 25th Degree, which continued to be conferred under Templar Charters, and in that form is not yet quite extinct, applied to Brother John James Joseph Gourgas, of New York, for a Charter to practise the Ancient and Accepted Rite of 33rd Degree -- the pupil and amanuensis of the notorious Emanuel de la Motta in 1813. The Rite, as we have seen, dates from Charleston in 1802; Ireland had obtained a Charter from Charleston in 1825, Scotland from France in 1843. Accordingly the following English brethren obtained a Gourgas Charter 26th October, 1845, namely: -- R. T. Crucifix; George Oliver, D.D.; Henry Udall; D.

W. Nash, of Bristol, who was expelled by his confreres in 1858 because he had the audacity to attend meetings of the Templar bodies from which they had each and all received what degrees they individually possessed when the Charter was granted. Brother D. W. Nash then reorganised the old Templar body and pushed it as a System of seven degrees. The S.G.C. is said, however, to have freed itself from the Morin-de la Motta frauds by registration as a Limited Liability Company. The reader may consult the two exhaustive Histories of Robert Folger, M.D., and Wm. H. Peckham, of New York, as to the discord created by Charleston.

The seven degrees of Nash in 1858 were as follows: -- 1st Degree, Knight Templar; 2nd Degree, Knight of St. John; 3rd Degree, Knight of Palestine; 4th Degree, Knight of Rhodes; 5th Degree, Knight of Malta; 6th Degree, Rosae Crucis of Heredom; 7th Degree, Grand {485} Elected Knight Kadosh. To obtain a union of Bristol Knights with the Grand Priory of England that body in 1866 agreed to allow the practise of the old degrees of Heredom Kadosh, by its older Encampments, now termed Preceptories. Manchester revived the old

Dunckerley degrees of Red Cross, Heredom, Kadosh, 1869-70. The trouble with Bristol led to a similar trouble at Bath in 1871, and they revived their old degrees together with the whole of the degrees which they had had from 1811 Of the Scottish Rite. In 1872 they received and certificated seven "Noble Knights" of the Manchester Chapter, and formed an alliance with them, their Certificates including the whole of England, Scotland, and Ireland and an alliance was formed.

When Harry J. Seymour, the S.G.C. of the Cerneau S.G.C. of New York, was over in Manchester in 1872 he received as 33rd Degree of that System the writer, John Yarker, and on his return to New York had him created an Honorary Member, 15th November, 1872, and Representative of Amity, and the same was renewed in 1880 by his successor W. H. Peckham, S.G.C. 33rd Degree. On the other hand Dr. R. B. Folger established a S.G.C. in Canada with Bro. G. C. Longley as S.G.C. 33rd Degree, and, 23rd July, 1882, Hon. Membership was conferred upon Yarker with a request that he would send on two other names for the same rank. Again on the 11th July, 1882, Peckham established a 2nd S.G.C. 33rd Degree in Canada with Bro. L. H. Henderson as

G.C. 33rd Degree. Canada had also two bodies of the Rite of Memphis which were united in 1882, and from the combined bodies Theo. H. Tebbs visited Manchester, and formal documents were drawn 12th January, 1884, since which time the Scottish Rite has been in occupation.

It may be mentioned here that, January, 1903, Mrs. Annie Besant established in London a S.G.C. 33rd Degree, conferring all degrees from the 1st to the 33rd indiscriminately upon Men and Women; she received her constitution {486} from India, a S.G.C. which had its authority from a dissension in the S.G.C. of the 33rd Degree for France, Tilly s constitution.

THE TEMPLAR.

The new Templars assembled a Grand Conclave 27th February, 1846, and elected Sir Knight Charles Kemeys Kemeys Tynte as Grand Master, and revised their ritual, as a single ceremonial in 1851. On his death, 22nd November, 1860, the ensuing Grand Conclave elected Brother William Stuart who was Installed Grand Master 10th May, 1861. On the death of this brother in 1870 the Order was placed under H.R.H the Prince of Wales with H.M. the Queen as Grand Patron, and attempts were made to unite with Ireland and Scotland under a General Chapter, or Convent General, with National Grand Priories in each country, but Scotland posed as a superior System though they had accepted a Patent in 1811 from Edward Duke of Kent, the Grand Patron of English Templary during the Grand Mastership of Bro. Alex. Deuchar, and hence the full scheme fell through. Other changes in clothing, nomenclature, and ritual were introduced, which met with scant approval. On the 12th December, 1895, the Prince of Wales dissolved Convent General, which had been utterly without success, and was proclaimed Sovereign of the National Great Priory, and the Statutes of the Order were revised accordingly. England has had as Gd. Priors, Earl of Limerick, 2nd April, 1873; Shrewsbury, 8th December, 1876; Lathom, 5th October, 1877; Euston, 8th May, 1896.

THE RITE OF MIZRAIM.

As to its origin and history something may be gathered from the French historians of the Rite. It may be added that the Hermetic Scottish body named the Illuminati of Avignon was founded by Dom Pernetti, and Gabrianca, and thence spread to Montpelier in 1760. Gad Bedarride {487} of Cavillon went in 1771 to Avignon, where (he says) he was Initiated into Masonry by one Israel Cohen surnamed Carosse; and, after a few years, he obtained (the equivalent) 77th Degree, at Toulouse. In 1782 an Egyptian of the name of Ananiah visited Cavillon, and gave Gad an "Augmentation of Salary," which means a higher degree, and perhaps we owe to this "augmentation" the Talmudic and Cabalistic degrees of the Rite. In the troubles of the time, Gad became a Captain of Artillery at Nice, and here he united himself with G. M. Blanc, and became 87th Degree, and was afterwards made a Sovereign Grand Master, 90th Degree, at Naples, by G. M. Palambo. The great authority of the Rite, Marc Bedarride, together with his brothers Michael and Joseph were born at Cavillon in 1766, and Marc became a soldier, and was Initiated at Cesina, 5th January, 1801; at Paris he received the 18th Degree Of Rose Croix (his 46th Degree), and also the 31st Degree Of the A. & A. S. Rite, and he says the 70th Degree of the Rite of Mizraim.

At this time the Chief of the Rite was Bro Le Changeur, of Milan, who is said
to have systematised the 90th Degree in the year 1805. Ragon seems to have examined a certificate granted to B. Clavel in 1811 by a Chapter of Rose Croix meeting in the Abruzzes, and which Marc Bedarride signs as 77th Degree. In 1813 Milan granted Patents of the 90th Degree to a few brethren in Paris, and the Grand Orient accepted the authority, but on the 22nd December, 1817, the Rite assumed independence. Marc Bedarride himself states that he received the 90th degree at Naples, and he seems to have taken an active part in the Masonic Lodges of Italy and France. With varying fortunes the Rite continues to meet in Paris, and has recently exchanged Representatives of Amity with this country. Rebold says Jacques Etienne Marconis (surnamed de Negre), and founder of the Rite of Memphis, was at one time a member of Mizraim.

The "Rite of Mizraim" was first cumulated and established in Italy in 1804- 5, and consists of 90 degrees, collected from all sources, and is not without value; it {488} was then taken to Paris by the brothers Bedarride. At one time it was looked upon favourably in this country, the Duke of Sussex was its recognised head in England; the Duke of Leinster in Ireland; and in Scotland the Duke of Athol was succeeded by Walker Arnott of Arleary, Esqre.; but eventually they came to an agreement to abandon the Rite. No doubt they were influenced in this step by financial difficulties in Paris; some one has observed that it needs the fortune of a kingdom to carry on a Rite of ninety degrees with the necessary splendour. Some of the Templar Conclaves continued to confer it till recently; in Italy and some other parts it has been reduced to 33 degrees, and designated the "Reformed Rite of Mizraim." In a quiet way it is still conferred in this country under its own Supreme Council.

THE ANTIENT AND PRIMITIVE RITE.

The "Rite of Memphis" has a similar record to that of Mizraim, and was established on the basis of the Rites of Primitive Philadelphes and the Primitive Philalethes; occult branches of the systems of Paschalis and St. Martin, in which the grades were not clearly defined, but each of the three sections into

which they were divided had power to add any suitable degrees useful for its aims. An Egyptian system of Masonry was foreshadowed in the pamphlet of "Master of Masters," Paris 1815. Freemasonry had been introduced into Egypt by the armies of Buonaparte, and from thence, where it gathered some additions, was transplanted to Montauban in France, 1816, by the Brothers Marconis, Baron Dumas, Petite, Labrunie, Sam Honis of Cairo etc. After an interval of sleep it was revived at Brussels and Paris by Jacques Etienne Marconis, surnamed de Negre, son of Grand Master Marconis; its revival at Brussels took place in 1838, and at Paris in 1839, with the assistance of the elder Marconis, under the designation of the Ancient and Primitive Rite of Memphis divided into three Sections, and 95 or 97 degrees. At an early period it was introduced {489} into America, Egypt, and Roumania, the former Chartered a Sovereign Sanctuary for Great Britain and Ireland in 1872, and in the two latter countries it is the only Rite held in much esteem. It requires, in this country, that its neophytes should already be Master Masons, and in this year of grace is spread into almost all countries, with whom Representatives are appointed. It introduced the Rite into Germany in 1905, where it has numerous Craft Lodges, and Paris is in course of re-establishing itself.

THE SWEDENBORGIAN RITE.

The Swedenborgian Rite was revived in the United States and Canada by Brother Samuel Beswick. It consists of three elaborate and beautiful ceremonies for which the Craft is required. A Supreme Grand Lodge and Temple for G.B. & I. was chartered by Brother Colonel W. J. B. McLeod Moore, 33rd Degree, &c., of the Canadian body, on 1st October, 1875, with Bro. John Yarker as G.M. A Charter has recently been issued by this country for a body in Paris, and previously to Roumania and Egypt.

MARK MASTER.

In the old arrangement there were, as we saw, two ceremonies of Mark Man and Mark Master, and at its early establishment a cubic stone of the Craft was used, then changed to an arch key stone. There was also a Fugative Mark conferred upon Royal Arch Masons, as well as a Christian Mark. It has also been worked in conjunction with the degrees of the Wrestle, the Link, and the Ark. One version which was practised in Yorkshire last century, say 1780, is based upon the older Red Cross of Babylon and the Second Temple. The ceremonies must have arisen from the discontinuance by the Speculative Masons of the old Operative Mark. A Grand Lodge of the Degree was established by Lord Leigh in June 1856, and has now a very numerous following. {490} The present Ritual is a revisal of an old Aberdeen one; in Scotland the Marks are often hereditary.

RED CROSS OF CONSTANTINE.

This Order was revived in 1870; it had been formerly worked under Lord Rancliffe, and Judge Waller R. Wright; it enjoys consideration. Newcastle has not been dormant.

ROSICRUCIAN ORDER.

The Rosicrucian Order in IX. degrees was revived in 1866, chiefly by the exertions of Brother Kenneth Mackenzie, who had resided in Germany; it has made itself most useful to Freemasons by the publication of papers upon occult and abstruse subjects, of a superior kind, emanating from Scotland, Newcastle, York, and London. The first Supreme Magus was Bro. R. W. Little, whose successor was Dr. Woodman, and the present Chief is Dr. W. Wynn Westcott.

THE CRYPTIC RITE.

This is an American importation, and is the revision and rearrangement of certain ceremonies of the Ancient and Accepted Rite, as well as those of Mizraim and Memphis, and therefore was scarcely necessary in this country.

THE ORDER OF ST. MARTIN.

This Order has its Supreme Council in Paris, and its members are scattered all over the world. It has bodies in this country and a Sovereign Inspector and Delegate. Each of its members are supposed to contribute a paper annually upon the aims of the Order, and in affinity with those of its founder the Marquis de St. Martin. In Paris, its members are republishing the works of that author.

ALLIED DEGREES.

In 1884 a Grand Council of the Allied Masonic {491} degrees was constituted in London; taking over the Red Cross of Babylon; the Knight of St. Lawrence, which claims an operative origin; the Knight of Constantinople, an American invention; the Grand High Priest, a degree in part referring to the Head of a Chapter prior to 1838, and in part to the Chief officer of Knight Templar Priest; there is also the Secret Monitor, and other degrees have recently been added, such as the Red Branch Knights of Ulster.

ORIENTAL SOCIETIES.

THE SAT B HAI. This is a Hindu Society organised by the Pundit of an Anglo- Indian Regiment, and brought into this country, about the year 1872, by Major
J. H. Lawrence Archer. The name alludes to the bird "Malacocercis Grisis," which always fly by "sevens." It has seven descending degrees, each of seven disciples, who constitute their seven; and seven ascending degrees of Perfection, Ekata or Unity. Its object is the study and development of Indian philosophy. Somehow its "raison d etre" ceased to be necessary when the "Theosophical Society" was established by the late H. P. Blavatsky, which at one time at least had its secret signs of Reception.

AUGUST ORDER OF LIGHT. This Order was introduced here in 1882 by Bro. Maurice Vidal Portman. The Altar is that of "Maha-Deva," and had a Ritual of 3 degrees -- Novice, Aspirans, Viator. The writer arranged with Bro. Portman to amalgamate it with the Sat B hai Rite of Perfection, but it seems to be continued separately at Bradford, Yorkshire, as the "Oriental Order of Light."

Its early certificate adopted the forms of the Cabala, with which the Theosophy of India has some affinity. In the East ceremonial degrees are not valued, the object being the development of practical Occultism, which was the purpose of the establishment of the Order of Light, governed by a Grand Master of the Sacred Crown or "Kether" of the Cabala. The writer has a letter from Bro. Portman in which he says: "The Sat B hai rituals are {492} without exception the finest and best suited to an Occult Order of anything I have ever read," and he leaves all arrangements in the writer s hands.

ADOPTIVE MASONRY.

This Chapter would be incomplete without some mention of Adoptive Masonry. Societies admitting females as members were established in France early last century, and spread to other countries. One of the first to admit ladies were the "Mopses," who reorganised after the Papal Bulls of 1738 against Freemasonry. The "Felicitaires" had a nautical character, and existed in 1742. In 1747 Brother Bauchaine, the Master of a Paris Lodge, instituted an Order, admitting ladies, called the "Fendeurs" or Woodcutters, modelled on the Carbonari a class of men who would seem to be a branch of the ancient Compagnnonage; the popularity of this Order led to the creation of others, to wit, of the "Hatchet," of "Fidelity," etc. This popularity induced the Grand Orient of France, in 1774, to establish a system of three degrees called the Rite of Adoption, with the Duchess de Bourbon as Grand Mistress of All France; the Rite has been generally adopted into Freemasonry, and various degrees added from time to time, to the number of about 12 in all. The "Ladies Hospitallers of Mount Tabor" added to the original plan, a recondite System called the Lesser and Greater Mysteries. The French Lodges of Adoption were patronised by the highest ladies in the land; and there is evidence that the Rite of Mizraim held androgynous Lodges in 1819, 1821, 1838, 1853; and the A. & P. Rite of Memphis in 1839; of these two last there are handsome certificates in the museum of the Lodge of Research, Leicester. America has a system of her own called the "Eastern Star" in 5 points. In all systems admissions are usually restricted to the wives, widows, sisters, or daughters of Master Masons. Scotland has attempted {493} the working both of the "Order of the Eastern Star" and "Adoptive Masonry," but not successfully.

SUMMARY.

To sum up this chapter, it advances that prior to Grand Lodges there were Masters of Masters and duly Passed Masters or Harods, who had controlling power over the ordinary Craftsmen, and that the chief Rites of the speculative system of which there is evidence may be thus summarised: --

1. The Guild Rite of four working and three official degrees -- Judaic.
2. The Craft and their ruling Harods in the Co. of Durham.
3. Three Craft degrees, and the Red and Rosy Cross, Judaic and Christian.
4. Ancient Masonry of the Moderns, three Craft, and the higher degrees of Holy Royal Arch, Knight Templar, Priest.

But outside all this, numberless degrees which we have not space to mention, in some cases derived from the Mystic Schools and adopted into the Masonic System. In many cases new degrees were but variants of the different

Rites, readopted by others with a new name; the ruling degree of one Rite becoming a mere ritualistic ceremony in another. In other words, a constant revision by ignorant Rulers, making confusion worse confounded.

14

CHAPTER XII. FREEMASONRY IN THE GRAND LODGE ERA

" **A** nd therefore what I throw of is ideal --
Lower d, leaven d, like a history of Freemasons, Which bears the same relation to the real,
As Captain Parry s voyage may do to "Jason s." The Grand Arcanum s not for men to see all;
My music has some mystic diapasons;
And there is much which could not be appreciated In any manner by the uninitiated."
-- Byron s " Don Juan. " "Canto" xiv., Stanza xxii.

The Guild Assembly is supposed to have been revived as the Grand Lodge of London in 1717, and according to the account of Dr. James Anderson, by four old Lodges, which met for that purpose at the Apple-tree tavern; but another account, of 1764, states that six old Lodges took part in the proceeding but gives no evidence. The first Grand Master may be considered a member of the old operative body, namely Brother Anthony Sayer, of whom a very excellently executed portrait has recently been published by Brother Henry Sadler; the election of this first Grand Master took place at the Goose and Gridiron on St. John s Day, 1717; he was followed by George Payne, a gentleman of antiquarian tastes, who was elected G.M. on the 24th June, 1718. In the year 1719 Bro. J. T. Desaguliers was elected Grand Master, he was a man of some scientific eminence, and visited Lodge Mary s Chapel, Edinburgh, where he was received, "after due examination;" it has been suggested that he may have exemplified the London working, but the facts are such that it is much more probable that he went to learn and not to teach, moreover, the Grand Lodge terms, "Cowan" and "Fellow-Craft" are Scottisms. {495}

Of late years the more critical historians have expressed themselves as very dissatisfied with the account which Anderson has given of himself and of the establishment of his Grand Lodge in 1717, and if the statements which appear in our pages are unassailable, -- as we believe them to be, -- he had every reason for prevarication and reticence. He says that the Grand Lodge was established because Wren neglected the Lodges, that is the Lodges which were established by the dissidents who left the operative Guilds in 1715. Under the circumstances whatever legitimacy the Grand Lodge of London had it derived it from the old operative Lodges, chiefly in the North of England, which united with it. The Guilds assert that it was Anderson who abrogated the seven years Apprenticeship and changed the seat of the Master from West to East.

In 1720 Brother George Payne was elected for a second time, and compiled a code of regulations for the Grand Lodge which was passed on the 24th June 1721, and forms the first Constitution. Several old MSS. were burnt in London

by scrupulous brethren in 1720, one of them being by Nicholas Stone, who is said to have been a Grand Warden of Inigo Jones. The office of Deputy Grand Master was instituted.

In 1721 the antiquary Dr. William Stukely was made a Mason and records the circumstance thus in his "Diary:" -- "6th January 1721, I was made a Free- mason at the Salutation Tav., Tavistock Street, with Mr. Collins and Captain Rowe who made the famous diving engine." In his "Common-place" Book he records; that: -- "I was the first person made a Free-mason in London for many years. We had great difficulty to find members enough to perform the ceremony. Immediately after that it took a run, and ran itself out of breath through the folly of the members." In his "Autobiography" he again refers to the matter: "his curiosity led him to be initiated into the mysteries of Masonry, suspecting them to be the remains of the Mysteries of the antients." These {496} references are very valuable in the inferences to be drawn from them. As there were few members in 1721, it is clear that under Anderson and his friends much progress had not been made, but from some old members, he must have received the impression of the great antiquity of Masonic Rites. On the 10th March, 1721, he says -- "I waited on Sir C. Wren." At a meeting of the 24th June 1721, at which were present the Duke of Montague, Lords Herbert and Stanhope, and Sir Andrew Fountain, Stukely saw the "Cooke M.S.," which he says Grand Master Payne had obtained in the West of England, and Brother Speth points out that Stukely made a copy of the first and last page. There exist two other copies of it made at this period; Stukely considered the MS. 500 years old. Grand Master Payne read over a new set of Articles and Dr. Desaguliers pronounced an Oration.<<Vide Gould s "Hist. Frem.">> From this we gather that Speculative Masonry was rising into importance.

On the 24th June, 1721, at the Grand Lodge held by G. M. Payne at the Queen s Arms, St. Paul s Churchyard, at the request of the Duke of Montague, Philip Lord Stanhope (afterwards Earl of Chesterfield), and several gentlemen attended; after usual proceedings the Brethren adjourned to Stationers Hall, and in the presence of 150 brethren the Duke of Montague was proclaimed Grand Master and Brother Beale, Deputy. Dr. J. T. Desaguliers delivered "an eloquent oration about Masons and Masonry," which is said to have been printed.

Stukely records that on the 25th May, 1722, he met the Duke of Queensboro, Lords Dunbarton and Hinchinbroke at the Fountain s Tavern Lodge to consider the Festival of St. John s. Philip Duke of Wharton was elected G.M. 25th June, 1722, and Brother J. T. Desaguliers Deputy. Brother Gould has given good reasons for believing that Anderson s statements of 1738 on this point, as well as upon others, are unreliable.<<"Ars Quat. Cor." viii.>> Brother William Cowper was appointed Grand Secretary, {497} and G.M. Wharton approved a Ceremony for Installing the Master of a Lodge. Wharton at this time was much embarrassed having inherited an impoverished estate, and was himself a man reckless in his expenses. Stukely records that on the 3rd November the Duke of Wharton and Lord Dalkeith visited the Lodge of which Stukely was Master. In this year J. Roberts printed the version of a MS., in which are the "New Regulations," as to one Master and Assembly which his copy says was passed 8th December, 1663; it contains the Clause that a Freemason must be fully 21 years of age. At this time the Grand Lodge claimed the sole right to confer the grade, or grades, of Fellow and Master; it is thought that one grade is implied, if

it is two it indicates the sense in which they regarded the rights of Assembly given in the "Cooke MS."

In 1723 Francis Earl of Dalkeith was Grand Master, and in this year Brother James Anderson, a presbyterian divine, and a genealogist, published the first "Book of Constitutions," which he had compiled from the old MSS., and other sources, by order of the Grand Lodge. It was dedicated to the Duke of Montague by J. T. Desaguliers the Deputy Grand Master, and Brother Gould is of opinion that Anderson, as an Aberdeen Man introduced Scottish terminology into the English Craft. As a Scottish Antiquary the author would be well acquainted with the Customs of the Lodges and the Masters Incorporations, and whilst the early years of Grand Lodge resembles the Scottish Lodges, the grant of "Fellowcraft and Master," to the private Lodges, and the sending of Masters and Wardens to Grand Lodge brings it into line with the Incorporations, but Desaguliers had also visited the Edinburgh Lodge. This year an engraved list of Lodges was begun by Brother John Payne, in a small volume; the "Freemason an Hudibrastic Poem," appeared, and attacks on the Society began in the Press.

In 1724, 1725, 1726,the Grand Masters were Charles Lennox Duke of

Richmond; James Hamilton Lord {498} Paisley; and William O Brian Earl of Inchiquin. In 1724 the office of Grand Treasurer was instituted. We gave particulars, in our last Chapter of a considerable Lodge at Chester of which Randle Holme was a member, and it is probable that admissions were continued, for in the year 1724 three Lodges were accepted at Chester and Brother F. Columbine was appointed the Provincial Grand Master. On the 27th November, 1725, Grand Lodge passed a Resolution granting the privilege of Masters to Private Lodges, -- "the majority of the members being Masters may make Masters at their discretion." No doubt Grand Lodge found its time fully occupied with affairs of the government; and this led, a little later, to the sanction of "Masters Lodges," or meetings for the sole purpose of making Masters.<<"Ars Quat. Cor." -- Lane.>> The lampoon on the Freemasons and Gormogons appeared, and in 1726 the "Freemasons Accusation and Defence." Anderson seems to have withdrawn from the Grand Lodge until 1730. A copy of the old Constitutional Charges appeared in 1726 which contains many additions and the name of Hermes is substituted for Euclid.<<Spencer s "Reprints," 1870.>> In June 1726 Dr. Stukely removed to Grantham and established a Lodge there.

In Ireland Masonry, as we have seen, was known at the University in 1688,

and there was a Grand Lodge of Dublin in 1725, having six subordinate Lodges of "gentlemen Freemasons." The first Grand Master was the Earl of Rosse who was Installed in the Great Hall of King s Inn 26th June, 1725. There was also a Grand Lodge at Munster in 1726, of which Brother James O Brian was Grand Master, and also member of the Horn Lodge in London. At Cork a Lodge is known to have existed in 1728. The custom of issuing Charters to Lodges began with the Grand Lodge of Ireland in 1729, and they were the first to Charter military Lodges, the earliest of which is 7th November, 1732, to the "First Battalion Royal."<<"Cem. Hiber." -- Crawley.>> {499} A copy of the English Constitutions edited by J. Pennell, with some slight additions, was printed by J. Watts of Dublin in 1730; and in 1734 Bro. Wm. Smith issued a "Pocket Companion," of which later versions appeared in England.

In the constant reception of noble brethren, changes in the Constitutions, and in the qualifications, coupled with the elimination of Christian references which had obtained admission in the course of ages we probably see, it is supposed in the first named case especially, the cause of the attacks made by the press between the years 1723-26, by a class socially inferior, but equally zealous for Masonry, of whom the old Speculative and Operative body had been previously composed. There are allusions in the "Praise of Drunkenness" by Robert Samber to catechisms then known in 1723; another appeared in that year; the "Grand Mystery" and praise of the Gormogons 1724, and a second edition in 1725; to this a short reply was printed by Dublin Masons, 1725, in which the Society is held to be of great antiquity and supported by superior persons. Some years ago the late Brother Matthew Cooke brought to light a very curious and important MS. book of this period which is now lying in the British Museum, being Add. MSS. 23002.<<"Frem. Mag." v, 1861. -- Old Lodges. Now facsimiled by Quat. Cor. Lodge.>> It is a minute book of the "Philo Musicae et Architecturae Societas" established at the Queen s Head, near Temple Bar, by seven members of whom two were made Masons by Mr. Thomas Bradbury and three by the Duke of Richmond. Other Initiates were afterwards made by the Society and we read under date 1724, -- "Mr. William Goulston, Court Nevit, Esq., Mr. William Jones, and Mr. Edmund Squire were regularly pass d Masters, in the beforementioned Lodge of Hollis Street, and before we founded this Society a Lodge was held consisting of Masters sufficient for that purpose, in order to pass Charles Cotton, Esq., Mr. Papillon Ball, and Mr. Thomas Marshall, Fellow Crafts; in the performance of which Mr.
{500} William Goulson acted as Senior Warden. Immediately after which, viz.
the 18th day of February A.D. 1724, the said Mr. William Goulson was chosen President of the said Society." These brethren, were visited amongst others by Past Gd. Master Payne, and the S. Gd. Warden Wm. Sorrel. As there are no minutes in Grand Lodge of any one being made Masters after 1723, and as it never had an actual body of "Passed" Masters the ancient Guild ceremony is in evidence. It is probable that the regulation of passing existed only on paper, for we see that officers of Grand Lodge were visiting and acting in private Lodges.
In the North of England, following a meeting evidently operative at Scarborough in 1705, and therefore unminuted; at Bradford in 1713; there are records of meetings in 1721, 1723, 1725, 1726, of Private Lodges at York, that mode being used to distinguish the Lodge from the General Assemblies on St. John s day. At a meeting in 1725 Francis Drake, the historian was made a Mason by Brother William Scourfield. A Code of regulations for their meetings was agreed upon and the Society now took the title of "Grand Lodge of All England." In 1726 Charles Bathurst was appointed President, and Francis Drake, Warden, and the latter at the Annual Assembly on St. John s day, 27th December, 1726, gave an address, which has often been printed, and always held to be of great interest; he speaks of the efforts to revive the Society in London; addresses the operative Masons, other trades, and gentlemen, and claims for York the undeniable Mastership of "All England." Brother Wm. Scourfield in 1726 was suspended for calling an unauthorised meeting, and making masons, and was probably acting with the operatives. The old body met till 1744, and then fell into abeyance until the year 1761, when Drake revived it. Besides York other bodies of an operative and indepen-

dent nature

existed in the North as at Swalwell, Alnwick, Hexham, Ford, Newcastle, etc.
{501}
At London in 1727, 1728, 1729-30, the Grand Masters were Henry Clare Lord Coleraine; James
King Lord Kingston; Thomas Howard Duke of Norfolk who held the position for two years. On
the 27th May, 1727, Hugh Warburton was appointed Prov. Gd. Master for North Wales; and on
27th December, 1728, George Pomfret opened a Lodge in Bengal. A copper plate of the "Mystery of
Free Masons," was printed by Andrew White -- "Taken from the papers of a deceased Brother"; and
we find Bro. Oakley quoting largely from Samber s Preface to Long Livers, 1721. Benjamin Cole
published in 1728, from copper- plate, the Constitution of 1726. It is noteworthy as illustrating the
state of things now existing that Past Gd. Master Sayer was censured for "behaving irregularly," and
what he did was probably to attend his old Guild as he was an operative. Brother Gould thinks he
may have been visiting the Gormogons. In August and September 1730 the "Daily Journal" printed
certain spurious rituals, and the "Grand Whimsey" of Masonry, by F. G., and these were followed in
the same year by a broadsheet reprint entitled, "The Mystery and Motions of Free-masonry discovered." In this year also Samuel Prichard published his "Masonry Dissected" (12mo. pp. 31, London,
1730) which led to an able "Defence," which Brother Gould has proved, from the Minutes of the
Lodge at Lincoln, was written by Brother Martin Clare. Also the censure of Grand Lodge fell upon
a Society of Honorary Freemasons. Also appeared in 1730 "The Perjured Freemason Detected." In
all this there was probably a Jacobite undercurrent coupled with High grade dissatisfaction, for the
sympathies of Grand Lodge was Hanoverian while York was essentially Jacobite. On the 29th January, 1731, the Duke of Norfolk presented Grand Lodge with the old sword of Gustavus Adolphus,
to be used as the Sword of State. It is worthy of note that in the few preserved minutes of Lodge
meetings, at this period as in those of Lincoln, there is but little mention, {502} and sometimes
none, of the degree of Fellow, now termed Fellow-craft, the minutes confining themselves to record
the making of Apprentices and Masters.
Faulkner of Dublin printed in 1731, Swift s "Letter from the Grand Mistress of
Female Freemasons."
There appears in the "Daily Advertiser" of 16th August, 1731, an advertisement to the public, that
there was on view a fine model of King Solomon s Temple, with 2,000 chambers and windows,
7,000 pillars, and models of the Ark and all the holy utensils; further stating that a printed description, with 12 fine cuts, might be had. This would be a model prepared by Councillor Schott of
Hamburg between 1718-25 and on exhibition 1725-31. There is mention 22nd September, 1732,
of the admission of Jews in the Rose Tavern in Cheapside, and the "Grub Street Journal" printed
letters attacking Freemasonry.
There are several interesting notices of meetings at Newcastle-on-Tyne, which we should suppose
from "Border Table Talk," to have had a succession from 1581, a tolerable antiquity for an English
Lodge, if the links were shewn. The Northumberland Calendar states that 1st July, 1674, the Society
met in the White Friar s tower; and no doubt the "Watson MS." written in 1687 by Edward Thompson was their Lodge document. On the 29th May, 1730, a Lodge of the "Honourable Society of Free

and Accepted Masons" was held at Mr. Barth. Pratt s "at which abundance of gentlemen assisted, wearing white leathern

aprons and gloves." On 28th December, 1734, the "anniversary of the Most Honourable and Ancient Fraternity of Free and Accepted Masons," was held at widow Grey s, "the Society consisting of the principal inhabitants of the town and country;" after this they attended church to hear a sermon by the Rev. Mr. Robinson, Vicar of Byewell, "their chaplain." On 27th December, 1737, Walter Blackett, Esq., was W.M.; Mr. Thoresby, Deputy W.M., Messrs. Newton and Graham, Wardens, for the ensuing year.<<Gould s "Hist. Freem." ii, p. 261; also "Trans. Newcastle Coll. Ros." pt. I.>> Richardson says that {503} in, "1742, the Company obtained from the Corporation a grant of the Cutler s tower in Carliol Croft (now Croft Street), which they repaired, and fit up in a handsome manner."

We have seen an old Craft certificate form used in the old Newcastle Lodge, under the Grand Lodge, which represented two pillars on one of which was engraved "Isk Chotzeb, Isb Sabhal, Giblim;" and on the other (facing right), "Bonai, Menatzckhim, Harods."

The Lodge of Alnwick preserved its minutes from 1700-55, and these have been handsomely printed by the Newcastle College of Rosicrucians. We find mention of the Entering of Apprentices; making of Free-brothers; of Brothers and Fellows; the annual elections of the Masters and Wardens; yet no word as to Rites and secrets. But the only inference we can draw from this is that the brethren were real Masons, not pretenders, innoculated with the new doctrines of 1717, and knew that such things could not be written about. Hence in the case of similar omissions in the minutes of York, Durham, Scotland, etc., no reliance can be placed, or arguments drawn from obscure allusions to matters of this nature. There was also, at this period a Lodge at Hexham, which would seem to have died out without at any time coming under the Grand Lodge of England. There was another at Swalwell, which will be referred to when it comes under the Grand Lodge in 1735.

We may add a few lines here in regard to Masonry in Scotland, which had many ancient Lodges at work; and which were societies sanctioned by law for mutual assistance and the regulation of business, and over which the Clare family had an hereditary jurisdiction, and had to be in possession of the "Masons Word." From early times they had admitted traders unconnected with building, and gentlemen of position; the one termed "Domatic" or operative Masons, the other "Geomatic," or Speculative Masons. These bodies met together in 1736, and established a Grand Lodge upon the London {504} system, and consolidated it by the election as Grand Master of Brother William St. Clair, who then resigned the rights if such still existed which he had from his ancestors who had been appointed in the 16th century Lord Wardens General, and patrons of the Masonic Craft; with the consent of Lodges, and sanction of the Kings, Judges of all matters in dispute.<<Vide the "Schaw Constitution," or rules, also previous chapter.>> From this period, Scotland gradually conformed to the ritualistic system of England, but as proved by the "Dumfries MS.," quoted in our last chapter, for a long period retained its Christian character.

In this condensed account it is unnecessary to repeat the mere names of the Grand Masters of England; these are found in any modern Cyclopaedia, or in the Grand Lodge calendars. Various old Lodges must have united themselves with the Grand Lodge, but as the entries are made from the date of admission, it is impossible in all cases to trace their origin by the Grand Lodge Register;

one notable exception is Lodge 65, of St. Rook s hill, Chichester, which is registered as dating from the time of Julius Caesar. An old Lodge of Swalwell, nr. Gateshead, with minutes from 1725, accepted a Deputation, or joined the Grand Lodge, 21st March, 1735, and the Earl of Crawford appointed one of its members, namely Brother Joseph Laycock of Winlaton, as Prov. Grand Master at the same date with a second Lodge at Gateshead, 3rd March, 1736, No. 256. The Lodge was frequented by "brethren from all the surrounding country as the Grand Master conferred the Harodim at his residence."<<"Freem. Mag." 1794, also "Kneph.">> That these Lodges had the Harodim is proved by an Address which he gave the Lodge in 1735, and which is printed in "The Book M, or Masonry Triumphant," Newcastle, 1736, and which contains subscribers from this Lodge at Swalwell, from Hexham, and Gateshead; but the minutes do not confirm the statement that Laycock continued the Harodim. It is the "Pocket Companion" of Brother Smith {505} of Dublin adapted to English use; its full title being: "The Book M: or Masonry Triumphant. In two parts. Part I. containing the History, Charges, and Regulations of FREE MASONS, with an account of Stately Fabrics erected by the Illustrious Society. Part II. containing the Songs usually sung in LODGES, Prologues and Epilogues spoken at the Theatres in LONDON in honour of the Craft, with an account of all the places where Regular Lodges are held. "Be wise as Serpents, yet innocent as Doves." Newcastle upon Tyne. Printed by Leonard Umfreville and Company. MDDCCXXXVI." It is dedicated to the Brethren and Fellows, "assembling in Lodges in the Northern Counties of England." In 1735 Anderson complained to Grand Lodge in evident allusion to it.

The Grand Lodge of London had now achieved high prestige, for in 1733

eighteen new Lodges were constituted in the London district alone, and the powers of the Committee of Charity were extended. In 1734 Prov. Gd.. Masters were appointed for Lancashire and Durham, Northumberland we have already named. This would not be likely to give much satisfaction to the Grand Lodge of All England at York, and may have contributed to its later relapse, and even in the South, 1735-8, dissatisfaction was spreading; Freemasons were being admitted in unchartered "St. John s Lodges," members dropped off, and Lodges began to be erased.

On the 15th April, 1736, the Earl of Loudan had Garter and Lyon, the Kings of Arms of England and Scotland, besides many titled persons, to attend his Installation as Grand Master, but his appointment of officers seems to have given dissatisfaction. In 1737 the Prince of Wales was made a Mason, at a private Lodge held at the palace of Kew. Under the Marquis of Carnarvon the Gd. Master in 1737 a Prov. Gd. Master was appointed for the West Riding of Yorkshire. A Papal Bull excommunicating the members of the Society made its appearance in 1738. In the same year Anderson issued a second {506} edition of the "Book of Constitutions" in which the history of architecture is much extended, but some changes were made in the wording of the Charges which were not altogether received with favour. In the same year the "Gentlemens Magazine" printed a pretended description of the ceremonies, and J. Wilford, the printer of Prichard s 7th edition,issued a 6d. pamphlet entitled, "Masonry further Dissected; or more SECRETS Of that Mysterious "Society" Reveal d. Faithfully Englished from the French Original, just publish d at Paris, by the Permission and Privilege of M. de Harrant, Lieutenant General of Police" (pp.xvi. and 32, London, 1738). This work of Heraut is given in "Masonry Trahi." 1745.

In 1739, the Holy Roman Inquisition ordered to be burnt a work, written in French, entitled, -- "The History of, and Apology for the Society of Freemasons, by J.G.D.M.F.M. Printed at Dublin by Patrick Odonoko, 1730." Oliver gives a professed translation in Volume III. of the "Remains;" and it has been erroneously attributed to the Chevalier Ramsay.

On the 30th June, 1739, Lord Raymond, G.M., there are complaints of irregular makings, and the laws are ordered to be enforced; and on the 23rd July, 1740, Earl of Kintore, G.M., there are complaints of brethren "being present and assisting at irregular meetings." In the year 1741 the Grand Lodge prohibited the publishing of anything concerning Freemasonry; and in the following year a mock procession was got up by people calling themselves Scald Miserable Masons, in imitation of that of the Grand Lodge which led to the abolition of the annual procession of Freemasons. A plate of this ridiculous procession was published 27th April, 1742, but this must not be confounded with Hogarth s embodiment of the Gormogon s slanders which had a third edition about the same year, and mentioned in our last chapter. On the 24th June, 1742, three Lodges were erased for not answering summonses to appear; and between 1743-7 there were 34 more Lodges erased, but No. 9 restored;

{506} next there were five Lodges erased, but two restored. Thus the basis was laid for the prosperous advent of a rival. A new "Book of Constitutions," the third edition, appeared in 1746, but Brother Hughan points out that it is but that of 1738, with a new title.

In 1736 "Le Franc Macon," appeared at Frankfort and Leipzic, and was dedicated to Count Bruhl. (Scott gives it in his Pocket Companion of 1757).

In 1737 "The Mysterious Receptions of the Celebrated Society of Freemasons." Also, in the same year, "The Society of Masonry made known to all men," by S.P.

In 1738, "Masonry further Dissected."

In 1745, The Testament of a Freemason or "Le Testament de Chevalier Graf." In 1747, "L Adept Macon, or the True Secret of Freemasonry."

In a work entitled "Magistracy settled upon its only True Basis," by Thomas Nairn, Minister of the Gospel at Abbotshall, printed in the year MDCCXLVII., for which I am indebted to my Publisher, there is a peculiar "Protestation" in the Appendix. At Kirknewton, on December 27th, 1739, James Chrystie, James Aikman, Andrew Purdie, and John Chrystie renounce the Mason-Word, to which John Miller, at Dalkeith, July 27th, 1747, adds his adhesion. All repudiate their oaths as members of "The Society of Operative Masons in the Lodge at Torphicen to meet at Livingston Kirk." They declare "When I was young at my admission amongst you, both as an Apprentice and Fellow Craft, wherein (upon very solemn penalties) I was bound to Secrecy and also to admit none but operative Masons into the Society." . . . "Kneeling upon their bare knee with the Bible upon the same, and the naked arm upon the Bible." . . . "Most of the secrets being idle stuff and lies." . . . "And as a further aggravation the idle and excessive misspending of precious time and money in superstitious observation of St. John s Day in idleness, drunkenness and profane jests and songs." Several particulars {508} of the old Operative Charges are quoted and they withdraw from the Society in favour of the

"Oaths of our National and Solemn League and Covenant."

In 1750, December 27th, A Sermon was preached at Gloucester, by F.M.:
printed and dedicated to "Henry Toy Bridgeman, of Prinknach, Esq.," High

Sheriff of the County of Gloucester, Master Mason, and Master of the Lodge of the Ancient and Honourable Society of Free and Accepted Masons, regularly constituted in the City of Gloucester. In 1751, "An Answer to the Pope s Bull, with a Vindication of the Real Principles of Freemasonry." Published by the assent and approbation of the Grand Lodge of Ireland. "Magna est veritas et proevalebit." Dublin, printed by John Butler on Cork Hill, for the author, 1751. Small 8vo., 64 pp. Dedicated -
- "To the Right Worshipful and Right Honourable Lord George Sackville, Grand Master of the Ancient and Honourable Fraternity of Free and Accepted Masons in Ireland." (Arms plate -- R. Close, Sculp.)

In the same year, "La Macon Demasque." By T.W. initiated at the Swan, in the Strand, thro his friend Mons. Cowen, a Mr. Fielding being the Venerable or Master. London 1751. (In Berlin 1757).

It is not difficult to see where the shoe pinched the "Modern Mason." An old broadsheet of 1755 says that, "the Moderns leave out at least one half of the Lectures" -- and this is confirmed, later, by a pamphlet of 1765 entitled, -- "A Defence of Freemasonry," the writer of which states that he visited a Lodge of the "Ancients," and he condemns their prolixity, and defends the abridged form of Modern ceremonies. In our days the Guild Free Masons have spoken, to some extent, and we know their process. What the founders of the G. L. of 1717 did was to do away with all technic, and revise what was left to make a new system; the Dermott body had Guild Masons to help them.

The general dissatisfaction thus shewn to exist, was {509} taken advantage of in the establishment at London of a rival Grand Lodge of which Brother Lawrence Dermott, an old Irish Mason, became the Grand Secretary. Their ceremonies were undoubtedly, as he states, remodelled by Ancient Guild Masons. Their affairs from 1751 were managed by a Committee of the Lodges until 1753 when Robert Turner, Esq., became Grand Master, and was succeeded by Robert Vaughan in 1754. In 1755 a Manifesto entitled "the Masons Creed" was issued. In 1756 Dermott issued their first Book of Constitutions under the title of "Ahiman Rezon," and certain rules are entitled, "Regulations for Charity in Ireland and by York Masons in England." The Earl of Blessington became Grand Master in 1757. Brother Henry Sadler in his work entitled "Facts and Fictions" has done much to disentangle the confused history of the period and he has shewn that this body was established by Irish Masons, reinforced by dissidents who had been Initiated in the unchartered "St. John s Lodges," and by members of the Lodges which had been struck from the Roll of the Grand Lodge of 1717. They claimed to have retained the full ancient work of York which had been curtailed by the Grand Lodge which they dubbed Modern.

The "Ancient," or the "York Masonry," by which the new Grand Lodge
distinguished itself, was an old Arch-Templar body, and the same system was worked by the London Grand Lodge of 1751. By their Charters the Arch was worked under Lodge authority, and though no prominence was given to the Templar, it was usually conferred with the Arch degree. At York itself, when a revival took place under Grand Master Drake, in 1761, the Arch was recognised by the

Grand Lodge and the Templar also, continuing in active operation until 1792, when they silently expired.

In 1764 Dermott published a second edition of the "Ahiman Rezon," in which comments are made upon three pamphlets of the period, namely: "Hiram, or

the Master Key to Masonry; The three Distinct Knocks;" and "Boaz" {510} "and Jachin;" these works seem to have given Dermott much annoyance, and he brings the author of the two last to untimely ends on the 23rd August, 1762, and 8th September, 1763. The Charity regulations of this new edition give in parallel columns the Dublin and London rules in force since 1738, and those of 1751 for his own Grand Lodge. In 1772 the Duke of Athol became Grand Master, after which they were usually designated "Athol Masons," and had formal recognition from the Grand Lodges of Scotland and Ireland. A third and enlarged edition of the "Ahiman Rezon" appeared in 1778.

We will now return to the Grand Lodge of 1717; and may mention that in 1746 a brother of the name of John Coustos published an account of the sufferings he had undergone by the Roman Inquisition for the crime of Freemasonry, and expressing his grateful thanks to the British Government for claiming his release from his abominable torturers. Complaints of irregular meetings reappear in 1749, and again in 1752. In 1754-5 there are proceedings against the members of a Lodge held at the Ben Johnson s Head in Spitalfields as "Ancient" Masons and the Lodge was ordered to be erased; Dermott says that some of its members had been abroad, where they received much favour from the fact of their following the traditional rites of the "Ancients," and therefore they resolved to practise "Ancient" Masonry every third Lodge night, to which meetings the ordinary Craft Mason was not admitted. The matter was not mended by Brother Spenser, who replied to a letter from an Irish petitioner for his relief that their Grand Lodge was "neither Royal Arch nor Ancient," and Dermott prints his letter in 1764. The progress of the "Ancients" has been attributed to the general mismanagement of the affairs of Grand Lodge and to the absence from England of Lord Byron the Grand Master, 1747-52, and a proposal was on foot to supersede him in 1751, but Brother Thomas Manningham interposed so judiciously that the proposal fell through, and he himself was promoted to the office of Deputy {511} Grand Master in 1752; various Lectures and Sermons, given between 1735-52, are printed by Oliver in his "Remains," and Brother Thomas Dunckerley delivered a Lecture "On Masonic Truth and Charity" at Plymouth in 1757.

A new edition of the "Book of Constitutions," edited by Brother John Entick, was published in 1756. In 1757 a list of 14 irregular Masons meeting at the Marlboro s Head in Pelham Street, Spitalfields, was ordered to be sent to each Lodge; and Brother Henry Sadler points out that they were working independently of any Grand Lodge. In 1760 J. Burd published a translation of "Les Ordre des Franc Macons Trahi" under the title of " A Master Key to Freemasonry;" by which all the Secrets of the Society are laid open, and their pretended Mysteries exposed to the Publick."<<"Ars Quat. Cor." 1896, p. 85; J. Bird, opposite St. Dunstan s Church, Fleet St., MDCCLX. 6d. viii and 48pp. 8vo.>>   This led in the same year to the publication of "The Freemasons Advocate, or Falsehood Detected."   In spite of this untoward state of affairs Freemasonry made progress. In 1764 appeared a work entitled "Multa Paucis for Lovers of Secrets," which is the basis on which is grounded the charge of negligence by Lord Byron. In Scotland Joseph

Galbraith, of Glasgow, in 1765, issued the "Free Masons Pocket Companion."   It contains an account of the "Acts of the Associate Synod concerning the Masons Oath," at Stirling in 1745, September 26th, and at Edinburgh in 1755, March 6th, and appended is an "Impartial Examination of the Associate Synod against Free-masons," reprinted

from the "Edinburgh Magazine" of October, 1759. In 1763 a Lodge at Durham which had met since 1738 went under the Grand Lodge.

The office of Grand Chaplain was instituted in 1765, and in this year a Lodge at Ford in Northumberland, consisting of 40 members, petitioned Grand Lodge for a Charter, "it being of old standing"; and between 1764-7 seventy-one new Lodges were established. Prince Edward Duke of York having been made a Mason at Berlin in {512} 1765 was constituted a Past Grand Master in 1766. The Steward s Lodge this year printed an "Address" of 16th November, 1763. Entick issued a new edition of the "Constitutions" in 1767. On the 16th May, 1766, William Henry Duke of Gloucester received the three degrees in a Lodge held at the Horn Tavern; on the 9th February, 1767, Henry Frederick Duke of Cumberland at the Thatched House Tavern. Thus the three princes, as Masons, attended a meeting of Grand Lodge 15th April, 1767, and were presented with their clothing, and the Duke of Cumberland was elected a Past Grand Master. Brother Thomas Dunckerley, who claimed to be an illegitimate connection of these princes, was present at the meeting, and from this period was a most active promoter of Freemasonry. The registration of Initiates commenced in 1768. In the year 1769 Brother Wellins Calcott, P.M., published "A Candid Disquisition of the Principles and Practises of the Most Ancient and Honourable Society of Free and Accepted Masons;" he dedicated the work to the Duke of Beaufort, and had the large number of 1,200 subscribers for the edition.

In these years, 1759-70, the opposition to the Grand Lodge, which had never

ceased from the time that they broke away from the Operative Guild in 1715, was in constant evidence, as witness the following publications:

In 1759 appeared in jocular evidence, "The Secrets of Freemasonry Revealed, by a Disgusted Brother."

In 1760 "The Three Distinct Knocks," by W.O.V.-N., member of a Lodge in England. Also a "Wou d Be s Reason," for and against; followed by a "Willingly Wou d Be," believed to refer to Dermott s Ahiman Rezon.

In 1762, "Jachin and Boaz," followed by "A Freemason s Answer to the Suspected Author of Jachin and Boaz."

In 1764, "Hiram, or the Grand Master Key, by a member of the Royal Arch." And in the same year, "An Institute of Red Masonry."

In 1765, "Shibboleth, or every man a Freemason." {513} Also, in the same year, "Mahabone, or the Grand Lodge Door Opened."

Also, "The Way to Things by Words." McClelland.

"Solomon in All his Glory" professes to be "Translated from the French original published at Berlin, and burnt by order of the King of Prussia, at the intercession of the Freemasons." London: Printed for G. Robinson and J. Roberts, at Addison s Head in Paternoster Row, 22nd April, 1766. 2s. 0d. viii. and 61 p. A second edition appeared in 1768.

In 1766, "Solomon in All his Glory, by T. W., an Officer in the Army, and late Member of the Swan Tavern Lodge in the Strand."

In 1767, a second edition of "The Three Distinct Knocks" appeared at London, Sargeant; the previous edition being "Printed by and for A. Cleugh, Radcliffe Highway; T. Hughes, 35 Ludgate St.; B. Crosby, Stationers Court. Price one shilling." N.D.

In 1769, "The Freemason Stripped Naked." Isaac Fell.

We may also mention here six valuable plates by Lanbert de Lintot: 1, Grand Lodge of England. 2, Chapter and Grand Lodge. 3, Foundation of the Royal Order. 4, Fourth and Last Stone. 5, Old and New Jerusalem. 6, Night; and also in 1770 appeared in London a Ritual in French, of the Rose Croix as the 7th degree, the 6th degree being Knight of the East.

An effort was made at this time to Incorporate the Society by Act of Parliament and to build a Hall; and, in reply to a circular letter, 168 Lodges expressed themselves in favour of the proposal and 48 opposed it. A bill was accordingly promoted in 1771, but the scheme was finally abandoned. In 1772 under Lord Petrie, G.M., a Committee was appointed for the purpose of erecting a Hall, and Preston s "Illustrations of Masonry" received the sanction of Grand Lodge. In 1775, "The Spirit of Masonry" was published by Brother William Hutchinson, F.A.S., of Barnard Castle; it bears the sanction of the {514} Grand Officers of England, and is dedicated to the Grand Lodges of England, Ireland, and Scotland, and the Craft in general. He is said to have revised the Old York Lectures and his system was used in Manchester. The foundation of Masonic Hall was laid 1st May, 1775, and was dedicated on the 23rd May, 1776. On 10th April, 1777, the first "Freemasons Calendar" appeared.

In 1778 a dispute occurred between the time immemorial Lodge of Antiquity
and the Grand Lodge. This resulted in an application from Brother William Preston addressed to the Grand Lodge of All England at York, which had met regularly since 1761, for the grant of a Charter to establish a third Grand Lodge in London. This was accomplished on the 19th April, 1780, and a Grand Lodge on the Ancient system was constituted, with jurisdiction south of the Trent, and Preston mentions it briefly in the 1781 edition of his "Illustrations." Now we have three Grand Lodges in London and one in York.

During the ten years existence of this new Grand Lodge it established only two subordinate Lodges in addition to the "Antiquity," and the authority came to an end with the readmission of Brother Preston in 1790 by the premier Grand Lodge. In 1783 Brother Captain George Smith published a work entitled, "The Use and Abuse of Freemasonry." The death of the Grand Lodge at York following shortly upon that of Brother Wm. Preston left only the two London rivals of "Ancients" and "Moderns," and efforts began to be set on foot to unite them. It is asserted by the Rev. Brother A. F. A. Woodford, on the authority of Mr. Walbran, the editor of the Chartulary of Fountain s Abbey, that the York Brothers were in possession of a Charter, now missing, which was supposed to be that of Athelstan; other brethren say the same, but assert that it was almost illegible.

On the 1st May, 1782, Henry Frederick Duke of Cumberland was nominated
Grand Master, with the Earl of Effingham as his Deputy. In 1784 a new edition of the "Constitutions" was issued by Brother John Northouck; the {515} chief change is that the word "Order" is

often used for the customary titles of "Society," or "Brotherhood." On the 9th March, 1786, Prince William Henry, afterwards Duke of Clarence, was initiated in Lodge No. 86 at Plymouth; and on the 6th February, 1787, the Prince of Wales, afterwards King George IV., was initiated by the Duke of Cumberland in a Lodge held at the Star and Garter, Pall Mall, London; and on the 21st November, 1788, Frederick Duke, of York was initiated by the same Grand Master, at the same place, the Prince of Wales, his brother, assisting at the ceremony. Sir Peter Parker, Admiral of the Fleet, had been appointed Deputy G.M. in November, 1786. The "Freemasons

School for Girls" was founded 25th March, 1788, mainly by the exertions of the Chevalier Ruspini; it now bears the title of the "Royal Masonic Institution for Girls."

In 1790 the Grand Lodge met under the auspices of the Duke of Cumberland, when Edward Duke of Kent and Augustus Frederick Duke of Sussex, both of whom had been made Masons abroad, were constituted Past Grand Masters. It was on this occasion that the old Lodge of "Antiquity" was reinstated. On the death of the Duke of Cumberland, G.M., the Prince of Wales was elected to the vacant throne, and was Installed Grand Master 2nd May, 1792, when he appointed Lord Rawdon as Acting Grand Master, and Sir Peter Parker as Deputy. The great extension of Freemasonry under the patronage of all these Princes is shewn by the fact that the number of Prov. Gd. Masters had increased, from eleven in 1770, to twenty-four in 1795, when Prince William of Gloucester was initiated, and Earl Moira appears as Acting Grand Master in 1795. A Masonic publication entitled, "The Freemasons Magazine" was begun in 1793, and continued for some years with a change of title in 1798. In this year Bro. Stephen Jones published his "Masonic Miscellanies."

In 1798 the Boys School was founded, and continues to the present day. On the 12th July, 1799, an Act was {516} passed for the better suppression of treasonable Societies, special exemption being made of the Freemasons Lodges then existing. Under the favourable influence of the Prince of Wales and Earl Moira, Freemasonry made progress, and the possibility of uniting the two rival Grand Lodges began to be seriously contemplated. On the 10th April, 1799, an Address was received from the Duke of Sundermania, Chief of the Order in Sweden, and a brotherly reply was reported by the Earl of Moira to Grand Lodge 9th May, 1799.

The first step towards uniting the "Ancient" and "Modern" Masons was made at a meeting of the latter body 20th November, 1801, when a complaint was made against Brother Thomas Harper and others for frequenting Lodges of the "Athol Masons." Harper then requested a delay of three months, promising to use the time in exerting himself to promote a union of the two Grand Lodges, and this delay was conceded. On the 4th May, 1802, the complaint against Harper was rescinded, and a Committee appointed, of which Lord Moira was a member, to pave the way for a union. From some cause or other Harper turned his back on this arrangement; the Duke of Athol s name was used in opposition to the scheme, and no progress resulted. On the 9th February, 1803, Grand Lodge passed a resolution condemnatory of the "meetings of persons calling themselves Ancient Masons," and threatening to enforce the laws against their own members attending such meetings. In 1805 the Duke of Sussex was elected a Past Grand Master. A pamphlet dated 9th February, 1804, by an anonymous author was issued entitled, "Masonic Union: An Address to His Grace the Duke of Athol, on the subject of an Union, etc." Although the writer was a member of the Grand Lodge of 1717, he closes his title with a quotation from the ritual of Templar Priest. He overruns Masonry from the time of Carausius to the period when Harper was expelled by his Grand Lodge.

Other steps were being taken in the meantime, and {517} on the 12th

February, 1806, the Earl Of Moira reported that he had exerted his influence with the Grand Lodge of Scotland in favour of the union of the two bodies; the same course was followed with the Grand Lodge of Ireland, and a similar report was made on the 23rd November, 1808. On the 12th April, 1809, a resolution

was passed that it was "necessary no longer to continue in force those measures which were resorted to, in or about the year 1739, respecting irregular Masons; and do therefore enjoin the several lodges to revert to the ancient landmarks of the Society." This refers to a change which the Grand Lodge of 1717 had made, during the period, of what they were pleased to term the advent of "irregular Lodges," and which is referred to in the pamphlet of 1804, by reversing the words of the Ist degree and 2nd degree, and which the pamphleteer alludes to as a dispute whether "Gog" and "Magog" were on the right hand or left, according to the position of the beholder. The reversal yet continues with many bodies of foreign Masons. This step was followed by the appointment of a "Lodge of Promulgation" as preparatory to the desired union. Generally it is considered that this change had given the Athol Masons the first handle for terming the Grand Lodge "Modern," but the distinction between the two sects had much wider grounds, as shewn in our last chapter.

On the death of Admiral Sir Peter Parker, H.R.H. the Prince of Wales

appointed his brother, the Duke of Sussex, 11th December, 1811, as Acting Grand-Master, and when the former became Regent of the Kingdom, the Duke of Sussex was elected Grand Master, and the Regent Grand Patron.

At a meeting of the Grand Lodge on the 27th January, 1813, there were present six Royal Dukes -- Sussex, York, Clarence, Kent, Cumberland, Gloucester; on this occasion Earl Moira, now Marquis of Hastings, was presented with a magnificent chain and jewel of office, as he was about to depart for India. The Duke of Sussex was installed {518} Grand Master on 12th May, 1813; and as Edward Duke of Kent had already become a member of the Athol Grand Lodge, their Grand Master the Duke of Athol, with the union in view, resigned his office and recommended as his successor H.R.H. the Duke of Kent, who was accordingly Installed as Grand Master on the 1st December, 1813, at Willis ooms, St. James Square.

There now remained no obstacle to the union of the whole Craft, and the formal "Articles of Union" were drawn up at Kensington Palace on the 25th November, 1813, and ratified at meetings of the two Grand Lodges held on 1st December, 1813; these Articles were signed on behalf of the Grand Lodge of 1717, by Augustus Frederick, G.M.; Waller Rodwell Wright, P.G.M. of the Ionian Islands; Arthur Tegart, P.G.W.; James Deans, P.G.W.; William H. White, Gd. Secretary; and on behalf of the Grand Lodge of 1751, by Edward, G.M.; Thomas Harper, D.G.M.; James Perry, P.D.G.M.; James Agar, P.D.G.M.; Robert Leslie, Gd. Secretary.

In accordance with this the two parties met at the Crown and Anchor tavern in Strand, when the Articles were accepted with Masonic acclamation and unanimously confirmed. A "Lodge of Reconciliation," composed of nine members of the Constitution of England, with Brother White as Secretary, and nine members of the old Institution, with Brother Edward Harper as Secretary, was then constituted with the object of mutually obligating each other, and affording the necessary instruction for amalgamating the two usages into one uniform ritual.

Although the 1717, or "Modern" Masons, had become zealous members of the Royal Arch and Chivalric degrees, yet such degrees were held to be outside their Grand Lodge. On the other hand the 1751, "Ancient" Masons, had from the first treated the Arch degree as an essential part of Masonry to be conferred on Past Masters under Craft Charters, and to meet this the following was made

part of the "Articles:" -- "11. It is declared and pronounced {519} that pure ancient Masonry consists of three degrees, and no more; viz., those of the Entered Apprentice; the Fellow Craft; and the Master Mason (including the Supreme Order of the Holy Royal Arch). But this Article is not intended to prevent any Lodge or Chapter from holding a meeting in any of the Orders of Chivalry, according to the Constitutions of the said Orders."

By this Article, which is obligatory upon the Grand Lodge in all time, the Royal Arch is the completion of the third degree, yet worked as a High-grade, and though all other grades are excluded from the new Rite, they are not prohibited but they are allowed to be practised.

At the period of this Chapter the official Catechisms had become elaborate, the Harodim of Brother Preston being of some note. They still continued to retain a considerable amount of Christian symbolism, confined chiefly to the spiritualisation of Solomon s temple, and the furniture and utensils.

15

CHAPTER XIII. FREEMASONRY UNDER THE UNITED GRAND

FREEMASONRY UNDER THE UNITED GRAND LODGE.
A MEETING of the "United Grand Lodge of Ancient Freemasons of England" was held at Freemasons Hall on the 27th December, 1813, to formally consummate the Union. The Masters, Wardens, and Past Masters of the two bodies composing this united Assembly had been obligated by the "Lodge of Reconciliation" on a uniform plan, and were admitted by tickets, signed and countersigned by the two Secretaries whose names appear to the Articles of Union mentioned in our last chapter, Brothers White and Leslie. The two Grand Masters, namely, the Dukes of Sussex and Kent, occupied equal thrones. The Rev. Brother Coglin, D.D., Grand Chaplain of the Grand Lodge of 1717, proclaimed the confirmation of the Articles to which the brethren signified their assent; then the Rev. Brother Barry, D.D., Grand Chaplain of the Grand Lodge of 1751, proclaimed the Union; after which Brother Wesley performed a symphony on the organ. Other symbolic ceremonies were gone through and the tests were pronounced pure and correct.

The Grand Officers of both bodies now divested themselves of their Insignia.

The Duke of Kent proposed his brother the Duke of Sussex as Grand Master of the United Fraternity. The latter was then obligated, placed upon the throne and proclaimed; after which the Grand Master proceeded to appoint his officers, the Rev. Bro. Samuel Hemming, D.D., and Bro. Isaac Lindo, Grand Wardens, and the two Grand Secretaries being those of the former Grand Lodges. {521}

The Register of the united List of Lodges was settled by drawing lots for precedence, and as that resulted in favour of the 1751 body its Charters obtained a rank in numerical order over those of the other, which still perpetuates a muddle in the chronological position of the Lodges. A reference

to Brother John Lane s valuable "Masonic Records" indicates that the revised list of the United Grand Lodge included 388 Lodges of the 1717 Constitution, and 260 Lodges of the 1751 Constitution, or a total on the new Register of 648 Lodges. A new edition of the "Constitutions" was edited by Brother William Williams and issued in 1815, and which inserts the declaration as to degrees with which we closed our last chapter.

The Arms adopted by the United Grand Lodge were a quartering of those of the Grand Lodge of 1717, and those of the Grand Lodge of 1751; the first being a differenced coat of those granted to the London Company of Masons in 1472, and the latter being derived from the standards of the four principal tribes of Israel, adapted by Christians to the four Evangelists, and forming the seal of the Grand Chapter of York, the Grand Lodge Seal being the three crowns attributed to Prince Edwin of Deira. Motto: Aude vide tace (Hear, see, and be silent.)

A revision of the Lectures of the three degrees of the Craft was committed to the Rev. Bro. Samuel Hemming, D.D., Chaplain to the Duke of Sussex, who made some progress therein, but is said to have been completed by the Rev. Bro. Williams. The system, though exhibiting no great amount of genius, has continued in use to the present day, and though preserving the main features of the older systems all Christian references were expunged, in order to adapt them, in an antiquarian sense, to the supposed constitution of the Society by King Solomon, whose throne every Worshipful Master is fabled to occupy.

For some years the United Grand Lodge continued the even tenor of its way, without much worthy of notice for the historian. On the death of Brother William Preston {522} in 1810 he left 300 Pounds in Consols the interest of which was to be devoted to an annual rehearsal of his own system of Lectures. On the 8th March, 1820, the Grand Master called the attention of Grand Lodge to the death of George III., who had occupied the throne since 1760, and an address of Condolence was voted to the Grand Patron of United Freemasonry, now King George IV.; this address was presented by the Duke of Sussex on the 10th May, 1820, and the Royal Arms were hereafter engraved on the head of the certificates. A similar address was presented to His Majesty, the Grand Patron upon the death of H.R.H. the Duke of Kent, Past G.M.

Between the years 1819-23 a regrettable misunderstanding occurred between the Prov. Gd. Master of Lancashire and some of the Lodges under his sway; the misunderstanding arising in Lodge No. 31, meeting at Liverpool. Blame seems to be attributable to all sides alike, and the Lodge was erased in 1822; it was followed in 1823 by the erasure of the Sea Captain s Lodge, No. 140 which had resolved to stand or fall by No. 31.<<Preston s "Illus.," Oliver s ed.; also "Hist. Harmonic Lo.," 163, Jos. Hawkins.>>

The death of the celebrated traveller Brother Belzoni in 1825, left his widow in straightened circumstances, and the Grand Lodge voted her the sum, of 50 Pounds, and has placed it on record that this Brother was made a Mason in the "Lodge of the Pyramids" at Cairo, and whilst resident at Cambridge had joined the "School of Plato Lodge," No. 549. Belzoni left behind him some little memento of his Masonic theories, in which he refers to the triangular and the serpent aprons of the Egyptian Kings, and their Initiations; he also expresses an opinion that the invention of the Level and Plumb, are due to Nimrod and Ashur.

In the year 1829 past Grand Stewards had permission to wear a Jewel. The death of the Grand Patron George IV. in 1830 was reported to Grand Lodge 17th July, 1830 by his brother the Grand Master, who then read the draft of an Address to be presented to King William IV. {523} condoling with him upon the loss of his brother, and soliciting that he would extend his Patronage to the Craft. To this a reply was received from Sir Robert Peel, dated the 28th July, 1830, signifying the King s consent to become Grand Patron.

At the beginning of the year 1832 Sir John Soane, the Grand Superintendent of Works, reported the completion of alterations which had been in progress to adapt the new Masonic Hall as a Temple exclusively devoted to Masonry, and as the expense of the alterations had been great he enclosed a draft for 500 Poounds towards the cost. In this year 1832 a renumbering of the Lodges took place to fill up the vacancies occasioned by Lodges which had become extinct. In March 1833 Lord Dundas, the Deputy G.M. presented to Grand Lodge on behalf of the Duke of Sussex, G.M., a bust of King William IV. the Grand Patron; also three gilt trowels which had been used on the occasions of laying the foundation stones of the London University; the Licensed Victuallers Asylum; and the Charing Cross Hospital.

In the year 1834 the "Freemasons Quarterly Review" was commenced and continued its labours down to 1850 when a "New Series" was begun, since which time the Craft has never been without one or more periodicals. The learned Brother George Oliver, D.D., whose father, the Rev. Samuel Oliver, had been a Mason of the "Ancient" school, since 1823 had published a number of Masonic works; he may be considered the father of Masonic literature, though his works, for want of critical attention, have fallen into much undeserved neglect.

Several new Lodges were constituted in the Provinces in 1834, when the Earl of Durham was Deputy G.M., and new Masonic Halls were opened at Dorchester and Tiverton. In the month of June 1835 a resolution was passed at a meeting of brothers favourable to the scheme in view, -- "that it is expedient to provide for the wants of the meritorious, but aged and decayed Freemasons, by {524} the erection of an Asylum to receive them within its Sanctuary."

In December 1835 the Grand Stewards Lodge celebrated the Centenary of its foundation in June 1735, at Freemasons Hall. Also the Grand Lodge of Scotland celebrated the Centenary of its foundation by a Festival on St. Andrew s day 1836. In this year 1836 several foundation stones were laid in England with Masonic ritual and solemnities. The Duke of Sussex, G.M., had been for some time in bad health, and the loss of his eyesight was feared, but on the 27th Jany., 1837, he was so far recovered as to make his appearance in Grand Lodge, when he received a most cordial and hearty welcome. The Grand Lodge at this period conceived the idea of forming a Library.

In the year 1838 a magnificent Candelabrum, the funds to purchase which had been raised by subscription, was presented to the Grand Master. The "Asylum for Aged and Decayed Freemasons," celebrated a festival in June of this year, but later on, in the same year, an opposition to the scheme was raised by the Grand Master, who had formed the impression that it would injure the other charities, but the opposition was withdrawn, after some very unpleasant scenes, which for a time affected the Masonic standing of Brother
R. T. Crucifex, one of its supporters and the Editor of the "Freemasons

Quarterly Review." This Asylum was brought into actual operation in 1839; and the Earl of Durham was appointed Pro-Grand Master in the same year. In 1842 the Male Annuity Fund of the Royal Benevolent Institution was established, the Grand Lodge voting it an annual sum of 400 Pounds.

The Duke of Sussex, G.M., died on the 21st April, 1843, and it then became necessary for the Grand Lodge to elect a Grand Master. Bro. Thomas Dundas Earl of Zetland was selected for that office, and his Installation took place in March 1844. In the same year a handsome testimonial was presented to Dr. George Oliver. Also the {525} Duchess of Inverness presented to Grand Lodge the Candelabrum which had been given to her husband in 1838. Between the years 1944-7, a certain amount of friction occurred between the Grand Lodges of England and the Royal York of Berlin, owing to the refusal of the latter to acknowledge any other than Christian Freemasons; the difficulty was finally arranged by the Royal York, acceding, in a limited measure, to the liberal views of this country. Previous to 1847 it was, from olden time, a necessity that a Candidate should be "free-born," but in this year it was resolved to substitute the qualification of "free-man." In 1849 the Masonic Widow s Annuity fund was established; and the Queen became Grand Patroness of the Boy s School in 1852. On the 7th December, 1853, the Grand Master reported to Grand Lodge that

he had been under the necessity of suspending Bro. William Tucker, the Prov. Gd. Master of Dorsetshire; the offence being that he had made his appearance in his Prov. Gd. Lodge wearing, in addition to his Craft clothing, the insignia of the Christian orders of Masonry. It is also on record<<"Freem Quart. Review.">> that Brother. Tucker had made a point in his Address of recommending those higher degrees of Masonry found in the Ancient and Accepted Rite of 33 degrees, which after having met with disfavour from the late Grand Master had been introduced into England from America within two years of the death of the Duke of Sussex.

On the 4th June, 1856, an attempt was made to foist the ceremonial of the Mark degree into the Craft series, but was rejected as an impossibility, as the "Articles of Union" state that pure Freemasonry consists of three degrees and no more; on this occasion Brother John Henderson, the Grand Registrar, said that, -- "no man, nor body of men, could make such innovation as that proposed, without endangering the whole fabric of the Institution." The Earl of Dalhousie was appointed Deputy G.M. in 1857. {526}

Between October 1855 and September 1857, many of the Canadian Craftsmen withdrew themselves from under our banner alleging neglect by the officials of Grand Lodge, and thereupon erected a Grand Lodge of their own. This led to the formation of a "Colonial Board" in 1856 by the Grand Lodge of England, and the establishment of a second Grand Lodge in Canada. On this occasion England lost the Canadian Lodges, save a few Masons who remained faithful to their old allegiance. The two Grand Lodges, thus formed in Canada united 14th July, 1858 under the designation of "The Grand Lodge of Canada." These troubles led to the resignation of Bro. Wm. Hy. White, who had been Gd. Secretary since the union of 1813, and to the appointment in 1857 of Brother William Gray Clarke.

The nucleus of a Masonic Hall was begun in Manchester 27th,June, 1857, by taking the upper floor of rooms over the shops with an opening at 78 Cross Street, and dividing the same into Refreshment room supplied by a back

staircase, a Lodge Room and a Tyler s Room; a club also was established. The Liverpool Masonic Temple was commenced in 1858 by the purchase of a building for 1,600 Pounds.

In April 1861 the Earl de Grey and Ripon was appointed Deputy G.M. On the 8th January, 1862, the Grand Lodge voted an Address of Condolence to the Queen on the death of her Consort on 14th December, 1861. In July, 1862, the Prov. Gd. Master of East Lancashire Brother Stephen Blair, laid the foundation of a Masonic Hall at Manchester, the necessary funds being raised by a Company of Shareholders. On the 3rd December, 1862, it was resolved to revise the numbering of the

Lodges, thus eliminating the vacancies occurring since 1832. The Masonic Hall at Manchester was opened by the Prov. Gd. Master 3rd November, 1864. It had been in contemplation to improve the Masonic Hall, London, by separating the Tavern entirely from that portion used for Grand Lodge purposes, and on the 27th April, 1864, the Earl of Zetland, G.M., laid the {527} foundation stone of the new building which was completed for Masonic purposes in 1866.

In 1865 a revision of the "Book of Constitutions" was made and it was

directed that the term Prov. Grand Master in England, should be District Grand Master in the Colonies and foreign parts. On the 7th June, 1865, the subject of the Mark degree was again brought under discussion and it was resolved to refuse recognition to the Mark Grand Lodge which had been established in 1856, the ceremonial being treated as comparatively modern. The learned brother Dr. George Oliver was interred with Masonic honours in 1867; and on the death of Brother William Gray Clarke in 1868, Brother John Hervey became Grand Secretary.

On the 2nd June 1869 the Earl of Zetland, G.M., informed the Grand Lodge that H.R.H. the Prince of Wales had been received into Freemasonry by the King of Sweden; and in September of the same year he was elected a Past Gd. Master of England, and the Prince attended Grand Lodge in December 1869. The number of Lodges on the Roll had increased from 723 in 1844, to 1299 in the year 1869. Freemasons Hall had now been separated from the tavern, and was formally inaugurated on the 14th April 1869.

On the voluntary resignation of the Earl of Zetland as Grand Master in 1870, a handsome testimonial was arranged and subscriptions obtained; the Earl accepted a silver inkstand, and directed that the remainder of the contribution, which amounted to 2,730 Pounds should form a fund for the relief of distinguished brethren who might be in distress and to be named the "Zetland Fund."

Earl de Grey and Ripon was now nominated to the office of Grand Master, and was installed as such on the 14th May 1870. The Masonic career of this Grand Master, who was made a Marquis for diplomatic services in the United States, was not closed in a manner equally distinguished, as upon his embracing the Roman Catholic faith he resigned his office of Grand Master 2nd September, {528} 1874. Arthur Duke of Connaught and Leopold Duke of Albany were initiated in 1874, the former in the "Prince of Wales Lodge," and the latter in the "Apollo University Lodge."

The Prince of Wales having already the rank of a Past Grand Master of England, a deputation was appointed to interview him upon the acceptance of the office vacated by the Marquis of Ripon. At the meeting of Grand Lodge in December, 1874, it was reported that the Prince would accept the Grand

Mastership, and would appoint the Earl of Carnarvon as pro-Grand Master, and Lord Skelmersdale as Deputy G.M. Accordingly the Prince of Wales was Installed Grand Master, with great pomp, at the Royal Albert Hall, South Kensington, on the 28th April, 1875, which was duly commemorated by a painting in oil, and an engraved copy of the same. In May of the same year the Prince was Installed G.Z. of the Supreme Grand Chapter. His brother Leopold Duke of Albany was Installed Provincial Gd. Master of Oxfordshire in February 1876.

At the meeting of Grand Lodge, April, 1877, the Prince of Wales, G.M., appointed his brothers the Dukes of Connaught and of Albany as his two Grand Wardens; and 4,000 Pounds was voted by Grand Lodge to the Royal National Life Boat Institution. On the 5th December in this year a Committee was appointed to consider the action of the Grand Orient of France in reference to the abolition of the requirement of any special religious belief from candidates for Initiation, or as the Grand Lodge preferred to put it, the removal of the name of God from their Constitution, and in March 1878 the Committee gave in a report denying recognition as "true and genuine" brethren to those so Initiated.

In 1879 Brother John Hervey, whose death took place the following year, resigned the office of Grand Secretary, and Colonel Shadwell H. Clerke was appointed. On the 1st June, 1881, the list Of Grand Officers was increased by adding a Deputy Master of Ceremonies and two Grand {529} Sword Bearers. In 1882 the Prince of Wales, G.M., was present at Grand Lodge, with his two brothers, when a congratulatory Address was voted to the Queen on her escape from the danger of assassination. In 1883 a new edition of the "Book of Constitutions" was issued; the great Hall at Freemasons Hall in London was destroyed by fire; and the Society lost the Duke of Albany by death, 28th March, 1884.

On the 28th November, 1884, a Charter was granted for the "Quatuor Coronati Lodge," 2076, Brother Sir Charles Warren being the first W.M.; the object of the Lodge, besides the ordinary routine of such bodies, being the increase of Masonic knowledge by competent Lectures at each meeting, the publication of the same in a journal entitled "Ars Quatuor Coronatorum," and the reprint of our ancient MSS., and other works in volumes designated "Quatuor Coronatorum Antigraphia." One of their first developments was the establishment, by the late Brother G. W. Speth, the Secretary of the Lodge, of a "Correspondence Circle" which now numbers over three thousand members.

In the year 1884 Grand Lodge passed a resolution of Remonstrance against the Pope s Encyclical denouncing Freemasonry; and a new edition of the Arch Regulations was prepared. At a meeting of "Royal Alpha Lodge," London, on the 17th March, 1885, the Prince of Wales, G.M., himself Initiated his eldest son Prince Albert Victor, and in 1887 conferred upon him the office of Senior Grand Warden. The new Great Hall was completed in 1885; and on the 22nd June, 1886, the Prince of Wales, G.M., Installed his brother the Duke of Connaught as Prov. Gd. Master of Sussex.

On the 1st June, 1887, Brother Henry Sadler was appointed Sub-librarian of Grand Lodge, which was a poor affair for so wealthy a body, but which Brother Sadler has done much to improve and is himself the author of some valuable works, as "Masonic Facts and Fictions; Life of Thomas Dunckerley; Notes on the Ceremony of Installation;" {530} Portrait of G. M. Sayer; Catalogue of Gd.

Lodge Library, etc. In this year, 1887, Brother R. F. Gould completed the last volume of his well-known "History of Freemasonry."

On the 13th June, 1887, a grand Masonic Celebration of Her Majesty s Jubilee was held at the Royal Albert Hall, under the presidency of H.R.H. the Prince of Wales as Grand Master, when an Address, handsomely illuminated on vellum, for presentation to her Majesty the Queen, was read to the Assembly and a special Jewel was presented to the Grand Master, such as might be worn by all Masons who were subscribing members of any Lodge at the time. At a meeting of Grand Lodge, 6th June, 1888, the rank of Past Grand Master was conferred upon Oscar II. King of Sweden and Norway, Grand Master or Vicarius Salamonis in those countries. Between the 4th and 7th of June in this year the Royal Masonic Benevolent Institution for Girls celebrated its centenary at the Royal Albert Hall; the 4th was the prize distribution day, at which were present the Prince and Princess of Wales, and the Princesses Louise, Victoria, and Maud. On the 7th the Prince of Wales presided, and was supported by the King of Sweden, and various notables of the English Craft.

In December 1890 the Prince of Wales, G.M., Installed his eldest son Prince

Albert Victor Duke of Clarence and Avondale as Prov. Grand Master of Berkshire; unfortunately his tenure of that office was very short as he died on the 14th January, 1892. The death of Brother Shadwell H. Clerke, the Grand Secretary, on the 25th December, 1891, led to the appointment to that office of Brother Edward Letchworth.

On the 27th January, 1892, the Grand Lodge voted an Address of Condolence to the Queen, and to the Prince of Wales, G.M., on the lamented death of the Duke of Clarence and Avondale, and the whole Craft followed this example. The Jubilee of the Royal Masonic Benevolent Institution was celebrated the 24th February of this year at the Covent Garden Theatre, with the Earl of {531} Mount Edgecombe as President, when the unprecedented sum of 59,593 Pounds 15s. 0d. was contributed. In December, 1892, Grand Lodge again agreed to enlarge the number of Grand Officers by the addition of a Deputy Grand Registrar, a Deputy Grand Sword Bearer, additional Grand Deacons, and Grand Directors of Ceremonies; the like appointments to extend to Provincial Grand Lodges, according to their numerical strength. During this year the question of admitting Jews as Freemasons was agitated in Prussia, and a new Lodge was established for the special purpose of such Initiations. It is, however, outside a work of this nature to print the ordinary and recent outline of the routine of Freemasonry, which must give the world the idea that all is pomp, parade, man millinery, and banqueting. Matters of this sort can be gathered from the ordinary Freemasons Journals, which make it their business to report every detail for the edification of the members of Lodges. With the great increase that is constantly taking place in the numbers of Lodges, innovations are constantly being introduced of a doubtful character, not calculated for the good of the Society. We will, however, mention a few more items of general interest.

At a meeting of Grand Lodge, 19th April, 1896, the rank of Past Grand Officer

was conferred upon 21 distinguished Masons, in commemoration of the 21 years during which the Prince of Wales had filled the Grand Mastership. A commemoration festival was held on the 14th June 1897 at the Royal Albert Hall, in honour of her Majesty the Queen having attained the 60th year of her reign, and which was one of the finest spectacles on record. Another, worthy of

record, was the Festival of the Royal Masonic Institution for Boys, on the 10th July, 1898, under the Presidency of the Grand Master at the Royal Albert Hall, London, when the unprecedented sum of 141,000 Pounds was reported as subscribed for the purpose of erecting new school buildings, and removing the School to Bushey, near Watford. At the meeting of Grand Lodge on the {532} 7th September, 1898, terms were proposed and passed for the recognition of the sometime established Grand Lodge of New Zealand.

On the 12th May, 1900, the foundation-stone was laid at Bushey of the New Royal Masonic Institution for Boys; the inscription upon the plate deposited was as follows: -- "This stone was laid on the 12th May, A.D. 1900, with Masonic ceremonial, by H.R.H. the Duke of Connaught and Strathearn, K.G., &c., &c., Grand Master, President of the Institution."

The death of H.M. Queen Victoria occurring on the 22nd January, 1901, With the accession of the Prince of Wales as Edward VII., caused his resignation as Grand Master, on the 15th February, upon which the Duke of Connaught was nominated as Grand Master and was Installed 17th July, 1901, in the Royal Albert Hall.

The prosperity of the Craft, for many years, has been progressive and uninterrupted in its numerical accessions, and since 1869, when the Lodges were renumbered, to the day we write, some 1,500 Lodges are added to the Roll. The advance in its literary efforts has kept pace with the numerical increase in its Lodges, though Freemasons as a body are very indifferent to its literature. The "Quatuor Coronati Lodge" has distinguished itself by the issue of numerous facsimiles of ancient MSS. reproduced with great care, and in the most beautiful style; it has completed twenty volumes of its "Transactions," Lectures and papers distinguished by the accuracy and soundness of their information, and the excellence of the workmanship, and it has thus been the means of spreading sound and reliable Masonic literature over all the world; and we have been much indebted to its papers in compiling this book. In equally good style the Newcastle College of Rosicrucians has produced facsimiles of ancient MSS. besides their ordinary "Transactions." The Rosicrucian College of London has also published valuable papers. The West Yorkshire Provincial Library, established by the exertions of Brother Wm. Watson, the Prov. Gd. Secretary {533} and Librarian, has reproduced nine copies of the Constitutional Charges at the cost of the Prov. Gd. Master, the late Brother Thos. Wm. Tew. The York brothers have published a similar volume of the old Charges by subscription. Other valuable works have proceeded from the pens of Brothers Wm. James Hughan, Kenneth R. H. Mackenzie, Robert Freke Gould, W. Wynn Westcott, M.B., G. W. Speth, John Strachan, Q.C., Henry Sadler, John Lane, W. J. C. Crawley, LL.D., G. W. Bain, and many others too numerous to mention; also some reprints of old plates, books, and documents. The Quatuor Coronati Lodge, 2076, however, has had the great misfortune to lose one of its most valued pillars, Bro. G. W. Speth, 19th April, 1901, in his 54th year, and the Lodge erected, by subscription, a monument. The death of the Treasurer followed on the 4th June 1901, viz., Sir Walter Besant in his 65th year. In 1905 Bro. R. F. Gould published his "Concise History of Freemasonry."

Another notable event of the time was the establishment, by Mrs. Besant, of a

S.G.C. 33rd Degree, in London, under authority from India, which received it from a dissension which occurred in the S.G.C. 33rd Degree of France. It

confers all its degrees indiscriminately upon males and females, and works the Craft degrees under the Ritual of the Grand Lodge of England, and at the present time has numerous adherents and Lodges. It has added only to the Ritual a "Dharma" Lecture which compares Masonry with secret societies of India, and takes the name of Co-Masonry.

Even this may aid in rousing amongst Freemasons a more intellectual standard of labour. Possibly, if Masonry was less of a political machine, officered from the Court, and its high officials elected by the Craft for "Merit" alone, we should see a better state of things than now exists. A section of the Press is now agitating against Freemasonry, assigning as grounds that the worst men are employed by our Municipal Councils to the detriment of non- Masons. On the other hand, a very worthy brother,

{534} who was initiated in the same Lodge as myself, was complaining against the carelessness in inquiry into the character of candidates. I replied that this was so, but although I had been fifty-five years a Mason, and had been deluged from every part of the world with unsolicited Honours, I was pleased to say that, in all these years, I never, in a single instance, met with any one Mason with an eye to my worldly interests, hence I utterly disbelieved those assertions that good men were ousted in the interests of Masons.

In all these years the old Operative Guilds of Free Masons have continued
their work without changing the secrecy of their proceedings. They have their Lodges in London, Leicester, Norfolk, Derbyshire, Holyhead, York, Durham, Berwick, and elsewhere. Some of these are in a languishing condition, but they exist, and are in course of galvanisation. Of late years they seem to have become disgusted with the vain pretensions of Modern Speculative Freemasonry, and under authority of the three coequal G.M.M. s of the South and North have to some little extent relaxed the secrecy of their proceedings; and though the greater part of their members are utterly averse to anything whatever being made public, possibly in time these restrictions will be further modified, to the advantage of the Speculative system of 1813, for many parts are quite incomprehensible, even to learned Freemasons, without the technical part which only the Guilds of the Free Masons can supply.

FINIS.

16

APPENDIX.

IT has been thought advisable to add here copies of the ancient MSS. referred to in the foregoing pages, reduced into somewhat more modern English for the comfort of the reader. No injury can arise from this procedure, as those who are interested in the exact verbiage will consult the facsimiles issued by Lodge 2076, and other printed copies. We have made use of certain emendations which have been shewn to be necessary by the best critics.

Attention was first directed to these MSS. by Brother William James Hughan, who printed, in 1872, a volume of the "Old Charges." For some years his efforts to direct attention to these MSS. met with slight success, as the bearing of them upon the present state of Freemasonry was not fully recognised; but to Brother Hughan belongs the credit of bringing these documents into prominent notice.

A few zealous brethren, amongst whom may be mentioned the Rev. A. F. A. Woodford, R. F. Gould, G. W. Speth, Dr. William Begemann of Rostock, C. C. Howard of Picton, N.Z., Wm. Watson, Henry Sadler, F. F. Schnitger, and others, have laboured to develop the work thus begun by Brother Hughan, and we must express indebtedness to their unselfish labours.

It is noteworthy that, with the exception of those MSS. which refer to Henry VI., all these documents close their Masonic history with the reign of Athelstan. Practically the "Regius MS." and the " Book of Charges " of the "Cooke MS." are identical, except that the versifier has lengthened the former MS. by his own comments, and we have therefore taken the prose copy, as probably nearer the Athelstan original; for most of the emendations (in brackets) we are indebted to Brother C. C. Howard. Brother G. W. Speth considered it likely that the nine ARTICLES were the legal enactments of the King, whilst the nine POINTS were those of the employers.

JOHN YARKER.

" West Didsbury,"

"near Manchester, 1909."

{537}

INTRODUCTION. I.
ANGLO-SAXON CHARGES.

This MS. as we have before stated is the "Book of Charges" attached to the "Cooke MS.," and agrees with the "Regius MS.," being complete in itself; and (our oldest MS.) is actually, with some additions, a rhythmical version of No. 1. When we come to the mention of "New Men," it is possible that the 9 Points may have been substituted for them by "Divers Congregations"; in later times they were read as the Charge of an Apprentice. It is even so to-day by Masons.

II.

ANGLO-NORMAN CHARGES.

There seems no reason to doubt that No. 1 is the original Saxon Charge, but as there was a constant influx of French Masons from the time of the conquest, a pure French Charge must at one time have existed, and which has clearly been added to the older English documents.

The 1316 document is extracted from Brother R. F. Gould s History of Freemasonry (Vol. ii. p. 341). It is of equal value with any that we have, and illustrates the old MSS. in an interesting way. In the first place the Laws are decreed by the very authorities which the Charges themselves appeal to, and "six or four ancient men of the trade" are required to testify on a Master taking on work. It settles the dispute between the Mason-hewers and the Light masons or setters, and places them both under sworn Elders or Ancients of the trade. It admits that there was no Court, and orders one to be sworn, which thus became the London Company of Masons, uniting Masons and Freemasons, of which the former had 4 representatives and the latter 2, but became now a United Company.

III.

The text of the "Cooke" preface, as far as the same is complete, has been used for this document, the remainder being taken from the "Watson MS.," which is a document complete in itself, but with many errors of the copyist. The author speaks of "old books of Charges," existing before his time, and he has possibly mistaken "Martellus" for "Secundus," inasmuch as Charles Martel was not King but Regent, and only "came to his {538} kingdom" in his children, Charlemagne being his grandson, who had a grandson Charles II.

IV.

MODERN CHARGES.

These modern Charges, of which there are about 70 copies, of which no two are exactly alike, are an abridgement of the "Watson MS." series, which had become too lengthy for use in Lodge work. The version given is a fair representative of all the others and is a York MS. circa 1600. The portion in brackets [ ], and Charges 19-25 are found in the "Tew MS.," West Riding of Yorkshire.

V.

The Southern Variation of No. 5 is peculiar and found in a few MSS. The evidence of causing Edwin to be made a Mason at Windsor shews that it was compiled in the South, though Winchester is probably meant, as King Athelstan had his royal residence in that city. The version is a late 16th century view found in the "Lansdowne MS.," the "Probity MS.," and the "Antiquity MS."

VI.

The "Apprentice Charge" attached to a MS. which contains the "New Regulations," are found in many MSS., and are those used in the written Indentures of an Apprentice. The "New Regulations" are found in the "Harleian MS.," which is the one we give; (2{1?}) the "Grand Lodge MS. 2," numbered 29

c. 33; (2) the "Roberts MS.," numbered 1 to 7; (3) the "McNab MS."; (4) a MS. seen by Dr. James

Anderson, number 1 to 7; but there must have been an older original. The Harleian, Grand Lodge, and McNab MSS. give no date of the Assembly; Roberts and Anderson give 1663; probably there was no date in the oldest original. The British Museum officials consider the "Harleian MS." to be early 17th century; it forms a species of Grand Lodge, and inaugurates a Charge for Apprentices. VII.

The Addition of 1663 to the "New Articles," and numbered 6, is given by Anderson in the copy he saw, and also in the copy printed by Roberts in 1722. But as it appears in "Grand Lodge MS. 2," as Article 32, it may have been omitted by accident from VI. version.

{539}

I.

"THE ANGLO-SAXON CONSTITUTION."

GOOD MEN for this cause and in this manner Masonry took its first beginning. It befell sometimes that great Lords had no such large possessions that they could well advance their free-begotten children for they had so many; therefore they took counsel how they might advance their children and ordain for them an honest livelihood. And they sent after wise Masters of the worthy science of Geometry, that through their wisdom they might ordain them some honest living. Then one of them that had the name of Euclid was the subtle and wise founder, and ordained an Art and called it Masonry, and so with this honest art he taught the children of the great Lords, by the prayer of the fathers and the free-will of their children; the which, when they were taught with high care, by a certain time they were not all alike able to take of the

aforesaid Art, wherefore Euclid ordained that they who were passing of cunning should be passing honoured, and ordained to call the more cunning Master, to inform the less cunning, Masters of the which were called Masters of Nobility of wit and cunning of that Art. Nevertheless they commanded that they who were less of wit should not be called servant, nor subject, but fellow for nobility of their gentle blood. In this manner was the aforesaid Art begun in the land of Egypt, by the aforesaid Master Euclid, and so it went from land to land, and from kingdom to kingdom.

After that many years, in the time of Athelstan King of England, by his Councillors and other great Lords of the land, by common assent, for great defects found amongst Masons, they ordained a certain Rule amongst them, once in the year, or in three years, as the need were, the King and great Lords of the land, and all the commonality, from province to province, and from country to country, Congregations should be made by Masters, of all Master Masons and Fellows in the aforesaid Art, and so at such Congregations they that be made Masters should be examined of the "Articles" after written, and be ransacked whether they be able and cunning to the profit of the Lords (having) them to serve, and to the honour of the aforesaid Art.

And moreover (that) they should receive their "Charge" that they should well and truly dispend the goods of their Lords, as well the lowest as the highest, for they be their Lords for the time of whom they take pay for their service, and for their travail.

The first "Article" is this, -- That every Master of this Art should be wise and true to the lord that he serveth, dispensing his goods truly as he would have his own were dispensed, and not give more pay to a Mason than he wot he may deserve, after the dearth of corn and victual in the country, no favour withstanding for every man to be rewarded after his travail.

The second "Article" is this, -- That every Master of this Art should be warned beforehand to come to his congregation, but they be excused by some cause. But nevertheless if they be found rebellious at such Congregations, or faulty in any manner {540} of harm to their lords, and reproof of this Art, they should not be excused unless in peril of death, and though they be in peril of death, they shall warn the Master who is Principal of the Gathering of his decease (disease).

The third "Article" is this, -- That no Master take no Prentice for a less term than 7 years at the least, because such as be within a less term may not profitably come to (knowledge of) this Art, nor able to serve truly his lord and to take as a Mason should take.

The fourth "Article" is this, -- That no Master for no profit take no Prentice to be learned that is born of bond blood, because his lord to whom he is bond, will take him, as he well may, from his Art, and lead him out of his Lodge, or out of his place that he worketh in; for his Fellows peradventure would help him and debate for him, and therefore manslaughter might arise; it is forbidden. And also for another cause; this Art took beginning of great lord s children freely begotten, as it is said before.

The fifth "Article" is this, -- That no Master give more to his Prentice in time of his Prenticehood, for no profit he might take, than he notes well he may deserve of the lord that he serveth; nor not so much (but) that the lord of the place that he is taught in, may have some profit for his teaching.

The sixth "Article" is this, -- That no Master for no covetousness nor profit take no Prentice to teach that is imperfect, that is to say having any maim, for the which he may not truly work as he ought to do.

The seventh "Article" is this, -- That no Master be found wittingly, or help to procure to be (a) maintainer and sustainer (of) any common nightwalker to rob, by the which manner of nightwalking they may not fulfil their day s work and travail, (and) through the condition their Fellows might be wroth.

The eighth "Article" is this, -- That if it befall that any Mason that be perfect, and cunning come for to seek work, and find an imperfect and uncunning (Mason) working, the Master of the place shall receive the perfect and do way with the imperfect to the profit of his lord.

The ninth "Article" is this, -- That no Master shall supplant another: for it is said in the Art of Masonry, that no man can make an end so well of work, begun by another, to the profit of his lord, as he (that) began it, to end it by his matters, or to whom he sheweth his matters.

THIS COUNCIL is made by divers Lords and Masters of divers Provinces, and divers Congregations of Masonry, and it is, to wit, that whosoe coveteth to come to the state of the foresaid Art it behoveth them: --

First, principally to (love) God and Holy Church and al-halows, and his Master and his Fellows as his own brethren.

The second "Point," -- He must fulfil his day s work truly that he taketh for his pay.

The third "Point," -- That he can hele the Counsel of his Fellows, in "Lodge" and in "Chamber," and in every place where Masons be.

The fourth "Point," -- That he be no deceiver in the foresaid Art, nor do no prejudice, nor sustain any Articles against the Art, nor against any of the Art, but he shall sustain it in all honour, inasmuch as he may.

The fifth "Point," -- When he shall take his pay that he take it meekly, as the time is ordained by the Master to be done, and that he fulfil the acceptations of travail and of rest ordained and set by the Master. {541}

The sixth "Point," -- If any discord shall be between him and his Fellows, he shall obey meekly, and be still at the bidding of his Master, or of the Warden of his Master, in the Master s absence, to the holy day following, and that he accord them at the disposition of his Fellows, and not upon the workday, for hindering of the work and profit of the lord.

The seventh "Point," -- That he covet not the wife, nor the daughter of his Master s, neither of his Fellows, but it be in marriage, nor hold concubines for discord that might fall among them.

The eighth "Point," -- If it befall him to be Warden under his Master, that he be true mean between his Master and his Fellows, and that he be busy in the absence of his Master, to the honour of his Master, and profit of the lord that he serveth.

The ninth "Point," -- If he be wiser and subtler than his Fellow working with him in his Lodge, or any other place, and he perceiveth that he should leave the stone that he is working upon for defect of cunning, and can teach him and amend the stone, he shall inform him, and help him, that the more love may increase among them, and that the work of the lord be not lost.

WHEN THE MASTERS and the Fellows be forewarned (and) are come to the Congregation if need be the Sheriff of the country, or the Mayor of the City, or Alderman of the Town, in which the Congregations are holden, shall be Fellow

and Sociate to the Master of the Congregation to help him against rebels, and (for) upbearing of the right of the realm.

At the first beginning "New Men" that never were "Charged" before (were) "Charged" in this manner, -- (1) That (they) should never be thieves, nor thieves maintainers. (2) And that they should truly fulfil their day s work and travail, for their pay that they shall take of their lord. (3) A true account give to their Fellows (as Stewards) in things to be accounted of them. (4) And to hear and love them as themselves. (5) And they shall be true to the King of England and to the realm. (6) And that they keep with all their might all the Articles aforesaid. (7) After that it shall be enquired if any Master or Fellow that is warned, have broken any Articles beforesaid, the which if they have done it shall be determined there. (8) Therefore it is, to wit, that if any Master or Fellow that is warned before to come to such Congregations, and be rebellious and will not come, or else shall have trespassed against any Article beforesaid, if it be proved he shall forswear his Masonry and shall no more use his Craft;

(9) the which if he presume to do, the Sheriff of the Country in which he may be found working shall prison him and take all his goods into the King s hand, til his grace be granted him and shewed.

For this cause principally were these Congregations ordained that, as well the lowest as the highest should be well and truly served in his Art beforesaid, throughout all the Kingdom of England. Amen, -- so mote it be.

SUPPOSED ASSENT OF ATHELSTAN. (REGIUS M.S.).

"These Statutes that I have here found,   Beseeching him, of his high grace, I will they be held throughout my land,   To stand with you in every place, For the worship of my Royalty,   To confirm the Statutes of King

That I have by my dignity.   Athelstan.

Also at every sembly that you hold,   That he ordained to this Craft, That ye come to your liege King bold,   for good reason."

(1-9) Possibly the ancient points, the Nos. 1 to 9, do not appear in the original MS.

{542}

"THE ANGLO-NORMAN CONSTITUTIONS"

II.

STATUTES OF A.D. 1356.

At a Congregation of Mayor and Aldermen holden on the Monday next before the purification of the Blessed Virgin Mary (2 Feby.) in the thirtieth year of the reign of King Edward III, etc., there being present Simon Fraunceys the Mayor,

John Lovekyn, and other Aldermen, the Sheriffs, and John Little, Symon de Benyngtone, and William de Holbeche, commoners, certain Articles were ordained touching the trade of Masons, in these words: --

1.   Whereas Simon Fraunceys, Mayor of the City of London, has been given to understand that divers dissensions and disputes have been moved in the said City, between the Masons who are "hewers" on the one hand, and the light- Masons and "setters" on the other; because that their trade has not been regulated in due manner by the government of Folks of their trade in such form as other trades are. Therefore the said Mayor, for maintaining the peace of our Lord the King, and for allaying such manner of dissensions and disputes, and for nurturing love among all manner of folks, in honour of the said City, and for the profit of the common people, by assent and counsel of the Aldermen and Sheriffs, caused all the good folks of the said trade to be summoned before him, to have from them good and due information how their trade might be best ordered and ruled, for the profit of the common people.

2.   Whereupon the good folks of the said trade chose from among themselves twelve of the most skilful men of their trade, to inform the Mayor, Aldermen, and Sheriffs, as to the acts and articles touching their said trade; -- that is to say Walter de Sallynge, Richard de Sallynge, Thomas de Bredone, John de Tyringtone, Thomas de Gloucestre, and Henry de Yevelee, on behalf of the "Mason Hewers;" Richard Joye, Simon de Bartone, John de Estoune, John Wylot, Thomas Hardegray, and Richard de Cornewaylle on behalf of the "light- Masons and Setters;" which folks

were sworn before the aforesaid Mayor, Aldermen, and Sheriffs, in manner as follows: --

3.   In the first place that every man of the trade may work at any work touching the trade, if he be perfectly skilled and knowing in the same.

4.   Also, that good folks of the said trade shall be chosen and sworn every time that need shall be, to Oversee that no one of the trade takes work to complete, if he does not well and perfectly know how to perform such work, on pain of losing, to the use of the commonality, the first time that he shall by the persons so sworn be convicted thereof, one mark; and the second time two marks; and the third time he shall forswear his trade for ever.

5.   Also, that no one shall take work in gross, if he be not in ability in a proper manner to complete such work; and he who wishes to undertake such work in gross, shall come to the good men, of whom he has taken such work to do and complete, and {543} shall bring with him "Six" or "Four" Ancient men of his trade, sworn thereunto, if they are prepared to testify unto the good men of whom he has taken such work to do, that he is skilful and of ability to do such work, and that if he shall fail to complete such work in due manner, or not to be of ability to do the same, they themselves who so testify that he is skilful and of ability to finish the work are bound to complete the same work, well and properly, at their own charges, in such manner as he undertook; in case the employer who owns the work shall have fully paid the workman. And if the employer shall then owe him anything let him pay it to the persons who have so undertaken for him to complete such work.

6.   Also, that no one shall set an apprentice or journeyman to work, except in
the presence of his Master, before he has been perfectly instructed in his calling; and he who shall do the contrary, and by the person so sworn be convicted thereof, let him pay the first time to the commonality half a mark,

and the second time one mark, and the third time 20 shillings; and so let him pay 20 shillings every time that he shall be convicted thereof.

7.   Also, that no man of the said trade shall take an Apprentice for a less time than seven years, according to the usage of the City; and he who shall do the contrary thereof, shall be punished in the same manner.

8.   Also; that the said Masters so chosen, shall see that all those who work by the day shall take for their hire according as they are skilled and may deserve for their work, and not outrageously.

9.   Also, that if any one of the said trade will not be ruled or directed in due manner by the persons of his trade sworn thereto, such sworn persons are to make known his name unto the Mayor, and the Mayor by assent of the aldermen and sheriffs shall cause him to be chastised by imprisonment, and other punishment, so that rebels may take example by him, to be ruled by the good folks of their trade.

10.   Also, that no one of the said trade shall take the Apprentice of another to the prejudice or damage of his Master, until his term shall have fully expired, on pain of paying, to the use of the commonality, half a mark each time that he shall be convicted thereof.

"THE ANCIENT CHARGES." III.

CHARGE, "circa" 1400, REVISED, "circa" 1475.

THANKED BE GOD our glorious Father and founder and former of heaven and earth, and of all things that in them is, that he would vouchsafe of his glorious Godhead to make so many things of divers virtues for mankind; for he made all worldly things to be obedient and subject to man; for all things that be comestible or of wholesome nature he ordained it for man s sustenance. And also he hath given to man wit and cunning of divers sciences and crafts, by the which he may labour in this world to get our living with (them); and to make divers things for God s pleasure and our (own) ease and profit; the which things if I were to rehearse them, it were too long to tell and to write. Wherefore I will leave (them), but I will shew you some part of them, and tell you how and in what wise the science of Geometry first began, and who were the founders thereof, and of other Crafts more, as it is noted in the Bible and other stories.

{544}

How and in what manner this worthy science of Geometry first began I will tell you, as I said before. Ye shall understand that there be seven Liberal Sciences by which seven sciences all the Sciences and Crafts in the world were first found, and especially the science of Geometry, for it is the cause of all other that be, the which seven sciences are called thus: -- As for the first, that is called the foundation of science, its name is "Grammar," it teacheth a man rightly to speak, and write truly. The second is "Rhetorick," and it teacheth a man to write formably and fair. The third is "Dialecticus"<<"Logic" (Watson M.S.)>>, and that science teacheth a man to discern the true from the false, and most commonly it is called the art of sophistry. The fourth is called Arithmetic, the which teacheth a man the craft of numbers, for to reckon and make accounts of all manner of things. The fifth is Geometry," the which

teacheth a man mete and measures and ponderation and weightiness, in all manner of crafts. The sixth is "Music," that teacheth a man the craft of song in notes of voice and organ and trumpet and harp and all others pertaining to them. The seventh is "Astronomy," that teacheth a man the course of the sun and of the moon, and all other planets and stars of heaven.

OUR INTENT is principally to treat of the first foundation of the worthy science of Geometry, and who were the founders thereof. As I said before, there are seven Liberal Sciences, that is to say seven sciences or crafts that are free in themselves, the which seven live only by one, and that is the science of Geometry. And Geometry is, as much as to say, the measure of the earth, "et sic dicetur a Gea graece quod est pro terra Latine, e metrona quod est mensura una Geometria ie mensura terae vel terrarum," that is to say in English that Geometry is, as I said, of "geo" in Greek earth, and "metron" that is to say measure, and thus is this name Geometry compounded, and is said (to be) the measure of the earth.

MARVEL ye not that I said that all sciences live only by the science of Geometry, for there is no artificial or handicraft that is wrought by man s hand but is wrought by Geometry, and a notable cause, for if a man works with his hands he worketh with some manner of tool, and there is no instrument of material things in this world, but it comes of some kind of earth, and to earth it will turn again. And there is no instrument, that is to say a tool to work with, but it hath some proportion more or less, and proportion is measure, and the tool or instrument is earth, and Geometry is said to be the measure of the earth. Wherefore I may say that men live all by Geometry, for all men here in this world live by the labour of their hands.

MANY more probations I could tell you, why that Geometry is the science that all reasonable men live by, but I will leave it at this time for the long process of writing. And now I will proceed further on my matter. Ye shall understand that among all the crafts of the world of man s craft Masonry hath the most notability, and most part of this science of Geometry, as it is noted and said in history, and in the Bible, and in the Master of Stories, and in the "Polichronicon," a chronicle proved, and in the histories that is named Beda " de Imagine Mundi, " et Isodorus " themolegiarum ." "Mathodius Episcopus et Martyrus," and others, many more, said that Masonry is principal of Geometry, as me thinketh it may well be said, for it is the first that was founded, as it is noted in the Bible, in the first book of Genesis in the 4th chapter, and also all the doctors aforesaid accordeth thereto, and some of {545} them saith it more openly and plainly right as it saith in the Bible -- Genesis.

ADAM S line lineal of sons descending down the 7th age after Adam, before

Noah s flood there was a man called Lamech, the which had two wives, the one called Adah and the other Zillah; by the first named Adah he begat two sons, the one named Jabal and the other named Jubal. The elder son Jabal, he was the first man that ever found Geometry and Masonry, and he made houses and is named in the Bible, "Pater habitanicum in tentoriis atque Pastorum," that is to say father of men dwelling in tents, that is dwelling-houses.<<And the fnther of Shepherds and Headsman (other MSS.)>> And he was Cain s Master Mason and governor of all his works when he made the city of Enoch; that was the first city that ever was made, and that made Cain Adam s son, and gave it to his son Enoch, and gave the city the name of his son and called it Enoch, and now it is called Ephraim, and there was the science of Geometry and Masonry

first occupied and contrived for a science and for a craft; and so we may say that was the cause and foundation of all crafts and sciences, and also this man Jabal was called "Pater pastorum."<<And the father of Shepherds and Headsman (other MSS.)>> The Master of Stories saith, and Beda "de Imagine Mundi Polichronicon," and others more say, that he was the first that made partition of land, that every man might know his own ground and labour thereupon, as for his own. And also he parted flocks of sheep that every man might know his own sheep, and so we may say that he was the first founder of that science. And his brother Jubal was the first founder of Music and of song as ("Pythagoras") saith, the "Polichronicon," and the same saith Isadore in his "Ethemolegies" in the sixth book, there he saith that he was the first founder of music in song and of organ and trumpet, and he found that science by the sound of ponderation of his brother s hammers, that was Tubal Cain.

SOOTHLY as the Bible saith in the same chapter, that is to say the 4th of

Genesis, this Lamech begat upon his other wife, that named Zillah, a son and a daughter, the names of them were called Tubal Cain, that was the son; and his daughter was called Naamah, and as the "Polichronicon" saith, that some men say that she was Noah s wife; whether it be so or no we affirm it not.

YE shall understand that this son Tubal Cain was the founder of Smiths Craft and of other Crafts of Metal, that is to say of iron, of brass, of gold, and of silver, as sundry doctors sayeth; and his sister Naamah was founder of weavers craft, for before that time there was no cloth woven, but they did spin yarn and knit it, and made such clothing as they could, but as the woman Naamah found the craft of weaving, therefore it is called women s craft; and these three, her brethren, had knowledge before that God would take vengeance for sin either by fire or by water, and they had great care how they might do to save the sciences that they had found, and they took their counsel together and by all their wits they said that there were two manner of stones of such virtue that the one would never burn, and that stone is called marble, and that other stone would not sink in water, and that stone is named lacerus (laterus). And so they devised to write all the sciences that they had found in these two stones, so that if God should take vengeance by fire, that the marble should not burn; and if God sent vengeance by water that the other should not drown; and so they prayed their elder brother Jabal that he would make two pillars of these stones, that is to say of marble and lacerus, and that he would write in the two pillars all the {546} sciences and crafts that they all had found, and so he did, and therefore we may say that he was the most cunning in science, for he first began and performed the end before Noah s flood.

KINDLY (intuitively) knowing of that vengeance that God would send,

whether it should be by fire or by water the brethren had it not by manner of prophecy; they wist that God would send one thereof, and therefore they wrote their sciences in the ii. pillars of stone, and some men say that they wrote in the stones all the seven sciences; but they had in their minds that a vengeance would come; and so it was that God sent vengeance by water, so that their came such a flood that all the world was drowned; and all men were dead therein; save viii. persons, and that was Noah and his wife and his iii. sons and their wives of which three sons all the world come of and their names were in this manner -- Shem, Ham, and Japheth. And this flood was called Noah s flood, for he and his children were saved therein. And after this flood, many years, as the chronicle telleth, these ii. pillars were found, and as the

"Polichronicon" saith that a great clerk that men called Pythagoras found the one and Hermes the philosopher found the other, and they taught forth the sciences that they found therein written.

EVERY chronicle and storiell, and many other clerks, and the Bible principally, witnesseth of the making of the tower of Babylon, and it is written in the Bible, Genesis, Capo. x., how that Ham, Noah s son, begot Nimrod, and he waxed a mighty man upon the earth, and he was a strong man like a giant, and he was a great king. And the beginning of his kingdom was the true kingdom of Babylon, and Erech, and Accad, and Calnah, and the land of Shinar. And this same Nimrod began the tower of Babylon, and he taught to his workmen the craft of measures, and he had with him many Masons, more than forty thousands, and he loved them and cherished them well: and it is written in the "Polichronicon," and in the Master of Stories, and other stories more, and this, in part, witnesseth the Bible, in the said x. chapter, where it saith that Ashur, that was nigh of kin to Nimrod, "yede" out of the land of Shinar, and he built the city of Nineveh, and Plateas, and other more, thus it saith -- "De terra illa in de Sennare egressus est Assur et edificavit Nineven et Plateas civitatis et Calen, et Resen, quoque est inter Nineven et Calen haec est civitatis magna."

REASON would that we should tell openly how, and in what manner the

Charges of Masoncraft was first founded, and who gave first the name to it of Masonry. And ye shall know well that it is plainly told and written in "Polichronicon," and in Methodius episcopus et Martyrus, that Ashur that was a worthy lord of Shinar, sent to Nimrod the king to send him Masons and workmen of craft that might help him to make his city that he was in will to make. And Nimrod sent thirty hundred of Masons; and when he should go and send them forth he called them before him, and said to them -- "You must go to my cousin Ashur, to help him to build a city; but look that ye be well governed, and I shall give you a charge profitable to you and me.

"WHEN ye come to that Lord, look that ye be true to him, like as ye would be to me, and truly do your labour and craft, and take reasonable for your meed therefore, as you may deserve; and also that ye love together as ye were brethren, and hold together truly, and he that hath most cunning teach it to his Fellow, and look ye govern yourselves well towards your lord, and among yourselves, that I may have worship and thanks for my sending, and teaching you the craft." {547}

AND they received the charge of the King that was their Master and their Lord, and went forth to Ashur and builded the city of Nineveh in the country of Plateas and other cities more that men call Calah and Resen that is a great city between Calah and Nineveh. And in this manner the craft of Masonry was first preferred and charged for a science and a craft.

REASON would that we should shew you how that the Elders that were before time had these Charges written (to them as we have now in our Charges of the Story of Euclid, as we have seen them written) in Latin and in French; and how that Euclid came to Geometry, we should tell you as it is noted in the Bible and in other stories. In xii. capitolo Genesis he telleth how that Abraham came to the land of Canaan, and the Lord appeared to him and said, "I shall give this land to thee and to thy seed," but there fell a great hunger in that land and Abraham took Sarah his wife with him and went into (the land of) Egypt in pilgrimage, while the hunger endured he would bide there. And Abraham was

a wise man and a great cleric, and he knew all the seven sciences, and taught the Egyptians the science of Geometry. And this worthy clerk Euclid was his scholar and learned of him; and he gave it first the name of Geometry, all be that it was occupied before it had the name of Geometry. But it is said in Isidorus, "Ethemolegiarum," in the 5th book, Capitolo primo, that Euclid was one of the first founders of Geometry and he gave it name; for in his time there was a water in the land of Egypt that was called Nile, and it flowed so far into the land that men might not dwell therein. Then this worthy clerk Euclid taught them to make great walls and ditches to hold out the water; and he by Geometry measured the land and apportioned it in divers parts, and made every man to close his own part with walls and ditches, and then it became a plenteous country of all manner of fruit and of young people, of men and women, that there was so much fruit of young people that they could not well live. And the lords of the country drew them together and made a council how they might help their children that had no livelyhood competent and able to find for themselves and their children, for they had so many. And among them all in Council was this worthy clerk Euclid, and when he saw that they all could not bring about this matter he said to them -- "Will ye (give) to me your sons in governance and I shall teach them such a science that they shall live thereby gentlemanly, under condition that ye will be sworn to me, to perform the governance that I will set you to, and them both." And the King of the land and all the lords, by one consent, granted thereto.

REASON would that every man would grant to that thing that were profitable to himself, and they took their sons to Euclid to govern them at his own will, and he taught them the Craft of Masonry and gave it the name of Geometry, because of the parting of the ground that he had taught the people in the time of the making of the walls and ditches aforesaid, to close out the water, and Isadore saith in his "Ethemolegies" that Euclid calleth the craft Geometry; and there this worthy clerk gave it name, and taught it the lords sons of the land that he had in his teaching. And he gave them a Charge, that they should call each other Fellow and no otherwise, because they were all of one craft, and gentle birth born and lords sons. And also he that were most cunning should be governor of the work and should be called Master, and other Charges more that are written in the "Book of Charges." And so they wrought with the lords of that land, and {548} made cities and towns, castles, and temples, and lords palaces, and did live honestly and truly by the said craft.

WHAT time the children of Israel dwelt in Egypt they learned the craft of Masonry. And afterwards, (when) they were driven out of Egypt, they came into the land of Behest which is now called Jerusalem, and it was occupied and Charges there held and kept. And (also) at the making of King Solomon s temple that King David began. And King David loved well Masons and he gave them Charges right nigh as they be now. And at the making of the temple in Solomon s time, as it is said in the Bible, in the third book "Regum in tercio Regum capitolo quinto" that Solomon had iv. score thousand Masons at his work; and the King s son of Tyre was his Master Mason. And in other Chronicles it is said, and in old "Books of Masonry," that Solomon confirmed the Charges that David his father had given to Masons. And Solomon himself taught them their manners, but little differing from the manners that now are used.

AND from thence this worthy science was brought into France, and into many other regions. Sometime there was a worthy king that was called Carolus Secundus, that is to say Charles the Second, and this Charles was elected King of France by the grace of God and by lineage also. And some men say that he was elected by fortune only, the which is false as by the chronicle he was of the king s blood royal. And this same King Charles was a Mason before that he was a King, and after that he was a King he loved well Masons and cherished them, and gave them Charges and manners at his device, whereof some be yet used in France, and he ordained that they should have reasonable pay and should assemble once a year and commune together of such things as were amiss, and to be ruled by Masons and Fellows.

EVERY honest Mason or any other worthy workman that hath any love to the Craft of Masonry and would know how the Craft came first into England, and how it was grounded and confirmed, as it is noted and written in Storialls of England and in old Charges of St. Alban s time and of King Athelstan (s reign<<In original the word is "declared.">> that Amphabell came out of France into England and brought St. Alban into Christendom, and made him a Christian man. And he brought with him the Charges of Masons as they were in France, and in other lands. And at that time the king of the land, who was a pagan, dwelt where St. Albans is now, and he had many masons working on the town walls, and at that time St. Alban was the King s steward, paymaster, and governor of the King s works, and he loved Masons and cherished them well and made them good pay, for (before that time throughout all England) a Mason took but a penny a day and meat and drink, and St. Alban got of the King that every Mason should have xxxd. and iiid. for their noon finding, and he got them Charges and manners as St. Amphabell had taught him, and they do but little differ from the Charges that be used at this time, and so these Charges and manners were used many years. AFTERWARDS they were almost near hand lost through barbarous wars,

until the time of King Athelstan<<Query, Edwd., and Athelstan (suggested by Bro. W. H. Upton, P.G.M., of Washington). May admit of interpretation as Edwd. the elder, and his sons Athelstan and Edwin (see IV. and V.)>> (who brought the land to rest and peace, and he loved well Masons and had a son called Edwin),<<Query, Edwd., and Athelstan (suggested by Bro. W. H. Upton, P.G.M., of Washington). May admit of interpretation as Edwd. the elder, and his sons Athelstan and Edwin (see IV. and V.)>> and the same (Edwin) loved well Geometry and applied himself busily in learning that science, and also he desired to have the practice thereof, wherefore he called to himself {549} the best Masons that were in the realm, for he knew well that they had the practise of Geometry best of any craft in the realm, and he learned of them Masonry and loved and cherished them well, and he took unto him the Charges, and learned the manners, and afterwards for the love that he had unto the craft, and for the good grounding on which it was founded, he purchased a free charter of the King his father that they should have such freedom, to have correction within themselves, and that they might commune together, to correct such things as were amiss within themselves; and they made a great Congregation of Masons to assemble together at York, where he was himself, and let call the old Masons of the realm to that Congregation, and commanded them to bring to him all the writings of the old books of the craft that they had, out of which book they contrived the Charges by the device of the wisest Masons that were there, and

commanded that these charges might be kept and holden, and he ordained that such Congregations should be called Assembly, and he ordained for them good pay that they might live honestly; the which Charges I will declare hereafter, and thus was the Craft of Masonry grounded and confirmed in England.

IN ENGLAND Right Worshipful Masters and Fellows that (have) been of divers Assemblies and Congregations, with the consent of the lords of this realm, hath ordained and made Charges, by their best advise, that all manner of men that shall be made and Allowed Masons, must be sworn upon a book to keep the same, in all that they may, to the uttermost of their Power. And also that they have ordained that when any Fellow shall be Received and Allowed that these Charges shall be read to him, and he to take his Charges. And these Charges have been seen and perused by our late Sovereign Lord King Henry the Sixth, and the Lords of the honourable Council, and they have allowed them well, and said they were right good and reasonable to be holden. And these Charges have been drawn and gathered out of divers ancient Books, both of the old Law and new Law, as they were confirmed and made in Egypt by the King and by the great clerk Euclid; and at the making of Solomon s temple by King David, and Salom his son; and in France by Charles King of France; and in England by St. Alban that was steward to the King; and afterwards by King Athelstan<<Query, Edwd., and Athelstan (suggested by Bro. W. H. Upton, P.G.M., of Washington). May admit of interpretation as Edwd. the elder, and his sons Athelstan and Edwin (see IV. and V.)>> that was King of England, and by his son Edwin that was king after his father<<Query, Edwd., and Athelstan (suggested by Bro. W. H. Upton, P.G.M., of Washington). May admit of interpretation as Edwd. the

elder, and his sons Athelstan and Edwin (see IV. and V.)>>; as it is rehearsed in many and divers histories, and storialls, and chapters, and ensueth as the Charges following, Particularly and severally. The first and principal Charge is: --

1.   THAT ye shall be true man, or true men, to God and the Holy Church, and that ye shall use neither error nor heresy, by your own understanding nor discredit wise-men s teaching.

2.   That ye be true liegemen to the King without treason or falsehood, and if you know any treason or treachery, look ye amend it if you can, or else privately warn the King, or his rulers, or his deputies, and officers.

3.   That ye shall be true one to another; that is to say every Master and Fellow of the science and craft of Masonry, that be Allowed Masons; and to do unto them as ye would they should do unto you.

4.   That every Mason keep true Council both of "Lodge" and "Chamber," and all other councils that ought to be kept by way of Masonry.

5.   That no Mason be thief, or thieves (maintainers), so far as he knoweth.

{550}

6.   That he shall be true to his lord and (to his) Master, that he doth serve, and truly look to his Master s profit and advantage.

7.   You shall call Masons your Fellows, or your Brethren, and by no foul name, nor shall you take your Fellow s wife in villany, nor further desire his daughter or servant.

8.   And also that you pay truly for your meat or your drink, wheresoever you go to board, also ye shall do no villany in the house, whereby the Craft may be slandered.

THESE be the Charges in general that every Mason should hold, both Masters and Fellows.

NOW other singular Charges for Masters and Fellows: --

1st -- THAT no Master, nor Fellow, take upon him Lord s work, nor other man s, but he know himself able and cunning to perform it; so that the Craft have no slander nor disworship; so that the lord may be well and truly served.

2ly -- That no Master take work but he take it reasonably so that the lords may be well and truly served with his own goods, and the Master may live honestly, and pay his Fellows truly their pay, as the manner of Craft asketh.

3ly -- That no Master, nor Fellow, shall supplant other of his work, that is to say, if he have taken a work, or stand Master of any lord s work, or other. Ye shall not put him out, unless he is unable of cunning to end that work.

4ly -- That no Master, nor Fellow, take no Apprentice, to be allowed his apprentice but for seven years, and that the apprentice be able, (and) of birth and living, as he ought to be.

5ly -- That no Master, nor Fellow, take no allowance (nor allow any) to be Mason without the consent of V. or VI. of his Fellows at least; and that he that shall be made Mason to be (amenable in all points), that is to say, that he be free born and of good kindred, and no bondsman, and that he have his right limbs, as a man ought to have.

6ly -- "That no Master, nor Fellow, take any lord s work to task that hath been accounted to be journey-work.

7ly -- That every Master) give pay to his Fellow but as he may deserve, so that the worthy lord of the work may not be deceived through false workmen.

8ly -- That no Fellow do slander another behind his back to make him lose his good name, or his worldly goods.

9ly -- That no Fellow within Lodge, or without it, do minister evil answers to another ungodly, without reasonable cause.

10ly -- That every Mason shall do reverence to his elders, and shall put him to worship.

11ly -- That no Mason shall play at hazard, nor at the dice, nor at any other unlawful games, whereby the Craft might be slandered.

12ly -- That no Mason be ribald in lechery, to make the Craft slandered.

13th -- That no Fellow go into town in the night time without a Fellow to bear witness that he hath been in honest company; for if he do so there is to be a Lodge of Fellows to punish the sin.

14th -- That every Mason and Fellow shall come to the Assembly if it be within five (fifty) miles of him, and if he have any warning to stand at the award of Masters and Fellows.

15th -- That every Mason and Fellow if they have trespassed to stand at the award of Masters and Fellows to make them accord, if they may, and if they may not accord then to go to the common law.

16th -- That no Master make no mould, nor square, nor rule, to layers (i.e., setters).

17th -- That no Master, nor Fellow, shall set a layer within {551} Lodge, nor without it, to shew any moulded stones, with any mould of his making.

18th -- That every Master shall receive and cherish strange Masons when they come out of the country, and set them to work, as the manner is; that is to say, if they have moulded stones in the place, ye shall set him a fortnight at the

least in work, and give him his pay, and if ye have no stones for him to work, then ye shall refresh him to the next Lodge.

19th -- That you shall truly serve your lord for your pay, and justly and truly make an end of your work, be it task or journey-work, so that you may have your pay truly, as you ought to have.

20th -- That every Mason work truly upon the working day, so that he may receive his pay and deserve it; that he may live honestly upon the holiday; and that ye, and every Mason, receive your pay godly of your paymaster, and that you shall keep due time of labour in your work, and of rest as it is ordained of the Master s counsel.

21st -- That if any Fellow shall be at discord or dissention, ye shall truly treat with them to make accord and agreement, and shew no favour to either party, but act justly and truly for both, and that it be done at such times as the lord s work be not hindered.

22nd -- ALSO if ye stand Warden or have any power under the Master, where you serve, ye shall be true to your said Master while ye be with him, and be a true mediator between Master and Fellows, to the uttermost of your power.

23rd -- ALSO if ye stand steward, either of Lodge, Chamber, or Common House needs, ye shall give a true account of your Fellows goods, how they are dispensed, at such times as they may take account; and also if ye have more cunning than your Fellow that stands by you at his work, and see him in danger to spoil his stone, and wants counsel of you, ye shall inform and teach him honestly, so that the lord s work be not spoiled.

THESE Charges that we have declared and recorded unto you, ye shall well and truly keep to your power. So help you God, and your Hali-dame; and by ye holy contents of this book.

IV.

"MODERN CHARGES." (ABBREVIATED, "circa" 1535).

The might of the Father of heaven, with the wisdom of the blessed Son, through the grace of God, and the goodness of the Holy Ghost, that be three persons in one Godhead, be with us at our beginning, and give us grace so to govern us here in this life, that we may come to His blessing, that never shall have ending.

GOOD BRETHREN and Fellows, our purpose is to tell you how and in what manner this worthy science of Masonry was first founded and afterwards how it was maintained and upholden by worthy kings and princes, and many other worshipful men. And also, to them that be here, we will declare the Charges that it belongs to every Free-Mason to keep sure in good faith; and therefore take good heed hereunto, for it is a science that is worthy of being kept, for it is a worthy Craft; and is one of the seven liberal sciences. {552}

The names of the seven liberal sciences are these: The first is "Grammar" that teacheth a man to speak and write truly; the second is "Rhetoric" that teacheth a man to speak well, in subtle terms; the third is "Dialectic," or Logic, that

teacheth a man to discern truth from falsehood. The fourth is "Arithmetic," that teacheth a man to reckon and count all kinds of numbers; the fifth is "Geometry" that teacheth a man to mete and measure the earth and all other things, on which science Masonry is grounded. The sixth is "Music" that teacheth the craft of song and voice, of tongue, organ, and harp. The seventh is "Astronomy" that teacheth a man to know the course of the sun, moon, and stars.

THESE be the seven liberal Sciences, the which are all grounded upon one, that is to say Geometry. And this may a man prove that the science of all work is grounded upon Geometry, for it teacheth mete, measure, ponderation, and weight of all manner of things on earth; for there are none that work any science, but he worketh by some measure or weight, and all this is Geometry. Merchants and all Craftsmen, and others who use the Sciences, and especially the plowmen and tillers of all manner of grains and seeds, planters of vineyards and setters of fruit, none can till without Geometry; for neither in Grammar, Rhetoric, or Astronomy can any man find mete or measure without geometry. Wherefore this science may well be called the most worthy science, for it foundeth all others.

HOW this science was first begun I will now tell you. Before Noah s flood there was a man called Lamech, as it is written in the Bible in the 4th chapter of Genesis. And this Lamech had two wives, the one called Adah by whom he had two sons, one called Jabal and the other Jubal. And his other wife was called Zillah, by whom he had one son Tubal-Cain, and one daughter named Naamah; and these four children founded the beginning of all the sciences in the world. Jabal, the eldest son, found out the science of Geometry; he kept flocks of sheep and lambs in the fields, as it is noted in the chapter aforesaid. His brother Jubal founded the science of Music, in song of tongue, harp, and organ, and trumpet. And the third brother Tubal Cain found the science of smith s craft, in gold, silver, copper, and iron. And their sister Naamah found the craft of weaving. And these persons knowing right well that God would take vengeance for sin, either by fire or water, therefore they writ their several sciences that they had found in ii. pillars of stone, that they might be found after Noah s flood. The one stone was marble that would not burn with fire, and the other called "latres" (latens, laterns, lacerus, &c.) because it would not drown with water. Our intent is now to tell you, how and in what manner these stones were found in which were written these sciences. After the destruction of the world by Noah s flood, as histories affirm, a great clerk called Pythagoras found the one, and Hermes the philosopher (who was Cush s son, who was Shem s son, who was Noah s son) found the other, and was called the Father of wise men. These two found the two pillars in which the sciences were written, and taught them to other men.

AND at the making of the Tower of Babylon masonry was much esteemed.

And the king of Babylon that was named Nimrod was a Mason himself, and he loved well Masons and their science, as it is said by Masters of histories. And when the cities of Nineveh, and other cities of eastern Asia, were to be built this Nimrod sent thither three score masons<<Other MSS. have it, sixty, forty, thirty hundred, see also No. 3 MS.>> at the request of the {553} King of Nineveh, his cousin, and when he sent them forth he gave them a Charge in this manner. That they should each one be true to the other; that they should love well one another; that they should serve their lord truly for their pay, that

the Master may have worship and all that belong to him. And other more Charges he gave them, and this was the first time that a Mason had any Charges of his Craft.

MOREOVER Abraham and Sarah his wife went into Egypt, and there he taught the seven sciences to the Egyptians; and ("he had") a worthy scholar named Euclid ("and he") learned right well and was Master of all the vii. sciences; and in his days it befell that the lords and states of the land had so many sons, some by their wives and some by their concubines, for that land is hot and plenteous of generation; and they had not a competent proportion of estates wherewith to maintain their said children, which caused them much care; and the King of that land summoned a great Council to consult how they might provide for their children to live honestly as gentlemen; and they could find no good way. And then they made proclamation throughout all the realm, that if there were any that could inform them therein he should come to them and would be well rewarded for his labours. After this proclamation was made the worthy Clerk Euclid came and said unto the King and the nobles -- "If you will accept of me to teach, instruct, and govern your children, I will teach them the vii. liberal sciences whereby they may live honestly as gentlemen. I will do it upon condition that you will grant me and them a commission, that I may have power to rule them, after the manner the science ought to be ruled." The King and all the Council granted him this and sealed the Commission; and then this worthy doctor took to himself these lords sons and taught them the science of Geometry, and to practise work in stones, of all manner of work that belongeth to building churches, temples, castles, towers, manors, and all other sorts of buildings, and gave them a Charge in this manner: First, that they should be true to the lord that they serve; that they should love well one another; that they should call each other Fellow or Brother, and not servant, knave, or other foul name; that they should truly deserve their pay of their lord, or the master that they served; and that they should ordain the wisest of them to be masters of the work, and neither to chose for love, nor affection, nor greatness, nor richness, to set any in the work that hath not sufficient knowledge or cunning to be master of the work, whereby the Master should be evilly served and they dishonoured; and also that they should call the governor of the work Master, during the time that they work with him, and other more Charges which is too long to tell here. And to all these Charges he made them swear a great Oath, that men used at that time; and he ordained for them reasonable pay that they might live honestly thereby; also that they should assemble themselves together once every year, and consult how they might best work for their lord s profit and their own credit; and correct within themselves him that had trespassed against the science. And thus was the science grounded in Egypt, and that worthy Master Euclid was the first that gave it the name of Geometry the which is now called Masonry.

AND, AFTER that, when the children of Israel were come into the land of

Behest which is now called with us the country of Jerusalem (Jewry), King David began the temple that is now called Templum Dei, as is called with us the Temple of Jerusalem, and the said King David loved well Masons and {554} cherished them much, and he gave them good wages, and also Charges and manners, as they had learned in Egypt ("from Euclid"), and other more Charges that you shall hear afterwards. After the decease of King David, Solomon his son finished the said temple that his father had begun, and he sent for Masons

out of divers countries and divers lands, and gathered them together so that he had four score thousand workers of stone who were Masons, and he chose out of them three thousand that were ordained to be Masters and governors of the work. And furthermore, there was a king of another region that men called Hiram, and he loved King Solomon well, and he gave him timber for his work. And he had a son named Aman (Aymon, Hymon, Anon, Adon, &c.) and he was a Master of Geometry, and chief Master of all his gravings, carvings, and all his masons and masonry, as appears in Scripture, in libro primo Regum and chapter 5th. And this Solomon confirmed both the Charges and manners that his father had given to Masons, and thus was the worthy science of Masonry confirmed in the country of Jewry, and city of Jerusalem, and in many other kingdoms.

CURIOUS Craftsmen walked about full wide into other countries, some to

learn more craft, and some to teach others that had little skill and cunning. And it befell that there was one curious Mason named Namas Graecas (Namus Graecus, Manus Graecus, Memon Grecus, Mammungretus, Mamus Graecus, Minus Goventis, Marcus Graecus, Namus Grenaeus, etc.) that had been at the building<<Building s (query of Bro. Schnitger) -- he had a Solomon s temple ritual.>> of Solomon s temple and he came into France and there he taught the science of Masonry to men of that land. And there was one of the royal line of France called Charles Martel, and he was a man that loved well such a craft, and he drew to this . . . . . abovesaid, and learned of him the craft, and took upon him Charges and manners, and afterwards by the providence of God, he was elected King of France, and when he was in his estate he took and helped to make men Masons which before were not; and he gave them both their Charge and manners, and good pay as he had learned of other Masons, and also confirmed a Charter from year to year to hold their Assembly where they would, and cherished them right well, and thus came this famous Craft into France.

ENGLAND in all this time stood void of any Charge of Masonry until St.

Alban s time, and in his days the King of England<<Carausius.>> then a pagan did wall the town (that is now called) St. Albans about. And St. Alban was a worthy Knight and Steward of the King s household, and had the government of the realm, and had also the ordering of the walls of the said town, and he loved and cherished Masons right well, and made their pay right good, for he gave them (3s. a week -- 2s. 6d. and 3d. for noon, 3s. 6d. and 3d., etc.), and before that time, throughout all the land, a Mason took but a penny a day, until St. Alban amended it; and he procured them a Charter from the King and his Council, for to hold counsel together, and gave it the name of Assembly, and thereat he was himself, and helped to make men Masons, and gave them a Charge, as ye shall after hear.

BUT it happened soon after the death of St. Alban that there arose great wars in England, which came out of divers nations, so that the goodly rule of Masonry was well nigh destroyed until the days of King Athelstan,<<Query, Edwd., and Athelstan (suggested by Bro. W. H. Upton, P.G.M., of Washington). May admit of interpretation as Edwd. the elder, and his sons Athelstan and Edwin (see IV. and V.)>> who was a worthy King of England, and he brought the land into good rest and peace, and {555} builded many great works, as abbeys, castles, towns, and other buildings, and loved well Masons; and he had a son named Edwin,<<Query, Edwd., and Athelstan (suggested by Bro. W. H.

Upton, P.G.M., of Washington). May admit of interpretation as Edwd. the elder, and his sons Athelstan and Edwin (see IV. and V.)>> that loved Masons, much more than his father, and he was a great practitioner in geometry, and delighted much to talk and commune with Masons and to learn of them skill and cunning, and afterwards for the love he bore to Masons and to their science, he was made a Mason, and he procured for them of the King his father a Charter and Commission to hold every year an Assembly, wheresoever they would within the realm of England, and to correct within themselves all defaults and trespasses that were done within the Craft, and he himself held an Assembly at York, and there he made Masons and gave them the Charges and taught them the manners and commanded that rule to be kept ever after, and also gave them the Charter to keep, and also gave orders that it should be renewed from king to king. And when the Assembly was gathered together he made proclamation, that all Masons who had any writings or understanding of the Charges and manners concerning the said science, that was made before in this land or any other, that they should bring them forth, and when they were viewed and examined, there were found some in French, some in Greek, some in English, and other languages, and the intent and meaning was found all one. [<<Added from "Tew MS." W. R. Co. York; also clauses 19 to 25.>> And these Charges have been gathered and drawn out of divers antient books and writings, as they were made and confirmed in Egypt by the King and the great Clerk Euclid; and by David and Solomon his son; and in France by Charles Martel who was King of France; and in England by St. Alban; and afterwards by Athelstan and Edward his son,<<Query, Edwd., and Athelstan (suggested by Bro. W. H. Upton, P.G.M., of Washington). May admit of interpretation as Edwd. the elder, and his sons Athelstan and Edwin (see IV. and V.)>> that was king after him.] And he had made a Book thereof, how the Craft was founded, and he himself counselled that it should be read when any Masons should be made, and the Charge given to them. And from that day to this the manners of Masons have been kept and observed in that form, as well as men might observe and govern it.

ADD furthermore at divers Assemblies there hath been added certain

Charges more by the best advice of Masters and Fellows. Tunc unus ex senioribus teneat librum ut ille vel illi potiat vel potiant manus sup librum et tunc precepta deberent Legi.

EVERY man that is a Mason, take right good heed to these Charges, and if any man find himself guilty of any of them, let him amend himself before God. And in particular, ye that are to be charged, take good heed to keep them right well, for it is perilous and great danger for a man to forswear himself upon "a book" (the Holy Scriptures).

1st -- The first Charge is that you be true man to God, and the Holy Church, and that you use neither error nor heresy, according to your own understanding, and to discreet and wise-men s teaching.

2nd -- You shall be true liegemen to the King of England without any treason or falsehood, and if you know of any that you amend it privily, if you may, or else warn the King and his Council of it by declaring it to his officers.

3rd -- Ye shall be true to one another, that is to say to every Mason of the Craft of Masonry that be allowed Masons, and do unto them as you would they should do unto you.

4th -- You shall keep truly all the counsel of Lodge and Chamber, and all other counsel, that ought to be kept by way of Masonry.

5th -- Also that you use no thievery, but keep yourselves true.

6th -- Also you shall be true to the lord, or Master, that you {556} serve, and truly see that his profit and advantage be promoted and furthered.

7th -- And also you shall call Masons your Brethren, or Fellows, and no foul name.

8th -- And you shall not take in villainy your Fellow s wife, nor desire his daughter, nor servant, nor put him to any discredit.

9th -- And also that you pay truly for your meat and drink where you go to table, and that you do not anything whereby the Craft may be scandalised, or receive disgrace.

THESE be the Charges in general that belongeth to every Mason to keep both Masters and Fellows. NOW come I to rehearse certain other Charges singularly, for Masters and Fellows: --

1.   That no Master take upon him any lord s work, or any other man s work, except he know himself to be of sufficient skill and cunning to perform and finish the same, that so the Craft receive no slander, but that the lord be well served, and have his work truly done.

2.   Also that no Master take any work at unreasonable rates, but so that the lord, or owner, may be truly served with his own goods, and the Master live honestly thereby, and pay his Fellows truly their wages, as the manner is.

3.   And also that no Master, nor Fellow, shall supplant another of his work; that is to say, if any Master or Fellow have taken any work to do, and so stands as Master of the said work, you shall not put him out of it, unless he be unable of skill and cunning to perform the same to the end.

4.   Also that no Master nor Fellow, take any Apprentice under the term of seven years, and that

such apprentice is sufficiently able of body and sound of limbs, also of good birth, free-born, no alien, but descended of a true and honest kindred, and no bondsman.

5. Also that no Mason take any apprentice unless he have sufficient occupation wherein to employ two or three Fellows at the least.

6. Also that no Master or Fellow take any lords work (in task) that was wont to be journey work.

7. Also that every Master shall give wages to his Fellows according as his work doth deserve, that he be not deceived by false work.

8. Also that none shall slander another behind his back, whereby he may lose his good name, or worldly riches.

9. Also that no Fellow, within the lodge or without it, shall misanswer or reprove another, without cause.

10. Also that every Mason shall reverence his elder brother, and put him to honour.

11. Also that no Mason shall be a common player at cards or dice, or any other unlawful game, or games, whereby the science may be slandered and disgraced.

12. Also that no Fellow at any time go from the Lodge to any town adjoining, except he have a Fellow with him to witness that he was in an honest place, and civil company.

13. Also that every Master and Fellow shall come to the Assembly of Masons, if it he within fifty (1, 5, 7, 10) miles about him, if he have any warning of the same.

14. And if he or they have trespassed or offended against the Craft, all such trespass shall stand there, at the award and arbitration of the Masters and Fellows there (present); they to make them accord if they can, or may, and if they cannot agree then to go to the common law. {557}

15. Also that no Master, nor Fellow, make any mould, rule, or square for any layer, nor set any layer (with) or without to hew any mould stones.

16. And that every Mason shall cherish strange Fellows, when they come out of other countries and set them on work if he can, as the manner is, viz. -- if he have no stones, nor moulds, in that place, he shall refresh him with money to supply his necessities until he come to the next Lodge.

17. Also that every Mason shall perform his work truly and not sleightly, for his pay, and serve his lord truly for his wages.

18. Also that every Master shall truly make an end of his work, whether it be by task or journey, viz., by measure or by days, and if he have his pay and all other covenants performed to him by the lord of the work according to the bargain.

19. Also that no Mason shall be a common ribald in lechery to make the Craft slandered.

20. Also that every Mason shall work truly upon the work day, that he may truly deserve his pay, and receive it so he may live honestly on the holiday.

21. And also that you and every Mason shall receive weekly (meekly) and godly (the) pay of your paymaster, and that you shall have due time of labour in the work, and of rest as is ordained by the Master s counsel.

22. And also if any Fellows be at discord you shall truly treat with them to be agreed, shewing favour to neither party, but wisely and truly for both, and that it be in such time that the lord s work be not hindered.

23.   And also if you stand Warden, or have any power under the Master whom you serve, you shall be true to him, and a true mediator between the Master and your Fellows, to the uttermost of your power whilst you be in care.

24.   Also if you stand Steward either of Lodge, Chambers, or common house, you shall give true accounts to your Fellows, at such time as they have accounts.

25.   And also if you have more cunning than your Fellow that stands by you, and see him in danger to spoil his stone, and he asketh counsel of you, you shall inform and teach him honestly, so that the lord s work be not damaged.

THESE Charges that we have now rehearsed to you, and to all others here present, which belongeth to Masons, ye shall well and truly keep to your power. So help you

God, and by ye contents of that book. Amen. (by your Haly-dome, Hali-dame, etc.).

V.

   "A SOUTH COUNTY VARIATION."

.   .   .   .

Afterwards, soon after the decease of St. Alban there came divers wars into England, out of divers nations, so that the good rule of Masonry was destroyed and put down, until the time of King (Knight) Althelstan.<<Query, Edwd., and Athelstan (suggested by Bro. W. H. Upton, P.G.M., of Washington). May admit of interpretation as Edwd. the elder, and his sons Athelstan and Edwin (see IV. and V.)>> In his time there was a worthy King of England that brought this land into good rest, and he builded many great works and buildings, therefore he loved well Masons, for he had a son called Edwin,<<Query, Edwd., and Athelstan (suggested by Bro. W. H. Upton, P.G.M., of Washington). May admit of interpretation as Edwd. the elder, and his sons Athelstan and Edwin (see IV. and V.)>> the which loved Masons much more than his father did, and he was so practised {558} in geometry that he delighted much to come and talk with Masons, and learn of them the Craft; and after for the love he had to Masons and to the Craft, he was made Mason at Windsor,<<Query -- Winchester.>> and got of the King his father a charter and commission, once every year to have Assembly where they would within England, and to correct within themselves, faults and trespasses that were done touching the Craft, and he held them at Assembly at York, and there he made Masons.

.   .   .   .

   VI.

   "THE NEW ARTICLES AND APPRENTICE CHARGE."

(Harleian MS., etc., early 17th Century).

   .   .   .   .

.   .   .   .

   (THE NEW ARTICLES).

(1)   26. No person (of what degree soever) bee accepted a Free-Mason unless he shall have a lodge of five Free Masons; at least where of one to be a Master or Warden, of that limitt or devision, wherein such lodge shall be kept, and another of the trade of Free Masonry.

(2)   27. That noe p son shall be accepted a Free Mason but such as are of able body, honest parent-

age, good reputation, and observers of the laws of the land.

(3) 28. That noe p son hereafter be accepted a Free Mason, nor shall be admitted into any Lodge or Assembly until hee hath brought a certificate of the time of accep con from the Lodge yt accepted him, unto the master of that limitt and devision where such Lodge was kept which say d Master shall enrole the same in parchment in a role to he kept for that purpose, to give an account of all such Accep cions at every general Assembly.<<See the acct. of such Roll at York, Ch. X.>>

(4) 29. That every person whoe now is Free Mason shall bring to the Master a note of the time of his accep tion, to the end the same may be enrolled in such priority of place of the p son shall deserve and to ye end the whole Company and Fellows may the better know each other.

(5) 30. That for the future the say d Society, Company, and Fraternity, of Free Masons shall be regulated and govern d by one Master, and Assembly, and

Wardens, as ye said Company shall think fitt to chose at every yearly general Assembly.

(7) 31. That no p son shall be accepted a Free Mason, or know the secrets of the said Society, until he hath first taken the Oath of secrecy hereafter following: -- I, A.B., doe in the presence of Almighty God and my Fellows and Brethren here present, promise and declare that I will not at any time hereafter, by any act or circumstance whatsoever, directly or indirectly, publish, discover, reveale, or make knowne, any of the secrets, priviledges, or counsells, of the Fraternity or Fellowship of Free Masons, {559} which at this time, or at any time hereafter, shall be made knowne unto mee. So helpe mee God, and the holy contents of this booke.

(THE CHARGE BELONGING TO AN APPRENTICE).

1. You shall truly honour God and his Holy Church, the King, your Master, and Dame, you shall not absent yourself but with the license of both, or one of them, from their service by day or night.

2. You shall not purloin or steal, or be privy, or accessory to the purloining or stealing, to the value of sixpence, from them, or any of them.

3. You shall not commit adultery, or fornication, in the house of your Master, with his wife, daughter, or maid.

4. You shall not disclose your Master s or Dame s counsels, or secrets, which they have imparted to you, nor what is to be concealed, spoken, or done within the precincts of their house, by them or either of them, or by Free Masons.

6. You shall reverently behave yourself to all Free Masons, not using cards, or dice, or any other unlawful games, Christmas excepted.

7. You shall not haunt, or frequent any taverns, alehouses, or such as go into any of them, except when your Master s business, or Dame s, their, or any of their affairs, or without their or any of their consent.

8. You shall not commit adultery or fornication in any man s house, where you shall be at table or at work.

9. You shall not marry or contract yourself to any woman during your Apprenticeship.

10. You shall not steal any man s goods, but especially your said Master s, or any of his Fellow Masons , or suffer any one to steal their goods, but shall hinder it if you can, and if you cannot, then

you shall acquaint your said Master, and his Fellows presently.
VII.

"ADDITION TO "NEW ARTICLES," IN" 1663.

6th. That noe p son be accepted a Ffree Mason, except he be one and twenty yeares old or more.
GRAND LODGE MS. No. 2, "circa" 1650.

32. The 6th. p. 559. (Hence the omission from Harleian MS., and some others may be an error by accident. No date.)

THE END.

www.ingramcontent.com/pod-product-compliance
Lightning Source LLC
Chambersburg PA
CBHW052109020426
42335CB00021B/2683